PRESSURES
and
PRIORITIES

*The Report of Proceedings of the
Twelfth Congress of the Universities of the Commonwealth
Vancouver, August 1978*

THE ASSOCIATION
OF COMMONWEALTH UNIVERSITIES
36 GORDON SQUARE, LONDON, ENGLAND WC1H 0PF
1979

Editor of Congress Proceedings
T. CRAIG, MA

Assistant Editor
EILEEN A. ARCHER, MA

CONGRESS ORGANISING COMMITEE

Dr. J. STEVEN WATSON, *Chairman*
Professor Ungku A. AZIZ
Professor Sir DAVID DERHAM
Dr. H. E. DUCKWORTH
Dr. PAULINE JEWETT
Dr. D. T. KENNY
Professor L. KERWIN
Sir DOUGLAS LOGAN
Dr. C. R. MITRA
Sir FRASER NOBLE
Dr. M. K. OLIVER
Dr. H. E. PETCH
Dr. A. T. PORTER
Dr. T. H. B. SYMONS
Dr. D. B. C. TAYLOR
Dr. C. J. THIBAULT
Dr. D. C. WILLIAMS
Sir CHARLES WILSON
Sir HUGH W. SPRINGER, *Secretary*
Dr. E. W. VOGT, *Chairman, Local Organising Committee*
Mr. J. E. D. PEARSON, *Administrator and Deputy Chairman, Local Organising Committee*
Mr. T. CRAIG, *Editor of Congress Proceedings*
Mr. J. A. WHITTINGHAM, *ACU Finance Officer*
Mrs. D. BLANCHE GUBERTINI, *Personal Assistant to Secretary*

Price £10 (Can. $26.40, US$22.60)

Printed in Great Britain by Hobbs the Printers of Southampton
Copyright © The Association of Commonwealth Universities, 1979
ISBN 0 85143 058 9   ISSN 0142–3584

TWELFTH CONGRESS OF THE UNIVERSITIES OF THE COMMONWEALTH
1978

Some other publications of the ACU:
COMMONWEALTH UNIVERSITIES YEARBOOK, annual. 1979 edition, £28.50 (£18.53 to staff of member universities).

RESEARCH STRENGTHS OF UNIVERSITIES IN THE DEVELOPING COUNTRIES OF THE COMMONWEALTH. Second edition 1978, £3.50.

ACU BULLETIN OF CURRENT DOCUMENTATION (ABCD), five times a year. Annual sub.: UK, £2.10; elsewhere, £2.95 (including 2nd class airmail).

AWARDS FOR COMMONWEALTH UNIVERSITY STAFF, every two years. 1978−80 edition, £2.75.

SCHOLARSHIPS GUIDE FOR COMMONWEALTH POSTGRADUATE STUDENTS, every two years. 1977−79 edition, £3.75.

FINANCIAL AID FOR FIRST DEGREE STUDY AT COMMONWEALTH UNIVERSITIES, 1977. 85p.

GRANTS FOR STUDY VISITS BY UNIVERSITY ADMINISTRATORS AND LIBRARIANS, 1979. £1.

LIST OF UNIVERSITY INSTITUTIONS IN THE COMMONWEALTH, annual. Single copies free.

COMMONWEALTH SCHOLARSHIP AND FELLOWSHIP PLAN: REPORT. Prepared by the ACU for annual publication, 1960−61 to 1975−76; latest, published by the Commonwealth Secretariat, is the Sixteenth Report (1976). Future triennial publication planned.

Reports of some previous Congresses are also available.
For a full list of ACU publications 1973−78, see p. 612

The Congress Symbol

CONTENTS

PREFACE *page* 7

OPENING OF THE CONGRESS (Dr. H. E. Duckworth [Chairman], p. 15; Chief Justice N. T. Nemetz, p. 15; Dr. D. T. Kenny, p. 16)   15

FIRST PLENARY SESSION

Reconciling National, International and Local Roles of Universities with the Essential Character of a University (Sir Charles Wilson)   19

The World Food Problem and the Universities (Sir John Crawford)   26

GROUP DISCUSSIONS

Topic 1: The World Food Problem and the Universities   53

Topic 2: Higher Education in Countries with Federal Systems of Government   185

Topic 3: Reconciling Equality and Excellence   285

Topic 4: The Public View of the Universities   385

Topic 5: Universities and Other Institutions of Tertiary Education   489

SECOND PLENARY SESSION AND CLOSING CEREMONY   573

APPENDICES

I   Quinquennial Report of the Secretary General 1973 – 78   579

II   General Meeting of the Association of Commonwealth Universities (Western Ontario, 16 August 1978)   614

III   A Statistical Portrait of Canadian Higher Education   625

COUNCIL OF THE ASSOCIATION   627

MEMBERS OF THE CONGRESS   629

CONGRESS COMMITTEES, OFFICERS AND SECRETARIAT   653

NAMES INDEX   655

PREFACE

The twelfth in the ACU's series of quinquennial Congresses of the Universities of the Commonwealth took place at the University of British Columbia from the 19th to the 26th of August 1978. The series began with the 1912 Congress in London, out of which the Association of Commonwealth Universities (the Universities Bureau of the British Empire as it was first named) was born, and has continued without interruption except during the two world wars. After world war II the decision was taken that Congresses should be held alternately in Britain and in another part of the Commonwealth; and so the 1958 Congress was held in Montreal and in 1968 the venue was Sydney.

A General Meeting within the week before or after the Congress is required by the Association's Statutes, and around it is arranged a Conference of Executive Heads of member institutions; it is customary also for the Council to meet before or after the Congress in the same country. Accordingly in 1978 there was a succession of meetings westward across Canada beginning with the Council at Université Laval in Quebec City. Excellent arrangements were made for the accommodation and entertainment of the Council by the Rector, Dr. J.-G. Paquet, and his staff; and the official social engagements included receptions and dinners by the University, the Provincial Government and the Lieutenant Governor of Quebec, the Hon. Hugues Lapointe. From Quebec the members of the Council went on to Montreal, where they were received and entertained at lunch by the universities located in that city, then to London, Ontario, to join the other executive heads for the General Meeting and Conference at the University of Western Ontario.

ACU Conference of Executive Heads

The members of the Conference were welcomed by the President of Western Ontario, Dr. G. E. Connell, and, with their wives, were entertained by the City of London, Ontario, at a reception, which was followed by a dinner given by the Provincial Government of Ontario, presided over by Her Honour the Lieutenant Governor, Dr. Pauline M. McGibbon, and by the President of Western Ontario. Speeches of welcome were made at the dinner by the President of the University, the Lieutenant Governor and the

Minister of Colleges and Universities, the Hon. Harry C. Parrott, and on behalf of the guests Dr. H. E. Duckworth and Professor Sir Arthur Armitage suitably replied. The Conference discussed a paper *University relations with staff both academic and non-academic,* presented by the Rev. Father R. Guindon and members took part in a case-study exercise, based on the topic *Universities in a changing environment,* prepared and led by Professor J. J. Wettlaufer and Professor C. B. Johnson of the University's School of Business Administration.

The statutory General Meeting was held on Wednesday 16 August, the main item on the agenda being the Quinquennial Report on the activities and affairs of the Association.

There was a programme of tours and visits by the wives and children of members of the Conference including a visit to Niagara Falls and the Kleinburg Village; the members of the Conference and their wives were the guests of the University at a performance of *Julius Caesar* at the Stratford Festival Theatre.

Excellent arrangements were made for the Conference and the social activities connected therewith by a committee under the Chairmanship of Professor R. N. Shervill.

The executive heads and their wives proceeded from London, Ontario, to Calgary where for most of two days they were guests of the universities in the Province of Alberta before going on to Vancouver for the Congress. The party of some 300 were welcomed by the President of the University of Calgary, Dr. W. A. Cochrane, and they greatly enjoyed the varied programme of entertainment which he and his helpers had prepared for them, the highlight of which was a visit by coach to Banff and Lake Louise.

Preparations for the Congress

The Congress Organising Committee was appointed by the Council at its meeting in Kuala Lumpur in April 1975 with Dr. J. Steven Watson as Chairman, the other members being: Dr. T. H. B. Symons (Honorary Treasurer), Sir Douglas Logan (Honorary Deputy Treasurer), Professor Ungku A. Aziz, Professor D. P. (later Sir David) Derham, Dr. H. E Duckworth, Dr. L. Kerwin, Dr. C. R. Mitra, Sir Fraser Noble, Dr. M. K. Oliver, Dr. A. T. Porter, Sir Charles Wilson and Sir Hugh W. Springer (Secretary General). The following members were later added: Dr. Pauline Jewett, Dr. D. T. Kenny, Dr. H. E. Petch, Dr. D. B. C. Taylor, Dr. C. J. Thibault and Dr. D. C. Williams. The Secretary General was Secretary to the Committee, which first met in

PREFACE

Wellington, New Zealand, in February 1976 and had five meetings in all. The fourth meeting was held in Malta and the rest in London.

The Canadian Committee for the Congress had been appointed shortly before the main committee and included Dr. H. E. Duckworth, Dr. L. Kerwin, Dr. D. T. Kenny, Dr. M. O. Morgan, Dr. M. K. Oliver and Dr. D. C. Williams. The following joined the Committee at later stages: Miss Joy McDiarmid, Dr. C. B. Mackay, Professor R. N. Shervill, Dr. C. J. Thibault and Dr. E. W. Vogt. Dr. Williams was Chairman until 16 April 1977 when Dr. Duckworth became Chairman and Dr. Williams Co-Chairman. President Kenny appointed Vice-President Dr. E. W. Vogt to take charge of Congress arrangements at the University of British Columbia and there was also a Local Committee including representatives of the other universities in British Columbia, namely Simon Fraser and Victoria, under the Chairmanship of Dr. Vogt, the other members being Mr. J. E. D. Pearson (Administrator and Deputy Chairman), Dean G. M. Volkoff, Miss A. Chasmar, Mr. J. Currie, Mr. M. Davis, Miss B. Fata, Mrs. M. Stovell, Mrs. B. Vogt and Mrs. A. Watt.

In late August and again in late October 1976, the Secretary General used the opportunities provided by his presence in North America on other business to have useful planning meetings in Toronto with members of the Canadian Committee, and a similar meeting was held in April 1977 at the University of British Columbia with members of the Local Committee of the British Columbia universities also present. On 30 September 1977 the Secretary General attended a third meeting in Toronto of the Canadian Committee and on 1 October he took advantage of his presence in London, Ontario (for the purpose of taking part in the installation of the new President of the University of Western Ontario) to discuss with Professor Shervill and others the arrangements being made for the Conference of Executive Heads. In April 1978 he visited Quebec to discuss with those concerned at the Université Laval their plans for the Council meeting to be held there; then Ottawa to discuss with the Executive Director and other officers of the Association of Universities and Colleges of Canada aspects of the Congress arrangements; and finally on 1 May he was present at meetings held at the University of British Columbia of the Canadian Committee and the British Columbia Local Committee.

A preliminary notice and an outline programme of the dates and places of the several meetings were sent to member institutions in April 1976 with a request for suggestions for topics for discussion at the Congress and the Conference. In November 1976 members received formal invitations to be represented by four delegates each at the Congress (the names of delegates to be submitted by July 1977) and by the executive heads at the Conference, together with a list of topics to be discussed at the two meetings. Invitations to both meetings were sent also to the executive officers of the inter-university bodies associated with the ACU. In January 1977 executive heads were invited to suggest the names of possible speakers.

Each opening speaker in the five Topic sessions was asked to make his paper available to the Secretary General in advance of the Congress, and 35 such papers were distributed to Congress participants by airmail several weeks before the Congress began. Speakers were asked not to read their previously circulated papers but instead to speak to them for a limited time.

Membership of the Congress

The total number of members of the Congress was 567, comprising 444 delegates and observers nominated by 186 member universities together with 123 representatives of other organisations and specially invited guests (their names are given on pages 629 to 652); about 360 of those who attended were accompanied by their wives or husbands.

His Excellency the Governor General, The Rt. Hon. Jules Léger, graciously consented to be the Chief Patron of the Congress, other patrons being the Chief Justice of Canada, the Rt. Hon. Bora Laskin, and the Lieutenant Governors of the Provinces of Alberta, British Columbia, Manitoba, New Brunswick, Newfoundland, Nova Scotia, Ontario, Prince Edward Island, Quebec and Saskatchewan. The Canadian Minister of State for Science and Technology was represented at the Congress, as was the Secretary to the Cabinet and the Department of the Secretary of State for Canada. Invitations were accepted by a number of national bodies and foundations in the fields of science and culture, both private and public, and by several provincial government departments.

The Commonwealth Secretary General and the High Commissioners in Canada of the following countries were represented: Australia, Britain, India, Lesotho, Trinidad and Tobago, and Uganda—the last three by their High Commissioners in person. Other representatives and guests included the executive officers of the national and regional university organisations in the Commonwealth, the chairmen of the University Grants Committees and equivalent bodies, and representatives of a variety of other

PREFACE

Commonwealth, non-Commonwealth and international organisations and foundations concerned with university education.

The Congress

Members of the Congress and their wives and husbands were accommodated in the Walter H. Gage Residence of the University of British Columbia and the meetings were held in the Instructional Resources Centre at the University. Delegates arrived on Saturday 19 and Sunday 20 August; and after lunch on Sunday they were taken by bus through the city of Vancouver to Simon Fraser University, where they were given a conducted walking tour of the campus followed by a reception and dinner. At the dinner they were welcomed by the President, Dr. Pauline Jewett, in the three halls where they were seated, and replies to her welcome were given by Professor J. F. Ade Ajayi, Dr. C. R. Mitra and Dr. J. A. Maraj.

The Congress was opened in the Students Union Ballroom by the Chief Justice of the Supreme Court of British Columbia, the Hon. Nathan Nemetz, who officially welcomed the delegates to the Province. Welcome addresses were given by the President of the University of British Columbia, Dr. D. T. Kenny, and by Dr. H. E. Duckworth, Chairman of the Association of Commonwealth Universities and Chairman of the Congress. After the formal opening the first plenary session followed under the chairmanship of Dr. Duckworth. Sir Charles Wilson gave the keynote address on the theme *Reconciling national, international and local roles of universities with the essential character of a university* and Sir John Crawford introduced the first topic, *The world food problem and the universities.* This and the other four topics, *Higher education in countries with federal systems of government, Reconciling equality and excellence, The public view of the universities* and *Universities and other institutions of tertiary education,* were discussed in groups on Monday afternoon, Tuesday morning and afternoon and Thursday morning. On Thursday afternoon the delegates of member universities assembled for a session on the domestic affairs of the ACU.

On Wednesday the members of the Congress and their wives and husbands embarked on the ocean steamship *Princess Marguerite* (for which our thanks are due to the Hon. Grace McCarthy, Provincial Secretary) and sailed, having breakfast on board, to Vancouver Island where they were entertained at the University of Victoria to lunch and a short tour of the campus, and given addresses of welcome by the Lieutenant Governor of the Province, Brigadier General the Hon. Henry P. Bell-Irving, and by the

President of the University of Victoria, Dr. Howard Petch. After a short musical concert by a university chamber ensemble they re-embarked on the *Princess Marguerite* for the return journey to Vancouver, during which they were served drinks and an excellent dinner.

On Friday morning the second plenary session of the Congress, at which the chairmen of the five topics – Sir John Crawford, Dr. J. Steven Watson, Dr. A. T. Porter, Dr. P. Lacoste and Dr. C. M. Li – gave short reports on the discussions, was followed by the closing session at which Dr. P. Lacoste, President of the AUCC, gave a valedictory address and Dr. J. S. Watson, Vice-President of the ACU, expressed the thanks of the Association and of the participants to all who had contributed to the success of the Congress.

A programme of post-Congress visits to universities across Canada had been arranged but had to be cancelled at the last moment because of the sudden suspension of operations of the principal Canadian airline.

The chief social events, in addition to the voyage to Vancouver Island on Wednesday, were a reception given by the University of British Columbia on Monday night, the Congress Dinner on Thursday night given by the Province of British Columbia and a salmon barbecue on Friday night followed by a performance of Canadian Indian dances. At the Congress Dinner the Chairman, Dr. H. E. Duckworth, presided and speeches were made by Dr. Duckworth, the Hon. Pat McGeer, Provincial Minister of Education, Dr. A. T. Porter, Dr. J. F. Leddy and Dr. C. M. Li. There was an orchestral concert on Tuesday night, and various groups of delegates were invited to smaller receptions on various days throughout the week.

There was a special daily programme for the spouses and children of members of the Congress which included tours of Vancouver City, Vancouver North Shore, Fraser Valley and Vancouver Gardens, a visit to the Centennial Museum in Vancouver and an all-day hike to Garibaldi Lake.

In spite of the distance between London and Vancouver, there was close liaison between John Foster House and the Congress administration at UBC. This was due to the excellent rapport between all concerned as well as to the great convenience of the international telephone service and timely visits by the Secretary General to UBC and by the Chairman and the Deputy Chairman of the Local Committee to London. The Association is much indebted to the University of British Columbia and to many of its members both on and off the Local Committee, of whom special mention can

PREFACE

be made here of only one or two. Our thanks then first to the President, Dr. Kenny, not only for creating a favourable climate for the whole operation, but also for a number of unobtrusive, but sometimes crucially important and sometimes generous, interventions. It was by his choice too that Dr. Erich Vogt was Chairman of the Local Committee and his name comes next on our short list for unstinted praise and thanks. With his I couple the name of Jack Pearson, his Deputy Chairman and Congress Administrator.

November 1978   HUGH W. SPRINGER
                                                   Secretary General

ACKNOWLEDGEMENT OF FINANCIAL SUPPORT

Generous and much-appreciated assistance towards the travel of delegates was provided by: —

The Canadian International Development Agency	Imperial Oil Limited
	INCO Limited
The Commonwealth Foundation	Kodak (Canada) Limited
Canadian Pacific	Mobil Oil Canada Limited
Imasco Limited	Southam Press Limited

The Conference briefcases were funded in part through a generous grant from the Bank of Montreal and the hospitality provided on the *Princess Marguerite* was aided by a welcome contribution from Joseph E. Seagram and Sons Company. The Province of British Columbia hosted the Congress Dinner, Calona Wines generously provided the dinner wines. The three British Columbia universities made substantial direct grants to the Congress and all of the universities of Canada supported the Congress financially.

OPENING OF THE CONGRESS
Monday, 21 August

Dr. H. E. DUCKWORTH (*Chairman of the Congress; President and Vice-Chancellor of the University of Winnipeg and Chairman of the Association of Commonwealth Universities*) opened the Congress by welcoming delegates from member universities and other representatives and guests on behalf of the Association of Commonwealth Universities.

He introduced the two Opening Speakers, Chief Justice N. T. Nemetz and Dr. D. T. Kenny.

The Hon. N. T. NEMETZ (*Chief Justice of the Supreme Court of British Columbia*): I am indeed honoured to be able to open this great assembly representing as it does the distinguished leaders of the universities of our Commonwealth. My good friend and senior colleague, the Right Honourable Bora Laskin, was to have been present today, but he is now convalescing from a brief illness and wishes me to convey to you his greetings and best wishes for a successful conference.

This meeting, coming so soon after the completion of the recent Commonwealth Games at Edmonton, reminds one again of the continued vitality of this voluntary assembly of nations. It is a symbol of the desire of those nations and races with differing cultures to meet and talk, and in their meeting and talking establish ties of friendship in a world where this commodity is in short supply.

In 1968 I had the pleasure of attending the Tenth Commonwealth Universities Congress in Sydney. I have never forgotten the exhilarating experience of meeting the stimulating representatives of so many different nations bound together by a lingua franca and reverence for education. As on this occasion, the first scheduled speaker, Sir Eric Ashby, was unable to be present. However, his remarks were read. I well remember his reference to the role of universities in the crisis which had arisen shortly after the events at Berkeley and Berlin. He urged that there be established a code which would lay down the university teacher's duty to his pupils so as to underline the distinction between the role of a university and that of a research centre. He felt that there was justification in the criticism that in some institutions the education of the undergraduate was no longer the primary interest of the university and hence the discontent.

I think that it would be wishful thinking to imagine that the student discontent of the sixties has completely disappeared. Instead, a disturbing cynicism is pervading our campuses and, I fear, too much of our society. I believe that young people want very much to learn and prepare themselves to enter a society in which justice is ranked with knowledge as twin supporting pillars of freedom and democracy.

You will be discussing many problems arising from circumstances within and without the university gates. But society looks to you to give the leadership to so instruct the youth of our many nations that they will have not only the knowledge to form sound judgements but to spend their lifetime as devoted servants of truth, freedom and justice.

Many years ago Albert Einstein, commenting on the attributes of leadership, said: '[It is] to be able to make men not look up or down at people, but on the same level — to help build a world in which all men can walk erect — a world uncontaminated by hatred.'

In opening this great Congress I wish you well in your deliberations.

Dr. D. T. KENNY (*President of the University of British Columbia*): May I begin by extending to you, on behalf of the University of British Columbia, Simon Fraser University and the University of Victoria, a very warm welcome and to express our deep pleasure at the event we are initiating today on this campus. It is an honour to welcome to the Twelfth Commonwealth Universities Congress all delegates and observers and so many friends who share so many common concerns and interests.

I have looked forward to this day ever since I attended the last Congress in Edinburgh. That Congress was an educational landmark in intellectual excellence and gracious hospitality. I sincerely hope this Congress will prove to be equally stimulating and that we can come close to the hospitality shown by the University of Edinburgh. We have come to expect, as a matter of course, that any Commonwealth Congress will be of great significance and benefit, and this one promises to run true to form. The architects of this Congress have arranged an agenda of topics that ensures this will be the case.

It is indeed a pleasure to be your host on this campus and in a corner of the Commonwealth where individualism, independence and self-reliance are not just catchwords but a way of life today no less than in the early years of our rugged province of British Columbia.

I wish to salute especially the many of you who travelled long distances in order to contribute to this Congress. By any measure, some of you are a long way from home.

Speaking of long distances brings to mind a story during the early days of air travel within the Commonwealth when saving time wasn't always what the airlines provided. In the mid-1930s England decided to link the empire with air transport. The equipment consisted of large but slow aircraft with limited range.

One of the first flights from London to Australia attracted a full passenger load. The plane flew to northern France where it was delayed by a long spell of bad weather. It finally arrived in southern France where one of the engines failed and it was necessary to wait for another engine to be shipped by sea from England. Other delays along the route occurred in Rome, Cairo, the Middle East and India. Finally the flight reached Singapore where more repairs were required.

At this point a lady passenger asked the manager in Singapore if he thought the airplane would arrive in Australia in the next few weeks because she was expecting a baby shortly. 'My dear lady', sniffed the manager, 'you should never have commenced your trip in that condition'. She replied: 'I didn't'.

I know that times have changed since then, but I hope that all of you arrived in Vancouver speedily and without any such events happening to you.

Besides officially extending warm greetings and welcome to you, I want to add a few other words on this hopeful occasion. I call it a hopeful occasion because it is not so much the promise of an interesting week as the *hope* which should be in our minds today.

This is an historic occasion for the University of British Columbia. It is certainly historic when so many distinguished people of the Commonwealth gather in Vancouver to inaugurate this Congress. And it is our shared common origin and common purposes which finally have brought us here.

We meet today in a beautiful land, a country known for its traditions of hospitality and a nation which has long maintained the strength of ties and warmth of friendships with other Commonwealth countries. We Canadians, I assure you, are no summer patriots on this. We cherish our connections with the Commonwealth.

I hope you feel very much at home here, and very much among friends. For those who are visiting here for the first time, I should note that the province of British Columbia and the University combine the dynamism of a frontier society and the cordial hospitality of warm people.

I hope that while you are here you will have the opportunity to experience other aspects of this University and this community. The strong — almost overwhelming — combination of rain, sunshine, ocean, mountains and forests is an influence impossible to ignore. Vancouver has always been a visionary city. From here men and women have looked to the sea, the mountains and the forests. Our dreams have centred around a mixture of hopes born of these influences.

These influences also gave rise to a native culture whose art and folklore is among the most interesting in the world and which you can study in our superb new museum of anthropology. Many of you would enjoy our Nitobe Gardens here on campus, a Japanese garden created as a symbol of friendship between two Pacific-rim countries.

You can see from our port a wealth of *raw* materials flowing out across the world. This means that we are embedded in a frontier society but we also look outward around the globe. Such impressions will convey to you, accurately, that you are in a developing university in a developing province, full of vitality and hopefully aiming for excellence. Some very bright people have come here for the first time and have never left. Even if you don't do that, I hope that you will feel very welcome here and enjoy your stay at the University of British Columbia.

May this Congress be one of the most exciting and challenging.

May you take away many golden memories and new friendships.

May this Congress provide you with intellectual and other kinds of refreshment.

May each of you wear well this week.

FIRST PLENARY SESSION

Monday, 21 August

Chairman: Dr. H. E. DUCKWORTH
Chairman of the Congress; President and Vice-Chancellor of the University of Winnipeg and Chairman of the Association of Commonwealth Universities

The first speaker (Sir Charles Wilson) was introduced by Dr. J. Steven Watson (Vice-Chairman of the Association of Commonwealth Universities and Principal of the University of St. Andrews).

RECONCILING NATIONAL, INTERNATIONAL AND LOCAL ROLES OF UNIVERSITIES WITH THE ESSENTIAL CHARACTER OF A UNIVERSITY

Sir CHARLES WILSON (*Principal Emeritus of the University of Glasgow*): It is now 66 years since the Congress of universities was held at which our Association was born. The chairman of the hatching committee was the then Principal of the University of Glasgow, Sir Donald McAlister. He spoke of the links between the different universities and went on to propose 'a permanent organ for the purpose of continuing that communication of knowledge and comparison of varied experience' which had been the objects of their coming together.

These are still our objects in coming together as we do now – though with many more participants in the discussions. In 1912 there were 51 universities represented: to-day there are 221 in the ACU. There is a correspondingly wider range of experience which can be brought to bear on the subjects which interest us. Yet I do not doubt that our founding fathers, if they could revisit, would recognise what we are at and feel at home.

In the course of the many Congresses since that early day the Association has explored and discussed almost every aspect of university affairs. Some topics, as Ashby noted when he wrote up our early history, proved to be regulars. In one form or another the relations of state and university appear on every Congress agenda. Almost as frequent are postgraduate training and research, the mobility of staff in the Commonwealth, aspects of the curriculum.

Apart from the perennials, we acknowledge that we are *Zeitbedingt* and there is a pattern of contemporary pressure and response to be discerned in our choice of topics.

We were all, for example, for many years, preoccupied with the problems of expansion, with the growth in the numbers of students, of staff and of buildings, with the addition of new universities. Now in some countries the concern is with a prospective decline in numbers and with the problems of contracting resources.

Again, for fully a decade we have discussed the place of staff and students in the internal government of universities — a topic which had not shown in our papers for 40-odd years before then. We dealt with student unrest, 'teach-ins' and 'sit-ins'. Now these 'ins' are out and the topic has vanished again, for the moment, from our agenda — to be replaced by the present theme.

It is an *omnium gatherum*, compendious sort of theme and as such slightly oracular. The key words are 'roles', 'essential character' and 'reconciling'.

First, 'roles' — this is a word which has been long in use before the sociologists made it one of their basic analytical tools and showed us its great value in that capacity. We need not aim now at a strict use but perhaps we should make two observations: —

(*a*) The first observation is that every role requires a setting, every part a scenario. To understand a role fully one has to know the setting to which it relates.

(*b*) The second observation is that there is a distinction between the role and the player. Always present to our minds, though often held long in abeyance, is the distinction between the real person and the part he plays, between the real thing and the function it performs. Our theme rests on this perception by speaking of 'reconciling' the essential university with the roles which it adopts.

What kind of roles do universities adopt and what are the settings in which they are performed? In the remarks that follow I bear constantly in mind that our universities vary, in respect of all our discussions, according to the position each of our societies occupies in the gamut of development. If I make only one or two references to this fundamental fact it is simply because there is no time to do more.

In our national societies the universities are major institutions, organised, as we know, for teaching and research. Research comes first in logic and in time but, in terms of size of operation and of scale of resources employed, teaching is preponderant. Let us begin with the teaching role.

In their 'teaching role' universities take in as students a proportion of the abler youth of a country, educate them over a period of years, examine them and graduate them. Courses and curricula offer advanced study in the various branches of knowledge, in an ascending order of specialisation. The graduates of the process pass into the professions of the country, its public services, and into business and industry. A small proportion returns for further study and research before ultimate employment. The framework or setting for this teaching role is the whole structure of educational opportunity in the university's society. This in turn depends on the social organisation, the economy and the political decisions of the society.

The research role of the university is still, in part, a teaching role, with postgraduate students. But the heart of the role is advanced study and enquiry with the object of gaining new knowledge and understanding. In the paradigmatic case the two roles are continuous, so that new knowledge and understanding first qualify the teaching of the research student, than later impose revisions of the undergraduate curriculum. A good example in our lifetime would be the case of molecular biology.

It follows that the setting of the research role is the setting of the teaching role, with additional elements. These are the state apparatus of research, from government research organisations to research councils—with their associated policies, the great charitable foundations, and whatever there may be in any country in the way of independent research organisations.

Teaching and research are the first-order roles of the universities. These are the services which universities, in a phrase of Scots law, 'hold themselves out as ready to provide'. In the performance of these functions, by the nature of what is involved in them, universities are inevitably cast in another, social, role—a second-order role. By second-order I mean that it is entailed by, is the effect of, the first-order roles. It by no means follows that it is of secondary importance. On the contrary, on any judgement this additional role is of the greatest weight. What is this third role?

In the nature of the case no one is likely to be able to do advanced work who has not shown himself, in the earlier stages of his education, to be up to it. Of those who are up to it a significant proportion is collected by the universities. Whatever the principle of admission, only the abler are retained and graduated. The universities thus emerge as agents for the recruitment and certification of a main proportion of those who are to take up the higher employments of a society. From a social point of view this is a major university role, even where, as in some of our societies, it is shared by other institutions.

If these three roles, then, are the principal university roles—though we may yet want to mention others—if these are the principal ones we have now to acknowledge that almost every element of their structure, operation and setting is the object of continuous argument and controversy, within and without the universities.

There is thus defined an arena of endless debate, in which the participants, apart from ourselves, are parents and schoolchildren, politicians, teachers, civil servants, scientists, farmers, doctors, business men and industrialists, etc., etc. Into the arena go the papers of this and other conferences, our own flow of reports and literature on what we do, streams of official enquiry reports, the literature of the educational press and of the professions—again, etc., etc. The outcome of it all is the changing adaptation of our roles and of their settings.

A look into the current state of the arena would show many topics germane to the roles we are discussing, which, under renewed examination, are being restated and perhaps renamed. (Of course, many of these topics are represented in our papers.) I choose two such for a brief comment. The first goes under the current name of 'relevance'.

The word 'relevant' itself is almost empty of meaning. It means 'bearing upon', 'pertinent to' something. But to what? 'Many things in a controversy', said Jowett, 'might seem relevant, if we knew to what they were intended to refer'.

Let me suggest three points of reference for the current use of the word: —

(i) It is argued that university teaching should take more account of, be more responsive to, local and national needs and problems, and that

(ii) its research should likewise be more closely related to these needs.

(iii) It is argued further that both university teaching and research should be more concerned than they presently are with world problems—such as global resources, population, environment.

Those who make a whole philosophy out of 'relevance' would, in general, like the universities to come closer to the world of action and practice and to sacrifice some of their detachment in favour of social involvement. The range of this view is vast. In the developing countries, for example, it presents universities with demands for programmes of teaching and assistance geared to the needs of the rural areas, for active participation in national policies of social and economic development, for a special contribution to national and cultural unity. In the developed societies proposals for closer social involvement of the universities are different but still have a very wide range. As far as the teaching role is concerned, they may ask for the adjustment of admissions and curricula to national requirements for particular kinds of graduates — manpower planning. In research they may ask for less pure and more applied research, related to established scientific and technological policies. In broader social terms they may demand that universities should contribute to major changes in society — for example, to greater social and political equality.

Many of these issues have figured before in our agenda, under our old headings 'Universities and the State' and 'Universities and Society'. Our debates have, often enough, distinguished the critical questions that should concern us. For example, who tells us what 'national needs' are? Is it simply 'the government of the day'? Are these short-term or long-term needs? Will students still be free to choose what they want to study? And those science policies, economic policies, welfare policies, manpower plans — how reliable are they?

To take a UK example, we know now from experience that there are intrinsic difficulties in forecasting manpower needs *and* in responding to such forecasts within the difficult timetables of higher education. In Chicago three months ago the present Secretary of State for Education and Science summed up her government's view as follows:

> 'It is probably fair to say that we are not very wedded to the concept of higher education being essentially related to employment and manpower planning. The reason we are not very wedded to that is because we have been so badly let down by the inability of manpower planning to . . . . match manpower needs . . . . . So while manpower planning is a factor, in other words it would be one of the factors we would take into account, we would not now try to wed very closely the planning of higher education with a highly sophisticated attempt to be very precise about manpower . . . . It must be a crude exercise'.

Over the last thirty years the main effect on the British universities of policies to meet national needs (leaving aside the general expansion itself) has been significantly to increase the proportion of places made available for science and technology, as compared with non-science subjects, in the total intake of universities.

'Manpower planning' may be a special issue but it has its place in the mainstream of this current debate on relevance. In the curricular field the debate concerns the standards which a discipline must exact in order that it may be adequately handled at an advanced level: again, proficiency in any subject of advanced teaching is grounded primarily on the state of knowledge in the subject and only secondarily on the connection with social utility. In the political field the debate is about organisation, about the variety of opportunity available in the educational field — for universities need partners in higher education. The situation of a university that has to be the maid-of-all-work for the whole range of tertiary needs is not to be envied.

There are plenty of stiff questions still, then, for the Relevantines as they press their views on the universities, but they will find, nevertheless, that the universities are deeply interested in the issues they raise.

'Relevance' is one current topic taken from the arena of debate on university questions. Let me take one other — again, for very brief comment — the topic of access to our universities.

I said earlier that our main roles, of teaching and researching, entailed a second-order role of great social importance, that of selecting and finally certifying a proportion of the appropriate age-groups in our societies. The setting of this role is the structure of educational opportunity in our societies. Both the role and its setting are the subject of continuing reappraisal in all our countries in the light of changing views of social justice and political equality.

After a long historical development, access to our universities had come to rest on a basis of individual equality of merit, measured by some minimum qualification of ability and free of any discriminatory bias on grounds of race, class, religion, etc. Recent years have seen this picture modified, in response to demands for equality of treatment, not for individuals, but for groups — groups which can be shown to suffer, as groups, under handicaps in their societies. Social justice is felt to require the rescue of those who find themselves disadvantaged by ethnic, tribal or class divisions. So a quota system for groups may be grafted on to the normal admission on individual ability. The pros and cons of argument on these policies are fascinatingly presented in some of our papers. And we should certainly note here the very interesting lecture by Professor Dore. The officers of the Association are to be congratulated on having made this available to us so timeously as an Occasional Paper.*

These questions of special access are not, of course, questions only for universities—they concern the other institutions of tertiary education also—but they may be thought to raise peculiar difficulties for the universities? These are the difficulties to be discussed under Topic 3 (Reconciling Equality and Excellence).

I have left till last the question raised at the beginning, in the theme—the relation of the roles to the player. In all these things we do, is there anything we do that, properly considered, is not reconcilable with our essential character? How are we to know what is inappropriate? What are the yardsticks? What *is* our essential character? As Sir Thomas Browne was wont to say: 'These are Questions'—and perhaps, as he would sometimes go on to say (obscurely): 'They may admit a wide solution'.

We all have colleagues who are prepared to tell us they know 'what a university is for' or 'what a university is all about'. These inexpressive phrases, which are not so much communications as a sort of grunts, nevertheless assert an intuitive understanding of our institutions. Should we leave it at that level, as a kind of *communis opinio doctorum*—a sort of 'general sense of the members'? Or should we try to be more explicit?

There is no Golden Book which tells us all we need to know. It must be true that all our models are drawn from history and experience. Reflecting on that long experience, we can say what the important marks are of the institution called a university.

● It is a device of men for their general advantage, a learning and teaching device.

● It operates at the advanced levels of knowledge and therefore, characteristically, with those able enough and willing enough to learn to an advanced standard.

● It operates over a wide range of disciplines and branches of knowledge so that, as much as possible, things may be seen in relation to other things.

● It pursues these activities in order that it may make statements about the realities which are studied which are valid statements and where, as in the sciences, the chief value is truth, true statements. Such statements are, of course, also useful. Unfortunately false statements are also often useful—so our criteria are truth and validity. 'Knowledge is a good before it is a power'.

● It pursues these activities of advanced study and teaching in an environment of freedom of thought and utterance, because these are necessary conditions of best performance.

The Role of Universities in National Development, Professor R. P. Dore, Institute of Development Studies at the University of Sussex. An ACU Occasional Paper, 1978.

These are all the important marks of a university—in a thumbnail sketch. Taken together they indicate the most important contribution that universities make to society and, therefore, the roles they should play. In the end, perhaps, we reconcile what we do with what we are by giving predominance to our first-order functions: this is our prime service to the world and to our respective societies.

Over time, as they pursue their fundamental activities of advanced study and advanced teaching, universities come also to acquire representative roles. They tend to be the focus of the intellectual life of a society and of some part of its cultural traditions. But these are not really roles, not even second-order roles, because they cannot be played deliberately or pursued directly. Rather they are representative or symbolic capacities. Universities come to stand in these capacities only because and only if they are effective in their first-order roles.

All that I have said is necessarily at a high level of generality. At a detailed and concrete level the problems of right roles are much more intricate and difficult. That more detailed examination I now leave to you.

* * *

The second speaker (Sir John Crawford) was introduced by Professor Sir David Derham (Vice-Chancellor and Principal of the University of Melbourne).

THE WORLD FOOD PROBLEM AND THE UNIVERSITIES

Sir JOHN CRAWFORD (*Chancellor of the Australian National University*): The title and the time assigned to me together present a dilemma. Thus, I could take the world food problem for granted and devote all of my forty minutes to the relationship of the universities to a problem which could, however, mean different things to us all. This seems too risky; so I propose to devote at least half of my time to outlining the nature of the problem as I see it. You will, hopefully, apply my remarks to your own university as I speak. In any case a statement of the problem will make more sense of my view of the role of universities. You will, of course, appreciate that the time constraint allows only the most dogmatic approach to both parts.

I. *The World Food Problem*

For any statistics in my statement of the problem I rely mainly on the work of IFPRI (International Food Policy Research Institute). I propose to confine my description of the world situation to those countries with low incomes (per capita incomes below US$300 per annum)[1]. In these terms the problem is very much an African and Asian one—including especially South Asia (excluding Pakistan), Philippines[2], Indonesia, the countries of the sub-Sahara region and in north-east and central and east Africa[3]. More than one billion people are located in these countries situated for the most part within the tropical belt. Alas, much of the area is identical with the British red so prominent in world maps of yesteryear! In them all rural poverty is especially marked and under-employment and unemployment rife. No one can or does claim that *average* food consumption levels in these countries were adequate in 1975. They were markedly bad both for the rural landless and the urban poor. Some countries had special food distribution schemes to help the poor but nowhere were they adequate to the need. Yet this year must be our benchmark for putting the problem in more dynamic terms[4].

Let us note a few characteristics of these low income countries—in statistical terms:—

(*a*) In the period 1960 – 75 average growth in production of cereals was 2.6% p.a., the same as the estimated population growth rate for the period. If we use data for all food staples (cereals, pulses and groundnuts) the comparative figures are 2.6% population and 2.4% for food production. There is not much room for optimism in those figures.

(*b*) If we use 1975 *consumption* figures as base and *project* both the production growth achieved in 1960–75 and estimated population growth trends to 1990, the deficit in staple foods in the non-exporting low income countries will be 36 million metric tons, or 16% of the production achieved in 1975. Put another way, the

---

1 Many of the problems of which I will speak are also present in the middle and higher income groups of developing countries but nevertheless less severely because of their more adequate foreign exchange situation.
2 Probably now a little above the US$300 mark.
3 *See* IFPRI Research Report 3, *Food Needs of Developing Countries*, December 1971, Fig. 1, p.28. Attached to this paper are some tables from it.
4 In what follows I have drawn freely on the IFPRI Report above cited and on remarks made by me at the seminar marking the centenary of Lincoln College, Christchurch, New Zealand, May 1978.

increase in production required by 1990 (assuming no imports) would be 119 m. tonnes or an annual growth rate of 3% as against the 83 million tonnes which will result if the 2.4% achieved in 1960–75 is merely maintained. If we now allow for a low growth in income per capita which would increase the demand for food, the deficit would be 69 m. tonnes. To eliminate this would require a production growth rate of 3.7% p.a. (If by some new miracle high economic growth rates are achieved, the deficit or measure of additional food requirements would be some 83 million tonnes.)[5]

Please remember that the figures are projections of the 1960–75 situation, *not* forecasts[6]. Moreover it is vital to remember that we have been talking of averages and trends. The use of trends conceals the economic and social problems created by seasonal variations in production performances; while the use of average consumption per head conceals the horrible reality that a great many people (more than half the population) enjoy less than the average consumption levels. The combined work of FAO (Food and Agriculture Organisation), World Bank and IFPRI staff suggests that at least 10% needs to be added to supplies to meet this problem, since direct transfer from above-average consumers is probably impracticable. The use of an additional 10% in supplies would require more effective employment policies for the poor and probably more highly developed special national distribution systems—not to mention the greater resources required to produce that extra amount.

There are some ameliorating features to be observed. Thus:

(*a*) It is inconceivable that there will be no imports—commercial and aid—of food into these countries, especially in years when production falls below needed trend. But such imports will not solve, and never have solved, the consumption problem. Nor should they be allowed to become a substitute for more self-reliance. I will argue this point later.

(*b*) We can be encouraged by recent experience in India where the record crops of two of the last three years cannot be explained simply by good monsoons[7]. Hard evidence is available of increased and more efficient use of water and inputs, together with significant developments in multiple cropping – especially in north and north-east India. Oddly enough, however, this very success has revealed the reality of the underlying and basic problem of poverty. Stocks have mounted not only because of good crops but

---

5 It is necessary to point out, however, that in most cases a high rate of growth is not likely to occur without a contributory higher rate of growth in farm production and incomes.

6. It is true that the population estimates for 1970 take into account the past judgement of changes becoming apparent in 1975.

7. The crops of 1975–76 and 1977–78 have raised the trend line perceptibly – but it is still below the trend required to make a major improvement in nutritional status and in rural incomes.

also because people in most need have not been able to buy them as freely as is desirable. This economic fact is at the heart of our general problem, as I will further comment shortly. Nevertheless, if India can more adequately feed itself a large slice of the world problem will be eased. I rate the omens promising – but only if India sustains its active and positive policies for agricultural growth.

(c) I am not competent to comment but I am impressed by the signs of a check in population growth rates in some of the low income countries. I gladly defer to Professor Borrie's judgement (*see* p. 92, permitting myself only the obvious comment: it will be some time before this is reflected in an equivalent fall in the rate of growth of the work-force needing both employment and food.

Before we can begin to ask the question 'where do the universities come in?', a good deal more needs to be said about the character of the problems these countries *and* the rest of the world face, if solutions are to be found. I propose first to suggest reasons why the countries most in need must aim at virtual self-sufficiency in food production and then, at greater length, to demonstrate the complexity of policies required for any solution. Not the least merit of adopting this approach is that the enormous scope for contributions from universities — both in developing and developed countries — is highlighted. There is no element in the policy complex that could not, with advantage, be subject to research in the universities.

There are three strong reasons for the view that developing countries in low income groups in Africa and Asia must strive for a high degree of self-sufficiency in staple food supply. The first is that there is little prospect that aid from traditional exporters — especially North America and Australia — in the form of direct transfer of foodgrains will ever be on a scale adequate for much more than relief of famine or partial relief of crop failures. Secondly, the prospects are poor that world trade will so build up that exports from these countries will buy all the food they need. All countries in the group have had, and must continue to have, foreign exchange problems. Even India, whose position is now much improved in this respect, dare not act as though she will not again have balance of payments problems. Moreover the third reason for urging self-reliance in food supplies is one that particularly affects India, regardless of the improved foreign exchange position.

This third reason relates to the need to provide greater employment opportunities to the poor, if consumption rates are to improve in a permanently satisfactory way. For adequate consumption rates are a function not only of increased production on farms but also employment (and income earned) both on and off the farm. The majority of people in these countries are in rural areas, and underemployment and unemployment are often more marked here than in urban areas. Most of us see more of urban poverty than we do rural. Yet even a great many of the small farmers are not always able adequately to feed their families. Farms can be efficiently run but be too small to produce the minimum required. Both they and the landless labourers together with workers in village industries need more employment opportunities than are available. More intensive farming generally increases employment opportunity and any attempt to replace farm production with imports is the very opposite of social and economic wisdom in these cases.

National policy in the poorest countries must, for all these reasons, give priority to measures which promote farm production and both on- and off-farm employment. Considerable investment resources will be needed to achieve self-reliance in food supplies—a point which will emerge in the next portion of my remarks. These remarks relate to the nature and complexity of solutions required if self-reliance is to be achieved. It is my wish to show how dangerous it is to look only for the desirable but insufficient single-factor solution—for example, the achievement on a research farm of new high-yield grain varieties. At the same time the very complexity of requirements widens the scope for interaction between universities and the policy-makers and programme administrators. I will present you a list of policy ingredients and then offer a few comments[8]. Only then will I speak about the opportunities for university participation.

Condensed remarks, such as these will necessarily be, tend to give the impression of a homogeneous mass of countries with no differentiation in resources or prospects. The truth is, of course, the reverse. The policy mix will vary in content from country to country in accordance with their resources. Some countries seem unlikely ever to be free of external assistance while others, for example Sudan and India, have a prospect of greatly reducing and even removing the need for external assistance. Nonetheless the elements of policy can be stated in terms common to all.

To begin with I assume (not always safely) that each nation has some clearly stated objective: *e.g.* raising food production and improving food consumption for the population as a whole. This objective calls for a farm and rural policy which includes the following ingredients:—

(*a*) *Research and extension*: designed to provide appropriate farm technologies for small and big farmers alike, for irrigated and

---

8. In this section I will follow closely a part of my Lincoln College address above cited.

rain-fed farms. Since, for the most part, land supply is now a constraint, yields per hectare must be raised by such technologies.[9]

(b) *Price policy* and associated storage facilities—together with welfare food distribution systems.

(c) *Provision of inputs:* seed; water; fertiliser; plant and animal protection (pests and diseases); power—*e.g.* for irrigation pumps.

(d) *Provision of credit:* for farm improvement and equipment and for seasonal purposes.

[(c) and (d) call for appropriate institutions designed especially to reach the small farmers.]

(e) *Public sector investment and capital provision:* not merely to support credit institutions but also to support expansion of water supply, fertiliser supply, research capacity, supply of power (*e.g.* for using irrigation equipment), and, not least, to provide rural infrastructure such as markets, roads, schools and improved village amenities (such as drinking water and waste disposal). The provision of basic needs and off-farm employment come together in such public sector activity.

Inherent in the foregoing is the allocation of scarce foreign exchange to *priority* needs within a total programme and the encouragement of trade as at least a partial means of securing essential imports of farm inputs not producible domestically. All this requires *political will* on the part of the national leadership and administrative skills to enforce the chosen priorities. However let us assume that all is well with the leadership and the priorities are right. To get closer to the role of the universities I will now enlarge on a few, but only a few, of the foregoing list of factors involved, noting as we do the interaction among all the factors. I repeat, no one factor is sufficient unto itself.

Research and extension. I do not have to enlarge on this topic except to remind us all that research is essential to provide and maintain technologies required in all major climatic zones and for irrigated and rain-fed conditions with appropriate adaptation for the location-specific factors (especially soil, rainfall pattern and farm sizes) in all areas. I shall not elaborate on the role of international and national research systems and the necessary interaction between them—great as is the temptation! However I do want to stress that, while improved extension systems are rapidly appearing in many countries, especially in Asia, no extension system can succeed unless sound and feasible technologies are available for extension. Feasibility implies incentives and readily available inputs—for, the world over, farmers will respond to new

---
9. Higher yields per ha. is an objective of research in all countries, but in some countries—*e.g.* Sudan, Indonesia—new land areas can be opened up. The objective of research here is to determine the proper use of the soils and other national variables in these areas.

technologies if these conditions are met. It is important to stress that less than adequate progress has been made in providing sure technologies for rain-fed (*i.e.* non-irrigated) areas. Even when advanced technologies are available there often remains a gap between research results and their application in the field. But while extension must bear some of the responsibility for this gap, we cannot ignore the farmers' conservative approach to risk-taking—a factor which gives added importance to the other elements in a total policy approach. Surely here I have clearly implied a major opportunity for the agricultural scientists and social scientists of universities to work together.

Price and storage policies. These are related. Prices have to cover costs or, better put, extra investment by farmers in a new technology must meet with profitable return. But price policies require grain storage to assure floor prices, to offset seasonal variations in supplies and, not least, to enable welfare food distribution on concessional terms to the very poor. And of course storage requires access to capital as does so much else in my recital of policy ingredients. Again it would appear that engineers and economists have useful scope.

Inputs: seed, water, fertiliser, plant protection materials, power. We talk much about new on-farm technologies but often fail to realise what national industries and/or special allocations of foreign exchange are required to support them. Clearly bad seed will ruin the whole effort: yet to secure a good national seed industry in developing countries is one of the toughest projects I know. Again, power failures can bring otherwise successful irrigation farming to nought. Planning for power has to be an integral part of the agricultural sector plans. Keep these two points in mind as I now indicate the large capital cost of irrigation (in all its forms—surface, groundwater, new projects and the improvement of old ones). IFPRI has estimated that to secure an addition of 90 m.m.t. of staples (in wheat-grain equivalent) to annual output by 1990 for some 35 low income, high food deficit, developing market economies will require some US$43 billion at constant 1975 US$![10] And this will not meet all their needs. Moreover the programme assumes good water management and the use by farmers of fertilisers at levels which I happen to think a little unrealistic.[11] Farmers do not quickly move to the highest yielding points on

10. My reference is to some unpublished IFPRI material. In India alone the output from improved and new irrigated areas looked for is 64 million metric tons, and will require some $26 billion of capital work and some 6.5 million metric tons of fertilisers (NPK) as compared with total usage in 1974 – 75 of 2.74 m.m.t. These figures dominate the total world picture, but this does not make the task facing other low income countries any easier for those smaller scale economies.

11. In making estimates of response to additional fertiliser and more assured water (irrigation) planners tend to use response ratios, *e.g.* of 10 kgs. of grain to 1 kg. of fertiliser nutrients, which are dependent on close to optimum usage of the input. Farmers tend, because they are conservative or cannot afford to raise the cost, to operate lower down the production curve.

production curves—a point social scientists and agronomists have made to policy-makers but will need continually to stress. Alas, irrigation is not and cannot be a mainstay in very many countries. Fortunately it is a major feature which can be enhanced in India and Bangladesh. Indeed in all countries the effort to make advances in rain-fed technology has to be stepped up with all the resources we can muster—a matter of considerable importance for priorities in allocation of research funds in which universities in developing countries should share.

Public sector capital. This heading may not seem germane to the role of the universities. However it is important to stress it, if only to make clear that no matter how great the contribution of the university in particular fields all will come to nought if the right priority is not given to allocating and securing the investment capital needed. I have indicated in one field only—irrigation—the large capital sums required. When we think of power, roads, transport, in addition to irrigation and not to mention basic human needs in rural villages and towns, we can readily recognise a major economic problem. It is here that foreign assistance assumes great importance in most countries—but it is rarely available to the extent of enabling any country to avoid the difficult issue of raising the bulk of capital internally. Fortunately the employment value of such investment is gaining better recognition, despite the difficulty that emerges when food is not available to meet the higher demand that flows from extra wages.

Land reform. This is a topic calculated to arouse the passions of some social scientists. If I have not made much of it, it is not to deny its importance in some countries. Thus land consolidation is vital in India and Bangladesh, countries characterised by a very high proportion of small fragmented holdings. In India as a whole some 70% of all operational holdings are under 2 ha. Of these only 60% of the holdings in each category are wholly or partially, mostly partially, irrigated. The greatest concentration of very small holdings is in the eastern states of Orissa, Bihar, West Bengal and Uttar Pradesh. The real point of stress here, however, is the fragmented nature of a very large proportion of the holdings—a fact which makes it difficult to apply policies which require whole farms for their application. It is not uncommon for very small holdings to be in six or more pieces scattered around the village concerned. Fortunately consolidation is proceeding and will steadily make it easier to adopt improved technologies.[12] But while it is going on

---

12. This problem of fragmentation does not exist in the collective holdings which characterise the farms of the production groups operating within the commune system in China. In this system the farms are collectives but the production teams in each case are the direct beneficiaries of increased productivity on the holdings.

much else can and must be done — even *e.g.* the provision of water to fragments of holdings not yet consolidated.

II. *Role of the Universities*

To follow the logic of what I have been saying would suggest some discussion now on the scope of international action on all these fronts. The need for large transfers from the developed world of capital and skills is apparent. Less apparent but no less real is the need for improved flows and pricing of goods in world trade. But these are not my subject. It is, indeed, high time to be more explicit about the role of universities in furthering the effectiveness of the kinds of policies I have outlined. I will now try to do so hoping and believing that many here will, during the week, add flesh to the mere skeleton I present. No doubt many will suggest that I have in any case omitted vital parts of the skeleton itself.

The customary and natural approach in talking of the public role of universities is through their seen responsibilities for imparting knowledge and for adding to it: teaching and research. This duality of functions covers much, if not all, of what needs to be said. But there is first a general point to be made. If allowed to function reasonably in a developing country, a university will almost inevitably have a pervasive influence in the social and economic development of its country, or of its region in the case of large countries like India. Certainly it is desirable, as the British Inter-University Council for Higher Education Overseas (IUC) has observed,[13] that the universities in developing countries provide leaders of thought and so act as agents of change. This will emerge in most Commonwealth countries in the civil service and in private and public enterprises where university graduates will be found. This is properly an important part of their role as agents for change. Another part of this role is to be found in their direct research activities and in the fact that they will train research workers for employment in public research institutions.

The emphasis on research as the root of change is not inappropriate, for, as I have earlier stressed, there is no escape from rural poverty and no progress to greater self-sufficiency in food production unless technologies are provided which will yield more per hectare of land or enable new lands to be opened up than can be expected from traditional technologies. But we have learned from the frustrations experienced in the development of the benefits of

---

13. *Rural Development Overseas:* First Thoughts on the Co-operative Role of British Universities and Polytechnics, 1976, p.9. This is a very constructive report which contains much that is relevant to the debate this coming week.

the 'green revolution' that much more than a new high-yielding variety of rice or wheat is required. My paper has been wasted if I have not convinced you that a wide array of policies and programmes have to be developed before real fruit comes from progress in the research laboratory. The scope for social science research is obvious. Indeed progress requires research and consequential investment and institutions to ensure the necessary progress. Naturally the whole responsibility for the decisions to be made lies outside the universities: but they have a large contribution to offer. I refer primarily to the universities in developing countries but, as will emerge, I do not exclude the universities in developed countries from an important role in support of the developing countries.

I have rather stressed the role of investment: the need is pervasive in all elements of the total solution. The universities are no exception to this need for investment if they are to function as a vital part in developing and applying new technologies. Governments cannot be blamed for requiring a mission-oriented approach in a sizeable part of university research operations; but these operations will fail without investment support. This admonition applies not only to the allocation of domestic resources but also to external support activities. Fortunately this recognition of the need for investment in universities is now an increasingly significant feature of the development assistance programmes of the developed country members of the Commonwealth. It is also a well-recognised part of major non-Commonwealth activity. I refer especially to US AID activities in research and to the World Bank. The latter is particularly stressing the role of universities in research and related activities and is suiting its actions to its words in its lending programme.

There is a danger that one exaggerates the possible contribution of university research to national economic and social development: this is because agricultural and rural research is rarely a full-time activity of staff. Nevertheless I am more concerned about underestimating it. Both the natural scientists and social scientists have a prime opportunity to adapt results from elsewhere (*e.g.* new high-yielding varieties) to the district and regional environment in which they operate. They may well also initiate promising results for testing on a wider scale at other centres. In short, universities can be part of a wider national and, I stress, international network, while concentrating on the region they serve.[14] This is the approach being adopted by the government of India and the World Bank in a

---

14. A region may, of course, be a whole country, depending on the range of environmental and social conditions in the country. In this respect countries like Nigeria and India must be seen as equivalent to many quite different regions.

currently evolving major project for developing the research capability of India's agricultural universities. Not the least reason for taking this approach is to provide a stronger location-specific research support to the efforts of the extension service to promote and adapt improved technologies for use by farmers in the field.

Altogether, I see the role of the university in research as both localised and as an integral part of a national and international system. Some of its better graduates can be encouraged to continue in research; the others must at least understand its importance for they will more than likely influence civil service and political understanding of its importance.[15] The more directly a university can contribute to regional and national problem-solving the more likely will it have influence on the course of policy.

I am not arguing that universities in developing countries should be wholly responsible for national research. For the most part I see the need otherwise. But I do see them as contributing trained research workers to the national system as well as making a direct contribution to solving some national and regional problems. There is today a growing network of relations between international agricultural research centres and national research systems in developing countries. I cannot say that the linkage with universities is as yet satisfactory: I would like to see this more strongly developed. One way to do this would be to encourage staff and postgraduate workers from the universities to spend time at these centres on problems of mutual interest. Again staff from developing country universities should be given opportunities to participate in network operations such as that of the International Rice Research Institute group which is studying the gap between promise and actuality in rice yields. This area of co-operation could be a fruitful project for assistance from development assistance agencies in the developed countries.

Role of universities in the developed countries. With exceptions, it is likely that universities in developing countries will be but moderately equipped for teaching and research. This statement, unfortunately, is just as true of many so-called national research systems in developing countries. This suggests an obvious backstop role for universities in developed countries. With the more sophisticated equipment available to them they can often better tackle, than can developing countries, basic problems standing in the way of solutions of field constraints on more productive

---

15. Professor McClymont of University of New England, New South Wales, puts it well in a 1975 report by him to FAO on Formal Education and Rural Development: 'If the University's approach to teaching is solely to produce specialized graduates in arts, science, economics, law, engineering, agriculture, etc. with *no shared understanding of the problems of rural development*, then the national approach to rural development is likely to be as deficient as the graduates' understanding of it' (Section 9, p.15).

agriculture. This same relation can usefully be available in respect of developed country universities and the international research centres. But our subject is the role of universities—especially those in the Commonwealth. My remaining few minutes will therefore be devoted to relations between universities in the developed and those in the developing countries of the Commonwealth.

Great Britain, Canada and—alas, so far much more modestly—Australia, are developing programmes which do encourage inter-university relations—both in the training of graduates (and sometimes staff) and in support of developing countries. The agencies concerned increasingly see the proper role for their own universities as:

(a) tackling, at the request of developing countries and universities, research problems beyond the capacity of the research centres and universities in those countries;

(b) sharing in research programmes on a university-to-university basis—in all fields of science pertinent to economic and social development; and

(c) offering training facilities in the advanced country in the interest of accelerating the build-up of research capacity in the developing countries.[16] Hardly less important is assistance in developing the training facilities available in the universities in the developing countries.

I have long been particularly impressed by the good sense that marks the United Kingdom's programmes for relating UK universities to those in the developing world,[17] but I will be readily understood if I refer especially today to the work of agencies and universities in our host country. CIDA (Canadian International Development Agency) has greatly strengthened university-to-university linkages; while IDRC (International Development Research Centre) has in its entire programme sought to encourage and facilitate capacity in developing countries for solving their own problems through their own institutions. It has also supported Canadian universities acting as backstops to the International Research Centre.

In a memorandum sent to me by Dr. J. King Gordon of IDRC my attention has been drawn to two points of change since Colombo Plan days. One is the increasing effort to strengthen self-reliance in developing countries—a process which has brought universities more to the front than they were. The second is the growing wish of universities in Canada (as also in Australia) to play a greater role as

16. Apparently not yet fully operational and in a somewhat uncertain state, activities under the Title XII Programme in the United States will finally amount to a massive effort to strengthen research capability in developing countries. Hopefully the universities in the Commonwealth developing countries will share in this.

17. See the reports of the Inter-University Council earlier cited and of the Ministry of Overseas Development (ODM).

principals rather than as adjuncts only to official assistance programmes. Alas, such ambitions are limited by funds. There is room for further rationalisation of their relationship with assistance agencies in the hope of providing more funds and more direct contact and negotiation between universities in the developed countries and those in developing countries. A step in this direction appears to have been taken by Canada in the establishment of an International Development Office (IDO), financed jointly by CIDA and IDRC. It is designed 'to facilitate co-operation and co-ordination of Canadian higher education institutions in international development programmes'. I very much hope that the committees this week will have an opportunity to pursue these matters further around the theme of how to mobilise developed Commonwealth (university) resources more effectively in support of 'research and university infra-structure of developing countries'.[18]

Here I stop. In the IUC publication earlier cited, dealing with the co-operative role of British universities, mention is made (p.10) of the moral responsibility of universities. Not being a professional philosopher I have not debated this question: I simply accept the view that a moral responsibility does rest with us to mobilise university resources for betterment. Moreover I believe it worthwhile in the sense that results are achievable. In this respect I think of India's improved position now in contrast to 1967 when one university leader in the developed world (Professor Ehrlich of Stanford) brashly and harshly announced that the battle of the 'imbalance between food and population' was lost, and that India and other countries like it should be written off as irredeemable. This is the philosophy of triage which is both completely immoral and, fortunately, completely wrong in judgement. Instead of urging the United States and the Commonwealth to cast our poorest nations adrift, I know all here will agree that the obligation of our universities is to play a positive role in development. We can be confident that success is achievable.

---

18. The words are King Gordon's used in the statement referred to above.

THE WORLD FOOD PROBLEM [Crawford]

ANNEX

The tables and charts in this Annex are (with one exception) all taken with permission from *Research Report No. 3* published by the International Food Policy Research Institute (IFPRI), 1776 Massachusetts Avenue, NW, Washington, DC, USA 20036. IFPRI is an independent non-profit organisation that conducts research on policy problems related to the food needs of the developing world. It is controlled by an international board and its staff is also widely international in composition.

Note.—Not all the tables and charts from Research Report No. 3 *have been reproduced, but cross-references to those that are omitted have been retained.*

TABLE 1: ANNUAL GROWTH RATES OF STAPLE CROP PRODUCTION NEEDED BY FOOD DEFICIT DEVELOPING MARKET ECONOMIES TO MEET CONSUMPTION REQUIREMENTS IN 1990 (by IFPRI category and region)

IFPRI category	Projected production growth rate 1975–1990	*Required production growth rate to meet consumption requirement in 1990[a]*			
		At 1975 per capita level	Low income growth	High income growth	At 110% of energy requirement
Low income	2·4	3·0	3·7	3·9	4·4
Middle income	3·5	3·7	4·3	4·5	3·9
High income	2·4	5·9	7·2	7·6	6·4
Total DME*	2·7	3·4	4·1	4·4	4·4
Region					
Asia	2·5	3·1	3·7	4·0	4·3
	(2·8)	(3·0)	(3·6)	(3·9)	(4·1)
North Africa/ Middle East	2·5	4·2	4·9	5·2	5·0
Sub-Sahara Africa	2·2	3·2	4·0	4·4	4·6
Latin America	3·7	3·9	4·5	4·6	4·1
	(3·6)	(2·6)	(3·2)	(3·3)	(2·8)
Total DME*	2·7	3·4	4·1	4·4	4·4
	(2·9)	(3·1)	(3·8)	(4·0)	(4·0)

Note.—The figures in parentheses include the grain-exporting countries.

(a) Based on the trend value of production for 1975.

* Developing market economies.

FIGURE 1: DEVELOPING MARKET ECONOMIES BY IFPRI CATEGORY

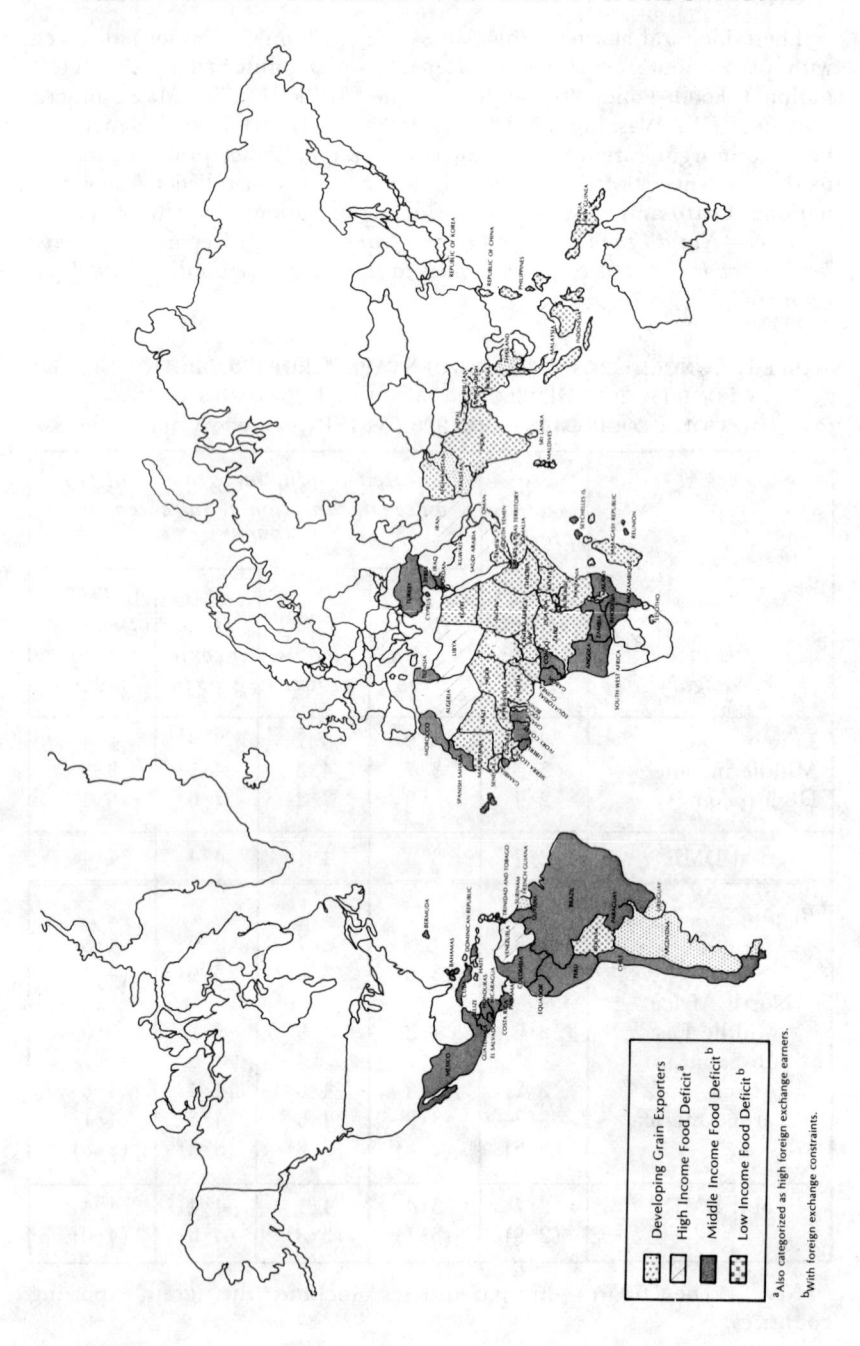

THE WORLD FOOD PROBLEM [Crawford]

FIGURE 2: DISTRIBUTION OF THE PRODUCTION OF MAJOR STAPLES IN DEVELOPING MARKET ECONOMIES, BY REGION, 1975 – 76*

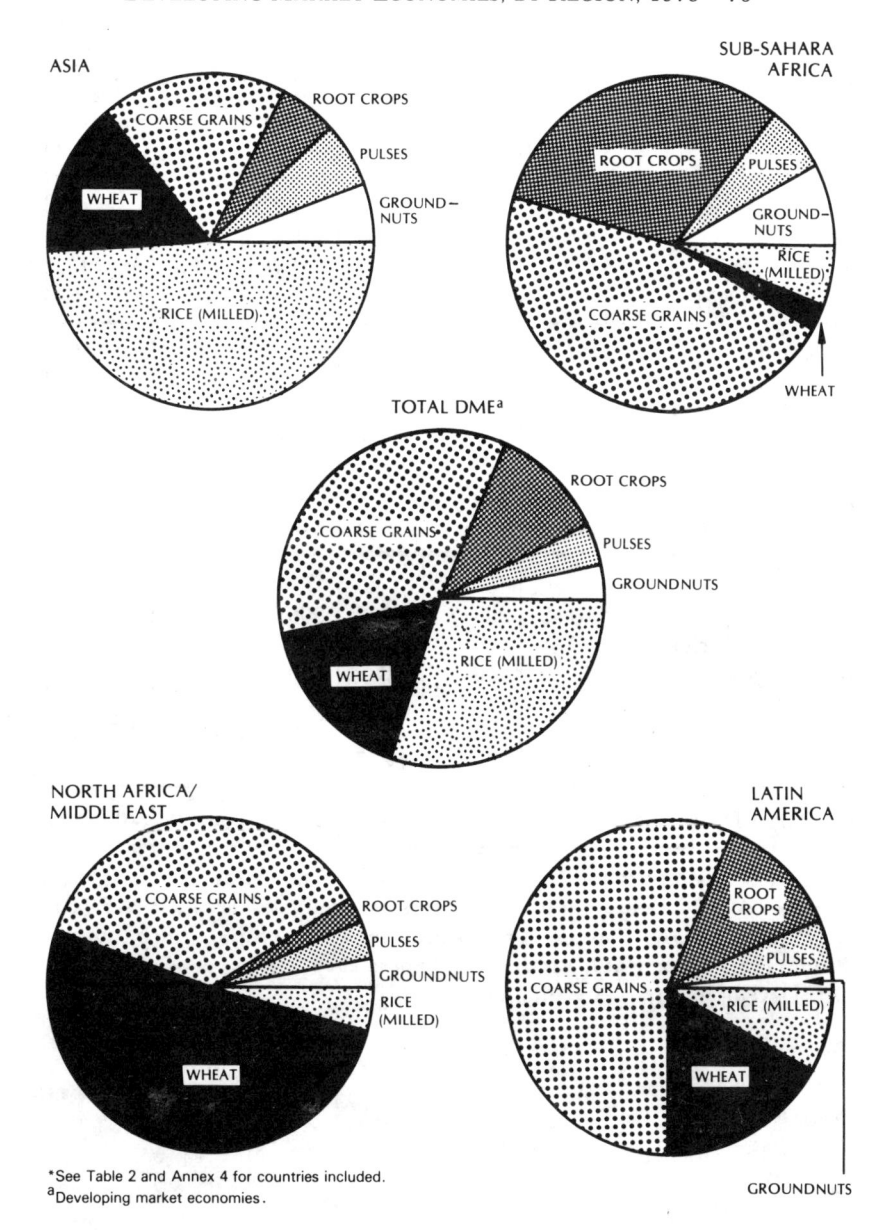

*See Table 2 and Annex 4 for countries included.
[a] Developing market economies.

TABLE 5: FOOD PRODUCTION AND CONSUMPTION IN DEVELOPING MARKET ECONOMIES, by IFPRI category and region, 1975 and 1990

(million metric tons)

	Food prodn.		Food consumption			
	1975	1990	1975	1990		
IFPRI category				At 1975 per capita level	Low income growth	High income growth
Food deficit	351·8	510·2	385·2	566·9	626·6	649·4
Low income	230·6	318·8	242·0	349·4	384·5	398·3
Middle income	99·2	160·0	108·6	165·1	179·6	184·5
High income	21·9	31·4	34·6	52·3	62·4	66·6
Grain exporters	47·2	88·4	34·9	51·9	55·6	56·5
Total DME*	399·0	598·6	420·1	618·8	682·2	705·9
Region Asia	201·8	298·2	211·2	305·7	336·6	348·1
North Africa/ Middle East	50·9	70·5	60·5	90·1	100·3	104·3
Sub-Sahara Africa	56·6	77·9	58·8	90·4	101·6	106·6
Latin America	89·7	151·9	89·7	132·7	143·6	146·9
Total DME*	399·0	598·6	420·1	618·8	682·2	705·9

Sources of basic data: UN Economic and Social Affairs Department, 'Selected World Demographic Indicators by Countries' (ESA/P/WP 55), May 1975; USDA, Foreign Agricultural Service, Computer Printout on Production, 1975; FAO, Production Tapes, 1975.

* Developing market economies.

FIGURE 3: ALL FOOD DEFICIT DEVELOPING MARKET ECONOMIES: PRODUCTION AND CONSUMPTION OF MAJOR STAPLES, 1960 – 75 AND PROJECTED 1990*

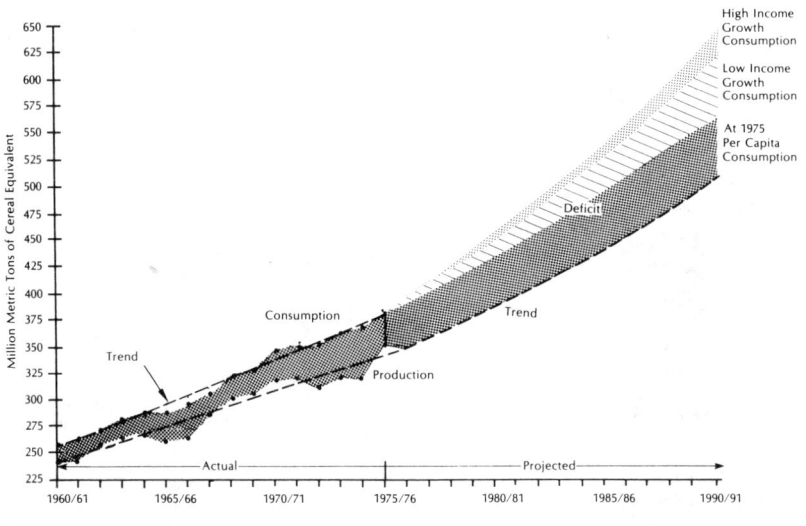

*See Annex 4 for countries included.

FIGURE 4: LOW INCOME FOOD DEFICIT DEVELOPING MARKET ECONOMIES: PRODUCTION AND CONSUMPTION OF MAJOR STAPLES 1960 – 75 AND PROJECTED 1990*

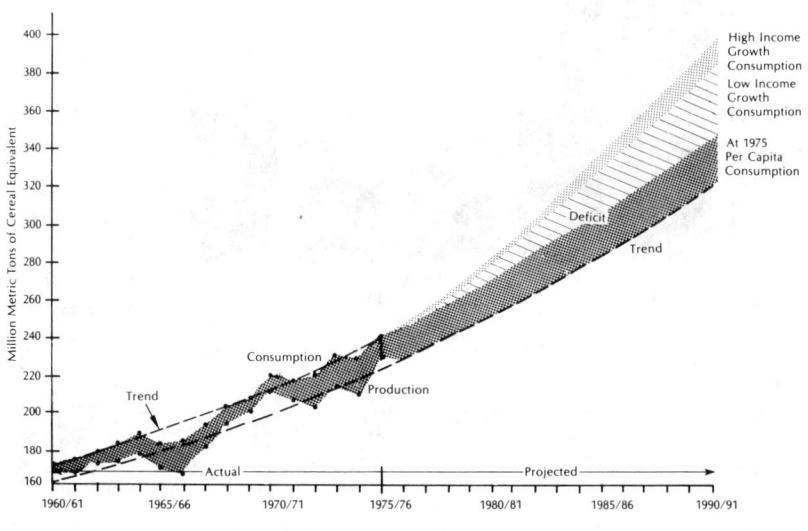

*See Annex 4 for countries included.

[Crawford]   FIRST PLENARY SESSION: ADDRESSES

FIGURE 5: DEVELOPING MARKET ECONOMIES: PROJECTED 1990 PRODUCTION AND CONSUMPTION OF MAJOR STAPLES, BY REGION*

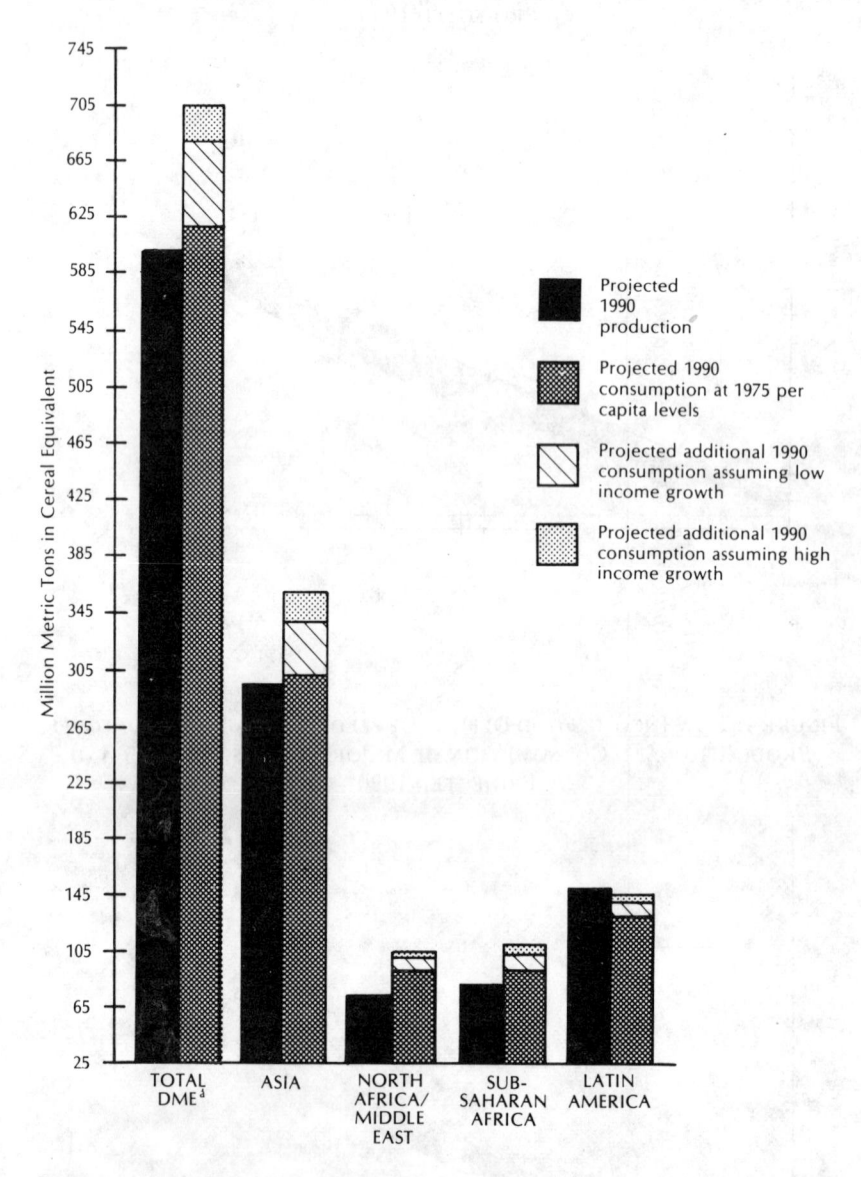

■ Projected 1990 production
▨ Projected 1990 consumption at 1975 per capita levels
▧ Projected additional 1990 consumption assuming low income growth
▦ Projected additional 1990 consumption assuming high income growth

(Y-axis: Million Metric Tons in Cereal Equivalent)

Regions: TOTAL DME[a], ASIA, NORTH AFRICA/MIDDLE EAST, SUB-SAHARAN AFRICA, LATIN AMERICA

[a] Developing market economies.
*See Table 5, above. See Annex 4 for countries included.

TABLE 6: GROSS AND NET DEFICITS OF MAJOR STAPLES IN DEVELOPING MARKET ECONOMIES, by IFPRI category and region, 1975 and 1990[a]

(million metric tons)

IFPRI category	1975 Gross	1975 Net	1990 At 1975 per capita level Gross	1990 At 1975 per capita level Net	1990 Low income growth Gross	1990 Low income growth Net	1990 High income growth Gross	1990 High income growth Net
Food deficit								
Low income	36.2	33.4	71.6	56.7	121.1	116.4	143.1	139.2
Middle income	12.1	11.4	35.9	30.6	69.0	65.7	82.6	79.5
High income	11.4	9.3	14.8	5.1	21.1	19.6	25.3	24.5
	12.7	12.7	21.0	21.0	31.1	31.1	35.2	35.2
Grain exporters	0.7	(12.2)	...	(36.5)	...	(32.8)	...	(31.9)
Total DME*	36.9	21.2	71.6	20.2	121.1	83.5	143.1	107.3
Region								
Asia	13.5	9.3	22.3	7.5	49.6	38.4	60.3	50.0
North Africa/Middle East	11.5	9.6	20.8	19.5	30.0	29.8	34.1	33.8
Sub-Sahara Africa	2.6	2.2	17.1	12.4	27.4	23.7	32.1	28.7
Latin America	9.3	(0.0)	11.5	(19.3)	14.1	(8.3)	16.6	(5.1)
Total DME*	36.9	21.2	71.6	20.2	121.1	83.5	143.1	107.3

Note.—The figures in parentheses indicate surpluses.
* Developing market economies.
(a) Gross deficit represents the sum of the production deficits of major staples in food-short countries of the indicated group of DMEs. Net deficit is gross deficit minus the surpluses of major staples of countries within the group; it is also equal to the difference between total production and total consumption of the group.

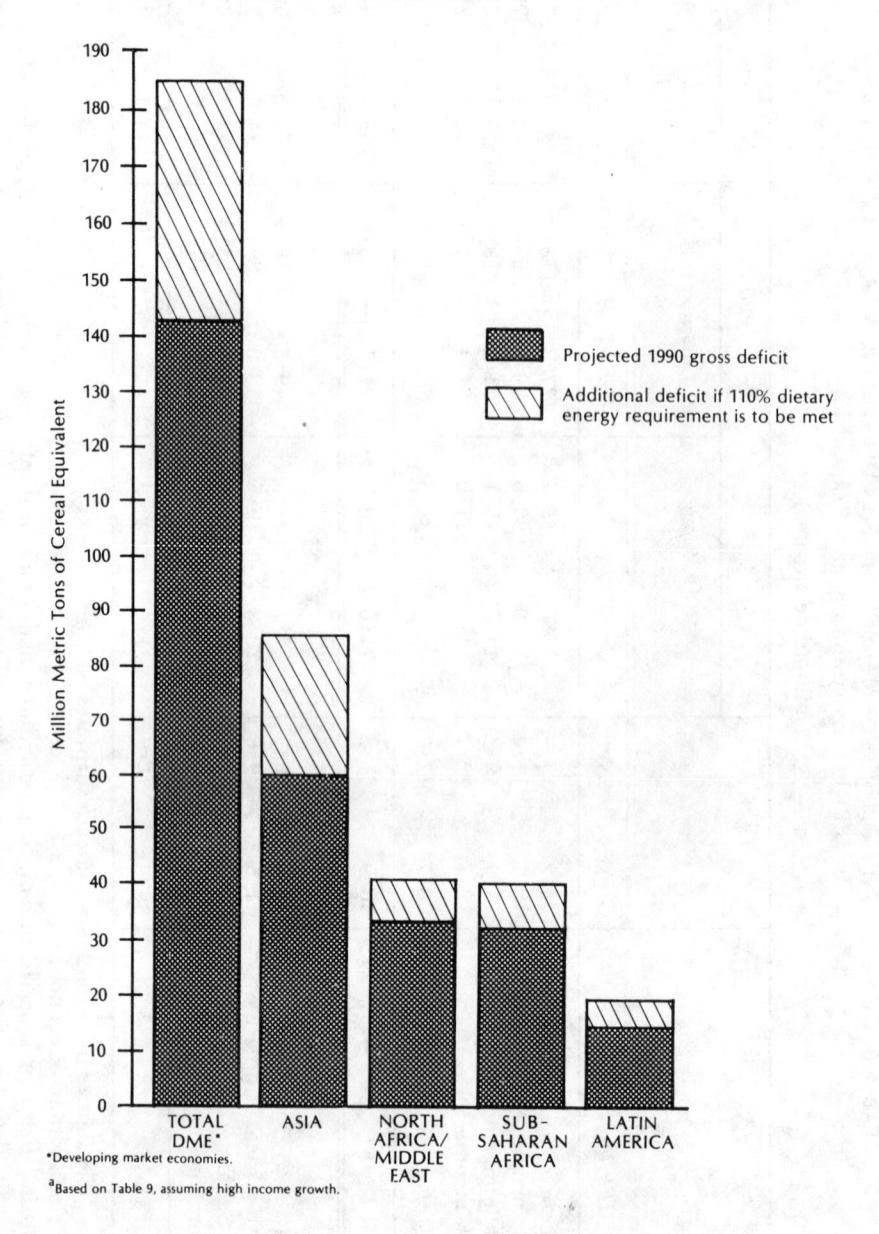

FIGURE 6: PROJECTED 1990 GROSS DEFICITS TO MEET MARKET DEMAND AND ENERGY STANDARDS IN DEVELOPING MARKET ECONOMIES, BY REGION[a]

[a] Based on Table 9, assuming high income growth.

*Developing market economies.

THE WORLD FOOD PROBLEM [Crawford]

FIGURE 7: PROJECTED 1990 PRODUCTION AND CONSUMPTION OF MAJOR STAPLES IN SELECTED ASIAN DEVELOPING MARKET ECONOMIES*

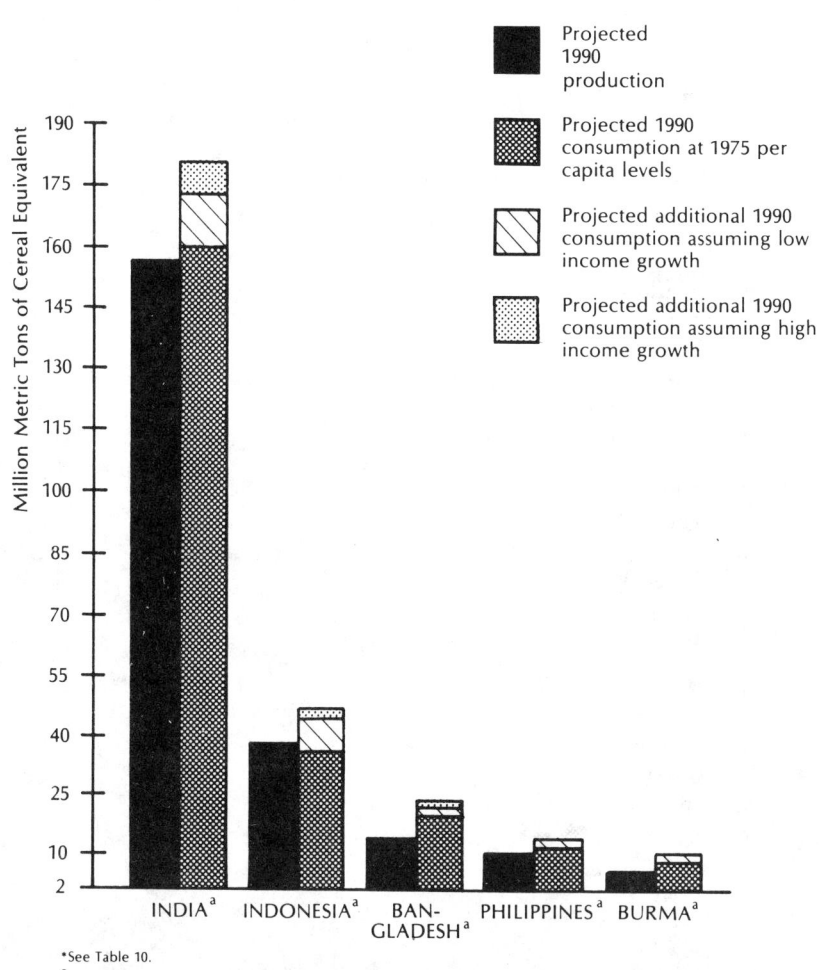

■ Projected 1990 production

▨ Projected 1990 consumption at 1975 per capita levels

◩ Projected additional 1990 consumption assuming low income growth

▦ Projected additional 1990 consumption assuming high income growth

[Bar chart: Million Metric Tons of Cereal Equivalent for INDIA[a], INDONESIA[a], BANGLADESH[a], PHILIPPINES[a], BURMA[a]]

*See Table 10.
[a] Low income countries.

ANNEX 3: IFPRI COUNTRY CATEGORIES

A. *Developed Exporters*
   1. Australia
   2. Canada
   3. South Africa
   4. United States

B. *Developed Importers*
  1. East Europe
     a. Albania
     b. Bulgaria
     c. Czechoslovakia
     d. East Germany
     e. Hungary
     f. Poland
     g. Romania
     h. Yugoslavia

  2. EEC: Euro-Six
     a. Belgium
     b. France
     c. Germany
     d. Italy
     e. Luxembourg
     f. Netherlands

  3. EEC: Euro-Three
     a. Denmark
     b. Ireland
     c. United Kingdom

  4. Japan

  5. USSR

  6. Other Importers
     a. Austria
     b. Finland
     c. Greece
     d. Iceland
     e. Israel
     f. Malta
     g. New Zealand
     h. Norway
     i. Portugal
     j. Spain
     k. Sweden
     l. Switzerland

C. *Developing Grain Exporters*
  1. Argentina
  2. Pakistan
  3. Thailand
  4. Other Exporters: Surinam, Uruguay

D. *Developing Countries with Foreign Exchange*[1]
   1. Asia Group
      a. Malaysia
      b. Republic of Korea
      c. Republic of China
      d. Other Asia, Brunei, Hong Kong, Singapore
   2. North Africa/Middle East (OPEC Group)
      a. Algeria
      b. Iraq
      c. Iran
      d. Libya
      e. Saudi Arabia
      f. Other OPEC: Bahrain, Kuwait, Oman, Qatar, United Arab Emirates
   3. Latin America: Venezuela
E. *Developing Countries with Foreign Exchange Constraints*[2]
   (Countries marked * are oil exporters which are likely to improve reserve positions.)
   1. Asian Market Economies
      a. Bangladesh
      b. Burma
      c. India
      d. Indonesia
      e. Nepal
      f. The Philippines
      g. Sri Lanka
      h. Other Asia: Bhutan, Macao, Pacific Islands, Papua New Guinea, Maldive Islands
   2. Centrally Planned Asia
      a. People's Republic of China
      b. Other Centrally Planned Asia: Cambodia; Laos; Mongolia; Vietnam, Socialist Republic of; Korea, Democratic People's Republic of
   3. North Africa/Middle East (Non-OPEC)
      a. Middle Income
         (1) Morocco
         (2) Turkey
         (3) Other Middle Income: Cyprus, Jordan, Lebanon, Syria, Tunisia
      b. Low Income
         (1) Afghanistan
         (2) Egypt
         (3) Sudan
         (4) Yemen Arab Republic
         (5) Yemen, People's Democratic Republic of

1. Also categorized as high income countries.
2. The developing market economies are grouped by income based on the average 1973 GNP per capita: middle income, US$300 or more; and low income, less than US$300. The Asian market economies all fall under the low-income group.

4. Sub-Sahara Africa
   West
   a. Middle Income
      (1) Ghana
      (2) Other Middle Income: *Angola, Cape Verde Isles, Ceuta and Melilla, Congo, *Gabon, Guinea-Bissau, Ivory Coast, Liberia, Namibia, Sao Toma and Principe, Spanish Sahara
   b. Low Income
      *(1) Nigeria
      (2) Sahel Countries: Chad, Mali, Mauritania, Niger, Senegal, Upper Volta
      (3) Other Low Income: Benin, Cameroon, Central African Empire, Equatorial Guinea, Gambia, Guinea, Sierra Leone, Togo

   East
   a. Middle Income
      (1) Mozambique, Rhodesia, Zambia
      (2) Other Middle Income: French Territory of Afars & Issas, Mauritius, Reunion, Seychelles Islands, Swaziland
   b. Low Income
      (1) Ethiopia
      (2) Kenya
      (3) Tanzania
      (4) Uganda
      (5) Zaire
      (6) Other Low Income: Botswana, Burundi, Comoros Islands, Lesotho, Malagasy, Malawi, Rwanda, Somalia

5. Latin America
   a. Middle Income
      (1) Brazil
      (2) Chile
      (3) Colombia
      *(4) Ecuador
      (5) Mexico
      (6) Peru
      (7) Other Latin America: Bahamas, Barbados, Belize, Bermuda, Costa Rica, Cuba, Dominican Republic, El Salvador, French Guiana, Guatemala, Guyana, Honduras, Jamaica, Nicaragua, Panama, Paraguay, Puerto Rico, *Trinidad and Tobago, other Caribbean Isles
   b. Low Income: Bolivia, Haiti

FIGURE 1: COUNTRY CLASSIFICATION†

	Falling per capita cereal prod. trend	*Increasing per capita cereal prod. trend*

I. Very severe food-deficit countries with very high potential intervention cost in relation to GNP and current imports:

Intervention cost is greater than 9% of GNP

high import burden	Rwanda Guinea Mali Ethiopia Upper Volta Yemen A.R. Chad Afghanistan Niger Bangladesh Somalia	Burundi

II. Serious food-problem countries with a high potential intervention cost in relation to GNP:

Intervention cost is less than 8% but greater than 3% of GNP

high import burden	Nigeria Burma Tanzania Haiti Nepal Bolivia	Zaire Pakistan Uganda India Sudan Sri Lanka Indonesia
lower import burden	Benin Sierra Leone Mozambique Kenya Gambia	El Salvador Philippines Malawi

III. Countries with an intermediate potential intervention cost in relation to GNP:

Intervention cost is less than 3% but greater than 1% of GNP

high import burden	Senegal	
lower import burden	Liberia Lebanon Malagasy R. Honduras Cameroon	Angola Colombia Guatemala

IV. Food-problem countries with a relatively low potential intervention cost in relation to GNP:

Intervention cost is less than 1% of GNP;
calorie supply is less than 106% of requirement

high import burden	Egypt	
lower import burden	Jordan Panama Syria Peru Guyana	Zambia Brazil Ghana Dominican Rep. Rhodesia Nicaragua Ivory Coast Surinam Tunisia Trinidad-Tobago

Note. — OPEC countries excluded.
†From IFPRI Report 'Recent and Prospective Developments in Food Consumption: Some Policy Issues', 6 January, 1977.

Group Discussions

TOPIC 1

THE WORLD FOOD PROBLEM AND THE UNIVERSITIES

Chairman: Sir JOHN CRAWFORD
Chancellor of the Australian National University

Editorial Co-ordinator: Mr. F. S. HAMBLY
Secretary of the Australian Vice-Chancellors' Committee

		page
Sub-Topic 1(a)	PRODUCTION POTENTIAL	
	Opening Speakers	
	Professor R. S. Musangi	55
	Sardar B. S. Samundri	63
	Dr. L. H. Shebeski	77
	Discussion	91
Sub-Topic 1(b)	POPULATION	
	Opening Speakers	
	Professor W. D. Borrie	92
	Professor S. Chandrasekhar	104
	Professor H. P. Oberlander	117
	Discussion	123
Sub-Topic 1(c)	ENERGY	
	Opening Speakers	
	Professor D. W. George	126
	Dr. B. D. Nag Chaudhuri	137
	Professor C. M. Switzer	146
	Discussion	155
Sub-Topic 1(d)	HEALTH	
	Opening Speakers	
	Professor J. D. Gillett	158
	Professor A. Omololu	175
	Discussion	180
Chairman's Response to Discussion		182

For index to names, see p. 655

Sub-Topic 1(a)

PRODUCTION POTENTIAL

Chairman: Professor Ungku A. AZIZ
Vice-Chancellor of the University of Malaya

Rapporteur: Professor J. D. STEWART
Principal of Lincoln College

Monday, 21 August

Professor R. S. MUSANGI (*Head of the Department of Animal Production, University of Nairobi*): The prevention of malnutrition throughout the world through the provision of adequate diets for a rapidly expanding population is a task of staggering proportions. Solution to this problem is perhaps the greatest challenge facing nations of the world today. The United Nations World Food Conference held in Rome in November 1974 called on governments and the international community to eradicate hunger and malnutrition in the world within a decade. In arriving at this decision the conference participants were well aware of the magnitude of the nutritional problems facing much of the world, especially the developing countries. In many developing countries the main problem is not only the periodic lack of adequate food supplies but also that, when the food is available, it is imbalanced in terms of proteins and energy. The main defect, however, is a shortage of protein, producing its most severe and tragic effects in children leading to a condition commonly known as Kwashiorkor (an extreme deficiency of protein in the diet).

This paper will, therefore, attempt to assess the production potential of world food and the role various institutions, including universities, can play in exploiting this potential in order to meet expected food production targets such as those set by the Rome conference.

The Status of World Food Supply

While most developing countries have increased their agricultural output, increases in production have not kept pace with rising consumption. It is now apparent that the world food and feed production barely keep pace with population growth and reserve stocks have declined. During 1960 – 74 the volume of food imports into developing countries grew at the rate of 4·4% per year. During the last four years of that period, at a time of rising prices, they grew at 6·2% annually. Thus the food's share of the import bill rose substantially during 1970 – 74. At the same time the oil import bill rose dramatically. These developments suggest that the problem of financing adequate food imports may become a major barrier to adequate consumption in many developing countries.

Leaving aside the problem of financing, it is difficult to foresee the needed supplies forthcoming. On the trade side, the major developed grain exporters (the United States, Canada and Australia) would need to approach annual increases in production of 4% compared with their long-term growth rate of 2·5% in order to accommodate only the aggregate market and calorie gaps of the developing countries. If such large supplies are to be produced, which is at least questionable, they would be forthcoming only at higher prices, thus aggravating the transfer problem between the exporters and the needy importers. The developing countries, for their part, need to increase their production growth rate from the present 3% to almost 6% annually to meet their food needs. This is an unlikely prospect considering the long gestation period between investment in agricultural projects and the realisation of significant gains in production. It is, therefore, true to say that, unless a concerted effort is made very soon by various governments, the international community and various institutions to increase food production, a calamity of major proportions may occur in the foreseeable future.

Increasing Food Production

The most important methods of increasing food supplies are to put more land into agricultural production and to increase the output per hectare of land through the increased use of inputs such as fertilizers, improved genetic strains of both animals and plants, mechanisation and skill. Many developing countries have applied a combination of these methods with great success. For example, national programmes such as the wheat programmes of Mexico and

SUB-TOPIC 1(A): PRODUCTION POTENTIAL

Pakistan, the All-India crops scheme and the Kenya maize programme should be considered as models for developing similar programmes in other countries.

There are, however, major problems limiting global food production, especially in the developing countries. These problems are broadly related to land availability, climatic changes, use of appropriate technologies to increase food production, and the availability of skilled manpower.

1. *Land availability.* Land is a major constraint on the production potential of food in that good farming land must first of all be available. There are several ways in which farming land is being diminished. However only two which are considered very important will be mentioned.

(*a*) Population Growth. As the population grows more land is taken up for housing and industrial development, especially in the big towns. The expansion of urban areas, due to population growth, onto adjoining land is particularly acute in small countries with limited land resources. It is noted in Cyprus that despite strategies for urban growth the spread of housing in the periphery of urban areas often involves the use of good agricultural land for development. In Trinidad urban sprawl around the capital region is not only pre-empting good agricultural land but is also creeping up hillsides and destroying natural vegetation. It is estimated in Egypt, for example, that cultivated land per person has fallen from about 0·39 acres in 1930 to the present 0·17 acres. In the corresponding period the population has increased from 20 million to about 70 million. The loss is believed to be mainly due to industrial and urban sprawl despite efforts to reclaim land by increased investment in irrigation facilities.

One other major problem which is very common in developing countries, especially in Africa, and which is an indirect consequence of population growth, is the practice of subdividing land among members of a particular family. It so happens that developing countries also have a very high rate of population growth and if the system of land subdivision continues without being checked there will eventually be only land for building the homesteads and nothing to cultivate. Studies should be made with the view to introducing legislation governing land use and planning in the rural areas in order not only to save farming land but also to preserve the environment.

(*b*) Desert Encroachment. The encroachment of the desert, which is now widely acknowledged, is due to many factors including overgrazing and tree-cutting. For example, it is known that the area between Alexandria and the Libyan border used to be well-populated and a prosperous vineyard of ancient Rome. Today it is a desert. Also, to the south of Khartoum in the Sudan, the acacia scrub-zone is known to have marched 90 kilometres southwards in the past 20 years. It is further pointed out by Flohn, 1977, that estimates of the areas of man-made desert, world-wide, are now over 900 million square kilometres of once arable land, representing a total loss of 40% of good farming land.

Whatever the reason for the loss of farming land, the most disturbing element is that the common factor in the pattern of desert encroachment is the hand of man. The destruction of natural vegetation either by tree-cutting or overgrazing leads nearly everywhere to an increase of the reflectivity (albedo) of the surface and thus decreases the amount of absorbed solar radiation (Flohn, 1977). It has been observed that increased reflectivity is associated with a drastic reduction in rainfall due to the loss of solar energy to space. For example, a typical reflectivity of a tropical rainforest is $0 \cdot 12 - 0 \cdot 14$, that of a humid grassland or cropland $0 \cdot 20 - 0 \cdot 22$, while that of a desert with bright sandy soil is about $0 \cdot 35$. These values are given for the visible part of the spectrum ($0 \cdot 35 - 0 \cdot 70$ μm). In the near infrared ($0 \cdot 70 - 3$ μm) part, higher values have been observed by Ottermann (1974). It is therefore necessary that land resources, especially vegetation and soils, should be properly utilized in order not to cause major changes in the climate, as we shall see later.

2. *Climatic changes*. Food production is very much dependent on the climate, especially rainfall. For example, in recent years the Sahel region of Africa has suffered from lack of rainfall. Whether these climatic changes are man-made, as indicated above, or natural, it is obvious that recent model simulations have led to a growing concensus that our climate cannot be regarded as stationary. There are constant climatic fluctuations or variations or changes, caused by natural phenomena such as solar radiation or by man through his burning of fossil fuel such as oil, gas and coal and his use of nuclear energy. For example, the burning of fossil fuel and forests does release a lot of CO_2 into the atmosphere. It is known that there is an annual increase of 1 ppm of CO_2 in the earth's atmosphere. This CO_2 has a major consequence for the climate in that, although it is transparent to visible light, it absorbs long-wave infra-red heat emitted by the earth's surface and re-emits it to the earth, thus causing a warming effect. It is estimated that by the years 2020 – 2050 low- and mid-latitude areas are likely to be drier and those of high latitudes wetter, if this process goes on at this pace.

SUB-TOPIC 1(A): PRODUCTION POTENTIAL [Musangi]

In view of the changes in the climate our farming systems must be constantly studied in order not only to keep pace with these changes but also to conserve natural resources, especially land. A specific consequence associated with climatic changes, especially rainfall, deserves mention here. In Africa rain is by far the most important element of climate and its distribution in both space and time not only determines the extent of human prosperity but also sets the limits for life itself on the continent. Studies need to be made, therefore, on how to adjust farming practices on the varying rainfall pattern in any one area. Rainfall changes will, for example, affect the level of fertilizer use. In Kenya, for instance, the amount of nitrogen recommended for wheat depends on the level of precipitation, as is shown in this table. If fertilizer use is limited owing to low moisture regime, crop yields will in turn be limited to some extent (Geus, 1973). Irrigation, where water is available, may be the answer.

Fertilizer recommendations for wheat in Kenya, related to precipitation

Annual precipitation in mm	kg. N/ha
<300	6·3 – 13
300 – 500	13 – 42
>500	32 – 42

3. *Use of appropriate technologies.* One of the major limiting factors in the production potential of food, especially in developing countries, is the adoption of appropriate technologies. We can come up with high-yielding seeds or livestock which can only yield their maximum genetic potential if high technologies and/or inputs are used. These may, in most cases, have other socio-economic consequences.

For example, in some developing countries of Asia the Green Revolution is failing to relieve poverty and malnutrition because implementation, according to the Asian Development Bank (Manning, 1977), was predicated on expensive capital-intensive methods, involving fertilizer and other inputs. Though the per capita income has increased in the majority of cases, the absolute number of people affected by malnutrition and other poverty manifestations has increased in many Asian countries.

4. *Manpower training and research.* In most countries of the developing world it would be difficult to effectively use additional massive aid in agriculture, owing to the limits to human capital and organisational capability required to handle the large tasks involved. There is a critical shortage of manpower in these countries trained and experienced in the sciences and technologies underlying crop and animal production. Although, therefore, the universities

have played and continue to play an important role in meeting this manpower challenge by training scientific staff to man agricultural extension, research, and to take up active farming themselves, existing agricultural and veterinary schools in these countries must be strengthened and expanded.

The aims of the universities the world over are threefold: the training of undergraduate and postgraduate students, and to carry out research. The undergraduate programmes in agriculture, whether general or specialised, are meant for the advisory services of both the public and private sectors and for active participation in farming. The postgraduate programmes, on the other hand, are meant to fill the more specialised areas in the above-mentioned sectors, especially research, and to provide academic staff replacements. The universities can also contribute significantly to research through their own academic staff research activities. This contribution to agricultural research is particularly important in the developing world where there is a shortage of qualified manpower in the many sectors of the economy.

The universities are particularly suited to carry out research in two ways: —

(*a*) In most universities, the world over, great emphasis is laid on the quality and to a lesser extent the quantity of publications a member of staff can produce. This tends to provide the necessary incentive for research by individual staff members. If indeed this research can be properly co-ordinated with national programmes, say in agriculture, there can be significant contribution to the economy.

(*b*) It is always encouraged that faculty members carry out research in order to keep abreast with new findings in their various areas of specialization. In this regard their contribution to agricultural research can also be very significant if this is directed to solving local problems.

The contribution of agricultural research by graduate students is important. In most developing countries it is advisable that graduate students are assigned projects aimed at solving relevant local problems. It is therefore stressed once again that facilities for such training should be developed in developing countries so that future agricultural scientists are trained in the environment where they are going to work. It has been argued in the past, with some justification, that students sent abroad are trained in an environment and using equipment which they are unlikely to find in their home countries on completion of their studies, thus making their training irrelevant in the immediate future. Since agricultural research is vital to the economies of many countries, especially those

SUB-TOPIC 1(A): PRODUCTION POTENTIAL [Musangi]

that depend largely on agriculture for their foreign exchange earnings, it is important that those scientific personnel who man it must be appropriately trained.

Food Storage and Processing

The world food problems relate not only to the production of food itself but also to losses in quality and quantity during storage and processing. Storage, for example, is a major problem in many developing countries of the tropics. The problems related to storage are two-fold: pests and weather.

Owing to the high humidity in some tropical countries food crops, particularly, cannot be stored for long without going mouldy despite having been dried sufficiently at harvest-time. These losses lead to food distribution throughout the year being difficult. Ways of ensuring that the harvest is not destroyed by humidity are being experimented upon in most areas of the developing world. For example, maize in Kenya is now partly being stored in air-tight cyprus bins.

The other major storage problem is pests. Pests, such as weevils and rodents, can destroy a big fraction of the harvest. It is estimated that in some countries up to 25% of crop harvests are destroyed by pests. If one considers that these are also the areas of the world well behind their safety food targets and, therefore, with a high food import bill, a loss of this magnitude is one they can ill afford.

Food and feed losses in storage could be reduced to some extent by processing, while the processing of crop residues, for example, could increase the amount of food available for human and livestock consumption. Milk may be stored very well when turned into milk powder, while there are a lot of crop and animal residues that would otherwise be useless if not processed for animal feeding and thus in turn be indirectly available to man. For example, sisal and pyrethrum residues, fish meal and bone meal are now so widely used for livestock feeding that at an FAO seminar held in Rome in January, 1977, it was suggested that it might be advisable for governments to aim that animal feeding be restricted to agricultural and agro-industrial residues, thus preserving grains for human consumption. It was noted at the same seminar that in India, for example, the rice grown throughout the country generates 270 – 300 million tons of straw, 20 – 23 million tons of husk, and 3 – 3·5 million tons of rice bran, which when treated would form good feed for livestock.

There are, however, a number of points which need to be reached in order to increase the utilization of these residues. These are: —

(*a*) the development of processing methods that are appropriate and aimed at specific products;

(*b*) the siting of recycling units of farm residues at the site of the industry that is producing them, in order to cut down on transport costs;

(*c*) a thorough study of the health aspects of these residues. For example, in feeding groundnut haulms there is a danger of aflotoxin poisoning, while in pyrethrum residue there is danger of high concentration of pyrethrin. In sisal residue, on the other hand, there is a danger of causing reproductive hormone imbalance.

A major factor in food production and preservation, however, is the maintenance of global reserve stocks to cover major contingencies, a matter which has been discussed for some time in international forums but which has not been agreed upon. The fact that grain stocks, for example, have risen substantially in major developed exporters makes it important to move towards establishing a global reserve before circumstances operate to dissipate them.

Food Marketing

Food marketing, especially the pricing system, in most countries needs thorough examination. The developing countries, for their part, should design their policies to ensure that prices paid to producers will encourage increased output. Food aid shipments to developing nations which bear down on prices pose a threat to maintaining such incentive prices. It is perhaps better still, in the long run, that unless there is a natural calamity needing emergency food aid the international community should aim at ensuring sufficiency in food production in countries prone to chronic food shortages, rather than in massive food shipments.

There is, however, a dilemma between the desirability of maintaining low prices to consumers, which also enable the poor in the community to eat better, and the need to establish incentive prices to producers. In the final analysis it would seem that adequate incentives to producers should not be sacrificed in the interests of food prices.

Conclusion

It is, therefore, reasonable to conclude that the end to the world food problem is unlikely to be reached in the foreseeable future unless rapid population growth and man's upper hand in the destruction of the environment, most apparent in all countries, are arrested. International co-operation in the marketing of food (particularly its pricing and distribution) and the development of appropriate technologies for increased food production and preservation must also be forthcoming in order to achieve this end.

REFERENCES

1. Geus, J. C. de (1973). Fertilizer guide for the tropics, *Centre d'Étude de l'Asote,* Zurich, p. 85.
2. FAO (1977). Residue utilization-management of agricultural and agro-industrial waste, *Rome,* 1977, p. 67.
3. Flohn, H. (1977). Some aspects of man-made climate modification and desertification, *Applied Sciences and Development* 9, 44 – 58.
4. Manning, R. A. (1977). Why the Green Revolution is not working out, *Development and Co-operation (D + C) P. 12/4/77,* Bonn, p. 26.
5. Ottermann, J. (1974). Baring high albedo soils by overgrazing: a hypothesized desertification mechanism, *Science* 186, 531 – 533.

Sardar B. S. SAMUNDRI (*Vice-Chancellor of Guru Nanak Dev University*): This paper is divided into three parts: the nature and extent of the world food problem; whether or not world agriculture can produce enough food for the expanding world population; and the role of the universities in removing constraints on agricultural production.

Nature and Extent of World Food Problem

Lord Boyd-Orr lamented in 1950 that 'a lifetime of malnutrition and actual hunger is the lot of at least two-thirds of mankind'. Since then there has been growing interest in the food problem. There was a sharp rise in grain prices following the food crisis of 1973 when there was a decline of 33 million tonnes in world foodgrain production. This brought the problem into sharper focus. The prices of wheat and rice rose from US$62 and US$129 per metric tonne in 1971 to US$139 and US$368 per metric tonne respectively in 1973. This created great difficulties for the food-deficit developing countries. In fact an FAO study has shown that, taking the world as a whole, the rate of growth of food production has substantially exceeded population growth. The data are given in Appendix I (p.72). It may be seen that in both the 1950s and 1960s, while the population increased at about 2% per annum, food production increased by 3·1% and 2·7% per annum respectively. The rate of growth of food production was about the same in both the developed and the developing countries. But, while in the developed countries the rate of growth of population was 1% per annum, it was over 2% in the less developed countries. The position in per capita terms was much worse in the latter group. Moreover many less developed countries were much worse off than the average position might suggest. An FAO[1] study showed that in many developing countries like Afghanistan, Algeria, Bangladesh, Cuba, Indonesia, etc., increase in food production did not match population growth. Sinha[2] reported that during 1952–72 the foodgrain production failed to keep pace with population growth in more than one third of developing countries. A recent study[3] has estimated the cereal shortfall in the developing countries to be of the order of $15 billion.

The same FAO study[4] reported that in 1970 the food availability in developed regions of the world was more than 20% in excess of the dietary energy requirements, whereas in the developing regions, in spite of some improvement during the 1960s, there was a deficit of about 3% in their requirements. In Africa, the Far East and the Near East, there were deficits of 6% to 8%. Average protein intake in developing countries was only about 60% of that in the developed regions. Furthermore, on the basis of clinical and anthropometric data, it was pointed out that about 10 million children under five years of age in the developing countries were suffering from severe malnutrition, 80 million from moderate malnutrition, and 120 million from less obvious, milder forms of malnutrition. Thus about half of all children in the developing world were inadequately nourished. In this context Ruth and Serrano[5] noted that in some Latin American countries more than half of all deaths of children under five years of age were directly or indirectly due to nutritional deficiencies.

An average person in a developed country consumes nearly three times as much sugar, more than four times as much meat, fats and

---

1. FAO. Population, Food Supply and Agricultural Development, *Monthly Bulletin of Agricultural Economics and Statistics*, Vol.23, No.9, September 1974, pp. 2–3.
2. Sinha, Radha. *Food and Poverty*, Croom Helm, London. 1976, p. 7.
3. University of California. *A Hungry World – A Challenge to Agriculture*, July 1975.
4. FAO, op. cit. (September 1974), pp. 5–6.
5. Ruth, Rice P. and Serrano, V. Carlos. *Pattern of Mortality in Childhood*, World Health Organisation, Publication No.262, 1973, pp. 164–66.

oils, and about six times as much milk and eggs as the average person in a developing country[6]. The average daily calorie intake in developed regions in 1969-71 was around 3,150 as against only 2,200 in the developing regions. The respective intakes of protein were 96 and 57 grams. A UN study[7] indicates that, excluding the Asian centrally-planned economies, about 460 million persons suffer from malnutrition. Up to a third of the Asian population receives inadequate supplies of food. The corresponding figures for Africa, the Near East and Latin America are 25%, 18% and 13% respectively.

The world demand for cereals is expected to grow from 1,207 million tonnes in 1970 to 1,725 million tonnes in 1985. During the same period demand in developing market economies and Asian centrally-planned economies taken together is expected to go up from 590 million tonnes to 929 million tonnes as against their expected domestic supply of 853 million tonnes. This is, indeed, a grim prospect. Clearly these countries will have to make strenuous efforts to develop their agriculture.[8] This is a big challenge.

Production Potential

In the past it has been common amongst the less developed societies to view agriculture as a lowly form of economic activity. Recently the thinking on this subject has undergone a change. The potential contribution of the agricultural sector has been recognised. Hayami and Rutton[9] have shown that agricultural development has no longer remained merely a pre-condition of total development; it has become a process of development in itself.

The production potential for food depends upon the scope for improvement in one or more of the following factors that affect agricultural production: cropped area, yield rates, cropping pattern and the inter-action factors. The potential for improvement in these factors is examined below.

According to a US government source[10], out of nearly 3,190 million hectares of potentially arable land in the world, 1,406 million hectares (44%) are currrently under cultivation.

---

6. United States Department of Agriculture. *The World Food Situation and Prospects to 1985*, 1974, p. 51.
7. UNO. *Assessment of the World Food*, World Food Conference, 1974.
8. Bhatia, B. M. *Poverty, Agriculture and Economic Growth*, Vikas Publishing House, 1977, p. 53.
9. Hayami, Y. and Rutton, W. Vernon. *Agricultural Development: An International Perspective*, The Johns Hopkins Press, 1971.
10. White House, USA. *The World Food Problem*: a report of the President's Advisory Committee, 1967, p. 434.

However, as shown in Table 1, below, this percentage varies among different regions. The greater part of the potentially cultivable but presently uncultivated land falls in Africa, South and North America, Oceania and the USSR. The most densely populated countries of Europe and Asia have only a marginal scope for bringing new land under cultivation. Myrdal[11] observes that in South Asia the increase in agricultural production in recent decades is attributable more to increase in the cultivated area than to improvement in yield per unit of land. The scope for expanding the cultivated area now being very limited in most underdeveloped ECAFE* countries, the central problem is: how quickly can these countries make the transition from the area-expanding method of increasing food output to the yield-raising ones? In India Rao[12] has reached the same conclusion. Not only is the scope for bringing new area under cultivation limited, the cost of this operation including reclamation of land, provision of infra-structural facilities and the settlement of new farm families is also prohibitive.

TABLE 1: POTENTIALLY CULTIVABLE LAND BY REGION

Region	Potentially cultivable land in million hectares	Percentage of cultivated to potentially cultivable land
Africa	733	22
Asia	628	83
Australia/New Zealand	154	2
Europe	174	88
North America	465	51
South America	680	11
USSR	356	65
TOTAL	3190	44

Myrdal[13] remarks that much that is relevant to a complete evaluation of the scope for expansion of cultivated area — particularly in regard to the quality of the untilled land — is still unknown, and in most South Asian countries the planner's interest in the problem has faded in recent years. We can, at best,

11. Myrdal, G. *Asian Drama*, Vol.II, Penguin Books, 1968, p. 1261.
12. Rao, C. H. H. *Technological Change and Distribution of Gains in Indian Agriculture*, Macmillan Co. of India, 1975.
13. Myrdal, G., op.cit., p. 1268.
*Economic Commission for Asia and the Far East (UNO).

say that the capacity of the land area has not yet been thoroughly tested. The social and institutional structure and the traditional agricultural techniques have stood in the way of increasing agricultural production through expansion of area under cultivation. Jacoby[14] mentions that in the Federation of Malaya, where extensive areas of waste land are available, land alienation procedures at the state government level have been a bottleneck.

With regard to improvements in productivity per unit of land, there is little doubt that there is considerable scope for this in the less developed countries even at the known level of technology. Yield rates in these countries are generally very low by international standards or in relation to technological possibilities. The average per hectare yield of major crops in selected countries is indicated in Appendix II (p.73). It may be seen that yields per hectare showed a wide range. In the case of wheat the yield was as low as 900 kg. in Australia and 1,382 kg. in India, while it was as high as 4,579 kg. in France, 4,378 kg. in Denmark, 4,224 kg. in the UK and 3,102 kg. in Egypt. In India the per hectare yield of paddy was only 1,616 kg. as against 5,334 kg. in Egypt, 5,847 kg. in Japan, 6,033 kg. in Korea (Republic) and 3,377 kg. in Sri Lanka[15], and of maize less than 1/7 of that in the USA. These are only rough comparisons and are, to some extent, accounted for by differences in climatic and topographical factors. They do, however, suggest that there exists tremendous scope for expanding agricultural production by raising yields to the highest known level in the world or to the level that known technology makes possible.

Swaminathan[16] has estimated that the yield per hectare of wheat and rice will increase from 14·1 and 12·5 quintals recorded in 1975−76 to 29 and 25 quintals respectively in 2000. Thus productivity improvement seems to hold the key to further advances in food production in India as in most other less developed countries, particularly the thickly populated ones.

The untapped production potential of rice has been explored by the International Rice Research Institute in the Philippines. It has termed the difference between experimental station yield and actual farm yield the 'yield gap', and the factors responsible for such a gap the 'yield constraint'. The operational research project of the Indian Council of Agricultural Research, New Delhi, has also made a similar exercise in assessing the production potential. The data have been analysed by Swaminathan.[17] He has found that the ratio

---

14. Jacoby, E. H. *Agrarian Unrest in South East Asia*, Asia Publishing House, London, 1959, p. 114.
15. FAO. *Monthly Bulletin of Agricultural Economics and Statistics*, Vol. 26, No. 9, September 1977, p. 8.
16. Swaminathan, M.S. Indian Agriculture at the Cross Roads, *Indian Journal of Agricultural Economics*, Vol. 32, No. 4, October−December 1977, p. 3.
17. Swaminathan, M.S., op.cit., p. 7.

between the average yield obtained by the farmers in different parts of the country and the yield of national demonstration plots ranged from 2 to 4 in the case of wheat and 2 to 5 in the case of rice.

The International Rice Research Institute, Philippines, sponsored a study of constraints on high yields in selected Asian countries. The study revealed a large untapped production potential of rice in these countries. In the case of Bangladesh it was estimated that the productivity of rice could be increased by about one tonne per hectare. In respect of Indonesia, the Philippines, Taiwan and Thailand, the yield gap was about 1·3, 0·4 to 2, 0·8, and 0·5 to 1·5 tonnes per hectare respectively.

Food production can be increased also by shifting land from non-food to food crops. But the scope for such transfer is very limited in the less developed countries, except in countries like Malaysia and Sri Lanka. In Malaysia more than four-fifths of the cultivated acreage is under non-food crops, and in Sri Lanka this proportion is nearly two-thirds. As against this, in India, about 74% of total area is already under foodgrains. Besides, non-food crops are important for exports and for producing essential raw material for industry. Some of the area under non-food crops is also not very suitable for food crops. The yield in terms of value is generally much higher in the case of the acreage under non-food crops than of the area under food crops.

The increase in yield rates involves massive increases in the use of modern inputs as well as more intensive and efficient labour. There are many instances where a country has overcome resource constraints by operating a sequence of innovations which led to the substitution of technical inputs for land and/or labour.

Assured irrigation has a crucial role to play in exploiting the available production potential in agriculture. It would not only increase the cropping intensities but also promote greater use of chemical fertilizers and new fertilizer-responsive high-yielding seed varieties. The intensification of agriculture thus achieved would inevitably raise per hectare yields. So far only about 201 million hectares or nearly one-seventh of the total world cultivated area is under irrigation. The low proportion of cultivated land currently under irrigation suggests that there exist immense possibilities of raising agricultural production through proper water management. The potentially irrigable area in the world is estimated at 260 to 470 million hectares. In India considerable progress has been made in the development of irrigation. The total gross irrigated area increased from 22·6 million hectares in 1950−51 to 41·7 million hectares in 1974−75. This is about 25% of the cropped area. It is now planned to raise the irrigational potential to 53·8 million hectares by 1977−78[18].

The contribution of irrigation in raising yields is well recognised. As an illustration, the yield of wheat in irrigated and unirrigated areas in selected states of India is given in Appendix III (p. 75). This shows wide gaps in the per hectare yield in the irrigated and unirrigated areas. Irrigation generally brings about dramatic improvements in agricultural production. It should, therefore, be the spearhead of a co-ordinated programme for exploiting the agricultural production potential in the developing countries.

The new farm technology based on high-yielding varieties of seeds requires intensive use of fertilizers. But unfortunately the use of chemical fertilizers has been rather low in most developing countries (Appendix IV, p. 75). Slowness in expanding soil-testing facilities, limited use of soil conditioners, poor extension services, lack of credit and purchasing centres within easy reach of farmers and high fertilizer prices are some of the major factors which inhibit fertilizer use in the less developed countries like India. There are often problems also on the supply side. It has been estimated that, if fertilizer application rates in India were to reach those in Japan, India's requirements of fertilizer would exceed the present world output[19]. Over the seven years from 1964−65 to 1971−72 the fertilizer consumption in India per cropped hectare quadrupled from about 4 kg. to 16 kg., but it was still only a fraction of the recommended dose. There is little doubt that if adequate supplies of fertilizer were available in the less developed world this would go a long way towards raising food output.

In order to unleash food and other agricultural production it is necessary also to reform and build up the rural institutional infrastructure. Progress in this respect takes time. It has, therefore, to be pursued with determination and with a clear sense of direction. Land reforms must be made an integral part of the new farm technology which has opened the gateway for rapid increase in agricultural production. Unfortunately progress in most developing countries like India has been tardy. It is equally necessary to create an adequate institutional structure for credit and extension. The extension of knowledge and the education of the farmer have an important role in reducing the gap between potential and actual output. Sustained increase in production also requires adequate control of the market so as to ensure remunerative prices to the farmers.

---

18. Swaminathan, M. S., op.cit., pp. 17−18.
19. Myrdal, G., op.cit., p. 1289.

Role of the Universities

Technological progress is an essential condition of sustained growth of food output. This, in turn, depends on research, education and extension. This is where the role of the universities comes in. Griliches[20] has rightly recommended that education should be included in the agricultural production function. In his research relating to the USA he found that new, variable, public investment in research and extension, introduced into the production function, is significant as a source of aggregate output growth. In an earlier study he estimated that at least 700% per year was being earned, as of 1955, on the average dollar invested in hybrid corn research.

There is need for large investments in research directed towards more profitable exploitation of resources and more even spread of the benefits of high-yielding varieties. The Green Revolution can hardly hold its own in the developing countries with only a few exotic varieties which do well in favourable conditions of soil and moisture. What is now needed is research on high-yielding varieties which could be grown in the areas lacking adequate and controlled water supplies and also some high-yielding strains of pulses and legumes which could be grown as a second crop.

Universities can make effective contribution by concentrating on problem-oriented research. Besides generating knowledge which is always of universal character, they should also devote their resources towards research meant exclusively for the solution of locally-felt needs of society.

Mellor[21] observes in this context that Japan is one of the few nations which have developed a successful approach to agricultural research. At a very early stage of Japanese agricultural development experimental stations were created at the prefectural level, and test and demonstration farms radiated out from these, providing wide coverage to specific physical conditions. A system of farmer education was then built upon the base of innovation and testing at regional experimental stations.

High yields in some areas in the developing countries have sometimes led to the conclusion that agricultural development requires merely the application of existing knowledge rather than development of new knowledge through research. Bradfield[22], an eminent soil scientist, has expressed a different view. He claims that

---

20. Griliches, Zvi. Research Expenditures, Education and the Aggregate Agricultural Production Function, *American Economic Review*, December 1964, pp. 961–64.
21. Mellor, John W. *The Economics of Agricultural Development*, Cornell University Press, 1966, p. 268.
22. Bradfield, Richard. 'Opportunities for Soil Scientists in Freeing the World from Hunger'. Presidential Address to the Seventh International Congress of Soil Science, Madison (Wis.), 1960.

further increase in yields would become possible in the wake of new knowledge and technology.

It is difficult to delineate the appropriate fields of research in the developing countries. But it is clear that research in biological sciences provides the prime basis for technological advance. Economics and the behavioural sciences can contribute only when the natural scientists have provided a stock of innovations. It is also important that research in biological sciences must be carried on in the country in which it is to be applied. This is because, first, problems of transferability are particularly great with research in these sciences and, secondly, the breeding of resistance and the development of other protective measures require a local research programme which can diagnose and even anticipate problems and go to work with counter-measures.[23]

The spread of higher education is the most important function of universities. They must devise their research programme to solve the felt needs of the community. It is difficult to disagree with Wellman[24] when he remarks that, if research in the areas of crop and animal production, insect control and aquatic food sources alone is pursued vigorously, it would easily double or triple the world's food supply within the next twenty-five years. Given the necessary measures it is realistic to conclude that for quite some time food production can be increased to make it commensurate with the growth of requirements. However a lasting solution to the world food problem would have to be sought not only in vigorous measures to enlarge and exploit the development potential in food production but also in effectively curbing the growth of population, particularly in the developing countries. In both these areas the universities, through their well-integrated education, research and extension programmes, have an effective role to play.

---

23. Mellor, John W., op.cit., pp. 279–280.
24. Wellman, R. H. Research Needed to Increase Food Production, *American Journal of Agricultural Economics*, Vol. 59, No. 5, December 1977, p. 847.

[Samundri]   TOPIC 1: THE WORLD FOOD PROBLEM

APPENDIX I

Rate of Growth of Food Production in relation to Population, World and Main Regions, 1952–62 and 1962–72

	1952–62			1962–72		
		Food Production			*Food Production*	
	Population	Total	Per caput	Population	Total	Per caput
	Per cent per year					
Developed market economies	1·2	2·5	1·3	1·0	2·4	1·4
Western Europe	0·8	2·9	2·1	0·8	2·2	1·4
North America	1·8	1·9	0·1	1·2	2·4	1·2
Oceania	2·2	3·1	0·9	2·0	2·7	0·7
Western Europe and USSR	1·5	4·5	3·0	1·0	3·5	2·5
Total, developed countries	1·3	3·1	1·8	1·0	2·7	1·7
Developing market economies	2·4	3·1	0·7	2·5	2·7	0·2
Africa	2·2	2·2	—	2·5	2·7	0·2
Far East	2·3	3·1	0·8	2·5	2·7	0·2
Latin America	2·8	3·2	0·4	2·9	3·1	0·2
Near East	2·6	3·4	0·8	2·8	3·0	0·7
Asian centrally-planned economies	1·8	3·2	1·4	1·9	2·6	0·7
Total, developing countries	2·4	3·1	0·7	2·5	2·7	0·2
WORLD TOTAL	2·0	3·1	1·1	1·9	2·7	0·8

Source: FAO. Population, Food Supply and Agricultural Development, *Monthly Bulletin of Agricultural Economics and Statistics*, Vol. 23, No. 9, September 1974, p. 2.

SUB-TOPIC 1(A): PRODUCTION POTENTIAL [Samundri]

APPENDIX II

Per Hectare Yield of Selected Crops (in kg.)

	Wheat	Paddy	Barley	Maize	Sugarcane
Egypt	3,102	5,334	2,816	3,747	96,053
Canada	1,680	—	2,229	4,985	—
Mexico	2,721	2,639	1,171	1,148	60,714
USA	2,196	5,250	2,347	6,084	92,560
India	1,382	1,616	1,028	865	47,716
Denmark	4,378	—	3,965	—	—
France	4,579	—	3,899	4,580	—
UK	4,224	—	4,039	—	—
Australia	900	—	806	2,744	—
USSR	1,467	—	1,348	2,450	—
Japan	—	5,847	2,678	2,900	—
Korean Republic	—	—	2,311	1,412	—
World average	1,628	2,251	1,793	2,785	—

Source:FAO (1973). *Production Year Book*.
(—) means figures not available.

Per Hectare Yield of Selected Crops in Punjab (kg.)

Year	Rice	Maize	Wheat
1960–61	1009	1135	1244
1965–66	1000	1653	1236
1969–70	1490	1469	2245
1970–71	1765	1555	2238
1971–72	2045	1564	2406
1972–73	2007	1612	2233
1973–74	2287	1348	2216
1974–75	2071	1720	2395
1975–76	2553	1467	2373
1976–77	2605	1144	2432

[Samundri]   TOPIC 1: THE WORLD FOOD PROBLEM

APPENDIX II (*contd.*)

Comparative Position of Yield Rates of Principal Food Crops in Ludhiana District and Overall Punjab State per hectare/kg., 1973–74 and 1976–77

Crop	Ludhiana 1973–74	Ludhiana 1976–77	Punjab 1973–74	Punjab 1976–77	Punjab Yield as % Ludhiana 1973–74	Punjab Yield as % Ludhiana 1976–77
Rice	3123	3614	2287	2605	73·23	72·08
Maize	1759	1776	1348	1144	76·63	64·41
Wheat	2929	3160	2216	2432	75·65	76·96

SUB-TOPIC 1(A): PRODUCTION POTENTIAL   [*Samundri*]

APPENDIX III

The Yield of Wheat in Irrigated and Unirrigated Areas in Selected States of India

	Grain Yield (Kg./Ha.)			
	1973−74		1974−75	
	Irrigated	*Unirrigated*	*Irrigated*	*Unirrigated*
Uttar Pradesh	1089	688	1283	744
Bihar	1235	840	1096	733
Madhya Pradesh	1400	720	1468	769
Haryana	1655	808	1831	1109
Punjab	2250	969	2475	1508

Source: *Estimates of Area and Production of Principal Crops in India 1975−76.* Directorate of Economics and Statistics, Ministry of Food and Agriculture, Government of India, 1977.

APPENDIX IV

Use of Fertilizer in the Different Regions of the World, 1972−73

	Kg. of NPK per hectare of arable land		Kg. of NPK per hectare of arable land
Western Europe	192	Latin America	30
North America	73	Far East	20
Oceania	36	Near East	18
Eastern Europe and the USSR	72	Africa	5
Other developed market economies	157	Asian centrally-planned economies	40
Developed regions	90	Developing regions	20
		World	53

Source: FAO (1974). *Annual Fertilizer Review.*

[Samundri]   TOPIC 1: THE WORLD FOOD PROBLEM

Consumption of Chemical Fertilizers in Punjab (thousand tonnes)

Year	Nit.	Phos.	Potassic	Total
1960−61	25	1	—	26
1965−66	214	21	1	236
1969−70	734	131	11	876
1970−71	1100	360	44	1504
1971−72	1122	331	20	1473
1972−73	1200	410	31	1641
1973−74	1123	427	35	1585

Consumption of Chemical Fertilizer (Nutrients) in Districts of Punjab, 1976−77

	NPK (000 Nutrient Tonnes)	Total Cropped Area (000 Hectares)	Kg./Hect.
Gurdaspur	28	411	68·1
Amritsar	42	631	66·5
Kapurthala	14	182	76·9
Jullundur	38	454	83·7
Hoshiarpur	13	387	33·5
Ropar	8	193	41·4
Ludhiana	52	536	97·0
Ferozepur	38	705	53·9
Faridkot	49	743	65·9
Bhatinda	23	707	32·5
Sangrur	31	714	43·4
Patiala	37	622	59·4
Punjab, Total	373	6285	59·3

Recommended Level of Fertilizer Use in Amritsar District of Punjab

Irrigated   Per Hectare

Wheat	123·5	61·75	29·64 = 214·89 Kg.
Paddy	123·5	29·64	29·64 = 182·78
Loamy Sand to			
Sandy Soil	39·52	19·76	14·82 = 74·1
Loam to Clay loam	79·04	39·52	24·7 = 143·26

Actual Consumption of Fertilizer in Punjab for the Year 1976−77: 90·5 Kg. per hectare sown area

SUB-TOPIC 1(A): PRODUCTION POTENTIAL [*Samundri*]

APPENDIX V

Net Area (Percentage) Irrigated to Net Area Sown in the Districts of Punjab, 1973−74 and 1976−77

	1973−74	1976−77		1973−74	1976−77
Gurdaspur	58	65·1	Ferozepur	71	77·4
Amritsar	94	94·9	Faridkot	78	82·8
Kapurthala	80	83·0	Bhatinda	68	69·9
Jullundur	81	86·6	Sangrur	81	83·3
Hoshiarpur	30	37·2	Patiala	69	75·9
Ropar	40	40·4			
Ludhiana	85	86·7	Punjab	72	77·0

Dr. L. H. SHEBESKI (*Dean of the Faculty of Agriculture, University of Manitoba*): The theme of this conference, 'Reconciling national, international and local roles of universities with the essential character of a university', strongly implies that the 'roles' of universities and their 'essential character' are at variance, and that reconciliation should be a major concern.

I interpret the national, international and local roles of the university, as seen by contemporary society, to be those of responding to the urgent concerns and needs of the societies that support them. For a definition of the essential character of a university I turn to a recent statement made by Professor Robin Harris[1], University of Toronto historian, and I quote: 'The essence of the University of Toronto, as of all great universities, is the intellectual experiences which are the outcome of the teaching and research functions. Everything else is designed to make such experiences possible.' Although there is much to commend in this description of the essence of all great universities (admittedly taken out of context), it is this kind of stated philosophy that leads many of the lay public to view the essential character of the university as that of the élitist pursuing esoteric problems and not concerned with the problems of the so-called real world.

For the past three decades world leaders, including Winston Churchill, John F. Kennedy, Albert Einstein and British historian

Albert Toynbee, have expressed deep concern about man's continuing ability to feed all his numbers. The United Nations, through its Food and Agriculture Organization, has continuously expressed the same concerns. If this is one of the great concerns of the human race, how well have the universities responded? Topic 1, 'The World Food Problem and the Universities', provides this conference with an excellent sub-theme to examine if, in fact, the roles of the university and the essential character of the university are in need of reconciliation.

I intend to convey my thoughts on this question in my closing remarks.

The Problem

As a preface to my remarks on my assigned topic, production potential, I intend to provide tangible evidence of the need to be concerned about the continuing adequate food supply for all the human inhabitants of this planet.

The concern was emotionally expressed in the last annual report put out by the Canadian International Development Agency (CIDA)[2], wherein it was stated that the year reviewed, 1976 – 77, was:

> '...a year of massive and disregarded human disaster, as the poor continued to die needlessly at an estimated rate of 10,000 a day from malnutrition and 25,000 a day from water-borne diseases. Even among the survivors, many—perhaps a billion—continued to live in what World Bank President Robert McNamara has defined as absolute poverty: "a condition of life so degraded by disease, illiteracy, malnutrition, and squalor as to deny its victims basic human necessities; so limited as to prevent realization of the potential of the genes with which one is born; so degrading as to insult human dignity".'

It can easily and truthfully be argued that the 10,000 who die per day from malnutrition do so not because of a world food shortage but because of their inability to purchase the food that they require for their sustenance. In the May 1975 issue of *Science*[3], dedicated to food, Dr. S. H. Wittwer, Michigan State University, wrote: 'There is enough food now produced to feed the world's hungry. That people are malnourished or starving is a question of distribution, delivery, and economics, not agricultural limits. The problem is putting the food where the people are and providing an income so that they can buy it.'

SUB-TOPIC 1(A): PRODUCTION POTENTIAL [Shebeski]

Grain production is stressed because, as can be seen in Figure 1, below, cereal and legume grains are the principal food crops of man, providing close to 70% of his sources of food energy. Even more important, the cereal grains are the non-perishable, readily transported components of the food chain. The cereal grains, legumes and oilseed crops occupy more than 90% of the cultivated lands of the world, as depicted in Figure 2, below, hence their importance.

FIGURE 1: MAN'S SOURCES OF FOOD ENERGY 1970[4]

FIGURE 2: WORLD AREA OF PRINCIPAL FOOD CROPS[5]

The proportion of the world's harvested cropland planted to cereal grains

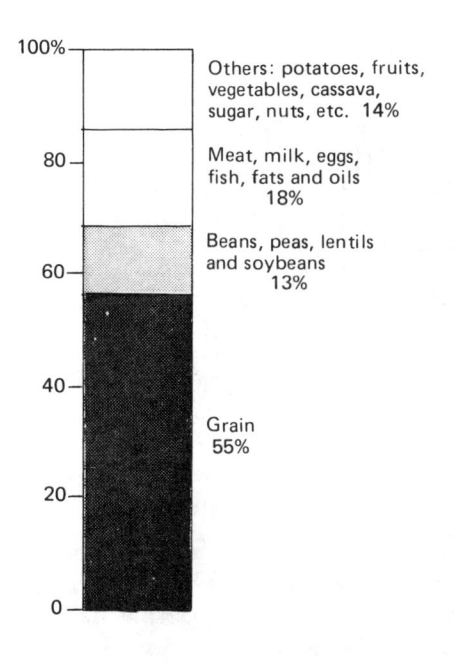

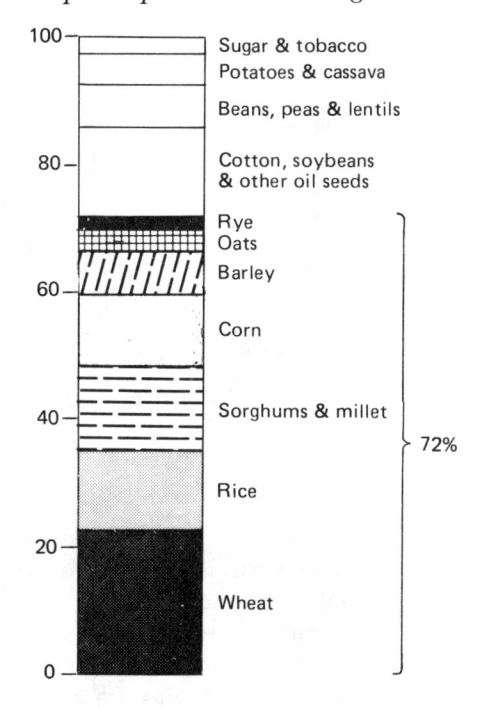

Figure 1 (bar chart, 0–100%):
- Others: potatoes, fruits, vegetables, cassava, sugar, nuts, etc. 14%
- Meat, milk, eggs, fish, fats and oils 18%
- Beans, peas, lentils and soybeans 13%
- Grain 55%

Figure 2 (bar chart, 0–100):
- Sugar & tobacco
- Potatoes & cassava
- Beans, peas & lentils
- Cotton, soybeans & other oil seeds
- Rye
- Oats
- Barley
- Corn
- Sorghums & millet
- Rice
- Wheat

(cereal grains total: 72%)

That grain production has not kept pace with population growth is depicted in Figure 3, below. Although 1976 was a record production year it would still be regarded as below the trend line for keeping up with population growth. Although Figure 3 does not show the production of grain for 1977, it was below that for 1976 and therefore the gap between production and population requirements widened.

FIGURE 3: WORLD GRAIN PRODUCTION COMPARED TO POPULATION GROWTH[6]

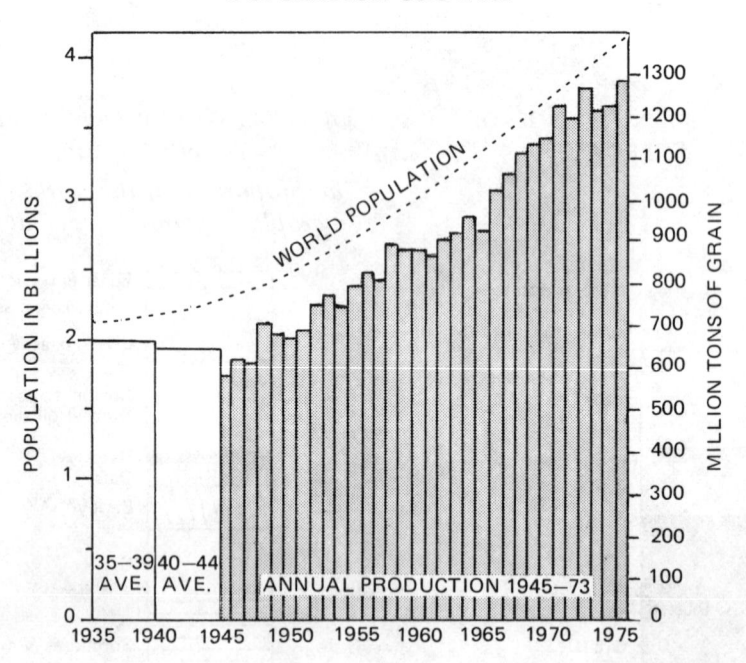

The fact is that for the past five years the food consumption, inadequate as it has been for so many of the world's people, has been based on production plus a component from the reserves that had been built up in the preceding decades. The depletion of reserves is indicated in the following table based on data extracted from Lester R. Brown's *Worldwatch Paper* # 2[7] — a drop in the past half-dozen years from 188 million metric tons to 100 million metric tons, or from 87 to 31 days of reserve, as based on annual grain consumption. Unfortunately the shortfall of cereals is becoming increasingly pronounced in the developing countries wherein more than half of the world's people live. Prior to the second world war the developing countries as a group were net exporters of grain. By

SUB-TOPIC 1(A): PRODUCTION POTENTIAL [Shebeski]

TABLE 1: DEPLETION OF GRAIN RESERVES

Year	Reserve stocks of grain (million metric tons)	Reserves as days of annual grain consumption
1970	188	87
1971	168	71
1972	130	69
1973	148	55
1974	108	33
1975	111	35
1976	100	31

1950 the developing countries had become net importers of grain, importing 12·4 million metric tons. By 1967 their net imports had more than doubled, reaching 31 million metric tons, and by 1976 their net imports had doubled again, totalling approximately 60 million metric tons. These figures do not include the massive food aid which, for the last decade, averaged 10 million metric tons annually.

The International Food Policy Research Institute[8] recently made two points: first, that the volume of food imports into developing countries, which grew at 4·4% per annum from 1960 to 1974, increased during the last four years of that period to 6·2% annually, and this increase took place at a time of rising prices; second, that unless there is an almost immediate reversal to the growth of food imports by the food deficit nations their production of cereals will fall short of meeting their food demands by approximately 100 million metric tons by 1985.

I would be remiss if I were not to indicate the tremendous strain that an ever-increasing population puts on the farmers of the world who are expected to increase production commensurate with population needs. To illustrate: in any one year Canada's total grain production is very little more than the grain requirements of the added world population. In other words, the world each year must add the grain production of an additional Canada.

The changing situation in Mexico serves as an example of what happens when the farmers cannot keep pace with population growth. The highly publicized Green Revolution, the development of the Mexican dwarf wheats, for which Dr. Norman Borlaug was awarded the Nobel Peace Prize, had its initial impact in Mexico,

[*Shebeski*] TOPIC 1: THE WORLD FOOD PROBLEM

permitting that country to change from a grain importing to a grain exporting country. This is depicted in Figure 4, below.

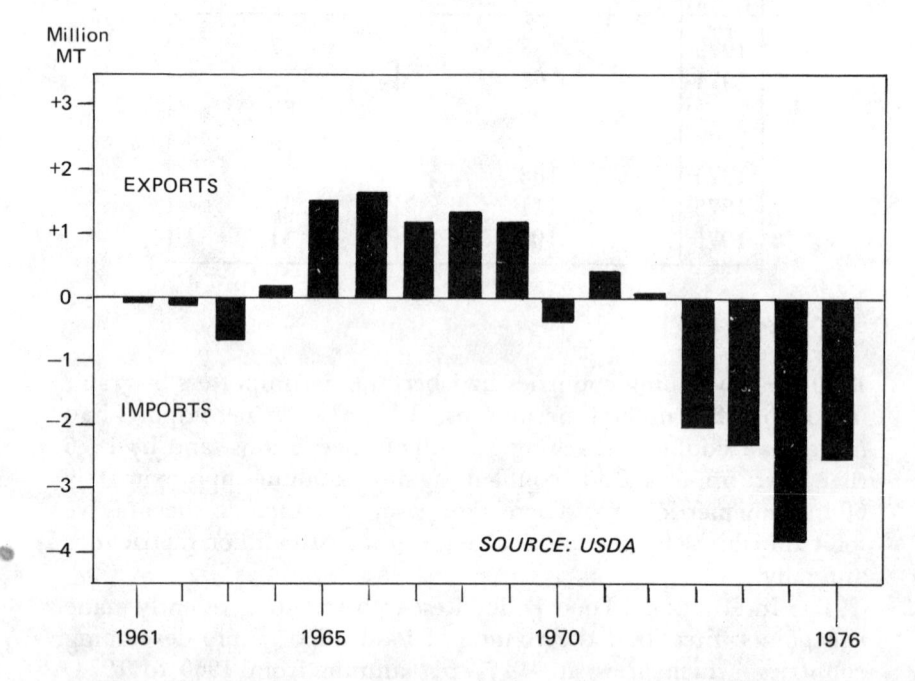

FIGURE 4: MEXICO: NET GRAIN TRADE, 1961 – 76[9]

According to Lester R. Brown, 'Mexico exported 10 per cent of its grain crop between 1965 and 1969, though the production gains were eventually overwhelmed by one of the world's fastest population growth rates'. Mexico currently imports 20% of its grain needs.

With the problem thus defined, what is the food production potential of this world? How many people can be adequately fed on this planet?

Production Potential

Probably no greater diversity of opinion exists on any topic than that of the food-carrying capacity of the earth. Estimates have ranged from a low of between 6 and 8 billion people, made by Barry Commoner, to that of 146 billion people made by DeWit. Colin Clark, Dr. Piel and others have estimated the supportive capacity to be in the order of 35 billion people.[10] According to reports emanating from the Eleventh Congress of the International Society of Soil Science held in Edmonton in June of this year, 'there is enough soil around to support 40 billion people'. Irrespective of which of these various estimates come closest to the true potential there can be little doubt that tremendous increases in food production are possible.

There are essentially two ways of increasing the supply of land-based foods: either by expanding the land resource on which food is produced, and/or by increasing productivity per unit land area. I will discuss each in turn. Since approximately 97% of man's food supply is obtained from land resources my remarks will be confined to land-based foods.

Global land resources and their productive potential are fairly well known. Literally every square mile of the earth's surface has been photographed and its physical characteristics examined and

FIGURE 5: GLOBAL LAND INVENTORY (13·3 BILLION HECTARES)[11]

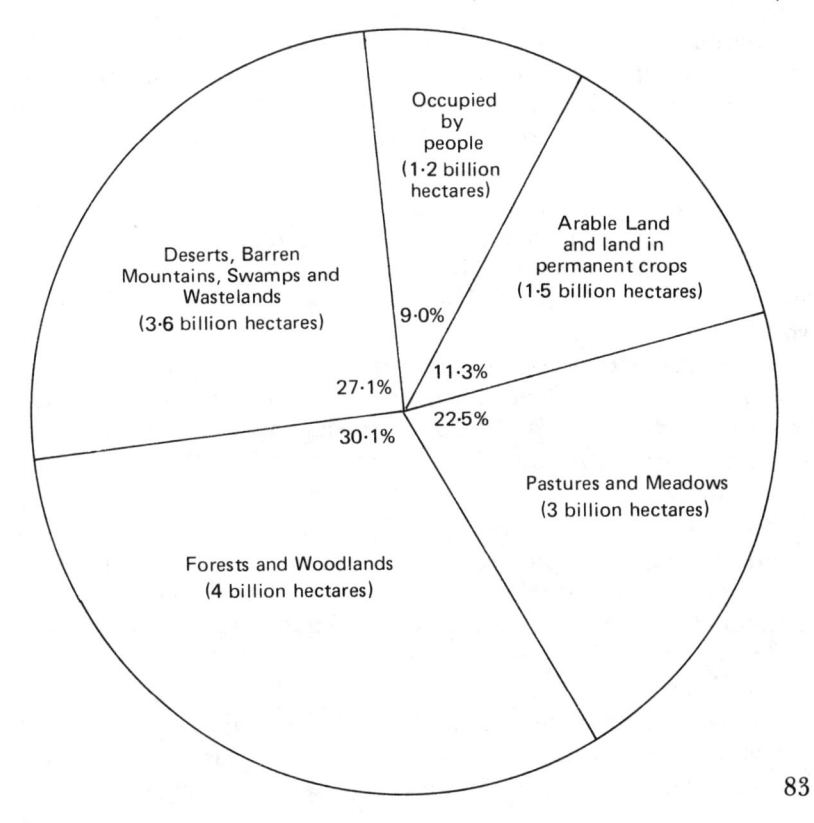

- Occupied by people (1·2 billion hectares) — 9·0%
- Arable Land and land in permanent crops (1·5 billion hectares) — 11·3%
- Pastures and Meadows (3 billion hectares) — 22·5%
- Forests and Woodlands (4 billion hectares) — 30·1%
- Deserts, Barren Mountains, Swamps and Wastelands (3·6 billion hectares) — 27·1%

described. In brief, as depicted in Figure 5, below, 13·3 billion hectares of the earth's surface (30%) is land. Of this, 9% or 1·2 billion hectares is occupied by the earth's 4 billion inhabitants, for their homes, for transportation, for commerce and industry, and for parks and recreation. The arable land and the land in permanent crop occupy 1·5 billion hectares, or 11·3% of the land surface. Four billion hectares are in forest and woodlands, and 3 billion hectares are in non-arable pastures and meadows. The remaining 3·6 billion hectares, more than twice that of the land currently in agriculture, is covered by deserts, barren mountains and wasteland.

It should be obvious from the foregoing, or from anyone's personal observations, that the land resources of the world are not equally productive and unfortunately the arable lands are not distributed on a world-wide basis according to the distribution of the world's population. The distribution of cultivated land and the land that could still be brought into production for different regions of the world were well documented and illustrated in the November-December 1974 issue of *Ceres*, published by FAO.[12] According to the FAO analysis, South Asia and China, with a combined population of 1·5 billion people, have virtually no more land that could be brought into production. This is also true of Japan. But on a world basis one billion additional hectares could be brought into production, a large proportion of which is in the tropical rainforests of Central Africa and South America.

At least three major problems are associated with bringing new land under production. The first is that potentially arable land is remote from the nations requiring arable land, and remote from the sources of energy and technology. Secondly, farmers throughout the world have traditionally farmed their best land before using land of lesser productivity. Seven hundred million hectares of the potentially arable lands are classified as podsolic or lateritic which are low or very low in fertility and thus, if developed, would require large amounts of fertilizers and other capital inputs. The third problem is that of the very high costs of bringing new land into production.

The secretariat of the World Food Conference suggested that it would cost the developing countries more than $30 billion in order to bring into production an additional 150 million hectares of land considered necessary for supplying their food requirements over the next ten years.

Some soil experts have estimated that in 35 years, and with an investment of $500 billion, an additional 420 million hectares could be brought into production. But should such a plan be undertaken and completed in 35 years (which is highly unlikely), an extra

SUB-TOPIC 1(A): PRODUCTION POTENTIAL [Shebeski]

420 million hectares would not have materialized. In the 35-year span the population would have doubled, and people occupy space. I have already indicated that the current world population occupies 1·2 billion hectares. The historical pattern of land settlement throughout the world has been predominantly on good agricultural land, and human expansion for at least the next two decades can be expected to continue to take place on agriculturally productive land. Thus the incoming additional billions of people, even assuming much greater crowding with less demand on space, will surely take out of production as much land as may conceivably be brought into production. In fact, according to an FAO official, in the last 15 years, during which time a billion people have been added, the additional food required came largely from the products of technology rather than from bringing an appreciable amount of additional land into production.[13]

It seems highly probable, therefore, that the future world food demands will have to be achieved by increasing production on not much more than the equivalent of current cultivated acreage, and thus the limits we face will be largely determined by productive capacity. The challenge, then, for the nations of the world, with greater life and death implications than any other current issue, is that of providing a political, technological, economic and social climate that will result in at least a doubling of productivity per hectare of land under cultivation in the next 30 to 35 years.

Despite the current food crisis man has hardly begun to develop the productive capacity of his arable lands. With known technology, fully utilized, the current agricultural land area of the world should be able to provide the food requirements of from three to four times the present population. This can be done by the increased use of fertilizers and pesticides, by greatly expanding the areas under irrigation, by developing higher-yielding and more disease-resistant varieties and species of crop plants, by increasing the number and kinds of crops grown per year in areas of the world where climate permits it, and by reducing the land in summer-fallow in the more temperate regions. Total food availability could be further increased by simply reducing the tremendous amount of spoilage and waste that takes place in many parts of the world.

Just one grandiose scheme alone, described by W. David Hopper[14] when President of the International Development Research Centre (IDRC), could virtually provide for a doubling of world grain production. According to Dr. Hopper there is, in the Indus-Ganges-Brahmaputra plain of North India, an area of more than 100 million acres of rich alluvial soil which, if multiple-cropped, is capable of producing as much as ten tons of grain equivalent per acre per year, or a total of more than one billion tons of food grain; an amount almost equal to the present total world grain production, and far beyond the projected needs of India for year 2000.

In many of the developing countries, where subsistence agriculture has been practised for centuries and where the chronic food deficits occur, the per hectare yields are only 20% to 25% of the yields obtained in Western Europe or North America. In these countries it should be possible to increase production by at least 50% during the next ten years, and in some cases even double production. The potential for such increases has already been well demonstrated by scientists working at a number of the World International Agricultural Stations. As an example, I will describe the mandate and some of the results of the work of the International Institute of Tropical Agriculture (IITA), located at Ibadan, Nigeria.

IITA's stated objective is the improvement of the quantity and quality of the major food crops in the lowland humid tropics of Africa, Asia and South America. In its mandate IITA has international responsibility for research on cowpeas, yams and sweet potatoes, and regional responsibility for research on rice, maize, cassava, pigeon peas and soybeans. This does not preclude exploratory work on other potential food crops.

Most of the agricultural areas in the lowland humid tropics are characterized by soils of low fertility on which a bush fallow or shifting cultivation is practical. Thus there is a very low usage of agricultural land for food production—seven years of bush fallow, three years of cropping with largely one crop per year during those three years. Therefore, in addition to the improvement of food crops, IITA has concerned itself with a study of cropping systems, and with the development of tools and small field equipment that would permit the predominantly subsistent farmers to increase the area they can crop, and this with less drudgery.

Perhaps the most significant of the emerging technological developments by IITA is that continuous cropping is possible, and could replace the traditional practice of bush fallow and shifting cultivation. By the input of high levels of fertilizer and by multiple cropping, the organic matter of the soils can actually be increased. With irrigation during the dry season three crops per season can be harvested annually, rather than the traditional one or two crops in three years out of ten.

I was in Ibadan last spring when the worst rain-storm in the station's recorded history occurred. More than six inches of rain fell in the fairly short period, with a maximum intensity of seven inches per hour. Land under traditional farming practice was severely eroded and numerous gullies had been formed. But under zero tillage and continuous cropping land in its seventh consecutive crop of maize, even on moderate slopes, showed no signs of erosion. This provided almost irrefutable proof that, with proper soil management, continuous cropping is feasible in the tropics.

I regret that time does not permit me to indicate some of the significant advances made in varietal improvement or yield stabilization of the food crops for this largely unexploited agricultural land area of the lowland humid tropics. The potential for increasing food production in these areas, according to Dr. W. K. Gamble, Director of IITA, will come from the application of a combination of improved technologies that are already available: high-yielding disease- and/or insect-resistant varieties, fertilizers, herbicides, insecticides, and light mechanization for better land management, all superimposed on greater and continuous land utilization.

For the root and tuber crops, cassava and sweet potatoes, with high fertilizer input, 300% increases in yield can be attained over the locally-grown varieties not fertilized. Two hundred per cent increases can similarly be expected in yams. In maize the current average yields of one metric ton per hectare could be increased to five metric tons per hectare. Thus in the next decade or less production could be more than doubled in those areas of the world, but only if the transfer of knowledge can be made to reach and be utilized by literally millions of subsistence farmers.

On the negative side, despite the rapid development of improved and appropriate technologies and the demonstrated potential for increasing production, there are serious constraints to the application of technology in the developing countries, and certainly in those countries that come under IITA's mandate. There is almost a complete lack of marketing structures. Storage facilities are inadequate, as are transportation facilities. There are no pricing policies which would assure the subsistent farmers a fair return even if they were capable of making the investments necessary to increase production. There is a lack of capital required for even the low-cost technological inputs such as improved seed, and there is a decided lack of other essential inputs—fertilizers, insecticides and herbicides. Energy costs have escalated to an alarming degree. Probably the greatest constraint lies in the lack of trained personnel at almost every level in the food production chain, and in particular in the lack of management skills at the largely illiterate, subsistent farmer level.

Although it is relatively easy to contend, and to provide strong supporting evidence, that global food production can be doubled by the turn of the century, the World Food Conference that was held in Rome in October 1974 was called because of the inability of the world to feed satisfactorily its present population of four billion. The World Food Conference made several points pertinent to the problem under discussion, and particularly to the constraints.

- Briefly, the Conference indicated that no single developing nation, or for that matter developed nation, had put its priority on food production. The Conference recognized that the rapidly rising food deficits in the developing nations would reach 85 million metric tons by 1985, and this could constitute an almost insurmountable problem in food transfer and in financing.
- The secretariat of the World Food Conference suggested that it would cost more than 30 billion dollars to bring into production an additional 150 million hectares of land necessary for supplying the food requirements of the developing countries over the next ten years.
- The Conference recommended that the flow of capital for agricultural development should be stepped up at least threefold, to about five billion dollars annually.

There should be little doubt that there is an untapped production potential that could be developed at a rate that would ensure an adequate diet for all the earth's inhabitants. Claiming this potential, however, will require that kind of enlightened and dedicated leadership in the nations of the world that will recognize and place agriculture at or near the top of its priorities for legislative attention and resource allocation. The limits of food production development are unwittingly set by the leaders of nations. The recommendation by the World Food Conference that the flow of capital for agricultural development in the developing nations should be stepped up at least threefold, to five billion dollars, is far too low. A world that can afford the luxury of an annual defence or arms budget of 400 billion dollars should be able to use at least 5% or 20 billion dollars annually to wage war on hunger.

In all of this, what is the university's role and is the role compatible with the essential character of the university?

Essential Character and Roles of Universities

The extent to which a university is able to respond to the urgent concerns and needs of the local, national or international community is largely determined by the essential character of the university—its philosophy, the strengths of its academia, the relevance of its research.

SUB-TOPIC 1(A): PRODUCTION POTENTIAL [*Shebeski*]

The essential character of a university, its philosophy and the strengths of its academia are in turn merely a reflection of, and determined by, its academic structure. All great universities of the Commonwealth are based in large part on the classical concepts of traditional British universities in which the primary pursuits are excellence and truth for truth's sake. These hallmarks of the classical university have in turn determined the primary roles, strengths and research priorities for all other Commonwealth universities that have adopted this classical model. It is significant also to observe that this classical model has always gained its greatest support from, and best serves the interest of, such faculties as arts, science, theology, law and, in more recent years, medicine.

It is the self-perpetuating strength of these faculties that has dominated the university scene and, as a consequence, has influenced and moulded the political, educational and social leaders of contemporary society. If there is a major weakness in the classical university, it would be the marked tendency to downgrade applied and technological pursuits. Agricultural education and research in the classical university has, at best, been tolerated, but has had little priority. It has lacked the prestige and support that would attract the better students. The complexity and importance of agriculture is not appreciated or understood in the classical university, and this is reflected in the relative size of budgets accorded to medicine vis-à-vis agriculture in any university where both have been established, in developed as well as developing countries.

In Canada, with approximately fifty universities, only seven include faculties of agriculture. All have faculties of arts and science. Sixteen of the universities have faculties of medicine—but medicine has largely been accepted and accorded the prestige it richly deserves.

I mention medicine because, as a professional faculty, the problems it attempts to resolve, complex as they may be, are essentially the same but much narrower in scope than those that come under the jurisdiction of agriculture. Medicine concerns itself primarily with one species, *homo sapiens*, and the interaction of that species with its environment. Agriculture must concern itself with many complex species in both plant and animal kingdoms, and their interactions with each other and with man. In addition agriculture deals with the economic and social impacts of plant and animal species and their pests. Agriculture must also concern itself with a thorough understanding of the uppercrust of the earth's surface—the soils in their many varied forms—and learn to manage those soils.

The developing nations, where the urgent increases in food production must take place, where the leaders of nations must be influenced to accord the same recognition and support to agriculture as they rightfully accord to medicine, should pattern their universities after the 'land-grant colleges' system in the USA rather than after the classical tradition. The wisdom of the land-grant college approach may be seen in the tremendous success of American agriculture, which has provided virtually 90% of world food aid in the past decade and which currently safeguards the food requirements of the food-deficit nations.

In my view, particularly insofar as the profession of agriculture is concerned, the inherent character of most universities in the Commonwealth continues to be at variance with the roles expected of universities by contemporary society and dictated by the urgency of third world food and related problems. The roles and essential character of Commonwealth universities are thus indeed in need of reconciliation.

REFERENCES

1. The University of Toronto *Bulletin*, 17 July 1978.
2. *Canada and Development Cooperation*, CIDA Annual Review 1976—77.
3. S. H. Wittwer. Food Production: Technology and the Resources Base, *Science*, Vol. 188, 9 May 1975.
4. L. M. Thompson. Weather Variability, Climatic Change, and World Grain Production, *Proceedings of a Seminar on Food and Climate Change*, Science Council of Canada, 13 January 1977.
5. Ibid.
6. Ibid.
7. L. R. Brown. The Politics and Responsibility of the North American Breadbasket, *Worldwatch Paper #2*, October 1975.
8. *Meeting Food Needs in the Developing World*. International Food Policy Research Institute, Washington, D.C., Research Report #1, February 1976.
9. L. R. Brown, op. cit.
10. L. H. Shebeski. Agricultural Resources—The Limits We Face. *Mankind's Future in the Pacific*, The University of British Columbia Press, August 1975.
11. D. G. Aldrich, Jr. Global Land Resources and Their Potential to Meet Future Demands. *Agriculture in the Whirlpool of Change*, Proceedings, Centennial Symposium, Ontario Agricultural College, University of Guelph, 1974.
12. The Fields of the World, *Ceres*, November-December 1974.
13. G. Hutton. *Canada's Role Countering the World Food Crisis*. The Natural Resource Institute, The University of Manitoba, February 1975.

SUB-TOPIC 1(A): PRODUCTION POTENTIAL [Shebeski]

14. W. D. Hopper. *To Conquer Hunger, Opportunity and Political Will*. International Development Research Centre, Ottawa, 16 May 1975.

DISCUSSION

While it was acknowledged that there are many aspects to this topic, the principal ones considered were: (i) the problem of reconciling the need to provide producers with prices that operate as an incentive with the known fact that the main cause of starvation is inadequate purchasing power; (ii) the question of whether the solution to the food problem lies in self-sufficiency or in importation; and (iii) the possibility of the sea, which provides only 3% of the world's food supplies, being developed more as a food resource.

It was concluded that the problem of food production and potential is global in character and that universities have both special responsibilities and a special role to play.

The universities should address themselves to the question of how best to utilize science and technology, with the objective of meeting production potential. The American land-grant college system, with its emphasis on combining teaching, research and extension, was cited as a useful model for developing countries. As opposed to this objective, it was contended that, in general, the classical United Kingdom university model tends not to place sufficient emphasis on the agricultural sciences and technology.

It was generally agreed that the prime role of universities in developing countries should be to train people with ability to undertake appropriate research, teaching and extension, at both low and high technology levels. While it was suggested that specialized research institutes with international funding were needed in particular areas (for example, the Rice Research Institute), because universities have the capacity to provide education and research of a multi-disciplinary nature they have a crucial contribution to make in solving the problems. Moreover universities in developing countries are more able to obtain resources for agricultural research than for research in other areas. Also, universities should recognize the critical importance of sub-university training in agriculture and food production in such places as rural institutes, and they should do all they can to nourish such developments.

Universities in developed countries can contribute significantly to the attainment of the productive potential of developing countries, by such means as the exchange of faculty; direct consulting services; and the training of students from developing countries. It is critical, however, that the need is appreciated for teaching and research to be undertaken in the appropriate physical and cultural environment. It was concluded that the Association of Commonwealth Universities has a responsibility to help promote the development of universities in the developing countries.

Sub-Topic 1(b)

POPULATION

Chairman: Sir GORONWY DANIEL
Vice-Chancellor of the University of Wales and Principal of
University College, Aberystwyth

Rapporteur: Professor A. N. BOSE
Vice-Chancellor of Jadavpur University

Tuesday, 22 August

Population: an Overview

Professor W. D. BORRIE (*Research School of Social Sciences, Australian National University*): The sub-topic for which this paper is written is 'Population'. This forms part of Topic 1, 'The World Food Problem and the Universities', in which other related sub-topics are 'Production Potential', 'Energy' and 'Health'. There has also been a principal address on the subject of Topic 1 before the session on population began (*see* p. 26), and my own remarks will be followed by those of two experts in the areas of high population growth and the spatial distribution of people. With this sequence of topics I have therefore interpreted my role as providing a broad commentary upon the present and immediate future demographic scene in areas relevant to this conference. What is happening to population? What are the current and likely future growth patterns? What are some of the implications of these actual and expected demographic trends and patterns for education?

Past, present and future demographic events have been, are being and will continue to be determined to a major degree by the levels of production and nutritional quality of food, by the accessibility of energy resources, and by the capacity of each cohort of births to survive through the years of reproductive life. These factors are crucially interdependent and failure in one will have a major effect on the others. Recognition of this interdependence was the main theme of the debate—sometimes acrimonious—at the United Nations World Population Conference held in Bucharest in 1974.[1]

At the one extreme stood the neo-Malthusians who still saw family planning as the big batallion that should lead the crusade against want and poverty. But they came under heavy bombardment from those who urged the case for economic development as the prime weapon: give the developing nations access to resources and capital, their argument ran, and they will achieve their own demographic transition from large families and high growth rates to small families and low growth rates, just as most developed nations have already done. High fertility is the product of poverty: abolish poverty and low fertility will follow. In the middle stood the majority who sought an integrative approach in the development of policies in which the aim was economic and social betterment—an approach that involved more extensive international efforts to bring about a more equitable distribution of, and access to, all relevant resources, including family planning resources as well as food and energy.

At the Bucharest Conference poor Malthus took a beating, as did the neo-Malthusians, for no developing country was prepared to accept the view of some Jeremiahs from developed areas that starvation through overpopulation was staring in the faces of some developing countries, and would inevitably soon do so in other cases unless population growth rates were drastically and rapidly reduced. Did all this debate over-simplify the complexities of the population issue?

So often the population issue, like so many other issues, including food and energy, is judged as static at a given moment without sufficient regard for the historical antecedents which must provide the basis for an assessment of the levels and directions of change. It is true that knowledge of causation of current demographic patterns is still far from adequate, but when these patterns are compared with the past it is clear both that they have unique as well as traditional elements, and that they neither have endured for very long nor can persist for very long. They must soon yield one way or another to the more traditional global pattern of very slow growth rates.

The world's growth rate today is estimated to be about 1·9% a year. As such a rate doubles a population every 36 years it clearly could not have existed far into the past and cannot persist far into the future.[2] Nor does the evidence suggest such a possibility. That global average growth rate of 1·9% is made up of a vast variety of demographic situations ranging all the way from population decrease on the one hand in some developed countries to growth rates exceeding 3% a year (a doubling time of only 23 years) in some developing countries.

In the former category the decreasing situation is associated with expectations of life exceeding 70 years and extremely effective and widespread fertility control which results in an average completed family size of not more than two children. This demographic situation, which is certainly unique in human experience, may be regarded as the terminal point of the demographic transition, a point at which the prolongation of life has been so successful that it is completely out of harmony with human biological reproductive potential, so that the only means by which the achievements and goals of such societies can be met and sustained is by bringing *natural* fertility down by a factor of about three, so that the forces of decrement and increment are brought back again into a new and, historically and biologically speaking, highly artificial balance. There is no other choice open to affluent societies which have attained expectations of life of 70 and more years and, as all the evidence indicates that longevity is what such societies covet above all else, their path to survival at current or better standards of living is being, and must continue to be, determined by extremely efficient fertility regulation. Without this their growth rates could jump to 4% a year, an exponential rate that would soon lead to chaos and destruction.

The path towards this new and unique biological equilibrium seems to be the chosen course for almost all countries of European origin, whether within Europe or overseas.[3] It seems also to be the path being followed by Japan, the first major non-European country to 'modernise' in the European tradition. Such statistics as there are also suggest that the onset of extensive and efficient fertility control may be close to being the rule rather than the exception in China, which probably carries about one fifth of the world's population.

Some years ago the emphasis in the study of demographic patterns of the developed countries was upon their growth potential emanating from the high proportion of their populations growing into the child-bearing age groups because of the baby booms which most of them experienced after the second world war. It is now clear that a major force in these baby booms was the emergence of new marriage patterns, typified by younger marriage and by very high proportions marrying, compared with the patterns prevailing before the second world war, rather than any breakdown of their small biologically-controlled family systems which had been amply apparent in earlier years. So when the marriage booms flattened off, so did the baby booms, but simultaneously there was also a widespread decline in marital fertility with the consequence that birthrates came tumbling down all over the developed world, in a few countries to the point of generating population decrease.[4] The extent of the decline in the birthrates of selected developed countries is estimated in Table 1, below.

SUB-TOPIC 1(B): POPULATION [Borrie]

TABLE 1: POPULATION IN 1975 AND CRUDE BIRTH-RATES PER 1,000 OF POPULATION IN 1950 AND 1974, IN SELECTED COUNTRIES

Country	Population 1975 (in thousands)	Crude Birth-Rate 1950	Crude Birth-Rate 1974	Per cent change 1950−74
Developed countries				
The Americas				
Canada	22,801	27·8	15·4	−44·5
United States	213,925	24·8	15·0	−39·5
Asia and the Pacific				
Australia	13,809	23·0	18·9	−17·9
Japan	111,120	23·7	19·4	−18·0
New Zealand	3,031	25·7	19·5	−24·2
Europe and the Soviet Union				
Austria	7,538	15·6	12·8	−18·0
Belgium	9,846	16·9	12·6	−25·4
Czechoslovakia	14,757	23·3	19·8	−15·0
Denmark	5,026	18·7	14·2	−24·1
France	52,913	20·5	15·2	−25·8
Germany, Dem. Rep.	17,194	16·9	10·1	−40·2
Germany, Fed. Rep.	61,682	16·5	10·4	−37·0
Greece	8,930	20·0	16·1	−19·5
Ireland	3,131	21·3	22·3	4·7
Italy	55,023	19·5	15·7	−19·5
Netherlands	13,599	22·7	13·8	−39·2
Norway	4,007	19·1	14·9	−22·0
Portugal	8,762	24·3	19·3	−20·6
Spain	35,433	20·2	19·3	− 4·5
Sweden	8,291	15·6	13·4	−14·1
Soviet Union	255,038	26·7	18·1	−32·2
United Kingdom	56,427	16·3	13·9	−14·7
Large developing countries				
China	823,000	37·3	26·0	−30·2
India	613,000	42·3	36·0	−15·0
Indonesia	136,000	45·0	40·0	−11·1
Brazil	110,000	41·4	38·0	− 8·3

contd. overleaf

[Borrie] TOPIC 1: THE WORLD FOOD PROBLEM

TABLE 1: POPULATION IN 1975 AND CRUDE BIRTH-RATES PER 1,000 OF POPULATION IN 1950 AND 1974, IN SELECTED COUNTRIES (*Contd.*)

Country	Population 1975 (in thousands)	Crude Birth-Rate 1950	Crude Birth-Rate 1974	Per cent change 1950–74
Large developing countries—(contd.)				
Bangladesh	76,000	49·2	49·2	0
Pakistan	71,000	49·6	47·0	−5·2
Nigeria	63,000	49·1	49·1	0
Mexico	59,000	46·6	41·0	−12·0
Smaller developing countries				
Africa				
Mauritius	899	46·2	27·5	−40·5
Egypt	37,543	44·9	34·8	−22·6
Tunisia	5,747	46·4	37·0	−20·3
The Americas				
Puerto Rico	2,902	36·6	23·3	−36·3
Trinidad and Tobago	1,009	37·7	26·5	−29·7
Venezuela	12,213	46·5	37·7	−18·8
Cuba	9,481	30·3	25·3	−16·4
Honduras	3,037	54·6	47·8	−12·5
Jamaica	2,029	34·8	30·6	−12·1
Asia and the Pacific				
Singapore	2,248	44·4	19·5	−56·1
Taiwan	16,198	45·8	23·4	−48·9
Hong Kong	4,225	33·1	19·3	−41·7
Fiji	577	44·3	28·0	−36·8
Sri Lanka	13,986	38·5	27·2	−29·4
Thailand	42,093	46·9	34·0	−27·5
Malaysia	12,093	45·4	33·0	−27·3
Korea, Rep.	33,949	37·0	25·0	−32·4
Vietnam, Dem. Rep.	23,798	41·3	32·0	−22·5

Source: adapted from figures in W. Parker Mauldin, 1976. 'Fertility Trends: 1950–75' in the Population Council, *Studies in Family Planning*, Vol. 7 No. 9, September, pp. 243, 244, 247.

SUB-TOPIC 1(B): POPULATION [Borrie]

What a contrast to the demographic situation of the developing nations! Here growth rates go soaring on, few get below 2% a year, some rising over 3%.[5] Yet there is nothing static about their situations either, which are also unique in terms of human experience but for a reason opposite to that of today's developed countries. In the developed countries reproductive control is the unique element: in the developing countries the unique element is mortality control. Expectations of life below 40 years, and sometimes below 20 years, have been the rule rather than the exception through most of human history, but these are rare in today's world and the whole thrust of national health policies and international health efforts is to ensure that such expectations never return. Already many nations of the ESCAP* region, for example, have expectations of life around 65 years, and the expectation of life in India now exceeds 50 years compared with only about 30 years about forty years ago.[6] It is this thrust to lower death-rates that drives up population growth rates and the direction of this thrust, now affecting every developing country, cannot be changed. The achievement of the low mortality levels now enjoyed by the developed nations is seen as an integral part of the processes of development in the mortality-disadvantaged countries; and of course an essential element in pressing towards this goal is adequate nutrition, without which the short-run gain to be derived from applied medical science rapidly becomes a chimera.

The opening of this gap between the forces of life and death is the meat of the argument of the population pessimists—of whom there are many—who see the human race rushing to its own destruction.[7] It needs only a simple bit of exponential arithmetic to show that the estimated annual growth rate of 2.3% a year between 1970−75 in the world's less developed regions would lead to destruction in a few years *if sustained*. But human societies are not composed of lemmings—and one of the safest predictions that can be made is that major parts of the human race will not hurl themselves to destruction over the cliff of overpopulation.

This is not to say that there are not, and will not continue to be, major problems arising from the maldistribution of resources. Famines arising from droughts, crop failures and other vagaries of nature will recur, and the maintenance of substantial global food stocks and international machinery to deliver the goods when and where catastrophy threatens will continue to be needed; but the basic solution can only lie in the reproductive patterns voluntarily chosen by the world's population of child-bearing age. Reference has already been made to the pattern that now appears to dominate the behaviour of these groups in the more developed sections of the

*Economic and Social Commission for Asia and the Pacific.

world. As yet the reproductive patterns in the less developed regions are, on average, vastly different, with completed family size about double that of the more developed regions.[8]

Yet change does seem to be occurring, in some instances dramatically. Declines in birth-rates in what are termed 'developing' countries today began to be apparent almost thirty years ago. Many of these countries lack the sure statistical data which permits precise measurement of trends, but from the evidence available, much of it based on surveys rather than vital registration systems, it does appear that the birth-rate was falling between the 1950s and 1960s in Brunei, Hong Kong, India, Indonesia, Japan, Republic of Korea, Malaysia, Philippines, Singapore, Sri Lanka, Taiwan, Thailand and Turkey. On the whole the downward shifts were slight, but in some of these and in other countries the downward movement has gathered pace since the 1960s. A recent assessment by W. Parker Mauldin is that the birth-rate of twenty-seven smaller developing countries declined by more than a quarter between 1950 and 1974. This is an impressive statistic, but it covers a population in 1975 of only about 319,000 people. But he also concludes that the birth-rate of the world's eight largest developing countries, with 1,951 million people or close to half the world's population in 1975, also came down between 1950 and 1974 by about a sixth, again an impressive statistic.[9] (*See* Table 1, *above*).

This downward trend does not mean that the majority of these countries are yet anywhere near a zero growth situation, like some of the developed countries. For most of them their expectations of life at birth are up to twenty years below those of the European peoples, although some are catching up fast. The developing regions also still have a majority of countries with birth-rates over 30 per 1,000 of population, whereas Europe has only one such country, Albania.[10] Yet the downward trend seems clear and strongly suggests that the developing world's growth curve *is* turning downwards, quite substantially. The most resistant region is clearly Africa, but here there is perhaps a higher potential of resources enabling the estimated current growth rate of over 2.5% to be absorbed a little longer. The same applies to most of the larger countries of Latin America. Also, the Chinese delegation to the World Population Conference in 1974 at Bucharest asserted that China could manage any expected increase in its population, and the concensus of current estimates is that China's birth-rate is under 30 per 1,000 of population, with some even placing it below 20.[11] The hard core of population growth viewed in its relation to resources remains in the massive populations of the Indian sub-continent, even although there are some signs there of slower population growth rates.

This short paper cannot go into an assessment of probable causes of these changes. Undoubtedly technological innovation, the revolution in the communication of ideas, rising economic expectations, changing social aspirations, the innovation of family planning policies, and the Green Revolution are some of the many inter-related factors involved, but in what proportions they have operated in specific situations is still largely unkown. The hope — and indeed reasonable expectation, judged from the history of fertility decline — is that once the downturn in birth-rates starts it will go on through the thirties into the twenties per 1,000 of population. There are no significant cases of fertility rising again in today's developing countries after the initial breakthrough has been thoroughly established, and no cases to my knowledge where the birth-rate has remained above 30 per 1,000 for any sustained period where expectations of life at birth have remained above 60 years. The association here, of course, is less between fertility and a specific level of mortality as such, than between fertility and the levels of *actual* social, economic and health developments, and economic and social *expectations* that go with such a mortality decline, both as cause and effect.

But a note of optimism, justified though I believe it to be, should not be allowed to cloak stark reality. The developing regions of the world are far from zero growth levels. Declining mortality and high fertility have created age structures which must ensure the continuation of massive growth over the next forty to fifty years. Their baby booms of the past make the mini-booms that worried many of the more developed regions through the 1950s and 1960s pale into insignificance. Compare the following figures of the broad age distributions of the more developed and less developed regions as assessed around 1970.[12]

	Percentage of Population in Each Age Group			
	0 – 14 years	*15 – 64 years*	*65 & over*	*Total population*
More Developed Regions	26·7	63·7	9·6	100·0
Less Developed Regions	40·5	55·7	3·8	100·0

The burden of young dependency is immediately apparent in the less developed situations, as is the potential for further population growth as the young grow into the marrying and child-bearing years. So great is the impetus to growth in the age structure of most of the less developed countries that only a continuous decline in fertility can prevent birth-rates rising. In retrospect, therefore, the declines in birth-rates discussed earlier become all the more impressive in view of the increasing growth potential that has been evolving in the age composition of these countries. Given constant levels of fertility birth-rates would have been rising, but the declines, once initiated, have more than counteracted the potential growth impetus in these age structures.

The other significant aspect of the age structure of the developing countries is really the mirror image of this high juvenile dependency pattern, that is the relatively low proportion of populations in the broad working age groups, compared with the age profile of the developed countries. However a direct comparison of the two situations in the 'more developed' and 'less developed' regions can hardly be made from this simple model, because almost no young people of the developed countries enter the workforce below the age of 15 years whereas young children are a significant component of the workforces of many developing countries. This is where 'development', however desirable in the long run, imposes real hardship upon the developing countries, for education tends to decrease the workforce and increase the dependency ratio. Consequently achieving a basic level of education to the end of primary or first level (around 12 years of age) is costing many developing countries as high a *proportion* (often around 5%) of their Gross Domestic Product (GDP) as do the complex and prolonged educational systems of the developed regions.[13] Striking although the developments in education have been in many developing countries, to the point of substantially increasing the *proportions* of children of school age who actually receive instruction, the demographic growth rate of successive cohorts of children has been so great that in some countries the *numbers* who remain illiterate are still increasing.[14]

Another way of looking at the educational problems created by these high growth situations is to examine the numbers of educable age against the numbers of working age. In developing countries the numbers aged 5 – 14 years are often half the numbers of working ages, 15 – 59 years, compared with less than a third in developed countries.[15] With earnings little above subsistence levels in the former category, education is clearly a major burden on the worker, both because of current costs and because it tends to reduce the GDP by deferring entry to the workforce. This problem becomes particularly acute with regard to education to higher levels, beyond the age of about 15 years. As one commentator has put it, simply because of the high proportion of populations of developing countries of educable age, 5 – 14, education has to be for economic reasons alone highly selective at higher ages, and depend rigorously on merit and potential, tailored to the emerging technological needs of the country as a whole.[16] Otherwise there is a danger of a large population in the age-bracket 15 – 24 years, which is the most productive among young and relatively short-lived populations, being supported at the cost of the working population, whose proportion and output will tend to diminish.

Yet basic and universal education is surely fundamental to the processes of development, which in turn may be fundamental to the processes of changes in social expectations and attitudes which can initiate and spread downturns in fertility.[17] The complex interaction of these variables is not yet fully understood but, assuming that universal basic education must be given a high priority in the development process, the export of talent for higher training in the tertiary institutions of developed countries at their expense may still be one of the most valuable forms of technical assistance, for these older students are not a burden on the domestic labour force while they are training abroad. But the catch is, of course, that many do not return to serve their own countries but remain in the developed regions. How to attract them back to serve their countries of origin is a very difficult question, but if they have no place in those countries for the skills they have acquired, and so remain abroad, are they really a net loss? They may at least be serving abroad the advancement of knowledge which is universal in its application. Moreover the permanent drain may be much less in the future than it was in the past, because in almost all professional and highly-skilled occupations in the developed countries the shortages of the past have suddenly become surpluses, partly for demographic reasons and partly because of rapidly rising higher education participation rates in past years. Thus employment opportunities for foreign students will be much scarcer in the future than they have been over the past few decades.

Indeed the surpluses, on the one hand, of the output of highly trained personnel in the developed countries, which have now emerged from their affluence and increased capacity to continue the full-time educational processes to over half the life-time of an Asian or African peasant, and, on the other hand, the continued incapacity of many of the developing countries to attain even basic universal literacy, are still telling illustrations of the maldistribution of resources; and it is submitted that the problems discussed here arising from the unique elements of today's demographic patterns are fit and proper subjects for present and future discussion in universities in both developed and developing regions.

[Borrie]   TOPIC 1: THE WORLD FOOD PROBLEM

People are an important resource: the trouble is they never seem to be around in the right numbers; but that they will be around in massive numbers cannot be gainsaid. The processes of retardation referred to in this paper may defer the doubling of the world's population, now slightly over 4,000 million, but for good or for ill, double it will, and that probably well within the next fifty years. Such is the momentum of growth generated from past years. And from an examination of the growth patterns that have emerged over the past generation or so, there seems no doubt whatever that the greater part of the world's growth for the rest of this century will be in the less developed regions. Table 2, below, illustrates a possible path to the year 2000, based upon the UN's most recent 'medium' variant.

TABLE 2: ESTIMATED AND PROJECTED WORLD POPULATION IN MAJOR AREAS, 1950, 1975 AND 2000

Major Area	Numbers (millions) 1950	1975	2000	Distribution Per Cent 1950	1975	2000
World Total	2505	3988	6406	100·0	100·0	100·0
Northern Group	1411	1971	2530	56·3	49·4	39·5
Northern America	166	237	296	6·6	5·9	4·6
Europe	392	474	540	15·6	11·9	8·4
USSR	180	255	321	7·2	6·4	5·0
East Asia	673	1005	1373	26·9	25·2	21·4
Southern Group	1094	2017	3876	43·7	50·6	60·5
Latin America	164	326	625	6·5	8·2	9·8
Africa	219	402	834	8·7	10·1	13·0
South Asia	698	1268	2384	27·9	31·8	37·2
Oceania	13	21	33	0·5	0·5	0·5

Source: adapted from UN Department of Economic and Social Affairs, 1974. *The World Population Situation in 1970 – 1975 and its Long-Range Implications,* United Nations, New York, pp. 59, 60.

My own feeling is that these figures, showing a world total of 6,406 millions in 2000, may be too high, primarily because they underestimate the extent of the decline in fertility in both developed and developing sectors of the world; but whatever total does emerge the bulk of the world's growth during this period will be in the developing regions, with a consequent marked shift, approximately in the proportions indicated in Table 2, above, as between the 'Northern' and 'Southern' groups, with the massive populations of South Asia (India, Indonesia, Bangladesh, Pakistan) and the burgeoning countries of Africa and Latin America well in the lead for the rest of this century in the world's growth stakes.

NOTES

1. See UN Department of Economic and Social Affairs, 1975, *The Population Debate, Dimensions and Perspectives,* Population Studies No. 57, 2 Vols., New York. For a perceptive comment upon the interrelation of population with other factors of development, particularly with relation to the Bucharest debate, see Gavin W. Jones, 1978 'Population and Development: Fact, Fancy and Politics', *The Australian Outlook,* Vol. 31, No. 2, August.

2. For a review of recent trends and an assessment of future prospects see UN Department of Economic and Social Affairs, 1974, *Concise Report on the World Population Situation and its Long-Range Implications,* Population Studies No. 56; and, 1977, *Population Bulletin of the United Nations,* No. 8, 1976, New York.

3. For reviews of recent trends and their implications in developing countries see US Commission on Population Growth and the American Future, 1972, *Population and the American Future,* the Report of the Commission, New York; UN Economic Commission for Europe, 1975, Economic Survey of Europe in 1974, Part II, *Post-War Demographic Trends in Europe and the Outlook until the Year 2000,* New York; and The National Population Inquiry, Australia, 1975, First Report, *Population and Australia, A Demographic Analysis and Projection,* Parliamentary Papers No. 6 and 7, 1975, Canberra.

4. Countries which have recently experienced some decrease in population include the Federal Republic of Germany, the German Democratic Republic, Austria, Luxembourg and Great Britain. In many other countries of northwestern Europe fertility is now so low that actual decrease seems imminent.

5. UN, 1974, op. cit., estimated that the annual growth rate of the world's 'less developed' areas in 1960−70 averaged approximately 2·3%, with the highest regional rate in Latin America (2·8%) and the lowest in East Asia (1·7%). Examples of individual countries with rates exceeding 3% were Mexico, Morocco, Uganda, Southern Rhodesia, Philippines, Thailand and Pakistan.

6. The expectation of life at birth of the 'less developed' regions around 1970−75 has been estimated at about 54 years, with rates varying from under 40 years in some countries of tropical Africa to more than 65 years in some of the smaller countries of East Asia. See UN, 1974, op. cit., and UN *Demographic Yearbooks.*

7. One of the most scholarly analyses with a pessimistic view about population growth is Paul R. and Anna H. Ehrlich, 1970, *Population, Resources and Environment, Issues in Human Ecology,* San Francisco.

8. A common measure of fertility is the female gross net production rate, which was estimated to be 1·13 in the more developed regions of the world around 1970 – 75, compared with 2·60 in the less developed regions. These figures imply completed family size of about 2·2 children in the former region and 4·4 children in the latter.

9. W. Parker Mauldin, 1976, 'Fertility Trends: 1950 – 75' in The Population Council, *Studies in Family Planning,* Vol. 7, No. 9, September.

10. Department of Medical and Public Affairs, the George Washington University Medical Centre, 1976, *Population Reports,* Series J, No. 12, November, p. 207.

11. Ibid., pp. 208 – 213.

12. UN Department of Economic and Social Affairs, 1974, p. 25.

13. For a comparative study see Ta Ngoc Chau *et al.*, 1972, *Population Growth and Costs of Education in Developing Countries,* UNESCO, Paris.

14. For example, it has been estimated that between 1960 and 1975 the numbers of children in schools in the less developed regions showed a massive increase from 99 to 205 millions, but that the numbers not at school would still increase from 118 to 128 millions. See UN 1974, op. cit., p. 27.

15. Ta Ngoc Chau, 1972, op. cit., p. 21.

16. UNESCO Regional Office for Education in Asia, 1974, *Population Dynamics and Educational Development,* Papers presented at a Regional Seminar, 10 – 18 September 1973, Bangkok, p. 41.

17. For a discussion of the effects of education on population trends see H. V. Muhsam (ed.), 1975, *Education and Population,* International Union for the Scientific Study of Population, Belgium, Part Two.

India's Population and Food Problem and the Role of Indian Universities

Professor S. CHANDRASEKHAR (*Vice-Chancellor of Annamalai University*): The world has been made aware since the termination of the second world war of the existence of two great threats to mankind and modern civilization: a thermonuclear war that may be triggered off by the world's two major technologically advanced countries, and the current population explosion in the developing third world. There is, however, a profound difference between these two grave dangers. A modern nuclear war would be so disastrous that it would perhaps rule out the survival of the human species as we know it today, but it would be a one-time phenomenon, which is its 'saving grace'. But the population explosion, in which man could inevitably breed himself to decline, degeneration and decay as an organism, would, unlike a nuclear holocaust, be a continuous phenomenon so long as there is no control of human fertility.

Fortunately, it may be pointed out at the very outset, there are workable answers to both these threats to our survival. If man can consider the world as a neighbourhood, treat all human beings as 'brothers and sisters under the skin', and grow in ethical and spiritual values to even a quarter of the heights of his scientific and technological advancement, peace can not only be achieved in our times but can also become a permanent possibility.

Similarly, if there is political will and national determination, and if cultural chauvinism and religious obscurantism can be eschewed, national birth-rates in poor and underdeveloped countries can be cut by half in a decade or two, as many nations both in the West and Asia, among both the free and the communist countries, have already demonstrated. Low birth-rates, like peace among nations, are achievable. It is not impossible to accomplish dramatic and definitive social change even when it involves intimate human behaviour.

World Population Growth

The familiar facts and figures of the world's runaway population growth can be recalled very briefly. Today the world's total population is just a little over 4 billion. Currently we are adding (despite inadequate data from certain countries) about 75 million people every year; that is, about 200,000 new mouths every day, 4 babies every second. And most of this in countries which can least afford them. At this rate of increase of about 2% per annum we would, on the basis of certain assumptions of current fertility and mortality, reach almost 7 billion by the end of this century, only 22 years away, and within the lifetime of a majority of people already on this planet today.

However this tremendous explosion is a recent phenomenon. According to some 'guesstimates' there were no more than 10 to 15 million people in the whole world at the end of the stone age. During the time of Christ the population had grown to about 250 million. Roughly it took a little more than a million years (and according to certain other sources nearly two million) for the evolution of man to his present position as *homo sapiens* and *homo faber* and for him to multiply to a billion (a thousand million) by the year 1830. This includes the transition of man all the way from the primitive 'hunting and gathering stage' to his becoming a town-dweller, including, of course, the domestication of animals and the all-important long-drawn-out agricultural revolution.

The second billion was reached in a century, by about 1930, during which period the industrial revolution had gradually made its way all over Europe, to North and South America, and finally to Asia and Africa.

It took only about thirty years to reach the third billion, by about 1960. The reason behind this exponential growth was simple enough: the health revolution (which can be summarised in one word—asepsis), launched by Jenner, Pasteur, Lister, Koch, Simmelweis and a host of other medical pioneers a century earlier, began to spread all over the world—and is still spreading. Its efforts to save man from the micro-organisms brought about a dramatic and definitive decline in the death-rate and its various components, particularly the infant mortality rate; and, since the birth-rate continued to be high and stationary, the enormous jump in the population to three billion.

And in 1975, just fifteen years later, when all the four major revolutions of mankind—agricultural, industrial, communication and transport, and the health revolution—had permeated to nearly every nook and corner of the world in varying degrees, the world's population passed the fourth billion. The rate of world population growth had become really staggering.

What of the Future?

What of the future? A few years ago a UN agency projected that under certain assumptions mankind might well double its numbers and become 8 billion by 2000 A.D. But since several countries, large and small, have effectively lowered their birth-rates, thanks to the global family planning campaign both under governmental and private agencies, the world's total population is now expected to reach instead about 7 billion by the end of the century. But there is a possibility of the redoubling of the population by 2052 A.D.

It is hoped that this figure for the year 2000 may prove reliable, for official population projections have a way of going awry. Even this, however, is an enormous population for this one world of ours with its finite resources to support. But the fact that the birth-rates in various countries are being successfully lowered gives us hope that we can, if we will, cope with the problem.

SUB-TOPIC 1(B): POPULATION [Chandrasekhar]

India's Population Growth

A few facts concerning the magnitude of India's population growth and the problem it poses may be briefly stated. In the world today India ranks second in population numbers, with 630 million by mid-1978. (Communist China tops the list and has touched the one billion mark, according to one reliable calculation.) India ranks seventh in land area (about 3 million square kilometres). That is, India has to support about 15% of the world's population on 2·4% of the world's total land. And this population lives on less than 2% of the world's income. Although India is only about two-fifths the size of the continental United States of America she shelters more than two and a half times the population of the United States. In the last 31 years, since India became independent in 1947, she has added more than 250 million to her total population, which is roughly about the total population of the Soviet Union. But the USSR, which is the world's largest country in terms of land area, has six times the land area of India.

And to this vast population India continues to add monthly more than a million, or about 13 million annually, which is about the total population of such countries as Australia, Taiwan or Sri Lanka, and about half the entire population of Canada. And according to a conservative projection based on current trends of fertility and mortality India's population may pass the 885 – 900 million mark at the turn of the century.

India's Food Situation

Overpopulation of any nation or region, meaning too many people in terms of available land area, renewable and non-renewable resources and the given level of technology, or the area's total carrying capacity, is still not recognized as a major destructive problem by millions of common people who create the problem and by some governments who appear to be anti-natalist but do not have the necessary political clout to do something tangible about it.

India's population growth is more than a mere numbers game. It involves directly the question of the quality of life for a great majority of her people and assuring them the basic, irreducible minimum decencies of civilized existence in terms of food, clothing, housing, education, health and some leisure and recreation. Of these fundamental needs perhaps the most pressing and formidable is an adequate food supply. As the population problem is most pressing in the tropical world, the poor can do without much clothing, housing or even education, but not without sufficient food—sufficient calories and needed protein—a simple but balanced diet to enable them to do a day's work. In terms of calories an adult in most of these areas needs about 2,300 – 2,500 calories to perform a day's labour in a field or a factory, a home or an office. And judging by the total food production in certain developing countries, and the poor distribution and want of purchasing power, millions go to bed literally hungry. This is true even in areas where there is relatively plenty of food as such, but people cannot afford to buy it at current prices.

No matter what any politician or government in power says, India's common people have been hungry for at least a thousand years, according to the available historical evidence. The golden age of the past is a comforting myth. People faced periodical famines and perished without protest or murmur, under the Moghuls, the British, and twice during the present three decades of freedom.

Today there is no famine in India, but hunger in the countryside continues to be endemic. For thirty years, since India regained her political freedom, we have been talking of 'freedom from foreign bread' and 'national food self-sufficiency'. And during this short period the country suffered two of the worst famines in her long, chequered history; but the toll was fortunately lessened by the timely and dedicated assistance of certain UN agencies, the US government, and certain Commonwealth countries such as Canada and Australia, as well as several voluntary international relief agencies.

Today (1978) the government of India has forecast a record foodgrain output of 125 million tonnes for the current agricultural year (July 1977 – June 1978). The available evidence shows that we may well reap a bumper harvest. If this happens it will be 7 million tonnes more than the official target and 4 million tonnes more than the previous record foodgrain yield of 121 million tonnes in 1975 – 76. But the point is that if the nation does not keep up the tempo India may easily face a famine in a year or two. For India's agriculture is still a gamble in the monsoon, as it has always been over the centuries.

Even the current expected bumper harvest is not really a great achievement, for if every Indian of all age groups and both sexes (women are always underfed in India—voluntarily) were to eat as much as he or she should according to nutritional standards, the surplus year of 1978 would really be a 'bad' year for the country.

Such unexpected yields have happened in the past owing to a variety of favourable conditions of nature. The result was official complacency and relaxation all round until the monsoons failed in a year or two and the nation did not have sufficient buffer stocks, and government officials had to scurry from Canada to Argentina arranging for foodgrains to be imported and expending precious foreign exchange. We have not yet learnt the lesson of the need to work continuously on an agricultural revolution, persevering until the problem is permanently solved. One swallow does not make a summer and this year's unexpected bumper harvest should hardly make us believe that Indian agriculture has come of age and hunger and shortages have become a thing of the past. This is a dismal sentiment but there is no absolute guarantee that there will be no famine or shortages in India in the near future.

The reasons are that the Green Revolution in India has proved to be little more than a useful gimmick. The revolution is confined to the North Indian wheat belt and particularly to the progressive province of the Punjab. Lack of space prevents the presentation of the available official evidence, but even here, the Green Revolution has meant that the rich farmers who could afford fertilizers, irrigation facilities and even a modicum of farm machinery have become richer, and the poor capital-less farmer with less than a few acres has been reduced to greater penury. The successful farmer is visible to the tourist, but the plight of the latter is latent and invisible.

Apart from wheat, the productivity of rice and maize (corn) continues to be low and Bengal and the entire South are rice-consuming areas. Periodical and haphazard official attempts, which began during the second world war years, to change dietary habits from rice to wheat have proved a total failure. And the average yield of rice (of all varieties) per hectare is less than a fourth of Japan's and half of that in Korea and Taiwan (countries which do not use any large-scale machinery).

Even in the case of wheat, because it has been grown intensively the traditional balance between it and various pulses has been upset. Now that returns from wheat are such a paying proposition to the rich farmer barley and pulses have been neglected. The per capita availability of pulses has gone down and the country is scouting for imports of pulses—pulses which used to be one of India's major agricultural products, supplying much-needed protein in the largely vegetarian diet of the majority of Indians.

Population Classification on the Basis of Food Consumption

If India's population is expected to reach between 900 million and a billion by 2000 A.D. India should produce, or must afford to import, about 150 million tonnes of foodgrains, on the basis of current levels of consumption (which are far from satisfactory).

From the point of view of current patterns of food consumption, India's population is normally divided into four classes: —

1. The rich, consisting of about 5% of the population, eat well. They can afford to eat adequate amounts of balanced food. But affluence is no guarantee of knowledge of nutrition, and a part of this sector suffers from the effects of malnutrition resulting from both traditional dietary prejudices and eating 'rich' foods.

2. The middle class consists of some 25% of the total population. This largely urban group enjoys what might be termed a near-optimum diet, in terms of both calories and protein, in the context of existing food habits, preferences and the availability of certain foods. This class is really the educated upper class which can be looked upon as a quasi-ideal norm in terms of both knowledge and financial resources. The Punjabi population contributes a disproportionately large share to this class.

3. The urban and the rural poor class, consisting of some 30% of the total population, suffer from both under- and malnutrition. They are both illiterate and economically poor and this group is vulnerable to all the diseases caused by poor nutrition.

4. Last is the 'poorest' class, made up of the remaining 40% of the rural masses as well as the urban slum-dwellers. These people are the gaunt, skeletal 'pot-bellied' who live on the pavements or in the slums of the cities and villages. Hunger is literally their constant companion.

This rough division of population based on official statistics and ad hoc random sample surveys is given here only to identify to some extent the magnitude of the nation's food problem.

The Attempts to Solve the Food Problem So Far

As for various attempts to solve the food problem made during this century, we are primarily concerned here with education, particularly agricultural education, in the belief that once science and agriculture are married the problem of food supply would be solved.

A brief early history of these efforts may not be out of place here. The earliest attempt in this direction was the product of famine. As a result of the Famine Commission Report of 1901 the government of India started six regional agricultural colleges at Coimbatore, Kanpur, Nagpur, Poona, Sabour and Lyallpur (now in Pakistan). Postgraduate education and agricultural research were fostered by the establishment of the Indian Agricultural Research Institute at Delhi, the Indian Veterinary Research Institute at Izzatnagar and the Indian Research Institute at Karnal. During the second world war some impetus was given to work at these places by the national 'grow more food' campaign. According to all accounts the campaign has become a handy annual ritual. The governors of states are shown planting trees year after year, but the campaign organisers are apparently unaware of the existence of a virile goat population in India. (And, incidentally, India is the only major country in the world where all kinds of animals are free to roam where they like but the plants are fenced in — albeit often inadequately.)

When India became independent in 1947 some political leaders had not forgotten the Bengal famine and its aftermath during the second world war. The government of India decided to make a determined effort to solve the food problem, supply adequate food to all the people, and erase India's image abroad as a famine-stricken country with a perennial beggar's bowl. But because of other pressing political problems it was only in the early fifties that India took a major step by inviting the United States into the Indian economic picture with its policy of aid, technical assistance and co-operation. Two Indo-American teams of experts examined Indian agriculture and its problems in some depth and agreed with the government of India that a large and growing population could not afford to be dependent on food imports (under the Wheat Loan and P.L. 480, etc.). The rupee funds which were fast accumulating in India under P.L. 480 to the credit of the US were made available to start at least one modern agricultural university in each state on the lines of the US land-grant colleges established under the Morrill Act of 1862.

These universities received considerable American equipment, technical personnel and their expertise. As in the US, these new Indian agricultural universities emphasised teaching, research and extension. And the last, extension, was the most important. The concept of taking the latest scientific knowledge directly to the farmers' doorsteps had never been attempted.

There are today some 21 agricultural universities in India and they are doing their best to further agricultural research. There has also been a rapid increase in the number of home science colleges for women. The education of women in modern nutrition is essential, for they dominate the kitchens and dictate the family diet. But the graduates of these colleges constitute only a tiny fraction of the total population of Indian women.

Despite all that has been done progress has been slow and the total agricultural revolution still eludes India. The graft of twentieth-century technology on a four-millennia-old culture, some of which has outlived its utility, does not always work. India's bumper harvests are periodical phenomena, and the latent hunger of the silent majority has not been solved. Cattle continue to wander through the streets which have twentieth-century traffic mixed with traditional traffic, and the government is apparently helpless. Of late the traffic death toll in India has become alarming in relation to the number of vehicles and our total road mileage. Our national priorities are still lopsided. Our hospitals have isotopes but no fly swatters.

What is the Nation's Food Problem?

What is India's food problem? Some 80% of the population of about 630 millions live in more than half a million (560,000) villages. That is, the population dependent on agriculture is about 500 million, considerably larger than the *total* population of any country in the world today with the exception of communist China. It is a problem because the vast mass of illiterate, ignorant peasants live in huts, hovels and sub-standard dwellings devoid of any basic sanitary or hygienic necessities, not to speak of such modern amenities as electricity, running water, etc. The environment of the average village is depressing, the streets narrow, crooked and unpaved; and the total picture from the public health point of view is one of filth and squalor.

Whether the peasant works as an independent farmer—his farm is small and uneconomic—or as a landless agricultural labourer or a sharecropper, his income is meagre and in a majority of cases below the poverty line. His family size is relatively large; rural birth and death rates and particularly infant mortality rates are high. Rural girls get married in their early teens and women are physically exhausted by the frequency of childbearing before they are 30 years old. Expectation of life at birth for rural men and women is less than 50 years. The demographic profile of India's rural population reveals needless loss of life and hence the picture is one of considerable demographic wastage.

Thus, in a word, the rural problem is both a demographic and a food problem. It is one of too many births, too many deaths, and the surviving population living a primitive life on a meagre income with a low level of living and consumption, far removed from the main stream of Indian national life.

The overall agricultural 'technology', if it can be dignified by that term, is so primitive that it takes almost 70% of the nation's population in nearly half a million villages to produce foodgrains which are not sufficient for the nation's minimum needs. In Great Britain, for example, a mere 3% of the population produces more than half the nation's total food needs. In the United States about 7% of the population produces not only the abundant food needs of the country but very much more to spare and export to hungry nations of the world.

If this is the problem, what is the answer? What about a policy of national rural reconstruction—a programme that would rehabilitate the economy of rural agriculture and cottage industries and increase the land's productivity and lower the nation's fertility?

We must concede that some ground has been covered and a little progress has been registered as a result of government and voluntary effort in the past three or four decades. Today in some rural areas there is some kind of school, however unsatisfactory, where there was none before; there is electricity in some villages where even a kerosene hurricane lamp was a rarity; there is now in some areas a primary health centre with at least a paramedical worker and a peripatetic visiting physician where in the past the only para- 'medical worker' available was the *dai,* the ignorant, traditional midwife. We have today in some places some kind of link roads where in the past there were only footpaths. Today some villages have even a post and telegraph office whereas in the past communications were absent and isolation was complete.

This is true of some villages. And yet the picture of most villages today is not what it ought to be in terms of the amenities available in urban areas in India or in terms of the life enjoyed by the rural population in advanced countries. What then is the means of transforming the face of rural India? To me education (to be defined below) is the major key to the development of rural India. Of course at the outset I am aware that this sounds simplistic and betrays my bias as an educationist. But I am convinced that nothing works like real education to bring about a rapid and enduring qualitative change in rural society. Education of rural youth and adults of both sexes is the real answer to the miserable plight of our backward rural millions.

But what kind of education? If the key to the rehabilitation of the rural agricultural population and the reconstruction of the village economy is granted to lie in rural education, let us look into certain details of the proposal for a national network of centres for such education.

Rural Universities for India?

Rural universities, not unlike institutions in Taiwan, Mexico and elsewhere, which would ultimately lead to the solution of India's food problem are what the country needs. This certainly does not mean that we should duplicate the kind of universities already in existence in the country. It does mean that such universities would be *designed* for rural India and *located* in a rural area, serving a stipulated number of villages around the university.

A sketchy outline of the role and function of these universities may be offered here. It may be pointed out that the objectives and scope of these proposed rural universities would be quite different from our present agricultural universities which, with a few exceptions, are located in cities and urban areas far removed from the rural milieu, and which educate not the peasants tilling the soil but white-collared agricultural administrators. All rural young men and women who are agriculturists and artisans would be admitted to such rural universities, irrespective of age, caste, creed or religion, and classes would be designed according to certain broad age groups. Older-age adults could be accommodated in classes held whenever they are free.

There would be no prerequisites of any kind, academic or otherwise, for admission to such universities, beyond a desire to learn. Rural residence and possibly rural-based occupations would be the only criteria. To begin with, all those who are illiterate and those who have lapsed into illiteracy would be given a few months' or a year's course to make them functionally literate in their mother tongue and the regional language. While in a great majority of cases the students may be required to learn only one Indian language, it may be necessary in some cases to learn two not dissimilar Indian languages (in cases where the peasant's mother tongue is not the regional language).

Once students have learned to read and write, instruction, largely oral but buttressed by specially-prepared manuscript texts, could be undertaken on various relevant subjects. And the subjects taught would be directly relevant and oriented to rural needs and problems. In addition basic science courses, particularly applied science courses, may be taught.

As well as adequate functional literacy rural people need a basic knowledge of health and hygiene, diet and nutrition, improved agricultural methods, and whatever cottage industry they are in already, or would like to be engaged in. In addition to functional literacy the Indian peasant must be taught the basic, elementary principles of healthful living, how to remove and dispose of human wastes and garbage, to filter and boil water before drinking it, and to treat the fly, the mosquito and the rat as his mortal enemies—as indeed the Chinese peasants have been taught in communist China in less than a generation. Then half the battle of India's rural education and reconstruction will have been won.

SUB-TOPIC 1(B): POPULATION [Chandrasekhar]

Since even basic medical facilities are virtually absent in 80% of our villages the motto for the rural population should be 'prevention is better than cure' until the central and state governments are able to provide a network of skeletal health services for rural India.

Since population control for India is of such paramount importance our target should be to reduce the nation's birth-rate of about 35 to 25, if not 20, per 1,000 in about a decade. The death-rate of about 15 per 1,000 shows a slow decline but is still high in relation to other countries. The experience of certain other countries, relevant to India in this connection, reveals that a reduction of the death-rate (particularly the infant mortality rate, which is currently more than 100 deaths per 1,000 live births per year) is one effective and humane way of reducing the birth-rate. This may sound paradoxical but it is true. This reduction can be achieved, as several countries—big and small—have demonstrated during the last decade and a half.

We have already done a lot of work in India in both rural and urban areas on the need for family planning, and the response and actual practice in terms of sterilizations, for example, have been fairly encouraging in the nation as a whole. There are, of course, considerable differentials in targets achieved between one state and another. What is needed is adult population education, which the rural universities would impart, and persuasion supported by a set of incentives.

In the problem of balanced nutrition not only enough calories for all members of a family, particularly the female children who are invariably short-changed, but also sufficient protein is of particular importance. If all rural wives can be taught the basics of adequate diet for growing children, nursing mothers and working adults, then the perennial problem of hunger in the countryside can be solved. Nobody believes that the rural folk who raise the food and feed the cities should themselves go hungry, but such is the paradox of India all too often. The wife must learn to raise vegetables and green leafy plants, and if the family can be helped to maintain a cow or she-buffalo the problem of milk supply, not for sale but for family consumption, can be tackled. If the family is non-vegetarian chickens can be raised and the consumption of eggs as well as milk can take care of the protein gap.

In this connection there is a great need to evolve a national meal—cheap, nutritious and balanced—readily available all over India and widely publicised so that wherever people go in India they can ask for and obtain this standard, nutritional and taste-satisfying food. It is high time that India's nutrition experts tackled this.

All this is, of course, predicated upon the rural family owning a plot of land and having a little capital to own a cow, a plough, etc. As for landless families, some amount of external help is imperative. And the provision of water, better seeds, fertilizers, etc., must be an urgent function of the government.

Rural universities could play a crucial role in helping villagers in all these essential matters, as well as in the basic, essential matter of transforming Indian agriculture from a pathetic way of life to a successful business proposition. The peasant already has 'hereditary' knowledge acquired from generations, as well as considerable common sense. He may have to unlearn some of his knowledge but his readiness to reform and his willingness to learn must be encouraged. If simple, applied and directly relevant courses can be designed on soils, ploughing, water, seeds, crops, manure, botany, livestock feeding and breeding, public health, sanitation, family planning, etc., and imparted with care and imagination, agriculturists who are dealing with these subjects in their daily work will readily see where they can improve.

Such rural universities would effectively bridge the gap between the teaching of theory in the classroom and practical work on the fields outside the classroom. And the daily work of the peasant on the land would be enriched by what he learns in the classroom since he can put everything he learns into practice on the farm where he works and has his being.

And last, the mere presence of a university in the heart of a rural area surrounded by villages would have a beneficent psychological repercussion: it would help to overcome the current general apathy and inertia, and instil in the people an ambition for higher standards and better quality of life and the will and determination to work for such ends.

Each proposed rural university should be set up in a relatively good farming region, with room to expand, where there is a depth of fertile soil and a plentiful water supply. If possible the rural university should be built not too far from a main road, or a feeder or link road, or a railroad, within reasonable distance of the local town and market. The university will have cubicles, classrooms, workshops and laboratories—simple and functional—to meet rural needs. The university will have its own dairy and poultry farm, its garden for vegetables, flowers and fruits and its nursery for trees. With the supply of cheap electric power and the provision of some road communication with all the neighbouring villages, the university may well help the rural population identify their well-being with the rural university in their midst.

Conclusion

Thus, if India's colleges and universities can play a new, pioneering and unconventional role in gearing their instruction and research to India's current pressing twin problems of population control and efficient agricultural productivity, she can not only become self-sufficient in food supply but stabilise her population at a desired optimum level. This is within the realm of possibility in this generation if India can change her priorities in economic planning and engineer a farm revolution involving the farmer, the soil and the total cultural milieu. This, of course, is easier said than done; but then other countries have faced similar problems decades earlier and have solved them with dedication and determination. There is no reason why India cannot gain by their experience.

In a word, India's objective must be to educate mothers to have two or three children instead of the six or more they have today, and make every blade of rice and wheat yield ten- or twenty-fold what they bear today.

The World's Food Problems in the Context of Population Shifts and Changes — The Role of Human Settlements

Professor H. P. OBERLANDER (*Professor of Regional Planning and Director, Centre for Human Settlements, University of British Columbia*): It is a privilege to join a panel of distinguished colleagues in a discussion of the world's food problems in the context of population shifts and changes. But why was I asked to contribute to this discussion since I am neither an agronomist nor a demographer, not even an economist? My concerns are with human settlements and their strategic role in world development.

What is the relationship between human settlements and your concern for food throughout the world? It is my contention that human settlements and the production, the distribution and the consumption of food are interdependent and interactive and represent a cause and effect relationship of profound consequence.

Human settlements are the places throughout the world where people live and work; they have grown into a network of communities of varying sizes, diverse densities and multiple functions, but they all interact. Their common denominator is that they are linked locally, nationally, regionally and globally in a system which makes them interactive and interdependent. Human settlements are the result of interaction of geography, history and human endeavour. Historically they may have been the result of food production and distribution, but very quickly human settlements have in turn profoundly affected the ways and means of food-growing and its consumption and therefore are performing a central and cyclical role in regulating access to food across the world regardless of social, economic or political levels of development in any given nation state.

Settlements satisfy two essential needs for man: on the one hand the essential satisfaction of living in groups; and on the other hand the opportunities for organizing production, distribution and consumption, including food. It is in this sense that any consideration of the world's food problems must include a concern for the settlement system which generates food and ensures its distribution for survival and growth. In this system of interdependence universities have a special role to perform through research and education; both should be geared to enlarge the scope and satisfaction of production, distribution and consumption.

These relationships were clear and often self-evident when the world's population was small and constituted a rural society based on an agrarian economy. These essential linkages, while growing complex, have been obscured and distorted through the rapid march of industrialization and urbanization — first in Europe and North America and now in the rest of the world which seems intent on catching up with its neighbours through a relentless drive for industrialization. The location, size and growth of settlements historically have been based on quantity and availability of food production. Early settlements throughout history were determined entirely by the capacity of a given hinterland to supply food, transport it and store it for a given population. Settlements rose and fell on their access to food and flourished in regions where an assured food supply was available. This symbiotic relationship achieved an inherent balance of scale which benefited both food production and the supply and expansion of related human activities. That balance has been severely upset throughout the eighteenth and nineteenth centuries in Europe and the twentieth century in North America. Many of the developing countries are experiencing this radical change in the current decades. If history is any guide, it is essential to re-establish the balance between human settlement needs and food production capability. The two are clearly interdependent and concern for one without the other leads to disaster.

Man's conviviality and his ability to harness his environment for survival have produced settlements throughout history and throughout the globe. Parallel with the formation and expansion of settlements was man's growing capacity to raise food, store it and distribute it over time and considerable distance. It was in and through settlements that man was able to expand food production beyond survival and then ensure food availability beyond a particular season and beyond local geographic limitations.

The relationship between food production, population needs and human settlements is as close today as it was in the Nile Valley 5000 years ago, or the Indus Valley 8000 years ago, or in our own Fraser River Valley 9000 years ago. To survive man had to grow food, but to go beyond survival man had to depend upon others for help and sharing of tasks and responsibilities which involved the founding and expansion of communities. Rural land produces food but the settlements provide the community of men who can plant, harvest, store, distribute and increase production by learning from previous experience. It is gathering this experience, recording it systematically and building on it for increased food production that has been one of the traditional roles of the universities.

Our University is no exception to the fact that most western universities in North America started as agricultural colleges in response to the direct needs of the society of the day and the demands of the students of that period. The first substantive faculty of the University of British Columbia was the faculty of agriculture and UBC's first president was an agronomist who had been dean of agriculture.

The essential point is the intimate linkage between human settlements and food production and the responsibility that the universities have to focus upon that linkage and support it with continuing research and education. Food production clearly requires settlements that provide labour, material, equipment and the continually expanding knowledge to improve production. It is in these communities that the food products are stored, merged into new products, further refined and, above all, distributed. Without the settlements of varying sizes and their close network of commercial and industrial interchange, food distribution could not occur.

In addition it is clearly the settlements and their recently exponential growth that have created the enormous market for food products, and conversely it is in settlements that food consumption is very often a crucial economic and political issue. The characteristic relationship between settlements and food production, food distribution and food consumption is a universal phenomenon—universal across the globe and universal over time. The historic Greek city-states exemplified this relationship and the early development of the fertile crescent of the Euphrates and Tigris Valley is another obvious example. The great civilization of the Nile Valley was both cause and effect in the interaction between food production and settlement growth and expansion. When Britain still depended on its own domestic food production and distribution in the sixteenth and seventeenth centuries, communities survived and flourished entirely in relation to the oats, barley and hops that formed their food basis as well as provided a surplus for trade. The settlements, in turn, provided labour and employment. These relationships have survived and persisted and are still evident in Africa, Latin America and Asia today. Food production in the third world is closely linked to size and distribution of human settlements for the reciprocal dependency of production, distribution and consumption. It is therefore clear that only the most sensitive and careful examination of these reciprocal arrangements will be appropriate for managing human settlements in the context of ever-expanding and growing demands for food production and appropriate distribution for rising consumption.

To consider the world's food problems outside the context of human settlements is to isolate an essential human need from the human being itself. What we eat, how we consume it and how it is available to everyone is entirely a function of size and distribution of settlements. It is therefore critical in any strategy of economic, social or political development to recognize the communities' dependence on food production and its distribution. This has only recently been recognized amongst governments and agencies concerned with the strategy for international development.

Let me introduce three specific examples chosen from the current discussion on food and development. The United Nations Institute of Nutrition for Central America and the Philippines recently estimated that one third of the food produced in the developing world is lost before it reaches human mouths. Here we are dealing with the most direct relationship between production and consumption at the local or small-scale regional level. This attrition of a most precious commodity is clearly related to the inability of the settlements of the region as a network to facilitate distribution and consumption of foodstuffs. We are all familiar with the unnecessary loss of food in quantity or quality through poor transport, poor storage, exposure to weather and rodents, let alone the slippery hands of unaccountable middlemen. Cities and towns of a given region can clearly be organized to increase effective distribution and efficient consumption of a scarce commodity. Here we have a system of conduits or pipes that ought to be improved by stopping leaks and corrosion so as to distribute 100% of the commodity from input to output. The system can be improved by shortening it, by reducing friction and by giving it priority in maintenance and protective care.

Food production is primarily based on known plant material and traditional production and consumption habits. Here again, the settlements in which research and development take place and in particular their universities can make a unique contribution to improving the food supply. There are 200,000 known plant species of which only about 100 have been domesticated in the sense that they have been modified genetically to make them fully useful to man. Of these 100 only about 30 provide 85% of the food-weight eaten by us and 95% of the calories and protein. More specifically, three-quarters of all human food energy and protein consumption comes from a mere eight species: wheat, rice, maize, barley, oats, sorghum, millets and rye. These are all cereals and represent a dangerously precarious base from which we expect to feed the world's expanding population. Many more plant species can and ought to be enlisted in the struggle for expanding the food supply and enhancing its distribution and encouraging rising consumption to increase healthy human productivity.

Two things have to be overcome. In both instances settlements and their institutions, particularly the universities, can play a leading role. The first deals with man's perception that many of these plants, as yet undeveloped, represent 'poor man's crops', not worthy of domestication and large-scale production. The other is to encourage research and administrative projects for these unexploited food plants in the regions of food shortages and through the institutions that have credibility and recognition locally. It is now fifty years ago that the then disregarded and underestimated soya bean was lifted from obscurity by the University of Illinois research team into a position where it provides more protein than any other plant species.

The third example of linkage between settlements and food production is socio-political. Substantial increase in quality and quantity of production as well as local availability would occur through land reform. Land ownership and access to its use in the developing world historically was the result of the priorities of colonizing powers. Ownership and scale of land production were not related to the efficiency of raising food crops or providing easy access between consumer and producer. The need for radical land reform is an issue common to the future of improving settlements and food production. Access to the land has to be the basis of food production and its linkage with a network of settlements must form the basis for a new network of activities. Coupled with the need for land reform, based on function and social requirements, is the need for a reassessment of technology which again is common to both settlement and food production policies. There are others who are far more informed in these matters but realistic balances will have to be struck between appropriate technologies for food production and appropriate technologies for its distribution and consumption throughout and within settlements.

Perhaps the most obvious aspect of interdependence and interaction between human settlements and food production is the eternal push and pull between rural and urban life. The most characteristic frustrations of the developing countries are the drift and shift of population to major urban centres. Even the most valiant and progressive policies for national development are often frustrated by the flight of population from the country to the town. This magnetic one-way flow of energy and endeavour invariably leads to compounding problems in the city and compounding the difficulties of maintaining or increasing food production in the hinterland. The town will always have its inherent attractions and its mysterious promise of a better life, particularly for the young. It has recently become clear that, unless living in the country and its increased potential for the next generation is attacked vigorously, any real hope of meeting hunger, poverty or death at a young age is in vain. It is for these reasons that policies for food production and policies for human settlements must be framed jointly in full recognition of their interdependence.

Two years ago while meeting in Vancouver the UN Conference on Human Settlements: Habitat '76 summarized these issues under its major concern for land:—

Recommendation D.6 (a) In view of the limited availability of land for human settlements and the need to prevent the continuing loss of valuable natural areas due to erosion, urban encroachment and other causes, efforts to conserve and reclaim land for both agriculture and settlements without upsetting the ecological balance are imperative.

(b) *The supply of usable land should be maintained by all appropriate methods including soil conservation, control of desertification and salination, prevention of pollution, and use of land capability analysis and increased by long-term programmes of land reclamation and preservation.*

(c) *Special attention should be paid to:* .... (ii) control of soil erosion, *e.g.* through reforestation, flood control, flood plain management, changes in cultivation patterns and methods, and controls on indiscriminate grazing;.... (iv) reclamation of water-logged areas in a manner that minimizes adverse environmental effects; (v) application of new technologies such as those related to flood control, soil conservation and stabilization and irrigation;.... (vii) economizing land by fixing appropriate densities in areas where land is scarce or rich in agricultural value;.... (xi) expansion of agricultural lands with proper drainage.

DISCUSSION

The world's total population is just over four billion, with a growth rate estimated to be about 1.9% a year. Such a rate doubles the population every thirty-six years, and it was agreed that this could not persist far into the future without the most serious consequences to mankind.

The global average of 1.9% is made up of a vast variety of demographic situations, ranging from population decrease in some developed countries to growth rates exceeding 3% a year in developing countries. While in most of the developed countries reproductive control has brought down the growth rate to less than, or slightly above, the replacement level, mortality control brought about by better public health services but without significant birth control programmes has boosted the growth rates in many of the developing countries which also have chronic food shortages. Although there are also indications of declining birth rates in the developing world, the present size of the population and the growth rate place a considerable strain on world food resources — the rate of increase in food production having been marginally above the rate of increase in population. India's case was cited as an example. Even with a creditable sustained growth rate in food production over the years and a record recent harvest of 125 million tonnes of food grains, nearly 60% of her population go to bed hungry. It was acknowledged, however, that non-availability of the required amount of food to large sections of the population is not determined only by the availability of the food in the country but by various social, economic and political factors as well. It was also maintained that sufficient food is produced in the world to feed adequately every person on earth, provided proper distribution could be assured.

It was felt that the food and population problems of the world are such that every country should have comprehensive food and population policies. It was pointed out that an increase in food production would not necessarily lead also to an increase in population, as was suggested in some quarters. Countries, particularly in the developing world, should establish co-ordinated policies of food production and population control.

Human settlements and the production, distribution and consumption of food are interdependent and interactive, and represent a cause and effect relationship of great significance. Settlements satisfy two essential

TOPIC 1: THE WORLD FOOD PROBLEM

human needs: the basic satisfaction of living in groups and the opportunity to organize the production, distribution and consumption of food. It was acknowledged that the problem of human settlements relating to food supply have both macro and micro aspects. Human history is full of examples of the migration of larger sections of population from one area to another, for various reasons, but principally from more populated to less populated areas in search of a better life and the hope of freedom from hunger. The view was expressed that mass shifts in population are probably no longer possible, for geo-political reasons. But within the boundaries of a country such shifts at the micro level may be necessary in the interests of larger food production.

In many developing countries, particularly on the Indian sub-continent and in Latin America, a large percentage of the population lives in rural areas and depends on agriculture for its livelihood. In the developed countries fewer people are engaged directly in agriculture, yet produce more food per capita because of the scientific and technological developments in agriculture. On the other hand in many of the developing countries population growth has resulted in a larger number of people being engaged in agriculture, bringing down per capita economic return. The low purchasing power of the people in these countries sometimes results in the paradoxical situation whereby, although there is a surplus of food, a large section of the population goes hungry.

Crowding in urban areas has a different significance in developing and developed countries. In developing countries the backward economies cannot in general provide alternative employment in the industrial and commercial sectors for rural people who do not have a remunerative occupation. The push and pull mechanism—pushed by economic hardship in rural areas, and pulled by the hope of lucrative employment in urban areas—has resulted in large-scale human misery. It was agreed that the economic stimulation of rural areas, based on agriculture and associated industries, should be a very important national priority in the solution of food and population problems.

More fruitful utilization of land is another matter of particular significance. If history is any guide, it is essential to re-establish the balance between human settlement needs and food production capabilities. In the developed countries the agricultural landholdings tend to be relatively large, while in many countries of the third world the ceilings placed on landholdings are often determined by political considerations rather than by socio-economic factors. Rational use of land, which is becoming a precious commodity, will become an increasingly important factor in shaping the future of society. In this connection attention was drawn to the very valuable recommendations made by the United Nations Conference on Human Settlements: Habitat '76 on conservation, reclamation and stabilization of the land.

The universities should play an important role in helping countries to solve their population and human problems. There are areas such as nutrition, home gardening, birth control and hygiene in which school-age children should be educated, and universities should help to train teachers

SUB-TOPIC 1(B): POPULATION

who would offer such courses in schools. It was felt by some of the participants that traditional universities, and even agricultural universities, established in some of the developing countries are not aware of the real problems of agricultural production and its impact on population in rural areas. These universities, it was maintained, produce agricultural bureaucrats who are out of touch with the rural community. It was suggested that in countries like India there is a need to establish rural universities with no prerequisites of any kind, academic or otherwise, for admission, beyond a desire to learn.

There was a general consensus that universal education is equally, if not more important than university education for population control and agricultural development.

Some of the participants were of the opinion that universities in developed countries could help developing countries by offering training and research in population control and food production, including food conservation and food distribution. Students and research scholars from developing countries should be compelled to return to their home countries after training. In the developing countries themselves what is needed most is instruction at a lower level in rural areas, for which their own university systems are well equipped.

Sub-Topic 1(c)

ENERGY

Chairman: Dr. C. J. MAIDEN
Vice-Chancellor of the University of Auckland

Rapporteur: Sir SAMUEL CURRAN
Principal and Vice-Chancellor of the University of Strathclyde

Tuesday, 22 August

Professor D. W. GEORGE (*Vice-Chancellor of the University of Newcastle, New South Wales*): The provision of adequate, economic and reliable sources of energy in the many and varied forms in which it is required by societies has become one of the great world issues in recent times. Few countries find themselves in the fortunate position of possessing a sufficiently wide range of indigenous energy resources in adequate quantities to meet all their energy needs. International trade in energy commodities, notably oil, received a severe shock with the OPEC (Organisation of Petroleum Exporting Countries) oil embargo of 1973, with its consequential effects on the economies of both industrialized and developing countries. Energy independence, or at least a move towards a higher degree of independence than had hitherto been thought necessary, has become a priority objective of much national planning. Countries such as the USA, Japan and some western European countries have embarked upon vastly expanded programmes of energy research and development with the objective of developing new and alternative sources of energy as well as limiting energy demand through conservation programmes.

The relationship between the availability of energy and the production of food is the particular subject of this discussion paper. The problems to be faced by different countries in this regard naturally vary enormously depending on their geography, climate, population, stage of development, economic structure, whether they are net exporters or importers of food and their own particular energy situation. However it should be noted that even countries which are important food producers tend to consume a relatively

SUB-TOPIC 1(C): ENERGY [George]

small proportion of their overall primary energy demand in these activities. For example, in Australia it is estimated[1] that only 2% of the total primary energy consumption is associated directly with agriculture, forestry, fishing, etc., compared with manufacturing (33%), electricity production (28%) or transport (27%). It will be self-evident that some of the energy used in these latter categories, *e.g.* in the manufacture of agricultural machinery and fertilizers, in the use of electricity for food processing and in liquid fuels for transport purposes, is closely associated with the overall food cycle and must be taken into account in any total analysis.

The high rate of growth of world energy consumption typical of the fifties and sixties (about 5½% per annum) has now dropped and there is less talk of an imminent global energy crisis. However further disruptive events similar to those of the early seventies could plunge the world into a deepening recession and instability. Energy for food production would necessarily feature highly in national priorities but it is important to understand what options are available in the way of substitution for and reduction in conventional energy supplies. Competition for land usage arises with one particular possibility, *viz.* the concept of 'energy farming' or the growing of crops for energy purposes, particularly liquid fuels for transport needs. Clearly such matters cannot be considered in isolation from each other, or independently of the total global energy picture.

With energy a matter of such topical interest it is not surprising that universities have become deeply involved in expanded energy research programmes, and university scientists and engineers have committed themselves both to short-term applied research projects and to much longer-term, more fundamental enquiries. Moreover this involvement naturally extends through the social sciences and humanities into the broader questions of societal objectives and the nature of the relationship between energy consumption and the quality of life. Concern about the exponential growth of population and energy consumption, their effect on the environment and the predicament of mankind had been highlighted by the well-known Club of Rome study[2] prior to the OPEC oil crisis, although the latter event clearly crystallized much thinking about the issues and introduced a sense of urgency into the discussion.

It is tempting in a forum like this to move into the broader issues involved and discuss energy in its widest aspects. However we are primarily concerned with the capacity of the world to overcome its

---

(1) *Solar Energy*—Report from the Senate Standing Committee on National Resources, Australian Government Publishing Service, Canberra, 1977.
(2) *The Limits to Growth*, Meadows et al., Earth Island Limited, London, 1972.

food problems and the contributions universities might make to this particular issue. What *is* relevant is the debate taking place within the universities on the so-called 'soft-energy' paths to the future, particularly in the context of the widening gaps between developed and underdeveloped countries. The ideas of Schumacher, Lovins and Birch have an international currency and a certain attractiveness to younger enquiring minds (as they should have) and dedicated groups such as the Friends of the Earth constantly urge on us the environmental advantages of lower technology. When the unique and controversial features of one particularly important energy form, *viz.* nuclear power, are added to such debates and the perceived or imagined role of the multinational oil companies is included, it is not surprising that the energy issue is emerging as an increasingly prominent feature of campus life.

This paper is thus in two parts, the first dealing with the specific issue of energy in agriculture and food production and the latter with future energy options and the role of the universities.

Energy in Agriculture

The social development of man has always had a close and direct relationship with the availability of energy and an understanding of the ways in which it can be exploited for man's benefit. The use of fire initially for warmth, the prehistoric domestication of animals to extend man's food-growing capacity without depleting his own food supply, and finally the development of power machinery in quite recent times, are all well-known stages in man's progress. Interestingly, the use of water power for irrigation purposes can be traced back to pre-Christian times and by the fourth century waterwheels of as much as two kilowatts power had been developed for grinding cereals.[3] Windmills appeared in western Europe in the twelfth century, but the application of mobile power sources had to await the relatively recent developments of the steam engine—the first stationary steam engines in the eighteenth century merely augmented water and wind power for pumping purposes.

Chauncey Starr[3] has provided some graphic illustrations of the influence of improved energy conversion devices on agriculture and society generally in the twentieth century. Machines replaced animals at a rapid rate on US farms between 1920 and 1960. In the same period farm output more than doubled. In 1920 a fourth of US

---

(3) Energy and Power, *Scientific American*, September 1971.

SUB-TOPIC 1(C): ENERGY [*George*]

farm acreage was planted in crops required to feed the nation's 75 million farm horses and mules. Although the improved productivity was partly due to improved irrigation systems and the introduction of new higher-yield grains, insecticides and fertilizers, the adoption of mechanical farm power was the primary cause of the quadruplication of farm output per man-hour between the years 1910 and 1958. In turn, of course, the consequence of such technological innovations in society generally has been the exponential increase in energy consumption with all its attendant problems.

Whilst energy was relatively cheap and plentiful, agricultural science has tended to concentrate on the production of food as a function of the inputs of nutrients, water and chemicals. A parallel situation applied to industry generally, with most production activities optimized for factors other than minimum energy input, although energy-intensive industries have always been designed with their fuel requirements clearly in mind. We now have as an almost new field that dealing with the 'energy analysis' of systems, which is expanding rapidly and takes into account not only the energies involved in processes themselves but also in the production of the materials and machinery associated with these processes. For example, the question is asked how long a power station must operate before the energy sent out exceeds all the energy costs incurred in producing its materials of construction (mining of iron ore, steel production, etc.) and in erecting it? The answer varies with the type of power station and must be clearly acceptable, as otherwise the activity (with its energy gain) would not be undertaken —once, the question would not even have been asked.

Energy analysis of agricultural systems is still in its infancy, apart from the long-time study of the solar-energy relations of crops and the nutritional-energy relations of animals. As an example of the approach currently in use, Appendix I (p.136) reproduces the results of Gifford[4] from his analysis of the energetics of five national agricultural food production systems for the mid to late 1960s. Many adjustments had to be made to bring the original data to an approximately similar basis and elements of uncertainty remain. The output figures represent the potentially digestible human-food energy content of the farm produce with no deduction for subsequent wastage beyond the farm. The final line gives the so-called energy ratio (ER), *i.e.* the ratio of the energy content of the food output from the system to the gross energy requirement for its production. In discussing this analysis Gifford notes the remarkably high ER for Australia compared to the other four countries, all of

---

[4] **Energy in Agriculture**, *Search* (The Journal of the Australian and New Zealand Association for the Advancement of Science), October 1976.

which have similar values of around 0·6, despite markedly different environments and farming systems.

'The relatively greater energy intensiveness of agriculture in the USA, UK, Holland and Israel is attributable to different causes. In Israel, the energy requirement for irrigation dominates the gross energy requirement and is primarily responsible for low ER. Holland's dominant input, representing over 60 per cent of the direct fuel input, is for heating glasshouses. The USA and UK have no such single dominant input, but are more energy intensive per unit output than Australia throughout most of the list of inputs.

'An important contributor to the UK's low energy ratio is the high level of intensive animal production using home-grown feed (almost 50 per cent of the nutritional energy production, compared with 15 per cent for Israel and Australia and about 30 per cent for Holland and the USA). Seventy per cent of the land devoted to cereals in the UK is for stockfeed.

'It is remarkable that despite these wide variations both in energy intensiveness of agriculture (Holland, 60 GJ/a per hectare of arable land plus high-grade pasture; Israel, 47; UK, 24; and USA,< 13) and in the input mix and product mix, the net balance expressed by the energy ratio is almost the same for these four countries. The input intensity for Australia is lower still — 3 GJ/a per hectare of arable land plus high-grade pasture.[5]

'A most striking contributor to the low intensity is the low application of nitrogen fertilizer in Australia. Nitrogen is applied to Australian arable land and sown pasture at a rate equivalent to 0·1 GJ/a per hectare (one hundredth the intensity for Holland), despite the fact that Australian virgin soils are notably poor in nitrogen, as indeed they are in phosphorus. Legume-based pastures, sown mostly in rotation with crops, fix sufficient nitrogen under the stimulus of exceptionally high superphosphate application to alleviate the need for artificial nitrogen.'

The conclusion Gifford draws is that, because Australia has not adopted a nitrogen- and irrigation-intensive strategy or raised yarded cattle, it is in the fortunate position of being able to withstand increased fossil-fuel prices much better than the other countries reviewed. However it should be noted that this analysis proceeds only as far as the 'farm-gate' and that the energy required for transport of harvested products and subsequent food processing and delivery is not included. Here geographic and demographic

---

[5] 1 GJ = 1 gigajoule (10^9 joules). The energy equivalence of one gigajoule is approximately 35 kilogrammes of black coal or one-sixth of a barrel of crude oil.

factors could intrude as of first-order importance. A country like New Zealand, for example, in which primary products generate over 80% of the total export income and which depends upon these for its national wealth and standard of living whilst still having to rely heavily on imported oil, is extremely sensitive to energy costs, particularly for production and shipping purposes.

There is the further qualification that analysis on a national scale, as above, obscures the vast differences in character of various regions of large land-mass countries like the USA and Australia. The energy dependencies and sensitivities of particular regions can differ widely, as with climatic conditions, and shortages or disruptions of energy supplies could have local consequences of great social significance without necessarily surfacing as national or global issues. Here the scenarios for energy management adopted by national governments will need to reflect an awareness of energy flow patterns down to state, regional and local community groupings.

But such concerns, important as they are to the individuals involved, must surely pale into insignificance when placed alongside the global inequities in food availability, the recurrent famines experienced by whole societies and the gross differences in world standards of living. International trade in food as in energy depends upon the capacity to buy, a capacity not readily apparent in developing countries, and the only satisfactory long-term solution would seem to be to produce more food where it is consumed whilst at the same time curbing population growth. Technology transfer in the form of agricultural knowhow appropriate to the particular environment has had a priority place in many international aid programmes, but today these tend to include and emphasize agricultural methods that are economical in respect of energy input. The extensive and growing literature relating to 'appropriate' technologies for developing countries, with its emphasis on the use of renewable resources for village and rural communities[6], affords evidence of the progress being made in this direction.

Studies of the energy dependencies of developing countries feature in the proceedings and meetings of the World Energy Conference. For example, at the Tenth Conference in Istanbul in September 1977 papers were presented from India, Bangladesh and Nepal and parallels can be drawn between these and other countries which are in transition from the use of traditional energy resources (firewood, cattle dung, vegetable waste, etc.) to commercial energy.

---

[6] *Energy for Rural Development*, National Academy of Sciences, Washington, D.C., 1976.

In India, for example[7], rainfall occurs during four months in the year and in the areas which are not irrigated by canal water agriculture depends largely on well-water. The rapid replacement of traditional animal-operated water-raising devices by diesel and electrically operated pumping sets depends upon continuity of oil supplies and the priority given to rural electrification schemes. In addition high promise is held out for the generation of methane through anerobic fermentation of animal refuse and other organic wastes for domestic rural needs of cooking and lighting. The traditional burning of dry animal dung as fuel is wasteful both because of its low efficiency of conversion and loss of nitrogenous matters used as manure.

'India has a cattle population of 222 million which annually produce about 1,200 million tonnes of wet dung. Nearly 20 per cent of this is directly burnt at a conversion efficiency of only 11 per cent. If this dung is processed through the anerobic fermentation plants, an energy output of about 167×10^{12} kcal per annum or 195×10^9 kWh per annum[8] equivalent to 40,000 MW(e) at 50 per cent plant factor can be generated. These methane generating plants, popularly known as "Gobargas" plants in India, can be built in various sizes ranging from single family units, requiring 4 to 5 animals to supply the family's domestic energy needs, to all-village plants needing about 250 animals to supply energy needs for a typical village of 500 people. There are 10,000 of these plants operating in the country and it is planned to install 15,000 more during the next 3 years. These gasplants not only reduce the demand on commercial forms of energy thus aiding their conservation but also reduce the pressure on firewood.'

Energy analysis of the subsistence-farming systems, similar in kind to that now being carried out for the western societies, is important to permit judgements on priorities and strategies, but the situation is so different that direct comparisons with the latter are of little value. In the former, the energy content of the food output exceeds the muscular input of the workers by a factor of $10-30$[9] yielding high energy ratios. The ERs of less than unity characteristic of industrialized agricultural systems merely reflect the availability of plentiful external energy sources to run the systems. A return to pre-industrial systems for such countries is unthinkable and would in no way contribute to overcoming the world's food problems.

---

(7) 'Energy Conservation in a Developing Economy—India', Bose et al., Xth World Energy Conference, 1977, Paper 2.5.3.

(8) 1 GJ = 280 kilowatt hours (kWh) of electricity. Thus 195×10^9 kWh per annum is equivalent to 7×10^8 GJ/a or several times the gross annual agricultural energy input for Australia (Appendix I).

(9) Energy in Agriculture, op. cit.

SUB-TOPIC 1(C): ENERGY   [George]

Universities and the Energy Problem

After the spate of gloomy predictions of global energy shortages by the mid-eighties (or by the turn of the century, depending upon the degree of pessimism or optimism of the forecaster), there is now a growing feeling that the world will cope with its energy problems much better than first believed possible. Higher energy prices have already increased the investment in oil and gas exploration and hitherto undiscovered resources can be expected to be added to the known reserves. But the most significant changes have occurred on the demand side. The length of the economic recession has resulted in the shutting down or deferment of new refinery capacity and around a seventh of the world's oil tanker fleet is currently laid up. Demand has remained virtually flat for four years and is still one million barrels a day short of its 1973 peak of 15 million barrels per day.

Conservation programmes, aided by higher prices, have begun to bite. Smaller cars with greater fuel economy, reduced domestic demand by the cutting of central heating temperatures and greater industrial efficiency of energy use have led planners to reassess the relationship of energy consumption to economic growth. The cumulative effect of a reduction in the historic $1\cdot1\%$ rise in energy for each 1% of economic increase to the now foreseen much lower ratio of $0\cdot7$ or $0\cdot8$ to 1 would be enormous. But even if events transpire to prove such optimism unwarranted, it is clear that the OPEC oil crisis has presented the world with an unequalled opportunity—the time to take stock, to reassess future energy scenarios and to explore alternatives in a more measured and, hopefully, intelligent manner.

Much emphasis is now placed on the desirability of converting from the present almost total dependence of the world on fossil fuel resources to the renewable energy resources, solar, wind, tide, geothermal, etc.—in other words, living on our energy 'income' rather than our 'capital'. Progress will clearly be made in the development of technologies based on renewable sources even with our present scientific knowledge of conversion techniques (photovoltaic surfaces, etc.) and scientific breakthroughs could completely change the current predictions of reducing cost factors arising simply from improved production methods and large-scale manufacture. Nevertheless conventional fuel prices would need to rise considerably from their present levels before any of the new technologies could be economically competitive, apart say from specialized applications such as remote locations requiring relatively low power levels. Realistic studies of the maximum contribution to overall energy demand that might be expected by the turn of the century from renewable energy resources place this within the range of 5 to 10%, even allowing for the vastly increased expenditure on solar energy and related technologies.[10]

Since the energy position of individual countries varies so widely, most governments have drawn up their own national energy policies which reflect their particular problems and needs, and detail the priorities which they are giving to different strategies. Common features include the more effective use of existing resources through conservation and pricing policies, the full development of indigenous fuels through exploration and improved recovery techniques and substitution and replacement wherever possible of one energy resource for another. Serious efforts are being made to arrest the world trend away from coal to oil and natural gas, although the advantages of liquid and gaseous fuels are such that emphasis is being given to the production of synthetic fuels (coal liquefaction, alcohol production, etc.). Environmental issues feature strongly in most national planning, especially, but not exclusively, in respect of the substitution of nuclear energy for fossil fuels for electricity production.

Universities, through the skills and dedication of their staff and students, have unlimited possibilities to contribute to the solution of national and international energy problems. Specialized research contributions on the scientific and technological aspects of energy production, storage and consumption represent obvious areas for detailed work and much is already going on in these domains. As research moves away from the fundamental end of the spectrum towards the development and demonstration stages, university personnel may need to contribute more in governmental and industrial settings than within their own laboratories, but this is a familiar concept not restricted to energy research. The techniques of energy analysis and modelling (with a view to assessing the complex interactions of economic, social and environmental factors with medium- and long-term projections of energy supply and demand) are still at an early stage of their development and can present an intellectual challenge to the best of analytical minds. The particular problem of providing energy for developing countries is a challenge to the idealism (hopefully) in us all.

Unfortunately much of the energy debate in the developed countries, particularly on nuclear and solar issues, is ill-informed, emotional and political in context. Soft-energy paths are argued for the support they would give to providing decentralized energy solutions, avoiding the 'dangers' inherent in highly technical

---

(10) The USA, France, Israel, Japan and a number of other countries are presently spending the order of $1 per capita per annum on solar energy and related research.

centralized systems. The issue of civil liberties is raised, the morality and ethics of western societies are challenged and energy has become a convenient medium for fighting old political and philosophical battles. The immediate future of nuclear power may be uncertain, and the new 'sun-worship' may continue for some time yet, but the existing pattern of dependence on energy in the developed countries is unlikely, in my opinion, to be easily shaken. The observed correlation between per capita energy consumption and national wealth and prosperity will continue to be attractive to the eyes of developing countries, even in its moderated and more appropriate form when unnecessary energy wastage has been eliminated.

Conclusion

The usage of energy in food production has been seen to comprise a relatively small component of the overall energy demand of developed and developing countries. Nevertheless escalating energy prices and possible energy shortages will adversely influence the economic basis of their rural industries, even if other sectors of their economies may be more severely affected. The careful application of energy analysis techniques will ensure that energy is not needlessly wasted, or inappropriately consumed on the simple assumption that commensurate gains in crop productivity are automatically achieved in all cases.

The energy-intensive agricultural techniques characteristic of the developed countries are not necessarily transferable to, or desirable for, developing countries. Some countries, for example Thailand, are able to be net exporters of food to their neighbouring regions in Asia despite their almost total dependence on imported oil for their energy base. Each country has its unique problems and the larger countries may well have within their boundaries many different regions requiring different solutions. If the overall solution to the world food problem lies as far as possible in the growing of food where it is needed, appropriate studies are required of all the local factors, including the influence of changed technologies on employment patterns, environmental factors and, in the context of this paper, their particular energy requirements.

To make a contribution to these problems is a challenge which confronts all university people but especially those of the resource-rich countries of the world. It is a challenge which we ignore at great cost to the future peace and prosperity of mankind.

[George]

APPENDIX I

Energetics of Five National Agricultural Food Production Systems

Country	USA	Australia	UK	Holland	Israel
AREAS ($\times 10^6$)					
Cultivated and pastoral	530	490	19	2.3	1.2
Crops & fallow (incl. fruit & veg.)	184	20	4.5	1.0	.35
High grade pasture (incl. temporary)	?	21	8	1.3	.06
NUTRITIONAL ENERGY OUTPUT ($\times 10^{15}$J/a)					
Total	1750	270	135	90	9.9
as crop product	1260	230	70	60	8.4
as animal product	490	40	65	30	1.5
GROSS ENERGY REQUIREMENTS ($\times 10^{15}$J/a) for:					
Direct farm fuel & elec.	1186	55	108	98	3.2
Fertiliser — nitrogen	434	5.3	63	25	2.0
— phosphorus	36	13	6.7	2.3	0.18
— potassium	29	0.53	4.1	0.6	0.08
— lime	?	?	8.4	?	?
Machinery & metal products	410	18	32		0.43
Chemicals	150	4.4	8.5	14	1.2
Irrigation	146	?	—		12.2
Other miscellaneous costs	—	1	68		.2
Sum of inputs listed	2391	97	299	140	19.5
Energy ratio (O/I)	0.7	2.8	0.5	0.6	0.5

Source: R. M. Gifford. An Overview of Fuel Used for Crops and National Agricultural Systems — Energy in Agriculture, op. cit., pp. 412–417.

SUB-TOPIC 1(C): ENERGY   [Nag Chaudhuri]

Some Aspects of Energy

Dr. B. D. NAG CHAUDHURI (*Vice-Chancellor of Jawaharlal Nehru University*): Cavalier statements are often made in many countries, mostly by certain establishments of the developed countries — echoed in developing countries, that a new era is coming, the age of solar energy. It is at best a misleading statement. Most developing countries use solar energy indirectly by biomass combustion or directly for drying cereal and other food and have been using considerable amounts of solar energy in this fashion for millennia. The fraction of solar energy out of the total used varies amongst less developed countries (LDCs) from 5 to 60%. By a curious euphemism of technological jargon biomass used for energy is termed non-conventional energy sources in many techno-economic tracts.

In India, for example, nearly 48% of the energy currently used is solar energy in varying forms, from drying grain to cooking food with dungcake, wood and straw, at low efficiencies — around 7% in the case of the rural domestic stove (chula) compared to 15–20% for the European equivalent. Some developed countries, in contrast, quote target figures of 3 to 5% of total energy use being met by solar energy by 2000 A.D. at estimated 10–15% efficiencies. Solar energy in India may not be used efficiently, managed economically or within a sound ecological framework; nevertheless it is the largest single source of energy for our people. This is true in most of the developing nations in the tropical and subtropical belt, in varying degree. By the same token, the developed countries have used coal and petroleum profligately and inefficiently. They have not only saddled their own societies with high costs, they have thoughtlessly ignored ecological consequences in their own territories and that of others.

The dramatic reduction of energy consumption in Sweden recently by more than 20% without reduction in productivity and living standards and with improvement in quality of life is significant as a possible trend for the future. The high costs of non-renewable energy may be bearable to the 'advanced' nations. They tend to percolate with disastrous effect on the developing nations, creating severe economic and social stresses. The technological impotence of the 'less advanced' countries to resolve such economic stresses, on one side, and the resiliency of their 'primitive' socio-economic structures is a curiously contrastive situation. This has often led to many questions on alternative pathways to progress.

Nature, unfortunately, did not take into account current political boundaries in distributing non-renewable energy resources around the globe. The result is a disparate distribution. However, technologically and economically powerful nations seem to be able to get access to the non-renewable energy resources they need with comparative ease, whether from their own territories when available or from the less advanced countries when they choose. The United States is a prime example of import of vast quantities of petroleum even though her own known resources are some of the largest in the world.

The energy consumption per capita, excluding biomass energy, is exceedingly disproportionate between various countries. Table 1, below, gives some notion of the large unevenness in energy consumption and per capita GNP between the poor and the rich nations.

TABLE 1: AVERAGE POPULATION AND CONSUMPTION LEVELS FOR ENERGY AND STEEL IN 1970

	Classification of Nations		
	Rich	Intermediate	Poor
Population (millions)	954	224	2440
Energy (10^6 metric tons)	5680	384	717
Steel (10^6 metric tons)	507	38	51
Per capita energy*	—	1610	293
Per capita steel (kg./person)	537	158	21
Per capita GNP (US$, 1973)	2720	846	169

*In kilogramme coal equivalent per person.

CLASSIFICATION OF NATIONS 1970

Nations	Per capita energy consumption†	Per capita steel consumption†	Per capita GNP in 1973 (US$)	Population in 1973 (millions)
Rich	2,048–16,384	256–1,024	1,280–5,120	977 (25·4%)
Intermediate	1,024–2,048	64–256	640–1,280	250 (6·4%)
Poor	64–1,024	2–64	40–640	2,500 (68·2%)

†In kilogramme coal equivalent.

SUB-TOPIC 1(c): ENERGY [Nag Chaudhuri]

From all accounts petroleum, the major fuel during the past fifty years, is poorly distributed and scarce, with an estimated global resource that will last around thirty years at current consumption trends. Both these factors contribute to a potential for conflict in the face of rapidly increasing demand for this source of energy by the have-not nations. Natural gas is even more scarce and it cannot substitute for petroleum except marginally. Hydrocarbons in oil shale and tar sands have been mentioned as a possible source of energy because of their abundance. However they contribute little or nothing to present energy supply. Further research and development is required to bring them to a stage of economic and technological viability. Geothermal energy is similarly a possibility in some parts of the world, although its use is negligibly small at present. Rather extensive research and development efforts and money are needed to explore and develop technologies for its use. Coal is the most abundant of energy sources and more evenly distributed than petroleum and gas. Unfortunately it is now used to the extent of less than 30% to meet the world's needs of energy. The use of coal as a source of energy is likely to grow as petroleum becomes scarcer and its price increases.

Uranium is the normal source of energy of nuclear reactors. It occurs in rich deposits only in a few places but is widely dispersed at low concentrations. Unless breeder systems are used uranium reactors do not seem viable for more than a few decades. With breeder reactors, which are now technologically proven although more hazardous, both the uranium and the more abundant thorium can be used as sources of energy giving a more extended time-span for fission energy sources. However nuclear power from fission reactors is, in spite of early promise, still providing only a small fraction of energy. The inhibiting factors are radiation and other hazards of accidents, handling and storage of large quantities of long-lived radioactive residues or fission products, high price and sophistication of fission energy systems. These have retarded the use of nuclear fission energy. There has been also increasing concern because of the relation between fission reactors and the production of fissile materials which can be diverted to make atom bombs.

Nuclear fusion energy, on the other hand, although still unproven, does not suffer from the immediate risk of being used to make atom bombs. Recent progress with Tokamak-type fusion reactor systems shows promise in the USA and the USSR, as they have operated close to the sustainable reactor regime. There are, however, several scientific and technological problems still to be solved. In any event fusion energy, at best, will be more expensive than fission energy at the beginning of the twenty-first century.

[Nag Chaudhuri] TOPIC 1: THE WORLD FOOD PROBLEM

Research and developments to bring thermonuclear fusion to the stage of practical use will take up the rest of the century. However if and when fusion energy is harnessed a longer span of energy supply is assured, but not cheaper or easily handled energy. We can then think in terms of a span, perhaps in terms of millennia of costly energy.

TABLE 2: NON-RENEWABLE ENERGY POTENTIAL
(Estimated 1975)

Figures in MTCE

Resources	Estimated Reserves World	Estimated Reserves India	Estimated Current Rates of Consumption World	Estimated Current Rates of Consumption India	Estimated Life at Current Trends of Energy Use (in years) World	Estimated Life at Current Trends of Energy Use (in years) India
Coal	600,000	21,000	2,563	84·52	200	100–150
Natural gas	72,000	112	1,668	0·96	—	—
Oil	100,000	256	3,567	28·5	30·35	10
Nuclear Uranium + Thorium	~10^6	50,000* / 400,000*	—	2·00	—	>1,000

*In tonnes

No figures are given for current biomass energy in use such as wood, straw, dung or waste or the potential of fusion energy, as these at best are uncertain. Oil and nuclear power are exploited by a few nations because of the low dispersion of the concerned technologies amongst the LDCs who constitute the bulk of world's population. Coal is trapped sunlight by plant life accumulated over many millions of years. We consume perhaps in one year what nature took a million years to produce. Oil also is a product of past living organisms produced over many million years of geological processing.

Some 70% of the world's population, somewhat around 2,500 million people, have a per capita consumption level of goods and services less than a twentieth of their more well-to-do sister nations, who account for about a quarter of the world's population. The large difference is attributed mainly to their greater consumption of energy from the non-renewable resources of petroleum and coal. Essentially renewable, depending primarily on the sun and living processes, biomass sources of energy will not be depleted with time if managed along sound ecological and technological lines. Let us remind ourselves that until about three or four hundred years ago this was the only source of energy in use.

The poverty of nations, like that of human beings, unfortunately, often occurs together with ignorance which reduces access to energy and leads to greater waste and inefficiency in energy use. Not only has scarcity and anticipated scarcity of energy resulted in increased prices, scarcity has been manipulated to bring about price increases. Scarcity and technological sophistication are going to increase price and distort availability even further in the future to the disadvantage of the developing nations, except for the fortunate few who have large untapped mineable sources of these non-renewable resources. Under these pressures social, political and legal aspects of energy will increasingly claim attention, leading perhaps to attempts to formulate an international regime for energy, as is being now attempted in atomic energy through the International Atomic Energy Agency (IAEA).

A few years after the forming of the IAEA there was an attempt to set up an International Energy Agency (IEA) in 1964. Unfortunately it was still-born. It was the sudden increase in oil prices by the consortium of oil-producing nations of the third world in 1973 that not only led to petroleum becoming a matter of international concern but led the world to become energy conscious. While the new oil prices affected the poorer nations even more than the richer ones, the world settled down within a comparatively short time to the new regime, which reflects the bearability of the higher price of petroleum and perhaps of energy. Apart from the steep oil price hike in 1973 there has been slow but steady increase generally in the price of energy, including the price of petroleum. There have been since 1973 efforts by many nations to control, regulate and assure energy supplies by various administrative and legal devices. In future growing scarcity of various energy sources is likely to increase the price of energy even further, particularly as demand is expected to continue to increase throughout the world. The transnational transfers of non-renewable energy resources have not been solely determined by market forces—fair or manipulated. Threats of military, technological and political pressures have played significant roles in determining such transfers. This affects comparatively more adversely the developing countries, where energy consumption is quite low and where the demands of development are going to increase energy needs without concomitant technological or political ability to command it. The relation of energy use to energy price and their international aspects will have other consequential effects: on one side the economic and technological efforts towards increasing efficiency and exploring other energy choices; on the other, social, political, legal and international aspects of energy demands will receive greater attention. Inevitably there will be an increase of various international and national stresses. One factor that will affect the developing nations even more than the developed nations is the adverse effect of slowing down of rate of growth of the GNP. Unless decreasing population growths more than compensate the decreasing GNP growth rate, the internal stresses within developing nations may increase substantially.

Some of the concepts, or rather misconceptions, about energy use will possibly come under greater scrutiny in the future. One such misconception is the linkage between production of goods and services and energy, another is that energy is a relatively fixed factor in the GNP. There are other fallacies widely extant, such as that reduction of energy consumption means replacing machines with manual labour or that tropical nations need less energy or that they waste more energy. Even such assumptions as that jobs are inextricably linked to energy consumption — that is, more energy consumption means more jobs — will require re-examination. We have noted that there is a minimum energy requirement linked to domestic well-being such as cooking and lighting and, in the cold countries, room-heating. Such energy consumption is not related to jobs. It is a requirement of minimum living conditions. Improvements can possibly be made to diminish energy requirements for such purposes by increased efficiencies, new technologies and improved social organisation.

Looking at the not too distant future over a time-span of thirty to fifty years, energy consumption characteristics of such facilities as transportation and habitat can change greatly; so can social conditions, organisations and attitudes. Energy consumption in residential and commercial buildings can undergo a great deal of change with changes in social organisation and public transport system; changes in architecture and house-building technologies can substantially reduce demands of energy. On the other hand industry, transportation, house-building and agriculture will be greatly conditioned by the momentum of current practices and current investments which will tend to ensure that the future is a continuity of the past. Crucial to the changes that may occur in the pattern of industry, transportation and agricultural use of energy will be the question of equitable distribution, access and price of energy. Inevitably questions of price and access to energy and issues of equity in distribution and consumption will tend to influence how we look at energy issues. Such debates may well lead to social and eventually legal restraints on the nature and efficiency of energy use. The constraints on automobile exhausts is a pointer.

Many of our public policies and social attitudes developed when energy was cheap and available and distant signals of world-wide limits were not clearly visible. As these signals become stronger the existing regime in many nations where energy producers make investment decisions on presumed long-term incremental prices, and energy consumers determine their effort of conservation and efficiency on energy prices and what they can afford, will tend to give way to national legal regimes of mandatory conservation and efficiencies. Similarly international questions of access and equity may be sources of serious international wrangling, because of scarcity implications of energy, which could only be resolved by developing the concept of an international legal regime to ensure access, equity and security.

The price of energy will go up steeply in the next quarter of a century. However whether it will be at least twice or more than four times the present costs by 2000 A.D. is unpredictable in the Niels Bohr sense that 'it is difficult to make accurate predictions, especially about the future'. The very large increase in the price of energy will tend to be a strong factor conditioning technology towards more efficient energy systems, forcing the pace of innovation, and developing social attitudes towards greater rationalisation and efficient energy use. Many governments may try partially to absorb the price increase effects by introducing various incentives, regulations, standards and other elements of control. Social attitudes of the past, such as buying a less efficient air-conditioner or an electric fan because it was cheaper, in spite of the higher operating cost, will tend to change, not only owing to new social attitudes concerned with life-time costs of domestic equipment but also by governmental disincentives, standards and regulations.

Energy-saving technology will perhaps play an increasingly important role in households, such as pre-treating fish, flesh or vegetables biochemically with enzymes or micro-organisms before cooking to reduce energy requirements for cooking. Energy-intensive domestic consumer goods will tend to be discouraged. Systems which heat the entire house rather than a small and necessary portion of it in the cooler regions of the world, or the opposite in warmer parts of the globe, will find less acceptance. The developing nations will be under greater pressure towards these changes than the richer nations. Such pressures may well lead to a re-examination of various traditional practices because of their energy-saving characteristics or their use of renewable biomass energy resources.

The gradual shift to coal will probably be quite marked by the end of this century and the beginning of the next. Coal may be liquified for use in transport and may substitute as a base for chemicals instead of the current dependence on petrochemicals. However, biomass use of energy is probably not going to be a significant addition in the developed countries, although some rationalisation of its use for heating purposes seems to be in the offing. Some of the developing countries might begin to use biomass energy more rationally and systematically by cultivating energy forests. The developing countries under the pressure of energy non-availability may well be innovators in biomass use for energy and towards finding substitutes for liquid fuels and petrochemicals and biomass.

The energy price effect will probably be much more marked in the developing countries and may indeed increase the disparity between developed and developing countries over the next thirty years. On the other hand a low energy future offers strong incentives for technological innovation. It can also exert a pressure for social innovation. Throughout human history the growth of civilisation seems to run almost parallel with the use of energy. The use of non-renewable resources of energy came very late in human civilisation. Coal was mined and used only in very small quantities in the past, and started to be an increasingly important source of energy from about 300 years ago. Petroleum came on the scene somewhat later and its use is hardly 150 years old. The increasing population of Europe and the USA in the nineteenth and twentieth centuries contributed to the demand for energy. In the developing nations the population growth came in advance of the demand for energy owing to great scientific discoveries about diseases, their control, and consequent improvement in public health and increase in life expectation. Inevitably the almost neo-Malthusian growth of population and technology development, which has brought about expectations of a better life, have led to increasing demands on energy.

India, as a not atypical example of an LDC, has had a population growth in the last fifty years of about threefold to over 600 million people; the consumption of non-renewable energy (coal and petroleum) has increased sixfold (around 250 metric tonnes of coal equivalent) of which less than half today is coal. The biomass energy used is not recorded but is estimated to have increased by a factor of two over the same period. It has visibly increased pressures on land, caused denudation of forests and in certain areas given rise to desertification. The rate of regeneration of biomass has dropped below rates of current use of biomass for energy and is now a cause for concern. The pressure is now strongly felt by our rural population since 70% of their energy resource is still biomass combustion. The pressures on the ecological system will become increasingly serious in the next two decades. Unfortunately the biomass energy resource is largely outside the market economy. The deleterious effects of biomass energy use beyond the regenerative capacity of the land is often unnoticed until it is too late for simple management measures to be effective.

Energy saving through social organization and technological efficiency can have a substantial impact on the saving of firewood, straw and other renewable resources, with consequent reduction of ecological stresses in the developing nations. An example of social organization to reduce the need of domestic cooking energy is the Egyptian practice of the government selling an unleavened baked bread rather than wheat. Another is the Indonesian practice of predigesting fish by inoculating with micro-organisms and then sun-drying or storing before cooking. While most of the tropical and subtropical countries, India included, are using far more solar energy by using renewable biomass energy resources for domestic purposes, there is room for a great deal more improvement in the efficiency of energy use, and developing innovations to keep such use within the limits of the local natural regenerative capacity. Unfortunately nature makes no concessions either to the inefficient poor or to the profligate rich.

The variety, the richness and the relevance of energy-related problems make them singularly meaningful for study and research in university systems. Studies of energy problems are both universal and location-specific; they are scientific, technological, sociological and economic. The multidisciplinary nature of most universities gives them the basic ability to deal with many facets of such studies with synergistic advantages. A very few universities have indicated interest in taking up energy studies — mostly in their technological aspects. A more comprehensive aim of such studies is likely to be more rewarding. Moreover energy is an area where a university in a developed country can co-operate with mutual profit with another in an LDC because of the complementarity of situations, social and technological, to lend substance to such studies and underline the global nature of energy problems. Universities provide a forum of discussion for clarifying and sharpening arguments which will find their use later in international forums.

The environmental problems of large-scale energy use are beginning to be regulated by law in many nations to prevent damage to property and to people. Environmental considerations have already brought about consciousness of pollution of the sea because of disasters such Torrey Canyon and Amoco. Regulatory concepts with regard to access and equity in the international sphere have not yet come about. However the New International Economic Order (NIEO) has now become a topic in UN forums and new international regimes will be under discussion in the UN and other international forums. The disparities of resources, dangers of pollution and the crucial nature of energy will be noted and pressures will increase to bring about sooner or later attempts at the international level to regulate and protect energy usage amongst nations. The LDCs, particularly those whose access to energy is limited, will try to discover various ways of increasing pressure on international institutions to develop such a new order. Inevitably international legal provisions to apply to such situations will be debated. Equitable access to energy sources has been mentioned in UNCTAD (United Nations Conference on Trade and Development) and other forums. To support such debates and make further progress towards an NIEO, a body of international conventions and laws might well emerge during the next decade embodying national rights and obligations in the field of energy.

Professor C. M. SWITZER *(Dean of Ontario Agricultural College, University of Guelph):* Agriculture is an energy-dependent system from the production of food by the farmer to its use by the consumer. The main purpose of the agricultural system is to supply food — but increasingly there is recognition of the role played by the system in respect to the environment and to economic and social concerns of society. The processes of agriculture must be based on ecological principles that govern energy and nutrient flow, recognizing that men in the long term must live in equilibrium with the world's resources and with other living creatures.[7]

In the past thirty years we have largely replaced human energy on the farm with chemical and mechanical energy. This has allowed fewer farm workers using less land to feed more people. It has been stated that one farmer in North America could feed himself and five others in 1900, whereas he is now capable of producing food for more than fifty other people. This great increase in efficiency has resulted from mechanization and the use of fertilizers and pesticides. According to Heichel[4] feed for animals previously used on farms in the US required about 1/6 of the cropland now used to grow food. He adds: 'But when the American farmer traded in his 25 million horses and mules for today's 5 million tractors, he became increasingly dependent on petroleum'. In Canada agriculture is one of the largest users of petroleum products, consuming 8% of the gasoline and 12% of the diesel fuel[1].

Food costs to consumers have been kept low at the expense of non-renewable energy resources. As Macleod et al.[5] have stated: 'The pressure on agricultural production (in Canada) has been to produce food cheaply for our consumers. The pressure has *not* been on producing food using minimal energy requirements or inputs'. Undoubtedly these pressures will change, as energy-saving measures will have to be undertaken by all parts of society—including agriculture. However one major constraint to large-scale energy savings is the requirement to maintain or increase production. Another is the concern for environmental protection and the restrictions this may place on the energy-efficient use of pesticides.

It is estimated that the energy used on the farm to produce food is between 2·4% and 3·0% of the total energy used in Canada[6]. This is considered to be about 1/10 of the energy used in transportation, and about 1/7 of the energy used for heating buildings. Forms of energy used in production agriculture include natural gas as the raw material for nitrogen fertilizers and petroleum-based fuels for machinery operation, for the production of pesticides, to supply energy for heating and cooling of buildings, for on-farm transportation, and for crop drying and storage.

Although food production is energy-dependent and does require relatively large quantities of fossil fuels, it must be kept in mind that primary agriculture and forestry are the only two industries that show a net gain in energy. According to Blaxter[3], 'farming is basically a process of harnessing the energy of sunshine through the photosynthetic machinery of the green leaf.' The yearly conversion of solar energy through photosynthesis on a global basis is equal to the energy utilized each year from oil and gas—even though only a small part of the sun's energy is captured by plants (1 to 2%). A crop of corn, for example, with an energy input (in fertilizer, pesticides, tractor use, etc.) equivalent to about one gallon of gasoline, will return an energy equivalent of 4 to 5 gallons of gasoline. However by the time the corn is dried, transported, processed, distributed, sold to the consumer and used, the total energy used is greater than the food energy available in the finished product. Indeed a recent publication from Agriculture Canada[1] states: 'for each BTU of fossil fuel used in North American agriculture, it is estimated that we receive about 0·2 BTU in food energy, as compared to about 53·5 BTUs in food energy for each BTU of human energy expended in the Chinese wet rice agricultural system'. Blaxter[3] estimated that in the UK it takes twice this much support energy (10 joules for each 1 joule of food) and suggests that the figure would be even higher in the USA.

If one compares the total energy used in different parts of the world with the energy used in agriculture (Table 1, below), it is interesting to note that there is little difference in the percentage of total energy used in farming in the various countries. Both developed and developing countries use around 3·5% of their total energy in the food system. The difference, as pointed out by Blaxter[3], is in the amount of total energy consumed by people in the different regions. Also the differences in support energy per agricultural worker are obviously very great.

Blaxter asks 'whether the course of economic growth in the developing countries and in particular the growth of their food production will mimic that in the developed countries?'. His conclusion is that:

> 'at present we have no technologies which will enable people in the developing countries to augment yield and attain higher nutritional status for themselves, other than by using greater industrial inputs. In the immediate future there is no alternative to increased use of fertilizers, agrochemicals and application of mechanical power to increase farm production in the developing world, but in the longer term these practices will accelerate depletion of world fuel reserves. The longer term solution is to develop new technologies for farming which result in improvement of solar radiation capture but which are less dependent on an exploitive approach to nonrenewable world resources.'

In a statement prepared by the Ontario Institute of Agrologists[6] the energy used to get food to the table was broken down as follows:—

Production (to the farm gate)	18%
Processing and packaging	32%
Transport and distribution	20%
Household preparation	30%

It has been estimated that the total energy expended to get the food on the table represents between 12% and 15% of the total energy

SUB-TOPIC 1(C): ENERGY [Switzer]

TABLE 1: The Annual Support Energy used in Different Regions of the World in the Agricultural Sector

Region	Total consumption by region (J x 10^{18})	Consumption by agriculture (J x 10^{18})	% of total energy in farming	Support energy per agricultural worker (J x 10^9/man)
N. America	77	2·1	2·8	556
W. Europe	43	2·1	4·9	82
Australasia	2	0·1	5·6	247
E. Europe & USSR	50	1·6	3·3	29
U.K.	8·9	0·3	3·6	453
Developed countries	186	6·3	3·4	63
Africa	1·6	0·1	4·5	1
Latin America	8·1	0·3	3·8	9
Far East	7·0	0·4	5·3	1
Near East	2·6	0·2	6·4	4
Asian Centrally Planned	14·3	0·4	2·9	2
Developing countries	33·6	1·3	4·0	2
WORLD	219·6	7·6	3·5	10

Source: Blaxter, K. Energy Usage in Agriculture[3].

consumption in Canada. The 18% of energy consumed on the farm has been calculated as representing 2·4% of the total Canadian energy consumption[1]. This portion may be broken down as follows:

Fertilizer production	57%	Fuel and machinery	7%
Crop drying	24%	Pesticide production	2%
Crop production	8%	Transportation to storage	2%

It would seem obvious that in a time of energy shortages decisions should be made that will ensure a continuing supply of energy to the food production system. This might not happen. For example, in the particularly cold winter of 1977, when shortages of natural gas occurred in the US, rationing took place to ensure sufficient supplies for home heating. Fertilizer producers who use natural gas in making nitrogen fertilizers were well down on the priority list. This resulted in a shortfall in production of between 6% and 17% in various plants and a marked escalation of fertilizer prices to farmers that spring.

Even though given more priority in the future, agriculture must be energy conscious, and emphasis must be placed on research aimed at increasing the efficiency of food production and towards seeking alternate sources of energy. In considering alternatives we must continue to be concerned that the type of agricultural production is *economic*. Hand labour, for example, is much less energy-consuming than tractors but it does not seem reasonable for us to consider such an alternative. Blaxter[3] has stated: 'If we wished to halve the present support energy consumption in farming by substituting labour (in the UK), some approximate calculations suggest that nearly half our labour force would have to be deployed on farms if yield were to be maintained'.

One alternative as energy becomes less available and more costly to farmers in Canada would be for them to grow only those crops that are most efficient in energy terms. Pasture crops, for example, give maximum energy food output per unit of energy input — the production of beef and milk gives very low energy output per unit input — and grain crops are intermediate. Other examples are presented below:—

Crop	Energy output/input	Crop	Energy output/input
Pasture	100·0: 1	Apples	1·50: 1
Hay	8·5: 1	Milk	0·24: 1
Wheat (flour)	5·3: 1	Eggs	0·19: 1
Grain corn	4·9: 1	Broilers	0·13: 1
Grains	4·4: 1	Pork	0·06: 1
Potatoes	3·4: 1	Beef	0·02: 1

Thus it might seem that in an energy-deficient world we should not be producing animals or animal crop products for food. However there are other aspects to be considered. Animal wastes provide a potential energy source, and a large proportion of the feed used by cattle is made up of materials which would not normally make up part of the human diet. Also, of course, cattle and other ruminants may graze on land which is not suitable for the production of grains or other foods, and thus are converting energy from forage which otherwise would not be available for human use. It is estimated that some 60% of the world's ruminant livestock population graze lands which cannot be economically cultivated[6]. Also animal products are important in the human diet as a source of protein — and, obviously, people enjoy a good steak, or chop, or glass of milk.

As mentioned earlier, the major energy inputs into agricultural production are petroleum-based products to operate machinery and as the base for the production of fertilizers and pesticides. The greatly increased cost of petroleum in recent years has reduced fertilizer and pesticide sales in some areas, and hence has led to some reduction in crop yields. As the price of energy continues to escalate the price of grain and other agricultural products will be forced up, followed by the cost of food to the consumer. In an attempt to counter such changes scientists in universities and at research stations are studying various ways to increase energy efficiency on the farm. Some of the ways that are being looked at are: —

(i) Using soil testing to a greater extent to ensure that no more fertilizer than necessary is applied.

(ii) Using nitrogen-fixing legume crops whenever possible. Crop rotations using nitrogen-fixing crops should be stressed. Research is continuing on biological nitrogen fixation with the hope of developing other crops than can utilize nitrogen from the air.

(iii) Minimizing tillage operations to save fuel by reducing depth and number of cultivations, and by reducing the depth of seeding and fertilizer placement. It should be kept in mind that if tillage is eliminated completely, as it can be on some crops on certain soil types, the farmer will have to rely entirely on herbicides to control weeds. Thus herbicides, which require energy for their manufacture but which are more efficient than mechanical cultivation (Table 2, below), would have to be placed high on the energy priority list. It would follow that more research should then be carried out on the environmental impact of additional herbicide applications.

Another advantage of minimal tillage is the reduction of erosion related both to the reduced disturbance of the soil and the additional plant residues left on the soil surface as a mulch. Shaw[8]

TABLE 2: ENERGY BALANCE SHEET FOR VARIOUS WEED CONTROL METHODS IN CORN

	Cultivation	Cultivation + Atrazine	Atrazine	Cultivation + Hand Labour	Hand Labour
Input per acre, kcal					
Chemical	—	11	33	—	—
Mechanical	56	57	5	56	—
Labour	1	1	1	10	33
TOTAL	57	69	39	66	33
Labour input/acres, hr.	0·57	0·62	0·05	17·57	36
Output:input ratio	49:1	54:1	96:1	57:1	117:1
Corn required to pay for input, lb./acre	31	38	21	36	18

Source: Nalewaja, J. D. Weeds Today, Fall 1975.

has stated that 'erosion has destroyed the potential for food production on about 200×10^6 acres (in the USA) and removed about 1/3 of the top soil from land presently under crops, thus reducing its potential productivity for the future. This loss in productivity has been estimated at 10–15% and the energy input required to offset it is about 200,000 Kcal/acre. This is equivalent to 5 gallons of fuel/acre or 50×10^6 barrels of oil/year or 4% of the total imported by the USA in 1970'. Even though it is recognized that erosion would not be completely eliminated under minimal tillage conditions, it would appear that the total energy savings from minimal tillage would be much greater than just the savings in tractor fuel.

(iv) Growing varieties of crops that require a minimum of energy inputs. Such crops give maximum response to fertilizer, are adapted to minimum tillage, and do not require high energy inputs for drying or irrigation (that is, varieties that are low in moisture content at harvest time or that are drought resistant). Also such crops give maximum yield per unit area per unit energy input, and are adapted to maximum use of the growing season and therefore need less energy during harvesting.

(v) Giving special attention to the storage of fuel, maintenance of equipment, excessive weight of machinery and wheel performance in order to reduce high energy losses relating to field work.

(vi) Considering how best to reduce energy loss from buildings where supplemental heat is required, such as greenhouses, through use of insulation and/or ventilation control.

As indicated earlier, the production sector of the food system accounts for only 18% of the total energy used by the system. Thus, emphasis should be placed on energy-efficient practices in the food processing, distribution and home preparation sectors. The Association of the Faculties of Agriculture in Canada has offered several suggestions for using energy more efficiently in the food system[2]: —

(i) encourage the development and installation of food processing methods that have low energy requirements through incentives such as accelerated depreciation schedules;

(ii) examine the role of convenience foods as many of these foods have high energy requirements for processing, packaging and distribution. Frozen potatoes, for example, require 3.5 times more energy from the farm to the table than do fresh potatoes; and

(iii) ensure that good land is reserved for food production. High quality land may produce as much as 25% higher yields with the same energy input. Thus one of the best ways to use energy efficiently is to retain high quality land for agricultural use.

Alternative energy forms for use in the food system will be developed in the future. Emphasis will be placed on renewable energy sources, but considerable time is likely to elapse before there are any major breakthroughs. The Ontario Institute of Agrologists[6] envisages a four-stage transition, namely:

'1. conservation of energy without reduction in food production,
2. continued use of traditional energy sources, with assurance of adequate supply to meet the needs of the immediate future,
3. gradual reduction of dependence on non-renewable fuel resources and increased conservation of energy in the face of increasing prices, and
4. adaptation to alternate sources and forms of energy.'

There has been considerable discussion about the use of biomass as an energy source. Using the systems we have today, farm land could not be spared to grow plants as a source of fuel. As Blaxter[3] has pointed out, 'if we cropped all land for biological fuel production in the United Kingdom, we could meet only 7% of our national fuel needs and would simultaneously produce no food at all; hardly a solution to the energy problem'. However if through research we could develop plants that are more efficient in converting solar energy, and if we are better able to utilize marginal land that is not useful for food plants, then the concept of biomass energy may become more important.

The question remains as to what the Commonwealth universities can, and should, be doing about the world food problem. It would seem apparent that greater emphasis should be placed on research on the biological processes that control crop and livestock productivity. Wittwer[9] suggests that what is needed is research 'that will address the problems of enabling plants and animals to more effectively utilize present environmental resources through:

'1. greater photosynthetic efficiency,
2. improved biological nitrogen fixation,
3. new techniques for genetic improvement,
4. more efficient nutrient and water uptake and utilization, and reduced losses of nitrogen fertilizer from nitrification and denitrification, and
5. more resistance to competing biological systems and environment stresses.'

Hopefully the circle of university scientists interested in the food system will expand in the future. The availability of additional funding and an increasing awareness of the importance of research in this area will induce many 'pure' biologists, chemists and physicists to become involved.

Also I would hope that a greater proportion of food system research in the developed countries will have international implications in the future. There should be greater co-operation among scientists in different countries and an increased willingness to participate in the expansion of research and training institutions in the developing countries. Aid from the developed world should be primarily in the form of scientific and technological assistance for self-help – and this aid should be appropriate to the particular country: culturally, socially, economically and environmentally. This type of aid to help solve the world food problem would seem ideally suited to the resources available in many universities of the Commonwealth.

REFERENCES

1. Agriculture Canada. The Energy Situation and its Effect on the Canadian Food System, Food Systems Branch, December 1977.

2. Association of the Faculties of Agriculture in Canada. A Position Statement on Energy Use in the Food System, March 1978.

3. Blaxter, K. Energy Usage in Agriculture, Address to Farmers' Conference, Lincoln College, New Zealand, May 1978.

4. Heichel, G. A. Accounting for Energy Use in Food Production, Frontiers of Plant Science, Connecticut Agric. Expt. Station, 27:2, Spring 1975.

5. Macleod, L. B., J. H. Lavering and J. A. McIsaac. The Energy Situation in the P.E.I. Agricultural Industry, Canada Agriculture Research Station, Charlottetown, PEI 1976.

6. Ontario Institute of Agrologists. Energy and Agriculture in Ontario, August 1975.

7. Science Council of Canada. A National Statement by the Faculties of Agriculture and Veterinary Medicine at Canadian Universities (22 p.), 1975.

8. Shaw, Michael, L. M. Lavkulich and W. D. Kitts. Agro-ecosystems, Proc. Symposium on Canada and World Food, Ottawa, Canada, August 1977.

9. Wittwer, S. H. The Next Generation of Agricultural Research, Science 199, January 1978.

DISCUSSION

At the outset each of the main speakers on this topic (see above) provided fresh material on the central theme of food production and its relationship to energy. Professor *D. W. George* (Newcastle, N.S.W.) emphasized the relatively small percentage of total energy consumption that is used directly in agriculture. In the case of Australia it is 2% of the total, 2·8% in North America, and 3·5% for the world on average. Processing, packaging and transport to the market multiply this by a factor of varying value, but the factor is usually about 5 or less. This same theme was explored in more detail, particularly with reference to Canada, by Professor *C. M. Switzer* (Guelph). He provided values of 2·4% for Canada and 12 to 15% of the total energy consumption as the value consumed in the total food system. This 12 to 15% of the total energy was analysed in some detail both for the components used on the farm and the larger total of energy consumed between the farm gate and the consumer. It was clear from what was said that energy analysis techniques are of considerable value. Professor George compared and contrasted the analysis for five very different countries (USA, United Kingdom, Holland, Israel and Australia) showing that for four the ratio of the energy content of food to energy used in production was roughly constant at about 0·6, and for one, Australia, it was 2·8. He stressed that all were friends of the earth but that the environmental aspects required much study of an interdisciplinary nature which universities are uniquely qualified to provide. The papers of Professor George and Professor Switzer illustrated that the topics were complicated, and this analytical side of the subject was highlighted in the contributions made by several participants in the discussion. It was clear that relatively simplistic approaches to energy analysis are sometimes made in published studies and there is a case for an exhaustive input/output analysis to be made.

Dr. *B. D. Nag Chaudhuri* (Jawaharlal Nehru) stressed the triaxial dilemma that is evident in the relationship between population, food and energy. He was concerned with the fact that no less than 45 to 48% of the total energy consumed in the less developed countries is used for domestic purposes in cooking, lighting and heating. He noted the high cost of fission, fusion, solar and geo-thermal systems and, by way of contrast, the low efficiency (6–8%) of the essentially biomass method of energy production which is cheaper and thus open to the poorer nations. He took the view that much better values of efficiency of small-scale energy systems could be achieved by the application of sophisticated techniques of the right kind which could properly be explored by university scientists and technologists. Likewise the sociological, political and wide-ranging environmental aspects of energy, food and population merit much more detailed study by university experts.

During the discussion the gravity of the fossil fuel situation and the importance of a net analysis approach were stressed. Throughout the discussion it appeared that, although agriculture as such is not a large energy-consuming section of society, food production would fall if energy supply proved inadequate. University thought might be directed to exploring the less energy-intensive systems of agriculture.

It was acknowledged that universities are already making substantial contributions to the food and energy questions, but that they could do a great deal more. It is possible in a university setting to debate, to study and to research, without prejudice, the various options that present themselves

SUB-TOPIC 1(C): ENERGY

now and that might appear in the future. There is some political sensitivity in many energy alternatives, and university contribution to the United Nations Conference to be held in Vienna in 1979 could prove important. It will be concerned with food, population and energy, and five regions will be studied. It was understood that major matters for study include the question of the developing countries obtaining the necessary energy to sustain their populations, the cost in energy terms of food in the developed countries, and the relevance of soft energy paths which it was thought would have to be sophisticated. The wastage of food everywhere (including in the developing countries) was seen as complicating the main issues rather seriously.

Sub-Topic 1(d)

HEALTH

Chairman: Dr. G. RANGASWAMI
Vice-Chancellor of Tamil Nadu Agricultural University

Rapporteur: Dr. R. W. BEGG
President of the University of Saskatchewan

Thursday, 24 August

The Universities and Health in the Tropics: the Problem and an Answer

Professor J. D. GILLETT (*Pro Vice-Chancellor and Head of School of Biological Sciences, Brunel University*):

Abstract

Malaria, still the biggest cause of death (if we disregard starvation), results largely from man's own ways; he so often creates the conditions that encourage both the breeding and feeding of mosquitoes. In a recent paper I suggested that if we are to put a stop to this appalling loss we must now enter a new phase in our fight against mosquito-borne disease. First we must set up the machinery for studying the malariogenic and other disease-producing ways of man and then, when these data have been collected and collated, we must set about trying to change these ways. I suggested that this difficult task would best be done by indirect methods via the media of radio and television; it would have to be done by example and not by simple instruction.

These ideas can now be enlarged to include many other afflictions of man in the warmer parts of the world, for example some of the leishmaniases, schistosomiasis and many of the gut parasites. Equally important, they can be extended to inculcate changes in the *time-honoured methods of husbandry and a building up of awareness of the importance of agriculture in countries where 90% of the human population is on the land.*

While this paper has been well received, and the need to take into account the ways of man as well as those of the parasites and the vectors has been acknowledged, it has been rightly criticised for not dealing more thoroughly with the means of achieving this goal, that is of reaching the people and influencing their ways. In the present paper I attempt to make up for this deficiency and explore these aspects at greater depth.

Background

I first went to the continent of Africa in 1936. My main task was to assist Major H. S. Leeson on his researches on the *Anopheles funestus* complex in all the countries that politically made up East Africa: Kenya, Tanganyika, Uganda and Zanzibar. One of my responsibilities was to record some of the work on 16 mm film for the Ross Institute in London, but at the same time I made a record of the expedition for our own use. I showed that film recently to an audience which included some students from East Africa. They remarked afterwards how surprised they were to see life then very much the same as it is today. Admittedly almost all the film was about rural life. But forty years had passed — not long in geological time — not long even in the total historical context — but a very long time indeed in the middle of this fast-moving scientific and technological century.

I have since spent many years in Africa and in this paper I shall draw mainly from this continent. I have been back again several times recently and it is true and also astonishing that once one is away from the towns one can detect very little that is different. Indeed life goes on almost all over the continent in much the same way, if not exactly so. And death goes on in much the same way too. The people still cultivate the land by the same old methods using the same hand hoes, sowing the same old crops and bearing their same old load of parasites. Malaria still takes its annual toll of a million or so people before they have had any chance to fulfil themselves — most of those who die of it are under 15 years of age. And those who do not die, by far the majority, continue on with their parasites. They soldier on with a partial immunity, or what we used in earlier days to refer to as low fever.

[*Gillett*] TOPIC 1: THE WORLD FOOD PROBLEM

The Parasitic Load and Poverty

In addition to malaria and also remaining virtually unchanged we find filariasis, trypanosomiasis, onchocerciasis, schistosomiasis, hookworm, tapeworm, roundworm, dysentery and diarrhoea of many kinds, pneumonia, syphilis, yaws, gonorrhoea and a host of other afflictions that shorten expectation of life or reduce it to a sad reflection of the good life and health that most of us here take for granted. All this is well known, of course. My point is that in rural Africa conditions remain the same. Methods remain unchanged. And much the same could be said of rural tropical Asia and even of much of rural South and Central America. And so to the list we may add dengue, haemorrhagic fever, encephalitis, kala-azar, Chagas disease, scrub typhus, and other less well-known accompaniments to the song of life, to the life where ill-health is taken as the norm.

I have so far confined myself to what are mostly the endemic diseases. But from time to time, when climatic and biotic factors combine favourably, or unfavourably from our viewpoint, various explosive epidemics take the stage: cholera, yellow fever, o'nyong-nyong, chikungunya and so on, while plague lurks ominously in the wings. Only smallpox has left the scene (we hope permanently).*
But overshadowing all is simple undernourishment and starvation, the one leading to permanent impairment, the other still, alas, an even greater killer than malaria.

Why should this be so? Why should life in the sunnier countries be one constant struggle against poverty and disease? Is one the cause of the other and, if so, which? It is tempting to argue that life at the subsistence level, and below, paves the way for the parasites. Indeed this is how the argument is usually presented: poverty not only begets poverty but leads inexorably by overcrowding and a lowering of standards to the presence of parasites and disease. There is, of course, no denying the truth of this; the constant threat of famine alone makes any meaningful fight against parasitic disease well-nigh impossible. But I question whether it represents the whole truth. Certainly they interact, but not only is there a vicious circle of poverty leading to disease and disease to poverty, there is a third factor that interferes with the smooth running of the cycle, pushing it in the direction of disease first, poverty later.[16]

The warm equable climate in much of the tropics allows the presence of vast populations of fast-breeding insects and other arthropods on which so many of the parasites that afflict man in these regions depend for the completion of their life cycles. These

---

*It is noteworthy that of the six great pestilences of history smallpox is the only one depending on person to person contact; malaria, plague, typhus and yellow fever depend on insect transmission and cholera on water, food and flies.

arthropods act as the go-betweens carrying infection over distance and over time. Vast populations of insects occur in the temperate parts of the globe too and even in the arctic, but these are active for only a part of each year, in the far north for a few weeks only. The effects of winter, with its low temperature and poor conditions of light, serve as environmental bottlenecks; even in the summer there may be a significant fall of temperature each night which will slow things down. In much of the tropics, however, provided the relative humidity does not drop too low, insects are free to breed unhampered all the year round, each generation, in some species, taking a matter of a week or a few days even.

But there is another reason why high temperatures tend to push the cycle in the direction of disease first, poverty later. Arthropods are ectothermic animals, the body temperature being largely controlled by the ambient temperature in which they find themselves. But the parasites capable of completing their development and in many cases multiplying 20,000 × or even a million-fold within the tissues of these arthropods are also ectothermic. Thus while the rate of development of these parasites is predictable within fine limits when present in man or other endothermic vertebrate, this is far from being the case within the insect. It is possible to predict the time taken to complete schizogony by the malaria parasites within hours or even minutes (the intrinsic incubation period), whereas the time taken to complete sporogony within the mosquito host (the extrinsic incubation period) varies within very wide limits according to temperature, being about doubled for a decrease of 10°C.[11] It is the short extrinsic incubation period of the pathogens, coupled with the short turn-over time of succeeding generations of insects that ensures that *homo sapiens* in the warmer parts of the world remains barely at or even below the usually accepted level of subsistence. Theories about the causes of poverty have little meaning unless we can see them within the context of the overall picture—a picture of man weighed down by parasitic disease—of man playing host to a multifarious load of parasites with which his undernourished body is unfit to cope. It is this that separates tropical medicine from its counterpart in the cooler regions of the world where a blessed winter and cool nights intervene to slow things down.

Soil and Agriculture

Of course other factors play a part in keeping productivity down to a low level. The poor soil, for example, in much of Africa and the uneven distribution of rainfall are potent factors and may well be even more important than those we have been discussing—such things are not easy to quantify. Many other factors make up the complex picture, all helping to keep the population, which in some countries of Africa is all but about 10% on the land, at the bare subsistence level. The situation is not helped by the unchanging methods employed by these peasant farmers. Whereas a farm family in the industrialized countries supports itself and 10 to 15 or more non-farm families and has a correspondingly high income, in much of the continent of Africa each farm family supports itself and less than one non-farm family.[1,9]

Again man has to battle with the insects or accept that much of his crops—as much as 50% at times—will be eaten by these pests or destroyed or weakened by the pathogens they transmit. Even when he attempts to store what is left of his labour the losses continue: it has been estimated that losses of stored grain in East Africa range from 25 to 100% each season.[1] Again we come back to temperature, for what holds for human pathogens during their essential period of development and/or multiplication within the arthropod hosts applies equally to the plant pathogens.

In the more arid regions the poor land is valued more for the cattle it can carry or rather for the cattle it is made to carry. Poor land that requires up to 10 hectares to support one animal is overstocked to the tune of one head per 1.5 hectares.[20] Acock[1] in his admirable paper on agriculture in Africa makes a plea for the better utilization both of land and labour. But Brown[4] in a discussion of this paper asks 'how can one expect hard work out of millions of individuals who are carrying around parasites, who are suffering from one or more diseases, who are periodically attacked by communicable diseases? I don't see how one can expect anything except inertia and disinterest from people who feel rather like we feel when we have a bad cold—we just don't feel very much like going to the office. Most of the African rural population is chronically in this state'.[9] This brings me back to my original theme that in the vicious circle of disease—poverty—disease it is likely that chronic poor health is the foot that pushes the pedal. The economic consequences of man's unsought-for partnership with the malaria parasite have recently been highlighted in a detailed study of the 'slash and burn' farming communities of Paraguay.[6]

The Problem

The continent of Africa is made up of some 60 countries, some of them enormous, most of them large and a few small; Uganda, one of the smaller countries, is about the same size as Britain. Together these countries constitute somewhere between 22 and 25% of the land surface of the world, even when we include arctic Canada, Greenland and antarctica.

We recognize the problems of disease, poor soil, uneven and unreliable rainfall, low output husbandry, and over-stocking of the drylands. We recognize the difficulties arising from language and custom and poor communications. We recognize too the appalling poverty that is found everywhere outside the towns, the latter, incidentally, presenting yet further problems with their over-fast development.[19,25] And much of what applies to Africa applies also to large parts of South and Central America. It applies also to India and neighbouring countries and much of South East Asia; but most of these latter countries carry enormous populations of man, a factor creating its own problems. If it is true, as I have argued, that parasitic and other disease and general poor health are central to these problems, we seem mostly to fail to recognize, or we have forgotten, that much of the ill-health is a direct result of man's own way of life.

We tend to regard man as the helpless victim of insect-borne disease, even though by his own activities he so often creates the very conditions that favour the maintenance of and close contact with the insects he hopes to avoid. The truly extraordinary and perhaps the most important aspect of this whole question is that it is not so much through *ignorance* of the part played by, say, mosquitoes in the transmission of disease. No, man continues through time-honoured custom to provide the conditions to which rural populations of mosquito species and other pests long ago adapted. Man not only provides the ideal breeding places for the aquatic stages of mosquitoes but seems content to provide a steady supply of blood that female adult mosquitoes need if these breeding places are to be kept stocked with eggs. He may complain about being bitten, but wait for someone-else to wave the magic wand.

The classic example of the man-invited mosquito is, of course, *Aedes aegypti*, the yellow fever mosquito. Throughout much of its range this tropical and subtropical species is referred to as a domestic mosquito breeding almost exclusively in man-made containers of all types, both those in use in and around the house as water-holders and those scattered around outside or discarded. Indeed it is this well-known property of *Ae. aegypti* that led to the success of the early campaigns against it in Cuba, Panama and Brazil.[13,17] The important point for us to consider is that despite the ease with which domestic populations of *Ae. aegypti* can be dealt with it continues to be found in and around countless houses throughout the tropics, in villages and towns. A survey carried out in Bangkok in 1968 revealed nearly two million such containers with some 800,000 of them actually breeding *Ae. aegypti*. The WHO Aedes Research Unit in Bangkok estimated that the output from these entirely man-provided breeding places in the city was nearly two million adult mosquitoes per day. In 1962 some 20% of all children in Bangkok suffered an attack of *Ae. aegypti*-borne virus disease, that is some 175,000 cases—'all of it home grown'.[17] Man breeds his own *Ae. aegypti* and sits back either in ignorance or in the hope that someone else will do the tidying up.

Much the same argument goes for a number of other dangerous and well-known transmitters of disease: *Ae. simpsoni* takes over from *Ae. aegypti* in much of rural Africa, breeding in the axils of certain man-grown crops around almost every house; *Culex fatigans*, breeding in highly polluted waste-water including human raw-sewage throughout the tropics and subtropics particularly in the towns; *Anopheles gambiae*, the most important transmitter of malaria in Africa, breeding in every man-made puddle, whether large or small, even those in the middle of roads and fully exposed to the hot sun—or rather, particularly those exposed to the sun—including also every excavation, however large or small, at roadsides, brickworks, airports and alongside railways, breeding also in every exposed footprint in open muddy country, whether of man, cattle or goat, and in shallow wells, irrigated crops, derelict canoes, beer vats, and so on and so on. About a million people, almost all of them below the age of 15, will die before this time next year, almost all of them because of this one species and almost all resulting from the ways of man. I could go on: *An. albimanus* in the western hemisphere and *An. balibacensis* in South East Asia provide at times further examples of man-assisted malaria production. And there are many more. Disease and misery resulting from these are not merely man-assisted, they are man-generated.

It is a curious fact that these pests, and many more, and the human disease and suffering for which they are responsible, are largely a result of man's own habits, his time-honoured customs and ignorance—ignorance of the part that his own customs play in the maintenance of disease and not of the part played by the insects themselves, I must emphasize. Equally curious, however, is the fact that we who claim to be the repository of knowledge and advisers on these matters almost totally ignore this aspect, or rather we seem to have forgotten it, for it was a standard part of the teaching in the schools of tropical medicine 40–60 years ago. The part played by man disappeared from the curriculum when the residual insecticides first began to be splashed around the world, exactly in the same way that the discipline of aseptic surgery disappeared, perhaps for ever, with the advent of the antibiotics.[14,15] We used to teach these matters but two generations of malariologists, encouraged by the enthusiasm of the World Health Organization, have grown up since those days.

It is evident that we have failed in our attempts to wipe out malaria, indeed it is on the increase in many places. It is equally evident that a host of other parasitic diseases from viruses to trematodes still plague the peoples inhabiting the warm moist places of our world, parasites that may not kill but nevertheless serve to reduce man's energy output and keep it barely at or below the level necessary for mere subsistence. Little wonder that ancient and inefficient methods of agriculture persist. Little wonder also that productivity remains so low.[1,5,22,23,28] It is also evident that one of the reasons for this failure is our own shortsightedness in not recognizing the part played by man in all this. Or rather, as I have already said—our forgetting to take account of this part. Blinded by bright hopes that DDT and the synthetic antimalarial drugs brought to us, and later lulled into a sense of security by over-optimistic schemes of eradication, we have forgotten that all too often man himself breeds his own mosquitoes. Even when he is beset by species arising from breeding places outside his control he, too, by his own behaviour ensures that contact with these species is maintained: he may buy and even use a mosquito net, but more often than not he will use it in such a manner that this simple and effective device resembles more a mosquito trap, with himself and his family serving as the bait.[17]

The Universities

It is clear that education too has failed. By education I refer both to education of the people in the third world and the education we give to those who set out to guide and help those people. The first thing we need to do, however, is to look at our own education. We need first to educate people to study people. Universities concerned with tropical medicine need to create new departments and schools concerned with the training of people who will look professionally at the social and anthropological aspect of these problems. And the same applies to tropical agriculture. Elsewhere I have advocated the need for a new breed of experts—the social malariologist—a specialist with a sound and up-to-date undergraduate training in the biological sciences but with a thorough postgraduate training in the methods of social anthropology that will allow him to go out into the field and study those aspects of human behaviour and social custom that play such a vital role in bringing misery and death to so many. We shall need an army of the new experts, not to replace the entomologists and medically-qualified experts but to work alongside them. It will not be enough merely to study the behaviour of man in this or that country; often each population will have to be studied separately, not merely because behavioural traits may vary from one population to the next but, and probably more important, because the total ecological conditions including soil, climate, vegetation, as well as the potential vector species present will certainly vary between areas occupied by human populations. Thus, even when religious practice and other customs are uniform over a wide area, the impact that the local vector species may have will depend on the local environment in its totality.

The universities may have to consider producing some new hybrid graduates, well-trained people combining some of the qualities of administrator, biologist, doctor, economist, engineer, geologist and sociologist. Teams made up of separate specialists in each of these fields rarely if ever work in harmony; usually the administrator or the doctor or the economist feels that he alone should dictate the tune.

We have books dealing with the multiplicity of parasites that affect man in this region or that. We have books dealing with the local representatives of the 3000 and more species of mosquitoes so far discovered. Other books and papers deal in detail with the tsetse flies, or with the sandflies, or the fleas or bugs, or with the ticks and mites. But we have next to nothing dealing with the malariogenic behaviour of man. Here is the big gap. Here is the main reason for our failure. We need to collect and collate all this information in a systematic and professional manner. The universities should now create these departments to foster the study of the malariogenic and other disease-producing activities of man.

Failure to take these steps is to delude ourselves. We shall, to be sure, find out more and more about the parasites and the populations of insects responsible for their safe delivery to their human hosts. We shall do this with ever-increasing ingenuity and sophistication, adding to our knowledge in an ever-widening circle that gets further and further from the central problem—man. We shall, as I have said elsewhere, 'end up when all is said and done, and paid for, with pretty much the mixture as before'. Meanwhile one and a half million young people in the world will continue to die each year without a chance to fulfil themselves and four or five hundred times that number will continue to play host to these and to many other kinds of parasite, including at least nine genera of tapeworms, eleven genera of nematodes, five genera of trematodes, seven genera of protozoa and the various species of all these, not to mention bacteria, Rickettsiae, viruses and other groups including pentastomids, acathocephalans and so on. Who knows the immunological price man pays for this unhappy association;[26] sickle cell anaemia (and other haemoglobinopathies),[34] man's genetic answer to sharing this planet with *Plasmodium falciparum*, is a heavy price indeed and one that continues to be paid in the absence of parasite pressure even to the tenth generation. It is not so much the parasites which kill that drag man, the species, down but those he continues to carry.

This, then, is the first step which the universities must take: to train an army of people to study people. The second step, educating the people themselves, that is the peasant farmers that make up the bulk of the human population in these regions, comes later. Indeed it may have to be delayed until all this information is to hand and until we are ready to apply entirely new methods at reaching the people. We have the means now, but it is a question of harnessing them at the right time.

An Answer

What means are available at reaching the people and persuading them to change their ways? We shall probably have to dismiss the straightforward easy way through compulsion, threat and by the process of law; such methods will almost certainly be unacceptable in a democracy, although they are being applied with apparent success in Singapore and, I am told, in China. The printed word will not do since we have to deal with a largely illiterate population. But neither will lectures by visiting experts, the problem is far too vast and the communities too scattered for this approach to have any effect whatever. Nor, in my opinion, will travelling exhibitions and demonstrations have any lasting good effect, even with mobile cinemas; by the time any place is revisited, perhaps years later, any scratch on the surface that may have been made on the problem will have long since healed, almost certainly without leaving a mark. But such methods are no longer necessary in this age of mass communication by radio and television, media that can penetrate the very homes of the people and on a national scale.[13]

Radio receivers can be produced cheaply enough and even television receivers are not out of the question, judging by the widespread use they already have in many rural parts of Thailand, where every small group of houses in remote rice-growing areas nestles under a forest of television aerials and even the barges on the canals bear the tell-tale television mast over the living-quarters. Rural Thailand is, however, much more advanced economically than the areas that are our main consideration. Even so, it shows what can be done in provision and distribution and what might be done if properly organised. It is said that 100% of the Thai peasant farmers

[*Gillett*] TOPIC 1: THE WORLD FOOD PROBLEM

suffer from the lung-fluke *Paragonimus,* the eggs of which are broadcast every time they cough. Gravitating to the water that lies beneath almost every Thai house, the hatching parasites take up residence in the freshwater crabs that abound there. These in turn are eaten by the people—and they are eaten raw! In a similar fashion a small gut-fluke finds its way into the people by their habit of eating uncooked dragon-fly larvae, although it is not through coughing that the eggs of this fluke find their way back into the water. Neither of these parasites is of great medical importance, but how easily the cycle of infection could be broken if the people could be persuaded to cook their crabs and other delicacies.

Persuasion, however, will not come from preaching, whatever the medium used; people, as I have said elsewhere, will simply switch to the other channel.[15] People do not take kindly to being preached at, nor will they easily be persuaded to give up time-honoured ways, ways given a feeling of normality and permanency because they were the ways of childhood.[17] But people will copy, particularly if they can identify with attractive heroes and heroines in realistic and compelling stories of everyday life. Does anyone suppose that the conservative British workman on the construction site would have taken so readily to wearing protective head-gear had he not seen his counterpart heroes wearing them on 'the box'. When in the 1930s Britain, alarmed at the rising number of bicycle accidents as motor traffic increased on our roads, introduced a few cycle-tracks alongside recently constructed roads, cyclists refused to use them. They were not going to be ordered about even if in the interest of their own safety and, surely, pleasure. The same applied to a government request that they use red rear-lights, they were even instructed by members of their union to disregard the request; a red reflector was all that was necessary, they argued. Except in totalitarian states, persuasion must be done by example, not compulsion. It must be done by entertainment in place of any attempt at direct instruction. In other words persuasion must be by indirect methods; as I have also said elsewhere: 'People will not *obey,* but our primate ancestry ensures that they will copy'.[17]

What part can the universities play in this new strategy? We have already seen that they can play a vital role in the first part, that is the study of the malariogenic and other disease-promoting activities of man. But how can the universities help with the second part—a part that seems far removed from the traditional role of these institutions. Let us try to put this role in perspective. The growth of universities coincided with the comparatively new technology of printing and the production of books. Before then the repository of learning lay mainly with the monasteries. Books were the key to this growth, books that could be reproduced relatively easily, books that could record and pass on the achievements of former civilizations, books that could record and disseminate the discoveries pouring in from the new philosophy of science. The gifted orator with his group of devoted disciples was replaced by the gifted writer and widening group of readers. The former was not altogether lost but the two went together — a book becoming the symbol of learning.

Books, however, remain closed except to the literate, for a skill is needed for their use. The incredible transmutation of what are natural auditory stimuli to artificial visual symbols is apt to be taken for granted, particularly, perhaps, in university circles. The alphabet, with its small set of only 20 – 40 letters (according to culture) enabling one to make an almost unlimited number of words, must surely rank as one of the great triumphs of man, perhaps the greatest. But the skill to make use of this incredible code, whether by reading or in writing, has to be learned. Books are fine for those with the skill to use them. Our problem is how to establish contact with a huge and widely scattered peasant community lacking this skill. To be sure, individuals may be found who can just about read and write, but much more than this is required if books are to be the vehicle of learning.

We could, of course, embark on a gigantic programme of education with a massive increase in the number of schools. But who will teach in those schools? What will be taught? And what will be the result? These problems have been admirably set out by Sutton[29] in a review of the problems of education in Africa: 'So long as education is seen as a somewhat mysterious acquisition, it naturally has the effect of setting apart its products as people of different and special status. It cannot be accepted unselfconsciously and "naturally" to become a part of the normal equipment for everyday life'. Later he adds: 'A great part of the work of the world depends on qualities which are not easy to develop by formal education. Judgement, assiduity, initiative, integrity — one can readily make a list of virtues for which there is no obvious curriculum'. This important paper is further illuminated by the discussion which followed it: 'I recently heard a rural schoolteacher (in Africa) instructing his pupils on the seven wonders of the world: the hanging gardens of Babylon are completely outside the experience of the village youth and the incident brought home to me the artificiality of much of their learning';[18] and: 'At secondary school level the great difficulty is not only the recurrent cost of teachers' salaries but also the difficulty in obtaining and retaining teachers,..........one of the ways in which we can solve this particular problem is to spread the high cost of teachers over the maximum number of pupils, making full use of radio, television and programmed learning. By these means one can put the job in the hands of a few relatively highly paid people and counteract all the tendency in expanding education to a lowering of standards'.[24]

Radio and television require no skill whatever on the part of the listener and viewer and hence their wide appeal and enormous impact. They can be used not only to extend formal teaching but to reach the illiterate peasantry—in the home. They can be used to reach the children of pre-school age and to reach the mothers of these children who for one reason or another did not receive a formal education. They can also be used to influence the ways of those who did receive some sort of education, who may be able to read and write and who may even be able to list at least some of the seven wonders. Both media can be used not only to make man more conscious of the presence of the parasites that beset him at every turn but to show him how to avoid them; they can also be used to show him how to make the most of the wretched soil he has to work on and perhaps make the fullest use of the poorly distributed rainfall that is his lot. And, as I have indicated, this will best be done by example.

In the paper to which I have made frequent reference I elaborated on this aspect:[17] a regular programme dipicting in a simple story of everyday life the consequences of ill-health and the benefits of health; a continuing story with realistic heroes and heroines in which every facet of village life rings true and in which no part offends in any way the dignity and pride of the people. A continuing series in which each episode tells a story that is both colourful and compelling, a story with characters with whom the people themselves can identify, a story in which freedom from parasites means a sharpened awareness leading to increased wealth and greater success with the other sex, for whether we like it or not these are the two aspects that will appeal.

For the most part simple changes in the ways of man would remove or greatly reduce contact between man and mosquito. And much the same goes for many other insect-transmitted diseases (for example kala-azar and others transmitted by sandflies) and even to some of those that are not brought to us on the wing: hookworm, bilharzia, lung-flukes, and numerous parasites of the gut. The reason why visitors to the tropics, even those who stay to make a career there, remain relatively free from infection whereas the indigenous peoples continue to suffer, is largely because of differences in the ways of the two groups. Admittedly a high proportion of the expatriate population lives in urban areas and may thus be less exposed, but comparing urban-dwellers with urban-dwellers and rural-dwellers with rural-dwellers, the great differences found result mainly from differences in the habits of the two groups in each setting.

Step two, then, is to plan and set in motion programmes of compelling stories for each region, stories in which these principles are unobtrusively and painlessly introduced. The first part of this scheme, that is the planning of these programmes, will inevitably involve the universities, for, following step one, the universities will have become the repositories of knowledge about the ways of man that play a direct role in the generation of disease, poor performance and poverty. If such a programme seems far removed from education as we have come to know it, then too must books have seemed at one time. I can well imagine the pundits of the day deploring the spread of books, a new medium that threatened to replace first-hand experience by second-hand accounts at least by those who had acquired the skill to read. And now the new mass-media threaten to replace the written word. Ah, but the new mass-media are instantly available to those who have not acquired the skill to read, and, more important, the skill to read and to understand. We need, then, to continue formal direct education (whether by orthodox methods or assisted by radio and television) at least to give as many people as possible the chance to acquire the skills necessary to cope with the three Rs. But if we are to change some of the deeply entrenched habits of man we shall, as I have said, have to introduce a measure of indirect instruction as well, for despite the growth of schools, despite the growth of universities and the dignity acquired through independence, the bulk of man in the third world has not changed his lot one jot.

An ECA*-FAO meeting of experts sat in Addis Ababa in 1964 to promote transition from subsistence to market agriculture.[10] They concluded that powerful stimulation would be needed to bring the largely uneducated, often undernourished and perhaps disinterested rural peoples of Africa into a more commercial frame of mind. How can they be induced to produce more, market more both for domestic use and export, introduce new crops, sell their cherished cattle and so on? Dekker[8], in the discussion which followed a paper by Acock[1], urged that the rural areas in Africa should be made more self-conscious: the importance of being a farmer must be stressed and the importance of farmers to the country must be emphasised. To which Acock replied: 'Your idea of making agriculture a more attractive way of life constitutes the sixth major policy agreed upon by the ECA-FAO experts.... I am sorry to say', he went on, 'they weren't very explicit on how they proposed to go about it'.

*Economic Commission for Africa.

Earlier administrators in Africa felt that taxation would be the stimulus for increased effort. They were wrong. They were wrong because trying to induce a parasite-ridden population to work harder had as much chance of success as trying to wring water from a dry sponge.

The present emphasis in education may be suitable for the town-dweller but there is a limit to how many the towns can absorb; it is likely to become education for unemployment, as Sutton[29] has described it, whereas what is needed is education for living. The people themselves must first get rid of their parasites by changes in their ways of living, ways that at present ensure reinfection at every turn. The people themselves must be made aware of these things and at the same time made aware of their own potential. This, I claim, can best be achieved by indirect methods, that is by example. And radio and television are the media for stimulating this new awareness. Elsewhere I have referred to the beginning of a new phase in our fight against malaria and mosquito-borne disease in general.[13] The applications, however, go far beyond this and the universities will have to play their part. If this also means the beginning of a new phase in education then let us prepare for it, for the system that has stood so well the test of time in the developed world has clearly failed in the so-called third. These are strong words. But others are beginning to think along similar lines. Thus: 'No amount of talking or lecturing will persuade people on a very low economic level to adopt measures for which their social experience does not make the need clear'.[27] 'The problem of health education is to reach the population'.[3] 'All this involves a great social and economic transformation and [the italics are mine] *the education systems do not yet exist in Africa* which will produce the kind of people able to accept such technical and social innovation'.[23] By direct methods one has as much hope of persuading the pastoral peoples that inhabit the drier parts of the third world to replace their present symbols of status and wealth with, say, pieces of paper with a picture of a well-fed cow on the back as one has of persuading the people of the United States to replace their green-backs with cowrie-shells. But by indirect methods, such as I have outlined, much could be done.

There is, of course, the spectre of over-population to be faced; are we to save the people from early death from parasitic disease only to have them die of starvation? The problems of health and population must be considered together. But one thing is certain—we cannot simply let nature take its course; we would not tolerate this for ourselves, so how can we advocate it for others—simply because they live far away. Perhaps, as I have already suggested[17], we should even now be looking for some sort of combined pill, a contraceptive-anti-malaria pill, as a first step.

If what I am advocating seems to be far-fetched and unrealistic let us remember that it is now 15 years since the International Telecommunication Union (ITU) put forward detailed plans for a network of radio and television stations in Africa. These envisaged 4969 radio and 1082 television transmitting stations.[12] Gayer describes how this scheme was to take 10 – 15 years to complete and how it would allocate frequency assignments covering every country of Africa. ITU already had available a cheap television receiver and cheap radio receivers were no problem. In the following year UNESCO met in Lagos to see how television could be used for educational and information purposes and to see in what way funds could be applied to attract the necessary experts. Professor F. G. Young, a member of IUC and chairman at the Ciba Foundation Symposium in Addis Ababa when Gayer gave his paper, observed that the British Association would be wise to take note of the growing importance of television;[35] I would go further and say that WHO and FAO should take note and think seriously of using this already available tool, a tool that would allow us to get to the heart of these problems, that is to the people themselves in their homes. The knowledge of the peoples' ways will have to come through the universities, but the application of this knowledge must be administered by some supra-national body in collaboration with the universities.

We may not yet be ready for these ideas, they involve so much that cuts across our cherished notions. But the first step, that is the setting up of departments to study and teach malariogenic anthropology or whatever term we think appropriate, could be taken now. It is the second step that takes some stomaching. It is the second step too that will cost so much. But it really depends on how we count the cost, on how we assess the value of one and a half million young people who die each year from malaria alone and the 1000 million and more who continue their bare existence at or below the level of subsistence, scratching away at the impoverished soil, weighed down by their burden of parasites. The choice is ours, now; it depends on how we see our priorities. Can we afford it? The world now spends the equivalent of about US$360 billion (US) per year on defence[21], that is, more than $11,000 per second. Even one thousandth part of this expenditure ($360 million a year or nearly one million dollars per day) would go a long way towards making this new approach possible. The choice is ours now, but posterity will be the judge. The question really is, can we afford not to?

ACKNOWLEDGEMENTS

It is with great pleasure that I record my thanks to Mrs. Joy Greedy and Mrs. Jo Smithson for the help given in the preparation of this paper.

REFERENCES

1. Acock, A. M. (1965). Agricultural potentialities in Africa (Wolstenholme and O'Connor, 1965, pp. 239 – 257).
2. Bourgeois-Pichat, J. (1965). Problems of population size, growth and distribution in Africa (Wolstenholme and O'Connor, 1965, pp. 65 – 97).
3. Brown, A. E. (1965). In Discussion (Bourgeois-Pichat, 1965, p. 94).
4. Brown, A. E. (1965). In Discussion (Acock, 1965, p. 248).
5. Clark, C. G. (1963). Agricultural productivity in relation to population (Wolstenholme, 1963, p. 23).
6. Conly, G. N. (1975). The impact of malaria on economic development: a case study, Pan American Health Organization: WHO Scientific Publication No. 297 (117 pp.).
7. Dekker, G. (1965). Climate and water resources in Africa (Wolstenholme and O'Connor, 1965, pp. 30 – 64).
8. Dekker, G. (1965). In Discussion (Acock, 1965, p. 250).
9. Food and Agriculture Organization (1963). Report of the 4th Inter-African conference on food and nutrition, Rome: FAO.
10. Food and Agriculture Organization (1964). Report of the ECA-FAO expert meeting on government measures to promote the transition from subsistence to market agriculture, Rome: FAO.
11. Garnham, P. C. C. (1964). Factors influencing the development of protozoa in their arthropodan hosts (Taylor, 1964, pp. 33 – 50).
12. Gayer, J. H. (1965). Telecommunications in Africa (Wolstenholme and O'Connor, 1965, pp. 179 – 193).
13. Gillett, J. D. (1971). *Mosquitos* (274 pp.) (World Naturalist Series), Weidenfeld and Nicolson Ltd., London.
14. Gillett, J. D. (1971). Report of the 1st international seminar of the SEATO Medical Laboratory, Bangkok, pp. 53 – 54.
15. Gillett, J. D. (1973). The control of arthropod-borne disease – the next phase. In Vector Control in S.E. Asia, ed. Chan Yow-Cheung, Chan Kai-Lok and Ho Beng-Chuan, 1st SEAMO Workshop, Singapore, p. 31.
16. Gillett, J. D. (1974). Direct and indirect influences of temperature on the transmission of parasites from insects to man (Taylor and Muller, 1974, pp. 79 – 95).
17. Gillett, J. D. (1975). Mosquito-borne disease: a strategy for the future, *Sci. Prog. Oxf.* 62, pp. 395 – 414.
18. Goody, J. R. (1965). In Discussion (Sutton, 1965, p. 209).
19. Gratz, N. C. (1973). C.R.C. *Crit. Rev. Envir. Control* 3, p. 455.
20. Harroy, J.-P. (1962). Surpopulation en Afrique centrale. In Bulletin des Séances, Académie royale des sciences coloniales (d'outre-mer), 8, pp. 524 – 527.
21. International Institute for Strategic Studies (1977). The Military Balance, I.I.S.S. (111 pp.), London.

22. Kimble, G. H. T. (1960). Tropical Africa, Vol. 2, The Twentieth Century Fund, New York.
23. Last, G. C. (1965). The geographical implications of man and his future in Africa (Wolstenholme and O'Connor, 1965, pp. 6 – 29).
24. Last, G. C. (1965). In Discussion (Sutton, 1965, p. 212).
25. Mattingly, P. F. (1962). *Bull. Wld. Hlth. Org.*, 27, p. 578.
26. McGregor, I. A. (1972). Immunology of malarial infection and its possible consequences, *Brit. Med. Bull.*, 28, pp. 22 – 27.
27. Russell, H. B. L. (1965). Epidemiology and the provision of health services in Africa (Wolstenholme and O'Connor, 1965, pp. 146 – 169).
28. Stamp, L. D. (1964). The Geography of Life and Death, Collins Fontana Library, London.
29. Sutton, F. X. (1965). Africa's educational needs and opportunities (Wolstenholme and O'Connor, 1965, pp. 194 – 221).
30. Taylor, A. E. R. (1964). Host-Parasite Relationships in Invertebrate Hosts (134 pp.), Blackwell Scientific Publications, Oxford.
31. Taylor, A. E. R. and Muller, R. (1974). The Effects of Meteorological Factors upon Parasites (117 pp.), Blackwell Scientific Publications, Oxford.
32. Wolstenholme, G. (1963). Man and His Future, J. and A. Churchill Ltd., London.
33. Wolstenholme, G. and O'Connor, M. (1965). Man and Africa (400 pp.), CIBA Foundation, J. and A. Churchill Ltd., London.
34. Woodruff, A. W. (1972). Recent work on anaemias in the tropics, *Brit. Med. Bull.* 28, pp. 92 – 95.
35. Young, F. G. (1965). In Discussion (Gayer, 1965, p. 193).

Professor A. OMOLOLU (*Professor of Nutrition, University of Ibadan*):

> Know then thyself, presume not God to scan,
> The proper study of mankind is man.
>   Pope

The story is told of three blind men who were taken to a zoo. They were taken to a tame elephant and allowed to feel the animal. As they left the blind man who felt the foot of the elephant exclaimed: 'The elephant is like a tree trunk'. The one who felt the ear of the elephant said: 'The elephant is like a flat tray'. Whilst the third who felt the moving trunk of the elephant exclaimed: 'Truly, the elephant is like the moving branch of a tree'. They were all right — in part — depending on what and how they felt. The world food problem is, like the elephant, colossal, and it seems that most people see it only from one angle. Many books have been written on the subject—even a world conference has been held—but the problem is still with us. Many authorities and authors tend to see the problem, from their speciality's viewpoint or from their country's point of view. The problem is, however, an international one.

The facts of the problem are very simple and non-controversial. By nutritional standards evolved by the World Health Organization and the Food and Agriculture Organization of the United Nations, at least one-third of the world's population—mostly children—are not getting enough to eat. In different parts of the developing world, at different times, thousands of people are dying of hunger due to droughts, floods, poor harvests and wars. In May 1978, people of 17 countries in Africa were classed by the Food and Agriculture Organization of the United Nations as falling into this group. The most disturbing fact, however, is that the world production of food is more than enough to feed everybody in the world. There are countries—mostly in the developed world—that are producing much more than they need; whilst most countries of the developing world are not producing enough to feed their people. To most simple-minded people from the developing world the answer to the problem will be to move food from the country that has too much to countries where it is needed. This solution, however, does not fit in with international politics, commerce and finance. Someone has to pay. Unfortunately most of the countries that are short of food are also short of convertible currency for payment. So the world food problem is still with us.

One is easily tempted to discuss the international economic and political implications and complications—as well as solutions—of the world food problem. This session is, however, devoted to discussing the health aspects of the problem and the role that universities should play. Let us try to isolate the health aspects of the problem.

As a result of the world food problem as outlined above, there are two groups in the world affected by the problem. Those who live in countries where excess food is available and who thus overeat and those who live in countries where there is not enough food to go round. This, naturally, is an over-simplification as, even in those countries that do not produce enough food, we have a minority who owing to position or money can and do overeat, whilst in the countries that do produce excess food people who cannot get enough to eat may be found.

The health problems of the first group are well exemplified by the USA and Norway—two countries that are trying to solve their food

SUB-TOPIC 1(D): HEALTH

problems. In 1976 the average person in the USA consumed 125 pounds of fat and 100 pounds of sugar—not to talk of meat. The Norwegian government has produced a nutrition and food policy which aims at reducing the amount of fat, sugar and milk available to its population over the years. The health problems of overeating include obesity, heart disease, strokes, cancer.

Recent studies show that in the developed world the foundation of obesity is laid by overfeeding with formulas and modified cow's milk during bottle-feeding in infancy. This is one area in which the universities in those countries are playing and should play an important role. There is more than enough evidence to show that human milk is by far superior to cow's milk (or modified cow's milk) in baby feeding. Yet owing to convenience, vested interest and ease of manipulation feeding with modified cow's milk is the rule rather than the exception in the developed world. Much more tragic is the spread of this practice to the people of the developing world through example, improper training of medical personnel and forceful advertising. The universities of the Commonwealth can and should take the lead to educate in this important field. There is need for nutrition—especially infant nutrition and breastfeeding—to be adequately and properly taught, especially to medical doctors. For a very long time the education of medical personnel—including nurses—in nutrition has been left to the baby-food manufacturing houses that provide posters, samples, diaries and calendars for the health centres, clinics and consulting rooms. Most medical training institutions still do not give enough training in nutrition, especially child nutrition and breastfeeding, to medical students who form the team-leaders of our health teams.

The foundation of obesity is laid in childhood and nurtured by overeating and lack of exercise in later years. These contribute to the heart diseases, deposits in the blood vessels of excess fatty acids— long and short chain fatty acids, high cholesterol. These, with lack of exercise, lead to heart complications and stroke. The lack of adequate fibre in the 'convenience' foods, excessive smoking, too much intake of alcoholic drinks and non-use of the breast for breast-feeding contribute to cancer of the gastro-intestinal tract, lungs, liver and the breast.

The health aspects of undernutrition are very difficult to separate from the socio-economic background. The conditions that make for undernutrition in a country or family include not only the availability of food but also—and in most cases much more importantly—poor environmental sanitation; bad or non-existent water supply; infections and diseases; inadequate and poor housing; lack of money, education and opportunity for work. The health

aspects of chronic undernutrition are many and various. They include:—
- High wastage of pregnancy due to more abortions and miscarriages.
- High death-rate of mothers during childbirth due to complications and weakness.
- Small-size babies with greater number of illnesses and deaths during childbirth and the first month of life.
- High death-rates in infancy and childhood due to childhood malnutrition and its complications. In most parts of the developing world at least one-quarter of children born do not reach their fifth birthday. The rebound phenomenon is excess production of children.
- Inability to attain full mental development in spite of full educational opportunities due to severe malnutrition in infancy.
- Stunted growth and development because of inadequate food to satisfy hunger.
- Lack of working efficiency and low productivity because there is not enough food to supply the necessary energy.
- Increased proneness to accidents at work because of lack of concentration due to hunger.
- Higher rate of absenteeism from work.
- Low life expectancy—in most developing countries life expectancy at 5 years is only 42 years—thus the contribution by the average person to the country's development is low.

All these—and more—are direct and indirect results of undernutrition. With time they have become a vicious cycle which cannot easily be broken. In 1936, when the first thoughts of a world food problem surfaced at the League of Nations in Geneva, it was thought to be a protein problem—and the solution was extra cow's milk. Now we know better. Within the past ten years the thought has grown that the answer to the world food problem is food—more food from the developed countries to the developing countries. At the present time those who are in the forefront of the world food problem know that this is not the full answer. The only effective solution to the problem is the development of the developing countries—their infrastructure, technology, manpower, economy, agriculture and standards of living. No piecemeal method will bring a lasting solution. Isolating or concentrating our resources on the health aspect alone will not solve the problem.

What then can the universities do? First, and most important, as leaders of thought and scientists we must see the whole problem and let the truth be known. It is incumbent on us to let the politicians as well as the man in the street know the truth. The governments and people of the developed world are afraid that if food consumption is increased in the developing world they would have to reduce their food intakes and standards of life. This is not so. There is the fear that if technology, food production and consumption of the developing world are increased the governments and people of the developed world would suffer. As such, most developed countries try to placate the people of the developing countries by offering some excess foods, family planning, a few tractors or some training facilities in their universities. When, after the second world war, America decided to put life into Europe, she produced the all-embracing Marshall Plan. Today Europe is a partner with America. America has lost nothing — instead she has a market for her goods and a worthy partner for peace and prosperity.

Secondly, the universities of the developed countries must be ready to transfer knowledge, technology, expertise and equipment to the universities of the developing world where the problems are. The solution to the world food problem can only be worked out in the countries affected — not in the developed world. Technology must be adapted to suit local conditions. Cultural, social and traditional factors must be considered in deciding the best inputs. All these considerations need local expertise and are best done by local people. Doctors and other health personnel need to be trained in their surroundings or in a comparable environment. Vaccines need to be adapted to local conditions. Universities need to know and learn more about the people they want to help. The 'ivory-tower' concept of universities is giving way to a 'utilitarian' concept — governments and people want to know what the universities are contributing to development and well-being. Universities must contribute to the upliftment of the country and its people. We need to know the people, their problems, aspirations and ways of life so that our researches result in fruitful, practical and meaningful solutions. The Green Revolution is an example of a package deal which worked well in developed countries but became too expensive in developing countries. The inputs of fertilizers, machinery and expertise that had to be imported with foreign exchange earnings made the revolution too expensive.

Lastly, in solving the world food problem the universities must realise that health forms only one part of the answer. The health team has to work with the agriculturists, nutritionists, economists and others for co-ordinated programmes. Full immunisation of all children in the developing world will more than halve the incidence of malnutrition — but most of these countries cannot afford to buy the vaccines needed or provide the manpower necessary for this work. There is need to train more staff at the country and regional level — not a myriad of doctors but thousands of health assistants and nurses able to identify and treat common infections and diseases early; to give immunisations and deliver basic health care. There is a need for vaccines and drugs to be produced locally — the cost of these has been a limiting factor to good health care in most developing countries. There is need for good water supply at the village and urban levels; sources of energy — cheap solar or mechanised equipment — again at local levels. By co-operation between universities of the Commonealth in the two-way flow of expertise, technology and equipment a great impact can be made on the world food problem.

DISCUSSION

Professor *J. D. Gillett* (Brunel) gave a concise presentation of the highlights of his circulated paper (see above). He discussed health in the developing world, concentrating on Africa where 90% of the population live in a rural environment, and drew attention to the lack of change in rural Africa over the past forty years — same agriculture, same poverty, same parasites. He pointed out that starvation is the main killer in Africa, followed by malaria. There are one million deaths annually from malaria in Africa, and 1·5 million in the world, with the young being the major victims.

Professor Gillett said that one parasite which exists is poverty interaction: ill-health from malnutrition, and parasites sap the energy and drive of the peasants who then accept their lot. Further, insects destroy crops in the field or in storage, or breed a transmitting parasite.

Unfortunately man is viewed as the helpless victim of circumstances but, Professor Gillett stressed, he has created his own environment. The ways of man are a part of the problem.

Professor Gillett suggested that the universities could play a significant role in the conquest of disease and malnutrition by providing people to study people. A biologist trained in social anthropology may find ways to educate people out of their poverty and disease. Such a programme must be by example, not lecture. Radio and television should be used with heroes and heroines as examples, because while people will ignore legislation they will follow the example of the hero. The International Telecommunications Union recommended 4969 radio and 1082 television stations for Africa fifteen years ago. This would provide the necessary further education network, and while the cost would be substantial, this must be balanced against the cost of the current poverty and ill-health.

Professor *A. Omololu* (Ibadan) highlighted and expanded upon the content of his circulated paper (see above) and emphasized that the subtopics of food production, population, energy and health were interrelated. He made the following points: (*a*) breastfeeding is important in

SUB-TOPIC 1(D): HEALTH

the nutrition of infants and cow's milk is not an adequate substitute, particularly if pure water, sterilization facilities and cool storage are not available; (*b*) the role of over-eating and obesity in heart disease is being ignored; (*c*) universities should cultivate local foods and set an example for their use in the community; (*d*) the Green Revolution is not feasible in the developing countries which do not have the economic resources to provide the necessary fertilizers, machinery, etc.; (*e*) health problems relate to culture and should be studied *in situ;* and (*f*) universities are changing from their traditional role. They should accept responsibility for the diffusion of knowledge to the common people with a view to improving their lives.

Professor Omololu showed some slides to demonstrate that immunization is more important than protein intake in relieving morbidity and mortality in children, and also that an adequate intake of breast milk is related to the activity of the infant.

During the general discussion the following points were made: —
● the problems of malnutrition and disease are similar in India and Africa;
● the dead weight of the traditional approach interferes with the introduction of the preferred multidiscipline approach by universities to the study of these interrelated problems;
● universities in developing countries should adopt villages and help them to acquire good habits of food and sanitation;
● malaria is reappearing in some areas in India as mosquitoes acquire DDT resistance;
● universities in developing countries should establish malaria units to undertake public education;
● junk foods are making their appearance in developing countries and pose a problem;
● a balanced protein intake is required for adequate development, and relates to income;
● cultural practices must be changed, such as the licking of infants by dogs leading to hydatids disease;
● the introduction of new and cheaper foods may reduce the required roughage in the diet;
● the availability of a balanced diet may require a diversification of crops;
● the introduction of soybeans to Hong Kong did not make an impact until converted into acceptable foods, such as noodles;
● nutrition deserves more attention in the training of home science students;
● there are problems resulting from cultural food taboos which exist in areas where there is food available;
● it is important that governments of developing countries give top priority to health problems and health education.

*   *   *

TOPIC 1: THE WORLD FOOD PROBLEM

At the Second Plenary Session on Friday, 25 August, the Chairman of Topic 1 (Sir John Crawford) gave the following 'ten-minute response to the discussion on world food':

It is not my task to report the discussion in detail. To attempt this would be futile and the work of the rapporteurs will appear in the Proceedings in due course. My only hope of being useful is to underscore a few major points which seemed, to me at least, to emerge quite clearly from the papers and discussion.

I begin by noting the importance of the fact that the topic 'The World Food Problem and the Universities' appeared on the agendum of this Congress. It is not a characteristic item if one may judge from past agenda. It is a recognition that the role of the universities in relation to the world about them calls for some reconsideration. It represents the universities looking out at the world and not merely inwardly (although fully understandably) at the internal problems of finance, organization, staff-student relations, etc., etc. I am encouraged to think that the discussions within and about our universities will increasingly reflect this outbreak of social consciousness. I am hopeful that it will be seen to be related seriously to Topic 4 on our programme, namely 'The Public View of the Universities'.

The particular problem under discussion has been the world food problem: but in all sessions this was seen as part—a very large part, it is true, but nevertheless a part—of the widespread human degradation and social injustice associated with poverty, malnutrition and low health standards. The food problem has been seen as one of particular societies but also as a global problem both in its elements and in terms of solutions required. It is not surprising, therefore, that the role of the universities was discussed not only in relation to the particular needs of particular countries but also in terms of inter-university links and common philosophical approaches to their role in all our troubled societies.

What pleased me most was that the papers and the discussion did reveal a large consensus on the many-faceted and complex nature of the world food problem and also on the need (and possibility) of a more extrovert stance on the part of universities. On the first point there were many illustrations given in all the papers of the multiple causes of problems and of the complex interrelated factors necessarily to be dealt with in seeking solutions. Some of these factors were quite properly spelt out as constraints on the productivity of both human and physical resources engaged in food production. Three in particular—population growth, health, energy—were illuminated in the papers.

In all cases there was a recognition of the stark contrasts that exist in the world. Thus the contrast in health standards needs no further words here. Perhaps less widely understood has been the contrast between the poor and richer countries in available energy supply needed for food production; or again, between the investment resources available. In all the discussion of the parts of international life (even when limited to food production and distribution) there was the constant question: where do the universities come in as agents of change for the better?

CHAIRMAN'S RESPONSE TO DISCUSSION

The answers given were quiet and modest, but to me very definite. The traditional responsibility for teaching and research remained at the core. But, hardly surprisingly, it was seen that it was not enough for universities to provide trained graduates for the civil service or for the more erudite postgraduate pursuit of knowledge. Whether it was spokesmen for the universities within the developing country member of ACU, or those from the so-called developed members, the message — or perhaps it was a yearning — was the same: 'Let us look out at society about us and contribute more directly to its needs. Let us assist in providing solutions; and let us assist one another across national and cultural boundaries to the maximum extent possible'.

This was the desire and the hope. In terms of practical tasks ahead I believe that the energies of the ACU, of the IUC and of the vice-chancellors' committees and other inter-university bodies in each country must be directed with full recognition of two points: —

(i) First, there must be an improvement and expansion of support relations in teaching and research provided by the universities in the developed countries to those in the developing countries.

(ii) However, this relationship should not, and need not, qualify the fundamental task and responsibilities of universities in the developing countries to relate to their own societies and to offer leadership in solving problems local and national. In the second place, therefore, support from universities in Britain, Canada, Australia and New Zealand should be directed to strengthening the capacity of their sister (or is it brother?) universities in the Commonwealth to carry out this role. This can be done by offering support both to teaching and research. In some cases the more sophisticated resources of the universities in the developed countries can be brought to bear on particular problems in the developing countries — hopefully with a welcome spin-off to the less well-equipped research efforts of the universities in the developing countries.

Alas, I heard little discussion of the Canadian initiatives I mentioned in the opening paper (p. 37) nor of present British and Australian programmes. I heard some rumours of expanding the role of IUC to bring in Canada, Australia and New Zealand. At least I hope I did. I do earnestly recommend that the ACU secretariat gather and distribute information on these programmes and, not less important, encourage discussion in its executive. Not least, I repeat, is the need for the universities in each country to discuss these matters between themselves and formulate programmes accordingly. This can be done at meetings of vice-chancellors but also in the many other professional inter-university gatherings that occur.

I come back to where we started on Monday: there is a world food problem. It is complex and its multiple facets provide ample scope for all our member universities to become less introvert by responding in the many ways open to them to the demand that universities contribute to solutions. This demand will fully test all their resources available for teaching and research. From the discussion of this week I believe that our universities are willing and ready to respond.

Group Discussions

TOPIC 2

HIGHER EDUCATION IN COUNTRIES WITH FEDERAL SYSTEMS OF GOVERNMENT

Chairman: Dr. J. STEVEN WATSON
Principal and Vice-Chancellor of the University of St. Andrews

Editorial Co-ordinator: Mr. P. B. HETHERINGTON
Assistant Secretary General (Appointments), Association of Commonwealth Universities

		page
Sub-Topic 2(a)	FINANCIAL EFFECTS OF FEDERALISM: NATIONAL AND LOCAL CONTROL	
	Opening Speakers	
	Dr. H. I. Macdonald	187
	Professor B. R. Williams	200
	Discussion	205
Sub-Topic 2(b)	STUDENT AND STAFF MOBILITY UNDER FEDERALISM	
	Opening Speakers	
	Professor K. Satchidananda Murty	207
	Dr. M. K. Oliver	218
	Professor T. M. Yesufu	231
	Discussion	242
Sub-Topic 2(c)	ACADEMIC PLANNING IN A FEDERAL SYSTEM	
	Opening Speakers	
	Professor J. F. Ade Ajayi	245
	Professor L. Kerwin	253
	Professor R. H. Myers	269
	Discussion	279
Topic 2	CONTINUATION OF DISCUSSION	281

For index to names, see p. 655

Sub-Topic 2(a)

FINANCIAL EFFECTS OF FEDERALISM: NATIONAL AND LOCAL CONTROL

Chairman: Dr. R. L. WATTS
Principal and Vice-Chancellor of Queen's University at Kingston

Rapporteur: Professor T. N. TAMUNO
Vice-Chancellor of the University of Ibadan

Monday, 21 August

Dr. H. I. MACDONALD (*President and Vice-Chancellor of York University, Toronto*): However altruistic Canadian universities may be in their aims and objectives, they are dependent on public sources of funds for their well-being and even survival. The cynical view of the university would hold that the institutions are indifferent to the source of funds, the level of funding being the significant factor. The heroic view would argue that the source and the level are less important than the assurance of the university's autonomy and academic freedom in the use of the funds. In either case the interesting question is why there should be concern about the implications of federalism for university financing. Are there real or apparent consequences arising from the particular governmental source of funds? Does one level of government contain a greater intrinsic probability of seeking control over the universities? Does local responsibility for university financing imply a more parochial university system? Does financing from the central government ensure greater uniformity in the level of support across the country, broader equality of opportunity, and a higher likelihood of national centres of concentration and excellence?

These questions are difficult to answer and almost impossible to quantify. The answers depend on a variety of circumstances associated with the particular form of federalism and the political attitudes which influence the operation of federal institutions. They vary from province to province and from time to time, with the effects often revealed only indirectly and after a lengthy interval. In some situations the source of funding—national or local—brings in its wake a significant influence on the outlook and attitude of the university. In other situations the extent to which the funding is accompanied by 'control'—direct or implicit—is the more important factor.

In the case of Canadian federalism the issue is one of funding by the federal (central) government as opposed to the provincial (state) governments. The word 'control' is significant less in literal terms than in the sense of direction which the university imposes upon itself as a result of dealing principally with one level of government. The last two decades provide a particularly lively period in Canada, both for contrasting phases in university growth and consolidation and major shifts in federal-provincial financial arrangements. This paper will attempt to highlight the implications of those changes, and draw conclusions where appropriate or possible.

Confederation and Higher Education

As a result of the division of powers under the British North America Act and demographic change in the post-world war two era, Canada has a highly decentralized federal system of government with immense power in the hands of the provinces and their legislative progeny—the municipalities. Under sections 91 and 92 of the BNA Act the provinces were assigned responsibility for areas of government expenditure which expanded greatly over the past two decades, particularly education, health and welfare. As a result, approaching two-thirds of public expenditure in Canada is now in the hands of the provinces and municipalities, and nearly 80% of public capital investment is placed by those two levels of government.

Nowhere is the influence of the provinces more important than in education—the exclusive constitutional preserve of the provinces and one over which strong words have always been exchanged at the federal-provincial conference table. Education has been defined as including post-secondary education for this purpose and, as a result, the responsibility of the provincial governments for university affairs is now firmly entrenched. The universities and colleges certainly shared in the growth of provincial expenditures in the 1950s and 1960s. In Ontario alone the network of provincially-supported universities grew from seven to fifteen, accompanied by the creation of a system of twenty-three colleges of applied arts and technology. Indeed I recall calculating, when I was Chief Economist in the Ontario government, that the capital investment in universities in the period 1967 – 72 would surpass all that had taken place in the first one hundred years of confederation.

To understand universities in Canada one must comprehend confederation. To comprehend confederation one must appreciate the significant changes in federal-provincial financial arrangements over the past two decades. Those changes account in large part both for the current flavour of Canadian universities and for the difficulty of identifying an underlying 'Canadian university policy' either in government or among the universities themselves. This is not to suggest that universities are unique in this problem. In a nation of two official languages, many cultures, regional disparities, relatively small population and immense geography, national policy is not easily manufactured. In a federal system such as Canada's, national policy can never be the product of the central government alone. For that reason the current search for constitutional changes which might enlarge our capacity to produce true national policy (in support of national identity) is of the essence. The evolving role and responsibility of our universities should be viewed against that unfolding drama in Canadian nation-building.

The Evolution of University Financing

In November 1956 the National Conference of Canadian Universities (the predecessor to the current Association of Universities and Colleges of Canada) sponsored a significant conference in Ottawa on 'Canada's Crisis in Higher Education'. At that meeting Dr. N. A. M. MacKenzie, the President of the University of British Columbia, reported:

> '...the work of the universities does not end at the provincial boundaries either in its scope or significance. In each of the larger universities in Canada there are students from all the provinces. In some cases, the students from other parts of Canada constitute as much as one-third of the total enrolment. Similarly, the graduates of the universities are distributed over the entire country. Anywhere from one-fifth to more than one-half of the graduates of particular institutions live and work in provinces other than the one in which they received their education.'[1]

Although this tradition has tended to diminish, not only absolute numbers but the participation rates in Canadian universities have expanded greatly. 'The scale of post-secondary provision exemplifies the massive commitment being made to the educational base of an

---

1. C. T. Bissell (Ed.). *Canada's Crisis in Higher Education*, Toronto, 1957, pp. 187 – 188.

open, democratic society—a commitment that goes well beyond that of most of the other OECD Member countries'.[2]

At that conference Prime Minister St. Laurent announced a significant increase in federal grants to universities. He also took the first step along the road to what was to become, twenty years later, full provincial responsibility for governmental contribution in support of the operating costs of universities. The Prime Minister proposed that monies voted by parliament each year be handed over to the NCCU for distribution among the universities. Part of his purpose was reflected in the accompanying words: 'We think that this system will prove a sufficient guarantee for all our universities, which should be completely free from any kind of interference'.[3] At the same time, however, the government of Canada announced the formation of the Canada Council which served to strengthen greatly the federal government's support of research in the universities, a role that would become its main bridge to the university community.

The Federal-Provincial Fiscal Arrangements Act of 1967 was the significant turning point in the public financing of universities — the incorporation of the federal contribution into the system of fiscal transfers. The background was provided by a major study undertaken by the Tax Structure Committee (composed of first ministers and ministers of finance of the federal government and the provincial governments) of the revenue and expenditure forecast for each level of government for the period 1967 – 72. Although the negotiated revenue-sharing fell short of the Tax Structure Committee's diagnosis and of provincial demands, it did provide a substantial transfer of fiscal resources to the provinces in lieu of the existing federal grants to the universities. Under the provisions of the 1967 act a province could receive a fiscal transfer equal to the greater of $15 per capita of provincial population or an amount equal to 50% of the eligible operating expenditures for post-secondary education in the province in 1967 – 68. For subsequent years the provinces to which the 50% formula applied would continue to receive transfers on that basis. Newfoundland, New Brunswick and Prince Edward Island (having opted for the $15 transfer) would receive yearly increases in the transfer comparable to the increase in eligible post-secondary operating expenditures in the provinces combined, until the other formula produced a higher entitlement.

The act was revised for the 1972 – 77 period in response to the federal government's anxiety over an 'open-ended' formula in times

---

2. OECD. *Reviews of National Policies for Education: Canada*, Paris, 1976, p. 34.
3. Ibid., p. 255.

SUB-TOPIC 2(A): FINANCIAL EFFECTS [Macdonald]

of steep inflation. The two basic formulae were retained, but a maximum of 15% in the yearly rate of increase of the total federal contribution was set. For a government not 'visibly involved' in the financing of post-secondary education the pressure on the federal treasury had become severe. Meanwhile the provinces were facing rising participation rates, costlier programmes and general inflation in carrying out their responsibilities. Consequently their objective continued to be a greater share of overall government revenues according to their perceived entitlement. Federal-provincial financial arrangements were once again on a collision course with the universities in a highly vulnerable position.

Meanwhile the Canadian universities were seeking to find the means of collaborating on their future direction and to have some input to and influence over the form and substance of university financing. The goals and objectives of the universities should be an ingredient, at least, in the ultimate financial formulae. However the negotiations prior to 1967, 1972, and again in 1974, were conducted entirely as federal-provincial fiscal matters. The ministers of education (or university affairs) were virtually silent partners in the prolonged and complex arguments about finance and fiscal federalism. Educational policy was not even confined to the bleachers; in fact, it failed to secure entry to the stadium.

Many leaders of the Canadian university community were determined to ensure that this would not occur in the future. The AUCC established a special committee to prepare a brief to the Prime Minister of Canada and to the premiers of the provinces prior to the negotiation of the post-1977 fiscal arrangements. It also encouraged the provincial and regional bodies to make similar submissions. Meanwhile serious efforts were under way to re-think the future of the universities, beginning with a symposium co-sponsored by the AUCC and the Royal Society of Canada in May 1976.[4]

The objective of the AUCC submission and the proposed approach was the following:

> 'After eight years of comparative neglect or piecemeal consideration, the Canadian dimension of university policy needs re-examination. Before major changes are made in the financing arrangements, policy objectives must be specified and the division of fiscal responsibility for achieving these objectives re-assessed. The universities, through the Association of Universities and Colleges of Canada, wish to assure that there is a national university "voice" to make representations and to be consulted

---

4. *The University of the Future,* Summary of Workshop Discussions and Recommendations, May 4 – 7, 1976 (Chairman: Dr. H. I. Macdonald).

continuously and systematically on all policy issues of a federal-provincial or interprovincial nature affecting universities. They are equally concerned that a way be found to bring together federal and provincial spokesmen in a forum to which their "voice" may be addressed.

'The need for such a policy is the central recommendation of this brief. Indeed, consultations should begin immediately amongst representatives of the universities, the provincial governments and the federal government with a view to establishing a national policy for universities consonant with the plans of the provincial and regional university systems. AUCC is prepared to initiate these consultations.'[5]

While preparing for the major discussions envisaged, the AUCC submission proposed, as interim recommendations, that: —

(i) the Fiscal Arrangements Act be renegotiated for a two-year period ending March 31, 1979, allowing sufficient time for federal-provincial-university consultations;

(ii) the federal government re-affirm its policy of participating fully in the financing of Canadian universities, and eliminate the 1972 restriction to unconditional payments, thus taking into account increased costs because of inflation and growth in student enrolment;

(iii) consultations begin immediately amongst representatives of the universities, the provincial governments and the federal government with a view to establishing a national university policy consonant with the plans of the provincial and regional university systems;

(iv) the federal government and the provincial governments, in consultation with the universities, identify existing and potential centres and programmes of excellence in fields corresponding to national priorities and assure that resources are made available for their development through special grants;

(v) the federal government in consultation with the provinces and the universities support the further development of programmes of university library and computer co-ordination and accessibility;

(vi) the federal government provide sufficient new funds to the granting councils to permit them to (*a*) increase funds for the direct grants they make for research in the universities and (*b*) add 35% for indirect costs to the grants without any diminution in the number or size of such grants;

5. *A Canadian Policy for Universities and Their Financing*, AUCC, January 1976, p. 1.

(vii) both the federal and provincial governments cover full costs, direct (including all salaries) and indirect, of contract research undertaken for them by the universities;

(viii) the universities of Canada continue their efforts to share resources with a view to achieving greater efficiency and working collectively in the national, regional and provincial interests.[6]

The objectives and the recommendations remain valid but the hopes and good intentions were swept aside by the fast-running currents of federal-provincial financial affairs. For some years several provinces, led by the government of Ontario, had been arguing for an end of the so-called 'shared-cost programmes' which had become a large element of total governmental expenditure in Canada. The proposal was that the federal contribution should be replaced by a transfer of tax points to the provinces, with programme administration becoming the sole responsibility of the provinces. Although not strictly part of a shared-cost programme, the federal contribution to post-secondary education was included in this proposal. There were a number of compelling arguments for the change: administrative simplicity, allocation of revenues to the government responsible for expenditures, a truer cost picture for the taxpaper, and so on. Consequently, when the provinces took a united stand at the First Ministers' Conference in Ottawa in December 1976, the federal government concurred. The new agreement, which took effect on April 1, 1977, converted one-half of the federal contribution into a transfer of income-tax points with the other half a cash payment to be escalated according to changes in the gross national product. In other words the new arrangement provided for an unconditional fiscal transfer, unrelated to the operating costs of provincial programmes. The provincialization of university financing had been completed.

The Consequences for Canadian Universities

As I suggested, it is difficult to assess the total consequences of the changed governmental orientation of universities over the past two decades. Moreover there is more to be said than this brief survey would allow. The federal government remains highly active, through a variety of departments and agencies, in the support of research. In the long term that relationship will probably strengthen and broaden. The variety of federal government support — direct

---
6. Op. cit., pp. 15–16.

and indirect—has had the effect of developing and improving the quality of university resources, both physical and human, through programmes of library grants, sabbatical leave fellowships, grants for special facilities, bilingual grants and other direct programmes. In terms of direct student assistance, it also operates the Canadian Student Loan Plan to which the various provincial governments have added their own support.

However in the course of the past ten years a subtle and important shift has taken place in the character of universities—nationally and internationally—as a result of changes in the intergovernmental process in our confederation. Although long an exponent of a greater measure of decentralization in our federation and the bringing of government and their bureaucracies closer to the people, I have always felt a sense of unease in one area—university affairs.

As the very name implies, the university belongs to the universe—there can be no barriers to the exchange of ideas, nor to the exchange of university people. Our universities had established a glorious tradition for openness and mobility throughout the world. The amendments to the Fiscal Arrangements Act in 1967 had the effect of placing the universities much more directly under the provincial governments. The changes agreed upon in December 1976 further reduce the financial assurance of the universities and increase the provincial governments' capacity to shift resources to fields other than the universities.

The result—although difficult to prove—has been to make the universities, at least in administrative outlook, much more provincial in their orientation and, in turn, less national and international. I do not believe students think as readily of studying in another province, and certainly we are making it increasingly difficult for foreign students to study in Canada. Parochialism has never been a prescription for greatness.

Similar concern was expressed in the brief of the Council of Ontario Universities in January 1976.

> 'An attractive feature of the fiscal transfer scheme is that it has left provincial governments free to design a network of post-secondary institutions appropriate to cultural and social conditions and serving special provincial needs. It is none the less obvious that the population of some provinces is too small to sustain extensive post-secondary systems, and the interprovincial mobility of students is a means of equalizing educational opportunity. Such mobility has further advantages in increasing intellectual stimulus by encouraging diversity amongst students' backgrounds, and it supports national unity by fostering mutual

understanding among the regions of Canada. Thus interprovincial mobility of students should be taken as a major concern of the Government of Canada in its policies for the support of post-secondary education. Indeed, it is already the case that some universities serve an interprovincial clientele, and the provinces in which those universities are located have a disproportionately large share of the national university student population. The fiscal transfer scheme, however, does not adequately compensate those provinces which bear an additional burden in educating a large number of students from outside the province, and it increases the difficulty of creating interprovincial systems except on the basis of a delicate trade-off in which, for each province, the influx of students is presumed to be balanced by a comparable efflux.

'The considerations mentioned in the previous paragraph are especially serious where specialized programmes, such as those in forestry or criminology, are involved. Such programmes, if they are to be viable must draw upon an interprovincial and perhaps an international clientele. Indeed, graduate work is typically interprovincial and even national or international in terms of the clientele it serves and the training it provides.'[7]

These sentiments are echoed in the AUCC brief:

'Increasingly, too, questions are being raised about limits on enrolment from other countries and from other provinces. At the same time the universities, seeing the extent to which the provincial governments have become the source or route of their revenues (including the regulation of their fees), have come to focus their attention upon their relations with the provincial governments as their primary interface with government. The last decade has consequently seen the rapid development of provincial and regional organizations, as exemplified by such bodies as the Conference of Rectors and Principals of the Universities of Quebec and the Ontario Confederation of University Faculty Associations, and their relative influence compared to such national organizations as AUCC and the Canadian Association of University Teachers has grown enormously. The general effect of federal funding by unconditional transfers has thus been a provincialization of universities to such a degree that there is little assurance that national objectives will receive attention commensurate with their importance for balanced university development.'[8]

---

7. *Brief to the Canadian and Ontario Governments on the Financing of Higher Education in Canada*, Council of Ontario Universities, January 1976, pp. 20–21.
8. *A Canadian Policy for Universities and Their Financing*, op. cit., pp. 4–5.

Circumstances in Canada today are such that a major objective of education should be the provision of opportunities for Canadians to learn more about all parts of their country, at first hand. This is particularly true of the university student community in terms of its responsibility for future leadership. To support that objective we should be seeking to ensure a national university community by all possible means. Student mobility—including international mobility—is the subject of another session of this conference, but it is appropriate to note the warning sounded in the AUCC brief:

> 'The national university policy vacuum is particularly vexing as it affects international, inter-regional and inter-provincial student mobility. As inflation and market instabilities strain budgets at every level, cries of alarm are heard about the numbers of foreign or extra-provincial students whose university education is being financed by public funds. If financial constraints continue and governments become less willing to fund growth in student numbers, available places in many programs will be limited and the question of which students occupy those places will become more acute.'[9]

Guidelines for the Future

'Indeed, who can maintain seriously that the fathers of the BNA Act had ruled against sensible inter-provincial and federal-provincial co-operation in the field of educational policy.'[10] That is true but, in fact, the record of co-operation falls short of any reasonable target. Perhaps the 'disentanglement' resulting from the 1977 fiscal arrangements will have cleared a path for more effective and complementary measures in support of higher education. However that will require a much more relaxed stance on the part of the Council of Ministers of Education than has been apparent in the past. This body of provincial ministers, founded ten years ago, has great potential but it has demonstrated two shortcomings: first, excessive sensitivity to perceived 'federal intrusions'; and second, insufficient interest in the university sector.

Canadian universities can still flourish under our present or potential federal arrangements, but they will require some guidelines. The division of responsibilities suggested by the COU is a helpful beginning.

---

9. Op. cit., p. 9.
10. OECD. *Reviews of National Policies....*, op. cit., p. 96

SUB-TOPIC 2(A): FINANCIAL EFFECTS [*Macdonald*]

FEDERAL RESPONSIBILITIES

(i) The equalization of educational opportunity for all Canadians at the university level, either by enabling provincial jurisdictions to support complete services, or by supporting arrangements that provide partial services plus interprovincial mobility, or by some combination of these;

(ii) the assurance of accessibility to university education for the economically disadvantaged Canadian students through a minimum-level guarantee of student aid;

(iii) the interprovincial mobility of the highly qualified manpower produced by universities;

(iv) the assurance of the existence of some programmes and institutions of international repute, and of some first-rate work in fields where only one or few programmes can be supported properly;

(v) the amount, scope, distribution and quality of research both basic and applied, and of literary and artistic creativity and scholarship;

(vi) the support of university programmes related directly to national purposes, such as bilingualism;

(vii) the support and (where appropriate) co-ordination at the national level of unique academic resources such as archives, museums and rare book collections, and of costly academic services such as library, audio-visual and computer networks;

(viii) the fulfilment of international obligations involving university personnel, such as assistance to third world universities and governments and teacher and student exchanges.

PROVINCIAL RESPONSIBILITIES

(i) The provision of access to university courses for qualified and desirous students to the extent that this lies in provincial competence and fits with provincial priorities;

(ii) the equalization of individual opportunity for higher education within the province including distribution and/or supplementation of federal student aid;

(iii) the countering of geographic barriers impeding accessibility either by broad distribution of university facilities or by enabling the mobility of prospective students, or both;

(iv) the provision of adequate facilities for the training of highly qualified manpower in the numbers and to the levels likely to be required in the province;

(v) more specifically, the provision of facilities for training the numbers of highly qualified manpower required for the operation of provincial services such as schools and health services;

(vi) where applicable, the provision of university facilities for francophone and anglophone citizens of the province;

(vii) the support of religious, cultural and educational diversity to the extent that these are provincial objectives and attainable through the province's system of higher education.[11]

The formulation of a national university policy for Canada remains an elusive, but an exciting, goal. Universities have a responsibility to ensure that it finds a place both in federal-provincial consultation and constitutional reconstruction.

TABLES

I. TOTAL INCOME OF CANADIAN UNIVERSITIES BY SOURCE: 1961/62 to 1975/76
($ millions)

	Operating Income	Sponsored Research Funds	Miscellaneous Income	Total Income
1961 – 62	159·7	26·5	24·3	210·5
1962 – 63	185·0	30·7	24·6	240·3
1963 – 64	219·7	36·8	26·7	283·2
1964 – 65	255·7	47·6	39·4	342·7
1965 – 66	321·4	61·4	43·4	426·2
1966 – 67	450·5	80·7	50·3	581·5
1967 – 68	579·0	104·2	57·3	740·5
1968 – 69	710·6	127·3	67·5	905·4
1969 – 70	871·9	143·1	70·0	1085·0
1970 – 71	995·2	151·8	75·8	1222·8
1971 – 72	1171·2	174·0	58·0	1403·2
1972 – 73	1213·4	184·1	58·3	1455·8
1973 – 74	1338·8	196·7	77·5	1613·0
1974 – 75	1547·1	233·9	87·0	1868·0
1975 – 76	1836·9	254·9	87·8	2179·6

Source: Statistics Canada.

11. *Brief to Canadian and Ontario Governments*...., op. cit., pp. 5 – 8.

SUB-TOPIC 2(A): FINANCIAL EFFECTS [Macdonald]

II. OPERATING INCOME OF CANADIAN UNIVERSITIES BY SOURCE: 1961/62 to 1975/76
($ millions)

	\multicolumn{4}{c}{Government}	Fees	Sub-total	FTE* Enrolment
	Fed.	Prov.	Municipal	Total			
1961 – 62	25·1	77·8	0·6	103·5	56·2	159·7	128,630
1962 – 63	31·8	90·2	0·6	122·6	62·4	185·0	153,686
1963 – 64	34·4	109·1	0·6	144·1	75·6	219·7	174,224
1964 – 65	35·9	129·6	0·5	166·0	89·7	255·7	195,813
1965 – 66	36·5	173·8	0·5	210·8	110·6	321·4	225,109
1966 – 67	81·6	237·3	1·7	320·6	129·9	450·5	254,562
1967 – 68	12·5	420·2	1·8	434·5	144·5	579·0	281,447
1968 – 69	14·9	531·7	1·7	548·3	162·3	710·6	294,890
1969 – 70	16·2	674·2	2·7	693·1	178·8	871·9	329,005
1970 – 71	15·7	788·3	0·7	804·7	190·5	995·2	354,205
1971 – 72	2·3	950·7	0·4	953·4	217·8	1171·2	367,422
1972 – 73	2·1	985·3	0·4	987·9	225·5	1213·4	366,113
1973 – 74	5·6	1093·1	0·4	1099·1	239·7	1338·8	378,171
1974 – 75	5·6	1284·7	0·6	1290·9	256·2	1547·1	395,930
1975 – 76	6·2	1555·2	0·8	1562·2	274·7	1836·9	423,926

*Full-time equivalent

Source: Statistics Canada.

[Macdonald]   TOPIC 2: COUNTRIES WITH FEDERAL GOVERNMENTS

III. SPONSORED RESEARCH FUNDS OF CANADIAN UNIVERSITIES
BY SOURCE: 1961/62 to 1975/76
($ millions)

	Government Federal	*Government* Provincial	*Other**	*Subtotal*
1961 – 62	16·8	1·1	8·6	26·5
1962 – 63	18·7	1·4	10·6	30·7
1963 – 64	22·7	1·7	12·4	36·8
1964 – 65	27·3	7·1	13·2	47·6
1965 – 66	36·6	9·4	15·4	61·4
1966 – 67	52·1	11·8	16·8	80·7
1967 – 68	71·2	15·3	17·7	104·2
1968 – 69	86·2	19·8	21·3	127·3
1969 – 70	98·4	23·9	20·8	143·1
1970 – 71	105·0	23·0	23·8	151·8
1971 – 72	122·5	14·5	37·0	174·0
1972 – 73	125·8	19·5	38·8	184·1
1973 – 74	133·3	27·2	36·2	196·7
1974 – 75	147·5	32·7	53·7	233·9
1975 – 76	158·4	42·3	54·2	254·9

*Funds received from corporations, foundations, religious organizations, etc.
Source: Statistics Canada

The Australian Case

Professor B. R. WILLIAMS (*Vice-Chancellor and Principal of the University of Sydney*): Australian universities, other than the Australian National University, were established by acts of state parliaments. The constitution of the Commonwealth of Australia does not confer on the Australian government any responsibilities or powers in education, excepting the power given by constitutional amendment to grant benefits to students. However section 96 of the constitution provides that the Commonwealth may make financial grants to a state on such terms and conditions as the parliament thinks fit. Parliament has seen fit to make great use of section 96 grants.

SUB-TOPIC 2(A): FINANCIAL EFFECTS   [*Williams*]

Before the second world war the six Australian universities derived their income from state grants, fees and other income in roughly equal proportions. The financing role of the Commonwealth was trivial. The eighteen universities in the states, and the National University, are now almost completely dependent on Commonwealth grants. By agreement with the states, from 1974 the Commonwealth assumed full responsibility for government grants to universities. It makes section 96 grants which specify the general recurrent grants, the special research grants, the equipment grants and the building grants to be made to each state university. The Commonwealth government at that time made another change of great significance — it made these grants for universities conditional on the abolition of tuition fees.

Shared Funding

Apart from the post-war reconstruction training scheme, under which it provided student assistance and some associated capital grants, the first Commonwealth initiative in the field of higher education was the appointment of the (Murray) Committee on Australian Universities in 1956. Following the report of that committee in 1957, the Commonwealth government established the Australian Universities Commission to advise it on financial grants to universities. Shortly after, a system of shared funding was evolved. Up to a limit decided by the Commonwealth there were matching recurrent grants of one dollar for each one dollar eighty-five cents of state grants plus fees and matching capital grants of $1.00 per $1.00. In the period from 1957 to 1968 real resources per student increased by 40%, from a level that the Murray committee had judged to be much too low.

The universities pressed for an increase in the Commonwealth role in financing. There were two main reasons for this — first, that the Universities Commission was thought to bring its recommendations for universities in the richer states somewhat into line with the financial capacity of the poorer states; and second, that the universities saw themselves as national institutions and preferred national financing.

Change to Commonwealth Funding

The change to full Commonwealth financing less than twenty years after the Murray committee report was not, however, caused by university preferences. The two major factors were the response of the Commonwealth government to the report of the (Martin)

Committee on the Future of Tertiary Education in Australia, and the centripetal influence of the Australian Labour Party.

The Martin committee, which reported in 1964, recommended a great expansion in tertiary education, especially in institutes of technology and teachers' colleges. It proposed an extension of Commonwealth finance to these institutions and colleges on the same basis as for the universities, and the creation of a Tertiary Education Commission to co-ordinate the financial grants to the three sectors. The Commonwealth agreed to extend financial aid to the institutes — or, as they were now named, colleges of advanced education — but not to the teachers' colleges, and perhaps because of this did not create a Tertiary Commission but a separate Commission on Advanced Education. In so doing the Commonwealth created an unstable system. Teacher education was established in the universities, some states had already made plans to free teachers' colleges from departmental control and to convert them into multi-purpose colleges, and all states now had a strong financial incentive to follow suit. By 1972 it was clear that the Commonwealth's decision had become nonsense, and financial aid was extended to the teachers' colleges as part of the advanced education sector. But instead of a three-sector arrangement and one Tertiary Commission as proposed by the Martin committee there was now a two-sector arrangement and two separate commissions.

Instability

The instability of these arrangements was increased by the origins of the advanced education sector. Whereas the universities had always been independent institutions, almost all the colleges had once been administered by state departments of education. These colleges were re-established as self-governing institutions under the general direction of state boards of advanced education. The issue of state rights, and the influence of state ministers, was far more important than it had ever been in the care of universities. For this reason alone the Commission on Advanced Education was inclined in a regime of shared funding to adapt its general plan to the various plans of the state boards. This arrangement did not work well with shared funding, and the end of shared funding gave state ministers and boards an incentive to make very expansive plans, and in effect to undermine the whole system.

The decision of the Whitlam government to establish a single commission to co-ordinate tertiary education and to end shared funding was not simply a consequence of a breakdown in federal arrangements. These decisions, like the decision to abolish tuition fees, were a consequence of long-established Labour Party policies. But these decisions created new centripetal forces in the system. The Commonwealth budgetary burden was considerably increased by the policies on education and this created an incentive to look for economies from the direct co-ordination of the two sectors of tertiary education and from measures of 'rationalization'. This incentive was increased by the recession which reduced tax yields and increased the need for welfare payments.

Effects of Commonwealth Action

Until the second world war there were separate Commonwealth and state income-taxes. Under war-time powers the Commonwealth assumed responsibility for all income-tax. After the war the Commonwealth retained full responsibility for income-tax and the states were content to make annual bargains on tax reimbursement formulae. In this situation the decision of the Commonwealth to enter the field of higher education was an important factor, and probably an indispensable factor in the growth of higher education.

In 1957 there were 9 universities and 36,500 students. Twenty years later there were 19 universities and 156,000 students. The number of undergraduates rose from $4 \cdot 7\%$ to $9 \cdot 6\%$ of the $17-22$ age group. In the same period the number of students in colleges of advanced education rose from 3% to $9 \cdot 5\%$ of the $17-22$ age group.

This increase in access was made possible by an increase in the capital and recurrent funds of the universities and colleges, and by the provision of scholarships. Until quite recently the states, through their education departments, provided the bulk of the finance for scholarships in the college sector, and the Commonwealth in the university sector. Now the Commonwealth provides almost all of the financial support to needy students. Access was also increased by the wider geographical distribution of universities and colleges, though the Commonwealth influence was not powerful enough to equalize access in the different states. Participation rates in universities are 30% greater in New South Wales than in Tasmania; and in colleges 100% greater in Western Australia than in New South Wales. For universities and colleges combined, participation rates in Western Australia and South Australia are 60% greater than in Tasmania and Queensland.

The Commonwealth had a strong influence on the growth of research, through the special research grants to universities (which at one stage it made although the states refused to match them) and the finance of the Australian Research Grants Committee and the

National Health and Medical Research Council. In Australia research and development in 1973 – 74 was 1·3% of the GNP and university research was 0·3% of GNP. The Commonwealth influence was not, however, directed towards the creation of centres of excellence. Until 1972 the Universities Commission assumed that there were economies of scale and did not even make allowance for the greater cost of students in the high-cost faculties such as veterinary science, medicine, dentistry, agriculture and engineering. The large universities with a full range of faculties were handicapped by this approach and their research capacity was not fully developed.

There are so many different factors at work that it is wise to be cautious in making generalizations. From 1957 to 1968 there was increase in real resources per student by 40%, but after 1968 there has been an average decline of 1% per annum and that decline has been greatest since the Commonwealth assumed the full responsibility for finance. How far that decline was due to the concentration of university and college finance in one budget (instead of as formerly spread around seven budgets) and how far to the recession it is not possible to say. But I have no doubt that the concentration of expenditure in one budget played a significant part in the financial squeeze.

The Universities Commission was formed in the image of the University Grants Committee in Britain to advise governments on grants and to protect university autonomy. The Commission performed both functions very effectively. There are already signs that the Tertiary Commission will be less concerned to protect autonomy, and there is reason to believe that the moves to erode university autonomy in the interests of 'co-ordination' and 'rationalization' will be more powerful under full Commonwealth funding than would have been the case under shared funding. The role of the Commonwealth Minister for Education and his department has become much stronger than it could have been under shared funding. Shortly after the end of shared funding, though seemingly in response to the recession, the Minister provided the Universities Commission with guidelines which specified the level of finance and the number of students. Annual ministerial guidelines greatly restricted the role of the Commission, and have been with us ever since, though it was announced recently that the Commission would soon be allowed to return to the custom of making triennial plans for recurrent grants.

Another sign of the times was the decision of the government to have an inquiry into study leave. I doubt whether this would have happened under shared funding. but it may have happened. The shift in public opinion on universities may have been more influential than the sources of finance.

DISCUSSION

In his preface to the discussion the group chairman (Dr. Steven Watson) called for a comparative analysis of the experiences of Commonwealth universities in relation to federal and local financing. Within a federal jurisdiction, he contended, higher education and such associated problems as research and manpower planning could give rise to friction between governments, which pointed the need for machinery to ease such friction. The sub-topic chairman (Dr. Watts) suggested links between, on the one hand, the constitutional responsibility of each order of government and the funding of universities, and, on the other, the overlap of policy interests at the two levels of government; he invited members to work towards an analysis that would exhibit similarities as well as differences in the experiences of Canada, Australia, India, Malaysia and Nigeria; he suggested that a contrastive approach of this kind might, for example, illuminate the United Kingdom's present concern with matters of constitutional devolution.

In presenting his discussion paper (see above), Dr. *H. I. Macdonald* (York, Canada) rehearsed briefly the developments to the present time in the financing of university education in Canada; he reiterated that the basic trend in Canada had been the transfer to provincial governments of the federal government's responsibility for university education; under current arrangements universities, he contended, lacked fiscal security and it was important to find means of giving Canadian universities adequate voice in matters of funding, and for the universities themselves to reassert their national and international, rather than purely provincial, role and status. The proper interests of universities were something which neither provincial governments nor the Council of Ministers of Education could protect, the latter exhibiting more interest in primary than in higher education and the former being now a party to an arrangement which provided for unconditional fiscal transfer which had no direct relationship to the costs of operating provincial programmes. He called for a strengthening and expansion of the basis for research funding, and concluded that both the funding and status of universities were bound to be affected by the outcome of current debate on constitutional review in Canada.

Professor *B. R. Williams* (Sydney), in presenting his paper (see above), distinguished Australian from Canadian experience, arguing that there had been constitutional room for the Commonwealth (federal) government to support state universities and that, furthermore, the Whitlam government had pursued a policy of centralisation which in 1974 had led to the substitution, for joint funding by federal and state governments, of funding entirely by the Commonwealth government. It was both internal

TOPIC 2: COUNTRIES WITH FEDERAL GOVERNMENTS

and external factors which had affected development in Australia, and what had imposed sharp constraints upon universities at the present time was not a policy of federal funding but world recession and consequently reduced tax revenue, and a revision in the federal government's estimate of demand for university graduates. Universities, he emphasised, saw themselves as national rather than parochial institutions and recognised a definite balance of advantage in having a federal rather than a state government as a source of their funds; thus academic salaries were determined in line with general and national salary trends and this had helped the university system in Australia avoid the development of the intense academic staff unionism which was to be seen in Canada.

Haji N. A. Noor Muhammad (Calicut) and Professor R. Joshi (Bombay) spoke of the role of the Congress Party and the consequences of its dominance of the Indian political scene for several years after India's independence. Regional parties were now calling for greater regional autonomy in education and other matters, though the central government had now been strengthened in relation to the state governments through its constitutional power to determine national standards, through the advantages which it enjoyed in finance and personnel, and through the role played by the University Grants Commission.

Professor O. Aboyade (Ife), Professor J. O. O. Abiri (Ilorin), Dr. J. Aminu (National Universities Commission, Nigeria) and Dr. C. E. Abebe (U. of Nigeria) spoke of the way in which developments in Nigeria had been influenced by the histories of the different universities, by changes in constitution and in the relationships between federal and state governments, by modifications in methods of fiscal allocation and revenue-sharing, and finally by the vicissitudes of the national economy. Nigerian universities suffered from a notable paucity of money from the non-governmental sector, a low ratio of student fees to federal subsidies, and the 'one-line' character of grants to universities through the National Universities Commission. There was discussion of the effect on educational policy and programme of calls for national unity and for the redress of educational imbalance, and there was reference, too, to the policy of deliberately harmonizing university salaries, both academic and non-academic, with the salaries of workers in other parts of the public sector.

Members gave some time to a discussion of university salaries, for which, it was clear, the initiative in Australia lay with the federal government, whereas in Canada it was much more dependent on the results of local collective bargaining and only informal contact between presidents and vice-chancellors constituted any attempt at consensus. The implications of this and other aspects of the discussion were a matter for comment by Mr. A. Davies (University College, Swansea) who voiced misgivings about the possibility that in the United Kingdom devolution might, through federal-local funding, cost the universities their national and international perspectives.

There was no discussion of developments in the West Indies and Malaysia.

Sub-Topic 2(b)

STUDENT AND STAFF MOBILITY UNDER FEDERALISM

Chairman: Sir JOHN LLEWELLYN
Director-General of the British Council

Rapporteur: Dr. AMRIK SINGH
Vice-Chancellor of Punjabi University

Tuesday, 22 August

Professor K. SATCHIDANANDA MURTY (*Vice-Chancellor of Sri Venkateswara University*):

I. Mobility in connection with education means 'a free movement of students, teachers and other personnel among educational institutions within a country and across national boundaries'.[1] The following kinds of mobility are theoretically possible for students in higher educational institutions. *First*, students can work, or take courses required, for a degree at more than one institution over a period of time and then appear for the necessary examinations at any one of these institutions and take the degree from it. This means for the same degree one can work or receive instructions at more than one university in a country. *Second*, those taking a first degree in a subject from one institution can join another institution to take a higher degree in that subject, or a first degree in another subject. These institutions may be within the same state/province in a country or within different countries, and these provinces/states or countries can either be neighbouring or distant ones. This is the more usual kind of mobility. I would have liked to deal with three or four countries such as West Germany, India and the USA with federal systems of government and discuss the types of student mobility available in them. But, except in the case of the USA, there does not seem to be enough available material, at least in India.

Similarly, mobility of teachers also is theoretically possible among universities in a state/province or a country, or among universities in different countries. Regarding this, too, there is a paucity of material except in the case of the USA. It is interesting that right from the time when the Allied Colonial Universities Conference was held in 1903 in Burlington House the question of 'circulation of teaching staff' among colonial/Commonwealth universities has been discussed a number of times in Commonwealth universities conferences, and every time it was unanimously decided that there should be 'close and intimate relationships' among universities for enabling circulation of students and teaching staff among them.[2] Still all sorts of rules and regulations and political and other impediments remain as barriers for the complete realisation of this ideal, which was once a reality in all universities in medieval Christendom and in all higher educational establishments in ancient and medieval India.

In the East as well as the West, in late antiquity as well as in the middle ages, in the proto-universities and universities it was the custom for students to receive education at more than one of them. For example in India a student could study Mimamsa (hermeneutics) at, say, Kumbakonam or Kanchipuram, then Nyaya (logic and epistemology) at Mithila or Navadvipa, and after that Vedanta (metaphysics based on Upanishads) at Varanasi. Similarly for alchemy and metallurgy one could go to Nagarjunakonda as well as Nalanda, and for medicine to Takshasila, Nagarjunakonda or a place near Madurai. Like their Indian counterparts, between 400–700 A.D., Chinese scholars like Fa Hsien, Sung Yun, Hsuan Tsang and I Tsing could travel all over India, going from one Buddhist university to another, staying for different periods at each, hearing lectures, holding discussions and copying manuscripts. In Europe also 'the tireless scholars of the Middle Ages were not content to study at a single university, they travelled far afield in search of teachers—"wont to roam around the world.... till much learning made them mad".'[3]

Thus students in those times were highly mobile. They moved from teacher to teacher, crowded at the lectures of the great masters and travelled widely to sample the wares of many universities. As universities became more established and institutionalised student life became restricted. In Europe 'nations' developed and in England 'colleges'. The colleges became like monasteries and each college tried to give a complete education to its students, discouraging them from moving to other institutions. The collegiate system encapsulated the students and became widely prevalent in England, North America and India. This deprived the students of the freedom to move from institution to institution and get the benefit of instruction from the best living masters in different institutions and countries, and made them more dependent on, and more subject to, the discipline of the university to which they belonged. In a way with the development of universities the *Lernfreiheit*, *i.e.* the student's freedom to choose his own programme of study living independently of any university and to move from university to university, became restricted.

But to this day students of West German universities continue to attend a number of universities during their four or five years' course, and so are able to come into contact with great scholars in different institutions and imbibe the academic atmosphere of different places such as Hamburg, Heidelberg, Tübingen and Munich. Thus in German universities the student is more free than elsewhere. He attends lectures if he wishes, can postpone examinations for years or for ever, his private life is not controlled by anybody, he can roam about the country sampling various universities, and decide where, if anywhere, he can take his final examination and degree. To a lesser extent this custom survives in Switzerland also.[4]

In addition there seems to be also more mobility than elsewhere among teachers in West Germany. Even after one has been nominated as 'ausserplanmässige Professor' by the ministry on the recommendation of a university faculty, 'no faculty worthy of the name will appoint one of its own graduates to a professorship if he has not already held a post at another university'. His appointment at another university depends on the recognition of his intellectual and teaching abilities in the academic world and the number of vacancies available owing to either retirement or death. After one has been appointed and accepted the appointment, one leaves the public service of one Land for that of another.[5] To all other countries what Caplow and McGee said about the USA seems to be applicable: inbreeding is commonly disapproved but widely practised.

The British universities with their collegiate system did not have any scope for student mobility till 1919 when the PhD degree was established in Britain, which as Ernest Rutherford then said was an 'entire innovation' and the 'greatest revolution of modern times'.*
This was done principally to attract to British universities postgraduates from the USA, other allied countries and the empire; it also enabled graduates of one British university to go to another for postgraduate work. Speaking in the Home Universities Conference in 1924, A. N. Whitehead hoped that this would revive 'one of the best institutions of the Middle Ages, the wandering scholar'.

---

* He meant this for Britain, for Germany, America and some other countries had doctoral programmes long before that.

There is no comprehensive study of teacher and student mobility in Indian higher education. In India in the beginning, when universities were few in number, students from different provinces (some consisting of more than one linguistic area) went to them for study and teachers from different provinces were able to obtain posts in them. This gradually declined even in the pre-independence days as more and more masters and PhDs were turned out by every university, increasingly enabling each one to have as teachers persons belonging to the province in which it was situated. In the post-independence period after the formation of linguistic states and adoption of Indian languages as the media of instruction up to the first degree level in most universities, the migration of students for study from one state to another has become very much restricted. In the state universities which constitute the majority of Indian universities men from other linguistic states, however qualified, are unfortunately not usually appointed as teachers. A more recent undesirable tendency gaining ground is the preference in appointment which these universities are showing for people who are not only their alumni but who in addition belong to the state, and preferably even to the area in the state, in which they are located. Thus it is difficult for, say, a man from eastern Uttar Pradesh, however well-qualified he may be, to get an appointment in a university in western Uttar Pradesh, and a man from Telangana area has a similar difficulty in getting a teaching post in any university in the other two areas in Andhra Pradesh, and vice versa; nor is it easy for a Rajasthani to get a job in a Bihar or Madhya Pradesh university, and vice versa. In each of the eight central universities, also, the number of teachers coming from the state and the area in which it is located is generally more than that of those coming from other linguistic states and areas. In spite of its motto *Yatra visvam bhavati eka nidam* (where the universe becomes a single abode), a non-Bengali finds it very difficult to get an appointment or promotion in Visva-Bharati. However in the two central universities at Delhi perhaps Bengalis and South Indians are found in considerable numbers, though the Hindi-speaking people constitute the majorities; and the recently-started Central University of Hyderabad is not so far giving any preference to those who belong to the state in which it is situated.

Syllabuses and courses of universities even in a single state differ, and a migration certificate* from the university one leaves has to be submitted to the university one joins. Moreover in most states universities give preference in admission to students who come from

---

* This, however, is only a formality, readily issued on payment of a certain fee.

colleges in their own area. For admission to postgraduate courses and doctoral programmes universities generally prefer their own alumni. In view of this, in India, compared to its size and the number of its universities, there is practically little migration of students from university to university. However there has been a mushrooming of institutions of higher education in some states like Madhya Pradesh, Uttar Pradesh and Orissa. In a number of them there is quite a surplus of seats and some of them levy capitation fees. So a number of South Indians unable to secure admission in universities in their own states migrate to them. What has been said in this paragraph does not apply, to a large extent, to the Indian Institutes of Technology, etc., which admit students on the basis of nation-wide entrance examinations and also recruit their teachers from all over the country.[6]

II. Studies of academic mobility in the USA are available. One of the earliest and most popular among these is that of Caplow and McGee.[7] Their sample consisted of liberal arts departments in nine major universities during the academic years 1954−55 and 1955−56. The conclusions of their study may be summarised as follows:−[8]

(i) *Rank*. Assistant professors have the maximum free and compulsory mobility, while for associate professors, because they have tenure, mobility is not compulsory, and because immobility is more advantageous to them it is also not free for them. Full professors have very little compulsory mobility though in rare cases some of them may be forced to quit, and few care to move out of their own accord, except in cases listed in (v) below, and that too is very difficult. In all cases mobility is limited by available openings.

(ii) *Age*. Free mobility is relatively easier for the younger assistant professors; while the older usually quit or get thrown out, and in such a case they may go to smaller institutions and get higher rank and better pay. Associate professors too old for their rank may go to similar institutions, or linger where they are till the end. The mobility of full professors, as already stated, is very much limited.

(iii) *Institutional prestige*. 51% of the total mobility observed by Caplow and McGee occurred in departments which their chairmen rated as among the first five in the country, 36% occurred in departments rated better than average for major institutions, and only 13% in departments rated as average or poorer than average.[9]

(iv) *Involuntary termination*. 74% of the vacancies occurred because of resignations and dismissals. The most common cause of this was that one either had to go up or get out. Other causes found by Caplow and McGee were: simple incompetence, social ineptness or quarrelsome disposition, lack of budgetary provision, firing or non-sanction of leave by the administration. Termination on grounds of race and sex was very rare, though there was such discrimination while hiring. Sometimes teachers leave because of non-promotion or because they are conveniently got rid of by negotiating for them positions in other universities, even without their asking and knowledge. Persons who are dismissed may drop out of the profession or may go from major universities to smaller ones.

(v) *Voluntary termination.* Six factors seem to be operative in this matter. (*a*) The most common thing is discontent and discord within the department. (*b*) Some have to leave because they outgrow their institutions, some leave in search of a better climate or cultural setting, and others when they get a chance may go back to their alma mater which is usually a great university. (*c*) Some drift away from the department into administration or research. (*d*) Personal motives are responsible in the cases of some leaving their departments. (*e*) While it is certainly true that money lures many, it is more often combined with prestige advancement, work duties and location. (*f*) In some departments its tradition and ethos favour collaboration between its members. People who cannot do collaborative research and prefer to work in isolation may like to leave such departments. Conversely, some people who find collaborative research or team-work congenial may not like to stay in departments which are not conducive to that.

According to Caplow and McGee: 'The "push" of academic migration is stronger than the "pull". The majority of vacancies cannot be attributed to the lure of opportunities elsewhere but to dissatisfaction — either the failure of the incumbent to please his associates or their failure to please him or both. These dissatisfactions can be most economically explained by reference to the system of disciplinary prestige.'[10]

R. M. Pankin who studied the structural factors in academic mobility in the USA found that job changing for 76 to 78% of college faculties involves some dissatisfaction with their work or institutions. Fifty-seven per cent of those who indicated some dissatisfaction refer to some feature of the internal structure of the institution. According to Pankin professionalism and bureaucratisation grew out of essentially the same set of social conditions, and developed along parallel lines. Organisation needs both expertise and management. Both are compatible, with no *inherent* conflict present. Yet Pankin raises the question: why is there a conflict between professionalism and bureaucracy? His answer is on the following lines. Professionals relate to each other as a group of equals on an informal 'primary-like' level. They resist the imposition of more formal relationships. But it is the tendency of an organisation to impose formal relationships on professionals, while they prefer 'collegial' relationships. This preference is pre-established and develops through a long process of professional socialisation. But to function at its most efficient level an organisation requires relationships which are the opposite of 'primary-like' informal relationships. Thus, he says, the conflict is due to the operation of different types of social relationships. Formalisation pushes people out of their jobs because it imposes on them non-preferred relationships which interfere with their creative process. Professionalism also pushes people from their organisations, as it provides the expectation for upward mobility which may be gained by changing organisations. On the other hand 'collegiality' is a retentive factor. So Pankin explains academic occupational mobility in terms of the three structural variables—formalism, professionalism and collegiality. When the first two increase the third decreases. He concludes that even if market conditions are poor the level of mobility does not come down, because when the market is tight administrators increase their control over faculties, and to escape from such a situation teachers have to publish or perish. This increases professionalism and decreases collegiality.[11]

Studies of college and university student migrations in the USA are also available. According to one such study on college and university student migration between states in the USA in the period 1938 to 1968, the total number of migrant students increased by 868,188 from 236,444 to 1,104,632. But when the number of migrants was converted to a percentage of total student enrolment it was found to have steadily decreased, particularly during the period 1963–68. In 1968 only 16.8% of the total number of students enrolled in all US universities and colleges were migrants. Also the percentage of migrants in public institutions steadily decreased while in private institutions it increased, especially during 1963–68. Some states were found to be major importers of students and others major exporters of them. Why do students decide to migrate and how do they adjust themselves in the new communities to which they migrate? There has not been enough research on this. Migrant students are exposed to different value patterns and different intellectual orientations in their new institutions, while these institutions benefit by a cross-fertilisation and free exchange of new ideas, and lose their parochialism. Migrants also form a substantial element of the consumer market, benefiting the local retail merchants and apartment owners. But student migration is not always an unmixed blessing. It results in additional costs to the local institutions, puts an additional burden on such services as the police and public transport and on the local job market, and gives rise to a greater incidence of crime.[12]

As other investigators have pointed out, in the USA in these days of relative affluence, high mobility and easy communications, the more rebellious students are likely to cluster on certain campuses. Thus Berkeley and San Francisco State have attracted large numbers of unconventional and rebellious students. In previous times such personality characteristics as rebelliousness and unconventionality were more evenly distributed than at present. Migrations have probably increased imbalance among campuses in personality characteristics, giving rise to social problems of some consequence.[13]

A national longitudinal study to compare the background characteristics of students who began college in their local community with those who migrated from their home community to a college within the state, in an adjacent state, or in a state beyond those contiguous to their home states, revealed that from fall 1956 to fall 1958: (*a*) inter-state migration declined significantly; (*b*) the proportion of those attending local colleges increased significantly; and (*c*) there was no statistically significant change in the proportion of those enrolling within the home state but away from the local home community. According to the investigators who undertook this study, decline in inter-state migration was due to: (i) many states putting up a variety of barriers (*e.g.* higher tuition fees, higher admission standards and quota restrictions) to prevent the influx of college students from other states; and (ii) rapid proliferation of public junior and community colleges and consequent increase of enrolments by leaps and bounds. It was also found that students who migrated had better school grades, higher educational aspirations, a rural or suburban home community, a moderate-to-higher family income, and no plans to work part-time; and also they were not much concerned with the cost of education but were influenced by the national reputation and special curriculum of the institutions they joined. Non-migrating students had a profile opposite to this. This means, the study concluded, that American higher education might become sharply stratified purely on socio-economic bases—a trend counter to democratic ideologies.[14]

III. From the foregoing accounts it is clear that, compared to the country's size, total student population and number of universities and colleges, there is little teacher and student mobility of any type among Indian universities either within a state or within the country.* In India it is not easy for a student to take a degree after

---

* In this paper the migration of students from one country to another, especially from the developing to the developed, for higher or specialised studies, is not considered. On that, see article on 'Migration of Talent', *The International Encyclopaedia of Higher Education*, Vol. 6, San Francisco, 1977, pp. 2731 ff.

taking the requisite courses at more than one university in a state or in the country, because regulations, syllabuses, curricula and examination systems differ even among the universities in a state; and every state university prefers to admit students of its own area or state, and each encourages students who join it to complete its own courses and take its own degrees. Some states have also barriers against the migration of students from other states through quota systems. Such mobility as is available is possible only for the affluent students. Teacher mobility is also becoming restricted day by day as Indian states have adopted different languages as the media of instruction and prefer to appoint as teachers men coming from their own states, communities and areas.[15] But it must be emphasised that in principle and in law no Indian university discriminates on the basis of one's religion, caste or home state.

In West Germany it is not difficult for a student to join a university, then take required courses in a number of other universities and finally take a degree from whichever he likes whenever he likes. Universities there have also the practice of giving the first appointment to persons who take their doctorates from other universities.

The situation in the USA has already been discussed in considerable detail. There has been in that country a decline in student migration since world war two. However affluent students with higher aspirations who wish to join institutions of great repute and students with particular characteristic traits appear to be resorting to certain universities. As in India, in the USA also there are barriers in some states against migration of students from other states, and in both countries proliferation of higher education institutions everywhere discourages inter-state migration and even migration from one part of the state to another. In the case of teachers mobility seems to be easy from major universities to smaller universities at the level of assistant professor, whereas at higher levels it seems to be rather difficult. American universities also prefer to have their own alumni for tenure posts whenever possible, whatever they may proclaim.[16] If this is the case in a society where, it is said, mobility is the norm and moving is an expected part of everyday life, and where for the past 50 years about 60% of all its males have moved at least once during their adult lifetime,[17] it can be imagined how far other countries would be from realising the ideal of the medieval wandering scholar.

I wholeheartedly echo the following sentiment: 'It will be a great disappointment for everybody if, ten years from now, it is not possible for a would-be student from (say) Manchester to sign up as if by right for a university course at Nancy or Munich, and if graduates from Rome cannot with equal ease take PhD degrees at Birmingham'.[18] That was written eight years ago; but is there any possibility of this being fulfilled? Today this is not easily possible even between, say, Banaras and Burdwan, Bombay and Patna, or even between Sri Venkateswara and Osmania which are in the same state. It would be a great accomplishment if our discussions culminated in practical proposals for reviving the institution of the wandering scholar and the peripatetic professor.

NOTES

1. *The International Encyclopaedia of Higher Education*, Vol. I, San Francisco, 1977, p. 359a.

2. Eric Ashby. *Community of Universities*, Cambridge University Press, 1963, pp. 49–52. Of course since the sixties several schemes for interchange of teachers and students among Commonwealth universities and universities of other countries have been in operation; but such official and formal interchange cannot be considered as free mobility or free circulation of teachers and students. Within the countries themselves there has not been any significant and steady acceleration of mobility (see, however, below).

3. C. E. Mallet. *History of the University of Oxford*, New York, 1924, Vol. I, p. 138.

4. Anthony Kerr. *Universities of Europe*, London, 1962, p. 65.

5. *The Staffing of Higher Education (Some European Situations)*, International Universities Bureau, Paris, p. 42.

6. S. M. Dube analysed the different aspects of mobility among professions in Gorakhpur City. He found that the spatial migration among university teachers in that city is 98%, even though 70% of them belong to joint families. S. M. Dube, *Social Mobility among the Professions*, Bombay, 1975.

7. T. Caplow and R. J. McGee. *The Academic Marketplace*, New York, 1958.

8. Almost the same causes of mobility as given below are given by others also; cp. *The Encyclopaedia of Education*, Vol. I, ed. L. C. Deighton, Macmillan and The Free Press, 1971, pp. 26–27. This source states that moving from one institution to another is not so difficult. The quality and quantity of published research and one's ability to continue to publish are the bases on which migration becomes possible, and a would-be migrant's qualifications are more rigorously scrutinised than those of new entrants (ibid.).

9. 'The amount of faculty turn-over', observes H. L. Hodgkinson, 'is a definite function of institutional size. . . . As the size of the institution grows, so does the amount of faculty turn-over, and rather startlingly (again, one of the largest jumps is between the medium and large institutions)'. This is because larger institutions attract the more highly mobile PhD professor involved in research and consultation who, travelling around the country a good deal, becomes aware of desirable

posts in other institutions. *Institutions in Transition* (Carnegie Commission Report), New York, 1971, pp. 76-77.

10. Caplow and McGee, op. cit., p. 80.

11. R. M. Pankin. Structural Factors in Academic Mobility, *The Journal of Higher Education*, Vol. XLIV, No. 2, February 1973, pp. 95 ff.

12. This paragraph is based on T. E. Steahr and C. F. Schmid: College Student Migration in the U.S., *The Journal of Higher Education*, Vol. XVIII, No. 6, June 1972, pp. 441 ff.

13. E. E. Sampson, H. A. Korn and associates. *Student Activism and Protest*, San Francisco, 1970, p. 154.

14. R. H. Fenske, C. S. Scott, J. F. Carmody. Recent Trends in Studies of Student Migration, *The Journal of Higher Education*, Vol. XLV, No. 1, January 1974, pp. 61 ff.

15. It must be mentioned that the Indian Education Commission (1964-66) strongly recommended the exchange of teachers wherever possible to break down regional and linguistic barriers, and also recommended establishment and maintenance of all-India institutions which would admit students from different parts of the country. The IITs, etc., are doing this, but *on the whole* not the universities. The UGC is making laudable attempts to permit interchange of teachers among universities through the programme of visiting professorships (of short and long duration) which it is financing, and through research fellowships (junior and senior) available to students of any university. Often the money allocated for the former purpose remains unspent, and the best teachers (unless retired) do not usually accept long-term visitorships of even an academic year's duration. And in practice fellowships are awarded by the universities to their own students. All this, however, cannot be considered as free circulation of students and staff.

16. For example Harvard, which maintains the most elaborate existing system of evaluating candidates and surveys the entire discipline to discover the best man in the country whenever a vacancy is to be filled, finds that the best possible candidates are found to be already at Harvard for 79% of its associate professorships and 88% of its full professorships. See 'The Recruitment of Personnel', *The Behavioural Sciences at Harvard*, Report of a Faculty Committee, June 1954, pp. 197-209.

17. See item on 'Geographic Mobility' based on the work of J. H. Tropman, *Intellect*, Society for the Advancement of Education, New York, January 1975, Vol. 103, No. 2362, p. 216.

18. *Nature*, 27 June 1970. The report of the Council for Cultural Co-operation of the Council of Europe, *Mobility of University Staff* (Strasbourg, France, 1973) has put forward worthwhile ideas to advance mobility of teachers and research workers in Europe.

[Oliver]   TOPIC 2: COUNTRIES WITH FEDERAL GOVERNMENTS

The Canadian Case

Dr. M. K. OLIVER (*President and Vice-Chancellor of Carleton University*): The free exchange of ideas, the search for truth whereever it may be found—these concepts lie at the heart of the university. Their first line of defence is assertion of academic freedom. The second is the maintenance of the right, and the ability, of scholars to move freely and easily from one intellectual centre to another.

Usually, when we think of freedom of movement for scholars, we have in mind the right to travel and visit, to move for a year or two to another laboratory or library or programme, or to register or to take a post in some other university. This mobility within the charmed circle of universities is our first concern. But there is another kind of mobility that will require brief attention: the ease with which one can move into the university world or move (or be moved) out of it.

International movement is fraught with difficulty, although organizations like the ACU help to remove the obstacles and lower the barriers. Within states, movement from one university to another is usually quite simple. Federal states, especially those in which jurisdiction over higher education is a provincial matter, are in an intermediary situation. This paper will look at Canada. It will attempt to describe the patterns of mobility in this particular federal state and to assess likely trends for the late 1970s and early 1980s. It is hoped that other participants can do the lion's share of the work in pointing out in discussion the relevance (or lack of it) of the Canadian experience to other federal situations.

Student Mobility in Canada

The movement of university students from one province to another may be set against the background of general interprovincial migration in Canada. Out of a population of 23,000,000, nearly 400,000 adults and children (or about 2% of the population) moved from one province to another in 1976–77. Levels of movement relative to provincial population were highest in Alberta and Prince Edward Island. The net effects were most striking in Alberta (with a gain of 27,500) and Quebec (with a loss of 23,300).[1]

Interprovincial movement of university students is much higher than for the population as a whole, reaching a peak in New Brunswick where, in 1975–76, 23·4% of the students registered in

---

1. Source: Government of Canada. *Statistics Canada daily*, Tuesday, April 25, 1978, Catalogue 11–001E.

SUB-TOPIC 2(B): STUDENT AND STAFF MOBILITY [Oliver]

New Brunswick universities came from other provinces and 23·8% of all students with homes in New Brunswick were registered in the universities of other provinces. The mobility of graduate students is, as might be expected, much higher than that of undergraduates. In most provinces, as Table 1 below shows, between one-fifth and one-third of their residents who were pursuing graduate studies in Canada did so in another province. The major exceptions were Prince Edward Island, where there are no graduate programmes, and Ontario, the province in which graduate studies are most highly developed. Less than 10% of graduate students of Ontario origin studied in other provinces.

Provinces which fund higher education keep an eye on the balance between those of their students who are studying in other provinces and the out-of-province students who register in their provincial universities. For the four western provinces the flows in and out balance fairly well and, compared with those of the maritime provinces which must be looked at more carefully, these flows do not loom large as a factor in university enrolments. Language difference alters the picture in Quebec. The unwillingness of predominantly anglophone non-Quebeckers to pursue studies in the French-language universities of Quebec brings the proportion of out-of-province undergraduates down to 3·0% (the second lowest after Newfoundland's 1·9% where geographic isolation is a factor) and the proportion of out-of-province graduate students to the lowest figure in the country, 4·9%. Both the comparative willingness of Quebec's francophones to study in English and the fairly high interprovincial mobility of Quebec's anglophones bring the proportion of Québec students studying out-of-province to the third highest level in the country. By contrast Ontario students, both undergraduate and graduate, show the least tendency to look outside their province's 15 universities for their higher education. In absolute numbers if not in percentages, however, Ontario's universities attract the most students from other provinces.

A remarkable mobility pattern characterizes the three maritime provinces, Prince Edward Island, Nova Scotia and New Brunswick and, as Table 2 below indicates, it has remained fairly stable during the 1970s. In each province a very high proportion of students studying in its universities comes from other Canadian provinces. In two of the three, PEI and New Brunswick, a very high percentage of their own students are registered in the universities of other provinces.* In Table 3, below, where the maritime provinces are

---

* The different pattern in Nova Scotia applies only to the undergraduate level, according to 1971–72 figures. At the graduate level, Table I shows that 38% of its graduate students study in another province.

TABLE 1: CANADA 1971–72

	Undergraduate Students		Graduate Students		Total Students	
Province	% of out-of-province students in provincial universities	% of provincial students in out-of-province universities	% of out-of-province students in provincial universities	% of provincial students in out-of-province universities	% of out-of-province students in provincial universities	% of provincial students in out-of-province universities
Newfoundland	1·9	9·5	16·1	31·1	2·4	10·4
PEI	15·2	31·5	--	100·0	15·2	34·1
Nova Scotia	21·4	8·4	34·6	38·0	22·1	10·1
New Brunswick	22·1	17·2	42·4	44·6	23·1	18·7
Quebec	3·0	15·8	4·9	19·4	3·2	16·2
Ontario	7·3	3·1	22·7	9·5	8·6	3·6
Manitoba	7·7	4·6	20·5	27·6	8·5	6·1
Saskatchewan	4·9	7·9	19·1	36·3	5·5	9·2
Alberta	6·0	5·7	14·6	14·5	6·8	6·5
British Columbia	6·2	6·8	27·6	21·6	8·5	8·3

Source: Max von Zur-Muehlen. *The Development of Canadian Education in the sixties and seventies*, AUCC file No. LA 412. V6, Tables 14 and 15.

SUB-TOPIC 2(B): STUDENT AND STAFF MOBILITY [Oliver]

TABLE 2: MARITIME PROVINCES

(1) *Percentage of Out-of-Province Students in Provincial Universities*
(2) *Percentage of Provincial Students in Out-of-Province Universities*

Province	Total (Undergraduate and Graduate) Students					
	1971–72		1974–75		1975–76	
	(1)	(2)	(1)	(2)	(1)	(2)
Nova Scotia	22·1	10·1	21·5	10·1	21·6	10·2
New Brunswick	23·1	18·7	22·6	23·3	23·4	23·8
Prince Edward Island	15·2	34·1	16·4	44·0	13·8	44·2

Sources: 1971–72 figures, Table 1; 1974–75 and 1975–76 figures calculated from Maritime Provinces Higher Education Commission, Second Annual Report, 1975–76, Fredericton, New Brunswick, September 1976, pp. 22–23.

221

[Oliver] TOPIC 2: COUNTRIES WITH FEDERAL GOVERNMENTS

TABLE 3: MARITIME PROVINCES

(1) *Percentage of Out-of-Maritimes Students in Maritimes Universities*
(2) *Percentage of Maritimes Students in Out-of-Maritimes Universities*

Province	Total (Undergraduate and Graduate) Students					
	1971–72		1974–75		1975–76	
	(1)	(2)	(1)	(2)	(1)	(2)
Nova Scotia	11·3	4·5	9·7	5·8	10·0	5·4
New Brunswick	14·6	5·3	14·0	7·6	15·9	8·0
Prince Edward Island	8·2	5·3	6·1	6·8	8·6	6·9
Maritime Totals	12·4	4·9	11·0	6·4	12·1	6·5

SUB-TOPIC 2(B): STUDENT AND STAFF MOBILITY [Oliver]

grouped together, it becomes evident that many students may leave their own province to go to university but stay within the maritime region. The proportion of those who study outside the maritimes lies within a range very comparable to that of each western province taken separately. The inflow of students whose province of residence lies outside the maritimes remains higher than the Canadian average, but considerably less so than when viewed province by province. Inter-regional mobility thus accounts for a considerable part of interprovincial mobility. The fact that only the maritime provinces have established an interprovincial planning body, the Maritime Provinces Higher Education Commission (MPHEC), is a reflection of the tendency of students to see the region rather than the individual province as the system of higher education within which they will make a choice of institution.

Formal barriers to the movement of Canadian students from one province to another for undergraduate and graduate studies are rare. Alberta has provincial and out-of-province quotas for every field of study, but in most cases the latter quotas are high enough to accommodate other Canadian applicants. The exceptions occur in admission policy to professional programmes, which will be reviewed below. Admission standards are set by individual universities rather than by provincial policy and, although the fact that each province has its own system of secondary education means that 'equivalency' definitions have to be established to compare the state of preparedness for university studies of entrants from each province, these definitions rarely discourage mobility. Indeed an odd situation prevails with respect to Quebec and Ontario which makes it possible for a student from either province to shorten the time required for a first degree by one year by entering university in the other province.

Once a student is registered in university he or she is counted in the same way for provincial funding of the university in question, no matter what his or her province of origin or residence may be.

Should a student decide to transfer from one university to another in mid-programme problems of transfer of credits arise. It makes very little difference in the magnitude of the problems, however, whether the university in which the student originally studied is in the same or another province.

The decision to go to university in another province will be affected by financial considerations including the level of fees, the availability of scholarships and eligibility for loans and grants.

Three Canadian provinces now charge considerably higher fees to non-Canadians than to Canadians (Alberta, Ontario, Quebec). These fee differentials were opposed by the university community both in themselves and because they might be the harbingers of interprovincial fee differentials. This latter concern has thus far proved to be unfounded and no province charges higher fees to students from another part of Canada than to its own residents. Fee levels are not identical across the country, however. They are lowest in the western provinces and highest in the Atlantic region.

The Canada Student Loan Plan, based on federal government legislation, provides a common minimum level of student assistance tenable anywhere in Canada. In addition the provinces have their own schemes of grants and/or loans for their residents, integrated with the federal scheme. (Quebec has a purely provincial scheme which nevertheless matches in most respects the federal element that enters into the other provinces' programmes.) Both the level and the kind of support available to students thus varies from province to province. So do rules regarding eligibility. In the western provinces provincial assistance tends to be provided only for residents of the province attending a provincial institution, although exceptions are made when no provincial university offers the programme desired. In Ontario *grants* may be held in a ministry-approved college or university anywhere in Canada, but Ontario student loans and special bursaries apply only to students studying in Ontario. Quebec gives *loans* for anywhere in Canada, but with rare exceptions gives bursaries only to students enrolling in institutions east of the Ottawa River (except for Laurentian, Carleton and Ottawa universities, in Ontario) but excluding Memorial University in Newfoundland. The maritime provinces make most assistance available anywhere, although the level of support may be low.

Federally-sponsored graduate scholarships and fellowships (from the National Research Council and Canada Council) are available to outstanding students and are tenable anywhere in Canada (or in the world). The graduate scholarships provided by some provinces usually will not finance out-of-province studies. In some provinces, however, non-residents are eligible to apply for scholarships to pursue graduate studies within the province, although preference is given to residents.* Finally, each university has its own scholarship, fellowship and bursary funds which are rarely restricted to residents of the province in which the university is located.

There can be little doubt that the tangle of student assistance provisions inhibits interprovincial mobility. The only public body that deals with higher education on an interprovincial basis, the MPHEC, has set itself the target of rationalizing both the rules

---

* Ontario and Quebec have established an Ontario-Quebec Exchange Fellowship Programme which provides generous support for ten students from each province to pursue graduate studies in the other official language in the other province (*i.e.* Ontario students study in French in Quebec; Quebec students study in English in Ontario).

regulating eligibility and support levels and the administration of these rules. It believes that a common regional approach to student aid is essential.

Graduate student support frequently takes the form of payment for services as a teaching assistant or research assistant. At present most universities with a major programme of graduate studies assign students to these posts according to criteria which combine considerations of need, competence, and complementarity with the student's academic pursuits. At the urging of some provinces, however, the federal Department of Employment and Immigration is now contemplating policies which will restrict access to these posts by foreign graduate students. Each post would have to be advertised and only if a qualified Canadian was unavailable to fill it would a foreign appointee be permitted. As in the case of differential fees for foreign students, the universities' concern about this policy change derives in part from the fear that interprovincial restrictions on access to graduate support may follow on the heels of international restrictions.

Access to professional faculties and schools is an extremely complex matter, often involving a multitude of quotas and restrictions. Barriers to interprovincial movement of students are sometimes insuperable. In the heavily populated central provinces of Quebec and Ontario, each with many universities linked in a provincial system that covers a very broad range of programmes, students' problems are manageable. Almost every form of professional training is available within the province. In the west and in the east difficulties abound. Not every province can support a faculty of veterinary science, or a forestry school, or a programme in agricultural engineering. If home province demand for access to places in such programmes is so high that out-of-province applicants are excluded, students from a province that lacks such programmes face a dead-end. Partial remedies are found in a maze of interprovincial agreements which characterize both the Canadian west and east. Some of these are extremely informal inter-institutional accords ('we will take some of your music students if you take some of our home economics students'); others involve high politics. In the latter category arrangements for veterinary education provide telling examples in both the Atlantic and western regions.

In the west, the decision to establish a college of veterinary medicine at the University of Saskatchewan was made after a federal task force studied the needs of British Columbia, Alberta, Saskatchewan and Manitoba in the 1950s. The college's policy is strongly influenced by an advisory council composed of four representatives from each of the four provinces. The council considers entrance qualifications, quotas from each western province and from other provinces and foreign countries, the college's programme of studies and the adequacy of physical facilities. Only three of 66 students admitted in the current year came from outside the western provinces. The college is financed both by student fees and by payments to Saskatchewan from each of the other western provincial governments. The provincial payments are calculated on the basis of 50% of costs less tuition fees per student enrolled.

In the Atlantic region the controversy over where to locate a school of veterinary medicine has raged for several years. Four provinces — the three which have joined to form the MPHEC, plus Newfoundland — are involved. The process of reaching a decision has followed a typical Canadian pattern: a commission report, followed by a report on the report from an augmented committee of the MPHEC, followed by political negotiations amongst the provincial premiers. Plans are going ahead to build the college in Prince Edward Island, over strong protests from Nova Scotia.

Staff Mobility in Canada

The movement of faculty amongst Canadian universities has always been free and frequent. University professors do not see their careers as linked to a provincial system of higher education and there is little evidence that interprovincial movement is contemplated with any more hesitation than movement from one university to another in the same province. The exception is Quebec. Movement from one French-language university to another within the province is much more frequent than movement out of the province to an English-language institution. The reverse flow — professors coming from a non-Quebec university to teach in French in a Quebec university — is a barely visible trickle.

In the years that preceded the great expansion of Canadian universities of the 1960s a singular pattern of movement was established. Doctoral programmes were concentrated in two Canadian universities: McGill in Quebec, the University of Toronto in Ontario. Graduates from these universities, even though the PhD was by no means a requirement for a university appointment, formed a considerable element in the Canadian staff of every other university in the country. (There were, of course, many other Canadians who had done graduate work outside Canada.) Something resembling the 'farm' system of sports like hockey emerged. Young academics went out from Toronto and McGill to the farm teams of the minor league universities where their performance was assessed. If they seemed to have 'star' potential they were brought back to Toronto or McGill after a few years to fill a vacancy. Provincial boundaries meant nothing in the operation of this system.

During the 1960s and 1970s other universities developed graduate schools and the old pattern faded. Moreover much of the staff recruited for the years of expansion came from outside the country, and particularly from the United States. Staff interchange persists in more complex forms, however, and in 1974−75 over half the appointments made at Canadian universities were simply shifts from one university to another. Among newly appointed staff with PhDs, the percentage of those who had previously been employed in another university or college was as high as 66·8%. Appointees who were former PhD students or postdoctorals made up only 17·5%.*

Many factors will enter into the decision of a university professor to move from one province to another, including provincial tax differentials, differences in housing costs, the ease with which his/her children can transfer from one provincial school system to another, and the cultural and physical amenities available. More directly related to the university world are factors like library and laboratory facilities, relative salary scales, moving costs, comparative rates of promotion, tenure provisions, the availability of consultancies, fringe benefits, and particularly the transferability of pension rights.

Salaries tend to cluster by province, but variations amongst provinces are significant. The most readily available, although not the most satisfactory, information is on salary minima. For 1977−78 there was a spread at the assistant professor level from less than $15,000 in Nova Scotia and Newfoundland to nearly $19,000 in Quebec. Ranged in between were, from low to high, the other maritime provinces, Ontario and the western provinces. Comparable differentials occur for the other ranks. Quebec's high salaries are the result of a provincial policy which adjusts salary levels to changes in the cost of living. There is good reason to believe that the outflow of anglophone professors from Quebec's English-language universities, provoked by recent changes in the province's language laws which limit the use of English in schools and in business, was checked by the prospect of salary sacrifices if a move were made to another province.

Most universities have their own pension schemes and limits on portability, both from institution to institution and from province to province, affect decisions to move, particularly for senior staff. Tenure is not usually transferable and a willingness to forego job

* Max von Zur-Muehlen. *Profile of university teachers in the mid-seventies: selected characteristics* (Part II of *Characteristics of Teachers at Canadian Universities*), Ottawa, Ontario, Statistics Canada, 1977, Table I, p. 6.

security is declining as the prospects of falling university enrolments in the 1980s, with the possibility of consequent staff reductions, grow ever more probable. Indeed the growing sense of insecurity among Canadian academic staff is quite likely to affect appreciably the rate of mobility in the 1980s.

For the moment, however, the feared approach of a shrinkage in university staff is, for one group of university teachers, forcing an undesired mobility rather than lowering the rate of movement. Universities which foresee staff reductions seek to reduce appointments in the tenure stream and to maximize term appointments with no promise of renewal. The phenomenon of the scholar-gypsy is upon us. Young PhDs traipse across the country picking up a one-year term appointment in one university, then another, and another, with little prospect of stability for years to come. A recent study describes the effects of Canadian universities' current reluctance to give long-term, tenure-stream appointments poignantly: —

> 'They [the policies] tend to the creation of a group of highly qualified young people, faced annually (or even more frequently) with the prospect of being forced to move or of being unemployed; implicitly warned against developing any strong commitment to a particular university or its environment; as a consequence, obliged to function as second-class citizens of the university community, unable to participate fully in various aspects of its life and work or to plan their lives and careers with reasonable hope. One must ask not only about the equity of such conditions, but about their effects on the ability of universities to attract to their faculties the most able people—indeed, whether able people are likely to wish to enter university teaching or to go through the difficult and expensive process of qualifying themselves for it.'*

The relevance of Canadian federalism to this situation is still tenuous but may become real. Two sets of possibilities will be examined, but first some other aspects of the situation Canadian universities may face in the 1980s must be outlined.

In brief, the Canadian 18 – 24 age cohort will begin to decline in numbers in about 1982. Unless the rate of participation in university studies increases for this age group, and/or the post-24 population increases its demand for higher education on a part-time basis, university student numbers will also decline. Not until about a decade later will student numbers in the traditional university

---

* *Academic Career Planning: The Ivory Tower and the Crystal Ball,* Report of the Joint COU/OCUFA committee on the study of academic career planning in Ontario universities, Toronto, May 1976.

recruitment pool regain the level of the late 1970s. At present participation rates for the 18 – 24 cohort are declining; thus hope from that quarter is dim. Those of sanguine temperament await an economic recovery or a revaluation of higher learning.

The pattern of decline in the 1980s, however, will be far from uniform across the country. It is steeper in the Atlantic provinces and Quebec than in Ontario; steeper in Ontario than in the prairie provinces. And in British Columbia the 18 – 24 demographic curve simply flattens briefly before resuming its upward trend.

Let us assume, first, that remedial action to raise the level of demand for newly-minted PhDs is taken neither by governments nor by the universities. Job opportunities in universities will nowhere be high, but they will be considerably higher in the west than in the east. Will western provincial governments be tempted to restrict entry by non-residents into the universities under their jurisdiction? A few years ago this would have been a wholly fanciful suggestion; it is still a highly improbable response. The last few years have seen a considerable tightening of rules governing the employment of non-Canadians in university posts, however, and sympathy for such a protectionist attitude is quite high. Moreover the erosion of national feeling and the withdrawal of the federal government from the direct financing of universities open the door to provincial protectionism. We are currently wrestling with the problem of Quebec legislation that restricts entry of construction workers from other provinces and the threat of retaliatory legislation from Ontario. One hopes that a free national labour market will be preserved and that even if restrictive exceptions creep in they will affect last of all the university world.

The realm of probability is approached more closely if it is assumed that restrictions on the interprovincial movement of university teachers will *not* be imposed, but that provincial university systems may act to increase the chances of young PhDs entering university careers by upping the exit rate among senior academic staff. Schemes of this kind are in the air. Early retirement policies are being examined, generous 'separation' allowances are contemplated, plans for secondments to government or to industry or to universities in countries where student numbers are still expanding are being studied. But if the problem of low job opportunities is pressing in one province (Ontario) and negligible in another (British Columbia), can one assume that remedial policies would be introduced with the same range and vigour in both? And if such policies loom large in one province and hardly put in an appearance in another, what would be the effect on interprovincial mobility? Would senior professors from Queen's (Ontario) or

Dalhousie (Nova Scotia) who dislike early retirement or do not want to be seconded seek posts in Alberta and British Columbia? What would be the effects on the quality of university teaching and research from one province to another?

It is time to descend from the airy realm of speculation and admit that very little is known about the factors that affect decisions in Canada to move into or out of a university career or, indeed, to move from a university in one province to that of another. Two Ontario sociologists, Dr. Morris Berkowitz and Dr. Linda Moffit, are at present engaged in an 'Ontario faculty mobility study'. They aim to discover why professors leave universities, what characteristics the leavers may share and where they go for subsequent employment. They will also look at the university career prospects of Canadian graduates and at the career patterns of newly-appointed professors. It may be hoped that other Canadian provinces can be studied in like fashion. Whatever emerges is sure to be complicated and will probably be depressing.

Concluding Comments

The complexities and imperfections that federalism brings in university life are easy to identify. Yet it is important to underline the advantages as well. In vast areas like India, Australia, Nigeria, Canada or the United States, federal forms permit a degree of mobility for scholars and students which would not readily be attained if national barriers intervened. Those tempted to yearn for the simplicity of unitary regimes are simply unrealistic.

Canada's universities benefit from fairly easy movement from province to province. The United States practice of charging higher fees to out-of-state students is absent. Within the country academic standards are tested by continuous interchange, both through shifts of persons from one province to another and through country-wide associations based on disciplines or, like the Association of Universities and Colleges of Canada, on institutions. The integration of the anglophone and francophone academic communities is far from complete, but provincial jurisdiction over Quebec universities protects the French-language universities and scholars of that province from relegation to minority status.

Maintaining the mobility that characterizes higher education in Canada will be a challenge for the 1980s.

SUB-TOPIC 2(B): STUDENT AND STAFF MOBILITY [*Yesufu*]

The Nigerian Experience

Professor T. M. YESUFU (*Vice-Chancellor of the University of Benin*):

Federalism and University Education in Nigeria

The effect of federalism on universities depends very much on the provisions of the country's constitution and the educational policies of the constituent governments as these reflect the prevailing economic and social milieu. Under the pre- and post-independence constitutions of Nigeria higher education was a concurrent subject. This meant that the federal and regional (later state) governments could establish and control universities subject to federal law overriding that of the region or state in case of conflict.

With the transformation of the colonial unitary system of government into a federation, as Nigerian independence approached, the University College, Ibadan, which was established in 1948, was retained as a federal institution. In 1955 the eastern regional government passed a law for the establishment of the University of Nigeria, Nsukka, but the university did not come into being until 1960. Following upon the Ashby Commission report (1959 – 1960), the University of Lagos (located in what was then known as the federal territory) was established in 1962 as the second federal university. In the same year the Ahmadu Bello University, Zaria, and the University of Ife, Ile-Ife, were established respectively by the northern and the western governments as regional (state) institutions. In 1970 the then Mid-Western State government established the Mid-West Institute of Technology which was transformed into the University of Benin in 1972. But the state government, for financial and other reasons, handed over the University of Benin to the federal government on 1 April, 1975.

Each university was established under a separate law and governed by its own statutes as laid down by or under that law. While there were differences of some detail, in fundamentals all the laws, both federal and state, exhibited a great deal of similarity, and the universities' institutional framework—council, senate, congregation, etc.—and their administrative procedures and governance were also very similar. Except for the University of Nigeria, Nsukka, Nigerian universities were conceived and patterned after the British model. Nsukka, on the other hand, was modelled along the American land-grant system which, when proposed, seemed so radical that it caused 'no small consternation at home and abroad'.[1] Over the years, however, the underlying concepts of Nsukka, particularly as regards the need to ensure local vocational relevance of curricula, and the course system, have influenced and been adopted (albeit in modified forms) by the other universities, while Nsukka itself has also been influenced by the strong British tradition of the other universities. Thus all Nigerian universities came to be marked more for their institutional and academic similarities than for their differences. Even their entrance requirements were, and have remained, basically the same.

After the change in the military administration in July 1975, the federal military government decided to take over all the state universities. Even under the previous dualism all state universities received federal grants equivalent to 30% and 70% respectively of their annual recurrent and capital development estimates. In 1967 the level of federal recurrent grant to Ahmadu Bello University was raised to 75%. During 1976 the federal government decided to establish seven more universities at Sokoto, Kano, Maiduguri, Jos, Calabar, Ilorin and Port Harcourt. The thirteen universities existing in Nigeria today are, accordingly, all federal institutions. Indeed the federal military government went so far as to pre-empt the power of the states to establish their own universities, so that under the present military administration the powers to establish, regulate and control universities have become exclusive to the federal government.[2]

The Concept of Staff and Student 'Mobility': Precept, Policy and Law

In spite of the background which we have sketched above, suggesting mutual interaction, and increasing uniformity or similarities both in institutions, academics and proprietorship, the question of university staff and student mobility has been a live and very controversial issue in Nigeria. It is necessary, however, to understand the sense in which the term 'mobility' is being used here. In respect of students 'mobility' implies: —

(a) the freedom of a student to attend any university of his choice, irrespective of his state of origin within the federation;

---

1. A. Babatunde Fafunwa. *The Growth and Development of Nigerian Universities*, Overseas Liaison Committee, American Council on Education, OLC Paper No. 4, April 1974, p. 14.

2. It may be noted, however, that with the recent student disturbances and the crippling financial burden of the universities, thought is again being given to sharing constitutional responsibility for universities with the state governments. The constituent assembly endorsed this by making education at this level once more a concurrent subject under the proposed new constitution for civilian rule in 1979.

(b) inter-university transfers of students either on their own initiative or on a co-operative basis between two or more universities under joint, complementary or reciprocal academic programmes; and,

(c) the acceptability of a student with, say, a first degree in one university to pursue a higher degree in another university (*i.e.* mutual recognition of degrees and other student academic awards and attainments).

As regards staff 'mobility' implies: —

(a) the freedom of a qualified candidate to teach in any university of his choice irrespective of his state of origin within the federation; and,

(b) the acceptability, and free transferability, of the service of staff, both as to level and duration, from one university to another.

With the British tradition as the model the issue of discrimination in respect of access, for groups or individuals, never arose with respect to the University (then University College) of Ibadan at its foundation in 1948. It was a national institution designed to serve national needs for higher education, without distinction of ethnic or geographical origin of its students or staff. The post-independence University of Lagos, Ife, Ahmadu Bello and the University of Nigeria, Nsukka, were conceived and established at the moment of the fruition of the nationalist struggle, and their underlying policies and perspectives were categorically national. As regards the University of Nigeria, Nsukka, its very name indicated its national outlook and aspirations. At the inaugural meeting of the council of the University on 2 March, 1960, Dr. Nnamdi Azikiwe, then chairman of the council, emphasized its national character and went on to add that the successful establishment of the University 'will have created an opportunity for the youth of Nigeria to give play to their talent which is latent'.[3] In respect to staff the emphasis of policy was equally on the training of 'Nigerian' scholars to man the institution.[4]

The Ahmadu Bello University was, among other things, designed 'to secure the diffusion of knowledge throughout Northern Nigeria'.[5] Nevertheless Sir Ahmadu Bello (after whom the University was named) at his installation as the University's first chancellor took care to emphasize that it shall be 'reflecting the needs, the traditions, the social and intellectual heritage of the land in which we live ... We shall be a *truly Nigerian Institution* and not the mirror of some alien body'.[6] Similarly the University of Ife

---
3. c.f. Okechukwu Ikejiani (ed.), *Nigerian Education*, Longmans, 1964, pp. 159–161.
4. Ibid., p. 162.
5. Ibid., p. 163.
6. Fafunwa, *The Growth and Development of Nigerian Universities*, op. cit., p. 15 (emphasis, the writer's).

indicated that 'its policy would be to open its doors to students from all parts of the Federation and the world'.[7] The policy and objectives of the University of Lagos, which was federal by proprietorship and cosmopolitan in its environment, were national from start. The University of Benin, first christened as the Mid-West Institute of Technology, was born in the throes of the civil war. It rode high on the crest of the sympathy of the nation at large, the Mid-West State being the only part of the federation that was, albeit briefly, temporarily overrun by the then rebel Biafran troops. The University was in part an expression of the internal solidarity of the people of the state in times of crisis and in part a symbol of equality with the other states, each of which had its own university. Like these others, its perspective and declared policies were national, as evidenced by the cross-national composition of its first council which drew membership from all parts of the federation.

In this way all the six Nigerian universities which existed up to 1975 lived up to the recommendation of the Ashby Commission, and accepted by the federal government, 'that all universities in Nigeria should be national in outlook'.[8] This was reflected in the governing law of each university which forbade it to discriminate against student or staff candidates on the grounds of place of origin, race, sex or religion. The following provision in the governing law of the University of Benin is typical in this respect:

> 'No person shall be required to satisfy requirements as to any of the following matters, that is to say ethnic grouping, sex, place of birth or of family origin, or religious or political persuasion, as a condition of becoming or continuing to be a student at the University, the holder of any degree of the University or of any appointment or employment at the University of any body established by virtue of this Edict; and no person shall be subjected to any disadvantages or accorded any advantage, in relation to the University, by reference to any of those matters.'[9]

All the seven new universities established since 1976 have been founded along the same tradition, and have been insistent that they are national or federal in policies, practices and orientation.

Student 'Mobility' in Practice

As already indicated, the issue of student mobility can be examined under three main headings: freedom of choice of

---

7. Ibid., p. 16.
8. Fafunwa, op. cit., p. 11.
9. University of Benin Edict, No. 3 of 1975, Section 18.

university; inter-university transfers; and mutual recognition of degrees and other academic awards. The last two have not raised any serious problems and can first be dealt with more summarily.

Inter-university transfers. In a country where universities are at different stages of development it makes sense for two or more of them to co-operate in training some categories of students under joint or reciprocal academic programmes. In the early years of the University (then University College) of Ibadan large numbers of its students went to London to complete their degree courses. This question has thus nothing to do with 'federalism' as such. However in Nigeria there have been instances of academic co-operation between a federal university and a state university, and also between two state universities. At the inception of veterinary medicine at Ibadan (a federal institution) and at Ahmadu Bello (then a state institution) there was an agreement for the students to do part of the course at Ibadan and part at the Ahmadu Bello University. Between 1973 and 1975 the Ahmadu Bello University received medical students from the University of Benin (then also a state institution) at a time when the latter's facilities were still inadequate to meet the course requirements in medicine. These were temporary arrangements which terminated when the institutions concerned were able adequately to develop their independent facilities.

The voluntary transfer of students from one university to another has however been on a relatively small scale. Such transfers tend to be more common when a student has failed in one university and is required to withdraw. He then applies to other universities and invariably has to start from scratch as the system of transfer of credits from one university to another has not yet been developed in Nigeria. This also accounts for the fact that there is hardly any mobility of 'successful' students between Nigerian universities during the degree term. There was, however, the historical exception when in 1967, as a result of the civil war, many students of non-eastern origin at the University of Nigeria, Nsukka, were displaced to other universities. Special dispensations were granted by these other universities in order to allow the students to matriculate at their respective levels and to graduate. Some students of eastern state origin also left the other universities at that time to enrol at Nsukka.

The main barrier to transferability, up till recently, was that most Nigerian universities patterned their courses and examinations on the traditional British system whereby courses taught throughout the year were examined at the end of the session as a combined package — a student either passed or failed that level of examination as a package. Only the Univesity of Nigeria, Nsukka, followed the

American model by instituting the 'course system' from its very beginning. Moreover there were, and still are, important differences of detail in the content of syllabuses of the different universities, and of combinations of courses at different levels of even the same discipline. This is characteristic of universities in most countries of the world; it promotes innovation and enriches the total academic experience and heritage. However most Nigerian universities are now adopting the 'course credit system' and this should enhance the transferability of students from one university to another in the future.

Mutual recognition of degrees and academic awards. The first two Nigerian universities, namely Ibadan and the University of Nigeria, Nsukka, were fostered by reputable foreign universities—Ibadan as a University College, by the University of London; and Nsukka, as a full-fledged university from its inception, mainly by Michigan State University. The other Nigerian universities (except Kano, Ilorin and Port Harcourt, which operated very briefly as university colleges) were, like Nsukka, established as full-fledged degree-granting universities. But a number of universities (such as Benin) were nurtured under teneral and special link and technical assistance arrangements with reputable universities abroad. Also, the use of external examiners by every university is institutionalized by its laws. Thus every university uses external examiners from other Nigerian universities as well as from overseas. In this way the development and maintenance of high and comparable standards are assured and Nigerian universities accept without question the degrees and other academic distinctions awarded by their counterparts. This mutuality of recognition of degrees has ensured free mobility of students from one university to the other, particularly at the postgraduate level.

Freedom of choice of university. Under a federal system students may be subjected to disabilities in the choice of university in a number of forms, such as:—

(*a*) differential fees, with rates imposed on students from other states being higher than those paid by students of the state which owns the university;

(*b*) a quota system of admissions, by which a certain proportion of student intake is reserved for students of the university's home state;

(*c*) a combination of (*a*) and (*b*) above; and,

(*d*) in respect of federal institutions, the use of a quota system of admissions so as to ensure student intake from all the component states.

SUB-TOPIC 2(B): STUDENT AND STAFF MOBILITY [*Yesufu*]

As already indicated Nigerian universities, whether they were federal or state institutions, proclaimed freedom of admission to all student candidates irrespective of their state of origin. The University of Benin, for a brief period, tried to give special consideration in admissions to students from certain disadvantaged areas of the Bendel State when the university was a state institution. When the way it operated tended to amount, in practice, to a quota system, it was abandoned. Even then candidates from other states of the federation freely applied to the University and the majority of students actually enrolled tended to come from outside the state.

In the light of the above it may seem paradoxical that nothing has perhaps bedevilled Nigerian university politics and administration, in the last three years, so much as the controversy over student admissions. The critics have held that student enrolments weighed too heavily in favour of certain (mainly the southern) states of the federation — namely the western states (now comprising Oyo, Ogun and Ondo), the eastern states (now Anambra and Imo states) and the Bendel (formerly Mid-West) State. In terms of primary and secondary education, however, these states have historically been the most advanced while the northern states, in particular, were highly disadvantaged in so far as western education in general was concerned. Coincidentally university places available annually had also never been adequate to absorb all candidates with the requisite minimum entrance requirements, particularly in the arts and social sciences. The combined effect of the above was that during the academic year 1974 – 75, for example, the six northern states (out of the then twelve states of the federation) which had more than 50% of the country's population accounted for only 5,764 or just under 22% of the national total university enrolment of 26,448.[10]

This disparity as between the states in respect of student enrolments raised much dust and very heated arguments in the press, and even at the highest levels of government. In September 1976 the head of state himself, Lt. General Olusegun Obasanjo, addressing the vice-chancellors of all Nigerian universities, felt constrained to emphasize 'the need for them to be more responsive to the needs of the Nation and to be more realistic in their admissions and other policies. He expressed the view that the universities must help to redress the country's educational imbalance by accelerating the educational development of the disadvantaged States of the country'.[11] Some people held that the prevailing system should be changed to a quota system to enable students from all states to get

---

10. National Universities Commission, Nigeria. *Annual Report, July 1975 – June 1977*, Table 4a.
11. Ibid., p. 53.

admission. They argued that the admissions system, which was essentially by competitive academic merit, was unfair to the disadvantaged states and detrimental to national unity. The main strands of the debate went along the following lines:
- universities are national institutions and should help promote national unity and the even development of the manpower resources as between the various states;
- every university should, therefore, reflect the federal character of the country in its student admissions by admitting students from all states; and,
- this could best be done by a quota system of admissions.

In what amounted to an indictment of the universities, some vice-chancellors felt constrained to comment. One vice-chancellor came out with a statement that his university had, more than any other university, always reflected the national character of the federation in its composition of both students and staff. Another, appalled by the prospect of the enforcement of a quota system of admissions, reaffirmed that his university had always based student admissions on competitive academic merit, without reference to the state of origin of the candidates, and would continue to do so. Another indicated that admissions to his university would be by competitive academic merit, modified to some extent by a quota system.[12]

It is accepted that universities are national institutions and should, particularly in underdeveloped countries, assist, within their manpower resources and terms of reference as educational institutions, to promote national development. They should also, by virtue of their apparent superior intellectual resources, assist in promoting national unity where the fabric of society, as in Nigeria, tends at times to be threatened by ethnic distrust and tribal differences. But it is equally true that, in the context of Nigeria, neither a quota nor a merit system of student admissions as such has any special merit for promoting national unity. Indeed, applied rigidly, each could only exacerbate national disunity.[13] For example, the merit system is academically unassailable — but, as already indicated, its effect has been an apparent weighting against the already disadvantaged states. On the other hand a quota system might have the advantage of 'balancing' the opportunity of university education among the states — but it would have the disadvantage of penalizing the bright student mainly because he had the 'misfortune' of coming from an educationally advanced state. In any case very few states in Nigeria are ethnically homogenous, and every state would have a problem sharing its quota among the component ethnic groups. A

---

12. Adeyemo Aderinto (University of Lagos). *Undergraduate Admissions in Nigerian Universities* (mimeo), pp. 2–3.
13. T. M. Yesufu. Vice-Chancellor's Address to the Congregation for the Conferment of Degrees, January 1978, University of Benin.

quota system of admissions would only, therefore, have fostered not only inter-state, but also intra-state disunity.

The federal government ultimately announced that it had decided against the introduction of the quota system of admissions into the universities. But it decided to set up a Joint Admissions and Matriculation Board (JAMB) to deal centrally with admissions to all Nigerian universities. Proposals for such a board were already being formulated by the Committee of Vice-Chancellors. But whilst the committee intended the board to be a central clearing-house for admissions and to avoid the problems that were inherent in the multiplicity of student candidates applying and getting admissions to more than one university at the same time, the board, as established by government, has been given statutory powers not only to receive applications but also even to determine the entry qualifications to the universities and select the students for each of them.

It appears as if government's original concept of the JAMB was to enable it both to ensure a fairer distribution of admissions among the states and, at the same time, to eliminate the polarization of students to universities located in their home states; in other words, to ensure an admixture of the students enrolled in each university in order to reflect the 'federal character' of the nation and promote unity. In practice, however, the JAMB has no way of meeting these expectations. To the extent that university admissions will continue to be by competitive examinations and merit, the number of students admitted into the universities from a state will reflect their performance in the examinations and the number of places available. As regards polarization of students to universities in or nearest to their home states, this will continue as long as students (as at present) are free to express their preferences and such preferences are respected. Indeed as it becomes more difficult for universities to guarantee hostel accommodation to students the pull of students to universities of nearest geographical proximity to, and preferably of, their home states is bound to become stronger. The economic costs of studying far away from home (*e.g.* the cost of transportation) as well as the social problems of finding suitable accommodation, whether independently or with a relative, and settling down in a different cultural milieu, are much greater the farther the student travels away from home. And too much can be made of the unifying effect of students from different states having to study together. Where the general political and social atmosphere in the country already reeks with mutual distrust and inter-state or ethnic hostility, these attitudes by forced interaction may only become more hardened to the greater detriment of national unity, rather than the other way round.

As regards the problem of inter-state imbalance, available statistics show that in recent years the proportion of university students from the disadvantaged states has been rising. At the time of independence in 1960 the proportion of university students from the then northern region was less than 10%. As we have already indicated, the figure was just under 22% during the academic year 1974 – 75. During the following session, 1975 – 76, the six states constituting the same area accounted for nearly 24% of enrolments.[14] For a country that is rightly concerned to promote national unity and even development there is still a long way to go to redress the imbalance. But the solution lies not in castigating the universities over admissions policies and practices but in developing a wider and stronger base of primary, secondary and basic education in the disadvantaged states, in order to enable more students from there to qualify for university entrance. This is now being done by the federal military government. A universal primary education scheme (UPE) has been decreed by the government, more federal and state secondary schools have been developed. In particular, special schools of basic studies have been established in the disadvantaged states under the tutelage of designated universities to prepare candidates from these states for university entry. Moreover more universities have been established and sited in these historically disadvantaged areas. This would constitute an added incentive for persons in these areas, who would normally otherwise be discouraged from attempting university entrance, to do so.

Staff Mobility

The problem of staff mobility between universities has never been a very serious one in Nigeria. In conformity with their laws the universities have generally thrown their staff positions open to competition by candidates from all parts of the federation, and even from abroad. Indeed there has always been a scarcity of qualified academic and senior administrative manpower available to fill requisite vacancies, and no university could afford to pursue a policy of ethnic or state discrimination in its staff recruitment.

Apart from first appointments, transferability of staff between universities has been enhanced by the fact that the structure of employment and the terms and conditions of service have always been similar. In the pre-independence days university staff, because of the relationship between the University of Ibadan and the University of London and also because most of the staff, then

---

14. National Universities Commission, *Annual Report, July 1975–June 1977*, op. cit., Table 4b.

expatriates, were seconded from British universities, were members of the British Federated Superannuation System for Universities (FSSU). After independence and with an increasing proportion of university staff being indigenous, the Nigerian Universities Joint Superannuation Scheme (NUJSS) was instituted, to which all the universities belonged. Following the Public Service Review (Udoji) Commission Report of 1974 the universities were brought under the unified public service system. The NUJSS was abolished and a non-contributory pensions and retirement scheme was introduced. This has, in fact, further enhanced mutual transferability of service for the purposes of calculating pension or gratuity.

It is an abiding rule of all the universities that all positions above the senior lecturer grade should normally be filled by advertisement. They also use external assessors for evaluating the qualifications, publications and other credentials of candidates at these levels. The chances of nepotism and practice of discrimination on the grounds of ethnic or state origin are, accordingly, extremely narrow.

There have however been two occasions in the history of Nigerian universities when the principle of free admixture and mobility of staff was badly shaken. The first was in 1965, during the rumpus that surrounded the change of vice-chancellor at the University of Lagos. The issue degenerated into ethnic polarization and animosity and inter-university movement of those concerned along tribal lines.[15] The second occasion was during the civil war, when the staff of the University of Nigeria, Nsukka, of non-eastern state origin, were required, or felt compelled, in the interest of their security to leave. Virtually all of them were absorbed in other universities. Some staff of other universities from the east also left for Nsukka. It is clear that these incidents were not voluntarily perpetrated in pursuance of any deliberate policy of discrimination.

It is highly symbolic of the prevailing situation that, over a period of one month during which the present writer collected data from the universities for the purpose of writing this paper, as many as nine of the thirteen universities could not produce statistics of the state origin of their academic staff. Three of the four that supplied such information were among the seven new universities, and were able to do so only because the staff numbers were still small. Significantly, in all the universities that supplied the relevant information staff from other states of the federation far outnumbered the ones whose states of origin were those in which the universities were located. Moreover a casual analysis of available data suggests that no university in Nigeria has staff from less than six states. This

---

15. For a detailed examination of this incident see T. M. Yesufu (ed.), Creating the African University, Oxford University Press/Association of African Universities, 1973.

[Yesufu]   TOPIC 2: COUNTRIES WITH FEDERAL GOVERNMENTS

provides clear evidence that universities in Nigeria do not consciously practise discrimination in staff recruitment.

It is nevertheless true that for each state of the federation the greatest proportion of university staff deriving therefrom tend to be concentrated in universities located in or nearest their homes. As in the case of students, the reasons are both economic and social, and derive from the free choice of the individuals concerned.

Conclusion

In Nigeria federalism has hardly ever operated as a conscious element in university student admissions or in staff appointments. In fact the laws governing the universities forbid them to practise such discrimination. Internal crisis at the University of Lagos in 1965 and the Civil War in 1967 led to mass movement of staff and students, on ethnic or state basis, between the universities. These, however, stand out as the historical exceptions that prove the rule of free access to and movement between the universities. There is mutual recognition of degrees awarded by the universities and reciprocity in the transfer of staff, the latter of which is encouraged by the prevailing uniformity of terms and conditions of service.

In practice student enrolments have shown an imbalance against some states. But this was due to the historical disadvantage they had suffered since the colonial times in the development of western education. This is now being remedied through special measures to expand education at all levels. There is tendency for the greater proportion of staff and students from a given state to polarize to a university in, or proximate to, their home states—mainly for economic and social reasons, and this has nothing to do with federalism as such, or any disabilities consciously put in their way to move to other universities. As the university system grows and interstate imbalance is reduced the recent controversy over student admissions and staff recruitment will largely die a natural death.

DISCUSSION

By way of gloss on the formal papers (see above), Professor R. H. Myers (New South Wales) spoke of Australian experience, distinguishing mobility among students from mobility of staff; Australia, he explained, was a large country in which there was little movement, whether interstate or indeed inter-city, of students, who normally sought places at their nearest university. Staff, however, were of very diverse provenance; the 1,300 staff

SUB-TOPIC 2(B): STUDENT AND STAFF MOBILITY

members at his own University come from perhaps as many as 80 universities and while, to lower levels of staff, recruitment was mainly local, at the level of full professor it was almost international. Free movement was seriously inhibited only by such factors as the transferability of superannuation rights.

Professor E. A. Ayandele (Calabar) spoke of the particular role to be played in such countries as India or Nigeria by university staff and students as agents of a national unity. In response to this point Dr. M. K. Oliver (Carleton) spoke of the response which the Symons report on the status of Canadian studies among Canadian universities* had elicited from the universities, and of the efforts which institutions were now making to redress cultural imbalance.

Professor R. J. Baker (Prince Edward Island) gave instances of the interchange of staff and students within Canada and expressed a general satisfaction with the characteristics and levels of mobility there.

Sir Douglas Logan (ACU) doubted the effects of federalism on mobility which, in his view, was much more affected by language. He found paradox in the United Kingdom's movement towards external federalism and at the same time towards internal devolution. The sub-topic chairman (Sir John Llewellyn) invited the group to extend the discussion to encompass the United Kingdom's involvement with the European Economic Community and the prospect of a growing need to encourage mobility of teachers and students between the United Kingdom and the rest of Europe. The topic chairman (Dr. Steven Watson) referred to French opinion, which rated the movement of students as more important than that of teachers, though it was impeded by differences between levels of tuition fees, higher in the United Kingdom than in France. The chairman, again, spoke of calls within the EEC for the equivalence of qualifications, which were leading to the establishment of bodies of information about grades and syllabuses. Dr. Oliver (Carleton) referred to the problem of professional programmes and qualifications in Canada, where it was not possible for small provinces to develop many specialist courses and where, in consequence, the application of provincial quotas became unavoidable. Professor T. M. Yesufu (Benin) argued that, while in the case, for example, of the EEC the pressure for easier equivalence and greater mobility was political in origin, universities should make it their business to seize initiatives in this kind of matter. Dr. J. Aminu (National Universities Commission, Nigeria) pleaded that the concern with mobility should not lead to over-centralisation.

Professor R. C. Mehrotra (Delhi), reverting again to Indian experience, agreed that language constituted a greater barrier to the mobility of students than any difficulties inherent in a federal structure. India had adopted a number of schemes to ease mobility; places at institutions of technology were open to national competition and regional engineering colleges had to draw something like half the student body from other than

---

*T. H. B. Symons. *To Know Ourselves: the Report of the Commission on Canadian Studies*, Association of Universities and Colleges of Canada, Ottawa, 1976.

TOPIC 2: COUNTRIES WITH FEDERAL GOVERNMENTS

local catchment. Similarly the UGC-sponsored Centres for Advanced Study also had to look externally for students. Mr. R. K. Chhabra (University Grants Commission, India) reported that a number of graduate places at Jawaharlal Nehru University were reserved for students from other states. Mr. K. S. Kolge (Bombay) referred to the efforts made by the University Grants Commission in seeking to establish uniform scales of academic salaries throughout the country; he added a reference to the obligation of universities, where posts were advertised, to announce them on a national basis. His experience in a metropolitan university was that universities exercised a unifying influence on society.

Dr. J. A. Perkins (International Council for Educational Development) spoke of the findings of his organisation that while federalism exaggerated division it also promoted mobility, in that industrial development followed trained manpower; the universities' necessary involvement with the training of manpower led to a situation in which federalism helped to promote local talent. He contended, against the argument of some earlier speakers, that language was no necessary impediment to mobility, but often helped in the spread of professionalism. His organisation had concluded that in a number of countries research councils, commonly a function of federal governments, had played an important role in uniting universities and in helping them play an important role in society.

Sub-Topic 2(c)

ACADEMIC PLANNING IN A FEDERAL SYSTEM

Chairman: Professor R. C. MEHROTRA
Vice-Chancellor of the University of Delhi

Rapporteur: Professor F. J. WILLETT
Vice-Chancellor of Griffith University

Tuesday, 22 August

The Nigerian Example

Professor J. F. ADE AJAYI (*Vice-Chancellor of the University of Lagos*):

Federal Structure

The University College, Ibadan, was established in 1948, consequent upon the recommendation of the Elliot Commission on Higher Education in West Africa, during the colonial era when Nigeria had a unitary system of government. Although it could grant certificates and diplomas its degrees were those of the University of London to which it was affiliated.

By 1954, in the process of decolonisation, Nigeria adopted a federal constitution initially with three regions: east, west and north. Higher education was placed on the concurrent list, that is, leaving it open for the federal and regional governments alike to establish and finance universities of their own. It soon became manifest that the dawn of independence would be characterised by intense regional rivalry and that university education in its relationship with manpower and economic development would be a prominent feature of that rivalry. Already in 1955 the east regional government had passed the University of Nigeria Act and was seeking external assistance to finance it. Other regions were also soon to begin to initiate their own plans. It was clear that if the central federal government was to play a co-ordinating role and avoid an imbalanced development and wasteful duplication, some central planning and direction must be given to higher education throughout the country. It was in pursuit of this that the federal government set up the Ashby Commission in 1959 to review the manpower needs of the whole country and make recommendations for a structure of post-secondary and higher education to meet those needs in the 1960s and 1980s.

The Ashby Commission[1] recommended the establishment of a second federal university to be located in Lagos to cater for commerce, business studies and law, not available in Ibadan, as well as for regional universities in the east and north where no universities then existed. It also recommended that all the universities should be national in outlook and subject to some central planning and direction, with the bulk of capital grants and a proportion of recurrent funds coming from the federal government. However this attempt at a fair distribution in the location of new universities failed to take account of political realities. The west regional government, led by the party in opposition at the federal level, regarded the proposals as discriminatory against the west and pressed for a west regional university. Hence, between 1960 and 1962, the University of Nigeria (Nsukka), the Ahmadu Bello University (Zaria), the University of Ife and the University of Lagos were established, and the University College, Ibadan, made into an autonomous university. In 1963 the mid-west region was carved out of the west and it also began to demand its own university. It was the national crisis, 1966 – 70, that delayed the establishment of the University of Benin till 1972.

The controversy over the establishment of the University of Ife had shown both the necessity for and the political constraints over central planning of higher education in a federal system. In a White Paper[2] on the recommendations of the Ashby Commission report the federal government had proposed that while each university, federal or regional, should have autonomy in the management of its affairs, the 'overall national interest' should be safeguarded through the establishment by law of (i) an inter-regional manpower board, (ii) an all-Nigeria academic council and (iii) a national universities commission. The National Manpower Board was established in 1962 but it has not been effective in exerting any significant influence on the planning of higher education. The academic council was never established. The National Universities Commission appointed in

---

1. See *Investment in Education:* the Report of the Commission on Post-School Certificate and Higher Education in Nigeria (1960), Lagos.
2. *Educational Development, 1961 – 70*, Sessional Paper No. 3 of 1961, Federation of Nigeria, Lagos, 1961.

1962 was through an administrative action and not by act of parliament. The twelve members, appointed in their personal capacities, were largely officials. There was not a single Nigerian academic on it, though Sir Eric Ashby was retained as honorary adviser.[3]

Non-Statutory NUC

The National Universities Commission was based in the cabinet office and directly responsible to the prime minister. Its terms of reference were: —
- To inquire into (and advise the government on) the financial needs both recurrent and capital of university education in Nigeria.
- To assist in consultation with the universities and other bodies concerned in planning the balanced and co-ordinated development of the universities in order to ensure that they are fully adequate to the national needs.
- To receive annually a block grant from the federal government and to allocate it to universities with such conditions attached as the Commission may think advisable.
- To act as an agency for channelling all external aid to the universities throughout the federation.
- To take into account, in advising the federal government, such grants as may be made to the universities by regional governments, persons and institutions both at home and abroad.
- To collate, analyse and publish information relating to universities' finance and university education both in Nigeria and abroad.
- To make, either by itself or through committees, such other investigations relating to higher education as the Commission may consider necessary and, for the purpose of such investigations, to have access to the records of universities seeking or receiving federal grants.
- To make such other recommendations to the federal government or to universities relating to higher education as the Commission may consider to be in the national interest.

Soon after its inauguration the Commission embarked on its major assignment of preparing a quinquennial programme for university development in the country, as part of the first National Development Plan 1963 – 68. This programme was eventually

---

[3]. Offices held by the original members of the Commission were as follows: Emir of Yauri, a traditional ruler (chairman); president, Nigerian Union of Teachers; secretary, Nigerian Union of Teachers; secretary to the prime minister; chairman, Federal Board of Inland Revenue; provincial secretary, Sokoto; resident engineer, Sokoto; minister of education, Eastern Nigeria; chief secretary to the premier, Eastern Nigeria; medical practitioner, Benin City; executive director, Western Nigeria Development Corporation; secretary to the National Universities Commission; master of Clare College, Cambridge (honorary adviser).

embodied in the Commission's report entitled *University Development in Nigeria: Report of the National Universities Commission*, 1963. The main recommendations of the report can be summarised as follows:

(i) that the universities should aim at a maximum enrolment target of 10,000 by 1967 – 68;

(ii) that priority should be given to the development of the scientific and technological departments of the universities, and that of the total student population of 10,000 recommended, 7,580 should be taking courses in the sciences, pure and applied;

(iii) that for the present only three engineering faculties should be developed, *i.e.* the engineering faculties at Ahmadu Bello University, Zaria, the University of Nigeria, Nsukka, and University of Lagos.

(iv) that veterinary science should be developed jointly by the University of Ibadan and Ahmadu Bello University, the pre-clinical course being given at Ibadan and the clinical at Zaria;

(v) that there should be only two faculties of medicine this quinquennium, at Ibadan and Lagos;

(vi) that all Nigerian universities except Lagos should develop strong faculties of agriculture; the University of Ibadan should build up a vigorous postgraduate school in agriculture and the three regional universities should each develop an agricultural extension department in co-operation with the appropriate regional ministry of agriculture;

(vii) that all the governments of the federation should make most of their undergraduate scholarships tenable in Nigerian universities in order to increase the number of scholarships available to Nigerians and in order that the income of the universities may be increased;

(viii) that the University of Lagos Act should be amended to enable the senate of the University to have an overall responsibility for the academic affairs of the University of Lagos Medical School.

(ix) that the University of Ife should move to its permanent site at the earliest practicable date and that it should be compensated for the loss of its Ibadan campus buildings, which should be taken over by the University of Ibadan;

(x) that the universities should be assured of a capital grant of £17·63 million and a recurrent grant of £30 million during the quinquennium 1963 to 1968;

(xi) that the federal government should provide the entire financial needs of the universities of Ibadan and Lagos together with 50% of both the capital and recurrent needs of three regional universities;

(xii) that there should be a national universities fund into which all grants and subventions to the universities should be paid;

(xiii) that the National Universities Commission should be converted into a statutory body with the same terms of reference as those set out at page 2 of the report and with responsibility for the management of the national universities fund;

(xiv) that each of the laws establishing the regional universities be amended so as to provide for nominees of the federal government universities.

Most of these recommendations with the exception of recommendations (xiii) and (xiv) were approved by the federal government. Recommendation (xiii) was not implemented until much later, in 1974. But this bold attempt at co-ordination was unsuccessful for a variety of reasons.

Limiting Factors

Until quite recently, as stated earlier, the Commission was not a statutory body and had no statutory authority for the exercise of any measure of control over the financial policies and procedures of the universities, nor had it the statutory power to ensure that public funds, once allocated to the universities, were spent only on the objects for which they were voted. Contrary to the recommendations of the Ashby Commission, and in spite of expert advice to the contrary, the National Universities Commission was established by administrative action and remained in an advisory capacity to the federal government in the same way as the Universities Grants Committee is advisory to the British government. But whereas in the United Kingdom the sole governmental responsibility for the finance and operation of the universities rests with the single central government, in Nigeria the responsibility was a concurrent one shared by the federal government and the then existing regions (now states). Many of the problems of university co-ordination in Nigeria have arisen from this transposition of a system of co-ordination designed to operate within a unitary system of government to the federal system of government in Nigeria, where university education was a concurrent responsibility of both federal and state governments.

For these reasons, and also because of the failure to establish the national universities fund recommended in the Commission's report (1963), it was not possible for the Commission to implement effective procedures for the administration of capital and recurrent grants to the universities. In the Commission's report under reference, the recommendation was made that 'although the National Universities Commission was established to advise the

Federal Government on university development, the system we propose to operate would not be wholly effective unless there is cooperation between the Federal and Regional Governments in the consideration of that advice. For instance, in order to ensure financial stability for all the universities, it was necessary for the universities to look to one source for their funds—the National Universities Commission Fund—to which all governments will contribute according to some agreed formula'. Although this recommendation was accepted by the federal government in Sessional Paper No. 4 of 1964, it was only after much protracted correspondence and as late as 1965 that the regional governments accepted in principle the proposal for the establishment of the fund. Draft rules for the creation of the fund were under consideration by the cabinet office and the ministry of finance when the national crisis broke out in the country and up till now the fund has not been established, even though the NUC now operates its own bank account. The result of operating without the proposed fund was that the Commission did not exercise control over regional (state) governments' grants to their universities nor, until 1975, did it hold and operate federal grants, a situation which made it impossible for it to introduce effective procedures for the exercise of necessary control over capital developments and recurrent expenditures in the universities.

The major problem arising from this lack of centralized control over recurrent expenditures was that the universities, with the encouragement of their councils and regional governments, were establishing courses not approved by the Commission and duplicating each other in most of the courses they offered, despite the fact that the Commission repeatedly urged a rationalization of the university system so that, rather than duplicate one another's efforts, universities in Nigeria might complement one another in the interest of national needs. This state of affairs continued even though the burden of financing the universities was progressively falling more and more heavily upon the federal government, which by 1967 was contributing not less than 70% of the total annual cost of university education.[4]

4. By 1964 the funding of various universities by the federal government was as follows:

University	Federal support (*percentage*)	Regional or state support (*percentage*)
Ibadan	100	–
Lagos	100	–
Nigeria	30	70
Ife	30	70
Ahmadu Bello	50	50

In 1967 an amendment was effected to this scheme only in respect of Ahmadu Bello, which was henceforth to have a federal financial support of 75% and state support of 25%. Since 1975, with the placing of all universities on the exclusive federal list, all the six universities and the seven new ones have been funded 100% by the federal government.

The Interim NUC, 1968 – 74

The take-over of government by the armed forces in January, 1966, the transition of four regions to twelve states in 1967 (and nineteen in 1976) and the civil war of 1967 – 70 had important consequences on the fortunes and the planning of higher education in Nigeria. It was clear that the advisory NUC had been unsuccessful and other models were sought, notably in the University of California and the Swedish university systems. These were canvassed but considered unsuitable in the context of the strong regional and state-centred feelings generated in the civil war period. Indeed attention had to be focused elsewhere and the secretary of the NUC had to double as the commissioner for external affairs, leaving only a skeleton staff to carry on the work of the NUC during the war years.

In 1968 an interim NUC was established and its membership took account of criticisms of the earlier NUC.[5] Its chairman was a distinguished lawyer and former pro-chancellor and chairman of council of the University of Ife. There were only two civil servants. There were four university professors, a representative of the principals of secondary schools, two businessmen and another legal practitioner. It remained an advisory body, suffering from the basic limitations of the earlier NUC. It was as a result of state political pressure rather than an act of deliberate planning of the NUC that the Mid-West Institute of Technology founded in 1972 became recognised as the University of Benin. The main difference from the earlier NUC was that the interim NUC had access to increasing levels of federal government funding, but that only increased its frustration at its inability to enforce central planning. In the meantime also, the Committee of Vice-Chancellors emerged as an informal but effective co-ordinating body, with a modest secretariat to collate and present the joint opinion of the universities.

With the end of the war came increasing prosperity from oil revenues which greatly enhanced the spending powers of the federal government. The increasing dependence of the state governments on federal grants which resulted came to reinforce the unified chain of military command which bound the state military governor to take orders from the supreme headquarters. Without the federal structure of higher education being abolished, the federal government saw the way clear to a unified planning system that was not possible in 1960 – 65. It therefore decided to create a statutory NUC

---

5. The occupations of the eleven members appointed by name were as follows: legal practitioner (chairman); chief federal adviser on education; permanent secretary, federal ministry of economic development; secondary school principal; professor of political science; professor of mathematics; professor of education; professor of pathology; personnel director, UAC; assistant general manager, KCN; legal practitioner.

with its own bank account, place higher education on the exclusive federal list, and establish a central admissions and matriculations board.

The Statutory NUC

By a decree of the federal military government of January, 1974, a statutory NUC was created, even though it did not begin to function until April, 1975. Its membership is similar to that of the interim NUC, but with heavier bureaucratic representation. Besides the functions of the earlier NUC, the new NUC was charged additionally with: —

(*a*) Preparation of periodic master plans for the balanced and co-ordinated development of universities in Nigeria. Such plans were to include: (i) the general programmes to be pursued by the universities; (ii) the recommendations for the establishment and location of new universities as and when necessary; (iii) recommendations for the establishment of new faculties or postgraduate institutions in existing universities and the approval and disapproval of proposals to establish such faculties or institutions.

(*b*) Undertaking periodic reviews of the terms and conditions of service of university staff and to recommend thereon to the federal government where appropriate.

(*c*) To recommend to the visitor of a university that a visitation be made to such a university as and when it considers it necessary.

The NUC began to function against the background of a vigorous attempt on the part of the federal government to exploit its new position to define a new national policy on education, using education as a unifying force, correcting the imbalance in the accessibility of higher education throughout the country, insisting on greater relevance and directing universities towards set national goals.

With an expanded and growing secretariat, its own bank account, close accessibility to government either directly or through the federal commissioner for education, central control of admissions and federally-financed chain of schools of basic studies especially in the disadvantaged areas, the NUC is well set to achieve a better co-ordinated university system and reduce imbalance in the educational development of the country. It is, however, faced with a number of problems. The powers are such that conflict with the university councils and senates, the Committee of Vice-Chancellors and the federal ministry of education can hardly be avoided. Besides there is the very haste with which the NUC has been expected to move and haste does not always produce the best atmosphere for planning. Within a few months of the new NUC beginning to function, the federal government announced the establishment of four new universities at Sokoto, Maiduguri, Jos and Calabar, and three university colleges at Ilorin, Port Harcourt and Kano. A year later, even the three colleges were declared universities. The task of seeing the new universities grow has not left much room for the proper planning and phasing of their development. In spite of the statutory powers, political realities and the strength of individual leaders and personal relationships, and not rationalisation alone, exert undue influence on development.

The powers of the NUC are, I repeat, such that it can hardly avoid conflict with various other statutory bodies like university councils and senates and the federal ministry of education. Its relationship with the Committee of Vice-Chancellors in the co-ordination of university activities is also far from clear. There is also room for conflict from state governments with unfulfilled university ambitions.

Within two years of the establishment of the statutory NUC the slump in oil revenues has necessitated cutbacks in expected grants to the universities. This has not helped the cause of rational planning. While free tuition has been retained, increased charges for boarding and feeding have had to be imposed. State governments are being asked to find more resources and to expect less from the federal government. Diminished resources have increased the necessity for judicious planning but weakened the ability of the federal government to sustain centralised planning.

The constituent assembly, which has just approved the new constitution under which a civilian government is expected to take over power from the military in October, 1979, has already decided that higher education should return to the concurrent list. The future civilian government is thus unlikely to accept the recent centralised approach to the planning and control of higher education. It seems therefore that the search is to continue for the most efficient and acceptable formula for planning higher education in a federal Nigeria.

Professor L. KERWIN (*Professor of Physics and Past Rector, Laval University*): A long, long time ago a traumatic experience was visited upon the university. Organized society became interested in it, and it has not been the same since.

I say *organized* society, because of course the university was always the product of society *tout court*. When the first person who had found out something interesting and made a note of it was approached by another person who wished to learn it the university was born, and it has since scarcely reached a higher state of perfection. This eminently social intercourse still constitutes the essence of a university. For a generation now there has been a great increase in the analysis and criticism of the idea of a university, and its role in society has been advanced in thousands of ways—I myself have contributed dozens of statements and speeches about it, as have all of you. But shorn of the frills and technical language, disabused of the pleading for local socio-economic justification, the essential character of the university is still unshakeable: it is an institution for the preservation, increase and dissemination of knowledge. This essential character is the theme of this Congress.

Thus the national, international and social role of the university is still basically that of facilitating exchange between individuals: between the professor and the student, between the master and the apprentice, between the learned and the learning, between the curious.

The traumatic experience came about when organized society—groups representing or controlling other groups—governments—perceived that the university dialogue led to benefits which should be multiplied and extended. Governments began to approve of the professor and the student, then to encourage them, then to assist them, then to direct them, then to command them. However the direction and commanding of intellectual enterprise inhibits it, and so universities have had to try to devise ways of remaining free of such constraints—of remaining universities. The benefits of being a kept institution are very considerable however, and this brings us to the other half of the theme of this Congress: the *reconciling* of the role within organized society with the essential character of the university. I am most interested in the results of our discussion. Shall we surrender some more? Rationalize some more? Or get back on the end of the log opposite the student, where we belong?

It is possible that the national role of the university, and possibly even its international role, is conditioned by the structure as well as by the ideology of the government of the country in which it functions. Of the various structures of government in the world there is a widespread one called 'federal' and this provides the more restricted framework in which our particular group is working. This afternoon we are considering a most important aspect of a university's life with government: how academic planning is carried out. Presumably our hope is that we shall end up better informed as to how planning is done in a federal system, whether it succeeds in reconciling the social role of the university with its essential character, and whether a university is better or worse off in this respect than is a university under some other form of government structure. These are the three points to which I shall address myself.

There is no typical federal country, and so in the course of the analysis which he made in giving me invaluable assistance with this paper, Dr. Marino Kristjanson of the Association of Universities and Colleges of Canada examined a cross-section of them, nine in number: Australia, Canada, Czechoslovakia, Germany (FDR), India, Mexico, Switzerland, United States of America, Yugoslavia. We have also included Denmark, a non-federated state, as a control.

All of these are federal states in the sense that their citizens live under at least two levels of government, each with considerable powers: a state or provincial government with relatively regional powers, and a federal government with jurisdiction in matters considered of broader national interest. There is obviously great variety under this umbrella, even in the cross-section selected.

This variety appears in the basic data. Figure 1 (p. 261) shows the populations of these countries, which vary from 6 millions to 600 millions. The area of the countries also varies considerably, from $0 \cdot 04M$ km^2 to 10M km^2. These two parameters make for varying population densities (Figure 2, p. 261): from $1 \cdot 8$/km^2 to 250/km^2 (Figure 3, p. 262). Data such as these may eventually be advanced to explain certain national characteristics of universities.

The educational systems of the countries considered provide varying pools of resources from which they draw their university populations. The numbers of primary and secondary school students are shown in the next Figure (4, p. 262), together with the numbers of teachers available. The percentage of the total population in this part of the school system is moderately constant, and varies from 15% to 23% (Figure 5, p. 263). The number of students per teacher varies from about 11 to about 36 (Figure 6, p. 263). All of these data contain arbitrary factors concerning level, classification, etc.

Another index of the potential level of general information is the number of radio and television sets available to the population. In the next Figure (7, p. 264), we see how many sets there are per 100 citizens in each country. The number varies from about $2 \cdot 5$ to about 250.

The next Figure (8, p. 264) shows the numbers of students at universities and other institutions of what is called 'higher learning'. The percentage of the population so engaged varies from $0 \cdot 4$ to $4 \cdot 6$

(Figure 9, p. 265). The number of students per professor varies from about 9 to about 20 (Figure 10, p. 265).

The economic resources which a nation may draw on may be measured, according to one point of view, by the gross national product per citizen (Figure 11, p. 266). This may be compared with the expenditure per university student. We see that this varies from 63% of the gross production per citizen to 138% (Figure 12, p. 266). The absolute expenditures, however, vary considerably — from about US$500 to about US$8400 per university student. An interesting statistic is the number of university students supported per million dollars of GNP. As shown in Figure 13 (p. 267) this hovers around 3, with some exceptions.

It is not evident that these figures provide very many indices concerning the condition of universities in a federal state. First of all, the difficulty that plagues all statistics seeking to make international comparisons is very much present: that of obtaining comparable data. Most of the data which I have used could be contested on one point or another, but also defended. Secondly, there is great variety to be found in the figures for federal states. Thirdly, if we take Denmark to be a reasonable representative of a comparable group of non-federated states, we see that the data for it are not particularly distinguished from those of federal states. However further refinement might make the analysis of basic data more profitable insofar as the subject of this paper is concerned.

Data more particular to the nature of the federal state is indicated in the next Figure (14, p. 267). We see that the number of governments involved in legislating about universities varies from about 9 to about 50: presumably this means that there is more than an order of magnitude difference in the co-ordinating process. The sources of funds for the university budgets also vary considerably, from 100% federal to almost 100% state or province, with the notable case of the United States, where 50% is from private sources (Figure 15, p. 268).

The planning and co-ordinating process for universities also varies widely in federal states. Here are some salient facts for each country.

In Australia, the states are responsible for legislation, the federal government for financing. This has produced some conflicts, and may lead to some state financing. There is a federal Tertiary Education Commission which advises the federal government of the aid needed by the states for universities. The interaction of the two levels is claimed to have been a powerful source of change for the universities. A Committee of Vice-Chancellors has been very active in lobbying the federal government. A federal committee of inquiry is currently examining university evolution until 2000.

SUB-TOPIC 2(C): ACADEMIC PLANNING [Kerwin]

In Canada interpretations of the situation vary. Provinces are responsible for education, and some interpret this as including all of the activities of a university. Funding is about 40% provincial, 40% federal and 20% other, but here again some provinces consider the federal share to be in fact theirs. There exist university planning commissions in most provinces, a national Council of Ministers of Education, four regional organizations of vice-chancellors, a national association of universities, various federal commissions which investigate fields involving universities, and several federal ministries which deal directly with universities as regards research.

In the German Federal Republic the Länder are responsible for the bulk of the legislation and also the financing. However federal law imposes a certain amount of federal-Länder and Länder-Länder co-operation, and the federal government sees to some equalization. There was relatively little national planning before 1973, when the Federal-Länder Commission for Educational Planning and Research Promotion proposed a harmonized development of the entire educational system up to 1985. Most planning appears to be effected by federal-Länder joint agencies, with effective input and lobbying from the Conference of West German Rectors and the Conference of Ministers of Education. Generally speaking, however, planning has been minimized.

In Mexico, where there are federal, state and private universities, financing is largely federal. Most of the planning agencies are national: the National Association of Universities and Institutions of Higher Education and the recent Office of General Co-ordination of Higher Education, Science and Technology being prominent. The universities' association also has seven regional councils. There also exists a National Council of Science and Technology which co-ordinates research and exerts a certain influence on the universities as a result.

In the United States of America we find an enormous variety of institutions, many governments, and many co-ordinating associations and agencies, from state to regional to national. However the national planning agencies have so far played relatively minor roles, and it is the institutions themselves or small regroupings which have dominated the planning and co-ordination, which must be said to be low-key. Adaption rather than planning seems to be the practice. The federal government provides funds for planning, which have been accepted so far by 46 states.

In Yugoslavia there has been a trend to decentralization, with the federal government supplying equalization funds. The planning has been subdivided to the level of communities and basic organizations of associated labour in each sector. This has been criticized as producing interminable discussion with little action. Community-level planning is intense and continuous. There is also the League of Yugoslav Universities, the Yugoslav Students' Federation, and several federal agencies such as the Federal Committee for Science and Culture.

With 2.3M university students in over 100 universities and dozens of engineering schools, India has a great variety of institutions. The needs of various sectors of this vast country are so diversified that overall planning and co-ordination is difficult. In fact there is relatively little planning at the state level, although constitutionally the Indian states have a certain responsibility for higher education. At the national level there exists the University Grants Commission which co-ordinates the distribution of federal funds and also concerns itself with the rationalization of university research. Other federal agencies such as the Indian Council of Agricultural Research and the All-India Council for Technical Education do similar co-ordination in their spheres. The Association of Indian Universities is the leading institutional organization.

In Czechoslovakia the planning for universities is done by both the federal government and the state governments of the Czech and Slovak republics. The State Commission for Universities (federal) has a number of committees which prepare study plans and programmes for universities. There is also the Czechoslovak Academy of Sciences which co-ordinates most scientific research. In addition there is the state committee for universities and higher education institutions in each of the two constituent republics which advises the minister of education.

It is possibly in Switzerland that we find the universities the objects of detailed consideration. There are relatively few, and there is also a relatively low number of students. However these are extremely well supported, as we can gather from the budget spent per student and the student/staff ratio. The Swiss are interested in quality. Their universities fall under both federal and cantonal jurisdiction as well as that of the communes in some cases. There is also considerable private support. The planning and co-ordination is handled by various federal agencies, with some input from the Swiss Conference of Directors of Education of the 25 cantons or half-cantons. The Swiss Scientific Council co-ordinates research and the Conference of University Rectors exerts considerable influence. However the universities have wide autonomy and appear to be the main factors in their own planning.

In summary, as far as planning is concerned, the federal state offers a great variety of possibilities. These are summarized in the next Figure (16, p. 268) together with the preliminary indication of the extent to which they are used in the countries considered. One of the remarkable conclusions to which these incomplete data would lead us is the lack in every country of a tripartite planning mechanism involving federal and state governments as well as universities.

What is the result of the planning, or of the lack of it? In short, what is the performance of the university system in these countries? Here again we run up against the almost insurmountable problem of measuring yield, and of evaluating complex situations with the help of questionable data. One again has recourse to the arbitrary. A reasonable, but by no means exclusive, set of criteria for measuring performance might be the following:

Quality of scholarship	('Quality')
Contribution to the national cultural heritage	('Heritage')
Training of professionals for society	('Professional')
Provision of liberal education	('Liberal')
Provision of broad choice to total population	('Choice')
Service to all segments of population	('Service')
Constructive criticism of society and government	('Criticism')
Efficiency of administration of resources	('Efficiency')
Integration with entire nation	('Integration')
Popular support and approval	('Popularity')

These are indicated in the following Figure (17, p. 269), with a preliminary indication of what I judge to be the response of the federal system examined to these criteria. There is no doubt that some of the systems have a performance which is better than others.

However it is not a simple matter to correlate performance with planning. The variables are too numerous, too complex, and with many unknown interactions. Factors such as climate, population density, history and national character all may enter into the question. Economic development is obviously a major influence, as is political ideology. For every correlation which a researcher might suspect there are many factors which an adversary might reasonably invoke to prove it a mere coincidence. A proper analysis of the advantages and disadvantages of the federal state may never be possible, stemming not least from the great variety of constitutional arrangements in various federal states. Certainly this paper, which is one of the first to consider the problem, reveals itself to be at the merest beginnings of the preliminary examination of the question.

However, in spite of these reservations, I suggest that we have glimmerings of tentative answers to the three questions which I proffered at the beginning of the paper. We find, first, that there is now considerable data on how planning is done in federal systems: it is done at many levels, with rich interactions, and many possibilities for adapting to regional or other sectors of the population. We are also permitted to conclude in a tentative way that no planning is better than government planning, and that the individual university appears to be the optimum planning unit. Secondly, we may say that the universities in federal systems have not completely reconciled the social role of the university with its essential character: the social role is currently dominant and the planning of university systems usually emphasizes it, to the detriment of the essential role. As to the third question, I submit that the university is potentially better off under the federal system because it is more democratic in principle. The several levels of government are each responsible to the same voters, which may thereby keep them in check and balance. A balanced division of responsibility for the university thus keeps the citizen involved with university policy through at least two channels instead of one, and the university is at least partially shielded from the influence of a single all-powerful government, as the results of this study bring out.

This leads us to speculate that an optimum mix of influence and financial support for universities in federal states may eventually prove to be fourfold: three parts from the federal, state and private sectors of the nation, and one part, hopefully, from the international community of the utopic future.

GENERAL REFERENCES

E. F. Sheffield. *I.C.D.E. reports* on Australia and Mexico (other reports in preparation).

The Europa Year Book 1976 — A World Survey.

The International Encyclopedia of Higher Education, Asa S. Knowles, editor-in-chief, Jossey-Bass Publishers, USA, 1977.

Several OECD reports, *e.g. Educational Statistics Yearbook*, vol. 1, *International Tables* (1974).

Commonwealth Universities Yearbook, 1976.

Encyclopaedia Britannica — Book of the Year, 1978.

SUB-TOPIC 2(c): ACADEMIC PLANNING [*Kerwin*]

FIGURE 1: POPULATION

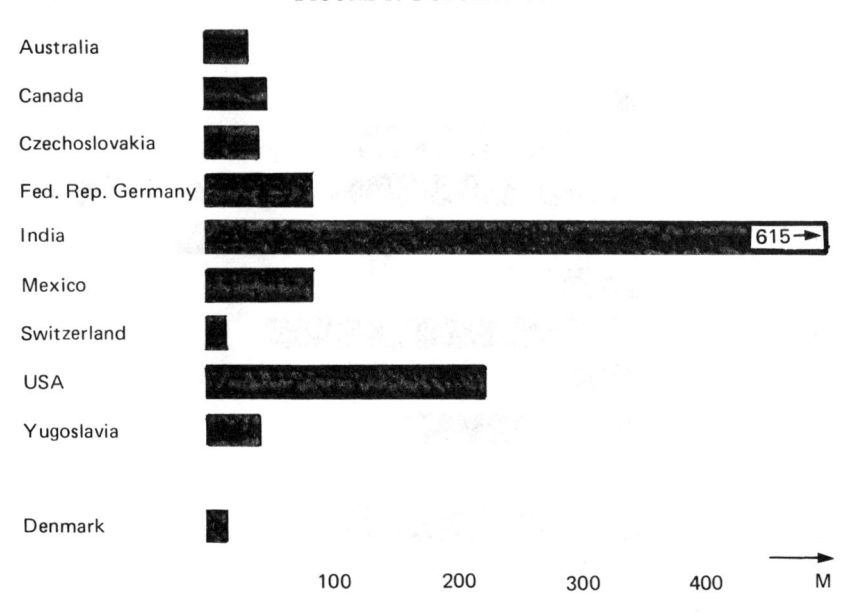

Country	Population (M)
Australia	
Canada	
Czechoslovakia	
Fed. Rep. Germany	
India	615 →
Mexico	
Switzerland	
USA	
Yugoslavia	
Denmark	

FIGURE 2: AREA

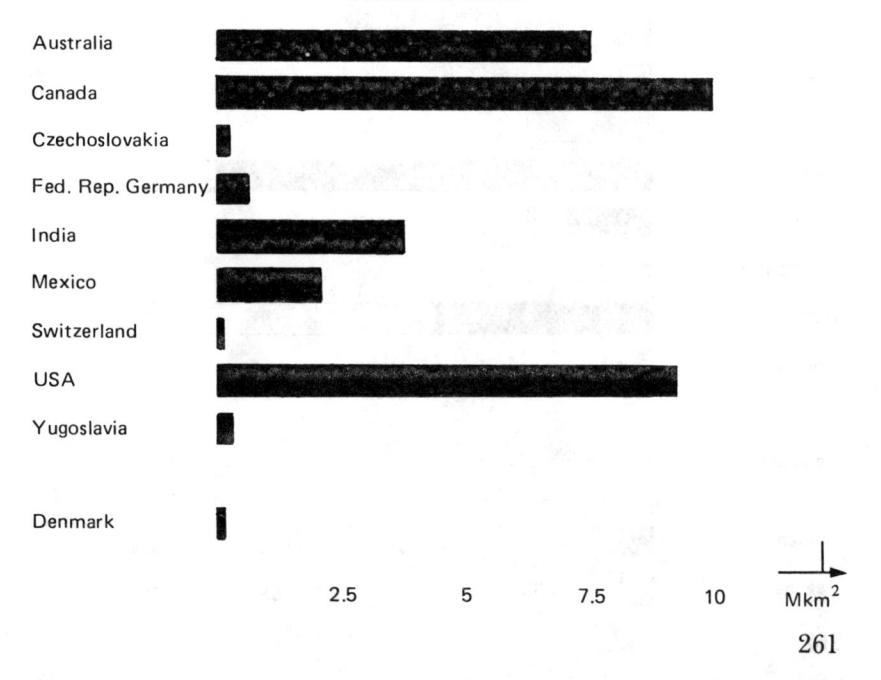

Country	Area (Mkm^2)
Australia	
Canada	
Czechoslovakia	
Fed. Rep. Germany	
India	
Mexico	
Switzerland	
USA	
Yugoslavia	
Denmark	

[Kerwin]   TOPIC 2: COUNTRIES WITH FEDERAL GOVERNMENTS

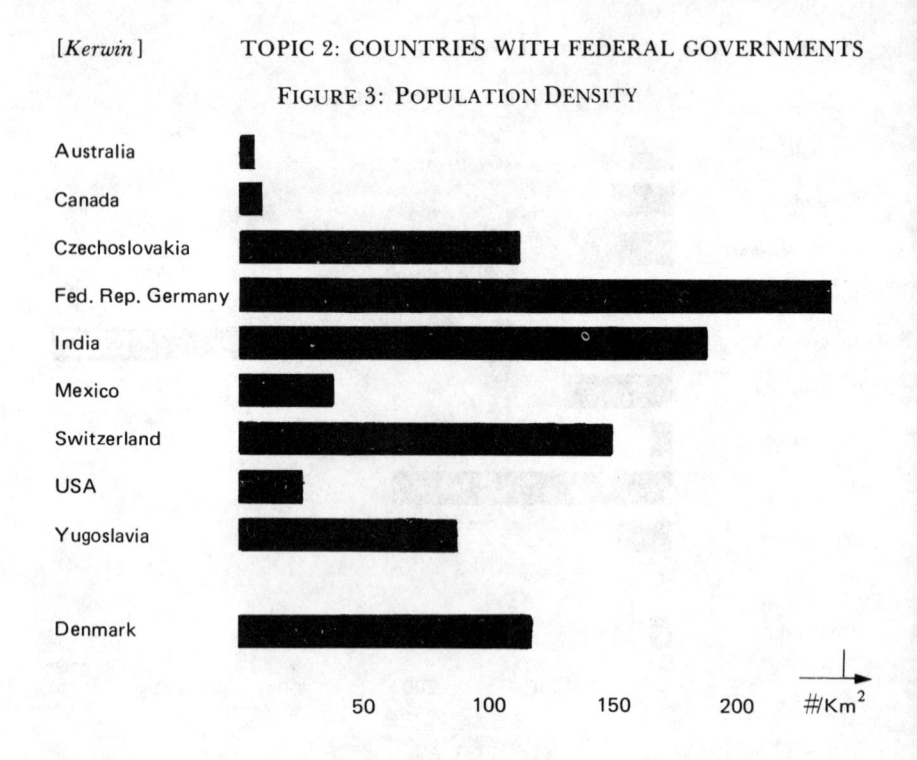

FIGURE 3: POPULATION DENSITY

FIGURE 4: STUDENTS AND TEACHERS: PRIM. + SEC. SYSTEMS

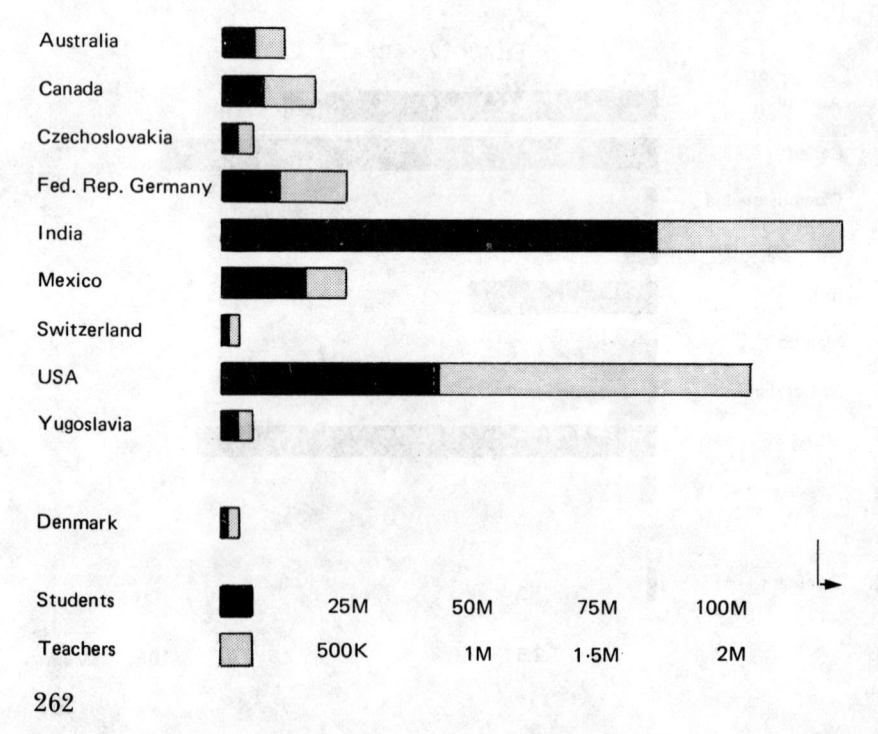

SUB-TOPIC 2(c): ACADEMIC PLANNING [*Kerwin*]

FIGURE 5: PRIM. + SEC. — % OF POPULATION

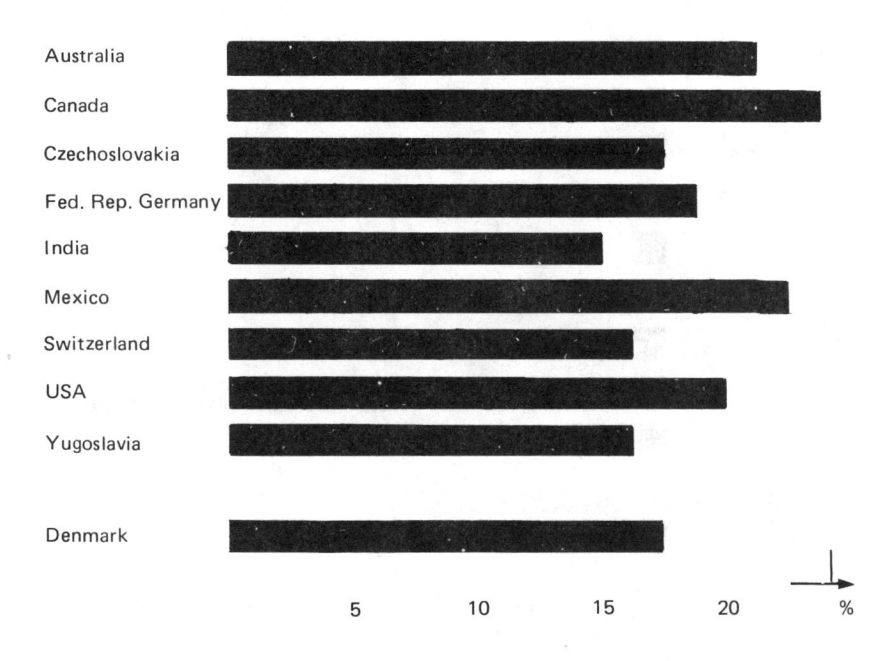

FIGURE 6: PUPILS/TEACHER: PRIM. + SEC.

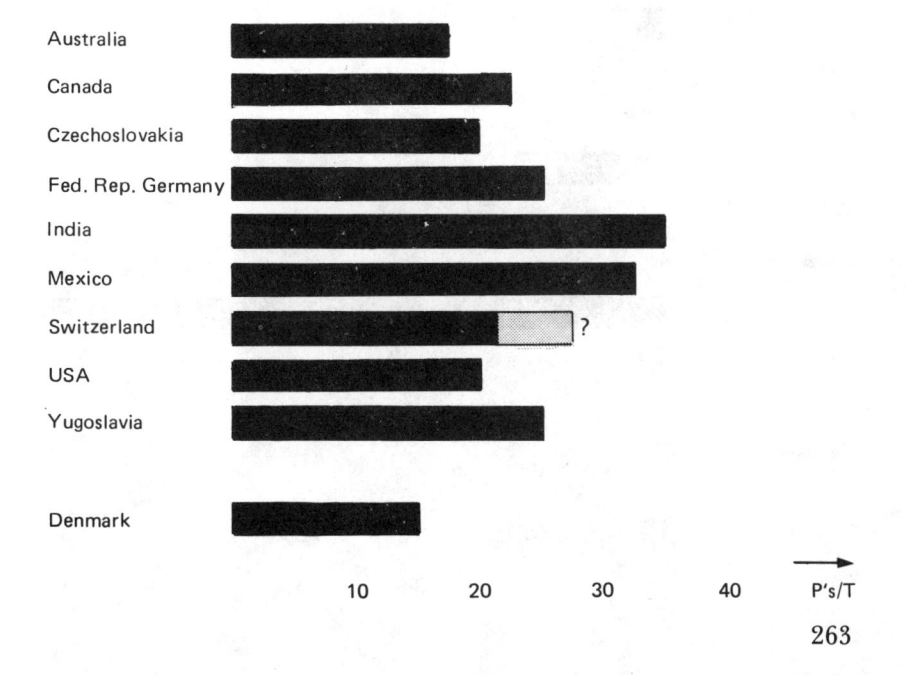

[Kerwin] TOPIC 2: COUNTRIES WITH FEDERAL GOVERNMENTS

FIGURE 7: RADIOS + TVS PER 100 POPULATION

- Australia
- Canada
- Czechoslovakia
- Fed. Rep. Germany
- India
- Mexico
- Switzerland
- USA
- Yugoslavia

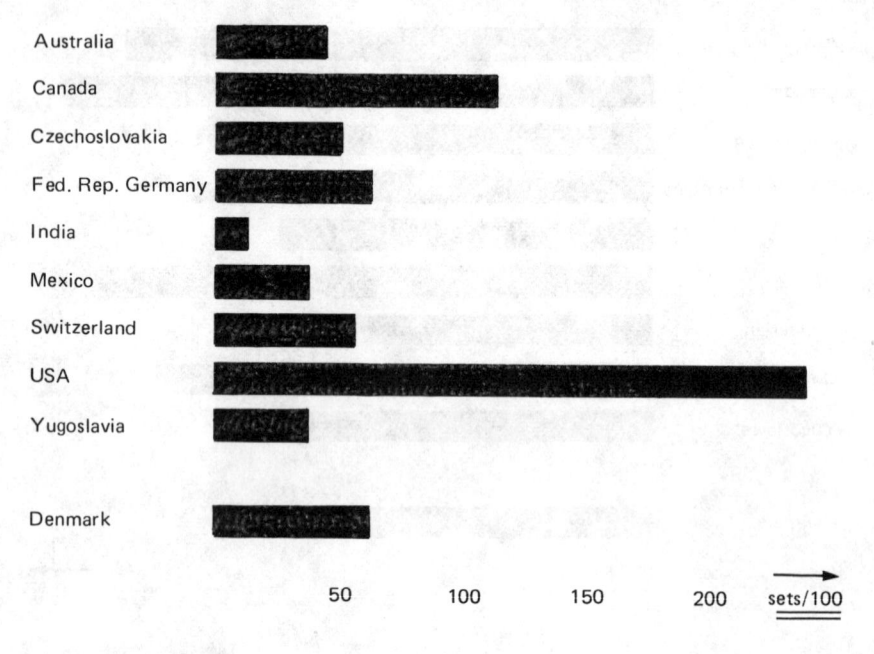

- Denmark

50   100   150   200   sets/100

FIGURE 8: PROFESSORS, STUDENTS, IN HIGHER EDUCATION

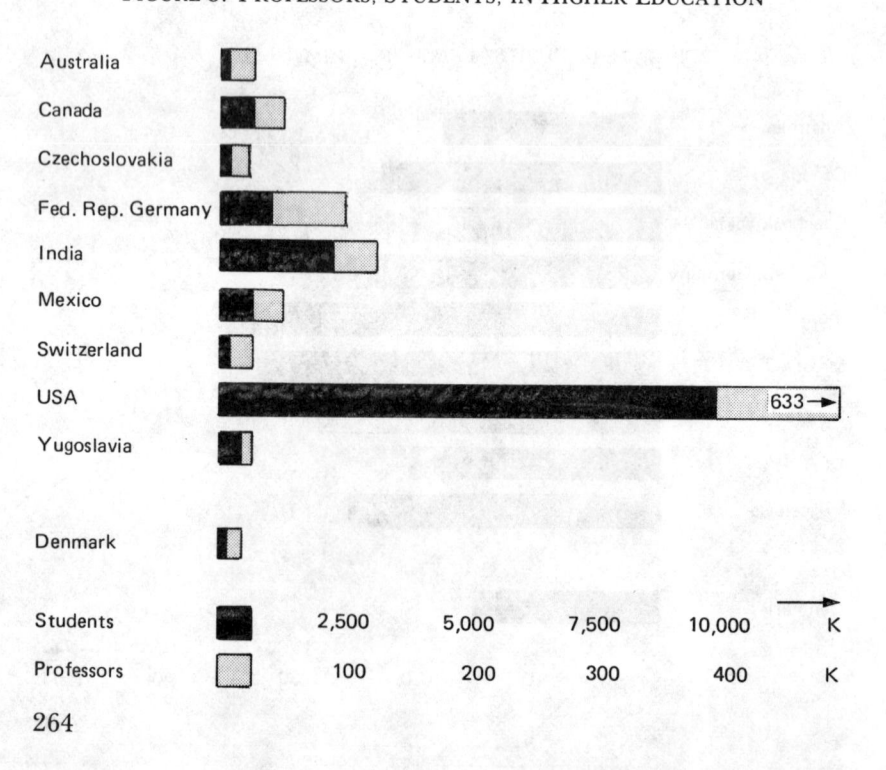

- Australia
- Canada
- Czechoslovakia
- Fed. Rep. Germany
- India
- Mexico
- Switzerland
- USA 633→
- Yugoslavia

- Denmark

Students   2,500   5,000   7,500   10,000   K
Professors   100   200   300   400   K

SUB-TOPIC 2(C): ACADEMIC PLANNING [*Kerwin*]

FIGURE 9: % OF POPULATION IN HIGHER EDUCATION

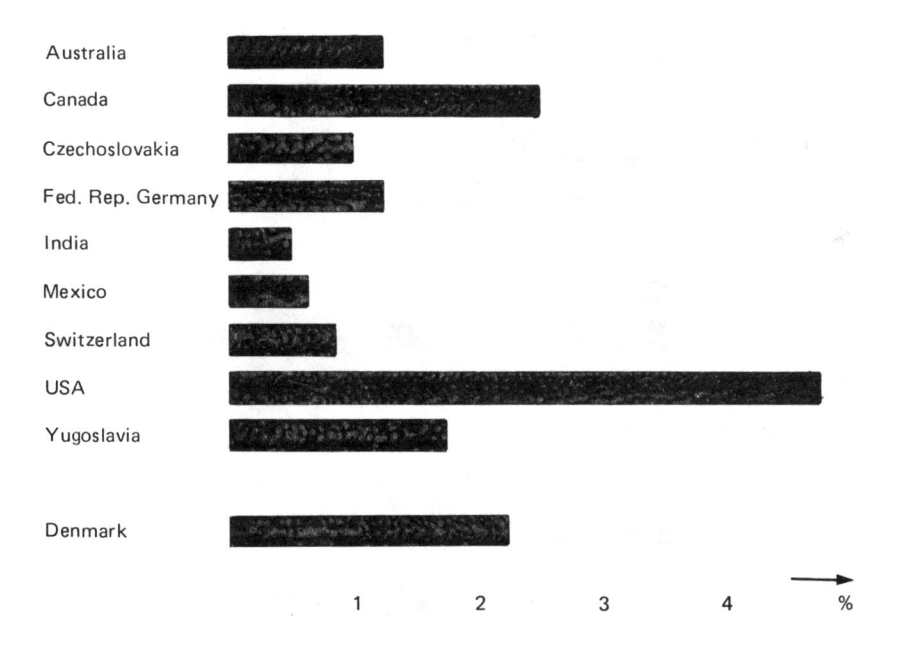

FIGURE 10: UNIVERSITY STUDENTS PER PROFESSOR

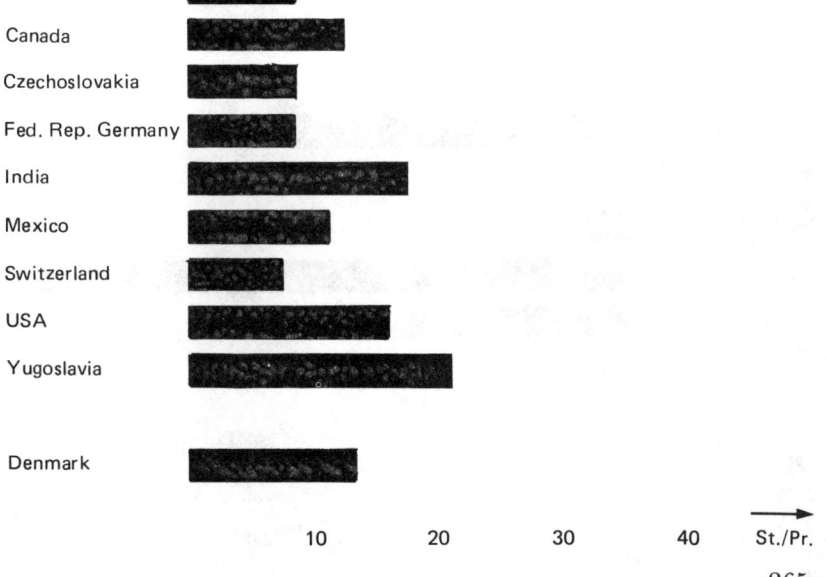

[Kerwin] TOPIC 2: COUNTRIES WITH FEDERAL GOVERNMENTS

FIGURE 11: GROSS NATIONAL PRODUCT PER CITIZEN

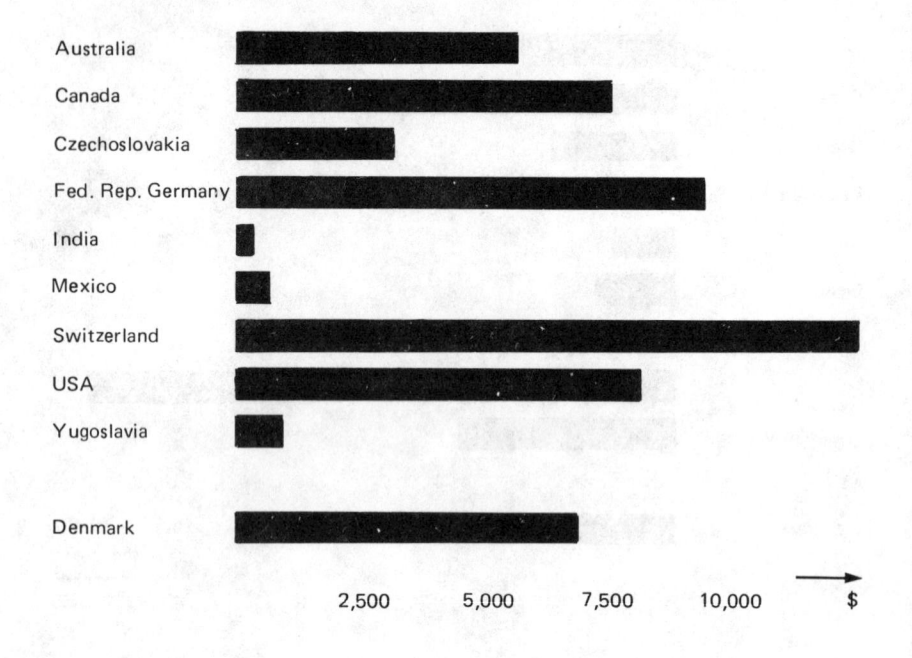

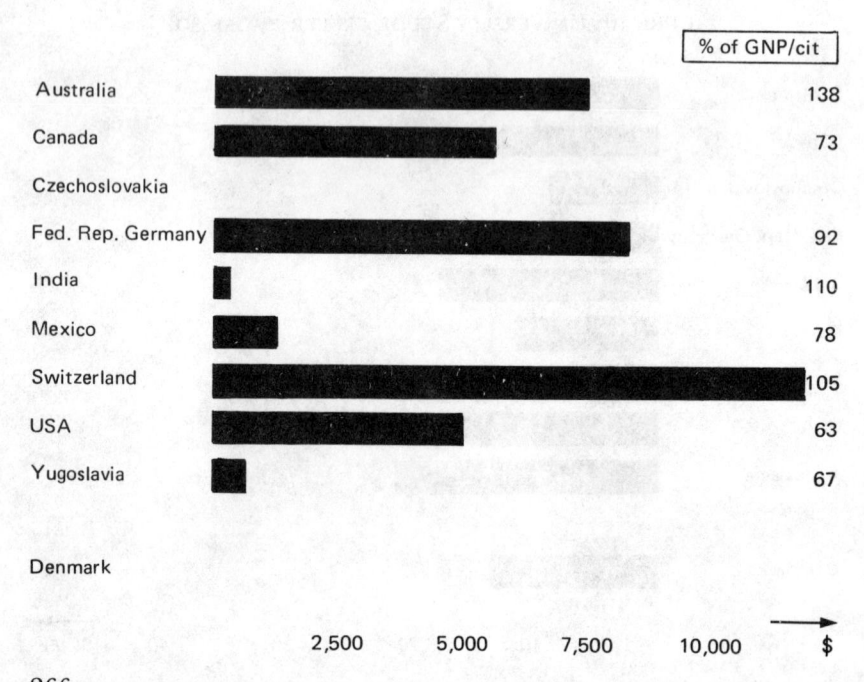

FIGURE 12: EXPENDITURE PER UNIVERSITY STUDENT

	% of GNP/cit
Australia	138
Canada	73
Czechoslovakia	
Fed. Rep. Germany	92
India	110
Mexico	78
Switzerland	105
USA	63
Yugoslavia	67
Denmark	

SUB-TOPIC 2(c): ACADEMIC PLANNING [*Kerwin*]

FIGURE 13: NO. OF UNIVERSITY STUDENTS PER M$ GNP

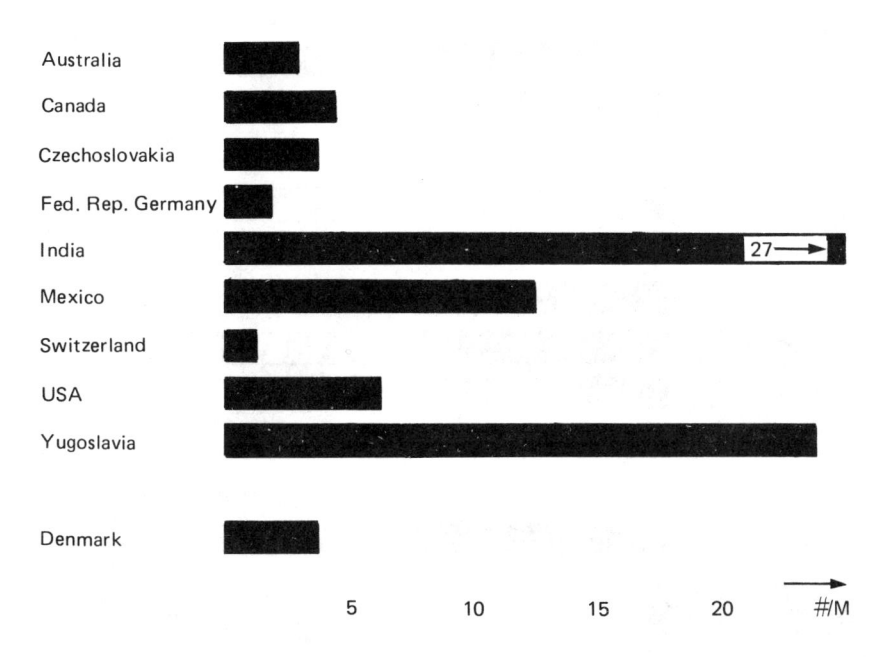

Country	
Australia	
Canada	
Czechoslovakia	
Fed. Rep. Germany	
India	27→
Mexico	
Switzerland	
USA	
Yugoslavia	
Denmark	

5   10   15   20   #/M

FIGURE 14: NUMBER OF GOVERNMENTS

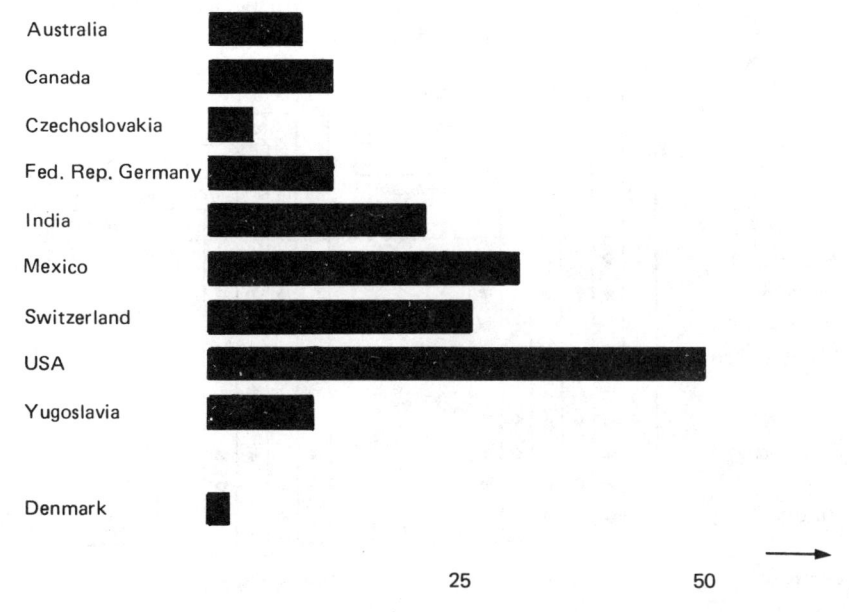

Country	
Australia	
Canada	
Czechoslovakia	
Fed. Rep. Germany	
India	
Mexico	
Switzerland	
USA	
Yugoslavia	
Denmark	

25   50

[*Kerwin*] TOPIC 2: COUNTRIES WITH FEDERAL GOVERNMENTS

FIGURE 15: SOURCES OF UNIVERSITY FINANCING

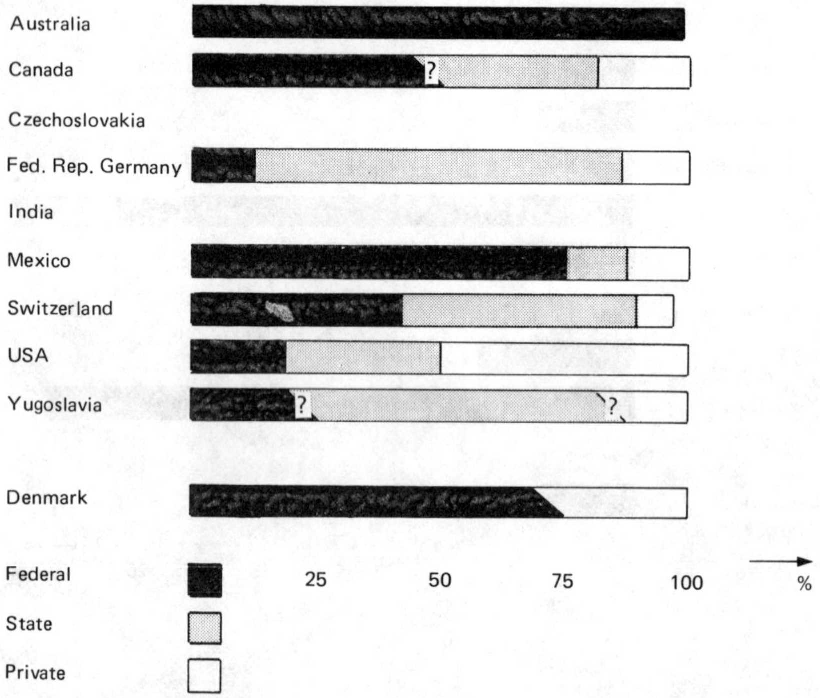

- Australia
- Canada
- Czechoslovakia
- Fed. Rep. Germany
- India
- Mexico
- Switzerland
- USA
- Yugoslavia

- Denmark

Federal ■ 25 50 75 100 %
State ▨
Private ☐

FIGURE 16: UNIVERSITY PLANNING AND CO-ORDINATION AGENCIES
(incomplete)

	Vice-Chancellors (National)	V.-C. (Regional)	V.-C. (State)	V.-C.+Federal	V.-C.+State	Federal	State	Fed.-State	State-State	V.-C. Fed.-St.
Australia	●	●	●			●	●	●		
Canada	●	●	●		●		●		●	
Czechoslovakia			●			●	●	●		
Fed. Rep. Germany	●	●				●	●	●	●	
India	●					●	●			
Mexico	●	●		●		●				
Switzerland	●			●	●	●	●	●		
USA	●	●	●	●		●	●			
Yugoslavia	●	●				●				
Denmark	● – – – –					● – – – –				

SUB-TOPIC 2(C): ACADEMIC PLANNING [Kerwin]

FIGURE 17: TENTATIVE ASSESSMENT

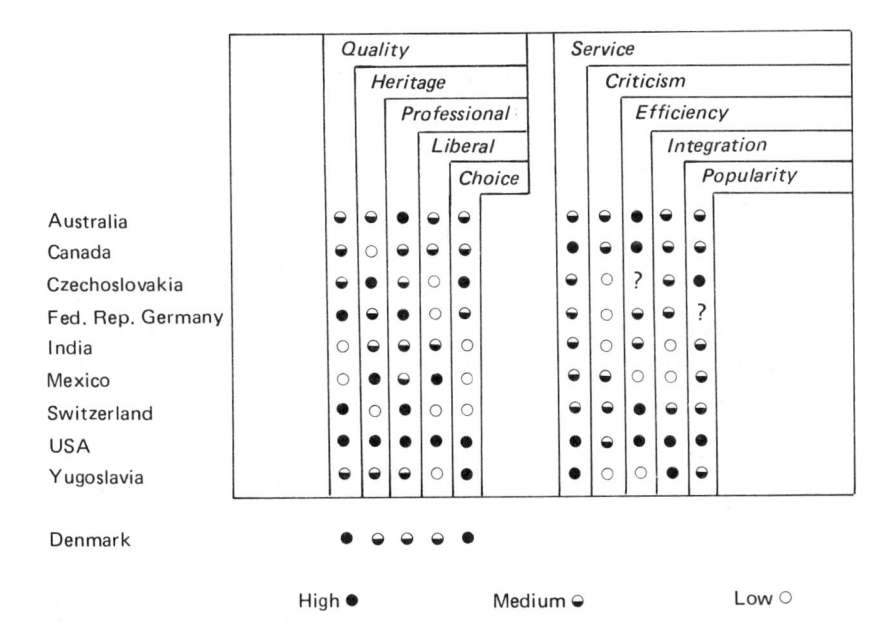

	Quality					Service				
		Heritage					Criticism			
			Professional					Efficiency		
				Liberal					Integration	
					Choice					Popularity
Australia	◕	◕	●	◕	◕	◕	◕	●	◕	◕
Canada	◕	○	◕	◕	◕	●	◕	●	◕	◕
Czechoslovakia	◕	●	◕	○	●	◕	○	?	◕	●
Fed. Rep. Germany	●	◕	●	○	◕	◕	○	◕	◕	?
India	○	◕	◕	◕	○	◕	○	◕	○	◕
Mexico	○	●	◕	●	○	◕	◕	○	○	◕
Switzerland	●	○	●	○	○	◕	◕	●	◕	◕
USA	●	●	●	●	●	●	◕	●	●	●
Yugoslavia	◕	◕	◕	○	●	●	○	○	●	◕
Denmark	●	◕	◕	◕	●					

High ●   Medium ◕   Low ○

Australia

Professor R. H. MYERS (*Vice-Chancellor and Principal of the University of New South Wales*): The Commonwealth of Australia came into being on the first day of this century, on 1 January, 1901. It brought together the six states which until then had been constitutionally independent. Under the constitution then adopted matters such as defence became the responsibility of the Commonwealth government; matters such as education remained with the states.

Education has continued to be, constitutionally, an area of state responsibility. In the last thirty years, however, the federal government has been increasingly concerned in the funding and planning of education. Its involvement began with universities; it has extended (but to different extents) to all levels of education.

This paper briefly traces the events of those thirty years, noting in them something of a pendulum movement—higher education at first entirely a state affair; then for a time and increasingly a federal matter; now an area of renewed interest and action by the states.

With the history brought up to date, the paper sketches some of the governmental agencies, federal and state, that now interact in the field of tertiary education; it notes how their activities affect academic planning and the affairs of the educational institutions themselves, and concludes with a glance at the future.

For the purposes of the paper three sectors of tertiary education are distinguished; universities, colleges of advanced education (the CAE sector) and colleges of technical and further education (the TAFE sector). Putting it very roughly, the universities provide for about 150,000 students in 19 institutions; the colleges of advanced education provide for about the same number in 88 colleges; the TAFE group cater for some 500,000 students in a large number of diverse institutions.

The paper is concerned primarily with the universities, secondarily with the CAE sector, and only in passing with TAFE.

The History to 1960

The first two of the Australian universities were founded in the mid-nineteenth century; they and those that came later were created, as self-governing corporate bodies, by acts of parliament. With the single exception of the Australian National University (set up by the federal government in Canberra, the national capital) they have been created by state legislatures.

Until the late 1940s the state universities were (apart from some private endowments, never large) state funded. State legislatures would occasionally comment on a university's affairs, but there was little state involvement in planning. Following world war two, as enrolments grew rapidly and the need for much larger numbers of graduates became apparent, the federal government began to interest itself in university education. Its role was limited to providing financial assistance. Planning was still left to the states, and, since the assistance was given on an annual basis, long-term planning was difficult.

There were, nevertheless, some important developments in this period; these included the creation or planning, by the states, of several new universities — my own university among them.

Shared Federal and State Responsibility: 1960 – 73

It was inevitable that the Commonwealth government, called upon for constantly increasing financial support of state universities, would involve itself also in the planning of university education on the national level. In 1959, following an inquiry chaired by Sir Keith Murray, then chairman of the UGC in Britain, the federal government established the Australian Universities Commission. The Commission was to concern itself both with funding and with planning the balanced and co-ordinated development of the universities.

The Commission operated on a triennial basis. Its financial recommendations covered the total financial programmes of universities, but the provision of full federal contributions depended on the payment of specified matching grants by the states. The establishment of this Commission began a period, which continued until 1974, of joint federal and state responsibility for the planning and financing of university education.

It was also inevitable that the Commonwealth would concern itself with other areas of tertiary education and in 1961 it appointed a wide-ranging inquiry 'to consider the pattern of tertiary education in relation to the needs and resources of Australia and to make recommendations... on the future development of tertiary education'. Following this inquiry the Commonwealth established an Advisory Committee (later to become a statutory Commission) on Advanced Education, with a role in non-university higher education parallel to that of the Universities Commission. A federal Commission for Technical and Further Education was also established in 1973 although its role was to assist the states in its sector rather than to be responsible for total financing and planning.

Federal Responsibility: 1974 and after

With the election of the federal labour party to government late in 1972 major changes in the Commonwealth role in education took place. In particular the Commonwealth assumed full financial responsibility for the university and CAE sectors from January, 1974.

This expansion of the federal role was generally welcomed by the states, although it greatly diminished their role in planning; indeed many decisions were then made by federal authorities and announced before the state bodies were aware of them. But with the return to government of the liberal-country party coalition in 1975 there has been closer consultation, especially because the new government has sought to contain public expenditure and to effect greater co-ordination and rationalisation.

While the universities generally have dealt directly with the Australian Universities Commission, the colleges have not dealt in a similarly direct way with the Commission on Advanced Education. In each state (but one) there has been, for some time, a state instrumentality to co-ordinate the planning of advanced education and to interact with the federal authority. This was partly because of their number—88—as compared with 19 universities, and also because they have always been state controlled and have not had the autonomy of the universities.

Tertiary Education Commission

The expansion of higher education in the 1960s and early 1970s resulted in much duplication of courses between the sectors and in the creation of an unnecessarily large number of CAEs and of courses in the CAEs. The procedures under which the three separate commissions operated made balanced and co-ordinated planning difficult, especially in such fields as teacher education which concerned all three.

For these reasons, and because the tightening economic situation called for even more careful use of resources, the Commonwealth government in 1977 established the Tertiary Education Commission (TEC) and replaced each of the three existing commissions by a council responsible to the TEC.

The prime function of the new Commission is to advise the Commonwealth government on the provision and allocation of financial assistance for universities, colleges of advanced education and institutions of technical and further education. It is required to promote the balanced and co-ordinated development of tertiary education as a whole.

State Government Authorities

The TEC is also required to consult the relevant state authorities responsible for co-ordinating tertiary education. These have, in most cases and for some time, been concerned more particularly with the colleges, but recent developments are tending to extend their responsibilities to all sectors of post-secondary education, including universities.

An illustration of the reasoning behind the establishment of state higher education authorities concerned with all post-secondary education is seen in Victoria where the minister for education, introducing in April, 1978, a bill to establish a state post-secondary education commission, said:

> 'The [Partridge] Committee concluded that co-ordination and rationalisation of post-secondary education was now of paramount importance to ensure that the resources available were

used to best advantage in serving the educational interest of the whole community.

Separate development of the several sectors in the past has led to duplication of courses and over-supply of opportunities and facilities in some fields of post-secondary education and insufficient development of others. To avoid continuation of these it was considered necessary to establish a single organisation with the capacity to review the whole of post-secondary education in Victoria and to evolve a coherent policy which would match resources for each sector to the real educational needs of the community.'

Planning within the Context of Federal and State Authorities

Finances. Triennial funding ended abruptly in 1975, when (at a time of financial crisis) the Commonwealth government put aside the Commission's recommendations for 1976–78 and approved funding for 1976 only. Since then funding has been on the basis of a rolling triennium: a firm level of funding for the first year, and the levels for the later years subject to annual review.

Longer-term planning under these conditions has been very difficult. In particular the planning of new programmes requires some assurance of funds for several years, since the full costs of a new activity are incurred two or three years after it has begun. Similarly some extended assurance is essential for the rationalisation of courses and institutions, where careful planning over lengthy periods is needed.

The TEC has recognised that funding on this basis 'makes considered planning virtually impossible' and that the tightness of the annual cycle of reviews does not permit proper consultation between the Commission, its councils, the state authorities and the institutions; it urged the Commonwealth government to return to triennial funding for recurrent expenditure. The government has just announced its adoption of this recommendation, a decision of great importance to the universities even though the recurrent funds now promised for the triennium will be virtually static in real terms.

The universities receive block grants for recurrent purposes and they have exercised considerable autonomy in developing new proposals, although they have needed Commission approval for major or expensive activities, such as a new faculty, or for activities which would duplicate work undertaken elsewhere. Generally speaking it has not been obligatory for them to consult state authorities.

The colleges of advanced education have not enjoyed any similar autonomy. For them funding has been related to enrolments in approved courses, with the Commission giving special weight to the views of state authorities.

Roles of state regulatory bodies. While the TEC is proposing to introduce new procedures for the approval of new programmes it still envisages dealing directly with universities but will deal with state authorities in relation to colleges of advanced education. It might therefore be said that, for universities, obtaining approval for new developments in the federal system has been little different from what it would be in a non-federal system, since only one approving authority has been involved. On the other hand colleges of advanced education have to deal with both state and federal authorities and it is more difficult for them to attain the degree of autonomy they consider desirable for an institution of higher education.

There are signs, however, that university activities also may come under closer scrutiny at the state level. The bill (mentioned earlier) introduced a few months ago into the Victorian parliament for the establishment of a post-secondary education commission provided for universities to obtain the approval of that commission for new courses of study and academic awards, for staff establishments and even for submissions for funds to the TEC. The universities objected vigorously to the proposed legislation and a revised bill was brought forward. In the new version approvals by the state body will not be required, but notice of proposed new courses or major changes must be given to afford the state commission an opportunity to comment.

In South Australia a committee of enquiry has recommended the establishment of a tertiary education authority with powers that include 'to approve any proposed new course in a tertiary institution'. And, again, the two universities in Western Australia have been advised by the post-secondary education commission in that state that universities would now be invited to submit new course proposals for its approval.

It seems probable, therefore, that Australian universities will have increasingly to deal with both state and federal authorities. Such an arrangement would be consistent with the developments taking place in federal-state relationships generally (the 'new federalism'), which envisage an increased role for the states — and more accountability at both levels in spending the taxpayers' dollars.

One of the difficulties of the dual system is that state and federal authorities may have different and conflicting aims for higher education. At present the Commonwealth government is looking especially at economic considerations in the planning of higher education and is setting financial limitations for its development, with rather less regard for research and research training and for higher education simply as an agent for the advancement of knowledge. But at the state level, where the costs of higher education do not have to be met, different aims may be in mind. The pressures of the electorate may be such that social demands and local needs will be given most weight.

There will be problems, again, where there are differences between the political philosophies of the Commonwealth and state governments. This would be reflected, for example, in differences between federal and state criteria for new academic programmes.

New institutions—test cases. Conflict between Commonwealth and state governments has generally been about the establishment of new institutions, or the amalgamation of existing institutions, rather than about new programmes or the expansion of existing courses. This might suggest, incidentally, that state involvement in the planning of higher education tends to be especially where political (electoral) considerations are seen to be paramount.

However that may be, with the move from shared funding to the assumption of full financial responsibility by the Commonwealth, the source of proposals for new institutions has shifted from the states to the federal authorities, with the latter exercising greater authority.

For example, the two federal commissions were asked late in 1972 to report on the location, nature and development of tertiary education institutions in and near the Melbourne and Sydney metropolitan areas and in the region of Albury-Wodonga, adjoining border towns between New South Wales and Victoria. The federal bodies in a joint report recommended that a university should be established in a region east of Melbourne. Their report noted that the Victorian government had already decided to establish a multi-campus university in three cities to the south-west, west and north-west of Melbourne; but the state's decision, although noted, seemed to have been largely ignored in the federal report. It was, however, acknowledged that the establishment of the multi-campus institution could influence the time of establishing the new university recommended by the federal authorities.

It was in any case necessary for the Victorian government to obtain federal funds (and therefore approval) for the multi-campus institution it had decided on. The Universities Commission considered the Victorian government's proposal and concluded that, on purely educational grounds, the Commonwealth government should not support the establishment of a university in any of the three cities but should rather merge the two existing colleges of advanced education in each city so that each would become a major college of advanced education. But, taking account of the Victorian government's decentralisation arguments, the Commission did conclude that federal financial support could be justified for a single-campus university in one of the cities, Geelong.

In the outcome a university, Deakin University, has been established in that city, absorbing the two existing colleges of advanced education, while in each of the other two cities the existing colleges have been merged into single institutions. But the significance of the example is that the notion of absorbing colleges into a new institution, or of merging the existing institutions in the three cities, was not part of the Victorian government's proposal but arose on the initiative of the federal Commission.

In New South Wales the state government decided that Wollongong Teachers' College should become part of the University of Wollongong and asked the Commonwealth to arrange for funds allocated to the Teachers' College to be paid to the University of Wollongong after the amalgamation. The federal Commission supported the amalgamation provided that 'the University were not permanently committed to the retention of the whole academic staff of the Teachers' College', such retention having been part of the state government proposal. This proviso was unacceptable to the state and the amalgamation did not proceed.

These and other examples where the Commonwealth government has overridden state wishes are clear cases where 'he who pays the piper calls the tune'.

Major new academic programmes. The provision of expensive programmes, for example in medicine, dentistry and veterinary science, has also been decided on reports of the AUC, admittedly after consultation with the states and the institutions involved. The AUC has also taken up the expansion of extra-mural degree courses, the expansion of the output of professional manpower in social welfare, the provision for training teachers of handicapped children, the teaching of community medicine in medical schools, the establishment of clinical pharmacology and of Asian languages and cultures and languages and linguistics in general. There are, on the other hand, few examples where academic programmes have resulted from state initiatives.

Industrial matters. During the last few years academic staff associations and other trade unions have become better organized; they are now in a position to exercise a significant influence in academic planning.

At first salaries were the main issue but recently security of tenure, fixed-term contract appointments, superannuation and study leave have come to the fore; also, with the stabilising of enrolments and the changing subject preferences of students, the prospect of some universities and colleges having to 'let people go' is causing concern. Issues such as these will greatly complicate the management of higher education in a dual system and in a no-growth era; they could seriously limit the capacity of universities and colleges to adjust promptly to changing community needs.

The complexities imposed by a federal-state system in these circumstances are well illustrated by the story of academic salary fixation during the 1960s and 1970s. Since 1964 there has been national uniformity in academic salary scales. Salaries were adjusted following federal reviews and then, in 1974, an academic salaries tribunal was established at the federal level. The tribunal cannot, as a federal body, determine the academic salaries payable to the states, but it recommends to the Commonwealth the salary scales to be used in determining the recurrent grants to universities. If universities decide to pay rates higher than those recommended they will not receive federal funds to meet the difference.

The tribunal's jurisdiction also covers CAEs, and here another difficulty recently came up. After a major review of salaries, the rates for college staff were challenged in the Western Australian industrial authority by a registered staff association. The state authority agreed to a variation from the national rates, a decision which involved additional salary costs for the colleges.

Recently in several states the academic staff associatic s have obtained registration with the industrial authorities and it is possible that other variations from nationally set salary levels, upon which recurrent grants are based, could develop.

Trade union action is also an issue of current importance in relation to salaries of non-teaching staff, the cost of which accounts for about 35% of recurrent expenditure of universities. There is an action before the federal industrial court to obtain national registration of trade unions covering non-teaching staff and to seek decisions on a nationally-based log of claims; the outcome might have serious implications for costs in universities. In one state the government is challenging the legality of granting federal recognition to a union in the 'industry' of education.

These actions vividly illustrate the consequences of operating in a federal system under economic and industrial pressures. On the one hand academic salaries and related matters, settled by individual universities in the light of federal decisions for two decades past, are now, because of constitutional limitations, likely to become the business of individual state instrumentalities even though the funding will still be from the Commonwealth government. On the other hand non-teaching staff, traditionally covered by state-based trade unions working to state industrial awards, are now moving into the federal arena where, as most believe, there is no constitutional barrier to the granting of a federal award.

Apart from the perplexities they generate, these complications of the dual system are imposing a heavy load on university managements and on academic planners generally.

The Future

There is likely to be increased pressure from the Commonwealth for co-ordination and rationalisation and for detailed financial accountability—even though universities already operate under stringent auditing procedures controlled by state governments. These pressures arise from the present economic situation and from the government's firm desire to contain and if possible to reduce expenditure for higher education.

The Commonwealth government's decision to hold an inquiry into study (sabbatical) leave for academics was an illustration of the present mood. This action, which could lead to significant restriction on the rights of universities to determine the conditions of academic staff employment, is being hotly contested.

It does, however, appear that in exercising a greater degree of control the Commonwealth government will be seeking the co-operation of state authorities and that the degree of involvement of the universities and colleges with both the federal and state authorities, on a whole range of issues which hitherto have not attracted their attention, will inevitably be greater.

Academic bodies will need to recognise that they can no longer count on the degree of insulation that has protected them from government and community probing. They will need to be more thorough-going in evaluating their educational programmes and in managing the resource re-allocation needed for new academic developments within a static, or maybe a reduced, budget. Universities will need to work even more closely together, in both state and federal groupings, if they are to succeed in maintaining their essential character in these challenging circumstances.

Conclusion

Although there is a thread of concern for the future running through this paper it would be unfair to politicians and governments not to record with gratitude the high degree of respect they have had, for well over a century, for the independence and autonomy of universities in Australia. If there is some faltering just now, perhaps the following quotation from a recent speech by the Hon. Harry C. Parrott, Ontario Minister of Colleges and Universities, will point out the way afresh to today's and tomorrow's holders of parliamentary (and academic) office:

> 'When tough decisions are needed, it's tempting to demand increased government involvement in setting the future direction and policies of the universities, but to start down that road — and I shall resist such a move every step of the way — is for the universities to abandon their essential academic freedom. If others insist on government involvement, they will find that government becomes empowered to question and regulate all aspects of university operations. Government scrutiny might fall, for example, on the rights of faculty members to tenure; the extent of university research; and how many new faculty should be hired, and who they should be. This is not government's role nor should it ever be'.

Postscript — The Williams Report

In 1977 the Commonwealth government set up an inquiry into education and training. The committee, chaired by Professor Bruce Williams, is expected to submit its report in July, 1978. Many matters important for post-secondary education will be covered: manpower planning, the roles of university, CAE and TAFE sectors, the roles of governments in education, the need for research, and the performance of educational institutions in teaching and community service. The report will certainly influence all educational planning in Australia for the rest of the century.

DISCUSSION

Presenting his paper (see above), Professor *L. Kerwin* (Laval) called members' attention to the very few — if any — examples of planning which involved a tripartite interaction between federal, state and institutional systems.

Professor *J. F. Ade Ajayi* (Lagos), speaking on his paper (see above), questioned whether within a federal system it was ever possible to separate planning from control; he expressed some doubt whether Nigeria, as one form of federal system, had yet evolved an effective planning system. Rational planning in a federal system, he argued, must be sharply circumscribed by the ways in which different levels of government interacted, and thus in Nigeria it was as much local interests as analytic deliberation which had affected decisions over, for example, the siting of the new institutions or the location of expensive academic enterprises. He was concerned that planning which was determined largely by political imperatives would be excessive and superficial.

In presenting and illustrating his paper (see above) Professor *R. H. Myers* (New South Wales) argued that the Australian system left university institutions with a fair measure of autonomy and with a modest level of state intervention; the alternative—college—system in Australia was subject to much closer state control.

Mr. R. K. Chhabra (University Grants Commission, India) outlined the formal processes of university planning in India and commented particularly on the correlation between quality and the wealth of the university, itself independent of government planning. He questioned whether the quality of American universities was a consequence of the federal nature of government in the United States.

In the ensuing discussion it was argued that in developed countries the quality of a university did not necessarily depend on the intervention of government, but there was challenge to Professor Kerwin's argument in favour of minimal governmental planning, as inapplicable to universities in the developing world. There was much discussion on the point that government planning and intervention was, within a federal system, inevitable and commonly necessary, but that it was not necessarily incompatible with the character of the university given that effective control over admission, over the content of courses and over the evaluation of results remained in academic hands.

Members were much exercised by Professor Kerwin's argument that 'no planning was better than governmental planning' and his claim for the status of the individual university as the optimal planning unit. In response to question he agreed that these judgements, which were both personal and subjective, turned largely on his own appraisal of the effectiveness of the university system in the United States, where planning by federal government was minimal. Several members of the group raised counter-argument to this point.

Topic 2

HIGHER EDUCATION IN COUNTRIES WITH FEDERAL SYSTEMS OF GOVERNMENT

Continuation of Discussion

Chairman: Professor O. ABOYADE
Vice-Chancellor of the University of Ife

Rapporteur: Mr. A. CHRISTODOULOU
Secretary of the Open University

Thursday, 24 August

There being no particular sub-topic for discussion, the group set itself the overall objective of (*a*) attempting to gather together the various threads of discussion over the previous sessions which had concentrated on questions relating to financing, mobility of staff and students, and academic planning; and (*b*) setting the points previously made in the context both of the overall theme of the conference and of the other main topics, with particular reference to: (i) reconciling equality and excellence; (ii) the public view of universities; (iii) planning across the whole sector, both university and non-university, of higher education.

In preliminary discussion it was generally agreed that if universities have an essential character that was worth preserving (and few, if any, speakers wished to challenge this) a key question to be answered was whether the fact that federal forms of government existed in some countries threw up special problems for universities in reconciling their severally accepted roles and obligations: to their local community and governmental agencies responsible for its affairs; to their national community and federal political institution; and to the international 'republic of scholarship and learning'.

Some speakers urged caution in approaching the problems in this way, since these roles could often be performed without tension and conflict between them; there was nevertheless a reasonable consensus that, in some developing countries with particular social and/or 'nationalistic' problems, particular forms of federalism could emerge where universities could only with extreme difficulty succeed in satisfying expectations held of them by state legislatures and their local communities and by federal government and overall considerations of national policy—largely because in such countries universities were seen as an essential element in regional development plans and overall national economic development plans, if not also as a prime tool in 'social engineering' in extending opportunities to wide sections of the community.

One general conclusion from which few demurred was that the meeting should be urged to avoid the dangers of formulating a broad generalisation to the effect that federalism posed for universities a unique and consistent set of problems in reconciling their various roles and preserving their essential character—(*a*) there were various forms of federalism, which differed from each other in the distribution of political powers and funding responsibilities as between federal government agencies and state/provincial government agencies; (*b*) within these different forms the expected or 'decreed' role for universities could be heavily influenced in diverse ways by factors other than simply academic ones. The situation in Canada could not, for example, be readily compared with that in the USA or Australia, if only because of the anglophone/francophone set of problems. Each country would therefore inevitably have its own set of problems depending on the nature of its federal structure and the underlying reasons that determined its objectives and its precise form.

Conversely it was also generally agreed that federalism could throw up a different range of problems for universities, the nature of which would vary from country to country according to its stage of development, the homogeneity or heterogeneity of its social structure and its immediate ambitions on a national as well as regional scale. In effect the only valid overall conclusion that could be urged on the meeting had to be along such lines, recognising that the more important considerations were likely to arise out of questions relating to whether there were particular language problems to be resolved (c.f. Quebec and Wales), culture traditions to be maintained (c.f. Wales and Northern Nigeria), regional economic imbalances to be resolved, etc.—all of which would need to be seen in the context of the actual distribution of constitutional power and authority between any one federal government and its constituent states or provinces.

A further major consideration would then be at what level—federal or state/province—was the educational system of the country being planned, effectively funded, and supervised, and the extent to which the universities in that country had an effective and persuasive voice in determining the shape of those plans. Without such dynamic participation in planning they could become mere creatures of current governmental policies.

Finally the group endorsed a proposal to urge upon the Congress the importance and value of special studies and research intended in each country to identify the critical factors affecting universities in countries with federal systems of government; and perhaps undertake a further examination of these on a co-operative basis at the next Congress. Though members thought this had been a less rarified and more practical topic than others at this Congress, the topic chairman (Dr. Steven Watson) argued that for any similar discussion in the future members might find it expedient to undertake more preparatory studies of their own: work on the

CONTINUATION OF DISCUSSION

report being produced by Dr. Perkins and his associates would, for instance, have been useful advance reading. He wondered if this discussion had not been the precursor of others, perhaps at the next Congress, on the general theme of the accountability of universities to their local communities, their country, and the international community of scholars.

Group Discussions

TOPIC 3
RECONCILING EQUALITY AND EXCELLENCE

Chairman: Dr. A. T. PORTER
Vice-Chancellor of the University of Sierra Leone

Editorial Co-ordinator: Mr. M. BAATZ
Registrar of the University of Leicester

		page
Sub-Topic 3(a)	STANDARDS OF ADMISSION AND THEIR EFFECTS ON SECONDARY EDUCATION	
	Opening Speakers	
	Professor Z. R. Siddiqui	287
	Mr. R. Toomey	291
	Professor R. F. Whelan	299
	Discussion	314
Sub-Topic 3(b)	WHAT RANGE OF LEARNING IS APPROPRIATE TO THE UNIVERSITY?	
	Opening Speakers	
	Dr. A. A. Bruneau	318
	Dr. J. M. Mwanza	324
	Professor N. M. Swani	332
	Discussion	340
Sub-Topic 3(c)	STANDARDS OF EDUCATION AND GRADUATION	
	Opening Speakers	
	Professor D. J. Gifford	344
	Dr. D. T. Kenny	348
	Discussion	355
Sub-Topic 3(d)	MOBILITY OF STUDENTS AND STAFF INTERNATIONALLY	
	Opening Speakers	
	Professor Sir David Derham	359
	Dr. J. A. Perkins	365
	Dr. F. Thistlethwaite	372
	Discussion	381

For index to names, see p. 655

Sub-Topic 3(a)

STANDARDS OF ADMISSION AND THEIR EFFECTS ON SECONDARY EDUCATION

Chairman: Dr. T. H. B. SYMONS
Honorary Treasurer, Association of Commonwealth Universities

Rapporteur: Mr. S. K. KWAN
Vice-Chancellor of the University of Singapore

Monday, 21 August

Professor Z. R. SIDDIQUI (*Vice-Chancellor of Jahangirnagar University*): In an international assembly like this a speaker is faced with one initial difficulty, irrespective of the topic of discussion. If his experience is limited to the situation obtaining in his country, as is the case with me, he can speak with reasonable certitude, keeping only that particular situation in view. His knowledge of other systems and other situations is more or less derived from second-hand sources. The awareness that systems and situations vary widely, and sometimes so widely indeed as to make comparisons almost irrelevant, can only add to his agony.

This is not to claim that the situation prevailing in the speaker's own country is free from complications. I shall soon be touching upon some of these in my own country—Bangladesh. Before I do so it seems I can, and perhaps I should, make one observation which, even with my limitations, appears safe. In some nations, euphemistically called 'developing', the present state of secondary education is so unsatisfactory that the nation's primary concern is taken up with issues more basic than the ones we have chosen for discussion. This will be true of many nations in South Asia and perhaps of Africa. Naturally enough the question of standards of admission at the secondary stage figures less prominently than it does for the tertiary system, in the less developed areas of the world.

I can try to explain this, without claiming any fullness for my explanation. In a backward economy education is only vaguely related to future career. In an agro-based economy this is all the more true. In a nation where at least 80% of the population is engaged in agriculture of a primitive sort even primary education is not considered necessary for a living. But since the country (I mean Bangladesh) is thickly populated and there is usually a village school within walking distance, substantially more than half the children of the relevant age group are actually enrolled. But the drop-out rate is appalling. It has been calculated that the drop-out rate is the highest in the second year, as high as about 40% of the original enrolment. By the time the student is in his fifth year it drops to somewhere around one third of the original number.

At the end of five years, therefore, with this reduced number of students and another substantial number finally stepping out of education, the pressure for admission to secondary schools is considerably less. But the urban situation here is markedly different from the rural situation. And within the urban areas, especially the larger cities, the pressure is considerably higher on the 'better' schools than on the average. In a recent survey conducted on the schools of the metropolitan city of Dacca this difference came out in sharp relief. It was found that no student was finally denied a place in one of the schools, though the school might not have been the school of his first or even his second or third choice.

In our Bangladesh situation the vast majority of the secondary-stage students are enrolled as day scholars in the local school, that is, the school within a few miles of their homes. The number of schools where a place is sought and has to be denied is comparatively small, perhaps not more than 15% of the total number. Tuition fees being the main source of revenue for the majority of the schools (virtually all the schools in rural areas), the concept of selective or competitive admission does not exist for these. It is only the better schools in bigger towns and the few residential schools (with board and lodging) that impose an admission test for the entrants.

As at the primary stage, so at the secondary, uniformity of curriculum has failed to ensure a reasonable uniformity of standard. And the reason goes much beyond the existing difference between the urban and the rural situations. Economic status and family background also play their parts. The better schools have little in common with the average, and even less in common with the below average. And this is inevitably reflected in the attainment of the student belonging to a particular school.

Under the existing situation only a fraction of the students at the secondary level in a developing country have a reasonable chance of attaining the excellence that nature promised them at birth. The rest cannot attain it for sheer lack of opportunity, for the simple fact that the only school their parents can afford to send them to is either poorly staffed or overcrowded or lacking in facilities, or all of these together. The secondary system itself, which provides for a diversity of streams from class IX onwards, aggravates the problem. The science stream, for example, draws about 15% of the students at this stage; the majority of the remaining opts for—as a matter of fact has no option but to go in for—the humanities; and the rest to some minor streams. Many schools in rural areas cannot offer science courses for lack of funds. Not only has the student—the average student coming from an average, that is, a poor, family—no choice of schools, he has in many cases no choice of courses either. The constraint has inevitably created a situation of inequality in a nation otherwise homogeneous—culturally, racially and linguistically—where all institutions are open to all.

The wisdom of this diversification has been challenged in recent years, though the Education Commission in its report (May, 1974) had endorsed it. The Curriculum Committee, an offshoot of the Commission's report, has reversed the existing scheme and has recommended a return to the general stream, seeking to strike a balance between the arts and the sciences, making both compulsory for all. This may, if the recommendations are accepted, strike at the idea of élitism in so far as it is enshrined in the curriculum, and ensure that the somewhat unfair basis of evaluation between students belonging to different streams is made straight.

But élitism has other sources more difficult to attack. In a situation where good schools are few and only a few in the community have the means to reach them, the élitist school is bound to prosper. The rub lies in this, that these again are the schools financed by the state exchequer, and the resources of the same, after meeting the demands of the government schools, are doled out thinly to the vast majority of the non-government schools. Contrary to the situation in many wealthy nations, the private school in a poor country is a school for the poor. The élitist school is in a position to ensure a reasonable excellence because its admission policy is determined by both merit and money. From the level of this school to the level of the poor school in a rural area the decline is disturbingly sharp. Naturally enough this is reflected in the results of the public school examination at the end of the tenth and twelfth years. The published results show at one extreme 100% success (or nearly so) with the majority in the first division, and at the other extreme 10% success with no-one in the first division, some in the second and the majority in the third. This means that all students from the élitist school will qualify for the tertiary stage of education, and hardly any from the latter. To any observer this is a reflection of the inequality more of opportunities than of merit.

I am aware that all I have said so far sounds like a country report which, as I warned you earlier, was unavoidable. The polarization of talent and opportunity, acceptable to a degree at the tertiary stage, is obviously intolerable in its present form at the secondary. Introduction of a uniform curriculum, mentioned earlier, will surely reduce the present inequality to a certain extent. But so long as the vast majority of the schools are not helped with money and materials the situation remains unchanged. A more balanced resource allocation to this sector, and a reasonable pay structure for the traditionally ill-paid schoolteacher, a more vigorous scheme for teacher training, are some of the remedies that are under the active consideration of the government. Further decentralisation of secondary education on the administrative plane has been suggested, in recent years, as one of the means to improve the lot of the rural school. But the basic difference between a school fully supported by the government and a school only partially and inadequately supported goes so deep that there are virtually two types of secondary education, judged from the point of view of quality. Even as a relative concept, excellence in secondary education in a developing country has a strictly financial connotation, irrespective of whether the point of reference is the school or the teacher or the student.

The span of secondary education, though basically a matter of educational structure, is also closely related to quality. It has been urged that five years of primary education is unsatisfactory and this should be raised to eight years. If it is also made through legislation both compulsory and free, as the Education Commission felt it should be, the secondary phase will automatically be reduced from its present seven years to a four-year span. This will also open up the possibility of converting the present intermediate colleges, identified with the last phase—classes XI and XII—of the secondary system, into full-fledged secondary schools with a four-year programme of study. The few existing institutions of this type all belong to the élitist group of schools. These are all superior schools with strictly limited enrolment, better finance and more qualified staff. Such standards with their accompanying excellence are not easily transferable to a large number of schools. Available resources, too, are not adequate for an immediate adoption of the scheme, but a phased adoption is both possible and desirable.

As long as this does not happen, secondary education in Bangladesh will continue to bear its present features, *viz.* deep inequality between the government and non-government schools, comparative backwardness of the village school, and a built-in disadvantage for the majority of students living in the rural areas. Phased nationalization is already an accepted principle but the pace is slow. There seems to be a consensus of opinion that the only way to reconcile the rival claims of equality and excellence in secondary education is through complete nationalization of the schools.

Mr. R. TOOMEY (*Under Secretary, Higher and Further Education, Department of Education and Science, Britain*): This paper looks at the question of standards of admission to universities and their effect on secondary education in the context of the position in Great Britain, and more particularly in England and Wales. This context, though restricted geographically, offers particular interest at the present time because the complex of issues involving university entrance requirements, the structure of school-leaving examinations, and the school curriculum, have for some time been under examination by the many interests concerned. This process is still going on and within a year or two crucial decisions have to be made. This is a good time to consider some of the problems involved.

Background

A distinctive feature of the British education service is that it works on the basis that responsibility for schools and further education is distributed between central government, the local education authorities and the teaching profession, while the universities, which are financed almost entirely from central government funds, operate as independent, autonomous institutions, solely responsible for deciding, amongst other things, which students to admit and what admission requirements to apply.

The curriculum in secondary schools up to the age of 16+ reflects the schools' traditional role of providing a broad general education. Legally the curriculum is the responsibility of local education authorities and school governors; in practice the content of the curriculum, teaching methods and the choice of teaching materials are left to the head teachers and their staffs. The Department of Education and Science does not, however, divest itself of responsibility for educational standards in the schools; within recent years, for example, it set up a committee of inquiry (the Bullock Committee) into reading and the use of English, and it has established an Assessment of Performance Unit (APU) within the Department. The task of the APU is to promote the development and use of better forms of assessment of pupils' achievement in schools, of monitoring standards, and identifying under-achievement among pupils of all levels of ability.

In general, secondary schools reflect the decentralised framework for the management of education and planning of the curriculum. But this is less true of education from the age of 16 onwards, that is to say, education in the sixth form, at least so far as those pupils undertaking General Certificate of Education (GCE) advanced-level courses are concerned. Somehow or other onto the flexible broad base of secondary education there has been grafted, one might say imposed, a rather narrow superstructure, closely related to the entrance requirements of the universities.

These requirements, which began to exert their influence towards the end of the nineteenth century, have themselves undergone significant changes. The early developments are well documented in a report on university entrance requirements in England and Wales issued by the UK Vice-Chancellors' Committee in 1962. After 1900, separate paths were followed by Oxford and Cambridge on the one hand and the other universities in England and Wales on the other. Outside Oxford and Cambridge the London matriculation examination provided the model on which university entrance requirements were based. Its essential components were a test in English, a foreign language and mathematics, designed to be taken after 4 or 5 years in secondary education, i.e. about the age of 16. It qualified the student to enter university and, in effect, take a bachelor's degree after 3 years. In 1918 the School Certificate examination, the precursor of the present General Certificate of Education ordinary level, was established by the central education department, then called the Board of Education. This was a school-leaving examination, but the universities agreed to accept it, with passes at credit level in stated subjects taken at one sitting, as exempting students from the matriculation examination. Then sixth forms began to be developed in grammar schools within the state system, and more and more pupils wishing to enter university started to follow a 2-year sixth-form course. Another tier was added to the school examination system, the Higher School Certificate, and a pattern developed whereby an increasing number of pupils in the grammar schools, after 2 years in the sixth form, presented 2 or 3 subjects in the Higher School Certificate at principal level. This gave rise to a situation where, in the 1920s and the 1930s, university entrance was obtained at two levels, i.e. by means of credit passes in the School Certificate and also by the Higher School Certificate, and sometimes by a combination of the two as prescribed by the university or the faculty. By 1950 or so the position had stabilised, and the normal pattern for those entering university was to do so after spending 2 years in the sixth form. The final stage, bringing us up to the present day, came with the introduction of the General Certificate of Education examination in 1950, at two levels, ordinary and advanced. This is a single subject examination, *i.e.* there is no compulsory grouping of subjects.

While these changes in the examination system were taking place an interaction was developing between that system and the entrance requirements of universities which influenced the shape and character of the sixth form in the grammar schools. These schools, for pupils up to the age of 16 or so, continued to provide the broad general education which was their main function; they carried these pupils up to the old matriculation standard. But increasingly, as universities refined their requirements and stated them in terms of performance at G.C.E. advanced level, education in the sixth form became more specialised, and was largely determined by these requirements. That is to say, examination performance served a double purpose — at the first stage it was a test of general education, but at the second stage it was a test of attainment in subjects that might be pursued in the undergraduate course at university.

Strands in the Present Pattern

It must, however, be recognised that university entrance requirements are only one strand in a complex pattern where responsibility for the school curriculum and examinations is widely dispersed, and where the nature of the sixth form is rapidly changing. Let us look briefly at these strands. Basic responsibility for the curriculum lies with the schools and the teachers, though, as I said earlier, legal responsibility lies with the local education authorities and the school governors. The General Certificate examination is operated by eight independent examining boards, of whom all except one have close links either with a single university or a group of universities; teachers are represented on the examining boards, and they exercise considerable influence. There is considerable variety in the syllabuses of the different boards, and a board may offer alternative syllabuses and papers in any one subject. Some co-ordination of the independent examining boards is carried out by the Schools Council for the Curriculum and Examinations, a body set up in 1964. One of its main responsibilities is to give advice to the Secretary of State for Education and Science on major policy issues relating to school examinations, and the Secretary of State must answer to parliament.

On the university side, each university has sole responsibility for prescribing its entrance requirements, but outside Oxford and Cambridge they now follow a common pattern of prescribing a general requirement, corresponding to matriculation, and a course requirement. In 1965, on the initiative of the Vice-Chancellors' Committee, the Standing Conference on University Entrance was established. This co-ordinates university policy on entrance requirements and acts as a link between the universities and the Schools Council.

The pattern is further complicated — and this may well prove to be a dominating factor — by the fact that university entrance requirements are, in effect, geared to a 3-year degree course, and the 3-year degree course is bolstered by the system of student support from public funds. That is to say, the student's grant is intended to see him through the course — in general, 3 years and no more. I am sure there would be strong resistance from central government to any appreciable extension of the length of the first degree course because of the vast additional expenditure that would be involved, both in supporting the students and in financing the institutions of higher education.

The various centres of influence and responsibility outlined above are probably having a greater effect than ever before in shaping the future pattern of the curriculum and examinations in the sixth form. What was formerly a process whereby universities exerted the dominant influence on sixth-form education is now a process of interaction between a number of different agencies.

Changing Pattern of the Sixth Form

The traditional sixth-form curriculum, then, is largely controlled by advanced (A) level examinations, and syllabuses organised by independent boards who are in turn subject to a variety of influences. Many students, after taking perhaps 8 subjects in the ordinary (O) level examination at the age of 16, are obliged to choose 2 or 3 subjects in an examination programme. The examination programme may be extended by a supplementary programme not leading to an examination, but the importance, and time, given to this supplementary programme vary considerably from one school to another.

At the same time the organisation and structure of secondary schools have changed considerably in the process of moving from a selective to a comprehensive system, and the A-level examination arrangements are not appropriate for all the pupils who now stay at school beyond the age of 16. Sixth forms no longer consist overwhelmingly of academically-minded pupils with the university as their goal. They contain in considerable numbers pupils who are staying on for one year only, following O-level courses or vocational courses leading to an examination; and, to a lesser extent, pupils studying post-O-level courses but without the university as their goal. So here we have a varied, and shifting, pattern while, on the other hand, the university interface has remained fairly stable. That is to say, admission to universities is still highly selective, there is competition between students and between institutions, and many degree courses are linear developments of sixth-form courses, *e.g.* mathematics, science and medicine.

Proposed Changes in the Examination Structure

A number of important proposals have been made by the Schools Council for changes in the national system of school examinations. Two were made in 1976. They were: —

(*a*) that a new examination, the Certificate of Extended Education (CEE) should be established. The CEE courses would be designed for young people who wish to remain in full-time education for one year after the age of 16, but who are not suited to A levels;

(*b*) that a common system of examining at 16+ should replace the present Certificate of Secondary Education (CSE), which is intended for less able students, and the General Certificate of Education O level.

But most important of all for our present purposes are the recent proposals to change radically the system of examination for sixth-form students at 18+ by basing it on five subjects to be examined at two levels—N (normal) and F (further). These have been developed because of dissatisfaction with the present sixth-form curriculum in that it is too narrow, forces pupils to make premature choices, and fails to take account of the widening range of ability in sixth forms as they grow in size. It should be emphasised that in all cases we are dealing with proposals which are at various stages of consideration, and that decisions on one set of examination proposals may affect the others.

Let us concentrate on the changes proposed at 18+. At present most sixth-form students take *three* subjects over a period of 2 years for examination at *one* level, *i.e.* A level. Under these latest proposals students would take *five* subjects to be examined at *two* levels, N(normal) and F(further). Each N subject would require half, and each F subject three-quarters, of the study time at present devoted to an A-level subject. It is intended that students should not take more than two subjects at F level. The total time given to three N and two F subjects would be the same as that now taken by three A levels. If this expectation were realised the present division between time spent working for examinations (about 70%) and time spent on other matters would remain unchanged.

So far as the schools are concerned the immediate issues which arise are whether educational standards would be affected, and whether additional pressures would be placed on resources available to the schools. So far as the universities are concerned the proposals call for a re-examination of their entrance requirements, and they could affect the length of first degree courses.

Implications for the Universities and Other Users

The educational arguments in favour of broadening the curriculum in the sixth form are very strong, but it is doubtful whether fundamental changes can be made in the curriculum unless they are matched by, or brought about by, fundamental changes in the examination system. Universities will no doubt be considering under what circumstances N (normal) and F (further) levels would be acceptable as a preparation for specialist degree work; and whether the normal length of a degree course could remain 3 years. Closely linked with this is the problem of the variety in existing A-level syllabuses in some subjects, and the need for some degree of standardisation. If greater progress were made towards a common-core syllabus, especially where degree courses build directly on sixth-form courses, it would mean that universities would be asked to take students who had a less extensive introduction to their degree subject, but one which was more uniform than at present, and less effort would have to be expended in bringing first-year students to the same starting point. If the proposals prove acceptable to the universities the extent of change in the curriculum could still be limited by the way in which entrance requirements were framed. For example, if entry to a science course required a concentration of N and F levels in science and mathematics, this would not be a very significant departure from the present system. In another direction, it would be possible for the universities, through their entrance requirements, to insist on a certain grouping or combination of subjects which do not form part of the present proposals.

SUB-TOPIC 3(A): STANDARDS OF ADMISSION [*Toomey*]

The Situation in Scotland

Hitherto I have been discussing the system in England and Wales. Scotland presents an interesting contrast because its 'sixth-form' examination system is geared to the tradition of a broad curriculum. The Scottish Certificate of Education (SCE) ordinary grade examination, which is of comparable standard to the GCE O level in England and Wales, is normally taken in the fourth year of secondary education (at age 16). In the fifth and sixth years pupils may take the SCE higher grade examination after essentially a one-year course. It is not unusual for an able pupil to obtain, in the fifth year, 5 or more higher grades in subjects spanning arts, social subjects and science. The sixth year may then be used in studies which entail some combination of: additional or improved higher grades, the Certificate of Sixth Year Studies (in at most 3 subjects for which a higher grade has already been awarded) or ordinary grades. Inevitably the broad span of subjects allied to the one-year course implies that the depth of study required for the H grade is less than for A level.

It is possible for pupils to enter university from the fifth year of secondary education, that is at age 17, though in practice the bulk do so from the sixth year. The general entrance requirement for a place at a Scottish university is 5 SCE passes of which at least 3 must be at the higher grade. Individual university or faculty demands are frequently for at least 4 passes at the higher grade and the majority of entrants offer this, or more—and at a high standard—for the more competitive subjects such as medicine.

At university the student may pursue either a non-specialised curriculum leading to the award after three years of an ordinary degree or, for those who choose to specialise, to the award after four years of an honours degree. Both types of course rest naturally on the generalist nature of the Scottish higher grade examination, but it is arguable that that characteristic has the advantage of making fifth- and sixth-year courses more suitable for those pupils who are not proposing to continue to university. This is evidenced by the higher proportion of pupils who leave the Scottish schools with post-O-level or O-grade qualifications.

Though the influence of the universities on school-leaving qualifications is important it should be noted that the Scottish Certificate of Education Examination Board which conducts the O grade, H grade and Certificate of Sixth Year Studies examination is not itself a university body. It is in fact a statutory body with members appointed by the Secretary of State for Scotland under arrangements which ensure that there is wide representation of the major partners in the educational system—the schools, the universities, the education authorities, the Scottish Education Department, the colleges of education, employers and others. The SCE is a national examination taken by pupils in virtually all schools in Scotland.

Changing Pattern of Higher Education in the 1990s

Looking ahead to the next decade and beyond, it is already certain that in the UK the 18-year-old population will rise to a peak in 1982, will then decline fairly rapidly, and very rapidly indeed from 1986. This has serious implications for the future development of the universities and other institutions of higher education.

The higher education system expanded enormously in the 1960s. In the early 1960s there were 23 universities and there are now 45. Student numbers continued to increase through the 1970s, though much less rapidly. However the participation of young people in higher education has not increased above its 1970 level (it was 13·8% in 1970, and is 13·5% now, having touched a peak of 14·2% in 1972), and the increase in numbers has been almost entirely due to the growth since 1969 in the population of 18–21-year-olds. This is in marked contrast to the position envisaged as recently as the 1972 White Paper—'Education: A Framework for Expansion'—which assumed a rapidly increasing participation rate, increasing to 22% by 1981 and still growing. With the very rapid decline of the 18-year-old population from the late 1980s onwards the number of young home entrants into higher education, on any currently plausible assumptions about the participation rate, will decline as well. In simplified terms, we face a period of continuing expansion in higher education up to the early 1980s, then a 5-year plateau, followed by a sharp contraction.

To encourage public debate on the issues involved, the government put out a discussion paper in February, 1978, entitled 'Higher Education into the 1990s'. This canvasses alternative ways of dealing with the situation. One question posed is whether there is likely to develop a significant change in the pattern and composition of the higher education student body, *e.g.* with more part-time and mature students so that the decline in the 18-year-old population might not lead to a decline in higher education student numbers. This suggests a flexible admissions policy. One question, however, which is not explicitly posed is the possibility of mitigating the effects of the prospective decline in numbers by extending the first degree course from 3 years to 4 years for some students. This seems to indicate that for the foreseeable future the 3-year first degree course is expected to remain the normal pattern in universities, in

England and Wales at any rate, for full-time students, and that an accommodation must be made between this, universities' entrance requirements and admissions policy, and the pattern of the curriculum and examinations in the sixth form.

The Present Position

As indicated earlier in this paper, responsibility for school curriculum and examinations is widely dispersed, and effective power to change the present situation is not concentrated at any single point. For a long time and somewhat haphazardly, without consciously willing it, the universities through their entrance requirements have exercised a dominant influence in England and Wales on the curriculum of the sixth form and the examination structure. We now seem to be moving to a situation where developments outside the universities are imposing change on the universities, and making it necessary for them to reconsider their entrance requirements. This involves the interaction of several agencies — the universities, schools, examining bodies, the Schools Council, and the central Education Department — with no single agency having the power to bring about radical change. So we are no doubt heading for a period of protracted debate and, possibly, negotiation.

Professor R. F. WHELAN (*Vice-Chancellor of the University of Liverpool*): In general this discussion paper will concentrate on the present educational system of England and Wales but it will also refer to the proposals which are under consideration for the future development of education in these countries. It is gratuitous to record that a different approach to secondary and tertiary education has evolved even in Scotland, close as it is to England, and that each member state of the Commonwealth has adopted its own educational policies and pursued its own academic goals. Despite these divergences it is hoped, nevertheless, that the English model will highlight some common experiences and point to some basic educational principles which transcend national boundaries.

Attention will be focused on the mechanism by which final-year pupils in secondary education become first-year students on a degree course in a university and on the influence which the institutions of higher education exercise on the schools as a result of this process. It is clear that, by virtue of their admission policies, the universities *do* impose some constraints on the sixth-form curriculum, although it is a far from simple matter to define closely the nature of these constraints. In addition, there is the danger of over-simplification if the inter-relationship of schools and universities is considered without reference to the many other interacting forces which propel our complex educational machinery. A complete analysis would need to review the roles of national and local government, the educational councils, the examination boards, the polytechnics, parents and employers, and many other groups, all of which impinge on our schools system. This paper largely ignores the influences of these bodies, but their omission is not a reflection on their importance.

Although universities do indeed influence the secondary schools, the constraints are by no means unidirectional. Universities may seem to enjoy a great degree of freedom in applying selective admissions procedures, but this freedom is to a large extent illusory. Maintenance of standards notwithstanding, the universities have to achieve a certain minimum student intake if they are to remain viable and the principle of 'supply and demand' exerts as strong an influence on university admission procedures as on other activities of our social structures. Ultimately the universities have to make do with whatever 'raw material' the schools provide and it is possible to conceive of a situation in which they would be forced to undertake a major revision of their degree courses as a result of curriculum changes agreed unilaterally by the schools. Such a consideration merely serves to emphasise that a national educational system has always to be seen as a unity and must take full account of the likely impact on one sector of changes proposed in another.

School Examinations

School candidates for university entrance in England and Wales most commonly offer two or three (occasionally more) subjects at the advanced level of the General Certificate of Education (GCE A levels). These examinations are normally taken in the summer term at the age of 18 +, after two years of sixth-form study. Examination results, published in August, are instrumental in determining university entrance in the following October. (In addition to A levels, optional special papers (S levels) are set in certain subjects. These papers are of a higher standard than A levels and are intended to test depth of knowledge and creative reasoning power as additional pointers to suitability for a university education. However S levels are taken by only a minority of candidates and play only a very peripheral part in the university selection process.)

A-level syllabuses are established, and the examinations are set and moderated, by eight independent GCE boards whose activities are co-ordinated by the Schools Council. The boards have established close links with the universities and also have a strong representation of schoolteachers on their governing councils. Passes at A level are accorded one of five grades, A-E. Generally about 10% of candidates attain a grade A pass, 15% grade B, 10% grade C, 15% grade D, 20% grade E (and 30% fail or are given an O-level pass).

University Admissions Procedures

Sixth-form pupils wishing to enter a university normally apply about one year before their proposed course is due to start. Each application is sent in the first instance to a centralised agency, the Universities Central Council on Admissions (UCCA), which distributes copies to the universities named on the application (up to five in number and usually ranked in order of preference). UCCA makes no decisions in the selection process but co-ordinates the complex exercise of matching applicants to available places and provides the essential channels of communication for this objective to be achieved as efficiently as possible.

The UCCA application form carries full details of the candidate, his academic and non-academic interests, the results of examinations taken to date (most commonly GCE ordinary (O) levels) and the subjects to be taken at A level. A report by an academic referee (normally the school headteacher) is appended and usually includes a prediction of the candidate's likely performance at A level.

The actual selection of candidates by universities is almost invariably carried out at departmental level and often only one or two members of the academic staff (the 'admissions tutors') are concerned in the selection process for each course. Admissions tutors are sometimes professors (17%) or readers (10%) but are more commonly senior lecturers (38%) or lecturers (35%).[1] The tutors normally interview some or all of the candidates for places in their departments. On the combined basis of (i) the examination results already obtained, (ii) the subjects to be offered at A level, (iii) the referee's report, (iv) the candidate's interview performance and, possibly, (v) the ranking given by the candidate to the course with which the tutors are concerned, the candidate may be accepted unconditionally for entry to the course or he may be rejected or, most commonly, he may be *conditionally* accepted. A conditional offer is dependent on the candidate's achievement of certain specified A-level grades in the forthcoming examination.

The competition for places on oversubscribed university courses and the resulting targets of specified A-level grades set by admissions tutors inevitably weigh heavily in the minds of pupils, teachers and headteachers in the schools, and are a major factor in the shaping of the sixth-form curriculum. The question of 'how' universities exert influence on the schools is thus broadly answered. However for a more complete analysis it is necessary to take into account the role of the examination boards and to investigate more thoroughly the status of entrance requirements in moulding the relationship between schools and universities and the extent to which it is desirable that the former should direct their activities to fulfilling the requirements of the latter.

University Entrance Requirements and Standards of Entry

The application of entrance requirements is a significant feature of the admissions process. Two largely unrelated sub-sets of requirements have to be distinguished. *General* entrance requirements stipulate the essential matriculation level for acceptance for a degree course. There are minor variations in the general requirements specified by individual universities in England and Wales but most commonly the stipulated minimum level of attainment is five GCE subjects, including at least two at A level. An additional requirement may be O-level English at grade C or better. *Course* requirements play a much more incisive role in the selection process than general requirements (which are only very rarely a significant factor in determining whether an applicant for a university place is successful or not) and are usually much more stringently defined. Thus, in considering the influence of admission standards on the school curriculum, attention needs to be concentrated on course requirements.

Course requirements are often stated both in terms of *named* subjects to be taken at A level and in terms of the *grades* of A-level passes to be obtained. It is clear that if a combination of A-level subjects is named as an essential requirement for entry to a particular degree course, a significant constraint is placed on a prospective applicant's freedom of subject choice in the school sixth form. Additionally it is often claimed that the attainment of high grades in the required subjects, essential for success in the often highly competitive university entrance process, militates towards an ever-greater concentration of teaching time on those subjects, to the progressive exclusion from the curriculum of other non-required (and usually non-examined) subjects. It is at these points of focus that the ideal sixth-form curriculum as perceived by the schools may not coincide with the combination of pre-course attainments perceived as most desirable by the universities.

The extent to which course requirements include specified A-level subjects is largely determined by the nature of the degree course itself. Some courses are 'sequential' in the sense that they build directly upon the basic factual and conceptual groundwork laid during A-level study. Examples are courses in mathematics, pure science and foreign languages. Other university courses are 'non-sequential' in that they do not extend a corpus of knowledge already acquired at A level but require their first-year students to grapple with largely unfamiliar concepts — law and philosophy, for example, would fall into this category. Generally the naming of A-level subjects tends to feature more prominently in the selection of candidates for sequential courses than of those for non-sequential courses.

It is rare for course requirements to demand *three* named A-level subjects. However the system has evolved in such a way that particular combinations of three subjects are regarded as the traditional passports to particular degree courses; other A-level combinations are often said to be treated by the universities as unusual, occasionally as 'awkward' and sometimes as completely unacceptable. Thus candidates for degree courses in chemistry will conventionally offer A levels in mathematics, physics and chemistry; for mathematics they will offer 'double maths.' and physics; and, for entry to a medical school, physics, chemistry and biology. Other single-subject degree courses have called forth equally well-established triads of A-level subjects.[2].

Although many course requirements name only one or two subjects at A level the candidate is often expected to obtain passes at a reasonable grade in other, unspecified, subjects. It has been claimed[3] that in practice the universities operate a discriminatory policy against some A-level subjects. Thus 'academic' subjects such as mathematics, physics, history and French are said to rank highly in terms of acceptability as entrance requirements, whereas admission tutors look askance at aesthetic or practical subjects such as music, art, 'elements of engineering design' and 'housecraft'. Such a policy, if it operates, presumably discourages university aspirants from taking A levels in the latter category. It is interesting, however, that schoolteachers themselves rank A-level subjects in an order of academic merit very close to that drawn up by admission tutors.[4]

The grades of A levels demanded of university applicants are largely a reflection of the relative numbers of candidates and available places. Generally the more popular a course the higher the grades required. In terms of A-level attainment the quality of candidates for most degree courses has been gradually rising over recent years, a reflection of the general increased demand for higher education. Superimposed on this trend, however, there have often been even more significant changes in entrance standards brought about by fluctuations in the popularity of particular courses. For example, over half of the entrants to UK degree courses in the 'medical group' in 1963 held A-level grades of only CCC or lower.[5] In contrast, no candidate was admitted to the Liverpool medical school in 1977 with an A-level performance lower than BBC and the average was ABB (there were 2,149 applications for 150 places, a ratio of 14·3 to 1).

Occasionally admissions tutors will offer a very good candidate a university place conditional on the attainment of relatively low A-level grades. This practice, which has been criticised, arises from the intricacies of the UCCA procedure. A candidate who is predicted by his headteacher to perform very well in the A-level examination is 'competed for' by the five universities named on his application. In accordance with UCCA rules, a candidate may accept a maximum of two offers; in the absence of complicating factors and a *firm* offer, he is likely to accept the lowest *conditional* offer, since his chances of going to university are thereby increased. In order to secure the candidate for his university an admissions tutor may demand from him less than the normal course requirements. In such cases the candidate usually achieves an A-level score much higher than that stipulated; it has been argued that his performance may even be improved through the absence of pressure to do very well.

Relevant Features of Undergraduate Degree Courses in England and Wales

Although the three-year honours degree course commonly offered by universities in England and Wales is of short duration by international standards, graduates from these universities do not appear to be less well qualified than their European and American counterparts. Conversely, however, universities in the latter countries find no difficulty in turning out graduates of a high calibre, despite the fact that their student recruitment is based on a much more broadly-based and less channelled system of secondary education. (Although as demand for university places in Europe increases there have been some moves to introduce specific entry requirements for certain courses.[6,7])

Some honours courses in England and Wales (and all in Scotland) extend to four or more years. Examples are medicine and dentistry in all schools, many modern language courses, classics and chemistry at Oxford and most courses at Keele (which include a 'foundation' year and require no *named* A-level passes for entry). Many universities offered four-year courses in several subjects until the pressures of increased demand and financial stringency forced a contraction to three years. The four-year course was particularly useful for students who had not already obtained a thorough grounding in their subject at school and were able in the first year to acquire the necessary foundation on which a three-year honours course could be built.

British universities, through applying much more stringent selection procedures than universities in Europe and America, tend to retain a much higher proportion of their students in the earlier years of the degree courses; the overall percentage of UK university entrants ultimately failing to graduate is low and is estimated to be about 7%. In contrast to the continental system, undergraduate mobility between institutes of higher education in the UK is very difficult and extremely rare.

In addition to the universities there are other degree-awarding institutions in Britain. The Open University offers its own degrees and the polytechnics offer courses leading to degrees validated by the Council for National Academic Awards (CNAA). It is becoming increasingly common for a sixth-form pupil to opt for a technologically-oriented polytechnic degree in preference to a traditional university qualification.

Historically honours degrees in British universities have been awarded on a single-subject basis. Recently, however, there has been an increasing demand for joint and combined honours courses reflecting the broader interests of students and the good employment prospects for graduates with expertise in several fields.

Recent Growth

Higher education in England and Wales experienced a decade of very rapid growth following the publication of the Robbins report in 1963.[8] More recently this expansionist phase has given way to a period of uncertainty dominated by the national economic climate and the resulting financial constraints. Nevertheless the trend, although slackening, is still upwards and the overall demand for places on degree courses shows no sign of decline. Some comparative statistics for 1954−55 (or 1964−65) and 1974−75 are given in Table 1, below. University admissions policies need to be considered in the light of these figures.

Pressure Points

In recent years, following the explosive growth in secondary and tertiary education, there has continued to be much questioning of the aims and methods of the British educational system and an increasing pressure for a revised curriculum to meet the challenge of expansion. Education is increasingly seen as a unity with the aim of granting to pupils of all ages and abilities the widest possible opportunities and freedom of choice to develop their particular interests and skills.

Most of the ablest pupils in the schools tread the traditional path of O and A levels to university. Now, however, as a result of the ever-widening application of the comprehensive principle, the raising of the minimum school-leaving age to 16, the increasing demand from employers for educational qualifications and the greater opportunities for higher and further education, it can by no means be assumed that all pupils who stay on at school beyond the age of 16 harbour university aspirations. (Indeed, in emphasis of this point, it has recently been reported[11] that one local education authority has introduced a system of grants of up to £7 per week to be paid directly to pupils to encourage them to stay on at school after 16 rather than join the dole queues; similar schemes seem likely to be adopted by other authorities.) Of the first-year sixth-form population in 1975 it has been estimated that 23·6% were studying no A-level subjects at all and 5·1% were studying only one.[12] Probably few of these 'new' sixth-formers were aiming ultimately to reach the minimum university entrance requirement of two A levels, implying that nearly one-third of the 17-year-old school cohort held no intention whatsoever of applying for a place at a university.

Since its introduction in 1951 the A-level examination has gained wide recognition as a yardstick of academic attainment and is much used as an indicator of a candidate's suitability for higher or further education, or for potential employment in a managerial capacity. The examination is not without its critics, however. Syllabuses have expanded to a level at which they are said to be overloaded with

SUB-TOPIC 3(A): STANDARDS OF ADMISSION [Whelan]

TABLE 1: COMPARATIVE EDUCATIONAL STATISTICS FOR ENGLAND AND WALES IN THE YEARS 1954−55 (or 1964−65) AND 1974−75

Figures in the first column relate to 1954−55 unless marked * when they relate to 1964−65

	1954−55 (or 1964−65*)	1974−75
No. of candidates sitting at least 1 A level[a]	55,991	250,523
No. of A-level entries[a]	137,867	498,883
No. of A-level passes[a]		341,297
No. of school-leavers aged 18 or over[b] as percentage of all school-leavers[b]	5·17%	14·45%
No. of school-leavers with 2 or more A levels (boys and girls)	68,000*	84,800
No. of school-leavers commencing degree courses at universities and polytechnics —		
From maintained and direct-grant schools — Boys	9,050	23,940
From maintained and direct-grant schools — Girls	3,170	14,570
From maintained and direct-grant schools — Total	12,220	38,510
From independent schools — Boys		5,210
From independent schools — Girls		1,840
From independent schools — Total		7,050
No. of universities[c] in England and Wales	21	43
No. of first degrees[d] awarded by universities[c] in England and Wales — Men	17,232*	30,574
No. of first degrees[d] awarded by universities[c] in England and Wales — Women	6,746*	15,124
No. of first degrees[d] awarded by universities[c] in England and Wales — Total	23,978*	45,698

(a) All candidates from schools, colleges, institutions and private backgrounds; summer examinations only.
(b) Excluding leavers from independent schools.
(c) Excluding the Open University.
(d) Honours, pass and ordinary degrees.
Sources: references 9 and 10 (p. 313)

factual content, thus placing an unreasonable burden of pure memory learning on candidates. There is great variation between the eight examining boards in the syllabus content of 'same-name' courses and a great proliferation of syllabuses within a single-subject classification (for example, there are between 50 and 60 different syllabuses available in the 'mathematics' group[13]). In addition there are sometimes claimed to be undesirable variations in the grading policies adopted by the boards; however it has also been claimed that a recent publication[14] issued jointly by the boards shows such suspicions to be largely unfounded.

Objections have thus been raised to A levels as qualifications in their own right, but criticisms have also been made of their pre-eminent role in shaping the sixth-form curriculum and the apparent domination of the latter by the exigencies of the university entrance process. It is claimed that the traditional course of three A levels leads to over-specialisation and premature commitment to over-narrow educational channels or limited employment opportunities. Schools are given little external incentive to extend the curriculum beyond the immediate demands of university entrance and the objective of a broad general education in the sixth form is very much subservient to the goal of enabling as many pupils as possible to gain places at university. Hence the established pattern of sixth-form studies is said to take no account of the needs of the 'new' sixth-formers, and may also not be in the best interests of those pupils who, although aiming at a university education, fail to reach the standard required and thus enter employment with what might be considered an unnecessarily restricted educational base.

The problems thrown up in the schools by specialisation sometimes surface in the universities also, despite the conventional assumption that a narrow sixth-form curriculum is a direct result of the entry requirement for higher education. Thus some students taking a degree in history are at a disadvantage through inadequate knowledge of foreign languages; some science and medical students have an insufficient grounding in mathematics; many students appear to have little knowledge of, or interest in, cultural and aesthetic subjects. And the disadvantages may persist after graduation—for example, civil servants enjoined with the task of unravelling the complexities of science and technology for policy-making purposes may have no scientific education beyond O level; engineers and industrial technologists may find themselves on important missions in Europe with no useful knowledge of languages; and medical practitioners increasingly involved in complex epidemiological studies or drug trials may wish that they had a more thorough acquaintance with statistics.

Proposals for Change

Dissatisfaction with the organisation of the sixth-form curriculum, with A-level examinations and with the university admissions process has led inevitably to the formulation of proposals for radical change. Some highly developed proposals[15] have been rejected — but only after considerable discussion. A new set of recommendations has recently been published[16] and is currently being evaluated in detail by all the interested parties.

The proposals, which aim to replace A levels with completely new examinations at N and F ('normal' and 'further') levels, follow recommendations made by a working party of the Schools Council and a joint working party of the Council and the Standing Conference on University Entrance. The proposals are based on three principles[17]: that changes are necessary to meet the needs of growing sixth forms of widening ability range, that reduction in specialisation is desirable on general educational grounds and that any narrowing of subject choice which restricts career opportunities should be deferred as long as possible. It has also been assumed that the 18+ examination has a dual function to act as both a measure of general attainment and as a specialised base for subsequent degree work.

It is proposed that sixth-form pupils should offer, in place of three A levels, five subjects of which three should be taken at N level and two at F level. It is suggested that the syllabus content of N and F levels should be respectively about ½ and ¾ of that of an A level in the same subject, but it is hoped that an F level, although carrying a lower factual content than the corresponding A level, might nevertheless retain an equivalent conceptual framework.

N and F courses would both be taught on a single-subject basis over two years, possibly with a common first year, a pupil's choice of which two subjects to offer at F level being deferred until the end of that year. It is suggested that 70% of the total teaching time be devoted to the five examined subjects, the remaining 30% of the curriculum being spent on private study and minority subjects. It is felt that much would be gained if the examining boards could establish N and F syllabuses with a much greater overlap of core content between boards than exists in the present 'same-name' A-level examinations. A survey has been conducted[18] of sixth-formers' potential choice of subject combinations: preference was shown for a range of courses from three or four different subject areas (this compares with the one or two subject areas normally represented at A level, suggesting that the objective of a broader curriculum would be achieved by the new system).

Consideration has been given to the framing of university entrance requirements in terms of N and F examination results.[19] It is suggested that *general* requirements should demand passes in all five subjects in the 18+ examination (but preferably with no F-level requirement and with the possibility of compensation for poor performance in one subject); naming of subjects should be minimised and passes in the 16+ examination should be acceptable in place of a named N-level pass. *Course* requirements should demand neither more than two F-level subjects nor more than three named subjects (at either N or F level) and again performance in a named 16+ examination might be acceptable in certain circumstances. Strong recommendations have been made for greater uniformity in the general and course requirements specified by institutions of higher education and, simultaneously, for a greater flexibility of approach to be adopted towards unusual combinations of subjects.

Individual universities in England and Wales are at present considering the implications of the N and F proposals at the secondary-tertiary interface; at the end of 1978 the views expressed will be sifted and welded into a corporate statement of university policy by the Standing Conference on University Entrance.

Inevitably the universities are paying close attention to the syllabus content of the N and F examinations. Approaching this issue on the basis of criteria of available teaching time and a reasonable burden of factual knowledge, the Schools Council has drawn up model syllabuses[20] which are shaped by these factors. The Standing Conference on University Entrance, approaching the question from the different standpoint of the minimal foundation of knowledge required as a basis for a university degree course, has published its own suggested syllabuses.[21] It remains to be seen to what extent the contents of these alternative syllabuses coincide and whether or not they are reconcilable where disparities occur.

The role of the F level as a specialist base for subsequent degree work will be closely scrutinised. In comparison with A level, the reduced factual content may prove to have a very significant impact on the shape of undergraduate courses and might result in a call to extend present 3-year degrees to 4 years, in order that standards might be maintained. (In this context, however, it has been pointed out that the large variation which exists between the present 'same-name' A-level syllabuses established by the different examining boards is already satisfactorily accommodated by the universities. Teaching time is used in the first year to bring all students to a comparable level of factual and conceptual knowledge, despite their divergent A-level backgrounds. Better rationalisation of F-level syllabuses would free this first-year teaching time for the covering of new material.)

The resource implications for schools of the implementation of the N and F proposals have already been analysed in detail[22]; however the extra provision which might be required by universities (particularly if it became necessary to introduce 4-year courses) remains unexplored. At a time when there is some suggestion that undergraduate degrees might be *reduced* from 3 years to 2 it is somewhat disquieting that changes in the schools might militate towards extended courses. It is to be hoped that universities will not find themselves throttled by, on the one hand, a lower educational attainment by their prospective first-year students and, on the other, by ever-tightening financial constraints.

The N and F proposals beg other questions. In a broader five-subject sixth-form curriculum would it be appropriate for 30% of teaching time to be devoted to non-examined minority subjects? Would the concentration on *two* F levels rather than *three* A levels in the second-year sixth lead to even greater specialisation and less freedom of choice? Would it be possible always to frame university entrance requirements in the terms proposed, or would the increasing popularity of certain courses or the need for specialist knowledge lead inexorably to the demand for three (or even more) F levels? Would it be possible to overcome satisfactorily the formidable problems of comparability and uniformity posed during the transition from A level to N and F levels?[23]

Future Movements

The next two decades are likely to witness as many rapid and far-reaching changes in our educational system as the past two and, inevitably, many of the changes will directly involve universities.

As already discussed, many of the pressures now building up in the schools as a result of the ever-widening application of the comprehensive principle and the consequent disaffection with the traditional 'academic' curriculum and examination structures will promote changes which will affect the universities as consumers of school-leavers. The proposals to replace the A-level examination at 18+ with the N and F levels, and the consequential need to rethink university entrance requirements and course structures, represent but one area of the system at present under close examination. Attention is also being directed at the existing divergent examinations of GCE O levels and the Certificate of Secondary Education (CSE) with a view to the possible introduction of a common system of examining of the 16 + age group.[24] Additionally a completely new examination, the 'Certificate of Extended Education' (CEE), is currently being evaluated as a possible objective for the 'new' sixth-formers.[25] It is clear that the universities will need to reach a consensus on the status of all the proposed new examinations both as formal entry requirements and as foundations for degree courses. It is equally clear that in the present highly dynamic climate it would be very undesirable for fundamental revision of single components of the system to be made in a piecemeal fashion without regard to the closely interlocking structure of the whole.

Other factors may prove equally significant in the future. The government has recently published a paper[26] drawing attention to the implications for higher education of the fluctuating birthrate in Great Britain. The 18-year-old population will rise to 941,000 in 1982 – 83 and then decline to 834,000 in 1989 – 90 and to 630,000 in 1994 – 95. Each year universities recruit about 70% of their new students from this group (as 'young home entrants') and it is suggested that the demographic patterns of the next twenty years may have an important impact on the demand for places in higher education. Although the 18-year-old population is closely predictable until 1996, the proportion of this group wishing to embark on higher education (the 'age participation rate') is much less amenable to accurate extrapolation. Hitherto demographic trends have played little or no part in determining student numbers in institutions of higher education; direct policy decisions (such as post-Robbins expansion) and changing attitudes to education in society at large have proved much more significant, as reflected in a rapid increase in the age participation rate. Whether or not a 'saturation level' has now been reached, rendering simple population statistics more important, is open to discussion. In any event it is apparent that the government's analysis and their various models for the future development of higher education are already being hotly debated.

It has recently been reported[11, 27] that in September, 1979, the government proposes to introduce a system of mandatory means-tested grants for 16 – 18-year-old students in full-time education at school or college. The details of the scheme have not yet been fully worked out, but this encouragement of young people to continue their studies may well result in increasing numbers of applications for places at universities and polytechnics.

Although universities are likely to continue to recruit most of their students from 18-year-old school-leavers, increasing attention will be paid to the claims of the 'mature student'. Particular consideration will need to be given to the accommodation of older students who, although willing and able to benefit from a university education, do not fulfil the formal entrance requirements and thus have to be admitted on different criteria.

Britain's strengthened relationship with the countries of Europe has already led to greater co-operation at all levels in the educational sphere. It is likely that such developments will accelerate over the next few years and that there will be general progress towards interchangeability of qualifications and student mobility across national borders. At present there exist considerable differences between the educational theories and practices of the EEC member states; it is to be hoped that in the immediate future all countries will adopt a receptive and flexible attitude to their neighbours' systems whilst seeking to preserve the best features of their own.

The inter-relationship of schools and universities will continue to be modified by a multiplicity of complex forces. Some future changes will be the result of policy decisions taken on the basis of informed opinion. Many developments will, however, be consequent upon much less easily defined undercurrents within society at large: economic uncertainty and altered manpower requirements and job opportunities, ever-increasing automation and more leisure time, changing attitudes to work and to the purposes of education. Ultimately we need to be sure not of the role and influence of university admissions procedures but of the role and influence of universities themselves.

REFERENCES

1. W. A. Reid. *The Universities and the Sixth Form Curriculum*, Schools Council Research Study, Macmillan, 1972, p. 22.
2. Schools Council Working Paper 60. *Examination at 18 + : the N and F Studies*, Evans Methuen Educational, 1978, p. 176.
3. W. A. Reid, op. cit., pp. 49 et seq.
4. Ibid., pp. 97 et seq.
5. Universities Central Council on Admissions. *Statistical Supplement to the Fourth Report 1965 – 66*, UCCA, 1967, Table D.
6. Schools Council Working Paper 47. *Preparation for Degree Courses*, Evans Methuen Educational, 1973, pp. 115 et seq.
7. Schools Council Working Paper 60, op. cit., pp. 246 et seq.
8. Report of the Committee on Higher Education (Robbins Report), Cmnd. 2154, HMSO, 1963.
9. DES. *Statistics of Education*, Vol. 2 – *School Leavers: CSE and GCE*, 1975.
10. DES. *Statistics of Education*, Vol. 6 – *Universities*, 1975.
11. The Times (p. 2) and The Daily Telegraph (p. 9), 8 June, 1978.
12. Schools Council Working Paper 60, op. cit., p. 8.

13. Ibid., p. 201; see also The Tenth Report of the House of Commons Expenditure Committee (Session 1976–77)—*The Attainments of the School Leaver,* HMSO, 1977, paras. 59 et seq., and 116.

14. G. S. Bardell, G. M. Forrest and D. J. Shoesmith. *Comparability in GCE: a Review of the Boards' Studies 1964–77,* Joint Matriculation Board, Manchester, 1978.

15. Schools Council and Standing Conference on University Entrance. 'Proposals for Curriculum and Examinations in the Sixth-Form: a Joint Statement', unpublished, 1969 (the so-called 'Q and F Proposals').

16. Schools Council Working Paper 60, op. cit.

17. Ibid., p. 4.

18. Ibid., pp. 138 et seq.

19. Ibid., pp. 183 et seq.

20. For references to Schools Council Syllabus Studies, see ibid., pp. 19 et seq.

21. For references to the SCUE Syllabus Studies see the Standing Conference on University Entrance, *Universities and the N and F Proposals,* 1978, pp. 47 et seq.

22. Schools Council Examinations Bulletin 38. *Examinations at 18+: Resource Implications of an N and F Curriculum and Examination Structure,* Evans Methuen Educational, 1978.

23. A. Hickey. *Qualifying for Higher Education under a New Examination System at 18+,* Report to the Schools Council by the National Foundation for Educational Research, mimeo, June 1977.

24. Schools Council. *Examinations at 16+: Proposals for the Future,* Evans Methuen Educational, 1975.

25. Schools Council. *CEE: Proposals for a New Examination,* Evans Methuen Educational, 1975.

26. DES and Scottish Education Department. *Higher Education into the 1990s—a Discussion Document,* HMSO, 1978.

27. The Times (pp. 1 and 2), The Daily Mail (p. 1), The Daily Telegraph (p. 1) and The Financial Times (p. 4), 13 May, 1978; The Times Educational Supplement (p. 3), 19 May, 1978; The Times (p. 2), 26 May, 1978.

DISCUSSION

In introducing his paper (see above) Professor Z. R. Siddiqui (Jahangirnagar) said that he had to widen the topic to include consideration of admission to secondary education. In some developing countries admission to tertiary education is of less prominence since secondary education is itself in a highly unsatisfactory state. In Bangladesh village schools provide primary education for more than half the children of the relevant age group, but there is a high drop-out rate and little pressure for

SUB-TOPIC 3(A): STANDARDS OF ADMISSION

secondary education in the rural areas. In the urban areas the situation is markedly different, and competition for entry to secondary schools, especially the 'better' schools, is very keen.

The diversity of streaming into science and arts and some minor streams from class IX onwards (9th year of school attendance) has aggravated the problem. Only 15% of the students make the science stream and many rural schools are unable to offer a science course for lack of funds. The curriculum committee of the Education Commission has recommended return to a general stream with a good mix of the arts and the sciences for all secondary students.

Students from the élite, government-supported, schools in the urban areas have a high chance of going to university. This is shown by the results of the public school examination at the end of the tenth and twelfth years. In this examination the public government schools will have nearly 100% success with the majority of results in the first division while, at the other extreme, schools will show 10% success with none in the first division, some in the second and the majority in the third. The poorly equipped and staffed village schools will continue to be disadvantaged unless all secondary schools are given better facilities through a nationalised system of resource allocation.

Mr. R. Toomey (Department of Education and Science, Britain—for paper, see above) said that in Britain the universities have for a long time been a dominant influence on secondary education through their entrance requirements. Schools gradually came to provide a broad general education up to the age of 16 and then specialised education for the age group 16–18 related to the entrance requirements of the universities. There is now a continuous interaction between a greater variety of agencies, exerting influences on the secondary education pattern. Among these is the fact that increasingly pupils are remaining at school beyond the age of 16 with other aims than entry to university. These varied influences have led to wide debate and discussion of proposals for changes in the national system of school examinations in England and Wales and these changes, if made, will have repercussions on university entrance requirements. One proposal is to replace the age 18 advanced level examination in 3 subjects at one level by an examination in 5 subjects at 2 levels. Another proposal is to have a common age-16 examination to combine and replace the Certificate of Secondary Education and the ordinary level examination. The proposals have developed because of the view that the present sixth-form curriculum is too narrow, tends to force pupils to premature choice of specialisation and is unsuited to the widening range of abilities of pupils staying at school in the sixth form. So far as the schools are concerned the immediate issues are whether educational standards would be affected and whether available resources would be sufficient for the changed teaching pattern. So far as the universities are concerned the proposals call for a re-examination of their entrance requirements.

The new system cannot come about without the willing co-operation of the universities, and universities will need to be satisfied that reasonably uniform standards are maintained in the new system of examinations. One

TOPIC 3: RECONCILING EQUALITY AND EXCELLENCE

likely effect of the change in the school curriculum and examination structure will be pressure to extend the degree course from 3 years to 4. This would mean increasing the recurrent grant to universities and additional grants for students as well as capital expenditure on buildings and equipment. Rough estimates suggest that pressures to extend the degree course would be necessarily strongly resisted by the central government.

Professor *R. F. Whelan* (Liverpool) in presenting a summary of his paper (see above) said that in England and Wales university admission requirements have exerted, and continue to exert, pressure on schools to adopt appropriate syllabuses and school work in the two sixth-form years is concentrated on 3 subjects relevant to a subsequent degree course. The pre-university preparation has ensured a very low failure rate—about 7%—among undergraduates and a degree course of 3 years which is of short duration by international standards.

Developments in the last two decades show that not all pupils who stay on at school beyond age 16 have university aspirations. Of the 1st-year sixth-formers in 1975, 26% were studying no A-level subjects at all and 5% were studying only one. Thus the A-level examination is no longer used for the purpose for which it was designed and the traditional pattern is being challenged in this and several other ways. The universities need to consider their responses to these changes.

The problems in the schools through early pupil specialisation sometimes appear also in the universities even though a narrow sixth-form curriculum is often said to be a direct result of higher education entry requirements. Some students taking degrees in history have insufficient knowledge of foreign languages, some science and medicine students have too little knowledge of mathematics, and so on. But the proposals to replace O and A levels with 'N' and 'F' must have significant impact on undergraduate courses. If universities maintain their intake, as they must, they will have to lower their admission standards. Some regard this as a small price to pay for a more homogeneous society. Another initial reaction to the lowering of entrance standards is to propose lengthening the degree course from 3 to 4 years, but this runs counter to another proposal that the degree course should be shortened to 2 years to cope with the population bulge of 18-year-olds and to reduce university expenditure. Alternatively the education system of England and Wales may move towards a pattern comparable to that of Australia, New Zealand and Canada with a larger number of students admitted and a larger failure rate.

The ensuing discussion was opened by Professor J. F. Scott (La Trobe) who said that in the state of Victoria in Australia developments similar to those in the United Kingdom have taken place. The pupils leaving school had widely different career intentions. A wide diversity of courses in the senior forms arose from the freedom of schools to devise their own curricula and there was a large amount of internal school-based assessment of pupils. It seemed inevitable that present trends would tend to either a lowering of standard of the 3-year degree course or a lengthening of the degree course to 4 years. Professor Scott asked whether the anticipated decline in numbers entering universities in Britain could not be offset by the otherwise additional cost of extending degree courses to 4 years.

SUB-TOPIC 3(A): STANDARDS OF ADMISSION

Professor (Mrs.) Madhuri R. Shah (S.N.D.T. Women's) outlined the problems experienced in India where universities frequently complained that secondary school leaving standards were too low. Secondary schools on the other hand wanted maximum educational flexibility to enable wide range of choices by pupils. Professor Shah suggested that the universities should decide what minimum test they require to judge the basic reasoning ability and intellectual quality of candidates. Dr. D. H. Irvine (Guyana) said that the ex-colonial UK school examination system further complicated the situation in his country where it was hoped to develop a school/university relationship on an N/F-type examination system.

Dr. C. I. H. Nicholl (Bishop's) said that a major problem was to have a system which helped pupils to make personally good career choices as early as reasonable. Some students realised their career intentions only after starting university. Dr. A. K. Dhan (North-Eastern Hill) and Mr. R. E. O. Akpofure (Commonwealth Secretariat) both referred to the dual function of universities in developing countries of producing trained manpower for national needs under government pressure for lower-level graduation and of ensuring graduation at the highest level to maintain science and scholarship. Sir Denys Wilkinson (Sussex) suggested that a 2-year course might gain a degree at technician level with the 3-year normal course leading to a general degree and a 4th year leading to a higher honours classification. Alternatively, he suggested, the range and content of subjects might be reduced to provide more specialised narrower science degree courses without loss of intellectual standard. Other speakers referred to the relevance of the structure of the International Baccalaureate to the question of broad school-leaving educational programmes: to other pressures for lengthening degree courses quite apart from a possible lowering of admission requirements, such as the demands of some professional bodies, *e.g.* a good honours degree required for membership of the Institution of Electrical Engineers; to improvements in teaching and learning techniques as a means to short duration of degree courses; and to the societal pressures for increasing educational provision.

Sub-Topic 3(b)

WHAT RANGE OF LEARNING IS APPROPRIATE TO THE UNIVERSITY?

Chairman: Dr. H. D. HICKS
President and Vice-Chancellor of Dalhousie University

Rapporteur: Mr. M SHOCK
Vice-Chancellor of the University of Leicester

Tuesday, 22 August

Dr. A. A. BRUNEAU (*Vice-President (Professional Schools and Community Services), Memorial University of Newfoundland*): In addressing the four functions of the university Professor Pierre Dansereau, in a presentation to a symposium on the future of the university, stated:

'Instruction, education, culture, and research offer four different missions respectively centered upon knowledge, understanding, practice, and discovery. Historical relays in the relative weight of each of these four endeavours may well be the result of shifting demands on the part of society who supported the universities. Thus, humanistic programmes strongly subjected instruction to education, whereas material progress put a greater stress on instruction. Democratization of access to the university emphasized culture. As for research, it has, more than any other university function, been highly vulnerable to national values and economic fluctuations'.*

Few would dispute that these — knowledge, understanding, practice and discovery — are the essential elements involving learning of those within the university community. Many, however, would question the relative merits of each and the appropriate emphasis required to achieve balance, if not equality and, although near unanimity could be reached on the goal of excellence in each, equally diverse opinions as to what constitutes excellence and how it might best be

*P. Dansereau. The Swinging Door, Symposium on the Future of the University, Royal Society of Canada, Ottawa, 4 May, 1976.

measured would soon be evident. Related as they are to subjective judgements that are conditioned by the diverse environments in which they have been formed, little useful purpose may be served in any attempt to reconcile all opinions. Rather, does the inclusion of this topic in the programme beg more the question of how the university can maintain what it perceives to be appropriate quality and balance in those activities involved in imparting knowledge, engaging understanding, encouraging practice and supporting and sustaining discovery in its traditionally-organized disciplines in the face of popular cries for relevance, than a defence of its applied and professional programmes?

The most pressing challenge today for many of us may well be directly related to the health, if not the survival, of those academic disciplines long considered the very heart of the university but perceived to be irrelevant in, and costly to, society. Their defenders should recognize that excellence in the eyes of society is likely to be more closely associated with apparent short-term usefulness than inherent merit, and equality more to do with currently perceived inequality attributable to the supposed misallocation of resources than any achievable state.

In Canada, and I suspect elsewhere, rather than this being the time to question again the place and role of professional schools in the university, it may well be the time in which we might more profitably explore the means by which those other disciplines, at least purportedly unrelated to professional pursuits and 'useful' contributions to society, might draw sustenance and strength through the linkages they might establish with the outward-directed 'relevant' activities of the professional schools. In doing so the university clearly will be challenged to re-examine and affirm its pursuit of excellence in those terms it best can define while ensuring that at least some of its activites are so coupled to society and presented in terms of relevance that society will perceive merit and ensure support.

In the most general terms much of the university's activity has been organized around disciplines that have provided the framework in which the activities of research and discovery could most effectively be promoted. The extraordinary increase of learning in depth this structure has supported, if not enabled, within a discipline is as remarkable as is its isolation from even its close neighbours. Tendencies within a discipline towards breadth typically are countered with subdivision into 'new' separate disciplines.

It is hardly surprising that the member of faculty, successfully engaged in research adding to the body of knowledge in a discipline, enthusiastically teaches in the discipline and encourages, through instruction and the study and research required of his students, the pursuit of his goals. The danger is that this process can, and too often does, become a self-reinforcing, ever-narrowing, activity, when isolated from society, that can ultimately lead to self-destructive introversion. The perception of usefulness, and consequently merit in society, intrudes in terms of the problems society perceives. These are not organized on a disciplinary base but rather are imposed by man's interaction within and with nature. They have a dimension of breadth.

Can we find those means by which we can synthesize approaches to learning that draw upon what is known, understood, revealed in practice, and discovered in research throughout the broad spectrum of disciplinary and professional activity within the university, that will impart a dimension of breadth to the structure of our learning processes, complementing the obvious depth made possible by the organization around disciplines? Should we add the establishing of such programmes to our goals? Surely it is time for our universities to add the dimension of breadth to that of depth in teaching programmes that are well-designed, articulated and presented.

No simple 'supermarket' approach of ill-advised sampling of the vast array of available courses is suggested. Rather a carefully conceived requirement to explore and develop the significant linkages between disciplines is required in a framework of goals sensitive to society's needs. The intellectual challenge and development of mental capacity in such programmes must at least equal that of our traditional courses, and there is no reason to anticipate any diminishing of excellence.

If our institutional goals, through the processes of learning, include the education of adults capable of functioning in our society and contributing to its goals in addition to the reinforcing and strengthening of our own internal pursuits, our role, however important, can be little more than to start the necessary processes, for ultimately their contribution will depend more on their behaviour after graduation than on what we may do in the brief student years.

Individuals so educated may well more clearly appreciate the long-term importance of sustaining those knowledge-oriented creative activities within the university than perhaps will be the case if the sometimes traumatic reconciliation of the isolated discipline orientation of their education and the demands of society is left entirely to them.

While it is predictable that society will perceive merit, and consequently value, or excellence, in efforts to synthesize knowledge and organize teaching in a more broadly-based society-oriented manner, such efforts, if seriously addressed, challenge the university to grapple with its concepts of excellence applied to such pursuits, for they cannot be identical to those internally useful within the established disciplines.

The essence of the problem faced has long been confronted within the professions. The fundamental prerequisites of knowledge and understanding through application and use grow and change in practice, which continuously challenges the practitioner to exercise judgement as he pursues solutions to problems not met before. Be those problems social, technical, legal or medical, the extent to which new steps can be taken towards better solutions more broadly applicable is dependent in no small measure on the stimulus provided through contact and interaction with those in pursuit of knowledge who provide new insight and understanding. Excellence here is more appropriately reflected in judgement than in knowledge and information and usually is associated with long experience.

If we can include a requirement for practice as part of the learning process, so that what is known is tested by application in society (where it so seldom fits as expected), we can be assured of the tension and stimulus which promote insight leading to discovery. The vital processes will be started.

The stretching of the intellectual capability of each and all those in the university community involved in such activities—undergraduates, graduate students, field workers, researchers, faculty members—must be a first prerequisite. The excellence—an elusive quality—that can be achieved is surely dependent on the ability, energy and creativity of those who are part of this community. Clearly inequalities will be apparent, not only amongst individuals but inevitably in the apparent and real support for, and strength of, particular pursuits. The degree to which these inequalities become issues as strengths or liabilities for the publicly-supported university has much to do with how the inequalities are perceived to match society's current fads and shifting demands.

Research, that university function most vulnerable to political action and economic analysis, has long attracted debate on the role and value of fundamental research concerned with the expansion of knowledge versus that of research applied to the pursuit of utilitarian goals. In Canada today, as in other nations, the pendulum is swinging in favour of the pursuit of utilitarian goals. Increased support of research is promoted as an economic investment rather than as a social overhead. What are the implications for our universities?

[Bruneau]   TOPIC 3: RECONCILING EQUALITY AND EXCELLENCE

In his pamphlet *Fundamental Research and the Universities*, Joseph Ben-David has eloquently addressed the issues we face:

'The link from economic and technological problems to fundamental research is more predictable than from fundamental research to economically useful technological innovation. As the range of science is much more limited than that of productive technology, it is easier to see which branch of science is relevant for the solution of any technological problem. Of course, from the point of view of any given branch of science the problem may be trivial in the context of existing paradigms. Still, a technologist in search of a solution to a basic problem will more easily find the proper address where to obtain either the answer, or the definitive denial of answer, than the basic scientist in search of a profitable application to his ideas.'

Continuing to address the issues raised, he goes on:

'The question, however, is not whether it is possible to redraw here and there the boundaries between some given scientific and technological communities, or where to turn for consultation. There have been, and there probably will be in future, cases of instant match between science and technology. But the restriction of research to such rare instances of immediate technological relevance would slow down the growth of scientific knowledge and make research extremely inefficient. Obvious leads to discoveries which might revolutionise broad fields of knowledge would be passed over for minor technological solutions, because there would be no professional scientists to pursue leads of merely theoretical significance. In the long run this would also be economically inefficient. Important theoretical advances usually have great indirect practical potentialities which can be exploited if there are entrepreneurs bringing them to the attention of technologists and others who may be concerned. But technological solutions, even if they have great potentialities for generalisation, will hardly reach that stage in the absence of professional scientists whose job is to theorize and generalize.

'...the optimal way to increase the uses of science is, therefore, not to select projects according to their supposed promise of applicability, but to increase the motivation and the opportunities to find uses for science, and to find practical problems which can stimulate research. The relationship between fundamental and applied research should not be visualised as a series of separate links between certain fundamental discoveries and their "applications". Rather, practical uses of science should be conceived as the result of chance interactions between fundamental discoveries on the one hand and practical interests on the other, which can occur in an infinite variety of ways. The purpose of policy should, therefore, be to influence the likelihood of these chance occurrences by increasing the density of both kinds of activities and the velocity of the circulation of ideas and problems from both areas of activity in spaces which ensure interaction. Increasing the density is a matter of investment, velocity is the result of entrepreneurship, and creating the properly enclosed spaces is a task for organisation.'

Can we rise to the challenge and opportunity presented? Throughout the university world many devices have been created to promote this interaction, and we are all familiar with research centres, institutes and programmes in which this has been attempted. In such organizations is there not an opportunity not only to strengthen the pursuit of goals of both our fundamental and utilitarian research but also to influence the organization and content of our instruction, education and cultural activities in many of our undergraduate activities? Within our professional schools this has long been so.

In this day of communications in which it is proposed, at least by the media, that we must know everything of significance and be capable of judging value to society, society will question and want simplistic generalizations which authoritatively express its values and goals and tell it what to think. The university sustained by the public will inevitably be judged by the public. It is vitally important that we play a role in determining what is evidence. If we retreat behind traditional values expressed in a language only we understand we are likely to be perceived as little more than an expensive social overhead, unjustly favoured in society. Rather, that amongst our activities which society may at any time consider irrelevant is probably best protected not by overtly arguing for our sacredly-held tenets but by emphasizing the support it provides those activities that interface with society through interpretative roles or by application and action. If we intelligently direct the spotlight, such activities can be well protected and free of external constraint.

But this requires of the university that it judge itself critically, and perhaps harshly, for if it so protects the second-rate and that which is incapable of excellence it does so at its own peril, whatever its defences. If we do exercise that judgement of excellence and act upon it, surely we can confidently explore a brand new range of approaches in our learning missions of instruction, education, culture and discovery, confidently interacting with and responding to society, unafraid of 'relevance' and committed as much to 'breadth' as to 'depth'.

Dr. J. M. MWANZA (*Vice-Chancellor of the University of Zambia*)*: The topic for this discussion—the range of learning appropriate to the university—is an extremely important one. It is important, first, because it goes to the core of the concept of the university as an institution of teaching and learning. Secondly, it demands of us the making of decisions as to the choice of what the university is to undertake and as to what is to be left out. The topic further forces us to consider as to whether what is appropriate to one university ought to be appropriate to all the universities in the world—in short, ought the concept of the university to be the same throughout the world?

I think it is important, before we go any further, to make the obvious point that a university does not exist in isolation. It is part of the entire educational system of a particular country. It therefore will reflect and, indeed, must reflect the values, the problems and aspirations of the country in which it exists. It must respond to the demands and exigencies of its society. But the demands of society are not everywhere the same, as societies differ in certain particulars. Thus it is clear that the problems that Great Britain, Canada and Australia face are to a large extent different from those that the so-called third world countries—such as Zambia, Ghana or Guyana—encounter. This is so because these groups of countries find themselves in different socio-economic circumstances, have had varied historical experiences and therefore face different problems. For example, as you know, Zambia became an independent state in 1964. At that time the educational situation was dismal. There were just over one hundred thousand School Certificate holders, the number of graduates with single degrees was computed at 104, and there was no university. And yet during the same period 3600 non-Zambians with degrees held jobs in the Zambian economy—and the civil service.[1] In 1972, 85% of the graduate secondary school teachers in Zambian secondary schools were expatriates; and up to the present the great majority of the secondary school teachers are expatriates. The *Zambian Manpower,* which made a detailed analysis of the requirements of university-educated manpower in

---

*This paper was produced with the help of Dr. L. P. Tembo, the Director of the Educational Research and Curriculum Development Unit of the University of Zambia.

Zambia, estimated that 'some 12,500 university graduates — almost one quarter of the new labour supply for professional and administrative jobs — will be needed by Zambian schools, professional offices, laboratories and businesses during the decade of the seventies. Somewhat more than half of the total will be needed to satisfy the requirements of economic expansion; the remainder to replace non-citizens in key jobs and fill unoccupied posts'.[2]

It can be clearly seen that for the Zambian government, and indeed other African and developing nations, the situation in which they found themselves at independence was quite serious. They had political independence, but the effective control and direction of the country and the educational system was still in the hands of the expatriates, some of whom were actually leaders of the economy, the civil service and education during the colonial period.

What I have briefly said is, I think, a pointer to the topic we are discussing. The range of what is to be learned in the university cannot be determined from mere theoretical abstractions. The range of subjects to be learned in the university is limited and delimitated by the priorities and demands of the particular society in which the university operates. In the case of the University of Zambia, and indeed other African universities, the demand for high-level educated manpower was obvious. The governments which build and finance the universities have an interest to see that what the students learn is of relevance in the alleviation of problems that the majority of the people face — poverty, ignorance, lack of shelter and disease. The Lockwood report, on which recommendations the University of Zambia was established, strongly advised that: 'The University must be responsive to the needs of the country....'[3]. These needs are developmental needs and the university is supposed to supply the necessary manpower to satisfy these needs. The African universities collectively have made an important observation: 'Since manpower training and development are, and will for long remain, an essential pre-requisite for national development, the establishment in each country of a National Manpower Board becomes of over-riding and urgent necessity, both as an aspect of development planning in general, and, in particular, to provide guidance to the universities and other institutions of higher learning, in respect of student admissions, and in the development of their courses and curricula'.[4]

I have talked quite a bit about the area of the importance of high-level manpower training and this may appear to be a digression from this topic — the range of learning appropriate to the university. The point I want to make here is that in developing countries the range of learning—*i.e.* the spread of subjects that are to be taught and learned—will be determined by what a particular country requires for its development. But this also means that, given financial constraints, the universities in conjunction with their governments will give certain subjects priority in the curriculum of the university. Thus almost all the students in the University of Zambia are on government bursaries. But there are conditions to their bursaries. They are not given bursaries because they have in general been admitted to the University '. . . but for admission in the first instance to defined areas of study. The intention is that bursary awards should be used, together with other means, to produce Zambian graduates in the categories of study which are based upon known manpower needs of Zambia'.[5]

This function others have felt to be important in the formation of human capital: '. . . attendance at university adds value to a person's potential productive contribution to the economic system and is to be regarded as an investment in one particular form of society's stock of productive assets or capital'.[6] In the universities of the developing countries this conception of the function of the university is seen by the emphasis put on professional education—in the University of Zambia, for example, priority areas are agriculture, education, engineering, medicine, mining, and the natural sciences. The assumption is clearly this: that economic and social development—the eradiction of poverty, disease, ignorance and hunger—are dependent upon relevant training in agriculture and on the development of technology.

From the manpower point of view, then, the range of teaching appropriate to learning in a university will depend upon the requirements of different countries. But different countries which are at different levels of development make different sorts of demands on a university. It is, therefore, clear here that in this particular area the range of subjects in the curriculum of different countries will vary.

What I have been describing so far can, I suppose, be said to contribute to the *horizontal* range of learning that is appropriate in a university. But I believe one can also talk about the *vertical* range of learning appropriate to a university. The question here is: what sorts of programmes are appropriate to the university? Should the university be involved in the teaching of certificate and diploma students, or should it only concentrate on graduate and postgraduate students? The answers to questions like this will, of course, depend again on the historical, social, economic and political experiences of the various countries. Some universities have no problem in this regard, for they may have sufficient numbers of other forms of tertiary institution which teach certificate and diploma courses. In most developing countries, however, the situation is largely different. Not only did some of these countries not have a university at all at independence, the facilities for training middle-level manpower were also almost non-existent. But, furthermore, the involvement of universities in the training of middle-level manpower makes sense. The argument which has often been proffered that middle-level training should be done in cheaper institutions specifically created for them does not make much economic sense, for in some countries university facilities are not fully utilized and can therefore be put to better use. Secondly, as has been pointed out, there is some training which is required but cannot be catered for in any of the institutions and yet is vital for national development. For example, certificates and diplomas in adult education, primary teacher education, social work and library studies, would not have been provided in Zambia had the university not accepted the responsibility of training people in these areas which provide important services to the community. Thus in a country like ours the university has no choice but to be responsive to the needs of the society.

In third world countries there is also the problem of recruiting expatriate staff to teach in institutions which train middle-level manpower. The inclusion of middle-level subjects within a university setting would attract better qualified tutors in this area as the university enjoys the status and prestige not accorded other tertiary institutions. We have found in Zambia, for example, that the three teacher-training colleges which train non-university graduate secondary school teachers and which are affiliated to the university for the purposes of curriculum development and examinations have no problems in recruitment—mainly because of this affiliation to the university. There is another important reason as to why it is not necessary to separate middle-level training from training that has traditionally belonged to the university. The separation is artificial, for in the world of work the two categories of people have to work together in co-operation. Thus, even where there are separate institutions of training for high-level and middle-level manpower, it makes sense to have these institutions co-operate with each other in mutual respect.

It is argued in certain quarters that bringing certificate and diploma subjects into a university would dilute the idea of excellence that the university is supposed to reflect. This does not appear to be a convincing reason to me, for surely the depth of the study of, say, economics in the first year of degree work will be less than that attempted or done at doctoral level. And yet we do not say that work in the first year will devalue that at the PhD level! Both levels demand excellence. Similarly there is need for excellence at the certificate level as there is at the graduate level. Indeed, as Ashby once put it, 'excellence, or quality, is a spirit of pursuit, not a milestone reached'.[7]

In some universities the range of learning has gone beyond the university walls. The universities provide extra-mural studies/ extension services as well as correspondence studies which sometimes lead to degrees. In the University of Zambia these services that the university provides are considered important. The Lockwood committee whose report I have already referred to was of the opinion that it would be wrong to restrict the activities of the university and its contribution to the development of the people by insisting on a formal association with the university to those who will spend years of full-time or part-time study on the campus. 'This', it reasoned, 'would deny opportunities to many potential students, especially mature students, who could benefit by the chance to read for a university qualification but who were prevented by their employment or by other considerations from pursuing a natural ambition to improve their education, competence and standing'.[8] The University of Zambia has found no cause to regret, over the past twelve years, the decision to implement this recommendation. Other countries such as Great Britain, and more recently Australia, may find the idea of the open university more amenable. Nonetheless the function of extra-mural education and that provided by the open universities is the same. Here continuing education is thought to be important.

Now it is very easy to be misunderstood with regard to what I have been saying in this section of the paper. I am not saying that the university everywhere ought to undertake all the programmes that have been mentioned. What I am trying to say is that the range of learning in the university can be very wide. What is appropriate to university learning is not necessarily tradition-bound. It to a large extent depends upon the needs and the requirements of society.

But it is important to emphasize that, in saying this, I am not asserting that all universities should take all these programmes as appropriate to them. The important thing is that the university should be able to discharge its duty with respect to the pursuit of excellence effectively, no matter at what level that discharge is called for. This means that the university must not be over-burdened financially or administratively, for this will affect the quality of its work. It also means that the university should leave out those functions which it can perform but which are already taken care of elsewhere. It is, for example, mainly for the reasons above that the University of Zambia did not take technical and commercial colleges

SUB-TOPIC 3(B): WHAT RANGE OF LEARNING? [Mwanza]

under its wing. The Lockwood committee argued that this would have 'meant a cumbersome hierarchy of control if all the many institutions doing this work were to be subject to the University Senate in financial control'.[9] The important point here is that the reasons for not absorbing these technical and commercial colleges were not strictly educational, but rather technical, administrative or financial.

The topic under discussion also calls for the consideration of another issue. The issue involves specialized training versus general education. The discipline approach to education is, as we all know, perhaps the most tradition-honoured in university education. This approach concentrates on a single subject area. The idea is this: that when university teachers in their research discover knowledge in their particular area they should straight away go and teach it to their students, for they are the only ones able to teach it. Further, there are certain subjects which are time-honoured and which have stayed as university disciplines since universities began. These subjects are important for their own sakes, and are therefore the best subjects for university education. What is more, it is argued, for the best education the disciplines should be studied for honours degrees.

The discipline-centred approach has not only been practised in older British and European universities: it was also introduced to universities in British colonies in both India and Africa. Eric Ashby, for example, has reported that in the 1959–60 academic year in the University of Ghana twelve undergraduates studied *nothing else* but Latin, Greek and history. This number was, of course, in addition to those who studied these subjects as well as others.[10] This approach to studies in the universities has its problems. One of the problems is that the teaching of these subjects does not take into account the needs of the individual and the society. The study of Latin and Greek has, for example, very little relevance to the problems of the African societies, especially when it is realized that very few African languges are taught in African universities. But even when the subjects being taught are modern and scientific, the fact that the decision to teach them is based on the subject itself may not render services to the student and the society—since seriously most students in most parts of the world would like to use some of the subjects they take at the university for their future career.

The other approach to university education is that which is often referred to as the problem-oriented approach. I have in part dealt with this problem when I was discussing the horizontal range of learning relevant in a university—*i.e.* when I was discussing the

329

selection of subjects to be taught in the university. But I think it is worth repeating this in the context of what is being discussed here. Those who argue in its favour begin from the point that the discipline-oriented approach is inadequate for solving problems which the world faces because it is not career- or vocation-directed. And yet the world faces various problems. The function of university education, it is argued, should be to prepare the students for future work in society. If the importance of the problem is put in its proper perspective, then it will be understood that various branches of natural sciences and indeed social sciences should be learned for the purposes of solving problems. It is further argued that the problem-oriented approach, having the advantage of being realistic, will necessarily deal with university learning in a multidisciplinary manner, since world problems are, necessarily, multidisciplinary. It is argued, for example, that if an engineer is to operate properly he has to have some knowledge of economics, business administration, accounting, etc. It is then concluded that the curriculum which will use the problem-oriented approach will necessarily be broader as opposed to the one that was the discipline-oriented approach.

Nonetheless the important point is that in general the university is considered to be a factory which will produce people for the purpose of servicing government bureaucracies, industries and corporations. In this conception of the university the humanities in the developing nations, being 'soft' and 'irrelevant' disciplines, are considered to be anachronisms. This is what Brzezinski was talking about when he said: 'The largely humanist-oriented, occasionally ideologically-minded, intellectual dissenter, who saw his role largely in terms of proffering social critiques, is rapidly being displaced either by experts and specialists who become involved in special governmental undertakings, or generalists—integrators, who become in effect house ideologists for those in power, providing over-all intellectual integration for disparate actions'.[11]

One of the consequences of this attitude to learning in the university is that the curriculum tends to be predetermined. This affects selection principles and procedures in such a way that students are supposed to fit the programmes instead of the programmes fitting the students. What has happened in the University of Zambia, as I have pointed out, is a case in point. What is perhaps more serious is that this attitude and policy in university education affects even other types of education. As Leo Marx has pointed out: 'An important function of primary and secondary education today is the "tracking" of pupils according to the presumed match between their abilities and the requirements of various departments within the multiversity. The end of the "track", of course, is a job or profession

— a slot in the system — and "getting off the track"...is a dangerous thing to do'.[12]

What principle or theory should the university adopt then? It is quite clear that choosing either the narrow, over-specialised, discipline-oriented curriculum or the predetermined job-oriented one will not do. It is obvious that jobs have to be done for development. It is therefore necessary to train high-level manpower. But this does not mean that this should be to the exclusion of everything else. At the centre of university education should be the individual and humanity. It is therefore important that university programmes should be relevant not only for livelihood but also a humane life. Students should not be forced to make a commitment for life at very early ages. They must be able to choose issues. I am here calling for creative flexibility in education. University students should not only be acquainted with the natural and social sciences but also with the humane culture of the societies in which they are going to live — aesthetics, literature, langauges and a sense for moral and social judgement, etc. As George Grant has observed: 'If we are to live in the modern university as free men, we must make judgements about the essence of the university — its curriculum. If such judgements are to be more than quibbles about detail, they must be based on what we think human life to be, what activities serve human fulfilment, and what place higher education should play in encouraging the realization of these activities'.[13]

I would like to say that this topic is not an easy one. It can be looked at from various viewpoints because the nature of the university itself is influenced by the environment in which it exists. Even in 'stable' societies the range of learning appropriate to a university cannot remain stagnant. There is therefore need for continuous research in university education. Despite differences among universities throughout the world, one limiting objective runs or should run through them all — pursuit of excellence for the good of the individual and humanity.

REFERENCES

1. *Zambian Manpower*. Government Printer, Lusaka, 1969, p. 48.
2. Op. cit., p. 46.
3. Sir John Lockwood (Chairman). *Report on the Development of a University in Northern Rhodesia*
4. T. M. Yesufu (ed.). *Creating the African University*, Oxford University Press, Lagos, 1973, p. 46.
5. John Mwanakatwe. The Growth of Education in Zambia since Independence, Oxford University Press, Lusaka, 1968, p. 193.

6. Henry G. Johnson. The University and Social Welfare: A Taxonomic Exercise, in Keith G. Lemrden (ed.), *Efficiency in Universities,* Elsevier Scientific Publishing Company, Amsterdam, 1974, p. 25.

7. Eric Ashby. Contribution to Dialogue on African Universities, in *Universities Quarterly,* Vol. 20, No. 2, December 1965, p. 82.

8. Sir John Lockwood (Chairman), op. cit., p. 4.

9. Ibid., p. 27.

10. Eric Ashby. *African Universities and Western Tradition,* Oxford University Press, 1964, p. 38.

11. Quoted in Leo Marx, Technology and the Study of Man, in W. Roy Niblett (ed.), *The Sciences, The Humanities and the Technological Threat,* University of London Press, 1975, p. 10.

12. Ibid., p. 10.

13. George Grant. The University Curriculum and Technological Threat, in Niblett (ed.), op. cit., p. 31.

Professor N. M. SWANI (*Professor of Textile Technology, Indian Institute of Technology, Delhi*): The task before the educationists today is to examine the system of higher education in the context of population explosion, need for economic development, scientific and technological revolution, explosion of knowledge and, finally, the demand for social justice and equality of opportunity for the masses.

The primary function of a university is to preserve, transmit and increase human knowledge. This classical concept of a university system has been widely accepted, since ancient days, in Greece, India and West Asia where university education is believed to have begun. In the ancient times the objective of higher education was to develop complete and harmonious personalities with balanced intellect. The supreme values of education, which was essentially designed for the elite, were knowledge, intelligence, appreciation of arts and spiritual values. The students were drawn primarily from the aristocratic classes of society, particularly those who were to perform the functions of providing leadership and governing the regions lying within its realm. The classical education in ancient western societies, for example, included grammar, rhetoric, logic, arithmetic, geometry, astronomy and music, aimed primarily at developing total personalities of individuals. The medieval higher education in both Christian and Islamic schools catered to the requirements of feudal societies in which religious doctrines played a dominant role. The universities then performed a very useful function as storehouses of knowledge generated in the ancient civilizations. The emphasis therefore was on the learning of classical literature, law, philosophy, theology, mathematics and astronomy. During the Renaissance and the Age of Enlightenment the personal development of young people, first through the study of the classical literature and moral principles and later through the teaching of natural sciences, became the major function of universities in Europe. The expansion of universities in Europe was, then, accompanied by significant diversifications of disciplines and faculties to keep pace with the rapid increase in scientific knowledge.

Prior to the industrial revolution the range of learning in the universities in both Europe and America had no relation to economic development. Training for scientific and industrial activities had not entered the high pedestals of the university. Technical education was mainly imparted through apprenticeship without an institutional framework. The education for 'noble' professions like medicine, law and religious ministry was alone considered appropriate within the realm of a university. For most European academics transmission of knowledge through teaching remained their sole purpose. This is evident from the fact that in Britain it was the institutions like the Royal Society and not the universities that proved to be fertile ground for scientific research during the early period of scientific advancement. It was only during the nineteenth century, under the presence of rapidly expanding industrial culture and advancement of science, that search for new knowledge became the dominant theme, and the advancement of knowledge rather than its transmission became the prestigious role of a university. The twin roles of teaching and research are still considered to be the principal feature of a true university.

A rapid social and economic transformation of society brought about in Europe after the industrial revolution initiated a movement for expansion in higher education. The whole range of professional training — engineering of various specializations, economics, commerce, sociology, which were earlier confined to trade institutions of lesser importance — was brought within the scope of university activities. However so strong was the élitist tradition in Europe inherited from the medieval age that the education in engineering was still not considered a scholarly pursuit in the true sense and the red-brick universities in Britain were, until the middle of the twentieth century, regarded as poor relations of those still wedded to the classical traditions and pursuit of knowledge as an end in itself. The emphasis has been on excellence and training of intellect, rather than service to the society. Subject to this supreme objective the universities have met the needs of the society by training graduates in various professional disciplines who could apply their skills and intellect in providing future leadership and who could adjust themselves to new and challenging tasks. However education for high-level manpower, though an indispensable function, is only an indirect contribution to economic development. The direct contribution can only result from activities which are of direct relevance to the problem of society, and providing extension services, that is, advice and instruction to persons and organisations outside the campus. This role of service to the society in a broader and more meaningful sense has been a feature of the American universities ever since the inception of 'land-grant colleges' in the middle of the nineteenth century. In the USA, where university education has remained more open to the masses, it is taken for granted that the activities of a college will be such that it would use the community in which it is located as an additional resource for teaching and research. The universities there have a long-established tradition of becoming deliberately involved in the current local urban problems as much as they were in the agricultural improvement in the latter part of the nineteenth century.

During the last quarter of a century the world has been going through a second scientific and industrial revolution. Through the tremendous rise in industrial production the western countries have been able to eradicate poverty for the first time in history, with the result that the income gap between the masses and the upper classes has narrowed considerably. The rise of a vast new middle class has led to a demand for substantial expansion of university education and research, particularly in science and technology with greater relevance to the needs of the society in an age of rapidly changing technology. In Britain a big expansion of technological institutions was launched in 1956. It was not until the Robbins report on higher education was presented in 1963 that decision was taken to found new universities, not so much because of fresh need for more places but in order to stimulate innovation and give a philosophical basis and framework for the new tasks before the universities. It is no longer disputed that the universities have a role to play in developing new ideas and new technology, which will be of direct value to industry and government. This concept of the 'popular' as distinct from the élite functions of the universities, which first took root in the USA and later, in the 1960s, in Britain and Europe, is now generally accepted both in the developed and developing countries.

SUB-TOPIC 3(B): WHAT RANGE OF LEARNING?

This growth of emphasis on social responsibilities of universities has important consequences. The demand for university education through formal or informal means will grow further because of the rising expectations of the masses. Research, particularly in science and technology, will become increasingly oriented towards projects sponsored by government or other user agencies. These will provide funds on the basis of the national priorities and the academic interests of the university staff are to be used as a resource for solving national problems. Purely academic research, unrelated to the needs of society at present and in the foreseeable future, is at a discount. This has implications for the academic freedom and autonomy of a university. Since fundamental research is the exclusive domain of the universities, a balanced approach has to be adopted and proper weightage given to this primary function. Most of the major problems of national or international significance are not confined to any particular traditional discipline and often their technological solutions have social implications. To solve any such problem in its totality in a meaningful manner a combination of inputs from various academic departments is called for. This poses a major organisational problem in old universities where barriers among strong academic disciplines cannot be easily overcome. The university scientists may be ill-prepared to take up such problems because of the traditional preoccupation of the university system in most countries with the importance of the individual scholar or student working in isolation. Status and advancement in the sciences are highly discipline-oriented. A scientist working on a practical problem with a colleague from another discipline often finds that such research is slow in yielding publishable results. However it is clear that the future activities both in research and teaching will tend to be interdisciplinary because of the complex needs of the modern society, and the older universities have to face this challenge by providing a system of co-ordination and constant evaluation of projects and curricula of this nature. The reward system, which is at present based principally on professional achievements in an academic discipline, has to be reviewed to encourage such innovative efforts in research and teaching.

In any system the implementation of change requires a great deal of commitment, planning and dedicated efforts. The degree of difficulty encountered is often directly related to the proportion of the existing system involved in the change. If in any change this proportion is high the effect on the entire system is considerable and often it becomes a formidable task to introduce major innovations affecting the entire university. It is noteworthy that in all countries the development of most of the new innovations in curriculum and management have occurred in new campuses. Priority is passing from conventional universities to other institutions of higher education, existing or newly created, such as the polytechnics in Britain, technology universities in France, Fachhochschulen in Germany, the district colleges in Norway and the Institutes of Technology in India. In some of these new institutions, like the IITs in India, the role and priorities are already defined. In some cases, for example the British polytechnics, the precise role is as yet difficult to clarify because of the uncertainty about their objectives. These new institutions combine the role of universities by offering a new type of engineering first degree course with the training of higher technicians by following a full-time or part-time pattern of post-secondary courses normally offered by technical colleges. As Anthony Crosland, the creator of polytechnics, stated in 1972, some of these have not yet outgrown the technical college tradition, while others seem determined on following the normal university pattern. To my mind their success will ultimately depend on the extent of their involvement in social and industrial needs of the regions of their location and the resources they are able to mobilise through part-time or full-time education to meet the professional aspirations of the masses in a highly industrial society.

In the developing countries the pattern of education appropriate to the universities has to be examined in the light of their socio-economic problems which differ considerably from the western countries both in their nature and magnitude. It would be pertinent to cite the example of India in this regard since the problems and their attempted solutions in this country might be of some relevance to other developing countries of the Commonwealth. During the colonial era education in the Indian universities was aimed at equipping the students with the necessary knowledge of science and arts subjects, in order to provide an intelligentsia with sufficient knowledge of English to cater to the needs for middle-level management personnel in the civil and military administration, and prepare a limited number of engineers, technicians, doctors and lawyers for supporting roles in their respective professions. After independence India opted for planned development through a series of five-year plans aimed at rapid expansion in industry and agriculture. The implementation of these plans demanded large numbers of engineers and technicians in all spheres of national activity. The existing pattern of technical education was not adequate for this task both in terms of the projected manpower needs and of the quality of scientists and engineers required for the purpose.

In order to develop the projected engineering manpower the first and second five-year plans gave high priority to the expansion of engineering education, and by 1971 the number of degree engineering colleges stood at 138 in comparison with 38 in 1947, with an annual enrolment of about 20,000 students. Also by that time about 280 polytechnics had been established to train skilled technicians for the industry at diploma level, with an annual intake of nearly 45,000. In addition a network of industrial training institutes was established on a very large scale to train skilled craftsmen and technicians at lower level. Such a large expansion of technical education in the country naturally called for large investment in terms of equipment, buildings and trained personnel. Since the resources in the country were limited a selective approach had to be made in the planning of our infrastructure for education in science and technology. The policy of the government has therefore been to equip the five Institutes of Technology, located region-based in the country, with the most modern facilities and staff of the highest calibre so that the output of the Institutes could compare with the best anywhere in the world. These were also declared institutions of national importance and provided with liberal funds from domestic sources as well as through collaborative assistance from more advanced countries. These Institutes are expected to act as leaders in the development of technological education by providing postgraduate and research facilities and innovative teaching programmes at both undergraduate and postgraduate levels. Major facilities for engineering research could only be provided for these Institutes and a few other universities having well-established engineering departments.

By 1971 the capacity of the industry to employ engineering graduates fell short of their output, causing widespread unemployment, and therefore the emphasis since then has been on consolidation, improvement of quality, and orientation of engineering education to the needs of the society rather than its expansion. A number of steps have been taken to make engineering education more meaningful and egalitarian, such as giving research experience and advanced courses to the faculty on full-time or part-time basis, providing means of greater interaction with the industry through supervised student training, consultancy and short-term programmes for serving engineers, curriculum reforms by establishment of special centres of curriculum development at selected universities and polytechnics, greater academic autonomy to affiliated engineering colleges on a selective basis, and introduction of co-operative programmes in some colleges in collaboration with the industry. In addition the resources of the Indian Institutes of Technology and other major institutions are mobilised for execution of research projects of direct relevance to the needs of the country. Such projects, especially those of interdisciplinary nature, are liberally sponsored by various public funding agencies, such as the Department of Science and Technology, Ministry of Defence and Department of Electronics, etc. In addition special centres of interdisciplinary research in fields like energy, materials, resources engineering, ocean engineering, etc., have been located in the Institutes of Technology. Various areas of research relevant to the needs of the country were spelt out in the National Science and Technology Plan prepared in 1972 after obtaining a large-scale concensus of scientists and engineers throughout the country. Similar reforms were introduced in the polytechnics for producing technicians with greater specialised skills to meet the requirements of middle-level manpower in the industry and government departments. A parallel growth has taken place in the development of agricultural universities which have played a leading role in developing the modern methods of cultivation and providing efficient extension services to the agriculturists in rural areas. As a result of these efforts India, since independence, has achieved a high degree of self-reliance in her scientific and industrial activity and ranks among the ten most industrialised countries in the world.

Admission to engineering programmes is strictly on merit and the fees for these courses (£25 per annum) are well within the means of low-income groups. A large number of undergraduates and all postgraduate and research students receive state scholarships. There are special statutory provisions for admission of students from socially backward classes, and their needs for extra coaching are catered to in a variety of ways. However opportunities for serving technicians for higher education through part-time courses are still very limited as compared to the western countries.

It would thus appear that in the field of technology the range of learning appropriate to universities has been more or less clearly defined in India. However, in strong contrast to such professional disciplines, the objectives of the university programmes in the field of natural sciences, commerce, social sciences and arts are still not clear. Corresponding to the bachelor's degrees in engineering and technology, the minimum professional qualifications required in science and arts are master's degrees which are awarded at the end of the same duration of study. The three-year programmes for bachelor's degrees offered in arts or science in a large number of colleges affiliated to the various universities thus lead only to intermediate broad-based qualifications which are of little use without pursuing specialised programmes at a higher level. For such courses at bachelor's level the universities merely act as examining bodies with little or no control on teaching. However in the case of research programmes the role of the university is more direct since most of research in science is concentrated in the university departments under their direct supervision. As the demand for higher education grew phenomenally in India after independence greater opportunities for university education had to be provided as a result of social pressures, with the result that at present about 350,000 graduates in arts, commerce and social sciences at the first degree level are turned out every year through full-time, part-time and correspondence courses. Since such courses are broad-based and lack depth these graduates do not easily find employment and most of them remain unemployed or at best are absorbed only in clerical and other general subordinate cadres. A comprehensive survey of the actual employment potential in the country of the first degree holders has yet to be carried out, and at present there is no relation whatsoever between the actual needs and the structure of courses in the colleges. It is a paradox in a country like India that while we face a tremendous shortage of schoolteachers, particularly in the rural areas, the university graduates remain unemployed or underemployed in various roles having no direct relation to the socio-economic development of the country. Often students holding an MSc degree have to go through a PhD programme before they can be considered for any position with good future prospects.

As against this picture, the educational development of the country is still in its early stages when only about 30% of the population can be called literate and the aims of universal primary education are still far from being realised. If and when our hopes to spread universal education in the country are fully realised, the student population in our schools, colleges, universities and other institutions would form a significant proportion of the total population of the country. As basic education spreads it is inevitable that the pressure on university and professional courses will also increase and suitable means have to be found to meet this challenge effectively. So far the economy of the country has not been in a position to absorb the large number of graduates pouring out of the universities. The basic problem of India is that still 75% of the population derives its sustenance from agriculture. Since there is not much scope left for employing more people in agricultural activity the only way to improve the situation is to supplement agriculture with small- and medium-scale industries. Although the government and other public agencies provide large-scale incentives for installing small-scale industries in rural areas, unfortunately the educated Indians, largely drawn from the urban areas, are not willing to take up the challenge because of the lack of the necessary infrastructure and poor availability of skilled manpower in the villages. One of the solutions of this problem is to generate technical manpower at the intermediate level locally in these areas. The needs of the rural areas and the industry that can be sustained there depend upon the local resources and environment and no unique educational recipe can, therefore, be used universally for this purpose. Such an effort would demand considerable flexibility and ingenuity in designing appropriate programmes for small-scale entrepreneurs. It appears that a system of community colleges based on local requirements is more suited to our social and economic needs than the present rigid and outmoded pattern of the university-affiliated colleges.

To determine the range of learning which would be appropriate at the university level against the background of such problems poses a great challenge to the university education system all over the world. Since the social and economic conditions are so varied from nation to nation there is no universal solution, and each country has to find its own answer as to how the system of university education can be best organised to meet the demands for equality of opportunity consistent with the high standards of scholarship and intellectual values traditionally cherished by it. It is the duty of any society to provide basic education and vocational training to every individual to enable him to maintain a reasonable standard of living, but it would be too much to expect the universities to be the sole agencies for meeting these universal aspirations. The real role of the universities lies in training of intellect to produce leaders of tomorrow. In catering to the growing demands for university education, therefore, a selective approach has to be adopted. Only talented students leaving the secondary school really have the capacity to go through any meaningful university programme. If under political and social pressures the aims of university education do not remain confined to the type of professional education most appropriate to its basic objectives, creation of future leadership of the right calibre in the society would become an impossible task.

DISCUSSION

Dr. *A. A. Bruneau* (Memorial, Newfoundland—for paper, see above) argued that universities were bound to respond to the emphasis of society and governments on utilitarian and short-term goals of return on investments, while striving to maintain those key elements in the programme of

SUB-TOPIC 3(B): WHAT RANGE OF LEARNING?

instruction which had long-term aims or were even esoteric. What society wanted was a greater concentration on problem-oriented enquiries that were often not discipline-based and Dr. Bruneau suggested that a synthesis was possible; programmes could be devised which would draw disciplines together and make them sensitive to society's needs. But this should never involve any dropping of standards; the stretching of ability should remain the prime aim of university education. Research provided different, though parallel, problems and it was here that Dr. Bruneau believed universities to be most vulnerable. The pendulum was swaying sharply to the utilities of strategic research and it was essential to lay the strongest emphasis on the fact that in science the most significant practical advances usually arise from chance interactions between fundamental work and practical interests. The universities must maintain their basic commitment to excellence and this remained possible while interacting with society and dealing with 'relevant' matters as well as with the fundamental.

Dr. *J. M. Mwanza* (Zambia — for paper, see above) began by stating that universities were bound to respond to the political, social and economic contexts within which they existed. What was appropriate for universities in developed countries was therefore unlikely to be applicable in the third world, particularly where there was no indigenous tradition of university education. In countries like Zambia it was essential that universities should concentrate on the frontier set by society, particularly for the training of high-level manpower. Training based on the old disciplines was almost always inadequate for such purposes and had given way to interdisciplinary programmes. The problem was one of balance. It was important to look for flexible solutions which made use of the stringencies of the disciplinary approach but tied them to the problems of society. Dr. Mwanza then turned to the question of levels of work. He argued that in the third world degree-level work was only one part of the university's responsibility which should cover a wide range, including considerable extra-mural and correspondence course work. The university should be able to discharge its duty with respect to the pursuit of excellence effectively, no matter at what level. As far as research was concerned, the task of the universities of the third world was to concentrate more on the betterment of the lot of their people by applications of knowledge than on pure research.

Professor *N. M. Swani* (Indian Institute of Technology, Delhi — for paper, see above), after a brief historical survey, pointed out that there was a growing emphasis on the social responsibilities of universities throughout the world. He said that only where they have excellence will universities effectively contribute to social needs. Research was increasingly sponsored by governments which were highly sensitive to its social and economic implications. The consequence was that research and instruction could be less and less confined to the old disciplines. Established universities often found difficulty in adapting themselves to change and innovation was largely to be found in the newer institutions. Professor Swani drew attention to the success of the schemes in India for the training of engineers and technicians under the five-year plan and in particular to the setting up of the five institutes of technology. Initial difficulty in the matching of

TOPIC 3: RECONCILING EQUALITY AND EXCELLENCE

manpower to needs had now been largely overcome. In the non-technological fields, however, India was still far from satisfactorily defining the objectives of university programmes and the large numbers of graduates found it difficult to find adequate employment despite shortages of teachers outside the urban areas. Professor Swani stressed that the central role of universities was to concentrate on the training of the most able to ensure that they are adequately prepared to be the next generation of leaders.

In the ensuing discussion: —

Mr. Justice G. J. Samuels (New South Wales) suggested that the universities of the third world should stress disciplines like philosophy and law, to train those called to make social decisions at a later stage of development when social problems became complex.

The Rt. Rev. Dr. E. R. Wickham (Salford) suggested there was an ambiguity in the title of the topic. He thought that courses should involve breadth of education but that in an increasingly specialised world this could not be satisfactorily achieved merely by adding 'cultural' options. It is more fruitful to explore the deeper social and human implications of the technological disciplines of the main course. Dr. Bruneau agreed and said that in Canada a good deal had been done in educating engineers in this way. It might well be that not enough was done in the more classical disciplines to extend knowledge of technology. Dr. M. Horowitz (Alberta) said that at Alberta many arts students now did courses in technology but that some initial knowledge was undoubtedly necessary.

Professor M. Mwanalushi (Zambia) said that students needed to understand the social implications of specialist scientific decision-making in the third world where knowledge of society, people and economics was essential. To produce students who were adaptive in the use of traditional disciplines was less promising than problem-oriented courses.

Professor S. Lal (I.I.T., Kharagpur) agreed, but argued that universities must also provide opportunities for individuals to develop the full potential of their talents and skills in extra-disciplinary activities and interests.

Professor F. R. Crane (London) pointed out the link between work done before the university and what was done there: if education at school had been broad there was less harm in specialisation at university.

Dr. D. H. Irvine (Guyana) noted that the distinction between universities and other institutions of tertiary education was relevant to defining appropriateness for universities and suggested that 'institutes of higher learning' might be more relevant to developing countries at present.

Dr. A. T. Porter (Sierra Leone) drew attention to a fundamental difference of view about the range of subjects to which universities should apply themselves. In the developed world universities had tended to remain narrowly concentrated and institutions such as polytechnics had been established. In the West Indies the concept of 'umbrella university' was favoured and he questioned the possibility of agreeing on a definition of what was not suitable to university learning. Professor Whelan agreed that there had been too little discussion of the binary system. He suggested

SUB-TOPIC 3(B): WHAT RANGE OF LEARNING?

that the criterion of a university discipline was that a portion of students returned to advance knowledge in it. Dr. Bruneau suggested that the specific attribute of a university was that it covered the complete range of knowledge from teaching to discovery.

Dr. D. R. Campbell (Manitoba) stressed the importance to university students of practical experience before admission and thought that universities in the third world could do more with mature and part-time students.

Professor J. F. Scott (La Trobe) drew a distinction between various aspects of the appropriateness of university studies: to the individual concerned with job prospects; to society where the manpower needs were dominant; to the pursuit of leisure interests which increasingly would concern the developed industrial societies; and to the university itself.

Lord Boyle (Leeds) said that the binary system had developed for two main reasons in Britain: the long history of involvement of local authorities in technical and other advanced colleges; and a strong political demand in the fifties and sixties for the expansion of a specifically university type of education. He suggested that it was probably impossible to define a university subject other than that it involved a particular way of teaching which was related to the expectation of derivative research and development.

Sir Hermann Black (Sydney) suggested that when attempting to define an appropriate range of learning there was an empirical test of what a university chose to include when resources were scarce. Sir Hermann then considered the constraints which universities impose on the student's choice of subjects in a degree course from one extreme of free à la carte choice to the other of the single rigid discipline and suggested that universities ought to take the middle position to provide flexibility and choice.

Professor A. E. Astin (Belfast) suggested that there was a basic distinction between sequential and non-sequential subjects which made it almost impossible for those without technical training to acquire much insight into *e.g.* the problems of engineering. Dr. Bruneau thought that the answer might be in interpretative courses which dealt with the implications of technology in application and could be understood by both engineering and humanities students.

Sir Denys Wilkinson (Sussex) said that universities should not lose sight of their high responsibility as transmitters of indigenous culture. At this time the responsibility was particularly heavy for the universities of the third world.

Sub-Topic 3(c)

STANDARDS OF EDUCATION AND GRADUATION

Chairman: Professor R. MUKHERJI
Vice-Chancellor of the University of Burdwan

Rapporteur: Professor P. P. G. L. SIRIWARDENE
Vice-Chancellor of the University of Sri Lanka

Tuesday, 22 August

On the Training of University Teachers

Professor D. J. GIFFORD (*Director, Centre for Latin-American Linguistic Studies, University of St. Andrews*): The following paper tries to tease out the threads of controversy that exist in a small university. It is given in the hope that a problem seen on a small and intimate scale may help others to get larger-sized tangles into perspective. I am a teacher of Spanish, and although I am aware that on the face of it this is a far cry from instruction in engineering or other technologies, political science or economics, my experience is that there are many considerations common to all branches of university teaching, be they in Asia, Africa or any other part of the world.

By way of preamble we start with the oldest questions of all: we are all—or have been all—university teachers. Are we teachers or are we researchers? How can we be assessed as teachers? Is university teaching something which can be measured?

In the past there has been little or no success in deciding what criteria really obtain in judging anyone's competence as a university teacher. Is he a lively-seeming man? Do students flock to his lectures, tell us later that they rolled in the aisles with mirth at his way of delivery, were utterly inspired by him? Alas, while often providing entertainment and interest such teachers do not appear to have imparted much by way of wisdom or knowledge, and subsequent examinations bear this out. Or take another man: does he not seem somewhat dull and morose? Do his pupils report him as reading out in quiet monotone as his class sit with collective eye on the clock? Yes, but the more ready-witted of the class also report that the stuff that comes out of his notes is concise and to the point, that his articulateness is, however drearily presented, something that can impart ideas and facts in sharply defined form. All the fireworks of his lively colleague are of little moment beside this serious and unexciting man, and examinations and subsequent pointers to educational success show conclusively that the students get far more from him than from the first.

It may be pointed out at this stage that lecturing is not just a matter of imparting facts or even ideas, but of lighting up the subject. But a *teaching* lecture is better if it is clear and useful to the student.

These two hypothetical cases are cited by way of starting point. Whether many colleagues would feel that the training of university teachers is only a luxury compared with the task of finding academically qualified men to fill the ever-growing number of posts in expanding universities—all that may in a sense be so. Yet whatever criteria we use, the question of excellence in teaching has to be raised some time: our own competence or incompetence in this matter is something that affects us intimately. To return to the first question—whether we are teachers or researchers: many may feel more confident in the matter of research than they may in teaching, and consequently do as little of the latter as they can get away with. For one's ability as a teacher is like one's ability as a lover or a friend: pull that thread and the whole pattern, as on a loom, starts to move. Whether we fail or not as teachers is something we care for, more than we would like to admit.

The ideal teacher in ancient times was the scholar or philosopher who, with some half-dozen disciples, talked and mused on his subject as well as on life in general. Students were amanuenses, their teacher an exemplar. To-day such a method is deemed to be impossible: getting 600 students through elementary engineering principles is not comparable with letting six students into the secrets of philosophy. Yet it does matter, 6 or 600, *how* we teach.

Our experience in St. Andrews involved a gestatory period in which we experimented with the idea of how to approach in-service training, that is, training in teaching methods while the teacher is at the same time doing his job. The compulsion to explore possibilities came partly from students, who thought that a young academic teacher should receive formal training rather than make all his growing pains affect his own pupils. Schoolteachers went through colleges of education—why not university teachers? The first attempt at discussion came through a day of lectures by senior university staff, where lecturing techniques, seminars, small teaching groups, tutorials, etc, were thoroughly gone into. Our Vice-Chancellor also took part, and also held a reception after the day's work in order to meet all the new lecturers. The next year (1971) a more ambitious series of training lectures was devised whereby the course covered every Saturday morning for eight weeks. The following session a party of 27 interested teachers met at a large house in the Scottish highlands for a week-end. Speakers were also invited in from outside. A psychologist talked about teaching assessment, a professor of Spanish about the assessment of students, a young social worker about the problems of young people, the Vice-Principal of an Oxford college on the analytical method in teaching, a teacher of German on uncongenial subjects and the ways used to interest students in spite of them, and our own Principal on academic teaching in general. Notes from the talks were then published in booklet form.

What emerged from these exploratory meetings was this: that although the young beginner-teacher would as often as not volunteer to come and take part in the discussions, those who had been teaching for some time were divided. The sessions were aimed at them as well as at the beginners but, whereas those who were well-known at being successful teachers would all attend, those who were well-known as unsuccessful ones nearly all stayed away. This on the face of it may seem an over-simplification, but on discussing the matter with them it appeared that they genuinely did not think they needed any improvement in methods. The conclusion one came to was that the worst offenders in university teachers are often those in their thirties, forties and fifties who have become used to bad teaching habits and are quite oblivious of the fact. One cannot get sacked for being a bad teacher, moreover.

The early seventies saw a lot of activity in the field of the training of university teachers. Many short courses were held, conferences organised and papers published. In Scotland a consortium of four universities decided to have an annual course which would be held in rotation. Stirling, Heriot-Watt, Dundee and St. Andrews formed this group. The following brief summary may give some idea of the substance of such a course: it pertains to that held at St. Andrews in 1973.

● First of all, one should emphasise that it was a cross-disciplinary course, that is, not subject-orientated. It was attended by some thirty new lecturers from the four universities I have mentioned.

- Secondly, it was residential.
- Thirdly, though not compulsory, it was strongly recommended for those starting their careers as university teachers.

This course lasted four full days, running from 9.30 a.m. till lunch-time, 4 p.m. till 6 p.m. and 8 p.m. till 10 p.m. The first day, after two introductory sessions, a professional actor gave a talk on lecture delivery and voice production; in the afternoon a panel of students and teachers discussed lecture techniques. This aired old criticisms. In the evening there was a discussion of the voice production lecture in the morning, again with the help of a student-staff panel. Students were encouraged to attend all the lectures on the course.

The second day we divided into groups for the morning, with sessions on video-taping specimen lectures. This involved a young lecturer being televised as he gave a 10-minute talk, and then having it shown back to him and the audience. Discussion of his technique followed. There were also sessions for the groups on programmed learning, seminars, practicals, lecturing techniques and tutorials. During the afternoon a talk on the Scottish educational system was given. This is an important issue, as school-leavers in Scotland are generally a year younger than in England, with the consequence that they start a year younger at university. In the evening small groups discussed objectives in teaching.

The third day the video-taping and other group sessions went on as before. In the afternoon there was a brains trust on advising students. This included a panel including the accommodation officer for students, the university doctor, the chaplain and various others. In the evening there was a general discussion on staff-student relationships.

The last day saw the final group of morning sessions, and the afternoon was spent hearing a lecture on the theory of aspects of learning.

So much for an example of a short four-day course. In other universities they might be more or less elaborately organised with varying emphasis on the differing teaching needs in each place. You will see that it was devised to cover both practical and theoretical approaches to teaching in universities, with a strong bias towards student participation.

A follow-up course was held at St. Andrews for a single day. This was three months later. Here are the topics discussed: university administration (by the Secretary of the University), student counselling, the assessment of students' work and means whereby they might be helped in this and a discussion of study methods. It was felt that these subjects would be of more use to the young lecturer now that his first term's teaching was over.

Such is a specimen attempt at solving the problem of training university teachers. It is one of many others and whether it is the right approach one cannot say. University teachers are not schoolteachers, for they have different objectives: colleges of education are therefore not the answer. For us, in-service training, with elder and more experienced teachers helping their younger colleagues—the old and traditional idea of apprenticeship—appears to contain the germ of a solution.

I should like to end on a different topic, that of the assessment of teaching. It is said that in various walks of modern society to get to the top of any one profession one needs to give up exercising one's basic skill and to take on the functions of an administrator. Nowhere so apparent is this than in the field of teaching at a university. Yet teaching is an art, and a sharing of that art. An actor, a painter or a musician can climb to the heights through the excellence of their technique and their genius, and remain actors, painters or musicians. It does not seem to be the same with the teacher. The answer lies of course in the fact that the artist can be assessed: the public at large can proclaim his excellence because it can perceive and appreciate it. Teaching cannot be assessed, and until it can it will not be rewarded or be taken seriously as an art. Our attempts at training the university teacher will only be accepted half-heartedly by the young beginner because his elders will in fact say to him: 'Don't waste too many hours teaching—there are better ways of getting on'. The bad teacher *can* rise to the top of his profession, that is, to heights of administration or to honours for research done, without doing more than the basic minimum required by contract.

This I feel is the great obstacle. The art of teaching is based on affection between tutor and pupil. Even to-day, for all our talk, it only enjoys an amateur status in the university.

Dr. D. T. KENNY (*President and Vice-Chancellor of the University of British Columbia*): Two decades ago universities lived in a straightforward world. Universities were at liberty to do pretty much as they desired. They were regarded as society's greatest hope. They set their standards of admission without giving any great thought to the declaration that equal access to higher education is the key to the future of youth and of nations. They were not convinced that admission policies or graduation requirements had to be bent in conformity with the social goals of society. If admission policies denied opportunities for advancement or upward mobility, it was not looked upon as a serious social or educational problem. If the requirements of education and graduation were overly demanding, major research universities did not perceive this situation as too serious for, after all, any displeased student, as a modern bedouin, could always hop a bus and find another institution with lower standards of exit — at least, this was the case in North America. Assumptions about the social purposes of universities were unexamined.

Then academic affairs began to become increasingly complex and mazy. The belief in our omnipotence was challenged in the turbulent and hurly-burly days of the late sixties. Universities became publicly vulnerable when they were bitterly denounced for denying opportunities for advancement in society. Universities were accused of racism, sexism and élitism.

These were serious charges since North American democracy has a deep passion for equality and social justice and special privilege for none. We are a compassionate society. For North Americans social justice represents a step toward a better world. Higher education was perceived to have a social responsibility to find a means to close the gap between promise and reality in order to improve societal well-being. The expanding expectations of egalitarian justice was to impose upon all institutions, including universities, the demand to examine and correct their priorities. Gradually the battle cry was heard that legislation might be the best democratic mode for correcting societal wrongs. It was proposed that progress by 'petty tinkering' was not a sufficient method for a civilized society.

Over the past few years these charges posed innumerable questions for higher education. The hard fact is that, by and large, the essence of higher education is to be selective. In accepting this truth most universities realized that their guiding principle was to enhance quality, while fully recognizing the importance of justice.

As the full flowering of the harsh debate about the priorities and standards of universities gathered full force, a wave of populist egalitarianism thrust three striking demands at higher education. Of first importance was the demand for equal opportunity of access to universities. This challenge took on added significance when equal opportunity was naively assumed to mean an 'open admissions' policy. This policy meant that anyone had a right to admission to higher education who happened to have the minimum qualification of a secondary school diploma. There was nothing new about this hope. After all it reflects the dream of universal access to post-secondary education. For all practical purposes, however, the full implementation of this policy would result in the political secularization of universities. Ultimately it also means that universities would take on the academic responsibilities of high schools. Viewed in this light any open admissions policy is a reaction to a social problem with a nostrum that doesn't remove the problem.

Second, there was the wistful demand that all individuals within the universities should be treated as equals and that higher education should give a guarantee of absolute equality of result. To fulfil this command, anyone would have the right to entrance and the right to graduate. In short, open admissions would lead to open graduations.

Unfortunately, in the zeal to better the social quality of life, all due care was not taken by some institutions in their respose to these twin anti-élitist demands. In fact certain universities effected a lot of buffleheaded and outrageous acts in the name of equality. In a very predictable manner, standards fell. As a consequence the broader national good and well-being was abused.

This brings me to the third salvo fired during the turbulent era of academic barricades. The demand went up for 'relevance' and for 'flexible innovations' in the curriculum. The predominant characteristic of this claim was the unquestioning belief in the new and the disparagement of the old. Change in the curriculum, rather than tradition, was to be institutionalized. The search for relevance and innovation often took on bizarre and faddish forms. In a time of uncertain standards and intellectual confusion, all too often the spun-sugar candy courses were based on nothing more substantial than the kind of information you use when you bet on a horse. Inconclusive and fragmented knowledge leads to the pooling of ignorance, and ignorance has never served universities and the nation well. No university or nation can build its destiny on individuals whose horizons are limited by self-evident realities.

As this decade draws to a close universities and the public are no longer so innocent on the issue of the reconciliation of equality and excellence. Against this backdrop of recent history, the remainder of my remarks has a certain kind of inevitability. It is the responsibility of all who seek a reconciliation of equality and excellence never to forget what the intellectual and academic essence of higher education is all about.

Fortunately the centuries-long history of universities has indicated that higher education's purpose has been, is and always must be unbiased critical enquiry. The university deals in ideas. That is what we produce and what we provide. It has often been said — and cannot be said too often — that a university is dedicated to learning.

This sounds thin, quaint, dull and limited. On the contrary, it is the one true and reliable source of intellectual excitement. The joy of the chase, the drive to discover is the fundamental reason for our existence.

Without a strong commitment to first-class learning a university will be committed to a second-class future. Our foremost precept has to be: what facilitates learning is beneficial, what hinders learning is harmful. There is no better guarantee against the undermining of this maxim than the 'grit' to maintain and strengthen standards. This test of excellence has to be the watch-concept of the university community in the allocation of resources, in setting entrance and promotion standards, in the approval of the curriculum, and in the recruitment and retention of faculty. In assessing the relative merits of competing needs within a university the answer can usually be ascertained by comparing the standards each claimant has. *What is important is that the side of high standards wins out.*

True, no university can claim perfection in the realm of high standards. Our reach for quality may exceed our grasp since perfection may never really be attained especially when financial resources are finite. It is also true that high standards of excellence are not reached at all times by every member of the university community, but it remains an objective. Our primary mission is to strive toward this golden vision. The progress of a university can be no swifter than its progress in excellence.

Without question, any trend to lessen excellence would be adverse to the academic and public interest. I remain convinced that our principal enemy is the failure to adhere to standards of excellence. In fact our case for public support and credibility rests upon our standards. They are the centrepiece of universities.

Unfortunately a portion of the public and some academics don't believe in this principle. Confusion has occurred in the public because no one seems to be in charge. This is not surprising in the light of various government edicts, the diverse views of university grant councils, the expansion of litigation, the passionate and often purple rhetoric of special-interest groups, and the rapid social changes in society. What the public requires are some broad guidelines that are clear. Without a public understanding and acceptance of the unique nature of universities in society, higher education cannot expect strong public support. As we come to the brink of the twenty-first century we must develop and adhere to policies that will permit the continuous strengthening of excellence. It is on this challenge that public and academic policy should now be focused.

There is no necessary incompatibility between academic excellence and the public interest. If universities are to serve the citizenry responsibly they must sharpen their emphasis on excellence. To illustrate, but by no means to limit, let me suggest some areas of concern to all people, whatever place they occupy in society.

Of all the social challenges a nation faces, equal opportunity is one of the most important. We all know that there are shocking inequalities and great social injustices in life, particularly inequalities in access to education. This is a common issue within nations and among nations. As I pursue this topic I remind you that we should not lose sight of one fundamental proposition: what a nation wants is a function of values and costs. If the value is known, then the public can decide if the product is worth the price. I cannot give prescriptions for any nation's values. The essential decisions about values must be made by your own society.

However there are three aspects one should keep in mind about public values and attitudes: first, the public is prepared to accept the reality that there are no free and quick fixes or solutions to knotty social problems; second, the public attaches great and cardinal value to responsibility; and third, the public rarely remains wrong for long when they realize the value of a product does not reflect the money spent on it. These are the enduring values that academics should keep uppermost in mind when they think of reconciling equality and excellence, for they are the standards by which the public will judge universities. Public confidence must not be weakened. To the contrary, the recognition of public accountability is part of the social costs of a public university. Universities cannot afford to have social objectives which are widely divergent from the larger goals of society.

Public and academic policy should ensure the implication of the principle of equal educational opportunity regardless of race or sex or religious belief or economic status. This principle simply means that we guarantee every person with the appropriate entrance requirements an equal opportunity to enter a university. This principle doesn't imply an open admissions policy. In fact entrance requirements assume an inequality based on intellectual and academic grounds. I do not believe that the public is prepared to support or value any university from which anyone could be exempted from admission regulations.

In 1978 it has become fashionable to link the promise of equality to the 'revolution of rising entitlements'. In the name of equal opportunity, the outcome of this linkage would be simple, but devastating. In effect universities would provide a built-in guarantee of equality of result. Some individuals in the academic and public community would, no doubt, applaud an announcement that universities were assuring equality of outcome. But the general public response would be entirely predictable—outrage. The thoughtful public never remains enthusiastic about the product which they know is worthless. The public is not prepared to accept the proposition that equality and academic success are correlated. Nor should universities.

There should be no doubt that our obligation is to oppose the establishment of mediocrity or undistinguished equality as the standard of performance in higher eduation. On balance the standards of education and graduation should be high and very demanding. Moreover universities should pay attention to a nation's long-term interests in the world of international scholarship. In the global competition that lies ahead nations will need more of excellence than mediocrity. For this reason alone no part of the world's intellectual capacity should lose ground because the standards of education and graduation are soft. The cost of excellence is high, but today all nations must be equal to the heritage of intellectual excellence.

I remain convinced that there is a deep yearning for excellence by most, if not all, modern societies. The public has a higher respect for intellectual exercise and discipline than we give it credit for. We do not need a constructive dialogue with citizens on this point. They fully acknowledge that our heritage of excellence is for the common good. They also realize that once standards start slipping they almost never stop.

Universities must build on this heritage of excellence, otherwise the failure on this score will increase their financial problems. With a sceptical public, universities would soon find their financial support shrinking.

The North American public is already disenchanted with the unenviable learning record of the elementary and secondary schools. A national consensus appears to exist concerning the decline of academic achievement in our schools. Moreover the public is even now starting to voice similar anxieties about some of our universities. These concerns are: the tragedy of grade inflation, the academic validation of non-academic experiences, the elimination of language requirements, the relaxation of curricular demands, and the cafeteria style of miscellaneous education. These afflictions are due to the attenuation of academic standards and the failure of some academics to recognize what a university should be.

Confidence in universities will be shattered if 'egalitarian excellence' becomes the accepted delusion in which we believe all are equal or nearly so. No university can hope to advance if it does not have the support of the community for, in the final analysis, much of what universities do is not exclusively 'our own business'.

The underlying reality to acknowledge is that society has given the universities a mandate to graduate individuals having the best qualities possible. Society expects our graduates to be brilliant — the best scientists, the most excellent researchers, the most wise humanists. There is persuasive evidence to believe that the public takes deep pride in first-rate universities. Just as banks must maintain selectivity among borrowers, the creditworthiness of universities will depend upon their resolve to preserve standards and to push forward a student's intellectual frontiers to the highest level before he is permitted to graduate. The university is damaged when students are not educated to the full measure of their abilities.

In this context, perhaps it is worth stating that students from minority groups who succeed will act as models for others, thereby increasing their numbers in the universities. In fact the acceleration of this trend is heart-warming. To the levellers and special-interest-beneficiaries in society I know that this view will be singularly unpersuasive since it appears to represent a slow movement forward.

So I come back to the need for excellence and sound academic judgement in those areas where the genuinely academic priorities are resolved. And this is where the relationship of faculty and students comes into play. Wherein lies the greatness and excellence of a university? It lies in those professors who are capable of excellence in their teaching and scholarship. The real challenge for any university is to recruit faculty members who believe in excellence, standards and scholarship. Critical to the success of excellence is faculty acceptance that the intrinsic mission of higher education can be attained. To accomplish most, if not all, of what I'm talking about, it is important that a university be able to attract and keep a distinguished professoriate which engages in sustained and deliberate scholarship.

The basic responsibility for stimulating and maintaining excellence in scholarship, teaching, the curriculum, entrance and graduation requirements, and the recruitment of professors must normally rest on the faculty, with help and strong leadership from faculty committees and the administration.

As universities and society pursue the debate over excellence and equality, universities should not lose sight of certain vital propositions, on which I believe most will surely agree.

SUB-TOPIC 3(C): STANDARDS OF EDUCATION [Kenny]

First, no matter what policies are set for admission and graduation, universities should understand that the most effective way of liberating a student's mind is to expose him to a faculty member of quality. The power of mind that is active in the development of a discipline is what begets excellence in students. This liberated effect is what graduation regulations undertake to assess.

Second, the faculty are the shapers of university policies. Accordingly the standards of education and graduation must be fashioned by the faculty. The reconciliation of equality and excellence must be shaped by each university. It would be foolish for me to provide prescriptions or specific norms on these matters. To be sure, a university cannot protect itself by hiding from excellence in an interdependent world. Hollow standards of education and graduation fall quickly when the question of excellence is at stake.

Third, the most direct method by which a university can uplift the academic standards of students and faculty is to enhance its own expectations of excellence and to sharply outline these expectations to the whole community. This is an important leadership role for strong heads, deans and the president or vice-chancellor.

Fourth, universities should avoid temptations and demands to compromise the traditional criteria in the selection and retention of faculty. With the 'revolution of declining opportunities' for faculty members, the temptation may exist to retain faculty on inappropriate grounds. Compromise is not always the best means for promoting the survival of a first-class university.

So, in closing, let me tell you about a classic remark made by the late Mayor Richard Daley of Chicago, one of the most powerful mayors in North America. In speaking to a political gathering, he remarked: 'We should all rise to higher platitudes together'. Undoubtedly he wanted to assert a great truth. We should all rise to excellence.

DISCUSSION

The paper presented by Professor *D. J. Gifford* (St. Andrews—see above) dealt with the training of university teachers and in his preliminary remarks he stressed points from his paper. Many university lecturers were not teaching properly and very little, if anything, was spent by universities in training them as teachers. He considered that one cannot train oneself and advocated an apprenticeship system. There should be an apprenticeship scheme in which senior staff can help juniors in their departments and there must be a system of evaluation (by examination or thesis) before tenure is granted, *e.g.* after a period of three years. If schoolteachers went through training, why was it not necessary for university teachers, even though the objectives of these two types of teachers are not always the same? He stressed that the art of good teaching was based on affection between teacher and pupil and such affection and dedication were necessary to make a good teacher.

Dr. *D. T. Kenny* (British Columbia), speaking next (for paper, see above), said that his comments related strictly to North American context but some of the conclusions were applicable generally. Universities must maintain standards even against society's wish to use them for the social advancement of the youth of the country. They have been accused of racism, sexism and élitism on account of their selection procedures. The essence of higher education is to be selective and universities had to maintain the guiding principle to enhance quality while fully recognising the importance of justice. Equal opportunity of access to universities is necessary but this should not be an 'open admissions' policy, nor can there be an 'open graduation' policy. Relevance and innovation in curricula were also demanded by society and sometimes these led students to inconclusive and fragmented knowledge. In the search for reconciliation between equality and excellence it was essential that the academic and intellectual essence of higher education was maintained. That essence was in unbiased critical enquiry and dedication to learning. Anything facilitating learning is useful; anything detrimental to learning is bad for the university. This is the *acid test* and this is what grants committees are for — to assess this test. The universities' case for public support and credibility rests upon the maintenance of their standards of excellence.

There is public concern on the lowering of standards in elementary and secondary schools and some similar concern is directed at some universities. There is persuasive evidence that the public takes pride in first-rate universities. Dr. Kenny suggested four general propositions as the foundation of the greatness and excellence of a university. First, high quality faculty is essential; secondly, faculty should be the shapers of university policy and maintain the high standards; thirdly, the vice-chancellors, deans and heads of departments must take responsibility for leadership in the institution and in society by constant drive for the excellence that has to be preserved; and, fourthly, staff must be retained only on the basis of excellence.

In opening the discussion the chairman (Professor Mukherji) expressed the need for cheaper textbooks which were lacking in developing countries and also the need for mobility of teachers to assist their training, and said that good course syllabuses were necessary if high standards are to be maintained in universities.

In response to the question 'what constitutes good teaching?', Professor Gifford said that a teacher should work with students to stimulate the students to start teaching themselves: the teacher's purpose is not merely to impart information.

There was general discussion showing many differences of opinion on the reward system for teachers and ways to assess good teaching. Professor

SUB-TOPIC 3(c): STANDARDS OF EDUCATION

J. H. Whitelaw (Concordia) said that the system of rewards in the academic profession must stimulate good teaching more strongly. Dr. Kenny stressed that assessment of teachers was a multi-dimensional problem solved mainly by senior staff observing the generation of student enthusiasm. He suggested that staff who concentrated on excellence in teaching might have tenure with the title of senior instructor. He expressed doubt whether there should be in universities staff who could only be manipulated to improve teaching by the outside reinforcement of a rewards system: only good staff with internal motivation to teach should be appointed. It was suggested that if a teacher was due for promotion or tenure, rather than the university attempting to assess him, he should be requested to submit details of his achievements. There were suggestions that a teacher could be observed while he was teaching and his notes could be examined. Student evaluation had defects since teachers could manipulate students in some universities. The chairman said that in developing countries the conditions were not suitable for student assessment of teachers. Professor G. J. Fraenkel (Flinders) said that if an institution is seriously committed to assessing staff it was not impossible to devise appropriate and effective methods. It was generally accepted that it is not possible to assess good teaching *exactly*. There were both the teaching and research dimensions when tenure or promotion were considered. A balance had to be worked out depending on the grade of teacher and the nature of duties entrusted to him.

Some felt that the fundamental criteria for a university teacher is excellence and knowledge of his subject, so that one sought master chemists and physicists or mathematicians and not master teachers.

Professor A. E. Astin (Belfast) said that although assessments cannot be quantified departments helped staff by having a junior attached to a senior member of the staff who gave informal guidance and advice.

Lord Boyle (Leeds) said that to maintain quality of faculty staff much effort was made by vice-chancellors when, for example, chairs are filled to get the best possible candidate. There should be more emphasis on the study of texts and dissertations in course work. He suggested that, while excellence is the right primary standard for graduation, regard should be given to the general contribution to his year of the less academically gifted student. Mr. W. Senteza Kajubi (Makerere) stated that, unlike professional people such as doctors or engineers, teachers work in isolation. He suggested that audio-visual methods for teaching helped learning because of the care taken in preparing material. He thought that with closed-circuit television a teacher can also assess his own teaching.

Mr. R. C. Connolly (Liverpool) agreed that the audio-visual system where one sees oneself was a good way to learn to teach. University teaching is very individual-oriented and one's personal style and techniques were important. There was a difference between schoolteachers and university teachers. The former require to be much more uniform and require training; they have similar teaching guides; the same material for teaching, etc. A university teacher, however, is more individual; he has to make his own interpretations and emphasis, to condense current literature, etc. Sir David Derham (Melbourne) supported this view. The child in school is a 'captive' audience and the school looks after him *in loco parentis*. Universities were the same some time ago but today there is freedom — a university student can approach his university teacher or move away from him at his discretion.

Professor W. A. C. Stewart (Keele) stated that university teachers also have the 'tutorial relationship' — the small group relation. There are obvious things a good teacher must possess — he must be audible, clear in what he says, and make a good contribution to scholarship. In summary he suggested that the good university teacher will be true to his own scholarship and thereby exercise a benign infection of the student with a like commitment.

It was clear from the discussion that it was not possible to assess a university teacher *exactly*. University teachers had different roles to play compared with schoolteachers. Different teachers would have different styles of teaching but it is essential that in whatever manner teaching is done it should be for the benefit of the student. Here the university teacher has the responsibility to seriously and honestly assess himself and take whatever steps are necessary to rectify his shortcomings.

Sub-Topic 3(d)

MOBILITY OF STUDENTS AND STAFF INTERNATIONALLY

Chairman: Dr. D. H. IRVINE
Vice-Chancellor and Principal of the University of Guyana

Rapporteur: Mr. E. E. TEMPLE
Assistant Secretary General, Association of Commonwealth Universities

Thursday, 24 August

Professor Sir DAVID DERHAM (*Vice-Chancellor and Principal of the University of Melbourne*): There are times when we should remind ourselves of things well known. This is one of those times. Nothing in this paper is new. All of it has been said before in one way or another; much of it a long time ago.

A sufficient movement of staff and students among the universities of the world is necessary for the health and strength of universities generally. Why this should be so, however, is not always easy to explain to regional communities at any particular time. To do so we should perhaps remind ourselves of some very general propositions about universities, about our recent past, and about the inevitable pressures to contain or restrict mobility. It is necessary to notice also that the reasons for the need for staff movement are in some respects different from, and more immediate than, those relevant to students, and that movement by postgraduate students is becoming much more significant than movement by undergraduates.

The idea of a university is controlling. When a university is established the idea proves to be the test of direction and development unless external controls are imposed of a kind which prevent the development of a real university and then perhaps, however slowly, the idea and the university die.

The idea is an ancient one. It has survived through times of troubles, and in spite of the forces of darkness, for many centuries; and it has worn many superficially different forms and colours. The central notion is clear nonetheless, and also that the family of man requires its preservation.

The purposes of a university are, of course, to acquire, to preserve and to disseminate knowledge. The first involves research, and the second and third involve teaching. But other institutions can claim those aims. The mark of a real university is made by a further statement about the nature of the knowledge to be pursued, and about the purposes of the dissemination of knowledge.

However important to its local community, to its state, or to its nation, may be the day-to-day or the year-to-year work of a university, its primary commitments with respect to the pursuit and dissemination of knowledge must be to the world, and not just to the community which gave it birth or which supports it. However we may fail in particular efforts, and though we may fail at particular times, a university must be committed to the acquisition and dissemination of knowledge beyond mere reference to the needs of particular times and places.

All nations to be truly independent in an international world need one or some universities which can satisfy that commitment.

The controlling idea of a university springs from the long lessons of history about the nature of human associations capable of pursuing the aims successfully. All societies are subject to processes of change in response to internal and external pressures which vary in intensity from time to time. Yet all societies, with varying success, seek to settle the disturbances which accompany change by ordering themselves towards a stable state in ways which involve resistance to change. To maintain their capacities for change, large and complicated societies in the modern world must consciously provide for special associations and special places in which restrictions upon the exploration of new ideas and the pursuit of new knowledge are reduced to a minimum. Those places need not, perhaps, be universities; but the idea of the university has produced for us, so far at least, the best answer to the need.

The university era in which we now live began, I suppose, in the first decade of the nineteenth century when Wilhelm Von Humboldt saw the realization of his dream for a university—'..... unattached to any particular creed or school of thought devoted only to the interests of science and learning'. It was those words that were used in the charter of the University of Berlin in 1809.

The development of universities like London, Birmingham, Toronto, Sydney and Melbourne, to name but a few, about the middle of the nineteenth century, carried through the notion and dream expressed by Von Humboldt. They responded to a technological and scientific age which, it was thought, would bring a remarkable, new and happy future for mankind. Let us remember that the new universities, called 'godless institutions' by the devotees of an older time, were established in the hope that all might benefit from an education designed to equip people to be citizens in an intelligent democracy. Those new universities provided for training in the technologies and in the sciences but, consistently with the ideals of their founders, theirs was no mere apprenticeship training to some skilled vocation. The hope was that it would be mellowed by the dreams of the poet and by the ideals of the philosopher.

Let me repeat that the nations in the interest of their own future must provide places where any subject and any question is open for rational inquiry. But most thinking and argument which goes on among men directly involved in the economic and political life of the community is tied closely to action. It is likely to be dangerous thinking if it is not limited to the reasonably possible in the light of society's structure as it is seen to be at the time. Thinking and argument which is intended directly to produce action is not only limited in itself by the immediately possible but it attracts limitations by society lest stability and security are too greatly disturbed. That is why the thinking and argument and research for which freedom ought to be provided in a university should be in some degree insulated from action taken in the community at large. This is not to suggest a retirement to a series of scholarly or monastic institutions cut off from community affairs. The days for such places are mainly gone. It would not be sensible nor desirable to attempt their recall.

This is not to say that the work to be done in universities should have no relevance to, or effect upon, those responsible for action in the community. Discoveries and new ideas, once published, stimulate changes in the community's ways of doing things in time. Similarly from time to time the problems incidental to changes in the community will be solved or compromised by the use of work and ideas which come from the universities. Nonetheless, with a grant of freedom to explore areas which may seem dangerous in the eyes of society as a whole, there is a concomitant restriction upon the explorers which removes from them the responsibility for taking action to promote the use of the results of their exploration. It is partly for this reason that universities as institutions should remain neutral, so far as it is possible to do so, in the great conflicts that arise in societies from time to time, whatever part their members as individuals might play in those conflicts.

It should require little reflection and less argument to conclude that universities with the high aims and purposes which I have outlined must enjoy a fairly high mobility among at least their senior academic members.

Such mobility is necessary if the highest standards of achievement, and the most promising methods and directions for the pursuit of new knowledge, are to be understood and available generally. If the necessary degree of mobility is not enjoyed naturally, as it were, then it must be achieved by deliberate planning. The first essential for its achievement is, of course, for universities to be free to seek appointments to their available academic posts from the best available in the world and for them not to be restricted by employment policies otherwise reasonable for their local community. Satisfaction of that requirement, however, may not be enough. Other devices and procedures must be used to ensure that the work proper to a university can be in touch with the best work anywhere in the world. Interchange schemes, study leave schemes, and the like, to supplement and enrich other means of communication, are required.

We should remind ourselves, however briefly, of some of the pressures which tend to impede mobility and to prevent the satisfaction of the commitments described for universities. Broadly speaking these are of two kinds; one is particular and tied to history; the other arises from changes which have been occurring throughout the world in this century. The first is peculiarly appropriate to be considered by this Association of Commonwealth Universities.

There are natural tendencies for local communities to preserve their own stability by drawing protective barriers around themselves. History shows these barriers being crossed, so far as knowledge is concerned, by connecting systems which drew channels and links through the boundaries of local communities. Those systems have been sacred and profane. It is not necessary now to consider which have been the more important or the more effective at different times. It is important to notice, however, that the system which produced communication channels and links to draw our members together was a profane one which became the Commonwealth. Many of us come from universities which had their origins in colonies of the British empire or in dominions of the British Commonwealth of nations. Some of those universities grew slowly and deliberately. Some of them were produced in great haste and with lavish support to achieve almost instant standing.

Most of them relied initially on the capacities of the central strength of the system to send qualified people to help them to see that the standards of their work would be acceptable to a world system, or they relied upon their own capacities to attract such people to new outposts of learning. However it was done, the aims were to achieve high standards on the one hand and to obtain recognition of achievement on the other hand.

In almost every case, however, one of the long-term and dominating aims of the enterprise was to raise the standards and the capacities of the local communities concerned. If not at once then as soon as it was possible, those local communities were called upon to support with money and effort the development of the universities concerned. It was inevitable, for it was intended that it should be so, that those communities should feel that the universities would serve their domestic purposes and, further, that people from those communities who achieved the desired standards should have the opportunity to lead the universities concerned and to conduct their work.

It was, therefore, to be expected that the expatriate teacher and research worker would be resented, if he occupied a place sought by qualified people from the local community, after the work for which he had been appointed during the developmental stages had been seen to be done. What could be more natural than for the claim that 'the days for expatriate appointments to our highest academic posts are over' to be made and to fall upon receptive ears. At certain stages in the history of any nation or any community it may be difficult to keep a desirable balance between the effects of pressures of that kind and the need to make important academic appointments in universities from the best people available in the world.

Similarly a local community, or even a large nation, not unnaturally may well say: 'We support these institutions, we pay the piper'; why should we pay for people to come from other communities to pursue their own purposes, whether they come to obtain postgraduate degrees and recognition for their research training or to obtain an undergraduate degree?

Here let me repeat that, in my opinion, where mobility is concerned the priorities in the interests of universities should be in the order: first, for creative and productive academic leaders whether by way of appointment or by way of travel and visits; second, for postgraduate students and research trainees; and third, for undergraduate students. At each of those levels a sufficient provision for mobility is important but if there are irresistible pressures for restrictions on mobility then, in defence, those priorities should be observed.

The second main pressure which tends to impede mobility is a very general one. It occurs throughout the world from time to time and it is occurring now. It arises, no doubt, from great changes in relations between nations and communities. The causes do not concern us particularly at this meeting. They flow from the creation of new empires and new trading associations, from the unwinding of old empires and old trading associations; they arise from wars and from the absence of wars. We seem now to be in the middle of a period when the identifiable controlling pressures arise from problems related to population growth and to economical and trading relations. Whatever the causes may be, we are going through a period when nations large and small are tending to look defensively to their own interests, to protect themselves from outside pressures for change, and to plan as best they can for the preservation of their own resources, in the face of a very uncertain future. Controls upon international travel, on the movements of people, on the movements of money and resources, are becoming more detailed and more intricate.

It should be expected that in such times, and particularly when there are wars and threats of wars, high arguments about the free movement of knowledge and the free movement of scholars and of scholarship will be questioned. Why should money provided by the taxpayer be put to support pampered academics from other countries? Why should money provided for university student places be put to support pampered university students from other countries? Such questions can be repeated for any country concerned in our Association. If the long-term aims outlined in this paper are to be kept alive for achievement, answers to such questions must be sufficiently persuasive to preserve the real role of universities in the world.

In the light of actual demand in many places, and of limitations imposed by the real resources available, it has to be accepted that universities cannot be open to all people who wish to come to them, without discrimination based upon origins. Nonetheless a sufficient number of people 'from other places' must be able to move through the universities of the world, else the blinds will come down too far and ultimately the lights will go out.

It is, of course, a nice question, for each category, to ask what is a sufficient number. The answer from time to time may not be capable of precise or logical demonstration so as to justify any precise figures. There might have to be answers which are seen to be arbitrary so far as the particular numbers are concerned. The need to ask the questions and to answer them is not thereby removed. The task is merely made more anxious.

Let me conclude this brief excursion into general theory by warning against those who would seek to solve some of the problems involved by co-ordinated planning of a statistically-based kind. Sometimes such people think that planning can be conducted as though the people with whom we are concerned are statistical units, to be moved like pawns on a board. The people we want, however, must be moved by their own choices and by their own interests. One aspect of the warning needed may be conveyed by this little fable.

The Hiver

Once there was a hiver, a beekeeper, who kept his hives in two places. Near a forest of leatherwoods he had forty hives. Some miles away, in mixed scrub, he had thirty hive boxes but in them were only ten active hives, and those not doing very well at that.

Concerned that he was wasting resources with his empty boxes he conceived the idea that he could improve the concentration factors at both places by forcing some of the swarms from the leatherwood forest to move to his empty hives. He did not really know much about the behaviour of bees generally. He also knew that the weapons he had to hand were limited. He therefore decided to smash ten of his hives near the leatherwood forest and to force bees to move to his empty hives.

The disturbed bees first attacked him, of course, but they then departed — perhaps to look for other leatherwood forests, who knows? He had succeeded, he found, in reducing his productive hives from fifty to forty — but of the other consequences of his action he knew nothing at that time; for many of the events in the complicated chain which followed his action could not be recognized for many years.

His production of honey dropped immediately, of course, and the cause was recognized. But the decline and ultimate demise of his leatherwood bees, and the failure generations later of his leatherwood forest, were not seen to be causally related to his actions except by a small group of scientists who examined the area long after the events which are here recorded.

Dr. J. A. PERKINS (*Chairman of the Board, International Council for Educational Development*): There are three stages in the development of student and staff overseas education and research. The first is the 'free market' or *laissez faire* stage where individuals select their own academic and research programmes, enter or associate themselves with institutions that will accept them, and are essentially accountable to no one but themselves. This first and primitive stage can be likened to the early automobile in open country—no traffic problems, few stop signs, no policemen and hardly any accidents.

As higher education expanded after world war two and the international dimension of higher education expanded at the same time, and as the purposes of international education became more differentiated and complex, overseas study and research projects became a matter of more than individual concern. They became a feature of both educational and national policy.

On closer examination questions began to arise about both the assumptions and the actual consequences of overseas educational activity. As a result Stop and Go signs begin to appear, dangerous curves are identified, and prospective hostels are marked for high standards of bed, board and room charges. Home institutions ask insistent questions about the way their overseas students spend their time. Academic credit is granted only after home authorities receive proof of achievement. Students are interviewed before entrance, language and course requirements are established and enforced, and financial solvency with local employment must be guaranteed. In short, an increasingly complex set of requirements and conditions has emerged to test those who would use the academic highways and to reduce the prospect that individual decisions would do the individual, the university and their societies more harm than good.

We have just described some of the features of stage two—known as the 'restricted market', where the individual is free to make the correct choices, choices he may disregard at his peril. But we have by no means completely moved beyond the 'free market' stage. The field abounds with the freelancer who moves on his own, dodges the traffic signs, travels by instinct rather than roadmap, and does not wish to be accountable for his performance to anyone but himself. It would be pleasant to record that our freelancer accepts the negative consequences of his independence. But, alas, our travelling scholar is all too human and frequently complains that he has been unjustly treated both at home and abroad.

We have not fully entered the 'restricted market' era because the guidance is imperfect, the purposes uncertain, the restrictions are full of loopholes and institutional and national differences vary so considerably as to allow great freedom of choice. However restrictions are on the increase everywhere. Differential tuitions penalize the foreigner, quotas are an established feature of the landscape, work opportunities and financial assistance for foreign students are progressively reduced and the choice of institutions is no longer entirely free.

SUB-TOPIC 3(D): INTERNATIONAL MOBILITY [Perkins]

We are now moving into a third stage that may well be a consequence of the second. As restrictions, rules, conditions and difficulties multiply, the 'planned market' emerges as the natural way to relieve the individual of having to deal himself with the complexities of stage two. By 'planned market' I mean the emergence of systems and arrangements worked out between institutions of different countries, generally with the blessing of their respective governments. Educational and national goals are established, appropriate preparation and reception is arranged in advance, funding and sometimes measurement of achievement is provided. By systems I mean regional and international organizations that supplement institutional arrangements like the Inter-University Council in the United Kingdom, the Fulbright programme in the United States, or the Deutscher Akademischer Austauschdienst (DAAD) in West Germany

There remains great freedom of choice for both students and staff but the wave of the future involves more structural arrangements with increased institutional responsibility to which students and staff will become increasingly accountable. Hopefully this process of organization will not too severely curtail the élan and spontaneity of the current scene. To return to the automotive analogy, we surely need the autobus and the railroad train but the private car will always have its uses. And footpaths must still be provided for those who wish to reach their destination by bicycle or even on foot.

Having laid the groundwork for the evolution of staff and student foreign experience, perhaps a more detailed look at the scene is in order. Student concerns will be followed by a brief reference to those of staff with a concluding comment on what is euphemistically called the 'brain drain'.

First as to students. We know that students seek foreign educational experience for a whole variety of reasons—some educationally respectable, some educationally neutral. We also know that there are a great many of them enrolled in foreign educational institutions. A reasonable guess is that there are over 700,000 students studying in countries other than their own. Some go abroad because there are literally no places for them at home. There are 5000 US students at the University of Guadalajara because they could not enter the narrow doors of US medical schools. Some go abroad because their governments find it less expensive to pay their costs in foreign universities than to expand their own.

Some wish to supplement their domestic education by continuing their studies in more sophisticated institutions, or to engage in graduate or professional studies, or to go to a country whose culture they wish to understand. Some are political or social refugees and wish to escape a hostile environment at home. This is a very sensitive problem but many countries make special provision for their attendance. Incidentally, it sometimes seems that governments encourage such an exodus as a way to be rid of troublesome persons.

Putting aside for the moment the controls of the receiving countries, let us consider the distribution of foreign students not only by the factors already mentioned but also by the financial resources available. The OPEC* countries send over 50,000 to the United States and possibly over 200,000 to foreign countries altogether. Nor should it be surprising that students gravitate to disciplines and professional programmes for which a particular country is well known—engineering and business management in the United States, humanistic studies in France, engineering and the humanities in Germany, and social studies in the United Kingdom. Language is also a great distributor. Students go to countries where they have some linguistic competence. Since English has become the most widely-used second language it is not surprising that the English-speaking countries—the United States, Canada and the United Kingdom—are three of the first four in numbers of foreign students. The UNESCO figures for 1975 report the foreign student population as shown in this table. Some comments on this table are in order. (a) The French figure includes about two-thirds from French-speaking former colonies which have woefully few of their own colleges and universities. (b) If foreign students as a percentage of total students were listed the USA would drop from first to twenty-first and our host country Canada would head the list.

Rank	Country	Thousands
1	USA	179·3
2	France	119·5
3	Canada	98·4
4	UK	49·0
5	Fed. Rep. of Germany	47·3
6	USSR	30·6
7	Italy	18·9
8	Japan	14·5
9	Austria	10·3
10	Switzerland	10·1

(c) Finally, the numbers of students reflect not only student choice but availability of places within a framework of ability to pay.

Two additional factors bear on the incentives for overseas study experience. The first is the extent to which a course of study is prescribed by a series of requirements for advancing through a discipline and receiving a degree. A free elective system makes a year or two of foreign study easier to manage. In the United States we have been passing through more than a decade of free electives and foreign education has been relatively easy. But even so some disciplines, particularly mathematics and the natural sciences, have

---

* Organization of Petroleum Exporting Countries

retained a tightly prescribed course of study and US students in these fields have remained at home.

The second point concerns employment prospects. Students seem to come to different conclusions as to whether an overseas experience in a tight job market helps or hinders their careers. Some believe that their chances of entry into their own professional schools are better if they stay close to home and personally cultivate their connections. Others believe that the academic records of applicants are so close that an overseas experience might be the deciding factor in their favour. Since there is no hard evidence either way everyone must make the best guess possible. Perhaps the only thing reasonably certain is the retarding influence of rising costs everywhere and, for US students, the decline of the value of the dollar. But in spite of all this over 110,000 US students studied abroad during the last academic year.

From the point of view of the receiving country there are also problems. Most countries want a substantial representation of foreign students for a variety of reasons. There is the belief that their own students will become less parochial, that graduates will return home as friends of their hosts, that some of the best will stay to add to the pool of high-level manpower and important artistic and cultural talent. For countries facing a surplus of places like the United States and others expecting a demographic decline there may, in time, be active recruitment of foreign students. They may become a source of educational income. Barbara Burn has suggested that in the United States this may amount to almost $700 million. But that time for other countries is not now.

At the present writing, foreign students are a substantial cost to many receiving countries that face a demographic bulge for the next decade or so. As a result some countries have established quotas for foreign students (7% in Germany), announced reduction in numbers (UK and France) and even threatened to cut them off entirely (Italy). Others have thought to apply the 'head and shoulders' formula (a foreigner must be 'head and shoulders' above a native prospect) to teaching assistantships which will directly affect the prospect for foreign would-be graduate students.

There are also cultural problems which can turn into psychological and political problems. Iranian students overseas seem to have a large complement of persons visibly and vocally opposed to their own regime. Since foreign students seem to swarm together, a large block of Iranian students on one campus can be a complicating factor for the local community. Even when relatively quiescent they can be a hard group to assimilate with consequent loss of the very values that underlie the whole arrangement.

Now turning from students to staff, we have some similar and some new problems. It has already been mentioned that the world has become a playground for the research scholar. Anthropologists who had been confined to studying native minorities can study more exotic tribes in Cuzco, Ching-mai and Ougadoogou. Teachers, burning their own pedagogical smoke, can experience the exciting novelty of teaching new students with brand new questions. Scholarly students of social and economic development can leave their ivory towers and try to put their theories into practice. Although few found brave new worlds, the widening of experience, the stimulation of novelty, the new perspectives on old problems—all led to increasing interest in overseas experience.

There are no reliable figures on the scope and content of the outflow of academic talent. An estimate has been made that over 100,000 US faculty members were active overseas in 1975 engaged in teaching, research or development activities—or only 1% of the total staff of US higher education. As in the case of students, the numbers continue to grow showing that in spite of increasing difficulties 'where there's a will, there's a way'.

Some problems can be identified. Many are similar to those of students. Lack of funds, inadequate leave policies, constraints of language, the fear of losing one's position on the academic ladder, the lack of the adventurous spirit, keep many staff at home. For those who do go the experience is cumulative—the second trip is easier than the first and by the tenth trip they are full-fledged members of the international intellectual community—sometimes inelegantly referred to as the international academic jet set. For those who have tasted the heady wine of international comparative study, confinement to one's own campus, or even country, can seem like a restriction hardly to be borne.

The receiving country presents problems also. Research that puts foreign countries under an academic microscope is not a very 'lifty' experience for the subjects of the inquiry. They come to resent it unless there is a chance for a reciprocal experience or at least one in which natives are partners as well as specimens. When there is a suspicion that the examination has political, or especially covert, purposes the whole overseas research process can be destroyed.

When research turns into participation in local economic or social development the process also becomes tricky. Here the auspice becomes decisive in order to establish a purity of purpose, a concern for the people to be aided, a willingness to work in harness with native colleagues, and a proven objectivity and insightfulness in reports on findings. Better to work quietly under the umbrella of a respectable native institution than to exercise visible leadership, however brilliant, a style not easily acquired by very successful scholars at home.

For those who would 'gladly teach', particularly for those who look for permanent positions in other countries, there are some hurdles. Short-term assignments for a quarter or semester present fewer difficulties but permanent positions are most frequently closed to foreign scholars except in the United States, the United Kingdom, West Germany and a few others. In most countries the professor is a civil servant, a post from which non-citizens are almost always barred. Efforts to liberalize and better arrange have grounded on the shoals of a diminishing job market. In a few cases, like the teaching assistant in Ontario, an appointment may be made if no competent native can be found. Rumour has it, however, that where there is a real readiness and desire to appoint a foreign teacher ingenuity has risen to the occasion. To reveal the means would endanger the laudable ends, so we shall turn to the special problem of the 'brain drain' or the movement of talent from less affluent and smaller countries to larger and richer ones.

For developing countries, and even for some developed ones, the movement of highly trained and scarce manpower to other countries assumes the dimensions of a large public problem. Now referred to as a 'brain drain', the loss can be as severe as the loss of capital, and perhaps more so. For the developed country it may involve a complicated social problem of digesting a foreigner with a different culture. Here we repeat the problems of the student with the great difference that the professor has his professional career at stake while the student, in most cases, plans to return home.

There is no way to remove the tilt towards the large affluent countries for posts in universities, hospitals and the like. The attraction is permanent and ineradicable. But the advantage can be and must be offset by vigorous measures to make more attractive the academic ambience of the home country, to have the obligation to return certainly on the part of the undergraduate student, and to grant graduate fellowships on the promise of return.

The international movements of students and staff are the results of tides in the affairs of educational and public affairs, as well as the changing aspirations and opportunities. On these tides students and staff range the world seeking ways to improve their knowledge and their training. Their numbers increase, their interests diversify, and the problems of their accommodation become painfully visible. But the tide increases and produces its own resistance. Efforts to eliminate barriers only increase the demands for countervailing measures. But the tide sweeps on, bypassing obstacles, rationalizing systems to make the currents more and more constructive and with less and less human wastage. The growth of the international intellectual community can scarcely be resisted. Do we really wish to?

Dr. F. THISTLETHWAITE (*Vice-Chancellor of the University of East Anglia*): The pursuit of education and scholarship has always extended beyond the boundaries of individual nation states. Since the middle ages students and scholars—traditionally highly mobile sections of society—have travelled to and fro across national frontiers with the purpose of seeking out the outstanding teachers of their day and studying at the important centres of learning. But only in this century—and really only in the period since the end of the second world war—has the movement grown to its present proportions. This is undoubtedly due in part to the rapid expansion of higher education and the foundation of new universities in many countries; and in part to the speed, economy and convenience of twentieth-century travel. Today the number of university students and staff moving between countries is greater than ever before, although the scale of the mobility varies considerably from country to country. In some it is very extensive, in others almost non-existent; sometimes—in the case of student mobility—keeping pace or growing faster than the numerical expansion of higher education at home, sometimes falling behind.

Academic mobility between countries takes place in many different ways. For staff it may range from permanent migration to the occasional attendance at international research symposia; for students, from full-time enrolment at a university abroad to a short exchange visit. But whatever form it takes few of us, I think, would deny its value. For the scholar and researcher—especially perhaps those engaged in advanced or highly specialised scientific research—travel abroad may be the only way to work with someone engaged in the same field of research. And for scholar and student alike, movement abroad gives the opportunity to live in a new country, to experience a different cultural and social environment, and to introduce some of his own country's ideas and traditions to his hosts. Nor are the benefits of this mobility limited to those who actually do the travelling: there are also important gains for nations and for the universities themselves. Most countries recognise this sort of movement as a way of improving international relations by encouraging a

SUB-TOPIC 3(D): INTERNATIONAL MOBILITY [Thistlethwaite]

cross-fertilization of cultures and ideas. For developing countries or those with small populations it provides a way of acquiring highly educated and trained manpower; and for larger and richer nations support for the international movement of students and staff is a generally acceptable form of activity with important economic, political or social effects. In the case of universities the movement contributes in many important ways to academic life, and helps to underline our position as international institutions with a common responsibility for the transmission and expansion of knowledge across the world.

Academic mobility is central to the interests and purpose of the Association of Commonwealth Universities. The primary aim of the Association is to promote co-operation and contact between the universities of the Commonwealth and there can be few better ways of doing this than by encouraging the interchange of staff and students. It is hardly surprising, therefore, that this theme, or some variation of it, has been a subject for discussion at most of the recent quinquennial Congresses. When I looked through the reports of the proceedings of these Congresses, one particular contribution caught my eye. This was from Sir Robert Aitken, then Vice-Chancellor of the University of Birmingham, who offered the 1963 Congress a broad statistical snapshot of the movement of students and staff between Commonwealth universities. The figures which he presented were for the first year or two of the 1960s and I thought that it would be of some interest to see what changes had occurred since then, bearing in mind the very rapid development of higher education in most countries during the intervening years.

For this purpose I have taken just two of the tables presented by Sir Robert Aitken in 1963 and slightly expanded and updated them. The first (Table A, pp. 376 – 77) shows the numbers of overseas students studying at universities in five Commonwealth countries in the years stated and gives some information about the continent and country of their origin. The statistics are taken from the *Commonwealth Universities Yearbook*. The second table (Table B, pp. 378 – 79) is a sampling exercise which Sir Robert employed to give some indication of the movement of academic staff. It examines a small number of universities in several Commonwealth countries and lists how many of their staff, as shown in the *Commonwealth Universities Yearbook,* took their first degrees in other countries and might therefore have been supposed to have started their academic life in those other countries.

Statistics have their value but also their dangers, and I am hesitant about drawing too many hard and fast conclusions from these two tables. They are compiled from statistics and listings

[*Thistlethwaite*] TOPIC 3: RECONCILING EQUALITY AND EXCELLENCE

which are not strictly comparable and they relate to years chosen simply because they happen to be the latest for which information was readily available. But a more serious criticism in the context of this discussion is that as a measure of total international staff and student mobility they are far from comprehensive. This applies especially to Table B which reveals just one small aspect of staff mobility. The table does not tell about staff moving between universities on one of the several international interchange or fellowship schemes. Nor about those who might be spending a term or two abroad on study leave from their own universities — and I suspect that this form of movement may be very extensive: a quick survey of the applications for study leave from faculty in my own university during the last three years indicated that nearly one-half intended to spend some of their leave abroad, often at a foreign university. Nor does the table tell us anything about staff who spend shorter periods in another country — perhaps following a particular line of research during a long vacation, or attending one of the growing number of international conferences and congresses. All these are part of the international movement of university teachers and should not be overlooked. Table A, which is concerned with student enrolments, is, I think, a rather more reliable indicator of student mobility between the countries concerned than is Table B of staff mobility. But even here the growing number of students on short-term study visits is ignored as are those who may be spending a period abroad as part of the degree programme which they are following in their own country. (This requirement, long regarded as essential for students reading for foreign language degrees, is, I sense, now becoming a feature of many other degree programmes).

So the figures which I have prepared need to be handled with care but I hope that they will provide a useful point of reference for our own debate.

I propose to devote the rest of this introductory paper to making one or two cautious comments on the trends revealed by the two tables and then to pose some questions about the future of academic mobility which we might consider in discussion. But first I would like to make one further general point about the factors which influence and control the mobility of staff and students internationally. It is that, whereas the quest for learning by individuals may have been the only force which determined the extent of the movement of scholars in the middle ages, today the picture is far more complex. Now, the state of the national and international economy, the political and social policies of national governments and the concerns and objectives of international agencies all play a critical part. Thus, for example, national immigration policies, the willingness of governments to issue work permits to foreign nationals, the availability of grants and scholarships, the level of tuition fees for overseas students and quota limitations all have a fundamental impact on academic mobility. This may be an obvious point, but it leads me to suggest that the movement of university students and staff internationally is now more than ever dependent on the attitudes which governments express in their home and foreign policy objectives. I am not suggesting that this is the only factor. The desires of individuals and the needs of research and scholarship will always be important. So, too, the ambitions of universities, and I am sure that there are still many things that we can do ourselves to encourage mobility—the recognition of periods of study abroad for credit, for example. But there is a limit to what can be achieved even by the most determined individuals or by the most outward-looking and autonomous universities. I would therefore suggest that any further extensive development of international academic mobility depends very largely on the sympathies of governments and their willingness to remove obstacles and provide incentives. The directions in which we might wish to influence governments is something to which I will return, but first a few comments on the statistics.

Looking first at Table A we can see the numbers of students who, in the years specified, came from five continents and from various Commonwealth countries to study at universities in Australia, Canada, India, New Zealand and the United Kingdom. The most obvious feature is the considerable increase in the total number of overseas students studying at universities in the five selected Commonwealth countries. The percentage increase over the period ranges from 96% in Australia to 343% in Canada. Although this is not shown in the table, there was a very rapid expansion in the number of home students in each of the five countries over the same period, so the proportion of overseas students in the total student population did not necessarily increase, although it certainly did in some countries—Canada, for example, where it rose from about 5½% to 9½%. In the UK the proportion of overseas students (defined for fees purposes) in 1974 – 75 was about 11%—the highest of the five countries selected, although what will be the impact of our government's present policies on overseas student fees and numbers is still most uncertain.

Turning now to the numbers of students coming from other parts of the Commonwealth we can see that this too increased although there are variations in the pattern from country to country. In three of the five 'host' countries the proportion of Commonwealth students in the total overseas student population increased. The

[*Thistlethwaite*]   TOPIC 3: RECONCILING EQUALITY AND EXCELLENCE

TABLE A: STUDENTS FROM ABROAD STUDYING IN NA[...]

	'HOST COUNTRIES'			
	United Kingdom		Canada	
	(a)	(b)	(c)	(c[...]
Students' Continents/ Countries of Origin	1961–62	1974–75	1960–61	197[...]7[...]
Asia	5,021	11,429	1,615	9,3[...]
America	2,571	5,351	4,049	10,2[...]
Africa	3,865	4,934	233	2,3[...]
Australasia	563	902	41	5[...]
Europe	1,364	4,247	1,282	9,5[...]
Stateless/unknown	1	1,477	31	
All students from abroad	13,385 (5,716)	28,340 (15,895)	7,251	32,1[...]
United Kingdom	—	—	582	5,8[...]
Canada	559 (442)	924 (686)	—	
Australia	380 (290)	662 (586)	31	3[...]
New Zealand	170 (128)	186 (172)	8	1[...]
India	1,660 (892)	987 (798)	288	1,0[...]
Ceylon/Sri Lanka	251 (147)	418 (276)	24	[...]
Hong Kong	275 (103)	877 (356)	676	4,3[...]
Malaya/Malaysia	303 (54)	2,358 (552)	42	4[...]
Singapore	131 (35)	502 (137)	5	1[...]
Jamaica	143 (40)	81 (35)	270	4[...]
Trinidad and Tobago	244 (43)	108 (37)	634	8[...]
Cyprus	142 (29)	408 (131)	3	[...]
Malta	48 (18)	33 (20)	2	[...]
TOTAL	4,306 (2,221)	7,544 (3,786)	2,565	13,7[...]
All Commonwealth students from abroad	8,086 (3,130)	11,106 (5,542)	3,294	15,98[...]
Commonwealth students as a percentage of all students from abroad	60 (55)	39 (35)	45	5[...]

* Perhaps a greater number of overseas students because no record [...] nationality—Canadian or non-Canadian—was held of 37,358 students.

Notes.—1. The numbers in brackets for the United Kingdom are those of po[...] enrolment in the United Kingdom (1961–62 and 1974–75), Canada (1974–7[...] time and external students, but it is likely that only a small number of overse[...] *Commonwealth Universities Yearbook* 1963, Appendix IV; cols. (b), (d), (f), ([...] and (i), *Commonwealth Universities Yearbook* 1963 [pp. 142–143 (c), pp. [...] and p. 902.

SUB-TOPIC 3(D): INTERNATIONAL MOBILITY   [Thistlethwaite]

1MONWEALTH COUNTRIES IN THE YEARS INDICATED

	'Host Countries'
	Australia		New Zealand		India
(e)	(f)	(g)	(h)	(i)	(j)
				1959– 60	1973– 74‡
,802	4,983	424	2,090	2,322	4,277
50	346	18	104	50	150
21	182	48	33	839	2,260
356	535	223	472	29	394
43	362	30	48	24	340
	10			107	374
,272	6,418	743	2,747	3,371	7,795
36	152	24	32	6	270
5	103	3	37		6
—	—	50	59		4
150	160	—	—		1
66	139	25	13		—
13	78	17	4	903	379
549†	399	6	23		
,143	2,429	139	1,611	273	1,124
495	395	32	130		
		1	3	} 21	30
	4				
	3	1		1	
,457	3,862	298	1,912	1,204	1,814
				at least	
,750	4,376	581	2,353	1,640	4,353
2–86	68	78	86	49	56

ncluding Macao and Taiwan.
Provisional data.

duate students *included in* the preceding figure.   2. The figures for overseas
India (1973 – 74) relate to full-time students. The other figures include part-
lents would be studying other than on a full-time basis.   3. *Sources:* col. (a),
(j), *Commonwealth Universities Yearbook* 1977 – 78, Appendix II; cols. (c), (e)
(e), and pp. 473 – 74 (i)]; col. (g), *Commonwealth Universities Yearbook* 1965,

377

[*Thistlethwaite*] TOPIC 3: RECONCILING EQUALITY AND EXCELLENCE

TABLE B: TEACHERS IN VARIOUS COMMONWEALTH UNIVERSI[...]
Survey of Sample Universities

	\multicolumn{12}{c}{Countries where First Degree Obtained}												
	United Kingdom		Canada		Australia		New Zealand		India		Tota
Country and University in which post held	1962	1976	1962	1976	1962	1976	1962	1976	1962	1976	1962	1
UNITED KINGDOM												
Bristol	—	—	2	9	6	10	2	5		4	10	
University College, London	—	—	7	12	17	21	3	14		4	27	
Manchester	—	—	5	12	13	14	1	10	1	17	20	
CANADA												
McMaster	34	204	—	—	2	23	1	7	1	27	38	2
Toronto	94	474	—	—	2	40	4	17	4	26	104	5
AUSTRALIA												
Melbourne	81	203	1	11	—	—	18	36	1	4	101	2
Sydney	104	193	2	15	—	—	27	38		7	133	2
NEW ZEALAND												
Otago	44	182	1	12	14	32	—	—		4	59	2
Lincoln College	10	38		3	3	13	—	—			13	
INDIA												
Aligarh	12	30		3		1			—	—	12	
Bombay	3	10		5		1			—	—	3	
OTHER UNIVERSITIES												
Hong Kong	67	91	3	20	6	22		6		3	78*	1
Ceylon/Sri Lanka	65	80		3		1		1	11	8	77	
Malaya	41	132	3	17	12	57	5	25	11	35	78†	2

* Includes 2 teachers who obtained their first degree in Malaya and Pakistan respectively.
† Includes 4 teachers who obtained their first degree in Ceylon and 2 who obtained their first deg[...] in Hong Kong.

Sources: statistics for 1962 from *Proceedings of Ninth Congress of the Universities of* [...] statistics for 1976 from *Commonwealth Universities Yearbook* 1977–78.

SUB-TOPIC 3(D): INTERNATIONAL MOBILITY [Thistlethwaite]

O HOLD 'FIRST' DEGREES OF OTHER COUNTRIES
Years 1962 and 1976

		Teachers with First Degrees from named Commonwealth Countries as approx. percentage of total staff		Teachers with First Degrees from Other Countries, including the named Commonwealth Countries— 1976 ONLY	
	1976	1962	1976	Total	As approx. % of total staff
4	1,233	Less than 2%	2·2%	73	5·9%
1	995	5% (Aust. 3%)	5·1%	176	17·7%
8	2,230	2%	2·4%	164	7·4%
9	977	19% (UK 17%)	26·7% (UK 20·1%)	537	5·5%
2	4,205	8% (UK 7%)	13·2% (UK 11·3%)	1,620	38·5%
8	1,054	14·5% (UK 11·5%)	24·1% (UK 19·3%)	374	35·4%
9	1,113	18·5% (UK 14%)	22·7% (UK 17·3%)	396	35·6%
2	699	22·5% (UK 16·5%)	32·9% (UK 26%)	305	43·6%
5	136	23·5% (UK 18%)	39·7% (UK 27·9%)	60	44·1%
2	847	4% (all UK)	4·3%	88	10·4%
1	180	4% (all UK)	8·9%	40	22·2%
0	482	32% (UK 28%)	29·5% (UK 18·9%)	246	51·0%
5	1,070	21·5% (UK 18%)	8·6% (UK 6·1%)	121	11·3%
2	644	64% (UK 33%)	41·3% (UK 20·5%)	509	79·0%

nmonwealth 1963, p. 194 (figures derived from 1963 *Commonwealth Universities Yearbook*);

exceptions were Australia, where it fell to 68% in 1975 and the UK where it fell from 60% in 1961 – 62 to 39% in 1974 – 75. Should we, I wonder, conclude that university education in the UK is becoming comparatively less attractive to students from the Commonwealth; or perhaps that this country's traditional links are slowly being replaced by new ones forged, for example, with our EEC partners? I will leave others to comment on the first question. The answer to the second is probably 'yes', although as far as the EEC countries are concerned the number of students coming to UK universities — and British students going to continental universities — is still very small. And this is true of all intra-Community movement, not solely that involving the UK. At present only about one half of one per cent of the total enrolment in EEC universities is accounted for by students from other member states. Different academic traditions, 'numerus clausus' restrictions, language difficulties, and complicated and unfamiliar administrative procedures present obstacles to student mobility which have never really existed, at least to such a degree, within the Commonwealth. During the last few years the first steps have been taken to overcome these obstacles. Information has been collected and disseminated about the admissions procedures in the member states and finance has been made available to develop joint courses offered by two universities in different countries. Grants to support short study visits by teaching, research and administrative staffs have been offered and more exchange schemes have been initiated between individual universities. These are all important and welcome moves to improve mobility, but the problems which still need to be solved are such that I believe it will be many years before the movement of students between Britain and her EEC partners begins to approach that which now takes place between the UK and the Commonwealth.

My final comment on Table A concerns the movement of students at the graduate level. Only figures for the UK are available and are shown in parentheses in the table. The proportion of graduate students in the total from overseas increased from 43% in 1961 – 62 to 56% in 1974 – 75 with a corresponding increase for the Commonwealth countries over the same period from 39% to 50%. Students from overseas now account for about one-third of the full-time postgraduate students at UK universities and those from the Commonwealth about one-third of that one-third.

Turning now to Table B — which, as I have said, is but a very small sample of one small aspect of staff mobility — the most interesting feature is the extent to which Commonwealth universities (except those in the UK — and I have no reason to suspect that the three institutions selected by Sir Robert Aitken are untypical) have recruited and continue to recruit staff who began their academic life in another country. The reason for this may simply be that the number of suitably qualified people coming from the home universities has been inadequate to cope with the very rapid expansion of university education in the last 15 or 20 years. If so we may expect to see the position change in the next decade or two as the expansion of higher education begins to fall, in line with demographic trends in many countries. I would be interested to know whether those who have recruited large numbers of graduates from overseas universities (and I do, of course, appreciate that they may not necessarily have been foreigners, but perhaps the members of an earlier generation of mobile students from home) have found this to be generally beneficial for their universities, educationally and socially, and whether they would wish to continue to recruit in this way in future. If so, what of the figures for the UK?

I said at the beginning of this paper that the international movement of staff and students could take many forms and I suggested that whatever form it took few of us would deny its value. Even so, I suspect that most of us would regard some forms of mobility as more valuable than others. And if, as I have also suggested, the further development of international academic mobility depends on the policies and attitudes of governments, then we would do well to consider our own priorities and those which we would wish to press upon governments. We might consider: —

- whether student mobility is more fruitful at the graduate level than at the undergraduate level;
- whether the benefits of movement for undergraduates (except perhaps those from developing countries) can be better achieved through university-sponsored exchange schemes or periods abroad as part of the requirement of a home degree programme;
- what are the most difficult obstacles to student mobility and whether there are any which are in our own power to remove;
- what are the most important incentives for student mobility and how significant is the availability of financial support;
- what are the principal obstacles and greatest incentives to staff mobility;
- which forms of staff mobility we would wish to see particularly encouraged.

DISCUSSION

In introducing his paper (see above) Dr. *F. Thistlethwaite* (East Anglia) said the topic of mobility was a perennial one in discussions between

TOPIC 3: RECONCILING EQUALITY AND EXCELLENCE

academics and especially within the framework of the ACU in view of the Association's aims of fostering contact and co-operation between its member universities. The academic Commonwealth is a free trade area within which movement, or the possibility of movement, is perhaps taken too much for granted. His up-dating of Sir Robert Aitken's statistics of the early 1960s (of movement *between* certain Commonwealth countries) pointed to a considerable increase in the number of students abroad, though the *proportion* of overseas students to the whole had fallen in some countries. Yet the numbers of such *postgraduate* students had increased both absolutely and proportionately. As far as the UK was concerned there had been no countervailing increase in traffic between the UK and EEC countries, thus the Commonwealth remained of high importance. Dr. Thistlethwaite commented it was *government* action today which shaped and dominated academic traffic. The movement of staff and student tended to be subject to distortion according to the dictates of 'relevance', aid policy or other non-academic criteria. One needed to watch for, and resist as might be necessary, the interventions of government.

Dr. J. A. Perkins (International Council for Educational Development — for paper, see above) concentrated upon six main points in his introduction of his paper. First, the rise in domestic institutionalised management of higher education was now extending to the international field. The move was away from individual initiative to a planned market often involving complicated regulations, though centralised planning could actually lead to an increase in academic traffic through minimum quotas, etc. Secondly, he regretted a general decline overall in foreign language instruction. Mobility in part depended upon the extent to which foreign languages were learned. The increased teaching of native languages and conduct of higher education in these languages could diminish mobility. English as a universal second language might be in decline also. Thirdly, finance was a factor in determining whether students and staff went abroad, and if so where. Fourthly, curricula (both contents and structure) and admission requirements affected the flow of overseas students. It was easier for a foreign student to be accepted in countries like Canada, the UK and the USA, having several levels and modes of provision of higher education. Fifthly, he pointed to the inflexibility occurring when academic staff are civil servants as contrasted with the free movement of staff members of autonomous institutions. Finally, Dr. Perkins referred to the complicated and sensitive subject of 'cultural confrontation'. Multicultural teaching tends to diminish reference to values or standards. Dr. Perkins concluded that the aim of the academic community should be to ensure that mobility is accepted and protected by governments, but managed by academics themselves.

Sir David Derham (Melbourne — for paper, see above) accepted the high importance, in mobility of staff and students among countries and universities, not of the same treatment for all but of fair and equal treatment of those who merited it. He detected pressures upon the academic community of a parochial kind and tendencies for countries to draw back and protect

SUB-TOPIC 3(D): INTERNATIONAL MOBILITY

themselves. In the last 25 years the demand generated by the expansion of secondary education had led many universities to see themselves only as part of a system of tertiary education. Sir David stressed, however, the historic identity and role of universities as places where any subject and any question is open for enquiry. Universities must preserve these central and enduring purposes which relied upon the mobility of intellectual interchange if international standards were to be reached and maintained. To Sir David the main question was not only to present the essential aim of the university to governments, but also to persuade the taxpayer what the purposes of the university are and that to maintain and fulfil them adequately requires interchange of ideas through mobility of, first, staff; second, postgraduate and research students; and third, undergraduates.

Professor U. F. J. Eyck (Calgary) saw no real alternative to English as the language of mobility. He considered multi-cultural institutions and teaching to be effective and stimulating so long as the sincerely held beliefs of each culture were unequivocally stated.

Dr. D. Kimble (Malawi) praised the work of the Inter-University Council for Higher Education Overseas and urged that developed universities might consider adopting or developing a link with a 'third world' university and from their own budget assisting the overseas university with resources in kind. Professor (Mrs.) Madhuri R. Shah (S.N.D.T. Women's) said that there was deep concern for values in multi-cultural teaching institutions: a deeper understanding of indigenous culture arose from understanding the cultures of others. Mutual benefits were gained from mobility. She regretted the increase in fees for overseas students on which academics had taken an insufficiently firm position. She suggested that if the number of potential university entrants were to decline in the developed countries the under-utilisation of resources could be avoided by admission of increased numbers of overseas students. Dr. C. R. Mitra (Birla I.T.S.) said that hitherto there had been mobility of Indian students to the west, but India now wished for a reverse flow. A long-term programme should be instituted to increase mobility and reduce the disparity in resources between developed and developing universities.

Dr. A. E. Sloman (Essex) said that, while all supported student mobility in principle, more thought should be given to practical planning. 11% to 12% of students in UK universities were from overseas but they were not distributed equally over all institutions nor over subjects (science and technology being predominant) nor as to the countries of origin. Further, there was a very small number of UK students who went to overseas universities. He urged that priorities for action be defined as to undergraduate or postgraduate mobility, the subjects most justifying mobility, whether the movement should be free-ranging or with bilateral arrangements, and whether the students from less developed countries should be assisted and encouraged by differential fees and how two-way flow could be increased.

Dr. M. K. Oliver (Carleton) and Professor J. F. Scott (La Trobe) agreed on the need for defining purposes and priorities and suggested that, with diminished opportunities for movement of staff within the universities of the developed world, self-interest could be served by international mobility

TOPIC 3: RECONCILING EQUALITY AND EXCELLENCE

and staff development programmes for universities in developing countries such as the Canadian International Development Agency supported. Dr. C. E. Young (California) and Professor D. A. G. Waddell (Stirling) urged that the university institutions accept responsibility for initiating two-way mobility through long-term bilateral arrangements which were the most productive. Professor A. M. Khusro (Aligarh Muslim) said that a marginal allocation of resources by developed institutions would be of major benefit to developing universities which were often experiencing a rapidly growing number of undergraduate applications for admission. Cultural problems of interchange were diminished if there were a firm requirement for the student or visitor abroad to return to his home country. Such arrangements made overseas students more welcome. Professor N. M. Swani (I.I.T., Delhi) suggested that bilateral research projects were a fruitful basis for staff interchange and maintained a high active academic involvement on both sides of the joint enterprise. Professor G. R. V. Mmari (Dar es Salaam), agreeing, pointed out that there were established centres of excellence in many developing institutions.

Mr. W. Senteza Kajubi (Makerere) urged the removal of barriers to mobility such as adversely differential fees which were a serious impediment to students from developing countries and produced very small additional income for the developed countries. Dr. D. A. Low (Australian National) suggested that not all the available opportunities for interchange were taken and urged that the academic community take the initiative in international relations which were too important to be left entirely to diplomats, civil servants and journalists. Mr. R. E. O. Akpofure (Commonwealth Secretariat) and Mr. R. C. Griffiths (Inter-University Council for Higher Education Overseas) agreed that not all was done that could be and that many awards offered by developing countries under the Commonwealth Scholarship and Fellowship Plan were not taken up, often because there were not strong institutional links to stimulate applications. In this connection Mr. E. E. Temple (ACU) drew attention to the Association's publication *Research Strengths of Universities in the Developing Countries of the Commonwealth,* which was designed to encourage such applications.

Group Discussions

TOPIC 4

THE PUBLIC VIEW OF THE UNIVERSITIES

Chairman: Dr. P. LACOSTE
Rector of the University of Montreal

Editorial Co-ordinator: Mrs. ROSEMARY A. CAVAN
Director of Information, Association of Universities and Colleges of Canada

		page
Sub-Topic 4(a)	THE RELEVANCE OF THE CURRICULUM TO THE NEEDS OF SOCIETY	
	Opening Speakers	
	Dr. A. G. Dickson	387
	Sir Fraser Noble	405
	Discussion	415
Sub-Topic 4(b)	THE RELEVANCE OF UNIVERSITY EDUCATION AND RESEARCH	
	Opening Speakers	
	Dr. C.-E. Beaulieu	418
	Sir Alan Cottrell	428
	Mr. J. K. Koinange	437
	Discussion	449
Sub-Topic 4(c)	DIRECT SERVICES TO INDUSTRY	
	Opening Speakers	
	Sir George Kenyon	452
	Professor E. Bamfo Kwakye	461
	Dr. B. C. Matthews	471
	Discussion	481
Topic 4	CONTINUATION OF DISCUSSION	484

For index to names, see p. 655

Sub-Topic 4(a)

THE RELEVANCE OF THE CURRICULUM TO THE NEEDS OF SOCIETY

Chairman: Dr. R. L. HUANG
Vice-Chancellor of the University of Hong Kong

Rapporteur: Professor W. A. MACKAY
Vice-President of Dalhousie University

Monday, 21 August

Dr. A. G. DICKSON (*Founder/Director, Community Service Volunteers, UK*): Never having been a vice-chancellor—indeed, never a junior lecturer nor even a lab assistant—by what chain of circumstances have I come to believe in the crucial importance of relating the curriculum to the needs of society?

For two decades it has been my concern to enable young people— over 30,000 of them—to engage in a period of full-time service, be it in Britain or in other countries, either on leaving school or after graduation. During these years two questions have increasingly demanded answers. First, must service, helping others, responding to need—call it what one will—always be regarded as an activity in its own right, separate from work, distinct from study, indeed capable only of being undertaken on completion of training (or in spare time)? Might it not be part of the educational process itself, an extra dimension of the syllabus, the social equivalent of apprenticeship in its most elemental form, whereby one contributes whilst one learns and learns whilst one creates—as the African boy, fishing beside his father, adds to the catch and the Asian girl, shown by her mother how to reap, helps with the harvest?

Second, must institutions serve one purpose only? Just as teaching hospitals both treat patients and train doctors, the two tasks complementing each other, surely we should be looking at how alternative uses can be developed for existing resources so that they reinforce each other—with the police post in a remote area operating also as a rescue station and information point, an army unit applying its manpower and training skills to aid the civil community, a college acting as a resource centre for help to the neighbourhood or nation as well as an institution for learning (just as many monasteries once did and some still do).

First let me eliminate several forms of response to the needs of society which do not meet my criteria. Thus Oxford, for example, has established a number of institutes—a Centre for Management Studies, a Transport Studies Unit, a Centre for Criminological Research, an Industrial Relations Unit, a Centre for Socio-Legal Studies and four or five others—but they do not impinge on ordinary student life and ordinary student life does not impinge on them. Whilst the pattern of community service in most secondary schools is that the pupils go out by themselves to assist those in need, leaving the staff back at base, here professors and postgraduate research workers wrestle with contemporary problems unhelped (or unhampered) by the great mass of the student body. This kind of approach—as the report of the International Council for Educational Development on *Education in the Nation's Service* pointed out—tends to isolate the generality of students and other faculty members from the social problems handed over to these special institutes, just as the institute personnel for their part become increasingly separated from the mainstream of teaching and university life.

When British vice-chancellors and principals were asked some six years ago for three instances each of what their institutions were doing 'to counter the argument that much university teaching is irrelevant to the needs of society', the answers included the introduction of Japanese studies (Sheffield), pharmaceutical studies (Nottingham) and a consultancy service charging commercial rates (Loughborough). Yes—but the provision of knowledge in accord with the forces of supply and demand, knowledge which is professionally marketable, may not be quite synonymous with responding to the needs of society. At least not in the sense that the late K. G. Saiyidain had in mind when, as Secretary for Education to the government of India, he declared: 'A university must accept the burden of social responsibility and act as the conscience of society'.

But neither, of course, is social responsibility the exclusive preserve of departments of social studies or social administration. In May I wrote individually to every university, polytechnic and college in the United Kingdom, asking in what ways they were involving their students in meeting community needs as an integral part of their course. This enquiry, which my organisation is undertaking with financial assistance from the Department of Education and

SUB-TOPIC 4(A): RELEVANCE OF CURRICULUM TO SOCIETY [Dickson]

Science, derives from a resolution, no. 1.181, passed unanimously at Unesco's last General Conference in Nairobi, urging the participation of students (and their teachers) in what was called study service. The replies received so far have, on the whole, been extraordinarily cheering. But too many appear to assume that it is only those pursuing courses in social administration—or directing extramural departments—whose work touches the life of individuals or the community. This clearly is a heresy.

One senses, too, that universities or colleges established originally to meet the particular needs of a region or city or category of student edge gradually away from this goal, as if to be specific were somehow to lose status (whether this is true also of the land-grant colleges in the United States today, I do not know). Their chastisement is best expressed in William Blake's *Jerusalem:* 'He who would do good to another must do it in minute particulars. General good is the plea of the scoundrel, hypocrite and flatterer, for art and science cannot exist but in minutely organised particulars'.

One other matter. In Britain the University Grants Committee is concerned about the student 'unit of resource', by which is understood the amount of money deemed necessary to provide adequately for the education of a given number of students. My disquiet, per contra, is that we fail to see students themselves—in the here and now, whilst they are still *in statu pupillari*—as units of resource capable of responding to the needs of society. In this respect the industrial nations have so much to learn from the developing countries. Some of these have already despaired of the capacity of institutions of higher education to make a direct practical contribution to development in their own community or further afield— and have set up national service corps and similar bodies, only rarely linked with the curriculum, to do just that. Equally many academics—a majority probably?—contend vigorously (as did Walter Moberley) that universities are essentially thought-organisations, not will-organisations, committed to detachment rather than action: and in referring one, in this context, to union presidents, some imply that this is no concern of theirs or the curriculum but rather of how students care to spend their leisure.

How, then, is it possible for the curriculum to have relevance to the needs of society? Not in one prescribed way, surely, but in an infinite variety of forms. Only one theme is common to them all: we do not have to choose between what is beneficial to the student and what is beneficial to the community. It is not a matter of either/or but of both/and. With intelligence and imagination, models can be developed which serve both, reciprocally. Here are some models, observed over a number of years in different countries.

Model I—The Humane Application of Knowledge

Model I is best described in the words of Herbert Thelen, Professor of Education at the University of Chicago, as 'the humane application of knowledge'. Without any change in the curriculum the students' learning is offered to those in need. Thus Dr. Rosen, at Chelsea College, University of London, has involved his students of basic medical science in discouraging younger teenagers in the locality from the use of drugs: perhaps because only five or six years separate their ages, the students eschew moral arguments but draw on their own knowledge of pharmacology to make clear the effect of narcotics on the human metabolism. At the London School of Economics, Michael Zander enables his law students to assist tenants in dispute with landlords when they are called to appear before rent tribunals: study or service?—surely a combination of the two.

Udayana University in Bali involves its law students in assisting villagers in any negotiations with expatriates over the purchase of land. Students of fine arts—understandably and rightly the largest faculty in view of Bali's unique cultural heritage—develop new dance forms for villagers so that they do not exhaust or prostitute their energies performing, say, the traditional harvest dance twice a day for the tourist circuit. Within the last few weeks, whilst some students of the Royal College of Art in London have been sculpting stricken elms in Hyde Park, others have been designing graphics to illustrate a kit on homelessness which we will be distributing to schools. The possibilities are endless. No model advocated in this paper represents the totality of the curriculum but only a part. But we should constantly remind ourselves that most students do not study subjects—they take courses, man-made and designed to provide a certain 'mix'. The opportunity to engage in the humane application of knowledge is one element with which to 'lace' a syllabus—an element that can motivate the dullest as well as the most brilliant.

Looking recently at the social education syllabus in the primary schools of Kano State, in Nigeria, it was apparent that, with only a slight alteration in emphasis, even young children could contribute to the betterment of the community. The teacher's manual advocated that they should inspect the famous wall which surrounds the city: would they not learn to cherish this more if they were to take a hand in restoring it? They were urged to write an account of a visit to a local hospital: might they not have written letters for illiterate patients? Their attention was drawn to the difference in dress between themselves, as Muslims, and children attending schools for southerners; would not an invitation to those other youngsters to visit their school or their homes have helped even more to bridge the cultural and social barriers?

If philosophers and mathematicians feel disquietened by the naïveté or simple practicality of these examples, let two sayings be recalled of one who was both a mathematician and a philosopher. 'Knowledge is for use', remarked Alfred Whitehead on one occasion, and wrote at another time: 'Our task is to keep unhappiness to a minimum'.

Model II—Where All is not Technical

Model II—perhaps a refined version or extension of model I—confronts students with contemporary issues which appear at first glance to be essentially technological but which on closer examination are seen to contain a social, human or political element that cannot be ignored. The department of electrical engineering at the Imperial College of Science and Technology puts problems of this kind to its students, in the conviction that outside the lecture room and the laboratory these elements are nearly always compounded. One such problem—a request from a London borough—was to find an efficient method of delivering hot meals to old people. Some of the questions which had to be answered were: How to keep food hot when a helper climbs four floors of a lift-less apartment to deliver meals? How to package food so that it can be easily transported but does not cut the hands of the kitchen staff and is easily opened by a 90-year-old woman with rheumatism? What is the optimal routing of vehicles, taking account of traffic lights and parking restrictions? Students had the capacity to tackle all the technological problems. But on accompanying the Meals on Wheels van they discovered that, for an elderly person living alone, the warmth of the meal was secondary in importance to the warmth of the conversation which accompanied it. Here they had to reconcile scientific requirements with human needs.

Another real-life request was to examine the feasibility of employing, in electrical engineering manufacturing work, residents of the London Borough of Camden who are chronically poor by virtue of social, physical, mental or other disability. The paper on which the project was based, written by the Director of Social Services for Camden, painted a moving picture of whole families living under conditions in which poverty becomes self-perpetuating. But equally moving were the summaries of the backgrounds of the students who were to tackle this project, combining as they did not only high achievement in mathematics and physics but deep involvement, even at their young age, in work with the scouts, their church, with handicapped children, with adults in distress. To have required them to concentrate on a purely technological problem would have risked withering this other side of their personalities. Fortunately the department is not guilty of this neglect. The students were told that their report would be simultaneously part of their degree studies at the University *and* a contribution to the solution of a poignant social problem.

Other projects have included an investigation of how far the law takes account of modern technology—tape-recordings, videotapes, laser holograms, computer printouts—as permissible evidence in court, and what technological steps can be taken to provide proper authentication of such evidence; investigation of new types of mass screening for heart disease—and the social/moral/political implications of compulsory screening and/or treatment; the compilation of a booklet which the Intermediate Technology Development Group in London might send to those many people enquiring how cheap, small-scale systems of electrical power can be brought to rural areas of developing countries—so that they could furnish the ITDG with the relevant details of their situation and enable an appropriate response to be given. In contrast to the sandwich course, this model—to pursue the culinary metaphor—might be described as a curry, where theory and practice are blended.

Some years ago I advised the vice-chancellors in a developing country regarding the involvement of their students in service to the rural areas, and advocated that this experience should be an integral part of their course. Eventually a national youth service corps was introduced, not by the vice-chancellors but by the government. Who would want to be operated on by a third-year medical student, or drive over a bridge designed by a second-year engineering student, asked the civil servants with some sarcasm. It sounded logical enough: so it was only after graduation that students were required to serve for a year in a region of the country not their own. But on a later visit I heard a professor (himself a citizen of the country) observing sardonically that by the time they had graduated students of architecture were so conditioned to design requirements such as are encountered only in the major cities that, placed in a village, they did not know how to help farmers construct a bridge with trees they had felled; as for the medical graduates, by the time they had qualified they could compete for appointments to London hospitals but were lost to the needs of the remoter parts of their own country.

A curriculum that bridges the two cultures by enabling the science student at least to relate the technical to the human in a real-life setting before the conclusion of his course may have much to commend it, from society's point of view as well as the academic. And awareness that their own lecturers may not know the answers to the problems—however much more experienced in the methodology of arriving at solutions—can evoke a sense of partnership that is valuable in itself: avoidance of confrontation is in the interest of the community as well as of the campus.

Model III—A Pastoral Role for Students

Model III enables students to exercise a pastoral role in caring for others. At the University of Hacettepe, on the outskirts of Ankara, students registering for the medical school are assigned responsibility for the health of a Turkish family living in a slum area of the city. Throughout their years of study they act as 'medical friend' of the family—and in this they have, naturally, the backing of the faculty. When they ultimately receive their degree their knowledge of community medicine has not been learnt from books or lectures: it has been acquired at first hand. Moreover the development of a sense of social responsibility towards the sick has not been left to chance: it has been built into their course of study from the very first day, through the inspiration of the Rector, Dr. Dogramaci.

At the New Paltz campus of the State University of New York young people in trouble are being assigned by the State Division of Youth—in America 'youth' appears to be a synonym for 'juvenile delinquency'—to the care of selected college students, as an alternative to their being sent to residential institutions. The student is expected to act as an advocate—'a person who will go to bat for someone who may never have had anyone to protect and fight for him'—and help the youngster through boyhood or adolescence by establishing a relationship of trust, friendship and understanding. This programme is based on certain assumptions, namely:

(1) there exist in colleges and universities vast and untapped institutional and student resources waiting to be used at the request of a social services agency;

(2) students can be identified who have the talent and organisational skill to implement programmes that not only render service but challenge the existing efforts of the relevant government department;

(3) an equal challenge exists for the institute of higher education itself as to its role within society and its definition of education.

In the United States—I wish it held true for the United Kingdom—more and more faculties are recognising the value (if not obligation on their part) of providing their students with some form of field experience to round out their academic study. How this fits into a student's course and whether it can or should be included in the ultimate assessment of his university work is obviously open to discussion. But to assume responsibility for the immediate destiny of a youngster in need, to be aware that he looks on you as a model, this contributes mightily to the student's maturing as a sentient human being.

Model IV — The Transmission of Understanding to Others

Model IV entails students transmitting their knowledge, in modified form, to others. To make the complex intelligible is an admirable way of reinforcing the student's own understanding of what he has been learning: and it is a task greatly needed throughout all parts of the world. At the Imperial College of Science and Technology, Dr. Sinclair Goodlad has been enabling students of electrical engineering to teach maths and physics to 15-year-olds in 'difficult' schools in Pimlico and Brixton. At the University of Papua New Guinea students (and faculty members) have formed the science demonstration squad, journeying by truck to remote high schools which lack the laboratory equipment to illustrate many theorems: bringing their own portable generator and calor-gas cylinders, they put on practical demonstrations which win over some of the high school pupils who might otherwise have concluded that science lacked the excitement of discovery.

At Strathclyde University students of architecture and planning help children at nearby junior schools to understand the difference between what is attractive and what is ugly in their surroundings, to see how buildings can embellish or desecrate a geographical setting, why Strathclyde has come to look like it does—and even what they themselves might do to improve the appearance of their own neighbourhood.

At Tirupati in Andhra Pradesh a system of adoption is being initiated by which every child in Vemuru, situated in an interior region without a motorable road, will be adopted by a student in Sri Venkateswara University, who will be responsible for the education and all-round development of the youngster: the student, when he graduates, will hand the child over to another in-coming student.

At London University's Institute of Child Health, Dr. David Morley runs courses for postgraduate medical practitioners where, amongst much else, they learn how they can use 9- or 10-year-olds in remote rural areas of the third world as allies. By measuring round the upper arm of a younger brother or sister with a length of old X-ray film (the 'Shakir strip'), these boys or girls, even if totally illiterate and innumerate, can discover whether the child is malnourished.

At York University, Professor Eric Hawkins, Director of the Modern Languages Centre, has regularly involved his students in helping Asian immigrant families to learn English: what they have discovered about the social inhibitions and sociological blocks in acquiring another tongue has compensated them for the time subtracted from their own studies.

At the University in Lae, Papua New Guinea, a commitment to the value of intermediate technology entails students learning how to invent devices and modify equipment which can be used by villagers. Students at Delhi University teach peons working on the campus to read. Managers in training at Plessey's, a major electronics company in Britain, are required to help an apprentice to pass the Duke of Edinburgh's Award—thereby establishing an infinitely more personal and human relationship than normally exists between executives and junior employees. We hear much today about continuing education or 'éducation permanente': what matters is that the educational process should be not only on-going but *on-giving*.

Model V—A New Concept of the Extra-Mural

Model V takes shape when a curriculum is designed for those who might otherwise never get to a university—and whose immense practical experience would thus be lost to society. Duke University in North Carolina is situated near one of the largest army bases, where thousands of medical corpsmen were trained for the war in Vietnam. Lacking the required academic background, they would be inadmissible today for training as doctors. The university developed, therefore, a special programme to enable returned corpsmen to build on their vast expertise in dealing with the sick and wounded, by upgrading their knowledge and skills so that they can make a significant contribution to community health care in the States. Surely this is a nobler memorial for those who strove to save life under battle conditions than the satirical, bawdy film (now a TV serial), M.A.S.H. Birkbeck College, London, and Ruskin College, Oxford—and now Britain's Open University—are examples of whole institutions designed for those who would otherwise probably never gain admission to a university.

Now that colleges in the United Kingdom are wondering whom they can attract when the number of 'ordinary' undergraduates decreases in the 1990s, perhaps there will be more special courses and new curricula organised that are relevant to the needs of society. Whilst they come outside the formal context of accepted university curricula, two further examples represent endeavours to bring into the college fold those who might not otherwise ever get there. For several years undergraduates at Balliol, together with two or three lecturers, ran three-week courses at the end of the summer term for 16/17-year-olds specially chosen by local education authorities as showing some intellectual promise yet who, on account of the socio-economic background, would probably have never considered going to university—least of all to Oxford. In these brief three weeks, undergraduates and lecturers strove to raise the aspirations of these boys and convince them that they could make it to university. Deep was the bitterness of the undergraduates when the dons withdrew after a few years on the grounds that it interfered with their vacation plans—and by their withdrawal invalidated the continuation of this endeavour in the eyes of the local education authorities and school heads.

Secondly I recall students in Northern Nigeria who, at the end of the civil war in 1970, offered to give up their own beds so that young Ibos from defeated Biafra could take their places again and make their institution once more a federal college. This is not the familiar concept of extra-mural studies: it is students going out and dragging those over the walls who might never have scaled them on their own.

Model VI—Design for Problem-Solving

Model VI concerns those courses which incorporate an element of design—with design seen as a logical approach to problem-solving in the interests of the community. If Victor Papanek, author of *Design for the Real World,* is still working at Carleton University, Ottawa, it is certain that he will have been encouraging his students to approach design as a means of relieving drudgery, avoiding danger, mitigating suffering, or assisting the survival of the poor. It could be a mechanism which enables the limbless to feed themselves; cooling devices, not dependent on electricity, to make life more tolerable in exceptionally hot climates; crates for the freightage of trucks to developing countries which, on opening up, provide shelter for an impoverished family in a shanty town at least more weatherproof than bits of corrugated iron and sacking.

When it was suggested some five years ago that they might design a solar heater for a self-help school in West Africa, students at Rolls Royce College, Bristol—boisterous and sometimes truculent industrial apprentices—made it clear that they cared little for the problems of the third world. Told by their supervisor 'there's the sun up there and the water down there—it's up to you', they moodily set about constructing a heater made out of wood, kitchen foil and copper piping. Then, returning from a lecture, they found that the sun's rays reflected off the foil had toasted the sandwiches which they had placed on the ground nearby, before setting fire to the wooden contraption itself. In a moment of time their sceptical indifference changed to enthusiastic commitment. Scrapping their first design, they went on to construct an alternative mechanism — and raised enough money to send two of their number to the Mayflower School in Nigeria to instal the heater and see that it actually worked. It is interesting that the initial attitude of the staff at Rolls Royce College had been that 'this kind of enterprise did not belong to the curriculum and should be undertaken in the students' spare time'.

At Queen Mary College, University of London, Professor Thring, convinced that examinations tend to discourage originality, confronts his students of mechanical engineering with open-ended problems such as the design of an early-warning fire system, remote control mechanisms for dealing with unexploded bombs, a diagnostic radio pill encapsulating a miniature transistor, a wheel-chair that will mount and descend staircases — or how to solve London's rush-hour traffic hold-ups. On one occasion he secured permission for a dozen of his engineering students to attend an operation at the nearby London Hospital. They watched with fascination the manual dexterity of the surgeon until, as he began to sew up the arteries, one student whispered to another: 'That can be done mechanically'. Back in their laboratory they designed an automatic sewing device to enable a surgeon to join two blood vessels together with a single movement. Lest it be thought that activities so immediately practical cannot be reconciled with the deeper concepts which should characterise a university — as compared with a polytechnic or college of technology — it is significant that Professor Thring has adapted the Hippocratic Oath for applied scientists and engineers:

'I vow to strive to apply my professional skills only to projects which after conscientious examination I believe to contribute to the growth of co-existence of all human beings in peace, human dignity and self-fulfilment... I vow to struggle through my work to minimise danger, noise, strain or invasion of privacy of the individual: pollution of earth, air or water, destruction of natural beauty, mineral resources, and wild life.'

Model VII—From Sandwich Course to Service

Model VII is the sandwich course — where the period off-campus is not just field work in its conventional form but entails students doing something of benefit to the community at the same time as learning from reality. Hundreds of courses now provide for students to put into practice what they have studied theoretically: the day is long past when the sandwich principle related primarily to engineering or other industrially-oriented courses. At Brunel University, at Uxbridge, every single course is structured on the sandwich pattern, with students spending five months of each year in a field placement.

Many community colleges and that (to British ears) oddly-named development, co-operative education, require or encourage students to spend a term or a year away from the campus. Since this movement (in both senses of the word) surfaced at a time when adult opinion thought that it would be beneficial if students simultaneously learnt the economic facts of life, importance was also attached to their earning their living during this period. The result is that thousands of students of management, applied economics, social studies, as well as of engineering and technology, secure attachments to well-established companies. But in fact the projects which could really profit from students' intellectual scrutiny and personal service (and provide, reciprocally, a profoundly educative experience)—projects struggling to cope with battered wives, homeless men, newly-arrived immigrants, unemployed youth, severely disabled people, the lonely and the old, industrial dereliction, housing problems, community relations—are rarely in a position to pay commercial salaries. Through this insistence on the rate for the job both students and the community are deprived of what each could give to the other: all credit to Durham University's business school for pursuing a different policy.

At the University of Bradford—committed by its charter to 'the application of knowledge to human welfare'—the students' manual suggests that they ask themselves: 'In what way has the academic study of the university enabled me to tackle the practical issues of the world?' (Some might think that the question seems premature before registration, and too late after graduation). More significantly and more refreshingly—in a study only just completed of 'The Year Away' element in Bradford University's school of interdisciplinary human studies—John Allcock robustly asserts that the real question to be asked should be: 'What can the student *give?*' and argues that the purpose to be served by a year of extra-mural experience is service. 'I would wish to say to students, "your education is a preparation for service".' Students, he asserts, do have skills which can be used for the benefit of others. As people they do have something to offer of value: and their exertions can make a difference to the satisfaction of the needs of other people.

SUB-TOPIC 4(A): RELEVANCE OF CURRICULUM TO SOCIETY [Dickson]

What marvellous opportunities are opened up by this sandwich concept — yet how prosaic and banal are most of the projects. Today the interdisciplinary approach is the 'in' thing — but that supposes a mingling only of academic perspectives. How much more challenging are undertakings that call for a combination of intellectual understanding, physical stamina and moral qualities (or attitudes of mind). In most educational institutions we take care to separate them, one for the lecture room, another for the sports field, with moral qualities probably left out on their own. Real life does not make these nice distinctions. Consider what Canada's Frontier College (admittedly not a collegiate entity) has asked of students and how they have responded, what working with prisoners in Manila's jails demands of Filipino students, what cyclone relief meant for students of Sri Venkateswara University and other colleges in Andhra Pradesh, what Thomas Gladwyn's study of navigation and logic in the Carolines involved ('East is a Big Bird'). I recall the defiant reply which my friend Muazim Husain gave, when he was head of UNESCO's mission in Southern Libya, to an enquiry from headquarters in Paris as to what qualifications were possessed by a young indigenous colleague whom he had warmly recommended for promotion: 'He is a graduate of the University of the Sahara!'.

Tranquillity and security did not characterise Solzhenitsyn's collection of data for *Gulag Archipelago*. Intellectual creativity may be the product of ferment as much as of seclusion. Implicit in this approach is the requirement that faculty members should have had comparable experiences themselves or be prepared to respond, alongside their students, to such challenges.

Model VIII — Response to Crisis

Model VIII — response to crisis — follows naturally from the previous paragraphs. When villages were razed to the ground by earthquake some years ago at Koina in India, students at the Institute of Technology, Powai, started at once to collect money for the destitute victims. But the Director pointed out that there was a contribution even more urgent that they alone could make: a design for quake-proof schools. Pooling their ideas, within twenty-four hours the students produced a flexible design, and local apprentices were mobilised to prefabricate parts — whereupon the Director put it to the students that they go to Koina to erect the construction themselves. Then he turned to the staff, asking whether they were content to sit back whilst their young people left to contend with this emergency on their own. So the staff laboured beside the students on the earthquake site in a joint project that is still talked about. When it was all over, reflecting on what it meant to students and staff to feel that they were responding to genuine human needs, the Director visited one government department after another in Bombay asking what were their unsolved technical problems—so that the students and staff could tackle these tasks as an integral part of their training.

Oklahoma University has been simulating hijackings, the seizing of hostages and kidnappings, in an effort to produce a basic primer of counter-terrorism. Former members of the US Green Beret special forces play the role of terrorists, students volunteer to be hostages, and the police play themselves. Under the direction of Professor Stephen Sloan of the political science deparment this study group on international terrorism has analysed over 200 cases of 'non-territorial terrorism' in which armed groups, operating on hitherto neutral ground, have seized hostages to promote a political cause. When I first learned of this, my initial reaction was: 'How typically Yankee!'. But then I reflected that our own planes had been hijacked in the Middle East, and that terrorism had erupted in recent years in our own cities. And if American students have been exhilarated by the part they have played in this programme, does this invalidate the experiment? Exhilaration at discovery resulted, so one is told, in Archimedes leaping from his bath.

A few years ago I addressed a gathering of teachers at Lerwick in the Shetlands on how they might involve their pupils in service to the community—not a particularly easy task in a cluster of islands set in the North Sea. Suppose a coupling broke when a tanker was discharging oil in their harbour, I asked—but then remarked that there was no need to consider hypothetical emergencies since the islanders themselves were already doing a grand job in polluting their shores. Their fish-processing ships were casting overboard cods' heads and tails plus pieces of plastic wrapping—all of it being washed up on the beaches on the next tide, stinking. Immediately a number of individuals rose to their feet, identified themselves as science teachers, and exclaimed: 'Let's have a major marine biology programme in our schools next term!' I congratulated them on their initiative, but even more on the fact that the nearest university was some hundreds of miles away on the mainland—for otherwise not only would no school pupils be allowed a look-in, neither would any first degree students: this would be appropriated as a postgraduate project to be funded by a grant from the Science Research Council.

I recalled this incident once last April, when a mechanical connection broke in the Ekofisk 'Bravo' oilfield and a sheet of flame erupted in the North Sea: we had to send to Houston, Texas, for 'Red' Adair and 'Boots' Hansen to put the fire out. I recalled it

SUB-TOPIC 4(A): RELEVANCE OF CURRICULUM TO SOCIETY [Dickson]

again this May when a Liberian tanker, Eleni V, broke in two off the Norfolk coast and revealed our unpreparedness to deal with such emergencies. What seems sadder than our unpreparedness is that in moments of crisis affecting the livelihood of thousands no public response is visible from our seats of learning — still less any suggestion that students themselves might have any contribution to make.

The value of emergencies is that they wrench us out of accepted modes of thought: pose dramatically the questions, 'What are we studying and why?'; reveal hidden resources in staff and students; and unite teachers and taught in a common response to need. As a friend remarked who had taken part in the Freedom Marches led by Martin Luther King: 'In times of crisis the middle-aged are rejuvenated, the young are seen to be capable of carrying adult responsibilities — and the barriers between the generations dissolve'. But this presupposes that institutions *want* to develop an extra dimension as resource centres of help to the neighbourhood or nation — and want to regard their students as constituting a vital human resource.

Model IX — When the Needs of Society Determine the Curriculum

Model IX accepts the needs of society as helping to determine the nature of the curriculum, indeed the nature of the university itself. From time to time the University of Toulouse in south-west France makes the resources of the campus together with the energies of younger students available to 'le troisième âge', the retired. Everything, from the academic facilities to membership of student clubs is open to them. The object is not just that they should go through a certain experience which is complete in itself and then have done with it, as with conventional courses. Rather it is that they should make use of the riches of the university so that these can be passed on to the outside community and be enjoyed for the remainder of their own lives. When they are following courses — in the welfare entitlements of the retired, for instance — they form small action groups with a view to sharing these benefits with other elderly people and thus improve the nature of the society in which they live.

At Bu-Ali Sina University in north-west Iran all the traditional faculties have been dissolved and stirred up to reappear as clusters — health sciences, education and ecodevelopment (a combination of economics and technology). Water is the kind of subject that makes sense in the curriculum for in spite of snow in winter there are no year-round sources of clean drinking water and most of the people in the area suffer from intestinal parasites of one sort or another. So students investigate water from all angles—chemical, geological, economic, and social—and undertake projects and research to seek new sources of fresh water. In view of the ritual significance of the communal bath in Persia's rural society, students of environmental engineering are working on solar energy panels which even in winter could provide the required hot water. Helping the villagers is not just a useful spin-off of university activity, it is its central purpose. 'We want to give our students new attitudes to development', says the Vice-Chancellor, 'whilst giving them a chance to work within the system'. Would Jowett have dissented?

The North London Polytechnic—at first surprised and then stimulated by Tower Hamlets Council declaring that their grant would be dependent on evidence of what the Polytechnic actually did for their borough—have in fact responded with a major effort to activate small businesses in an area where so many firms have closed.

But it is to India that one turns for the philosophy that underlies this model. Few have thought more deeply or based their thinking on harder practical experience than Professor Mabud Hasan of Aligarh Muslim University, who not only co-ordinates the contribution to development of students from each of his own university's faculties but also acts as an adviser to the all-India National Service Scheme. He feels that the changes endlessly pursued in the educational structure are seldom related to the developmental needs of the country. Making social service voluntary leaves the university's institutional stance and teaching approach untouched, he argues, and urges that courses should be so designed that participation by students (and lecturers, too) in community action programmes becomes an integral component of instruction itself. Then he declares:

> 'The philosophy that should guide educational planners is to restructure university courses around the problems of society. Thus each discipline or department of study should plan its curriculum with a view to identifying, from its special point of view, the social problems that clamour for solution and cultivate the requisite skills to attack these problems. The second important step will be to effect coordination between the approaches of different disciplines since a good number of problems are likely to require simultaneous tackling by more than one academic discipline.
>
> 'It goes without saying that the task of the faculties within the social segment selected by them will not be confined to study. The ideas and training in the classroom and laboratory must be

applied and tested in the field. These operations will enable students to re-evaluate their learning experience while, at the same time, the community will benefit by the solution of its problems. It is very important to keep this two-way benefit relationship in mind.'

This last point is echoed by Dr. Puey Ungphakorn—one-time Governor of the Bank of Thailand, for some years professor of economics and recently Rector of Tammasat University in Bangkok, now slowly recovering from a stroke in London—who pioneered the involvement of his own students in service to rural areas: 'We have been taught that the primary duty of students is to study, in order to render service to society. But, in fact, service itself has become study par excellence, and the simple truth is that a circle exists—study for service for study'.

They are not lone voices. It is my privilege to be currently advising the Vice-Chancellor of the University of the South Pacific on how students and faculties can combine study with service so that they make a deeper impact on the development of their island communities—in a phrase, that it may become more the university *for* the South Pacific. In Operation Bharani the University of Mysore has committed itself to a highly intelligent and compassionate endeavour to make itself a resource centre for the people of Hunsur Taluk: whilst, on a recent visit, my ears did detect the frequent intrusion of the word 'data-collection' in conversation with farmers—apparently Kannada has no word for this, though Canada may—I salute the Vice-Chancellor for establishing no less than 32 task forces in order that every sector of every faculty should consider how its knowledge and skills might contribute to the development of the surrounding rural area. The universities of Osmania, of Bombay, of Tamil Nadu, of Sri Venkateswara and others too numerous to mention by name are each, in their own way, doing everything in their power to link their curriculum to the needs of society. Whatever Newman may have said about the true purpose of a university, these vice-chancellors align themselves with Aristotle in their conviction that the end of life is not a thought but an action.

'Some people see things as they are and ask "why?" But I dream things that never were and ask "why not?"' This thought—the favourite quotation of Robert Kennedy—prompts the following questions:

1. Must everything taught in universities be assessable? No matter how great the educational validity of community-related curricula, it must be admitted that the reliability with which they can be assessed is low. Does this matter? Student profiles and other devices

to replace degree classification have been proposed. But if assessment for degree marks is insisted upon, how should it be done?

2. How can university faculty members be stimulated to introduce and supervise community-related curricula? Promotion usually depends on the results of research and contributions to learned journals—the publish-or-perish syndrome. Yet community-related curricula call for detailed administration by faculty members who not only understand the requirements of university teaching but are also well informed about social matters. Such people will not have much time or energy left over for scholarship or research. Are they to be self-sacrificial in a way that is not expected of their colleagues? Is a new university ethos desirable?

3. Although education creates economic benefits it is also a drain on the economy. To ease the situation and to raise the quality of education by improving the staff/student ratio each person enjoying full-time education might devote part of his/her time to helping someone lower down the ladder—with third-year students helping freshmen, second-year students helping pupils in their final year at school, and so on down to primary school level. How do we bring this about?

4. What are the academic and practical implications of making a 'sandwich' arrangement part of every type of university course? Some form of 'sandwich' arrangement may be an administrative necessity if students are to undertake community-related curricula. Such provision can be justified—in, for example, engineering or the social sciences—on the educational ground that theory is unintelligible without experience and experience is formless without theory. Matters are not so easy in the humanities, though there is value in personally experiencing social conditions which writers describe or historians chronicle. How best can this be done?

5. How can professional institutions and associations be encouraged to regard community service as a valid form of preparation for membership of their body? There are obvious advantages in arranging for intending professionals—doctors, lawyers, architects, teachers, engineers, etc.—to acquire direct knowledge of social conditions through participation in service to the community: such exposure to social problems may widen a student's whole perception of his role. But practice in most professions is controlled by professional institutions which define criteria of admission, educational standards, licensing or other formal entry examinations, career lines within the profession, et cetera. What can be done about this?

6. When there is everything to be said in favour of a break between school and university (Einsteins and Mozarts possibly excepted), why do not universities controlling their own admission

SUB-TOPIC 4(A): RELEVANCE OF CURRICULUM TO SOCIETY [*Dickson*]

criteria tell candidates: 'You will be welcome here — after a year of having done something positive for others'? To possess the authority to bring about a desirable end and not thus to use it is an abuse of authority.

7. Why does virtually no university faculty, department or institute of education make provision in the training of teachers for their learning how to involve their pupils in responding to the needs of the community?

8. Why do not more business management schools and departments of applied economics attach their students — instead of the conventional placements with commercial companies — to groups of unemployed youth, exercising their skills in identifying tasks/articles/services that these young people could undertake and helping them to form themselves into co-operative enterprises?

Sir FRASER NOBLE (*Principal and Vice-Chancellor of the University of Aberdeen*): When the organisers of this Congress invited me to speak on this topic I was put in mind of the response which the painter Matisse is reported to have made to a lady who asked him at a dinner-party: 'What do you think of Art' — 'Madam, don't you have an easier question?' It is a subject which has been debated ever since education was invented. 'Know thyself' (γνῶθι σεαυτόν) prescribed the Delphic oracle; and Plato explained that this maxim cannot be attained by an individual for himself in isolation, because man is a social animal and can only be known as a member of society. The quest for self-knowledge must, therefore, embrace the study of culture and the community, and this is the theme of the Commission on Canadian Studies whose report[1], written by this Association's distinguished Honorary Treasurer, was published in 1975.

The arguments about relevance have raged from Plato through the Renaissance and the Enlightenment and the nineteenth-century period of colonialism and urbanisation to the phenomenally rapid technological and social revolutions of the last thirty years or so*. As we have moved into a phase of deep uncertainty about ourselves and

---

*I have seen it recorded that there was a professor at Bologna who derided the study of Cicero (whom he professed not to have read) and promised to train his students in writing every sort of letter and official document which was demanded of notaries and secretaries of his day. He began one session by saying: 'Let us take as our theme to-day that a poor and diligent student in Paris is to write to his mother for necessary expenses'. Those were the days when tuition fees were paid direct to professors. Perhaps a return to that practice might encourage change towards a more relevant curriculum today, in the eyes of the student if not of society.

405

our future, anxiety about the objectives of the curriculum has become sharper. But it is not new, though it may have new aspects such as the fear of the dissent and social unrest that may follow from mass unemployment of over-specialised graduates.

In the medieval university the foundations of the curriculum were the *trivium* (grammar, rhetoric and logic) and the *quadrivium* (arithmetic, geometry, music and astronomy). They were the seven pillars of Wisdom, hewn out to build her house—and one that might be sounder and more secure than some modern institutions provide, with their chairs of effective living, cosmetology, and similar esoteric subjects (if we are to believe Jacques Barzun).[2] But even these foundations were constantly shaken by theological and other antagonisms between contending professors, as in Uppsala, recently 500 years old, where the university was disrupted by quarrels between the Aristotelian logicians and the disciples of the Socratic method. Yet, as the official historian of Uppsala (Sten Lindroth)[3] recently reminded us, with all its unpleasant features which at times assumed scandalous proportions the quarrel was, in a way, 'a sign of health: the minds of men were beginning to awaken at the University of Uppsala'. It was about this time that Francis Bacon, in England, surveying the European scene, complained that universities were too slow to change their curricula, failing to debate whether old courses might be 'profitably kept up, or whether we should rather abolish them and substitute better'.

The trouble, of course, with the *trivium* and *quadrivium* (as Asa Briggs[4] has reminded us) as it is with our curricular considerations today, is that there was a great burst of new knowledge outside the confines of these disciplines, and with it the emergence of new ideas concerning the purpose of university education. By the early nineteenth century, in Uppsala as elsewhere, the argument had changed. The status of the university in civil society was the issue between the academic romanticists, who condemned sordid utilitarianism and the empirical sciences 'with their accumulation of dry facts', and the minority who were 'faithful to the ideas of the Enlightenment and held fast to social utility as the lodestar of university education'. The latter saw the universities as serving the aims of economic progress and mankind's earthly happiness, in the age of incipient industrialism.

Round about this time in Germany a combination of factors, including industrialisation, urban growth, and nationalistic fervour, produced a new emphasis on specialisation and research, and set a pattern for mono-disciplinary study which remains of world-wide significance to this day. As we shall see, we cannot divorce consideration of curriculum from questions about the research function of the universities today. In Germany, because of social structures, political attitudes and other reasons, the promotion of basic research in the universities set them apart from government and from the industrial leadership, and subsequent history provides sufficient warning against a policy which enables the specialist to 'usurp the rank of philosopher and educator'. It is not healthy to promote a hierarchy of discontented intellectuals who are (in Barzun's phrase) only semi-educated, and to misuse the university for a combination of political ends and pure research.

In America the enlightened and farsighted ideas of Franklin and Jefferson favoured the application of knowledge by the university to the world which supported it, and advocated practical studies for the new age.[5] But in university terms the new age for universities which has been moulded in the classical tradition came only after the civil war, and the tremendous surge of new industrial energy. The Morrill Land-Grant Act of 1862 produced for American university institutions a mission of service to society to add to the European traditions of teaching and research. The public universities were to be an integral part of the community and to serve its needs. But how was service to the community to be construed? The radical Theodore Roszak[6] reminds us that Socrates had asked this question also! 'To which sort of treatment of our city do you urge me? Is it to combat the Athenians until they become as virtuous as possible, prescribing for them like a physician; or is it to be their servant and cater to their pleasure?' By 1870 Nietzsche was denouncing the subservience of the German universities to an inhuman scholarly technology. He wrote: 'The entire system of higher education has lost what matters most; the end as well as the means to the end. That education (Bildung) is itself an end — not the state — this has been forgotten'.

In the United Kingdom, if not indeed in the whole world, the debate has come to a head again over the last twenty years. The context has been the explosion of knowledge, the unprecedented rate of technological development and social change, the great expansion of higher education, doubts about premature specialisation in school curricula, questions about manpower planning and misfits between the needs of certain professions and the supply of graduates, frustrations about slow rates of economic growth in a consumption-oriented society compounded by acute inflation, chronic balance of payments difficulties and high unemployment. The debate began with the opportunities to establish many new universities and other institutions of higher education, and it continues in a phase in which there are severe constraints on society's ability to supply the resources needed to sustain them and doubts about the scale on which they should be maintained. There are doubts, for example, in relation to projections about numbers of potentially-qualified entrants to higher education and about the ability of the labour market to absorb them when they have graduated.

That the discussion is a continuing one is well illustrated by speeches made in the House of Commons in a debate held, ominously and perhaps appropriately, on a Friday the 13th—of January, 1978. One of the most remarkable things about this rather undistinguished debate was that it was the first to take place in the House of Commons[7] on the question of the universities for nine years! (The House of Lords is frequently more relevant in its themes for discussion). The chief spokesman for the Opposition said: 'We have far too much cant about the necessity of making universities relevant, but who can say what is going to be relevant in the long term or even in the medium term? To-day's relevance is to-morrow's irrelevance..... The only relevance that universities need to-day is to be faithful to the perennial values of truth, honesty and beauty, and to enjoy the freedom to pursue those values without fear wherever the path may lead'. This being a parliamentary debate, he was promptly accused of underplaying the contribution the universities make to industrial technology (which he then emphasised). He was later attacked (by the Minister of State, replying for the government) for seeming 'totally to dissociate the universities..... from the needs of the nation. One cannot do that [said the Minister]. One cannot pretend that universities exist in isolation either for their own good or for the good of the students within them..... [Students] intend to get a job that is economically useful to themselves and the nation. Therefore some regard—not manpower planning—must be paid to whether youngsters going to university will find employment when they leave'. The Minister went on to remark, perhaps with a sense more of hope than conviction, that students were already voting with their feet and moving into science and engineering courses which were likely to offer more security of employment than 'other courses' (one is left to infer that they would be courses in the humanities and social sciences) 'that they might have entered more readily or more frequently in the 1960s and early 1970s'.

Shortly before this debate in parliament, the minister for education herself had given some hint of her own views in a public lecture at Birkbeck College[8] when she said that she believes that 'we do specialise too young in the British educational system..... and have therefore created a very specific and therefore often insufficiently flexible system of secondary education running into higher education'. Referring to the expectation that people in future will move more from one career to another and from one skill to another, she argued: 'it does not make sense to educate for a flexible professional and industrial life if one has educated people, however well, in very narrow foundations of knowledge'.

Thirty years ago A. D. Lindsay made a brave effort to relate the curriculum to an understanding of the needs of society when he planned the foundation year at Keele (which was in a real sense the first of the new post-war British universities). This comprised a first-year course, taken by all students, 'designed as a whole to give an understanding of the heritage of Western civilisation, of modern society, and of the methods and influence of the experimental sciences'.[9] It has rightly been described as the most original innovation in British university education in this century. While in some respects it may not have been wholly successful, it was certainly influential in moving a good deal of the thinking about the curriculum in the new universities towards a general broadening and towards interdisciplinarity. It remains unfortunate that in the British system, in which we are rightly proud of the standards we achieve in turning out honours graduates in three years with low drop-out rates, government financial constraints have allowed no scope for further experimentation with four-year courses along Keele lines, but have at times presented a real threat of a reduction in the first degree course to two years, in spite of the continuing knowledge explosion.

From the faculty side the emphasis on the research function of the universities and the exponential growth of knowledge tends to produce greater specialisation in curriculum. Options proliferate, often reflecting research interests of staff. Disciplines split into sub-disciplines, and new departments arise more frequently than fusion occurs. New technology, like computing, produces new disciplines. Problem-solving creates new approaches in old subjects—from the whole animal to the cell in zoology, and back again in combination with the cell-biologist in ecological studies stimulated by problems of environmental pollution.

One of the Carnegie Commission reports[10] describes the schizophrenic tendencies in curriculum development in American universities in the 1960s. There are the conflicts between the pre-scribed curricula and the options, between the faculty's selection of what is essential from the widening range of things to study and the students' choice of what he wants to read. There are the conflicts between the concept of general education of the well-rounded man and the demanding professional requirements for a highly-trained engineer or physician or psychologist. To design a good general programme is difficult, both because of the overwhelming amount of knowledge that has to be taken into account and because of the zeal and enthusiasm of the specialists for their fields and for their 'professionalism'. Cross-disciplinary teaching is handicapped because pressures for promotion encourage effort within the departmental boundaries rather than outside. (I remember more than thirty years ago being rebuked by a senior university administrator for organising an interdisciplinary seminar, because it was not advertised in the prospectus and therefore did not attract a tuition fee!)

Perhaps because 'problems' are felt to be more relevant than pure knowledge, there has been a move towards more interdisciplinary teaching. You can learn a lot about the practical problems an engineer will encounter if you know something about the nature of choice in economics, but it is very hard to get the undergraduate to see this sort of thing, and hard to make economists enthusiastic about teaching bored engineering students. Sometimes one wonders whether the approach to interdisciplinary studies is not premature at the first degree level — yet postgraduate work inevitably tends to be even narrower and more specialised. In designing a general course, too, such as a broad introduction to the social sciences, one finds at the tutorial level if not at the lecturing level that the number of teachers involved for a large class is likely to be too large for any common understanding or acceptance of the objectives of the course to be possible — at least not without a great deal of effort by the course organiser, and a repetition of the effort year by year as the personalities involved change.

Towards the end of the 1960s we heard a great deal from students about the lack of relevance in the curriculum. Much of this criticism was opportunistic rather than idealistic but one cannot entirely withhold one's sympathy. There is an ever-present danger that scholarship will become too technocratic, even too professional, that the links between research and culture will be too tenuous. Nietzsche said: 'The advancement of learning at the expense of man is the most pernicious thing in the world'. This harsh judgement can be avoided if teachers, even if they are specialist researchers, can keep the true purposes of teaching in mind. In my own university there is still a chair of Latin — and it is called the chair of humanity. My former colleague Geoffrey Bantock once wrote: 'If one finds that Plato and Shakespeare are still important, it is because they raised questions or analysed states of mind which are relevant in the West, not to a particular phase of society, but to the human condition as it is likely to be lived within the foreseeable future'. I have never forgotten as an undergraduate in the 1930s being deeply moved and instructed by an article written by one of my predecessors as Principal of Aberdeen, Sir William Hamilton Fyfe, a former Principal of Queen's University, Ontario, in which he translated the famous passage in Thucydides on στάσισ (stasis—civil war or faction), substituting for the Greek names the appropriate Spanish ones.

What is relevant, both to the individual student and to society, is what is learned with a will. It is an illusion to think that you can devise a curriculum that is relevant to life and to society and can be kept relevant in that sense in the future. Relevant to whom, to which career, for how long? In a class of fifty there are fifty lives, probably many more than fifty careers, and many aspects of each life and each career. When we talk about the needs of society what sort of society do we mean? An open democratic society in which the interests of minorities are respected and protected, or a closed collectivist society in which the structure permits no options? I imagine that most of us here subscribe to the ideal of the open society, evolving by processes of continuous adaptation in which one of the basic needs (as Lord Hailsham has put it)[12] is that individuals and minorities are prepared to recognise their corresponding responsibility towards others as they expect their own rights to be recognised. Taking account, as he says of 'the fallibility of human nature, the impermanence and incompleteness of all political philosophies, and the inability of man to see far into the future', then relevance to the needs of society is a difficult prescription to write for a curriculum of university education, and a dangerous one to put in the hands of any particular group. The danger of talking about relevance to the needs of society is that governments, which by their nature tend to take short views, will be obsessed by some 'fantasy of instant utility', and prescribe a syllabus to be operated in a structure of credits and qualifications.

I agree with a comment by Jacques Barzun[13]: 'Relevance is in the mind, a perception of the ways in which ideas are related. It is not a connection between things'. He quotes Professor Jeremiah Day, writing in 1828 (150 years ago!): 'Our object is not to teach that which is peculiar to any one of the professions; but to lay the foundation which is common to them all..... But why, it may be asked, should a student waste his time upon studies which have no immediate connection with his future profession? Will chemistry enable him to plead at the bar, or conic sections qualify him for preaching? Or astronomy aid him in the practice of physic? The answer to this is: "Everything throws light on everything"'.

Sir Charles Carter, Vice-Chancellor of Lancaster, wrote in 1972 that the only true relevance for the student is concerned 'not so much with the content of studies, as with what they do to the mind', developing logical processes, stimulating the habit of questioning, strengthening the basic skills of literacy and numeracy, injecting a suspicion of the facile and the second-rate. That is not so very far from the *trivium* and *quadrivium* of the early *studium generale*. In his last annual report (December, 1977) Carter returned to the theme in the context of the argument that the curriculum does little to promote the material wealth of the country (what businessmen often call *real* wealth, presumably to distinguish it from the wealth of our cultural heritage). Carter says: 'learning is concerned with higher things than those of material welfare; its material benefits are purely incidental, and should never be elevated to become a primary purpose'. At the same time the university curriculum *does* achieve a great deal for society in terms of material benefit or the creation of wealth, and not merely through the education of members of the professions.

In the interests of society, which provides the funds for university teaching and research, it is perfectly fair to suggest that the curriculum should take some account of society's needs for manpower with special skills. Notions that students themselves may entertain about relevance may very well not fit with the needs of industrial society (whether capitalist or socialist) but caution is important. I remember a former chairman of the UGC warning vice-chancellors against talk of reshaping the curriculum because in the recession of 1971 British industry reacted (foolishly, as most people now accept) by cutting back sharply on its intake of graduates. He reminded us, rightly, that we were at that time discussing courses for new students who would not be graduating until near the end of the decade. As he said, who can tell what the labour market will be like then?

As it happens, after recovery, there has been a dramatic slump in employment, but the signs are that industry's recruitment policy for graduates has become less volatile and more far-sighted. So too have been the attitudes of young graduates. Whereas a few years ago student choice of course jumped around looking for the easy option and the job that meant 'working with people' (as though industry was not made up of people), now graduates seem rapidly to be becoming much more adaptable in their readiness to accept what the market has to offer. The important thing for the university planning the curriculum and the student choosing his course is not to think short, in terms of the first job the graduate is likely to take. Rather we must think long, appreciating that careers will change, that even in a given profession there will be new knowledge to acquire later, perhaps in a field undreamed of at the stage of professional qualification. Provided that we try to ensure that our graduates can adapt to new ideas, can think logically and realistically outside as well as within their own professional fields of expertise, can master complex issues and apply their minds in a wider context, we can avoid major problems of conflict between vocational or professional and liberal education, and keep our curriculum relevant to the needs of society.

I hope that I am justified in this rather optimistic conclusion. I am normally more inclined to pessimism in these matters, and a year ago at Oxford I heard Martin Meyerson of the University of Pennsylvania give a paper full of evidence of the overtraining of graduates in the USA and full of foreboding about the maldistribution, economically and geographically, of American talent. Although his statistics, profession by profession, were drawn mostly from the USA, and his projections of unemployment rates amongst PhDs made one's hair stand on end, his analysis appeared to apply equally well to most if not all of the advanced industrial countries.

As I have hinted, the most recent British evidence from the marketplace *is* much less gloomy. A young man or woman who has a degree certainly runs a much lower risk of being unemployed in Britain than a young person who has no higher education, and there is no hard evidence that Britain has been producing too many graduates or that our graduates are not adapting well to changes in the types of opportunity available to them.

What I am keenly aware of, however, is that my discourse has not been sufficiently relevant to the problems and concerns of many delegates from universities in developing countries of the Commonwealth. Their societies have special needs, and these needs may call for manpower trained along different lines from graduates of countries like my own. Often their universities will be confronted with more definitive instructions from governments about the interpretation of these needs through the curriculum than we in Britain, or indeed in Canada, Australia or New Zealand, would be prepared to accept even as guidelines from the University Grants Committee or its equivalent in these countries. I worry about this, because I hope that we can continue to contribute to the strength of the universities of the developing countries of the Commonwealth, and I am apprehensive about some of the criteria for aid which are now prescribed by the British Overseas Development Ministry and which increasingly circumscribe the help which we might, in free co-operation with you, extend to your colleagues and students. The criteria for aid should be the criteria for good education, judged by educationalists. I am uneasy when ministers of any government think that they can confidently and rigidly define the criteria of relevance to economic development for any university course or for the selection of students to follow it.

Whatever the context, I think that I have shown that the debate will go on, as it has done already for centuries. In 1974 the President of the United States[14] was acclaimed for saying that higher education is not practical enough, and proposed 'a great new partnership of labor and academia' through which programmes of education would emerge that helped students to acquire the abilities to think and understand 'while developing in them a sense of calling, in which life and career are integrated'. Two years later the British Prime Minister[15], in his Ruskin College speech which purported to set the great debate rolling, proclaimed that the goals of our education are 'to equip children to the best of their ability for a lively, constructive place in society and also to fit them to do a job of work. Not one or the other, but both'. So long as there are governments, politicians will go on begging the question. So long as there are universities, academics will argue the point. As they may yet say in Quebec: 'plus ça change, plus c'est la même chose'.

REFERENCES

1. *To Know Ourselves*: The Report of the Commission on Canadian Studies, T. H. B. Symons, Association of Universities and Colleges of Canada, 1975.

2. Jacques Barzun. *The American University*, OUP, 1969.

3. *A History of Uppsala University*, 1477–1977, Uppsala University, 1976.

4. *Interdisciplinarity* – Problems of Teaching and Research in Universities, Centre for Educational Research and Innovation, OECD, 1972.

5. James Perkins. *The University in Transition*, Princeton, N.J., 1966.

6. *The Dissenting Academy*, edited by T. Roszak, Random House, USA, 1967 (Pelican Books, 1969).

7. House of Commons Official Report Parliamentary Debates, Friday 13 January, 1978, HMSO.

8. Mrs. Shirley Williams, Birkbeck College Foundation Oration, 30 November, 1977.

9. See H. J. Perkin, *New Universities in the United Kingdom*, OECD, 1969.

10. Dwight Ladd, *Change in Educational Policy*, McGraw Hill, 1970.

11. G. H. Bantock. *Education and Values*, p. 122, Faber & Faber, 1965.

12. Lord Hailsham. *The Dilemma of Democracy*, Collins, 1978.

13. Jacques Barzun, op. cit.

14. President Gerald Ford. Speech at Ohio State University, 30 August, 1974.

15. James Callaghan, Ruskin College, Oxford, October 1976.

SUB-TOPIC 4(A): RELEVANCE OF CURRICULUM TO SOCIETY

DISCUSSION

In the summary presentations of their papers (see above), the two speakers emphasized the differences in their approaches to higher education. Dr. *A. G. Dickson* (Community Service Volunteers, UK) stressed the significance, for the student and for the community at large, of learning through service to people in the community as an integral dimension of any curriculum. Dr. Dickson warned that society is not satisfied by the current level of the university's service to the community. He felt it important for universities to inculcate this sense of service in undergraduate students and offered as an example the opportunities for service in isolated areas of countries.

Sir Fraser Noble (Aberdeen) emphasized the importance of education for its own sake, but not in isolation from society, to aid each student to develop to the fullest an inquiring mind, an appreciation of truth and beauty, and an ability to adapt to changing conditions and circumstances. He cautioned that it is unrealistic to attempt to devise a curriculum which is relevant to the individual and to the needs of society today and which will continue to be relevant to future needs. While university education should take some account of manpower needs, it must realize that careers will change and that today's education will not respond to all of the needs of future careers.

Most participants in the discussion suggested that the approaches outlined by the speakers were not irreconcilable. Each dealt with an aspect of higher education that would be of greater or lesser significance in each university's active pursuit of its own role in its own society. Examples were cited of changes that had been introduced in university curricula to meet society's needs. Professor C. M. Lanphier (York, Canada) pointed to the development of sociological studies, of statistics, of scientific and technical studies, as being crucial in modern social development. The importance of service to the local community was illustrated with reference to India by Mr. M. R. Apparow (Andhra). With only a minority in that society literate, the work of students and staff in promoting functional literacy through teaching programmes in surrounding villages had proved valuable and a substantial experimental programme was now to be greatly expanded. Universities were involved in developing and assessing measures to serve the surrounding community through student programmes, and a National Service Scheme now involved 50,000 students in summer projects serving rural areas. In dealing with social problems the role of students and of the minority who had enjoyed the benefit of higher education was most important. Professor M. Mwanalushi (Zambia) cited the great change in curricula in the universities of third world countries following independence, with emphasis now given to the human condition within the country concerned and not to the emulation of university programmes in developed countries.

On the role of the university generally, it was suggested by Professor E. A. Elebute (Lagos) that the development of attitudes, an inquiring mind, an appreciation of values and an adaptability to change was the most important function. When universities were small and dealing with

TOPIC 4: THE PUBLIC VIEW OF THE UNIVERSITIES

an élite student body much of this was gained informally, not in the prescribed curriculum of study but rather through the role model provided by teachers who readily became well known to their students. However, with the need to provide higher education to a much larger student body, the role model of the teacher is less evident and new means are required to develop attitudes appropriate for educated man, including attitudes about the necessity for universities to serve community needs. The emphasis on development of appropriate attitudes, including an acceptance of the necessity to serve people in the community at large, was supported by Professor J. Y. Ewusie (Cape Coast), Professor Mwanalushi (Zambia) and Professor K. V. Sivayya (Andhra). In this way the community and its more remote rural areas could be properly served by the university and its graduates.

A number of the examples drawn from local situations suggested a possible difference in the emphasis placed on service to the community among universities in developing countries when compared with those in more economically developed countries. It was pointed out by Dr. V. C. Kulandaiswamy (Madurai) that in developed countries universities had been able to adapt curricula and programmes more or less in pace with the gradual evolution of society from an agricultural to a highly industrialized economy. In developing countries the transformation to a highly industrialized economy must be accomplished very rapidly. High rates of illiteracy, extensive poverty and the accompanying social conditions presented special problems for universities in developing countries.

The last main issue dealt with in discussion was that of assessing community needs and the relevance of university programmes to those needs. Who should make such assessments – governments, the universities themselves, other agencies or the general public – and how the assessments should be made were recognized as difficult questions, the answers to which held importance for the university as an autonomous institution, as the chairman (Dr. Huang) pointed out. The group chairman cautioned that if universities fail to respond to the needs of their society someone else is likely to dictate a response on their behalf. This is bound to result in an erosion of the autonomy of universities. It was suggested by Professor Lanphier (York, Canada) that it was a task for the university itself to decide what programme adaptions it could undertake to meet community needs as assessed by the university. There was no ready agreement on this view. Some discussants, including Dr. Kulandaiswamy (Madurai) and Professor Sivayya (Andhra), felt that provision should be made for greater participation of the public in any assessment of the relevance of university curricula. Universities should use effective public relations to establish two-way communication with the public, to interpret community views about the university and to provide information as one means of accounting to the public for its programmes and its services (Dr. D. W. Bain (Lincoln College)). It was suggested by Professor Ewusie (Cape Coast) that it might have been appropriate to have more spokesmen from outside the university community address the subject under discussion.

SUB-TOPIC 4(A): RELEVANCE OF CURRICULUM TO SOCIETY

It was suggested by Sir Fraser Noble (Aberdeen) that these matters — the assessment of community needs, the determination of assumptions about the nature of the society to be served by the university, and the appropriate portrayal of the university's service to society — were of continuing concern to the university, and would be the subject of ongoing debate within the university.

Sub-Topic 4(b)

THE RELEVANCE OF UNIVERSITY EDUCATION AND RESEARCH

Chairman: Dr. D. B. C. TAYLOR
Vice-Chancellor of the Victoria University of Wellington

Rapporteur: Dr. A. N. BOURNS
President and Vice-Chancellor of McMaster University

Tuesday, 22 August

Dr. C.-E. BEAULIEU (*Vice-President, Academic Affairs and Research, University of Quebec*): The evaluation of the relevance of an operation is based essentially on a comparison of the objectives pursued with the interventions and anticipated or already observed results. When discussing the relevance of university education and research we can try to carry out this evaluation in a comprehensive fashion. We must then see how the university meets the broad main objectives it has established for itself or has been given.

We can also make this evaluation in a more specific and systematic fashion by examining how the university carries out the main functions it is generally acknowledged to have: general education, professional training and research. We would then study how the university meets these various demands by training scientists, high-level professionals and intermediate-level technicians, by accepting the simultaneous presence of basic and applied research and by combining research and teaching.

However, whatever method is used to discuss the relevance of university education and research, a major problem is soon encountered: obtaining among the different groups concerned — various members of the university community: students, professors and administrators on the one hand, and concerned groups of society on the other — a consensus on the needs and the objectives pursued — objectives which are so well-defined that they can be compared with interventions and results.

Indeed, who will be the final judge as to the relevance of university education and research? The answers given by the various groups noted above would probably be different because an evaluation of the needs would not be the same for each. Administrators, students and professors seem to belong to different worlds and have basic preoccupations which often represent positions that are difficult to reconcile. It is claimed that administrators are often involved in a somewhat utilitarian development policy, since they are sensitive to demands from different bodies which influence the development of their institutions and to the methods of funding used to assist them. On the other hand it is claimed that professors worry mostly about their professional status, at the expense of their students, while students see themselves sometimes as a developing social elite, and sometimes as promoters of the establishment of a new social order; but all are worried to various extents about their chances of finding a job when they graduate or of acquiring greater competency in the job they have.

With respect to the expectations which society has for the university, these are difficult to determine in a universal and explicit fashion, since the role of the university is not thought of in the same way in different countries, and its historical role has differed from epoch to epoch. In addition it is not always easy to find qualified groups or individuals willing to express and make known society's views of the university.

Because of these divergencies it is difficult to assign the objectives to be attained in any order of priority. In addition the extent to which these objectives have been attained, even if they are well known, also poses a problem for the evaluation of the relevance of university education and research, since such an evaluation is almost always based in large part on a subjective appraisal.

Faced with this state of affairs, and also considering the fact that the university has a spatial and temporal existence, the following discussion will deal first of all with the situation of the university in the province of Quebec, attempting to determine certain special features with respect to the relevance of its interventions in the society it serves most immediately, particularly in terms of accessibility. A second part will consider university education.

The Objective of Accessibility

During the last twenty years the province of Quebec has adopted a policy on a wider accessibility to university education, following in this respect policies advocated by most industrialized countries. This policy has been accepted implicitly or explicitly by Quebec universities and we may affirm that the University of Quebec itself, and probably the other universities as well, have made it a priority objective. In addition the province of Quebec has some catching up to do in this area, particularly with respect to its French-speaking population.

In fact, in 1961, full-time attendance at university for the 20–24-year-old age group was only 3% for francophones and 11% for the non-French-speaking population. One of the objectives of reform in the field of education at the beginning of the sixties was, on the one hand, to eliminate the relative under-education of the province of Quebec with respect to the rest of Canada and, on the other hand, to reduce the disparities between the various social and linguistic groups in the province of Quebec. After more than 15 years of efforts we can see how Quebec universities carried out this mission.

From 1966 to 1976 university enrolment in Quebec doubled for full-time students and quadrupled for part-time students. During this period the portion of enrolment belonging to French-language universities went from 53% to 67% for full-time students and from 37% to 71% for part-time students. Three times as many university degrees were granted in the province of Quebec during the last decade as during the previous decade.

Nevertheless, in spite of a rapid growth in enrolment in French-language universities, there is still a marked difference between linguistic groups. In the fall of 1976 it was estimated that 8% of the 20–24-year-old age group in Quebec attended university, either full-time or part-time. The attendance rate for francophones was 7%, for anglophones 15%. The gap of 8% which existed at the beginning of the sixties remained the same; considerably more effort will be necessary to close this gap.

In addition university attendance for the population group 15 years of age and above remains lower in Quebec than in Ontario; the rate in Quebec is also below the Canadian average and considerably below the American average. In fact in December, 1977, this rate reached 6% in Quebec, as compared to a Canadian average of 7·6% and an Ontario average of 8·8%. These figures show that Quebec universities have responded to the policy of making university education accessible in order to correct, to a considerable extent, an unacceptable situation with respect to the rate of university education for the population. These figures clearly show the relevance of action undertaken by Quebec universities in terms of the objective of accessibility.

It should be noted, with respect to this last element, that the policy of university accessibility has not only enabled more students to attend but it has also allowed new types of students to come into the university system, for the greater part adults already on the labour market. What we have here is a phenomenon of quantitative and qualitative change. As an example there is the University of Quebec, which has ensured the geographical decentralization of higher education.

On the other hand a policy of making the universities accessible leads to what some call mass education. This notion is based on the rather widespread belief that the individual and society gain certain economic, cultural and social benefits from a university education. This belief has now been questioned by certain groups, at a time when more people are graduating from university and employment conditions have deteriorated generally. Our society is faced with a problem heretofore unexpected: defining an 'optimal' level of university education which meets specific social and economic objectives. Since it is first of all through its teaching that the university contributes most directly to the cultural, social and economic development of society, we must first evaluate the relevance of university education in terms of the objectives of university education in order to answer these doubts.

We will now try to suggest a certain number of elements which relate to this question, elements which are defined largely within the framework of the traditional model of the university as an institution for training highly-qualified manpower. The fact that we are raising no questions with respect to the relevance of university research does not mean that we have given this a secondary place. Rather, a realistic choice must be made in considering a subject as complex as the relevance of the university with a minimum of rigour. We have chosen the education function especially because it is in this function that we find the main source of a considerable number of problems relating to changes in the conception of the traditional university.

General Objectives of University Education

Although there is no unanimity with respect to the combination or order of priority for the objectives of university education, at least two main classes or types of education can be identified. They are commonly acknowledged by everyone and are the natural extension of any system of education: these are the objectives related to the general education of man as an individual, and the objectives related to specialized training to meet manpower needs. Through the first group of objectives university education aims at promoting the individual's educational and intellectual development, shown by an ability to synthesize, think critically, judge, be objective, have an independent mind and what some call an aptitude for learning on one's own. It is in terms of this fundamental objective that the effects of the university on an individual are most lasting; they are also cumulative for the entire life of the student. This general education must also attend to the individual's cultural development, that is, encourage his sense of the aesthetic, his perception of man and the world, his understanding of historical evolution and his awareness of his own cultural identity. Another objective of an individual's general education, less often noted but more or less accepted depending on one's view of the role of the university, and which occupies an ever-increasing place in American literature on the subject, refers to the development of a person as a 'social being', someone with civic and moral qualities, someone with a sense of responsibility towards the community.

To this first group of educational objectives—the intellectual, cultural and moral development of individuals—must be added the objective of training highly-qualified manpower. The university must also transmit to the individual a set of technical knowledge and the mastery of a discipline enabling him to make a useful contribution (for himself and for society) to his profession. While these objectives are fundamentally complementary and not incompatible, there is always a certain tension between general education and specialized training. There is unanimity with respect to the necessity of ensuring both. However there is no universal and permanent balance between the two. This balance changes in accordance with historical circumstances, sociological characteristics of the various clienteles, contemporary institutional conditions, environmental pressures and individual experience. For example, studies carried out in the United States show that students entering university pursue personal objectives which are closely tied to career possibilities. Consequently it is possible that the desired education will be more technical and specialized. These same students, when they complete their studies, already perceive the importance of a good general education. After several years on the job market they tend to give this general education prime importance, not only because such an education is beneficial to their present development, but also because they see that it affects their professional performance. We therefore note that university students' perception of the preferred type of education changes with time, and that it is modified as these students acquire professional experience outside the university.

Many people question the benefits of a university education, general or specialized. We cannot help observing that this critique is made in a particular socio-economic context. The seventies have hardly shown themselves to be good times, economically speaking: severe unemployment, high cost of higher education, limited financial resources, strong inter-sectorial competition for these resources, crisis in the growth of the university—a host of elements capable of instilling doubt about the effects of a university education.

University Degrees and the Job Market

In a recent report entitled *University Degrees: Passports to Nowhere,* the International Labour Organisation estimated that underemployment, job dissatisfaction and often unemployment awaited young people upon graduation from university. It was reported that, in Canada, not less than 25% of spring '76 university graduates were still unemployed three months after graduation. A number of industrial countries were experiencing similar situations, as well as certain third-world countries. The ILO report concluded that in both developed and developing countries the surplus of graduates was 'out of proportion to the qualitative and quantitative needs of the national economies'. Consequently it would be the task of the universities to take the general employment situation into account and rationally guide the students in their choice of a field of study so that they might, if necessary, better adapt themselves to a fluctuating economic situation—if the recommendations of the report are followed. This is a considerable challenge to the university and implicitly gives to the university the main responsibility for the difficult employment situation for university graduates even if a variety of causes may be invoked to explain this situation, such as demographic evolution since the second world war, changes in the world economy and the policy of democratizing education.

When only the objective of preparing the student for a job is considered, the role of the university is seen as one of producing manpower. Within the framework of such a model of supply and demand (which is somewhat narrow) it will be said of the university that it produces too many or too few graduates, that it is adequate or inadequate with respect to the structure of the subjects studied, that the content of the educational programmes and the content of the requirements for the corresponding professions are more or less adapted.

Certain exaggerated ideas held by the general public about unemployment of university graduates must be dissipated at once. That there are more 'educated unemployed' than before is the case largely because of the increase in the number of graduates and the general increase in unemployment for the labour force. But the other side of the coin shows that university graduates are experiencing a rate of unemployment two to three times below the average for the labour force, whether it is in the US, Canada or Quebec. There is an inverse relation between workers' level of schooling and the rate of unemployment. We can cite some revealing figures from Statistics Canada's monthly survey of the labour force. In 1977 8·3% of the Canadian labour force was unemployed. But the average for university graduates was 3%. The rate of unemployment in Quebec was one of the highest in Canada: 11·2% in 1977. University graduates had an unemployment rate of 3·6%. Unemployment increased in Quebec from 1976 to 1977, going from 8·7% to 11·2%. But for university graduates it increased very little, going from 3·3% to 3·6%. Inter-regional comparisons show that unemployment does not first affect university graduates; in fact differences in the unemployment rates between the various regions of Canada were quite considerable for the entire labour force (for example: 11·2% in Quebec and 6·8% in Ontario), but quite small for university graduates (3·6% in Quebec and 3% in Ontario). Another interesting observation: there is a much higher rate of activity among university graduates (87% in Quebec) than in the entire population (59% in Quebec). There is a positive relation between the level of education attained and the rate of activity and this relation is even stronger in regions affected by unemployment.

Nonetheless it is clear that unemployment affects younger graduates more: 7·3% of those under 25 years of age were unemployed in Canada in 1977. But this situation is more attributable to their age. At a time of poor economic performance inexperienced workers are always more affected. In addition 14·9% of the labour force under 25 was unemployed: this is twice as high as for university graduates of the age group.

If it becomes more and more evident that the production of university degrees exceeds the immediate needs of the market in many professions, can we claim that this is more than a temporary phenomenon and that the situation will not right itself when better times come? Also, if the quantity corresponds poorly to the situation, can we think that the quality of university degrees is up to expectations? Is it not largely a question of quality rather than quantity, or of maintaining quality in education in the face of an increase in the number of students? The mass university has developed from the traditional model by adding and juxtaposing activities rather than by integration and conversion. McLuhan maintains that, faced with an explosion of numbers, the university responded by the implosion of its structures, that is, it quantitatively enlarged its older framework without much worry about adapting itself to new needs. Consequently there is no reason to be surprised that such a development brought about difficulties which went so far as to call into question higher education and the relevance of university intervention, not to mention the dissatisfaction expressed by the main interested party—the students.

In effect, many university professors are becoming more aware of the fact that students want to participate in useful work. This aspiration is not necessarily an answer to the overproduction mentioned earlier. Nevertheless it expresses a growing feeling among students that their education does not adequately prepare them to meet the problems encountered in the real world, either on the job they have or with respect to the social problems they see. On the other hand the acquisition of specialized knowledge at university does not correspond sufficiently to industry's expectations. It is estimated that in the United States industry spends approximately twice as much money as universities to train the managers and the professionals it needs. Consequently American universities have definitively lost a part of their monopoly in specialized training.

Adaptation of the University

Such observations, both in terms of quantity and quality, with respect to the production of university degrees and the recycling and additional training of adult students, invite the university continually to adapt itself if it wants to maintain the relevance of its interventions with respect to the present and future problems of society. Moreover this adaptation must be continuous, because we live in a world of rapid change in which the fallout from technological and economic development forces us continuously to question our way of life. Hence we should not be surprised that the university has been called into question. However this institution is doubtlessly well placed to adjust its operation to the new constraints it encounters. Indeed it would be something of a paradox if the university, which is itself a major factor of social change through its contribution to the development of science and technology, with their growing influence on society, were unable to adapt to the change which it has more or less provoked and encouraged, especially by welcoming new clienteles; it would be paradoxical were this university unable to find the means continually to adjust its role and mission to new situations which it has itself wanted to create.

The university has not been content with the mission of reproducing the present society; it has also wanted to take part in creating a new society. We could even examine the relevance of university education on the basis of its contribution to the realization of a new social order, as opposed to a reproduction of the existing order.

In this regard we should note that it would be difficult to organize and structure university interventions in terms of reproducing the existing society, since the knowledge we have of this society is more and more complex and its features are in constant evolution. Thus during the last fifteen years we have learned that we live in an extremely fragile, closely interconnected ecosystem which can be destroyed if we are not careful. Economically the interrelation between the economies of different countries are tighter and tighter. Technologically-advanced countries are much more diversified socially than two decades ago. They present a greater number of sub-cultures, interest groups and identifiable political forces. Regional differences are accentuated instead of disappearing. The appearance of this great diversity shows that society is detaching itself from its industrial foundation; in other words, 'that it is in the process of passing from the monoculture represented by industrialism to the polyculture which will be superindustrialism', if Toffler is to be believed. We are living in a world of change, voluntary or imposed by various external pressures beyond our control. These pressures are especially seen in the educational system: in student demands to better integrate university activities with social problems, in professors' attempts to redefine the way the university is run and how power is distributed, and in the more general questioning of the relevance of education.

The university is deeply affected by all these pressures for change. However, does this require that the university's traditional orientation and structure be changed? Is it not rather a question for the university of insisting on its mission of creating a new society rather than reproducing the existing society, which, in any event, will not be tomorrow's society? With this in mind it is not strictly necessary to call into question all the general objectives of university education, but rather to specify the importance given to both objectives, general education and training, and give general education more encouragement by adapting it to the new conditions.

Higher education must continue, as suggested in the ILO report earlier, to produce a limited number of high-level professionals and intermediate-level technicians to meet the predictable needs of the job market. It must also be able to produce more and more graduates with a certain intellectual independence and a creative spirit sufficiently developed to make it possible to take an active part in building a new social order. Higher education must also be able to integrate these characteristics into the framework of its job improvement and cultural development activities, which are becoming more and more important in the context of the new philosophy of continuing education. Among the specific objectives of university education it would be a good idea to attach more importance to those emphasizing the development of an individual's independence of mind and creativity. In fact we may ask whether the critical analysis which is a specific objective of university education is not in the process of causing some students to develop a negative attitude which often presents itself in violent demonstrations at certain universities. Certainly critical reflection is an important stage in the creative process, but we must continue beyond it. The university must encourage the development of an innovative and creative mind, which it makes one of its specific priority objectives. It would then be possible to see more graduates capable of contributing, through their work, to the realization of a new society. In this way the risks of producing unemployed graduates would be reduced.

Conclusion

Therefore, the university must give an increasing importance to general education and personal development programmes, programmes centred on independence of thought, an ability to synthesize, and fostering creativity. In certain areas employers show more and more interest in hiring graduates who have a good general education and whom they retrain during their careers, preferring this to hiring specialized technicians whose knowledge rapidly becomes outdated and who can become professionals only with difficulty. In addition general education brings the student into contact with certain fundamental values at a time when society no longer makes it easy for him to do so. This general education will also provide the student with good possibilities of improving the quality of life during his career.

General education must continue to be the object of cultural programmes at the university; it must also be an integral part of the various professional programmes. All higher education must succeed in reconciling its production function with its humanist function, even if it is not easy to find a lasting balance for this combination, which is a function of historical circumstances, sociological characteristics and institutional conditions. This is the challenge which the universities must meet so that their education and research will continue to be relevant.

[Cottrell]   TOPIC 4: THE PUBLIC VIEW OF THE UNIVERSITIES

Sir ALAN COTTRELL (*Vice-Chancellor of the University of Cambridge and Master of Jesus College*):

Calls for Relevance

There is an old story that Professor Chrystal, the mathematician, was asked by his university to teach a course of applied mathematics. At his first lecture he said: 'you cannot apply mathematics until you have some mathematics to apply', and on this basis he then taught pure mathematics for the rest of the course. That seems to me to have been a robust attitude to a problem which, in various forms, faces all academics. We should remember it when challenged by fashionable and occasional threatening talk about the relevance of university education and research. In saying this—and indeed throughout my talk—I am of course referring essentially to the position in Britain, for I cannot claim to have enough experience of universities in other countries to be able to generalize my remarks to them.

Of course universities have long endured criticisms, from some industrialists, that their teaching is not relevant to the needs of the practical world outside. The cry goes up, in the jargon of the critic's particular industry, 'why don't you teach your students how to make widgets' or 'train them to be good knurdlers'. I am glad to say, however, that in all universities which have successfully upheld their hard-won liberal academic traditions the professors have stoutly resisted such blandishments and have, instead, adhered to the view that all-round ability and versatility rather than a technician's skill is what they want to develop in their students.

Of course many employers understand the nature of university education and research as well as any academic and take a wise and far-sighted view. For example, I recall a train journey some years ago when I happened by chance to share a carriage with some of the senior people in Marks and Spencer, who were discussing their recruiting policy for future management. 'Our preference is for Oxford classicists', they said. 'That way we can be sure of getting people with first-class minds, able to think clearly about almost anything and to express themselves well. That's all we ask. We have years afterwards in which to teach them our own business, which we can do much better than anyone else.' It seemed to me at the time that that was a wise, intelligent policy and one which was in complete harmony with the great traditional idea of the university, expressed years ago by Newman as 'the high protecting power of all knowledge and science, of fact and principle, of enquiry and discovery, of experiment and speculation; it maps out the territory of the intellect and sees that... there is neither encroachment nor surrender on any side.'

But the cry for relevance has been taken up in recent years by other sections of the community. Regrettably one finds that some government ministers have echoed it; so much so that the Rector of Imperial College, London University, felt obliged to say about one of them, two years ago, that:

'it seems that he believes that important economies would result if the number of places in each subject were geared to national requirements for trained manpower, and if there were some controlling mechanism in the schools to ensure that the university places so calculated were filled according to plan. And so they would: except that manpower planning is a notoriously inexact science; and except that it is far more important to train people so that they can exercise their intellectual powers to the full over the whole of their lifetime than that they should instantly slot into a pre-ordained vacancy at the age of twenty-one; and except also that the country as a whole is more likely to benefit by encouraging the talents of its youth than it is by planning what talents it requires in order to meet some utopian ideal which will already have been abandoned long before it is attained.'

The other and more radical extension of the call for relevance came a few years ago from certain 'socially committed' students and academics. It is not altogether clear what they meant by 'relevance' for, unlike the industrialists and politicians, they did not call for education to be directed along more utilitarian channels, or to train students more specifically for immediate employment. They seemed to want the social significance of all knowledge to be taught; that is, for every academic subject to be converted into an aspect of social science. A few even seemed to confuse education with political indoctrination.

Looking back today, it seems that this movement was, in Britain at least, a short-lived product of the academically easy times of the early 1960s. Already by 1971 Mrs. Shirley Williams was telling scientists in Britain that 'the party is over'; but her prophetic words had a wider truth than even she may have suspected, for the pervasive and persistent economic recession which set in after 1973 has indeed confirmed that, not only for pure scientists but for universities and academics generally, 'the party is over'. In today's cold climate of financial stringency and high unemployment students have mostly become less interested in the political colour of their university record than in its job-winning potentialities.

University Education

Apart from lack of money, which in a direct, down-to-earth, way is *the* university problem of today, I think that two developments which have set the universities their most deep-seated problems are the growth in student numbers and the growth in university research.

In the 1960s most countries greatly expanded their numbers of university places. Britain, on the basis of the Robbins report which argued that everyone with ability should have the right to university education as a social benefit, opened 20 new universities (some of which were created from previously formed colleges of advanced technology) and more than doubled its student numbers. In other parts of the world even greater expansions occurred. The number of Commonwealth universities approximately trebled from 1959 to 1975; and in some European countries the number of students has multiplied fivefold, which has faced some of their universities with a near-impossible task. From the standpoint of 'relevance' it is very interesting to see what the President of the Royal Society of London, Lord Todd, said about the British expansion, in his Anniversary Address last November:

'It is too easily forgotten that between the 1940s and the Robbins Report in 1963, government, industry and, indeed, the country at large was crying out for more and more trained scientists and engineers. In the chorus of complaints about their irrelevance to the country's economic needs it is too often overlooked that the universities have discharged their responsibility superbly in this respect. In less than a quarter of a century the numbers graduating in science and technology from British universities have multiplied by three... And although many of these young men and women have been trained in institutions where people worry about such things as black holes or bacterial genetics... a very large proportion of them has found its way into the productive sectors of the economy. Indeed, for the first time in our industrial history, industry has enough technically trained people to satisfy its needs... Thise who claim that the universities have become 'irrelevant' forget that the universities have accomplished economically and without fuss the enormous task of expansion that they were set by the nation less than fifteen years ago.'

The universities have indeed accomplished that great expansion; and they have done it essentially by multiplying the numbers of places and centres available for their traditional types of courses.

And this is where the first of the problems comes in. For the traditional types of courses were designed primarily for dedicated and gifted scholars. For these rare individuals the great honours schools were and still are ideally suited. In the days when less than one per cent of the population had the opportunity to go to university, this was quite reasonable. For the child of a country vicarage, brought up with a love of books and serious studies, or the brilliant son of a coal miner, coming out the Welsh valleys with an entrance scholarship, the great honours schools were paradise. But such true scholars are as rare today as always. An honours class can count itself fortunate if it contains more than one or two of them at a time. But whereas before the expansion in university education these and perhaps half a dozen others made up a total such class, today these same few receive the same kind of teaching, still designed for them, but they receive it in classes of 100 or more others. The problem then is — what about the other 90%? Is the traditional honours school relevant for them? They are not born scholars, dedicated to a lifetime of learning, but simply fairly bright children who have gone to university either because it is fashionable to do so, or is thought to open the way to better jobs, or is merely a means of avoiding for a few more years the decisions they will eventually have to make about what they want to do with their lives. For these children, who make up the majority of the students in the universities today, the traditional honours course seems less like a guided walk through an enchanted garden of intellectual delights than a gruelling cross-country chase across a rugged and remote landscape, whose main value lies in its enabling them to say of it, afterwards, 'well, I had the guts to stick it out and here is my degree to say so'.

Unfortunately the discussion of this important and genuine problem has been sidetracked by the introduction of a political note centred on the word 'élitist', used accusingly as a term of abuse, and on the 'demand' (also a vogue word from certain quarters) that the universities should drop their academic standards, abandon examinations, and expound pop culture to all who happen to drop in. All I need say about this is that a nation which chooses to emulate the dinosaur, by neglecting its best brains, runs the risk of going with the dinosaur, all the way to extinction.

The problem of the honours schools in an age of mass education has another aspect. Honours schools are specialised. In American jargon they are 'discipline-oriented'. Depth, rather than breadth, is the quality prized by academics; and most university students are led to concentrate on single subjects. Departments of history prepare courses suitable for intending professional historians, those of botany similarly prepare the ground for professional botanists, and so on. In fact, in an unusual but justifiable use of the term, such honours courses are *vocational*, being designed to train people to be professional scholars and researchers. The problem is that most students going through such courses are not temperamentally inclined to become professional scholars; nor does society particularly want them as such. In the management of society's affairs, whether in government or business, the desired quality is the general all-round ability to cope with and somehow solve a great miscellany of problems. The professionalisms that may be needed for this are those not of the scholar but of, say, the farmer, accountant or personnel officer, which can only be learnt by practical experience.

Of course it is a long tradition in universities to cater for some well-established non-academic professions by schemes in which the student learns the scholarly side of his intended career in the university and the professional side outside, as an assistant in a working organisation. The great academic schools of medicine, law and engineering are based on this system; and for these professional subjects the relevance of university education is plain. The problem lies not here, but in those other faculties such as the arts, pure sciences and social sciences, which are not related to particular professions. Of course even in these faculties there are equivalent arrangements to enable students, through some associated professional training, to become schoolteachers; and the relevance of this part of university education is also clear.

But the facts remain that the numbers of students now entering many universities are too large to be absorbed by the professions; and that the traditional honours school, with its emphasis on deep, pure scholarship, is not really suitable for most such students. There is much to be said here in favour of the American system in which the first degree courses are of a broad and fairly elementary kind. The majority of students leave university at this point and go off into the professions, into business, into various jobs in the outside world; and only a small fraction, the true scholars, stay on to take master's and higher degrees in the postgraduate schools.

Some years ago Brian Pippard at Cambridge suggested a most interesting scheme of this kind, as an alternative to the traditional British honours school. The proposal was that all students, in for example a faculty of science, should spend their first two years taking a degree of a generalist rather than a professional kind. Most would then go out into the world, into various professions, business, public service, etc., as graduate apprentices. The minority of students who aimed to become professional scholars would then stay on to take a further two years of more intensive and specialised education leading to an advanced degree, followed by two years of research for the PhD.

This was a well thought-out scheme and developed in considerable detail. Whether two years is sufficient for a first degree is of course debatable and one might wish to explore alternatives, *e.g.* a three-year first degree course of a generalist kind, followed by a one-year course of a more specialised kind for the scholars, leading to a second degree, before these enter upon research. However it has not so far been possible to give such schemes a real trial. If and when the present financial straight-jacket in which universities now find themselves can be eased a little, I hope that some of them could be persuaded to use their unaccustomed freedom to try out a few such schemes. But I am not too hopeful of this, because the present trend is towards bringing all universities into a uniform pattern, suitable for collective national administration.

University Research

Over the past thirty years the most rapidly growing and costly – per capita – sector of higher education in Britain has been the postgraduate one, and the emphasis here has been on research work for higher degrees. Britain may be in rather a special position, here, in that most of its pure research is done in the universities, by academic staffs and their research students, rather than in separate research institutes. Thus the cost of postgraduate study is now about one-quarter of total British university costs. Most of the expansion has been in the natural sciences, although there are also large research schools today in history, social sciences and other subjects. The effort in scientific research is due partly to deliberate stimulus by governments, who have provided most of the money, and partly to the ambitions and drive of academic scientists. One can understand the scientists' motives, but what are those of governments? The answer goes back to the second world war and the tremendous impression that was made then, upon politicians and the public at large, of the power of science and technology to solve national problems.

Government policy for science in the 1950s and 1960s was the simple one of casting bread upon the waters. Large funds were provided for university research and a system devised, through semi-independent bodies such as the research councils and the University Grants Committee in Britain, for the distribution of these funds on purely academic criteria. Applications for research grants have been decided by the celebrated method of 'judgement by peers' and the only requirement has been that the proposed research should have 'timeliness and promise'. It has all been very civilised and in the best traditions of the liberal idea of a university. In terms of new fundamental knowledge and understanding gained, it has also been brilliantly successful. Mankind's view of the world has been extraordinarily enriched by modern discoveries of the structure of the universe, of the nature of matter, of the molecular basis of life, of the geological processes leading to the continental structure of the earth, of the early history of mankind, of the psychophysical basis of language structures, and of many other things in all branches of knowledge.

But disillusionment has set in amongst the politicians. Perhaps they expected too much. High scholarship brought deep knowledge, but not the wisdom for solving the great social problems of the day. Scientific research has won its Nobel Prizes but not large export orders. Instead there has been the 'anomaly' that Britain, one of the greatest spending countries on scientific research and technological development in relation to its gross national product, has remained stuck with one of the least impressive economies of the past quarter-century amongst the advanced industrial countries.

Dissatisfaction with low growth in the midst of high science has been the main reason for the criticisms by politicians and industrialists, in Britain at least, that university researches are 'irrelevant'. Although it can be proved, almost as a formal theorem in economics, that university research could never be a major contributor to national economic growth—just as a new spark plug could never by itself turn an old crock into a modern car—these criticisms persist and perpetuate the common view of universities as ivory towers addicted to useless studies.

I am glad to say however that governments by and large have not been persuaded by such criticisms. For example, clear, practical, evidence that it understood and agreed with educational and cultural purposes of university research was given a few years ago by the British government in its White Paper *Framework for Government Research and Development* (Cmnd.5046 : 1972). This paper laid down the general policy and administrative machinery for operating the so-called 'customer-contractor principle' which was to give various government ministries, such as the departments of health, agriculture, environment and industry, more control over the spending of governmental research funds in those particular applied sciences relevant to the executive functions of those departments.

The particular aspect of this policy which is of interest here was the channelling through these other ministries, instead of the Department of Education and Science, of certain portions of governmental funds paid to the research councils as a science budget. What was striking and significant about this (although it was largely overlooked in the general uproar amongst the scientific community about the imposition of the customer-contractor principle) was the actual distribution of the rechannelling. This was plainly designed to leave the universities as free as possible to pursue pure research as part of their advanced educational programmes. The Agricultural Research Council—which was heavily engaged in applied research of the kind that should be relevant to the agricultural ministries, which did little of its work in universities and had few educational responsibilities—was subjected to the largest proportion of rechannelling of funds. The Natural Environment Research Council and the Medical Research Council, with larger educational responsibilites, had smaller proportions rechannelled. But in the case of the Science Research Council, the largest of all, which is concerned primarily with pure science and almost entirely with research as part of higher education, *no funds* at all were rechannelled. That the government clearly understood what it was doing here is shown by the fact that it described the purpose of such research as 'to develop the sciences as such, to maintain a fundamental capacity for research, and to support higher education'.

The criticisms by politicians and others of university research led to an interesting study three years ago. Professor Linnett, then Vice-Chancellor, investigated 'Useful Research in Cambridge University', to quote the title of his paper. Engineering and medicine were omitted from the survey, because their usefulness was self-evident, but the report listed a number of researches being done in the natural and social sciences, history, languages, and in various other subjects, that were judged to be immediately and evidently productive in economic and social terms. It would be easy to quote the report's examples from the natural sciences, but the evidence from the arts departments is interesting—*e.g.* historians helping government archivists to digest massive recent public records, researchers in the English faculty dealing with problems of public communication by radio and televison, orientalists producing new dictionaries and computerising the Chinese language, and geographers studying underdevelopment and agricultural capacity in tropical countries. As Professor Linnett said, other universities would undoubtedly have no difficulty in producing similarly impressive lists of their useful researches in all subjects: and also that for useful basic research the universities, in his words, 'are the best and indeed, at the present time, the only places where significant amounts of research work of this kind can be done'.

Most university research is done for two purposes: first, to train graduate students in the methods of research and to enable academics to teach convincingly at the frontiers of knowledge; and second, to increase knowledge and understanding as an end in itself. Any additional benefits beyond these that the research may bring to society generally, are generally regarded as by-products, albeit extremely important ones in some cases. This raises several points. First, are the universities producing too many PhDs, or too many in certain subjects? I do not know the position in other countries, but in Britain I think that this is so, in relation to the number of research jobs available in the country. As a result many of the more bright graduates have been forced, after taking PhDs, to abandon their hopes of making careers for themselves in pure research, which has produced in some of them much disappointment and frustration at the start of their careers. For this reason I would much prefer any cut-backs in governmental postgraduate awards, if they have to be made, to take the form of a reduced number of grants, rather than a reduced payment per grant. Paying more to fewer may look like élitism but it is more humane than encouraging lots of the country's finest young people to enter a road that eventually leads nowhere for them.

Whereas universities can perhaps be fairly criticised for irrelevantly overexpanding their research schools, I am less sure that the more commonly heard criticism—that their chosen research topics are irrelevant to the needs of society—is altogether valid. Quite apart from the fact that, as Professor Linnett showed, much more university work is useful than is generally believed to be the case, there is the much deeper problem of what 'relevancy' is, in this connection. All too often being 'relevant' means engaging in the immediate public problems of the day. While there are occasions when this must sometimes be the right policy for a university, in times of great national upheaval—in wartime, for example, or in a developing country struggling for economic lift-off—and in fact universities generally do apply themselves wholeheartedly to the problems of the day in such circumstances; nevertheless under less turbulent conditions a university fulfils its responsibility to the community best, in respect of research, by tackling the more long-range issues. Having said this it must be admitted that universities often invite public criticisms of their research work because they generally do little to explain, publicly, what they are doing in simple and interesting terms. Universities could do much more to inform the public about their work.

A country groping its way forward into the uncharted future is like a caravan train of pioneers moving across an unknown land.

Not only does it need steersmen to keep it on its present course; it also needs outriders to go on ahead and discover its possible next direction. The highest social responsibility of its universities is both to train the steersmen and to explore the trackless ground ahead. The first is relevant education; the second is relevant research.

Mr. J. K. KOINANGE (*Principal of Kenyatta University College*):

The Nature of the Problem

Weinberg[1] has suggested that a major problem in assessing the contribution of a university can be traced to the fundamental difference between the universities' traditional view of what constitutes excellence and the societies' view of what constitutes excellence. To him universities are discipline-oriented, and their idea of excellence is whatever deepens understanding or insight into the problems generated or resolved within the various disciplines. In contrast to this view, society attributes excellence to whatever works. With this background, I would like to state the problem as it relates to African countries and, by extension and implication, to other 'third world' or developing countries.

In various African countries governments are under increasing pressure to find solutions to problems of hunger, disease, malnutrition, ignorance and other basic human needs especially in rural areas. Responses to these problems must include human resource development as a major component. The question becomes: to what extent have African universities responded to these needs? What is the role of African universities in development? How can they help to meet the societal needs of the communities within which they operate? Are African universities developing an identity of their own and are they capable of enriching the world-wide academic community?[2]

When we say that we should not only be concerned with quantity but with the quality of education, what do we mean by education and by quality? Does it mean more effective and economical ways of producing university graduates or does it also mean the production of mentally healthy, socially adjusted, progressive and productive individuals? How do we respond to some of these fundamental questions?

As Nevitt[3] has indicated, 'there is a connection between the functions of institutions of higher education and the stage of social development in the country that starts them. There are different conceptions at different times in different places'. This fact was acknowledged by representatives of African universities at a seminar organized by the Association of African Universities, held in Accra, Ghana, in 1973. To the participants the fundamental question seemed to be one of relevance.

'A truly African University must be one which, while acknowledging the need to transform Africa into the twentieth century, must yet realize that it can best achieve this result by completely identifying itself with the realities of a predominantly rural setting, and the aspirations of unsophisticated but highly expectant people. It follows that the emergent African University must henceforth be much more than an institution for teaching, research and dissemination of higher learning. It must be accountable to, and serve the vast majority of, the people who live in rural areas; it must be committed to active participation in social transformation, economic modernization, and the training and upgrading of the total human resources of the nation, not just of a small élite. The University must also concern itself with the inter-African and international problems.'[4]

In the light of these fundamental requirements the participants in the seminar suggested that the truly African university in the 1970s must perform, among others, the following functions:

(i) pursuit, promotion and dissemination of knowledge, especially the type of knowledge which is immediately useful to the generality of the people and therefore locally oriented and motivated;

(ii) research, both fundamental and applied, especially research into local problems that will contribute to the amelioration, in particular, of the life of the ordinary man and the rural poor;

(iii) provision of intellectual leadership;

(iv) manpower development, provision of secondary and primary schoolteachers, agricultural extension workers, ... ;

(v) promotion of social and economical modernization; and

(vi) promotion of intra-continental and international understanding.

I would now like to examine and illustrate how in Africa the universities are responding to the public's expectations in their education and research activities and cite my College as an example in this respect.

Kenyatta University College is perhaps one of the newest and smallest institutions of higher education in Africa, but it is at the

SUB-TOPIC 4(B): RELEVANCE OF UNIVERSITY EDUCATION   [*Koinange*]

same time one of the largest teacher education institutions on the continent, with a faculty nearing the 200 mark and an undergraduate and postgraduate student enrolment of close to 1,500. As a constituent college of the University of Nairobi its primary function is to provide graduate teachers for the 1,500-odd secondary schools in the country. Its role, however, extends far beyond the preparation of teachers and the traditional confines of degree-granting institutions. By virtue of the fact that we have our own governing council and academic board, and are wholly financed by government, we are at liberty to diversify our activities and develop our own programmes to meet the changing needs of our country. As a result the College has already made its presence felt in many areas of training and development in the country.

Without restricting my comments to the activities of Kenyatta University College I shall draw heavily upon its experience in attempting to show how an institution of higher learning in a developing country can and should participate in national and international development by:

(*a*) responding to the manpower needs of the country;

(*b*) relating its courses to prevailing conditions and situations;

(*c*) conducting research and initiating services which foster cultural identity, economic development and social well-being; and

(*d*) promoting international understanding and co-operation among nations.

Responding to Manpower Needs

Kenya's rapidly expanding secondary school system is making an enormous demand on trained manpower in the form of highly qualified and versatile educators. Several efforts have been made to fill this demand. A two-year post-'O'-level course leading to an S1 teachers certificate has now been phased out, except for the preparation of science teachers, 2,570 of which have been fed into the schools system through this channel. A two-year post-'A'-level diploma in education course, which has equally been discontinued, produced 458 teachers at a slightly higher level between 1975 and 1978. Two groups of BA or BSc graduates taking education as an option graduated in 1973 and 1974, and a few hundred arts and science graduates with a postgraduate diploma in education are now in the field, but this course is now in abeyance. The bulk of candidates wishing to become secondary school teachers have, since 1972, enrolled in a three-year post-'A'-level degree course; 1,277 such teachers are in service and the projected output of BEd teachers in coming years is 400 to 500 per annum.

TOPIC 4: THE PUBLIC VIEW OF THE UNIVERSITIES

To a country like Kenya, which in the past has relied almost entirely on expatriates to man its teaching force at secondary school level, this is an impressive achievement indeed. Equally important is the concern of the College continually to relate its programmes to the local situation which is characterised by rapid and constant social and economic changes.

Relating Courses to Prevailing Conditions and Situations

The present teacher education programme at Kenyatta University College consists of a three-year post-'A'-level course of study leading to a bachelor's degree in education. Generally speaking students major in two of the following teaching subjects: business education (accounting and/or secretarial), fine art, geography, history, languages and linguistics (Swahili, English, French), literature, music, philosophy and religious studies, mathematics, botany, zoology, physics, chemistry, home economics and physical education.

With a view to better preparing teachers for the role they are expected to play in schools, in their respective communities and in the nation, the University set up a committee consisting of the Principal of Kenyatta University College as chairman, the registrars and deans of faculties of arts, science and education at the University of Nairobi and Kenyatta University College, and heads of subject departments, a year ago to assess the adequacy of the present programme in attaining these objectives and to make recommendations thereupon to the University as well as to government. The University and the committee viewed its mission as an investigation into the expectation of the nation vis-à-vis education and the teachers who are largely responsible for bringing this education about. In order to do so it heard the views of the Ministry of Education and Teachers Service Commission (the body that employs teachers in the country), executives of the Headmasters' Association, provincial commissioners and those charged with education administration at provincial level. The committee interviewed 673 teachers currently teaching in a large cross-section of secondary schools throughout the country.

As a result of this massive exercise it is anticipated that the teacher education programme at the College will be modified to relate more adequately to the demands made upon teachers in schools, to equip them with knowledge and skills required to operate more effectively in society and, of even greater importance, to develop in them those professional and civic attitudes and values which give quality to education and life.

SUB-TOPIC 4(B): RELEVANCE OF UNIVERSITY EDUCATION [*Koinange*]

Research at Kenyatta University College

Research is another very important function of a university. Research at Kenyatta University College is focused on revitilization and promotion of traditional cultural values, economic development and social well-being. This can be amply illustrated by research currently in progress at the University.

The Humanities. At the University of Nairobi and Kenyatta University College the primary research obligations, especially in the decade after independence have been to focus on those areas where research was often neglected during the colonial era, or where, if it was done at all, it was often inadequate, distorted or even prejudiced. Which is to say that ours have not been the ivory-tower concerns and we have been keenly aware of our functional, albeit indirect, role in the society at large. Thus our historians, for example, have tried to focus on one of the great areas of misunderstanding about the African past or the precolonial period. Where the eye of the western scholar has often seen a dark landscape of dubious historical achievement or even inertia, such scholars as G.S. Were[5] have found that Africa was a place of great human activity and contributed meaningfully, throughout history, to world civilization. The impact of African arts on western civilization is a case in point and the contribution of Northern Africa to world agriculture and astronomy is, of course, another. The point here is that in order to begin to understand where we are going in the era of independence it is crucial to understand where we have been, what we have been, and what we have achieved in the past. This is as it should be. For what is at stake here is the question of our dignity. To ignore, for example, the fact that the Masai in Kenya had perfected techniques of amputation and the African peoples in general had some highly advanced medical expertise is itself to amputate an important aspect of our historical achievements.

What one can say about the new and refreshing research into history applies also to other areas of our arts faculty. Indeed what is interesting is the interdisciplinary approach to research. The Centre for Creative and Performing Arts, started recently at the College, is a case in point. Its aim is to combine those aspects in some departments under the faculty of arts which are of a creative and performing nature. Thus the department of literature which among other things teaches oral literature can work with the department of music to put oral poetry to music and offer a good evening performance to a varied audience drawn from all sections of the community. The actual performers themselves need not come from these departments only but the College body in general and indeed the society at large. Of interest here is that recently the Centre hosted a musical programme in which one of the conductors was a permanent secretary in government and a long-time civil servant. Others involved were well-known local musicians who are not themselves in anyway involved in intellectual life at university. This we feel is a most worthwhile extension of our obligations to the society at large.

One department under the faculty which has long recognized these obligations is the department of literature. The study of drama in that department, for instance, has never been a mere textbook affair. The department stages for the wider College community at least six plays a year. In addition it is notable that in the nation-wide schools' festival held each year at the Kenya National Theatre the schools that have performed best in the last three years are those in which Kenyatta University College graduates from the department of literature teach drama. In addition the departmental magazine *KUCHA*, which is aimed at a general Kenyan readership, has begun to preserve the best creative works and research by students, including essays, and it is gratifying to see that even at this level an attempt at contact with the larger society is being made. The point we are emphasising is that in a developing country like ours the universities cannot be islands unto themselves.

Working alongside the department of literature is the department of languages and linguistics. Formerly these two existed as one department, but with a great emphasis being put on other languages, international and local, it was felt that a department of languages had to be introduced. The most important languages taught in the department are English, Swahili and French. Swahili, which is spoken throughout Eastern Africa including such other countries as Zaire, is a very rich language with a strong culture and written literature dating back at least three centuries. Unlike English, which in many ways has been a medium for the educated, Swahili is spoken by all sections of the Kenyan society and deliberations in parliament in fact are carried on in Swahili which the society has adopted as our national language. As concerns the teaching of Swahili, the department of languages at Kenyatta University College has been carrying on a crash programme to produce teachers for our secondary schools, where there has been a great shortage of qualified teachers owing to the fact that the larger emphasis was always on teachers of English. Research into Swahili itself is going on all the time. One member of our languages staff is currently revising and updating the major English-Swahili/Swahili-English dictionary.

The Sciences. Although the science faculty of Kenyatta University College is primarily concerned with the training of secondary-school

SUB-TOPIC 4(B): RELEVANCE OF UNIVERSITY EDUCATION [Koinange]

science teachers in specific subjects, the programmes offered are essentially multidisciplinary. This flexibility enables departments to co-operate in both basic and applied research.

One important example is in the field of environmental and ecological studies jointly planned by Kenyatta University College and the faculty of agriculture of the University of Nairobi. As is well known, Kenya has some of the best agricultural lands to be found anywhere in the world. The Kenya highlands, though occupying only a small fraction of the country's landmass, are literally the breadbasket of the nation. Most of the remaining land however is arid or semi-arid and therefore of low agricultural productivity. To meet the challenge of increasing food demand by an increasing population the University is undertaking an ambitious research programme of arid farming. In recognition of the important part we are playing here, the government of Kenya has allocated 4,000 hectares of land to the University of Nairobi and Kenyatta University College. Among the planned programmes is the research into the development of arid farming and the breeding of drought-resistant legumes and grasses with high yield, ranching and utilization of the otherwise dry waste-land for intensive farming through irrigation.

Another pressing problem is the ever-increasing demand for more protein. In our studies of drylands research is directed towards wildlife ranching aimed at increasing the supply of animal protein. Already Dr. David Hopcraft of the Wildlife Ranching and Research Centre at Athi River has demonstrated the feasibility of this in low rainfall areas. Furthermore his work has shown that the meat obtained is lean with none of the saturated fats found in beef cattle. Besides, the cost of production is minimal compared to beef cattle. Co-operation between the faculty of science at Kenyatta University College and Dr. Hopcraft and his staff is already assured.

Extensive research on the incorporation of sisal-fibre reinforcement in cement paste and concrete is under way. Kenya is already using asbestos fibres in cement paste, and other fibres such as glass, steel and polypropylene are being used commercially elsewhere. However in Kenya sisal is in such plentiful supply that if its use in cement composites is found to have useful practical benefits, for example in producing low-cost roofing sheets that can be manufactured on a village-industry basis, this research project will have opened up a useful new industry in Kenya and in other countries where sisal is available in large quantities.

The physics department is establishing an Appropriate Technology Unit, the purpose of which is to research into the development of locally-relevant technology. Water-pumping, solar energy and construction materials are among the areas currently being investigated. The Unit is proving to be a useful training ground for student teachers of science. A conference to examine the possibility of linking appropriate technology and education at school level is being planned. A further extension of the project is a request to UNESCO for the establishment at the College of an Appropriate Technology Education Resource Centre for Eastern Africa.

Research work in the chemistry department includes the study of fluoride uptake by plants, both naturally and as a result of pollution, and the effects of this uptake on the plants themselves, and of animals and man eating the plants. A number of highly toxic fluorine-containing plants has been found in Kenya.

A study is also being made of the seed oil composition and concentration in Kenyan plants to see if they are of potential commercial importance for fat-making. There is a continuing programme for the synthesis of new organotin compounds which may be used as insecticides, fungicides, etc.; we are collaborating with the Coffee Research Station on this project. The organotin compounds are also screened for anti-tumour activity. Some organo-transition metal compounds are being synthesised with a view to making it possible to 'fix' nitrogen at room temperature. This could lead to cheaper production of nitrogen-containing fertilizers. A programme of analysis of Kenya's river waters to determine the extent of pollution is also in progress. Collaboration with colleagues in the department of zoology should reveal whether such pollution is harming wildlife.

Research is being carried out in the fields of taxonomy, medicinal plants, herbicidal weed control of both terrestrial weeds and aquatic weeds such as *Salvinia* found in Lake Naivasha. Other fields of research include genetics and cytogenetics. A recent work by a postgraduate student entitled 'A cytogenetic study of the effects of food preservatives, Sodium Bensoate and Sodium Sulphite' throws light on the effects of food additives.

Education. A number of research projects are also going on or projected in the area of education, some of which have a regional bias and others being specifically related to Kenya. The Intelligence and Development Tests for East Africa project, the Kenyan Tests and Norms project and the project on guidance and counselling are cases in point.

INTELLIGENCE AND DEVELOPMENT TESTS FOR EAST AFRICA (IDEA) PROJECT. Research workers at Kenyatta University College and the University of Nairobi in Kenya, Makerere University in Uganda and the University of Dar es Salaam in Tanzania, in collaboration with researchers in the Free University of Amsterdam,

Netherlands, are engaged in this project. The purpose of the project is to develop a number of test series for use in Kenya, Uganda and Tanzania. The need for psychological tests in these countries is felt most clearly at three different levels: at the beginning and at the end of the primary school, and after some years of advanced education. At those times important individual and institutional decisions have to be taken. Especially at the end of the primary school, tests can be of considerable assistance in determining the most suitable educational route to follow in choosing among alternatives beyond that educational level.

The IDEA project is entering its fourth year. During this time ability tests have been administered to samples of primary school children in their seventh year in school and to samples of secondary school students in their twelfth year in all three countries. Results of the performance of these schoolchildren at the examination at the end of the seventh and twelfth years in school have also been collected. The purpose is to determine the extent to which the intelligence or ability test is predictive of the performance of the pupil at the examination.

KENYAN TESTS AND NORMS PROJECT. In the more 'modern' and urban industrial world into which more and more people of Kenya are being drawn, as well as in the rapidly developing rural areas, the problem of the integration of the sub-normal children has become increasingly acute. Unlike in traditional societies, there are fewer useful functions they can perform and fewer people in their immediate environment to take care of them. The skills needed to live in a complex environment, with its increased social competition and physical dangers, are much more elaborate.

In response to the needs of sub-normal children it has become necessary to set up specialized institutions designed to take care of the problem children, the functions of which are to foster their optimal development and make their integration into the wider society easier. To be most efficient these institutions have to be capable of dealing with specific kinds of problems, handicaps or disorders. The specialized institutions set up lack the necessary diagnostic tools to identify and specify the problems, and provide an appropriate match with a possible treatment. These tools are psychological tests, which in many cases are needed to supplement a medical examination, or which may serve as a screening device for large populations so as to discover the individuals who need more specific attention.

If psychological tests are to be used it is important that they be adapted to the local situation and that local norms be used. For Kenya, in the absence of locally adapted tests, the situation is clearly unsatisfactory. This is why a group of specialists, including prominent representatives from Kenyatta University College, are developing a screening test for pre-school-age children for use in Kenya, with norms based on representative local populations. The instrument will cover a wide range of psychological functioning, including motor, perceptual, intellectual, linguistic and social development.

THE ROLE OF A SCHOOL COUNSELLOR IN KENYAN SECONDARY SCHOOLS PROJECT. There is a good deal of interest in Kenya at present in the establishment of guidance and counselling services in the school system. This is in recognition of the vital role that guidance and counselling plays in development. Through guidance it is possible to assist pupils to select an education route most suited to their capacities and specialized interests. This would reduce human wastage both in the school-going population and in the community at large.

In recognition of the role that guidance and counselling can play Kenyatta University College not only offers guidance and counselling courses to its bachelor of education students but it actively encourages research in this important area. One such research project is designed to discover the perceptions of secondary school students and teachers in Kenya of the role of the school counsellor and the problems the counsellor would have to deal with in Kenyan secondary schools. Another study is directed towards establishing counselling needs in Kenya secondary schools.

Negotiations are afoot to establish with the assistance of UNESCO a guidance and counselling centre at the College with a view to serving the College community and training teachers in counselling techniques.

The above-cited examples of research show that whatever goes on in the halls of the university in a developing country adds more to the meaning of life if it adds to improvement of the quality of living of the ordinary citizen.*

Promoting International Understanding and Co-operation Among Nations

In addition to contributing to economic development and the enhancement of the social well-being in the country in which it is situated, a university must also be concerned about the promotion of international understanding and co-operation among nations.

---

* For a full list of research in progress at Kenyatta University College, see: Ng'ang'a, J. M., *Directory of Research*, Kenyatta University College, 1975–

SUB-TOPIC 4(B): RELEVANCE OF UNIVERSITY EDUCATION   [*Koinange*]

Kenyatta University College has not been unresponsive to this concern. The Basic Education Resource Centre for Eastern Africa and the Environmental Education Centre perform this function.

Basic Education Resource Centre for Eastern Africa. All countries of the world are conscious of the universal need for education, which is at once an inalienable right of every citizen and a crucial force in development. Education, however, is no longer defined in terms of schools and classrooms, it transcends educational systems to the extent of involving 'all of one's life' in a 'learning society'.[6] Universities — and more especially teachers' colleges — can no longer isolate themselves from society which is rapidly becoming an educational institution in its own right. They have to participate, with all the talent, expertise and facilities at their disposal, in transforming society into a life-long learning experience.

The Basic Education Resource Centre for Eastern Africa (BERC) reflects Kenyatta University College's effort to bring education to the masses. BERC, which is largely financed by UNICEF (United Nations Children's Fund), acts as a regional information, research and training unit in the area of basic education. At present it serves the following eighteen countries: Botswana, Burundi, Comoros, Djibouti, Ethiopia, Kenya, Lesotho, Madagascar, Malawi, Mozambique, Mauritius, Rwanda, Seychelles, Somalia, Swaziland, Tanzania, Uganda and Zambia. It was instituted in 1975 in direct response to recommendations made at the July and October, 1974, Seminars on Basic Education in Eastern Africa, which called for a forum whereby countries in the region could exchange ideas and experiences in the all-important area of basic education. It has since been invited to become an associated institution of Network of Educational Innovation for Development in Africa (NEIDA), which is now being organized under the auspices of UNESCO at the request of the ministers of education of African states. In addition to meetings and the publications and the compilation of a directory of persons and organizations with interest and expertise in basic education, the most tangible result achieved through the Centre has been the emergence of a genuine concept of basic education as viewed by the countries of the region.[7]

Environmental Education. Environmental education is another area in which Kenyatta University College is playing its role in relation to problems of development on an intra-Africa and international basis.

There is an increasing concern about the need to preserve the natural environment. In September, 1974, under the auspices of the World Confederation of Organizations of the Teaching Profession

(WCOTP) and the International Union for the Conservation of Nature and Natural Resources (IUCN), a seminar was held in Mombasa, Kenya. The general objective was to frame guidelines for an environmental education methodology which would be applicable in both formal and non-formal educational situations. Seminar participants investigated the possible development of environmental education programmes for Africa based on the experiences gained through existing programmes. They sought also to stimulate the development of materials and methods usable in Africa and to provide guidelines for African environmental education programmes.

Arising from this seminar and subsequent meetings, Kenyatta University College, in response to the felt needs of the region, has put forward a proposal that a regional centre of environmental education be created at the College as an integral part of the UNESCO/UNEP* network of environmental education centres.

Concluding Remarks

The challenge which faces a university, especially in a developing country, is how in addition to fulfilling the traditional roles of the university it can respond to the development needs of the country in which it is located. Through my description of the functions that Kenyatta University College performs I have attempted to demonstrate that the College has responded to Kenya's need of highly qualified teachers to man its secondary schools. Through its basic and applied research programmes it is contributing to the solutions of problems associated with both social and economic development. And by establishing the Basic Education Resource Centre, the Environmental Education Centre and the Appropriate Technology Resource Centre for Eastern Africa, its activities go beyond the boundaries of Kenya, thus helping to foster international co-operation and understanding.

I conclude by recording concurrence with Wandira[8] when he says:

> 'In seeking an identity which can be developed by Africa herself, the African University seeks those qualities, structures and concerns which will distinguish it from other universities, and will better prepare it for service in its own continent. In asserting fellowship with other universities, however, the African University identifies itself with abiding concerns that transcend both time and space.'

Kenyatta University College agrees and abides by this dictum.

* United Nations Environment Programme.

SUB-TOPIC 4(B): RELEVANCE OF UNIVERSITY EDUCATION [Koinange]

REFERENCES

1. Weinberg, A. W. The Two Faces of Science, *Journal of Chemical Education*, 1968, 45 p. 74.
2. Wandira, A. *The African University in Development*, Raven Press, Braamfontein/Transvaal, 1977.
3. Nevitt, S. The Contribution of Higher Education to the Life of Society, in Niblett, W. R., *Higher Education: Demand and Response*, Tavistock, London, 1969, pp. 7–20.
4. Yesufu, T. M. *Creating the African University: Emerging Issues in the 1970s*, Oxford University Press, London, 1973.
5. Were, G. S. *East Africa Through a Thousand Years*, Evans Brothers Ltd., 1968.
6. *Learning to Be: The World of Education Today and Tomorrow*, UNESCO, Paris/Harrap, London, 1972, p. xxxiii.
7. Auger, G. A. *The Evolution of the Concept of Basic Education*, BERC Press, Kenyatta University College, 1977.
8. Wandira, A., op. cit.

DISCUSSION

A recurring theme throughout the discussion was the relationship between relevance and competence in both undergraduate programmes and research. Although few speakers were prepared to dispute the basic position of *Sir Alan Cottrell* (Cambridge) that competence must be given primacy (for paper, see above), the view was expressed that the two are not necessarily incompatible. Professor R. N. Haszeldine (Manchester, Institute of Science and Technology) maintained that a blending at the undergraduate level of basic principles with application can lead to enriched teaching and more highly motivated students. The difficulty is not that relevance undermines competence, but that faculty possessing purely scholarly attitudes have difficulty in making the necessary adjustment in their teaching.

While agreeing with this point of view, Sir Alan warned that relevance will detract from teaching if it is given too great an emphasis. It is essential to establish an appropriate balance. Professor E. B. Kwakye (Kumasi) suggested that the question of whether relevance or competence comes first may not arise at all. He felt that work in the area of appropriate technology can be as demanding as work at the frontiers of knowledge. It is an error to think that practical research—often related directly to local problems and concerns, particularly in the economically developing world—is not itself often at the frontiers of knowledge.

Professor C. Ake (Port Harcourt) and Professor R. Joshi (Bombay) suggested that the discussion of relevance versus competence had been in the context of conventional society and the conventional university, as though to imply that the direction of society is settled and all that is needed

TOPIC 4: THE PUBLIC VIEW OF THE UNIVERSITIES

are effective tools to advance that society. On the other hand, in addressing the question of relevance one is questioning the very nature of society and the role of the university within that society.

Considerable disagreement was expressed with Sir Alan's contention that, because of limited employment opportunities in research, the number of research students should be substantially reduced. Several speakers (Professor L. C. Holborow (Queensland), Dr. B. C. L. Weedon (Nottingham) and Professor Haszeldine (Manchester, Institute of Science and Technology)) maintained that, in addition to contributing to the development of the individual, doctoral training develops qualities which are extremely valuable in many areas of responsibility, including management. Students, however, should be given an opportunity to choose a research problem which may range from the very pure to the applied and, in the case of the latter, a working relationship should be developed with industry wherever possible.

Professor D. R. Stranks (Adelaide), on the other hand, drew attention to a recent Australian study in which general managers in the chemical industry expressed serious concern about deficiencies in the sociological skills of PhD graduates. Suggesting ways in which the perceptions of graduates might be broadened, he proposed closer links with industry, possibly through sandwich or co-operative programmes, and team supervision of research on problems which cut across traditional disciplines. Other discussants, including Sir Alan Cottrell, agreed that it will be necessary to substantially alter the nature of the PhD experience if universities wish to produce a more versatile graduate.

The question was asked: how much emphasis to place on applied research and how much on frontier research? To an extent, the answer to this question will depend upon the resources of the country concerned. Professor K. V. Sivayya (Andhra) stressed that the relevance of university research must transcend national boundaries; universities in technologically advanced countries have to contribute to areas of special relevance to developing nations.

In responding to comments related to his paper (see above), Dr. *C. -E. Beaulieu* (Quebec) reminded the group that the fundamental purpose of university research is to support university teaching. However, universities have allowed governments and the public to believe that university research is an immediate answer to economic development. Dr. Beaulieu cautioned against raising expectations for an immediate economic benefit from research, however relevant it may appear. He pointed out that research is only one factor, and frequently not the most important factor, in stimulating the economic development of a country.

Dr. Beaulieu also commented that the balance between pure and applied research will vary from institution to institution, often depending upon the age of the university. Newer universities may devote a greater part of their effort to applied research. Commenting upon the links between the University of Quebec and industry in the province, he pointed to his own institution as an example of this. Professor L. M. Birt (Wollongong) stressed the need for institutional role differentiation in

SUB-TOPIC 4(B): RELEVANCE OF UNIVERSITY EDUCATION

research, especially with respect to the relationship between small and large universities within a university system.

Mr. S. L. Martin (West Indies) drew attention to the dilemma facing young scientists, especially in small developing countries, who, at a critical stage in their academic development, undertake research projects which are directly relevant to their country's needs. It is often impossible to get such work published owing to the narrow application and interest of the research. And yet it is difficult to know what weight to give to unpublished research reports when evaluating academic achievement. Mr. Martin suggested that universities should themselves publish research results. Unfortunately, there is a problem obtaining financing for this activity.

Sir Frank Hartley (London) commented upon the use of 'taught' as opposed to 'research' master's degrees in British universities. These programmes provide for a deepening of the undergraduate work and their existence is dependent upon a flourishing research activity in the institution. He felt that greater use might be made of this opportunity, which was perhaps not fully understood or explored. Sir Alan Cottrell responded by pointing out that taught master's degrees were grafted on to the traditional honours programme, and he questioned whether this provides an appropriate foundation for a master's programme of this type.

There was some discussion of a restructuring of undergraduate education to make it a truly terminal education. One discussant was concerned that, at the present time, undergraduate work fits the student only for graduate work, and graduate work fits him only for research work.

Lord Alport (City) speaking, he said, as a layman expressed strong concern about the feeling of pessimism which seemed to permeate the discussion. A new society, he maintained, cannot be created in a mood of pessimism and defensiveness. Since universities represent the intellectual élite of our society we should not be surprised that today, as in the past, they are the subject of public criticism. Rather than being preoccupied with current attitudes they should be building for the future.

Sub-Topic 4(c)

DIRECT SERVICES TO INDUSTRY

Chairman: Professor W. AHMAD
Vice-Chancellor of the Bangladesh University of Engineering and Technology

Rapporteur: Dr. W. H. COCKCROFT
Vice-Chancellor of the New University of Ulster

Tuesday, 22 August

Sir GEORGE KENYON (*Chairman of Council, University of Manchester*): This part of the topic relates to the direct services to industry provided by the universities in the UK.

We all think we are special cases but there are grounds for suggesting that the social climate in the UK does affect relations between universities and industry because society has an ambivalent attitude to both. Universities have carried a smear of elitism and irrelevance (or irresponsibility); industry has been regarded as unattractive to intelligent people with aspirations to culture or service. Both are minorities—universities within the area of higher and further education and industry within the number of all people employed. Manufacturing industry in the UK already employs less than 40% of the working population and will rapidly employ fewer. Yet both universities and industry are vital to our future prosperity and well-being.

Even more unfortunately, they don't understand or much like each other. Those of us who work regularly in both the university and the industrial world are constantly having to take up the cudgels for one side against the other—either way. This does not induce any feeling of inferiority or superiority in either direction—simply an increasing realisation of the utter necessity of bridging this gap between the two most important elements in our society.

Before returning to these larger general issues let us try to assess the state of the game as it is. The best way of getting partners together and persuading two minorities to swim together instead of sinking is to cultivate the common interests and to enlarge the area in which they clearly help each other directly.

SUB-TOPIC 4(C): DIRECT SERVICES TO INDUSTRY [Kenyon]

What are these areas, how significant are they, and can they and should they be deliberately and substantially increased? Amongst the direct services to industry we may list: (a) supply of high quality people; (b) research—pure and applied; (c) co-operative ventures; (d) consultancies, research contracts, testing and intensive special courses.

Considering the question of *people*. The first degree in a UK university is generally accepted as amongst the shortest to complete and the best in the world. This is achieved by maintaining entrance selection standards and by not expecting or condoning any rate of drop-out beyond that due to special personal difficulties. Such a graduate being only three or four years out of school is in good shape to tackle life with enthusiasm having good reason to suppose that he is acceptable material.

This is where industry can fail so badly. The intake can be divided into:

(i) those who have clear vocational training, *e.g.* architects, engineers, doctors, lawyers;

(ii) those whose degree has practical application in a general sense to management problems, *e.g.* economists, social scientists;

(iii) those others who are drawn to try industry but with no direct qualification, *e.g.* history, English, languages.

There is no special difference between these categories as to the familiarisation and training procedure. There is first the particular problem of introducing the graduate to a new atmosphere where others have grown slowly into their background and are firmly embedded. University students are intellectually talented with exceptional skills of analysis. But these have to face the test of the market where other skills such as in personal relationships may be of greater importance. Universities encourage individual talents in an egocentric way whereas industry depends on team-work and a fair amount of suffering fools tolerantly if not gladly.

The social attitude to industry is perhaps more dangerously illustrated in the schools now than in the universities where the employment situation has introduced a cold douche of realism. However in assessing this difficult problem of adjustment from graduation to industrial humdrum I place responsibility for completing the closure of the gap at fifty-fifty. The graduate should be patient for a time and modestly try to learn the new tricks but equally industry should deliberately shorten its procedures and try not to present the indoctrination period as yet more 'training'. The graduate wants to be doing something obviously useful pretty quickly and should be allowed short-cuts. I have found that after a short period the

453

graduate will start to pull away from those who have been in the job years before him—other things being equal.

There is a lot of justifiable anxiety about the standard of qualified scientists, engineers and technicians being turned out. We are just starting a new 4-year course in several UK universities which is high-level and intensive and intended to combine engineering, management training and a practical attitude. This should go some way to remedying a serious weakness which largely explains why qualified engineers in Britain do not get through to higher management like their counterparts in Europe and America. The cry that industry is run by accountants and lawyers may be stilled in time.

Next *research*—pure and applied. Most pure research is done in the universities. The equipment and the physical resources are provided by government through research councils and other agencies and of course so are many salaries. As the government have pointed out, for example, the National Research Development Corporation in the last 27 years have considered 5,411 cases submitted from academic sources of which 1,892 were accepted for action and 205 became revenue-earning. This indicates that a good many ideas are given a chance and that only a small percentage seem to be viable. Nevertheless the ideas, the genius and the creativity can only come from a strong university atmosphere where teaching, research and administration are harmoniously balanced and each individual may pursue his natural bent freely, calm in the certainty that his contribution is accepted and welcomed as an essential element. The leaders of the British universities are quite capable of maintaining such a desirable judicious balance given the leeway with which to do it.

All UK universities have been most helpful in providing detailed information about the nature and amount of research and consultancy work commissioned from them. Some interesting tendencies emerge.

All universities seem anxious to develop these services and all have something going—but the pattern is very varied and it is impossible to generalise. The old-established universities have important and substantial arrangements which are clearly deeply-rooted and likely to increase strongly as time goes on. These however tend to be specialised and individual though often on a large scale, *e.g.* Oxford and London. Proximity to a specific industry leads to some spin-off, *e.g.* North Sea oil at Aberdeen—but this is only one example of a general effect.

Most universities keep a paternal eye on the efforts of individual departments to develop their contract work, without attempting much centralisation, but some have a strong central body which initiates new work through a separate small department but without interfering with individual initiative. Usually the contracts have to be vetted for legal and royalty purposes and to control the time of the academic staff. Several universities have formed separate companies for the purpose.

A useful booklet is the *Directory of University/Industry Liaison Services* (October 1977, fifth edition, from Brunel University, Uxbridge, Middlesex). It does not seem, apart from some well-known and very important exceptions (*e.g.* ICL and Manchester and ICI and Oxford), that much of the research contract money comes directly from industry.

Each university has taken the steps it thinks best to sell itself to industry in regard to its own local opportunities or its staff's capacity and a number of original developments have taken place with varying degrees of success. Perhaps Southampton with its ten industrial advisory units is the most outstanding example. They have raised their percentage income from such work to twice the national average and have clearly aroused a lot of widespread industrial interest. They expect to add an additional optional fourth year to their engineering course with encouragement from industry in the form of secondment and instruction by industrialists. It is quite common for the amount of all research money from outside to amount to 10% or more of total revenue and this is quite substantial. However of this 10% it is rare to find that more than a quarter comes from industry direct. There is nothing surprising in this because industry does not do much pure research and if it does so then it does it itself. So much applied research depends on its application at the point of production or use — on pilot plants and schemes. Since the 44 universities are well spread geographically and since all have clearly a positive view towards research and consultancy contracts with industry it seems that, without being complacent, good progress is being made.

Perhaps a more worrying thought is that there is not enough free movement, nor the means of achieving it, in the field of exploitation of the results of pure research. Industry has a problem of its own in the UK which is how to translate its developments into new products in the market-place fast enough to clean up before the international competition sets in. This will be helped by the better use of engineers and scientists in higher management with financial and marketing skills added to their technological expertise. They will thus play a more effective and more powerful role in boardroom decisions.

But deliberate manpower planning has proved difficult during the great expansion of the last twenty years and it is doubtful how closely output can ever be geared to employment needs and prospects. Consider the history of such recent attempts with town planners, civil and chemical engineers, teachers and earlier doctors. 'Manpower projections tend to assume the continuity of existing economic policies; experience indicates their discontinuity' (*see* University of Manchester appointments board's annual report, 1976–77, for this quotation and much else of great practical interest). The absolute numbers of scientists and technologists are limited by the intellectual demands of these subjects — only about 4% of the age group is able to reach graduate status in scientific and technological subjects. In terms of a broad match between graduate output and employment needs the UK universities have made a very real contribution to manpower planning. The proportion of first-degree graduates believed unemployed at 31 December, 1976, was 5·5% of the total of 1976 graduates; the corresponding figure for postgraduates was 1·6% — the figure for the polytechnics was 7·5%.

The UK universities are acutely conscious of national needs and their responsibility to contribute to those needs. They produce the highest proportion of science and technology graduates of any developed country, including the United States. The percentages are: 52% science-based (including medicine); 48% arts-based. This means that, of an estimated total student population of 282,000 in 1977–78, almost 147,000 are following sciences and technology-based courses. The projected expansion to 310,000 students in the universities by 1981 takes account of the swing back to science and will at least maintain the existing percentage distribution between arts and science.

At the postgraduate level the number of students engaged in postgraduate work represents about 19% of the total. Of these about half are taught postgraduate courses — including the postgraduate Certificate of Education and numerous other courses, many of a directly vocational kind. The remainder are receiving a valuable training in research methods and, in science and technology, are making an invaluable contribution to the research output of the universities.

In 1976 25·4% of graduates available for employment entered manufacturing industry compared with 22·9% in 1975. It is recognised that there is a need to attract more highly qualified scientists and technologists into manufacturing industry, *i.e.* wealth creation. It is likely that the problem is not so much one of quantity as of quality and universities can and do make a great contribution. They also have a responsibility through their careers and counselling services to encourage a responsible attitude among students towards industry. There are encouraging indications—the upward trend in applications for engineering courses, the new four-year manufacture and management courses already referred to and a strong demand from industry for graduates, but much will depend on the status accorded in society and the incentives offered to graduates to enter the wealth-creation process. 'The UK universities are passing through a series of crises from which they will emerge transformed. In the last 25 years they have increased by three times the numbers graduating in science and technology and have accomplished economically and without fuss the enormous task of expansion set them by the nation less than 15 years ago' (Lord Todd, Royal Society, November 1977).

What matters most in preparing the way for greater and more effective collaboration between universities and industry is the creation of the right social environment towards employment in manufacturing and especially in regard to the attitude of the schools who must provide the material for the universities. The government has put money, manpower and skills into research organisation of their own but it will always be through individual initiative and private ventures that the more spectacular and more risky but in many cases more successful and far-reaching developments will occur.

However, apart from what has already been discussed, there are several ways in which good progress is being made in providing the mechanism whereby the universities and industry can understand each other better and can work together on a larger scale. The first of these, which in principle has been going for a number of years, is the sandwich course. These are of many varieties, but overall in all higher education the number of people undergoing them per annum had increased between 1965 and 1975 from 4,000 to 47,000 of which 14,000 were in universities. Whereas only about 6% of undergraduates at universities take sandwich courses, in the polytechnics and other colleges the percentage of full-time students taking sandwich courses is as high as 35%. A growing number of students in the latter area are opting for a sandwich course in its own right as a first choice rather than as second best to a full-time degree course. Employers appreciate this and the motivation which goes with it.

The ten technological universities are very strong here and perhaps it would not be invidious to single out Bradford and Aston in particular. However, despite this substantial growth in the areas where it all began, there has been little expansion in the many other universities and possible reasons for this relative lack of growth are:—

(a) the technological universities, on their foundation, already had well-established traditions in education through the sandwich approach and had developed close links with employers willing to accept students for training; but a further phase of their expansion was postponed while there was a substantial increase in provision of sandwich courses in other institutions, especially degree-level courses in the polytechnics;

(b) in a period of economic fluctuations industry has found difficulty in keeping pace with the expansion in demand for training places for students—this may be the most important factor;

(c) institutions not traditionally involved in sandwich courses may regard them as a more expensive form of education in the short term, as an administrative inconvenience to set up on a significant scale in parallel with the normal full-term courses, and as the preserve of the 'technological' universities. However the sandwich course creates a bridge between education and the working environment. Its continued flexible development could do much for the common cause.

So far as the employer is concerned, it would be unwise for the universities to expand sandwich courses beyond the capacity of employers to collaborate because this would undoubtedly lead to a revulsion of feeling against the process. It is however a practical basis for providing the contact between academic and industrial staff who are inevitably involved in the placement and supervision of students during their training periods. It may however be wiser to leave the growth to those establishments already well developed in the field rather than to confuse the issue by spreading the idea too thinly throughout all the universities. Also some form of clearing operation to marry the two requirements together would be useful and there are advisory services where this could be done.

Another important development is that of teaching companies, the cost of which is shared between the Science Research Council and the Department of Industry. Seven of these relationships with companies in their own areas are in existence at Aston, UMIST, Salford, Birmingham, Loughborough, North East London Polytechnic and Strathclyde, and the plan is to increase these to 20 teaching companies by 1982.

The idea of SISTERS, special institutions for scientific and technological education and research, has been put forward but rejected. However, rather than the authorities discriminating by giving larger grants to all students in engineering and applied sciences, it is now possible for employers who wish to sponsor students to give them a £500 per annum grant without penalty.

SUB-TOPIC 4(c): DIRECT SERVICES TO INDUSTRY [Kenyon]

There is no space here to pursue the closely-written agreements about industrial contributions to university research and the relevance of the latter to industry which are developed in the Third Report of the Select Committee on Science and Technology and subsequent documents.

Within the limited scope of investigation of the present paper a certain perspective emerges. The universities will serve industry directly if: (a) they can give industry what it wants; (b) each knows enough about the other to be able to make the crucial contact; and (c) if there is enough money around from somewhere to oil the wheels. It was stated earlier that one should enlarge the area in which they can clearly help each other directly. One must ask how large can this area be? Could the contacts really be more significant than they already are? Or are we merely looking for a scapegoat for the alleged failure of the country to develop its potential faster and better?

We said that in terms of population universities and industry are minorities within their categories. Possibly each will comprise a reducing percentage of its category and of the population as time goes on. Within each there are sections which could never have recourse to the services of the other—whole areas of university life have nothing to do with industry and vice versa. We are really talking about top administration and vision (developed by cultivated minds) and about engineering and science. A tenth of a tenth of a tenth is a thousandth and so we are only talking about a few hundred people a year.

Are we therefore taking a sledgehammer to crack a nut? No—because a handful of men and women in one country in one generation can change its atmosphere and its prospects. This is where we come back to social attitudes and their effect on initiative and excellence. It is possible that a great state machine by constant churning can eventually produce the few ideas to transform a national attitude. It is also possible that, as mainly in the past, these will always emerge as a freak of individualism. The trouble is that western society is split fifty-fifty between these two conceptions. So we have compromise and uncertainty.

It looks as though most possibilities for liaison between universities and industry have been tried. There really are opportunities galore—and information lies around every corner. It is doubtful whether great geniuses lie undiscovered—no doubt some are on their way through because of the greatly expanded opportunities of the last fifteen years.

Whether their works or their products (even if appropriate) will be used by industry and developed commercially or practically is another matter. There is certainly room for improvement in the speed of industry's recognition of, reaction to, and development of technological ideas. But is our society any longer interested in such things? Is it not afraid of lasers, micro-processors, outer space and computers in everyday life?

The distinction between capitalism and socialism has long been blurred—and particularly in the west. Industry's only mechanism is the balancing of incomings and outgoings to achieve a sufficient reserve to continue the business by replacing assets, meeting inflation costs and servicing its capital. This calls for economy and control but the population are tending to think that industry is there to provide jobs at any cost and that the difference shall be made up by the state as 'social costs'. What significance therefore does the western system of state social responsibility attach to the nurture of excellence and the very special requirements necessary to bring it out and apply it?

These considerations go beyond the immediate discussion but few people in the UK remain unaware of their importance. What emerges is that the universities are in fact training the talent that comes to them and that there are plenty of ways of developing its passage into industry which are being pursued with reasonable energy and enthusiasm. The future of industry itself depends on the vision it displays in using this talent. But the needs of industry change as technological investment takes place. So a constant process of adaptation to the accelerating rate of changes is called for rather than yet another exercise in manpower planning.

Understanding and flexibility between the universities and industry and the realisation on the part of the community that both are vital to the country's future will make it possible to make the most of the already significant partnership between them both and the government. An opportunity for further broad discussion is afforded by the Department of Education and Science's recent discussion document on *Higher Education into the 1990s* and it is hoped that this will be searching and realistic. Its timing is right because we do now have a chance to pause and reconsider.

USEFUL DOCUMENTS FOR REFERENCE

1. Third Report from the Select Committee on Science and Technology: *University—Industry Relations*, 1976.

2. The Government's Reply (Cmnd. 6928), 1977.

3. *Industry, Education and Management: A Discussion Paper*, Department of Industry, July 1977.

4. Anniversary Address by Lord Todd to the Royal Society, 30 November 1977.

Also, by the Committee of Vice-Chancellors and Principals:—

SUB-TOPIC 4(C): DIRECT SERVICES TO INDUSTRY [Kenyon]

5. CVCP paper *Universities in a Period of Economic Crisis*, November 1975.
6. Memorandum from the CVCP to the Science Sub-Committee, June 1976.
7. Report of a CVCP Working Group on University—Industry Relations, May 1977.
8. A CBI paper on Qualified Scientists and Engineers, V.27.76.
9. Relations with Industry, paras. 111–114 of the CVCP *Report on the Period 1972–76*.

Professor E. BAMFO KWAKYE (*Vice-Chancellor of the University of Science and Technology, Kumasi*):

Introduction with Brief Background Information about Ghana

This report wants to be a brief case study of a university's 'direct services to industry' in a developing country. Ghana has been selected for the study because it is the country which the author knows best. The choice may not, however, be considered altogether unfortunate since it is claimed that most of the observations recorded in the paper would be valid or at least relevant in many other developing countries.

The Gold Coast, former British colony in West Africa, changed its name to Ghana after independence in March 1957. (Cynics say there wasn't much gold left anyway!) It is a tropical country with most of its 240,000 sq. metres divided between savanna and tropical rain forest. The population is estimated today at 10 million, most of whom farm in the rural areas. Cocoa, the most important crop, provides most of the foreign exchange earnings of the country. Besides the fertile land and the hard woods of the rain forest the country is endowed with considerable mineral wealth in the form of gold, diamond, bauxite, manganese, among others. Iron and oil deposits have been discovered but are not yet being worked. Agriculture remains the largest sector of the economy.

The Industrial Scene

Industrialisation was given high priority by the first post-independence republic. The efforts of the state in this direction culminated in the establishment in 1968 of the Ghana Industrial Holding Corporation to manage the state-owned manufacturing industries. Together with some joint state/private enterprises and the private industrial sector they produce goods categorised under food, drink and tobacco, building materials, chemicals and pharmaceuticals, electrical and electronic products, phonograph records, metals including steel cabinets and vehicle bodies, vehicles (assembled under licence), furniture, leather and plastics, toilet preparations, shoes, stationery, rubber products, textiles, timber products, aluminium, petroleum products and others. Small-scale industries are actively encouraged. They use mainly local raw materials and cover leather- and wood-work, food and oil processing, spirits, a wide range of bamboo articles, mats, baskets and similar products. Traditional craft and rural industries form an important arm of the small-scale sector.

Long before the major manufacturing concerns came to Ghana the mining industries operated with agriculture as the major sectors of the economy. The state's interests in mining are represented by the State Gold Mining Corporation which owns five gold-mining companies. The state has majority shares in all other mining enterprises. The gold, diamond, bauxite and manganese mined in the country are all exported without much refinery or processing.

The construction industry is often expected to achieve miracles in a developing country. In Ghana, especially in the last five years or so, it has flopped with a vengeance. So has the transport and communications industry. Domestic and industrial electric power is obtained principally from the hydroelectric generators of the Volta River dam project with an installed capacity of 750MW. Another dam is presently under construction. Pipe-borne water is available for domestic and industrial use in the cities and larger towns.

Problems of Industry

Ghanaian industry faces many problems which are inherent in the fact that Ghana, like other developing countries, is backward in the application of science-based technology to development. In the first place the machinery and processes of industry are imported. The manufacturing industry concentrates on consumer goods and accepts whatever technology is offered by the equipment manufacturer who succeeds in selling his machinery to the would-be entrepreneur or by the foreign company which allows its processes to be copied under licence. Assembly plants abound. The state-owned electronic company which assembles radios, TV sets and other electrical and electronic equipment from knocked-down parts supplied from Europe still functions the same way as it did some fifteen years ago!

A company usually begins by importing machinery. Experts accompany the machines to install and operate them for a period. The experts are expected to train local counterparts to take over from them. Here they encounter the second problem of Ghanaian industry, namely the scarcity of trained scientific and technological manpower. The directory of approved industrial enterprises lists 743 such enterprises as at 31 December, 1973. These enterprises were all in the manufacturing and construction sectors. By December 1973 the only faculty of engineering in the country had awarded 582 first degrees and sub-degree diplomas in civil, electrical, electronic and mechanical engineering. Most of the graduates were known to be employed in the service industries (hydroelectric power generation and distribution, water and sewerage works, etc.). Even when allowance is made for engineers trained outside the country and for expatriates in the manufacturing and construction enterprises, one would scarcely count one trained engineer, on the average, in each enterprise. One finds in many instances that the level of scientific and technological skills available to industry is low.

The importation of science-based technology into an environment which is poor in scientific and technological skills results in industrial plants whose operations are frequently interrupted by lack of maintenance, spare parts and the ability to resolve unexpected technical situations. Manufacturing programmes are often inflexible and innovation is always suspect.

Another circumstance attendant to the importation of technology is the necessity, in many cases, to import also the raw materials. In countries where foreign exchange is difficult to come by, as it is in most developing countries which do not produce oil, the importation of raw materials often creates a frustrating bottleneck in the smooth operation of industrial plant. It was reported during the last financial year (1977–78) that the manufacturing industry in Ghana ran at under 30% capacity. The leading culprits were identified as 'lack of spare parts and raw materials'.

For small-scale industries raw materials may not be a major constraint. They are more severely afflicted by the last though not the least of the problems of industry which will be listed: managerial skills. What is usually missing in this respect may range from simple technical or commercial information to modern management techniques. It is by no means rare to come across an entrepreneur who constitutes a one-man board of directors of his company and is its managing director, chief accountant and personnel officer all in one.

[Kwakye] TOPIC 4: THE PUBLIC VIEW OF THE UNIVERSITIES

Institutions Working to Improve Industrial Performance

Very few industries in Ghana have laboratories in the country which could help them maintain the quality of their goods or design and experiment with new lines. Factories which are associated with 'parent' companies in the developed countries usually obtain such services from the parent companies. The field is thus open for various institutions which have facilities for scientific and technological experimentation to offer much-needed services to industry.

The Ghana Standards Board was established in 1967 by government to ensure that Ghanaian enterprises maintain a reasonable quality of output. Specifically, the objectives of the Board are:—

(i) to establish and promulgate standards with the object of ensuring high quality in goods manufactured in Ghana, whether for local consumption or for export;

(ii) to promote standardisation in industry and commerce;

(iii) to promote industrial efficiency and development; and

(iv) to promote public welfare, health and safety.

To organise and co-ordinate scientific research in Ghana the government created in October, 1968, a Council for Scientific and Industrial Research (CSIR) as a statutory corporation. The functions of the CSIR include: advice to government on scientific and technological matters of importance to the utilisation and conservation of Ghana's natural resources; encouragement of scientific and industrial research of importance to industry, technology, agriculture and medicine; establishment, where necessary, of research institutes, units and projects; co-ordination of research in all its aspects in Ghana and collation, publication and dissemination of the result of research and other useful technical information.

The Council has a full-size secretariat through which most of its administrative functions are discharged. The secretariat also provides a number of common services including a scientific documentation service and a glass-blowing unit for the research institutes. Research institutes and units under the CSIR include Animal Research Institute, Crop Research Institute, Food Research Institute, Forest Products Research Institute, Institute of Aquatic Biology, Soil Research Institute, Building and Road Research Institute, Institute of Standards and Industrial Research and the Water Resources Research Unit.

The Ghana Manufacturers' Association has recently (1977) set up a research unit called the Manufacturers' Research and Technical Services Centre. The principal activities of the Centre have been stated in the following terms: 'to help the application of the results of research in industrial technology, provide on the spot guidance and consultancy services on technical problems, and very soon, build and demonstrate prototypes. The Centre also has a cooperative programme with the CSIR, the universities and other consultancy units to whom problems are referred when its own facilities are inadequate. It also provides the link between industrial research and industrial application of research results.' The Centre plans to promote efficient management practices especially in small-scale industries.

Indeed government has itself given some attention to the improvement of managerial skills available to industry. In October 1967 the government of Ghana, with the assistance of the United Nations Development Programme and the International Labour Office, established the Management and Productivity Institute (MDPI) in Ghana to improve and develop the standard of management and promote increased productivity. The Institute organises training courses, seminars, etc., and provides advisory and consultant services to all sectors of industry. It carries out studies, enquiries and research in the field of management development and productivity and serves as an industrial information centre.

The functions which the organisations described above, namely, the National Standards Board, the Council for Scientific and Industrial Research, the Manufacturers' Research and Technical Services Centre and the Management and Productivity Development Institute, are expected to perform could be reinforced and complemented by the universities. In most developing countries, especially in Africa, one often finds a greater concentration of experts at the university than in any other single organisation. The university thus has a unique potential to fashion a powerful interdisciplinary tool for problem solving. Moreover since most of the overheads of the university are provided for under the education budget the university can provide some services to industry at much less cost than any of the organisations listed above.

Ghana has three universities. The University of Ghana, the University of Science and Technology and the University of Cape Coast. Of the three, the one with the closest contact to industry is the University of Science and Technology in Kumasi. Founded in 1951 as a College of Technology, its training programme has been biased towards science and science-based professions. Its teaching and research programmes are organised in seven faculties of agriculture, architecture, art (fine and industrial), engineering, pharmacy, science and social sciences, and a school of medical sciences. To carry out its programmes for services to industry and the community at large the University has established a Technology Consultancy Centre, a Land Administration Research Centre, an Institute for Technical Education and a Centre for Cultural Studies.

Role and Organisation of University Services to Industry

It was stated earlier that universities could reinforce and complement the work of various agencies which offer services to industry. In addition to its primary function of training the required skilled manpower for industry the university could become directly involved in the various stages of industrialisation by: —

(i) offering advice on the type of technology (processes and machinery) to be imported;

(ii) assisting industry to improve the skills of its manpower by organising workshops, seminars and special courses for and jointly with industry;

(iii) devoting considerable research effort to the invention of new technology, adaptation of known technology, and improvement of products of industry;

(iv) disseminating relevant technical information in the industrial community;

(v) carrying out consultancy services, *e.g.* preparation of technical feasibility reports for industrial clients;

(vi) helping would-be entrepreneurs to set up their companies and acquire efficient managerial skills;

and in various other ways.

To do any of these things well requires some organisation of the resources available to the university. The scheme adopted by the University of Science and Technology provides a useful example. To act as a liaison between the University and industry a unit called the Technology Consultancy Centre (TCC) has been created. The Centre is manned by a director (with a deputy) and a small secretariat. It receives enquiries from industry and would-be entrepreneurs and brings them to the attention of the appropriate department of the University. In turn it informs the public in general and industry in particular about the results of research and development at the University which are considered to have commercial potential. The Centre employs a few research fellows to follow up projects initiated between clients and university departments. The research fellows also carry out research and development work on their own. The Centre maintains a workshop for developing prototypes and if necessary establishing a pilot plant.

SUB-TOPIC 4(c): DIRECT SERVICES TO INDUSTRY   [*Kwakye*]

Each faculty in the university is expected to set up a research committee to monitor its research efforts. The TCC liaises with the committee as well as with individual members of staff interested in industrial research.

The work of the faculties sometimes leads to the development of a marketable product or process. If the faculty considers the manufacture of the product a viable commercial proposition, but is not able to persuade an entrepreneur to embark on the new venture, it may decide to establish a small-scale production unit on the campus. The purposes of production units may be listed as follows: (*a*) to train craftsmen and managers in the skills of the new industry; (*b*) to complete product development under production conditions; (*c*) to test the market for the product in a realistic way; and (*d*) to demonstrate to entrepreneurs the viable operation of new industrial activity. Each production unit is managed by a management committee made up of the director of the TCC, the head of the department in which the prototype was developed, the dean of the faculty and the member of staff directly involved in the development of the unit.

To demonstrate the real life operation of the various ideas put forward above, case histories from the activities of the Technology Consultancy Centre as reported in its Annual Reviews will be described in the next section.

Case Histories of Direct Services to Industry

The Technology Consultancy Centre usually reports its technical operations under four headings, namely—
- consulting services for government departments, corporations and large industries
- production units on the university campus
- consulting services for small industries
- promotion of rural industries.

One or two examples from each area should illustrate the nature of the Centre's involvement.

(*a*) *Consulting services for government departments, etc.* (i) Repair of large hospital air conditioning plant. Early in 1972 the University discovered that the central air-conditioning plant at Korle Bu Hospital, Accra (the largest hospital in the country), installed at a cost of some $1m, had been out of repair for seven years. The TCC approached the Commissioner for Health with a three-stage programme proposed by the University's air-conditioning and refrigeration repair unit. The plan was accepted. The University's consultants worked on the plant during the long vacations and were assisted by students. Many parts were made in the workshops of the mechanical engineering department and the TCC including oil-coolers and portable equipment for clearing chilled waterpipes. Very few items were imported apart from refrigerant and cleaning fluids. On 25 April, 1975, at an official ceremony held at Korle Bu Hospital, the director of the TCC and the leader of the repair team handed the plant over to the Commissioner for Health. Local expertise and resources had been successfully employed to tackle a major task of considerable technical complexity at a fraction of the cost estimates provided for the ministry prior to 1972!

(ii) Operation 'make your own sugar'. Ghana has two sugar-producing industries which are notoriously over-designed and remain idle most of the time. Early in 1974 the government of Ghana introduced the 'make your own sugar' programme to encourage the local extraction of sugar from cane to supply the needs of rural areas. In response to this initiative the TCC offered the services of the University to develop a small-scale appropriate technology sugar-plant. After lengthy negotiations with the Ministry of Industries and the Sugar Industries Board, the latter awarded the TCC in April, 1977, a contract for the design of the plant. A member of the staff of the department of chemical engineering is undertaking the assignment. It is expected that a pilot plant will be constructed at a location with 100–200 acres of sugar cane.

(b) *Production units on the University campus.* A number of production units have emerged from the research and development efforts of various faculties and the Technology Consultancy Centre. The most prominent of these is the soap pilot plant which started with a project in the faculty of pharmacy and has resulted in a soap-producing factory outside the campus, owned by the Kwamotech Industries Ltd. A paper glue factory, Baffoe Manufacturing Enterprise in Kumasi, was also born out of the exertions of the University's industrial services. Schools Scientific Import Substitution Enterprises (SSISE), which began with the manufacture of simple school equipment—rulers, drawing-boards, T-squares, etc.—but has now widened its range of products, also started life on the University campus.

Production units in operation on the campus now include Steel Bolt Production Unit, Plant Construction Unit (for manufacturing tanks, pipes and other parts for soap, caustic soda and other chemical plants), Weaving Production Unit, Ceramics Production Unit (domestic tableware in stone-ware), Low-Cost Housing Materials Production Unit (Landcrete soil cement and cast-concrete sanitary ware), Air Conditioning Repair Unit, Electric Motor

Rewinding Unit, Traffic Lights Production Unit, Well Pump Production Unit, Electroplating Unit (about to start). These units are meant to be transferred or reproduced outside the campus for any seriously interested entrepreneur.

(c) *Consulting services for small-scale industries.* The type of request received varies considerably. Many small manufacturers seek testing and analysis of their products before starting production. Some seek a reassurance that their product will meet the requirements of the Ghana National Standards Board. Others need to know if their product is safe to use or could be improved. Some have been directed to consult the centre by a commercial bank or other organisation from whom they have requested a loan to start or expand their business. Advice is also sought on the selection and importation of machines and equipment. In trying to help entrepreneurs the centre also learns from their experience as the following example shows. The department of economics and industrial management proposed a closer management control system coupled with incentives for higher productivity in the University's Steel Bolt Production Unit. The department was asked to compare the effect of the new system with the performance of a similar enterprise in town (SSISE). It was observed that productivity at the campus unit doubled in a short time and profits increased. It is noteworthy however that the unit obtained the steel rods at controlled prices through legitimate channels. Labour was however dissatisfied and 7 of the 15 men employed in the unit left without giving any notice.

At the SSISE the pace was slower, machine utilisation was only 35% compared with 70% on the campus. But the entrepreneur was more nearly in harmony with the Ghanaian economic environment where everything is scarce and it is easier to produce a few items of high value than many items at competitive prices. The entrepreneur paid lower wages but bought his raw materials at black-market prices and sold his goods at high prices. His approach conserved scarce raw materials, reduced the consumption of cutting tools, minimised wear and tear on the machine (thus saving on foreign exchange for tools and spare parts), accommodated frequent power cuts and did not alienate the labour force!

(d) *Promotion of rural industries.* (i) Ashanti villages craft development project. The chairman of the Wonoo Village Development Committee felt the need to establish a centre with stores and showrooms for local craft products of his and two other neighbouring villages. The three villages specialised in traditional wood-carving, cloth-weaving and printing. The stores would undertake to purchase the work of the craftsmen on a year-round basis and sell yarns, tools and similar requirements to them. The showrooms would serve as a tourist attraction to the villages. As funds for the project became available the complex was designed at the department of architecture and built on low-cost building principles by the department of housing and planning research. The craft centre was designed as a focal point for the redevelopment of Wonoo and as a rest stop for tourists who could watch the local weavers at work on their traditional looms in congenial surroundings. When the building was completed a 120-feet borehole was drilled for water. A well pump made in the department of mechanical engineering was installed to complete the supply of pure drinking water.

(ii) Brass casting by lost wax process. At the village of Kurofofurom are many brass-founders skilled in the lost wax process of casting. Many traditional designs are cast including the famous 'gold weights' of Ashanti. One problem experienced by the craftsmen is shortage of raw materials and the TCC has been able to suggest an alternative source of supply.

An interesting development has been the attempt to introduce into the village the casting of engineering components. Some brass parts were required for the well pumps being made at the faculty of engineering and wooden patterns were sent to Kurofofurom to see if the villagers would be interested in supplying them to the University. Some trial items were produced and successfully finish-machined at the mechanical engineering workshop. It is hoped that quantity supplies can be obtained in support of the Well Pump Production programme.

The brass-founders have experienced some difficulty in adapting to geometrically symmetrical objects. Some assistance has been necessary in the preparation of the wax models, and moulds for these have been prepared at the ceramics section of the department of industrial art. It is expected, however, that with training and experience the craftsmen can adapt to new forms. The ancient, yet sophisticated, craft could then evolve into an engineering industry making machine components and supplying much-needed vehicle and machinery parts.

Conclusion

It is not claimed that the account given here does justice to the undertaking to describe the actual services of one university to industry. The general theme of direct services to industry would require several volumes to cover. The message that is being conveyed here is that the university in a developing country can no more ignore the incessant call on it to become directly involved in the socio-economic development of the community which sustains it. As far as service to industry is concerned no problem should be considered too simple to be heard, none too complicated to be tackled. The university's role should complement the work of agencies which support industry, guide policy-makers and inspire confidence towards self-reliance in the community. Its input should always have a quality of its own on the premise that from those to whom much is given, much will be required.

Dr. B. C. MATTHEWS (*President and Vice-Chancellor of the University of Waterloo*): The traditional roles of universities have been to serve as repositories of knowledge, to discover new knowledge and to teach. There is much evidence that universities over the centuries have performed these roles remarkably well. If they are to serve modern society, and the society of the future, the universities must not only continue with these traditional roles but also reach out to serve new needs. Universities must play a new role in the application of new knowledge. By assisting and actively promoting the effective use of new knowledge, universities can perform an important direct service to business and industry and to the economy of a nation.

The opportunities for direct service by universities to industry, and society in general, have never been more evident. By becoming more directly involved with industry and government in research and technology transfer, and by offering assistance and education for entrepreneurs, a university can provide a new service as well as enrich its traditional functions. With this as the central theme, I explore in this paper the opportunities and some of the mechanisms that a university may devise to perform this 'new' role.

The Past

Traditionally students in twentieth-century post-secondary institutions have represented a relatively small proportion of the total numbers of people of university age. To a large extent their purposes in attending a university were to prepare themselves to enter certain professions, *i.e.* theology, law and medicine, or, more commonly perhaps, to acquire the social graces and to make the personal acquaintances that would serve well in later life.

During the past three decades, however, increasing numbers of young people everywhere began to demand (and gain) access to the benefits of higher education. Governments responded to this unprecedented demand with massive financial support from the public purse for the expansion of entire university and college systems. The institutions struggled to retain their roles in liberal education and basic research while, at the same time, accommodating to the demand (sometimes explicit) for relevance — relevance in terms of the curricula so that students would be prepared to contribute effectively in the real world; relevance in terms of research and of the extent to which universities were involved in applied research as distinct from pure research. Ashby has pointed out that 'under the patronage of modern governments [universities] are [now] cultivated as intensive crops, heavily manured and expected to give a high yield essential to the nourishment of the state'.[1]

Yet universities are still often viewed as being remote from the real world, or at least not interested in being involved with real problems. In some measure that view may be accurate. Some people (faculty and administrators) in universities do seem to believe that to become involved with private commerce in solving real problems through research and the application of technology is something to be avoided, something not quite academically acceptable. I believe the function of a university cannot be limited to the discovery of new knowledge. It must extend to the application of that knowledge. Yet such an extended role for the university has seldom been acknowledged, and certainly has not been generally accepted within universities. We have paid and are paying a price for this neglect on our part — a price in terms of diminished public support for research in universities and few opportunities for young researchers upon graduation from our universities.

On the other hand one can observe some changes in attitudes that will lead universities in the future to provide greater direct service to industry and thereby support to the national economy in general. Partly as a result of the expansion of the universities in the sixties, large numbers of faculty members are now active in research in universities, many of them directing their efforts to the solution of problems in the private and public sector. Furthermore some universities, recognizing that involvement with business and industry in solving their problems can enrich their academic and basic research programmes, are developing policies and mechanisms and promoting attitudes that will foster and facilitate such involvement.

Co-operative programmes (pioneered in Canada by the University of Waterloo), carried out by various universities in several countries, provide excellent opportunities for mutually beneficial interactions of the university with the industrial and commercial community. The students benefit from intensive on-the-job experience while they are still undergraduate students; industry personnel can become involved in the development of relevant curricula, and at the same time benefit from close contact with the faculty and a greater knowledge of research work under way within the university laboratories.

Mechanisms for facilitating direct transfer of research and technology to industry are not so well established, but are being developed in some universities. The Science Council of Canada has made the case for the active involvement of government laboratories in the transfer of technology (developed in the laboratories) to industry.[5] Many of the arguments presented by the Science Council in support of the case apply as well to university as to government laboratories. The Association of the Scientific, Engineering and Technological Community of Canada (SCITEC) has recently stated: 'It is important that mechanisms and incentives be developed to transfer university technology to existing industry and to enable new technology to be introduced to the market through development of new enterprise . . . . Mechanisms must be established to encourage, through funding, development of university technology to stages of commercial interest'.[6]

Institutional Arrangements

If a university is to become involved in direct service to industry through applied research and technology transfer, it is imperative that specific internal arrangements be made to foster and facilitate that service. Faculty researchers must be relieved of much of the 'paper work' involved in grants and contracts acquisition and financial management, and the interests of the university must be maximized. Those in charge of research administration in the university must have the authority and the responsibility to develop contract research programmes, to make decisions on behalf of the university in the negotiation of contracts and to act as an information channel seeking out companies, agencies and individuals who may need the technical and scientific assistance that is available from faculty members.

The office of research administration (as the mechanism is called at Waterloo) should have extensive knowledge of patenting, the protection of proprietary rights, licensing, non-disclosure agreements and other legal requirements. Perhaps of fundamental importance is the role of the office in heightening the awareness of faculty and graduate student researchers of the need to consider ways and means by which newly-discovered knowledge can be put to use.

Contract Research

Contract research as a direct service to industry is especially important in Canada, where the research capacity in industry is relatively small. Contract research in Canadian universities is, however, a relatively recent development, but it is growing rapidly in importance. At Waterloo, for example, contract research began in 1967 when the University received a small grant from the federal government to establish the Waterloo Research Institute. From 1967 to 1974 the contracts tended to be small in size and the total value of contract research grew slowly, year by year. A substantial increase in the rate of growth of contract research became evident about 1974, and in 1977−78 the total value of such research at Waterloo exceeded $2,000,000, nearly double the figure of the previous year.

If a university is to develop contract research effectively and usefully, there are some preconditions that must be met.

(i) The individual faculty member must recognize contract research as being desirable and worthwhile.

(ii) The faculty member and the university must recognize and accept deadlines, and must produce results on time as specified in the contract. Success in this regard does much to ensure success in obtaining new and larger contracts in the future and to improve the image of the university.

(iii) The faculty members and the university must be prepared to recognize in some instances the need for 'secrecy' and the temporary withholding of publication. Any restraint on freedom to publish is considered anathema by many academics yet, in our experience, the fears in this regard are much exaggerated. Usually any clauses restricting publication are followed by a statement such as: 'these shall not be interpreted as imposing any restriction on the content or handling for academic purposes of the theses of students engaged in the research'. Thus contract research is not usually precluded as a vehicle for graduate student research. There are exceptions, of course, but they can usually be anticipated and accommodated through advance planning. Even in their normal non-contract research activity, university researchers sometimes delay publication until patents or other proprietary protection can be established.

(iv) The university must be careful in its contracting that it does not compete unfairly with private consultants and commercial laboratories or agencies. The university should, in fact, undertake research only when the necessary competence and facilities are not available in the private sector, or when the private sector is not interested.

(v) Discontinuity of income as research contract activity varies in volume from year to year requires special attention. For example full-time researchers may only be employed for relatively short periods during the course of the contract. Although this can cause increased administrative problems it does provide opportunities that might not otherwise exist for young people to work on significant industrial research. Furthermore the possibility exists for these researchers to move with the project to the industry concerned, if the research work moves from the university phase to the in-house industry phase.

University/Industry Joint Research

The joint involvement of university/industry in large research projects can have several beneficial effects not obtainable through ordinary contract research. Joint efforts that provide an opportunity for university researchers (faculty, graduate students, postdoctoral fellows and technicians) to join with researchers from industry can return great benefits to the industry and the university and also to society through effective technology transfer. Of course large-scale projects of this kind require sound and effective management and some flexibility of operation within the university. An interesting experiment along this general line is being tried in the United Kingdom. 'Teaching companies' analogous to 'teaching hospitals' have been set up. A 'teaching company' is one in which 'experienced practitioners, researchers, and students intermingle and cross-fertilize ideas while doing a job in a real environment connected with society where they can bring about changes which fit a real situation'.[4]

Another interesting example of university/industry involvement in research is a consortium arrangement, with the university and industrial companies in a practical partnership. For example the University of Waterloo is in a consortium with two companies—Electrohome Limited in Kitchener and Giffels Associates (an engineering consulting firm) of Toronto. The consortium has a contract with the government of Canada for research and product development in the solar energy field. In order to carry out its part of the work the University has hired a team of full-time researchers (all of them recent master's and doctoral graduates) who work under the supervision of faculty members active in solar energy research. Thus an opportunity is provided for young researchers to work within the university environment on a specific industrial problem, and in close consultation with companies involved in the practical aspects of putting the results of the research into the market-place.

The initial phases of the contracted research are being completed largely at the University, but as the work proceeds the industrial involvement will increase. As the project moves forward into the industrial 'in-house' phase some of the young researchers may move with the project into the companies concerned; others may move into other companies in the field. In any event, joint university/industry projects of this kind provide a useful bridge for newly-graduated researchers to make the transition from university to industry. Beyond that, such projects provide an excellent 'finishing-school' experience for new graduates, and indeed offer them an opportunity to create their own future career opportunities based on new technology. Contracts of this nature can also provide for senior faculty members to be released from regular university duties to work full-time on the contracted research, thus creating opportunities for newly-graduated PhD students to hold faculty positions at least temporarily.

Entrepreneurial Ventures

Much of the technology arising out of university research is in a very 'raw' state and must be developed much further before industry will accept it for still further development. In some cases it is technology 'looking for an application'. The university may be able to offer assistance in the further development of the technology to the point that an existing industry or a new company will take it and market it in the form of a new product. Yet it often happens (in our experience, at least) that no interest is shown because the market has not been identified, or because of lack of sufficient product development, poor timing, or other factors. Thus the university and the researcher(s) are left with few alternatives other than to seek out an individual entrepreneur who is willing to provide the venture capital.

Most Canadian universities have little experience in capitalizing on their research in this way. Yet new ventures are often the most appropriate means of putting new technology on the market. It follows, then, that education and research in new technology should include some training in entrepreneurship and preparation for starting new business enterprises. Such education and training can be done most effectively in conjunction with an innovative environment in which new enterprises are actually being created. Obviously the enterprises that would likely emerge from within a university would be technologically based, but they are precisely the ones that have the most potential to create social progress and employment. Indeed Zschau, Chairman of the Capital Formation Task Force of the American Electronics Association, has stated that an AEA survey revealed:

> 'the importance of young companies in solving the nation's unemployment problem. It shows that young companies create jobs much faster than mature companies.
>
> 'If we divide the companies in the sample into four categories — "Mature" (more than 20 years old), "teenage" (between 10 and 20 years old), "developing" (5 to 10 years old), and "start-up" (less than five years old) — the survey shows that the employment growth rate in 1976 for the teenage companies was about 20–40 times the growth rate in employment for mature companies. The development companies had an employment growth rate in 1976 that was nearly 55 times the growth rate in employment for the mature companies, and the employment growth rate for the start-ups in 1976 was 115 times that for mature companies.
>
> 'Even more startling is the fact that although the mature companies have on the average 27 times more employees than the young companies founded since 1955, in 1976 these young companies created an average of 89 new jobs per company versus an average of only 69 new jobs per mature company.'[9]

While these figures are for the United States, there is no reason to believe that the results would be greatly different in Canada or in other developed countries given the same opportunities.

At the University of Waterloo one can identify twenty-five companies which have been formed over the past few years by members and former members of the University (both faculty and students) who were enabled to do so by their research or other association with the University. Even more 'spin-off' companies might have been formed if the University had been more formally and effectively organized to support and encourage such developments, especially those based on new technology arising from research carried out in the University's laboratories.

In this context the 'innovation centre' concept seems worthy of development in Canada and perhaps elsewhere. It offers new avenues for the transfer of technology developed within the university to the market-place, and new opportunities for students, faculty or staff to establish their own businesses based on the new technology and to develop their entrepreneurial skills. Innovation centres already exist on an experimental basis in the United States. In June 1973 the National Science Foundation sponsored experimental innovation centres at three universities—Massachusetts Institute of Technology, Carnegie-Mellon University and the University of Oregon. The hypothesis of the innovation centre experiment is 'that formal training and experience in the process of becoming a technological entrepreneur will increase the quality of performance and quantity of students becoming successful technological entrepreneurs and concurrently increase the rate of introduction of new technology into the market-place'.[2]

A review of the innovation centre experiment after four years of operation indicated that (by January 1977) more than '700 entrepreneur-oriented students enrolled in 26 new venture courses, 53 faculty members and 46 community associates [were] participating in the experiment at the three universities. As a result of this participation, since 1973, 27 new products have been developed and 29 new venture businesses have been staffed with 33 Centre-trained entrepreneurs, having a total gross sale of $30 million in 1976. Almost 800 new jobs will have been created as a result of this performance . . .'.[2]

The MIT centre is involved in the establishment of new companies in which students or former students are the entrepreneurs in the development of new products in response to a specific need, with industry support, and in the licensing of developed inventions to existing businesses. Carnegie-Mellon's University Center for Entrepreneurial Development serves as an incubator for new business start-ups with a focus on technology transfer through entrepreneurship.[2]

These are serious attempts at making entrepreneurship an important outcome of university education. And they do succeed. A report by A. D. Little Limited on 'New Technology-Based Firms' has shown that many technological firms active today in the United States did not exist 20–30 years ago. 'The process of creating the next generation of technology-based firms must be carried on continuously in order to ensure the development of major new industries in the future.'[2]

Closely related to the 'innovation centres' concept, indeed an expansion of it, is the establishment of small business development centres at several universities in the United States. The successful launching of a new company based on new technology requires assistance from the business as well as the technological point of view. As Peterson[7] has pointed out, the linking of universities with business and industry through the small business development centre (and the innovation centre) is like the 'highly successful coupling of Faculties of Agriculture and agri-business some one hundred years ago'.

The idea of the innovation centre and the small business development centre, both closely associated with one or more universities, clearly offers a whole new dimension in education and service to industry through technology transfer, entrepreneurial training and the encouragement of new business ventures. Furthermore, by this means a giant step can be taken toward bridging the gap between the theory of the classroom and university laboratory and the reality of the business and industrial world.[3]

Inventors' Assistance

Obviously not all of the new technology and inventions occur within the university. Yet the university can provide a service to those inventors outside the university. Each year unknown hundreds of inventions never get beyond the 'idea' stage for lack of capital or even the confidence on the part of the inventor that the invention has potential.

I wish to mention two university programmes currently in operation to assist inventors. The University of Oregon Experimental Center for the Advancement of Invention and Innovation is under the direction of the College of Business Administration. Its focus is on idea and invention evaluation and upon transfer of technology to the entrepreneurial and corporate sectors.[4] Anyone can take a new product to the centre where students and faculty evaluate the product's potential market, costs and profits, and recommend procedures for marketing it.

The Inventor's Assistance programme offered by the University of Waterloo since 1976 and funded by Canada Patents and Development Corporation (a Crown Corporation), is unique in Canada. The programme provides an inventor (for a fixed fee) with an evaluation of an invention in terms of whether it merits the investment of time, money and effort in further development. As might be expected many of the inventions evaluated are judged to be unworthy of further investment. Of the 571 enquiries received by the Waterloo Inventor's Assistance office between April, 1976, and September, 1977, 167 actually registered and paid the fixed fee for evaluation, and of that number 108 have been evaluated. Of the 108, five have been evaluated as 'good'.[8] Often the inventor of a 'good' invention lacks the resources for further development. In such instances the University may join with the inventor in developing the invention.

Conclusion

The opportunities for direct service by universities to industry, business and society in general, have never been more evident nor have the needs ever been more urgent. I have reviewed some of the opportunities and some of the mechanisms that have been proposed and developed by some universities to meet these new challenges.

I do not suggest that all faculty and students should be involved in this extended role of the university. Many will not be interested in working at the interface of technology transfer or in entrepreneurial activity. Such people will continue (quite rightly) the research and scholarly activity that have been traditional in a university and which must continue if the university is to remain strong and vibrant. The presence of the 'traditional' scholars in the university is the best insurance that it does not stray too far in a 'non-academic' direction.

At the same time the benefits that accrue from the encouragement of technology transfer, entrepreneurship and new ventures development are large and real. The university has an obligation to support those whose 'bent' is in this direction, not for themselves but for the substantial benefits to society that can be derived therefrom.

While continuing its traditional roles undiminished, the university must serve the new realities of modern society. New services to industry and business and to the national economies of the kind I have discussed in this paper challenge our ingenuity and should excite our imagination.

REFERENCES

1. Ashby, Eric. Adapting Universities to a Technological Society, Jossey-Bass, London, 1974.

2. Burger, R. M. An Analysis of the National Science Foundation Innovation Center Experiment, Research Triangle Institute, North Carolina, July 1977.

3. Colton, Robert M. and Udell, Gerald G. The National Science Foundation's Innovation Centers—An experiment in training potential entrepreneurs and innovators, Journal of Small Business Management, Vol. 14, No. 2, p. 11, April 1976.

4. Holmes, E. L. Technology Transfer from Universities, Canadian Research, May/June 1976, pp. 33–34.

5. Science Council of Canada. Technology Transfer: Government Laboratories to Manufacturing Industry. Report No. 24, December 1975.

6. SCITEC. From Laboratory to Marketplace, Brief to Privy Council Office of the Government of Canada, February 1978.

SUB-TOPIC 4(C): DIRECT SERVICES TO INDUSTRY [*Matthews*]

7. Peterson, Rein. Small Business: Building a Balanced Economy, Press Porcepic, Erin, Ontario, p. 192, September 1977.
8. Phripp, D. Frank. Progress Report on Inventor's Assistance Program, Office of Research Administration, University of Waterloo, September 1977.
9. Zschau, Edwin V. W. Statement before (US) Senate Committee on Small Business, February 1978.

DISCUSSION

Sir George Kenyon (Manchester—for paper, see above) stressed the two direct services traditionally provided by British universities to industry.

(i) *Contract research*. This takes place to a smaller or larger extent in all universities in the United Kingdom; variations occur according to the type of industry located in the neighbourhood of the university. In particular, the new technologically-based universities have made great efforts to contact and co-operate with local industry.

(ii) *Provision of trained manpower*. Given that industry comprises so much more in its totality than just high technology-based manufacturing, Sir George said that graduates in all disciplines can secure jobs in industry if they have an interest in the industry and if they are of good quality. In his experience, the graduate requires a year or so to become established in industry. However, following this transition, the university graduate proves far more useful and advances more rapidly than the non-graduate. Certainly sandwich, or co-operative, programmes help a graduate to settle into industry more rapidly and an engineering student has more knowledge of industry. However neither of these factors is a necessary condition for employment in industry.

Sir George concluded by repeating his warning that, if high quality graduates come in increasing numbers into industry, society must recognize that this implies high standards and, possibly, 'élitism' which may or may not be acceptable to society.

Professor E. B. Kwakye (Kumasi—for paper, see above) outlined the industrial situation in Ghana and the work of his university in relation to this situation. The university is directly involved, under contract, in solving problems of maintenance of technological equipment and in evolving traditional crafts into technical processes of use in industry.

Dr. B. C. Matthews (Waterloo—for paper, see above) outlined work at the University of Waterloo in contract research and joint consortia with industry. He argued that he saw this type of activity not as being in competition with the traditional work of universities but as an extension of the role of the university in the community. In his view the moves towards 'innovation centres', where the raw technological research results produced in the university or elsewhere could be developed into marketable

TOPIC 4: THE PUBLIC VIEW OF THE UNIVERSITIES

products, were a natural extension of university-community involvement and a step already recognized by the Canadian government as worthy of support. He concluded by reiterating that, in his view, the thrust in these directions in recent years will enrich the universities, assist and support industry, and, in developing new processes, will create jobs and thus benefit the nation.

Professor K. V. Sivayya (Andhra) asked why no mention of agriculture had been made in the papers. He wondered how universities, particularly in developing countries, can assist their agricultural industry. Sir George Kenyon answered that he had regarded agriculture as outside his brief. However he pointed out that, in helping the manufacturing industry, for example, universities helped to support producers of agricultural equipment. Dr. Matthews had not mentioned agriculture because, in Canada, collaboration between universities and the agricultural community was of long standing and far ahead of university–industry collaboration. Indeed in some respects the present work with industry at the University of Waterloo was an attempt to catch up with what traditionally was done by agriculturalists in Canadian universities.

Mr. J. Chadwick (Commonwealth Foundation) confirmed Professor Kwayke's account of the industrial work underway at Kumasi and suggested that it could serve as a model for any university in an economically developing country. He suggested that international funding organizations, for example the Commonwealth Fund for Technical Co-operation, should be approached, if necessary through his own Foundation, so that publicity could be given to this type of work and encouragement given to others to follow the Kumasi example.

Professor J. C. Levy (City) suggested that an example of direct service to industry not yet mentioned was the provision of advanced courses. There was, however, a dilemma. Universities sought to provide one- or two-year programmes leading to master's degrees. However industry preferred short courses of one or two weeks' duration. Was the answer systematized, part-time degree programmes and, if so, would industry be willing to release qualified employees on a part-time basis and would government encourage this by paying fees and other costs? Sir George Kenyon replied that, in his experience of business schools, the answer was concentrated courses of about three months' duration. These appeared acceptable to industry. He also commented that the two-year master's programmes were being taken up quite adequately by immediate postgraduates.

Professor N. M. Swani (Indian Institute of Technology, Delhi) spoke of the wide gap between scientific attitudes and work in Indian universities, and field practice in his country. He felt that developed countries which had experience with the rapid transfer of technological innovation from research laboratory to practice could be of service to developing countries. They could assist in the design of a strategy to bridge the gap and accelerate the transfer of technology from universities in developing countries to the rest of the community.

Professor R. N. Haszeldine (Manchester, Institute of Science and Technology) asked if the University of Waterloo provided money for the

SUB-TOPIC 4(C): DIRECT SERVICES TO INDUSTRY

establishment of companies. Dr. Matthews replied in the negative. Laboratories and equipment are provided, but no money. The individual faculty member must raise the funds, where necessary, outside the university.

Sir Frank Hartley (London) asked a question related to the problem of patenting. There is not only the cost of establishing a patent, but also the cost of financing the inevitable gap between the invention and commercial exploitation. How had the University of Waterloo solved that problem? Dr. Matthews replied that in the first place, as a matter of policy, all rights to any discovery were given over to the individual who made the discovery. The university joined with individuals in sharing costs if necessary to obtain a patent, or encouraged the individual to obtain financial support from the Canadian Patent Development Agency Limited, a federal government organization. Sir George Kenyon agreed that the gap in time referred to by Sir Frank Hartley was indeed a problem. He was hoping to persuade large British companies to give financial and appropriate expert assistance to individual inventors faced with a need for time to develop their work in this way.

Professor R. E. Bogner (Adelaide) wondered how best to train an engineer for industry. Should there be a concentration on depth of study? Should breadth of knowledge and experience be stressed? Should humanities courses be added to the professional programme?

Sir George Kenyon drew attention to the new four-year courses recently begun in Britain. A selected number of universities were being asked by government to enrol prospective engineering graduates on special scholarships and to train them for industry in the broadest possible sense. These programmes used the extra time available to add training in managerial skills to the particular engineering courses being taken by these students.

In closing, the Chairman made a plea to developed countries not to add to the problems of developing countries by supporting students from these countries in work that is irrelevant to the real life in their home countries. The communications gap referred to by Professor Swani (Indian Institute of Technology, Delhi) was a very real one and could only be exacerbated by this kind of training.

Topic 4

THE PUBLIC VIEW OF THE UNIVERSITIES

Continuation of Discussion

Chairman: Dr. J. W. O'BRIEN
Rector and Vice-Chancellor of Concordia University

Rapporteur: Dr. A. J. EARP
President and Vice-Chancellor of Brock University

Thursday, 24 August

The fourth session on the main topic provided for further discussion of the subjects raised in the previous sessions. Mr. J. E. Madocks (Nottingham) launched the discussion by offering a mnemonic based on Vancouver, the name of the host city (vivacity/values; access; news; character; open-mindedness; universality; validity; education; reconciliation/reaffirmation). Mr. Madocks related the various strands from the previous dicussions to a central theme, suggesting that the group was introspective rather than reflecting upon the public view of universities. He stressed the need for universities to talk to their various publics in terms they understand.

Lord Hunter (Birmingham) warned of the dangers of élitism, of knowing what is best for others. Universities should examine society's suggestions humbly and objectively and must not expect to be placed upon a pedestal on the strength of the very few brilliant scholars who dwell within them. Dr. D. W. Bain (Lincoln College) expressed disappointment that the programme did not include speakers from outside the university community (*e.g.* a trade union secretary). He urged the universities to concern themselves with what non-academics feel about the institutions and to expand their public relations services.

Dr. J. A. Corry (Canada) suggested that, in Canada at least, the public's view of universities is not determined on the basis of what the universities are doing but rather by the public's judgement of their product. The situation has changed enormously in the past half-century. Fifty years ago there were few graduates and they were looked up to by the public. Now there are many graduates and the public has discovered that they are not very different people from the rest of society. Dr. Corry suggested that the prestige of the university in the larger community varies inversely with the number of graduates in that community.

Dr. W. C. Winegard (Ontario Council on University Affairs) pointed out that universities can benefit from the period of benign neglect by government that they are experiencing. Rather than dwell upon this situation the universities should get on with their job and do it well.

Professor D. R. Stranks (Adelaide) maintained that the public is very much influenced by the university. He believed that graduates do have a positive impact upon the community. Universities are an important part of the fabric of the community, essential for its development and evolution, and they are not a peripheral activity. He remarked that universities are not very proficient at knowing about the research going on within their own walls. They must rectify this situation and then describe their research projects to the community in palatable terms. Faculty is also an important source of expert advice to governments, corporations and others, and the service they provide to the community is real. The universities are also an important facet of the general cultural life of the community.

Dr. G. D. Saunders (Griffith) said that he thought it was well that emperors and vice-chancellors were seen on occasion without their clothes and he questioned the use of the vocabulary of power. He regretted the 'we/they' dichotomy and felt that the old myths of the separate nature of the university die hard. He commented that the sheer number of university graduates makes the university very clearly a part of the community.

Dr. B. C. Matthews (Waterloo) reminded the group that the public consists of many minorities: he identified such segments as politicians, alumni, parents. The universities cannot approach all of them in the same way. He felt it important for universities to reach the opinion-makers, the senior echelons of business and labour. He reported that he had found advisory committees a helpful mechanism in this regard.

Dr. W. F. Hitschfeld (McGill) stressed that professors should be competent on an international scale, must be able to project their competence, and apply it in the communities they serve.

The Rt. Rev. Dr. E. R. Wickham (Salford) suggested that the public was kind to universities because of a certain modesty on the part of these institutions, and less kind about the institutions with which they were more familiar, such as schools and hospitals. Self-criticism must arise within the university and he wondered whether it was undertaken with sufficient stringency.

Dr. V. C. Kulandaiswamy (Madurai) pointed out that in developing countries education is one major tool of economic development. Universities must play a more aggressive role as instruments of change in the developing world. Extension education has been effective in the field of agriculture; however, it is as important in the solution of social problems. Education standards may be similar throughout the world, but the application of them will differ. There should be both universal and local components in one discipline.

Professor E. B. Kwakye (Kumasi) returned to the issues of relevance and competence. Universities have an international role and therefore an even

TOPIC 4: THE PUBLIC VIEW OF THE UNIVERSITIES

wider responsibility than those already mentioned. Universities in the developed countries have a responsibility to those in developing countries, even if the developing countries, in the eyes of the developed world, represent constituencies of non-voters and non-tax-payers. There exists a broader responsibility to humanity as a whole.

Dr. R. L. Huang (U. of Hong Kong) reminded the group that there are some parts of the Commonwealth where the need to heed the public's view of universities is not so strongly felt as the universities become increasingly an arm of government. A decision laboriously arrived at in senate may be reversed by a single telephone call. Reaction to universities based upon colonial models might be partly responsible; but he felt there has been a tendency for universities in these countries to become too utilitarian and too politicized.

Professor V. K. S. Nayar (Kerala) said that in India, apart from questions of certification, the public was not widely interested in the orderly functioning of the university. Attention might be attracted in the press to the university if the vice-chancellor was rendered inoperative by a phalanx of students packed around him! Professor Nayar felt that there was a need to stress the role of the university in the process of development and this was a responsibility of faculty as well as of the vice-chancellor.

Professor J. M. Ham (Toronto) expressed reservations about the value of organized public relations. Universities will be known by their graduates. Relevance is not something that is imposed; instead it must come out of qualities of conscience and character. He commented that universities were becoming more concerned about certifying than civilizing. He pointed out that Canada is still developing. There is a danger in trying to make our universities perform functions which more properly belong outside the university. The relationship with industry was symbiotic; however, universities should carry their capabilities to industry.

Sir George Kenyon (Manchester) drew upon his own wide industrial experience in many countries of the Commonwealth to say that high technology industry does its own applied research. However small problems can be isolated and given to postgraduate students. In respect of public relations, he felt the group was too introspective. He cautioned that people will only take an interest in what interests them. Dr. H. Kay (Exeter) concurred, reminding the discussants that the public has always been ambivalent toward universities. Sir Theodor Bray (Griffith) pointed out that since universities are financed by public funds their public image will be increasingly important. He supported strong public relations departments within universities. Dr. P. P. M. Meincke (Prince Edward Island) said that if the public view of universities is incorrect it is a responsibility of the universities to point this out as part of their commitment to the truth.

Returning to the subject of direct services to industry, Dr. G. E. Connell (Western Ontario) asked to what extent a university can make commitments to industry without encountering administrative and other conflicts at a future date. Where does service to industry fall in a list of the priorities of the institution and of the individual faculty member? Can

CONTINUATION OF DISCUSSION

universities really exercise the kind of corporate discipline necessary to meet these commitments? Is there a basic issue of academic freedom involved? It was agreed that there are difficulties involved. Nonetheless this is a valid activity for a university and there will always be faculty interested in and committed to this function.

Group Discussions

TOPIC 5

UNIVERSITIES AND OTHER INSTITUTIONS OF TERTIARY EDUCATION

Chairman: Dr C.-M. LI
Vice-Chancellor of the Chinese University of Hong Kong

Editorial Co-ordinator: Mr. M. S. RAMAMURTHY
Secretary of the Association of Indian Universities

		page
Sub-Topic 5(a)	DIFFERENTIATION OF ROLES BETWEEN DIFFERENT INSTITUTIONS OF HIGHER EDUCATION	
	Opening Speakers	
	Sir Frederick Dainton	491
	Professor P. H. Karmel	504
	Professor J.-G. Paquet	511
Sub-Topic 5(b)	PROBLEMS OF CHOICE BETWEEN DIFFERENT INSTITUTIONS	
	Opening Speakers	
	Sir Walter Perry	516
	Mr. W. G. Pitman	533
Sub-Topic 5(c)	PROBLEMS OF TRANSFER AND COMMUNICATION AMONG DIFFERENT INSTITUTIONS	
	Opening Speakers	
	Sir Charles Carter	539
	Dr. L. Isabelle	544
	Mr. A. Z. Preston	552
Topic 5	DISCUSSION	567

For index to names, see p. 655

Sub-Topic 5(a)

DIFFERENTIATION OF ROLES BETWEEN DIFFERENT INSTITUTIONS OF HIGHER EDUCATION

Chairman: Dr. C. -M. LI
Vice-Chancellor of the Chinese University of Hong Kong

Rapporteur: Professor G. D. SIMS
Vice-Chancellor of the University of Sheffield

Monday, 21 August

Professor Sir FREDERICK DAINTON (*Chairman of the University Grants Committee, UK*):

I. *Introduction*

This is a very timely subject for the conference to have on its agenda if only because we have already burnt our fingers once when higher education was expanded dramatically in the sixties without any fundamental change in curriculum content or in the structure of the institutions (with the exception in Britain of the Open University as an example of the application of technology to the distant teaching of adults). We spent the vastly increased resources quickly as well as we knew how, which in fact meant simply expanding or replicating with minor modification universities of the kind we already had and were accustomed to, without ever considering whether the traditional functions of the university would suffice to serve society in the future as they had in the past.

No one can say for certain why governments were willing to make resources available at that time for this particular purpose. No doubt there were many contributory reasons. There was for example the notion that higher education in itself was a 'good thing'; that it would somehow improve society by increasing individual perceptions of its nature, that it would promote social mobility, add to personal growth, etc., etc.; and that, as Aristotle wrote, 'all men desire to know' and that the gratification of this desire was virtuous in itself. But governments also felt that it would be somehow financially advantageous in Britain, that it would fan the flames of the 'white-hot technological revolution' on which economic success was supposed to be critically dependent. Finally there was the evident demand from school-leavers to go on to higher education in what seemed to be ever-increasing proportions. In Britain we had our justificatory tablets of stone in the form of the Robbins report and even before the issue of that report government had already been advised by the UGC that it was necessary to create more universities.

Then came the actuality, which has made many people consider whether so rapid an expansion was wise. Students expressed their discontents, real or imaginary, in unacceptable and sometimes violent ways; faculty became unionised to an increasing degree, a process which called in question the very idea of professional commitment; everyone wanted to get in on the act of university government and the slogan 'participation' (Mitbestimmung) became a substitute for real thought about the purposes of universities and how these should be served, etc., etc. The disillusion of our political masters coincided with the onset of world economic crisis which provided the excuse for governments to demote higher education in priority compared with other pressing social problems such as inflation and unemployment—especially amongst youth.

Now, in our 'winter of discontent', it is time to see what new forms of higher education, what mutation, ought to be induced to flower in whatever chilly spring lies ahead. Old roles must be re-examined, scrutinised for possible future relevance, and possible new roles weighed in the balance for their value. Before doing this it is worth pausing briefly to learn from the history of the evolution of the universities in western civilisation, if only to avoid making the same mistakes again. The first point to emerge is that history teaches us that the purposes of universities can change because they have done so in the past.

The universities of the Commonwealth are the inheritors of a tradition going back seven-and-a-half centuries to Oxford and Cambridge universities which aimed to provide a common social, moral and intellectual experience for the sons of the ruling class and to provide training for the great professions of the law, the church and, latterly, medicine. The content of the curriculum was less important than the mental discipline it developed and its value as a vehicle for instilling moral and intellectual values. Not that those two universities always lived up to these high ideals! In the year that the founding fathers of the American revolution were working out the American constitution Edward Gibbon was constrained to refer to his own education in the following words: 'To the University of Oxford I acknowledge no obligation and she will as willingly renounce me for a son as I am willing to disclaim her as a mother. I spent 14 months at Magdalen College; they proved the 14 months, the most idle and unprofitable in my whole life'.

But by this time Scotland had its own four ancient universities the graduates of which, as 'dominies' in both rural and urban schools, had implanted a desire for higher education and a high degree of literacy in their pupils. There were no religious tests for university admission, access was both open and public and the universities emphasized practical subjects such as economics, medicine, law and divinity so that professors were valued for what they knew about their subject and the test of the professor's competence was the student's willingness to attend and pay his fee. Many years were to elapse before the achievements of the movement for non-sectarian higher education in England could match the accomplishment of Scottish universities. Only in 1826 was University College, London, founded. Today, one and a half centuries later, the only test to enter British universities is the assessment by the admissions tutor of the suitability of the applicant to profit from study at the university.

The idea of research as an integral part of university work entered British universities by a somewhat circuitous route. Its origin lay in the Humboldtian revolution in Germany which stressed scientifically conducted enquiry—even in the humanities—which aimed to enlarge and advance knowledge. The main aim of the professor was first to do research, secondly to publish and then, almost as an afterthought, to certify those who came to study with him as competent to enter certain respectable careers. Meanwhile the British universities went on their own tranquil way adhering to the ideals that seemed to them to be everlasting. It was not so in America. The land-grant colleges and state universities exemplified the adoption of the Scottish 'practical service' ideal. Research was perceived to be the working capital of the society, an investment in the development of America, and the idea that there should be research in universities became very pervasive not only in the state universities but also in the Ivy Leage colleges and created an entirely new structure of prestige which in turn led to the graduate schools and the structured PhD. In due course in the early part of this century, and in part impelled by the desire of colonial graduates to have some qualification after study in British universities, research as a *necessary* activity of British universities became firmly established.

The result today of this historical process and of the export of the British model is that within the Commonwealth we now see a great diversity of institutions serving many ends. They differ as to whether they are monotechnic or polytechnic, whether there is open access or selection at entry, whether the age participation rate is high (mass higher education) or small (élitist), whether the institution is small (measured in one or two thousand students) or large (measured in almost a hundred thousand), whether it is urban or rural in its location, whether it has great professional schools or not, whether it offers specific community services like extra-mural education; and they also vary enormously in the emphasis which is given to research.

II. *What Nations Will Expect from Their Systems of Higher Education?*

If this question had been put to academics in the last two decades the most common brief answer would have been 'the transmission, conservation, re-valuation (scholarship) and advancement (research) of knowledge'. But this will no longer satisfy the government as paymaster. Greater precision of functions is demanded, various categories of students need to be specified and catered for, research is no longer a completely self-justifying activity and each country perceives a different set of needs and possesses different resources with which to meet them.

May I spend a little time on this last point because within the Commonwealth we have as wide a range of countries in terms of degrees of economic and educational development as exist in the world, and the Commonwealth is a not very small microcosm of a world which I believe now faces a global watershed. The question of paramount importance is how to come to terms with our resources of energy and raw materials, *i.e.* how to achieve a rate of utilizing them which, allowing for recycling, does not lead humankind to a catastrophe in the twenty-first century when some essential component for which there is no substitute falls to an intolerable level, and how to use these resources without producing damaging environmental changes which go beyond the capacity of nature to repair. Ultimately this means nothing less than a limitation of human population and, because the only birth control method which works in democracies is that based on the raising of the standard of living to a level at which the potential parents realise that a plentitude of children is not essential to their own survival, every effort must be made to raise the standard of living to a point at which all man's biophysical needs are met. In Europe, Australia, New Zealand and North America all man's biophysical needs and most of his psycho-social needs are already met, whilst those of the third world are not. These facts lead to two corollaries: (i) that every help must be given to accelerate the increase of the standard of living of the 'have-nots' and (ii) that the 'haves' will move into the post-industrial society of Daniel Bell in which the creation of necessary goods and services will occupy less time thereby creating an opportunity to become 'learning societies'. At that stage further massive developments in education, especially adult education, can be foreseen as probable.

Thus higher education will have widely different emphases in the societies at each end of the economic spectrum and governments are likely to make these emphases explicit. This is the first differentiation of roles.

III. *Multiple Roles*

With this as a background let us now traverse the many possible purposes which institutions of higher education in the Commonwealth ought now be called upon to serve.

(i) The liberal education of selected 18-year-olds will remain a major objective in the wealthy countries but it may be questioned whether the same priority will be accorded to it in the poorer countries. It will still be true that the style of this education may be more important than the subject content; the aim being to implant in the student a lifelong desire for learning, objectivity in analysis, the power of critical examination of data and opinions and certain human values, so that he or she is a better citizen as well as helping to discover his/her own powers and limitations.

(ii) The continuing education of adults for their own personal growth and satisfaction. Again this may be of low priority in the third world and of higher priority in the wealthy nations. For these students the learning centre will necessarily be their home or near their home so that the institution cannot be a traditional university—though it may be an outpost of one. For most of the year the teaching is bound to make use of modern electronic devices to bring the information and learning materials into the home but, to avoid the problems of the isolation of the student, a local community centre or college will need to be provided.

(iii) Professional and vocational training will continue to have a very important place at the undergraduate (full-time and part-time including sandwich) and postgraduate (full-time and part-time 'end-on') levels. Universities may also be called upon to provide more extensively for part-time, post-experience short courses for re-training and/or re-orientation so that employed adults can meet their own career development needs and face successfully the rapid pace of technological change. Again the emphasis in the less developed countries will be greater on the undergraduate work and more on the postgraduate and re-treading in-service work in the highly developed countries.

(iv) As always, institutions will carry a responsibility for and be judged by the quality of their products. Certification of students in the above categories will continue to be a task which, however, may be discharged in a variety of ways, other than the presently prevailing methods of examination.

(v) Some nations may set additional goals for their higher education; for example, the relief of social stresses and personal injustice to disadvantaged (ethnic or otherwise) minorities for whom the school system has failed to compensate. How this is to be accomplished is another matter. For my own part I see little value in 'affirmative action' if it involves the admission of students who are ill-prepared educationally to benefit, but it may be that unless special remedial facilities are provided elsewhere the universities will have to perform this function themselves.

(vi) The activity we call 'research' if pursued for its own sake, *i.e.* merely with the object of advancing knowledge and understanding and to satisfy curiosity, requires not only long training and high ability on the part of the researcher and easy access to the means for his research (libraries, apparatus and materials) but also a supportive atmosphere which is not authoritarian or censorious and which is conducive to able minds to range over any part of knowledge which they deem worthy of their attention. For this reason, the university is the ideal environment for most researchers and one can safely predict that universities will want to remain the home of 'basic', 'self-chosen' or 'curiosity-oriented' research. But if, as Whitehead said: 'education is the acquisition of the art of the utilization of knowledge', then societies will also expect their universities to contain men and women skilled in the use as well as the acquisition of knowledge, and will remit to their universities certain research tasks. The way in which this is done without distorting the major purposes of the university is a matter of some delicacy which I cannot discuss now. I merely wish to register that there are problems here particularly when that research is in politically sensitive areas such as the social sciences or defence. But that universities should think about these problems and also make what contributions they can to the use of knowledge by society I have no doubt, and in the less advanced countries universities may expect to play a much larger role in applied research than might be thought reasonable in more advanced countries.

(vii) For somewhat similar reasons the universities will continue to be the home of scholarship, not only preserving the cultural heritage but also re-interpreting past values and their contemporary relevance. The more relevant the universities are the more likely they are to question established ideas and it will be a test of future societies that they can tolerate the inevitable criticism which must flow from the questioning of past values. To preserve their freedom to perform this critical role universities will need to show great sense of responsibility, otherwise the right to it may be endangered.

IV. *External Forces: The Government as Paymaster, Planner and Political Potentiator*

Peter Karmel was 'quicker on the draw' than I, sending me the outline of his talk (*see* p. 504) which placed the topic in the context of a comprehensive list of seemingly antagonistic functions to be performed within higher education. Whilst I should wish to comment on some of them a little later in this talk, before I do so I would like to discuss how any changes of role are likely to be initiated. Universities are self-governing institutions and have freedom to change many things themselves but it would be idle to pretend that any major redistribution of functions is not the business of government and therefore it is timely to ask what trends are to be discerned in the thinking of governments about higher education in the future.

Although the degree of local control of schools varies from country to country all governments have a near monopoly of financial responsibility for schools and further education. During this century the universities have likewise moved into the position where they derive most of their financial support in one way or another from the government and it is not surprising therefore that voices are heard calling for 'bringing the universities under proper democratic control'. Different meanings are attached to these words by different people. Leaving aside the question of mere financial accountability there are other accountabilities which the government may seek to impose on universities and other attitudes towards universities which the government may articulate and in the last analysis base their policy. It is therefore worth giving this some consideration.

All governments want value for money; by which they generally mean graduates at the lowest possible cost whose training nevertheless makes a contribution either to the economy by their subsequent employment in manufacturing industry or commerce or to the service industries (administration, local or national, health and social services, education, etc.). There are, of course, dangers here in that this attitude leads some legislators to ignore some important values. As an example I quote from a report of a recent speech: 'I cannot see why an ONC student [ONC is a qualification earned in a further education college to prepare a person to be a technician] in chemistry would only be entitled to a small discretionary (maintenance) award while some *obscure* student studying an *obscure* subject in an *obscure* university should be eligible for a mandatory award'. This remark, even allowing for the language of the impending hustings, smacks of obscurantism as well as exemplifying an extreme form of the utilitarian approach. In passing it is interesting to reflect that if the Aristotelian definition of education, 'enabling a man to make a right judgement in all things', is valid, then possibly the most valuable thing for society that universities can do is to help students to acquire this judgemental quality.

In a democracy estimates of expenditure in higher education no less than in any other field of government spending must be laid before parliament and justified by some kind of statement of the purposes for which the money is to be spent. Government is therefore actively involved in higher educational planning. This is bound to involve some consideration of manpower needs (to which subject I shall return a little later) leading to the setting of targets of student numbers, to the allocation of resources to meet these needs and, inevitably, to the kinds of institutions that should be established or modified to perform the different perceived functions. In this situation autonomous institutions can either submit passively to government diktat or, at an earlier stage, contribute from their own knowledge and experience to the shaping of opinion on some of these issues before decisions are reached. The latter is the better course and for this reason I should now like to turn to some problems all of which bear on the possible differentiation of roles of institutions and upon which I hope the university voice will be heard.

V. *Manpower Planning Revisited*

There is a temptation to governments to look on universities as factories manufacturing intellect workers—indeed the Swedish law U.68 expresses this explicitly. Even if governments do not succumb to temptation to this extent they are likely to wish to justify their expenditure on the basis of target student numbers in particular categories and for this they need some underlying rationale. Although nearly every manpower plan which has been invented has been invalidated by history, the lure of manpower planning as a siren song is one which some latterday Ulysses seem incapable of resisting. If universities are to escape from the rigidities which the manpower planners might seek to impose then it is important that they understand (*a*) why manpower planning cannot succeed in a mixed economy and (*b*) be ready with an alternative strategy which will give a better result.

Manpower planners aim to match the supply of qualified people to the demand for them. A 'perfect match' means that over a period of time (*a*) the annual output of higher educational graduates in each subject category matches exactly the number of new jobs available for that year and (*b*) that the stock of qualified manpower is all employed on tasks for which the higher educational training has been a uniquely appropriate preparation. Because employers cannot foresee their individual needs for a sufficient number of years ahead, because these needs are subject to fluctuation caused by technological change, international influences such as cartels, competition and world economic trends, a genuine national need cannot be specified sufficiently far ahead or reliably for adjustments to be made to the supply system in time. Even if that adjustment were possible a consideration of the flow of students through school into higher education and the choices which they make en route, as well as the allowances which have to be made for emigration and immigration, show that precise steering of the educational system is almost unattainable. Elsewhere I have shown that if one sets up the differential equations for the network of the interacting sub-systems with different variable time constants which bear some relation to reality, it would be miraculous if perfect match were achieved, even momentarily. Moreover even in those systems in which there is not a mixed economy, for example where the state is the sole employer of, say, teachers or doctors or social workers, attempts to get a good fit have in the past not been notably successful.

The better strategy is based on the recognition that the best guidance system of all is that of the intelligent young person faced with choices, but armed by as much information as can be produced about probable trends, plus an education which for most will inculcate adaptability, flexibility and the recognition of the need to continue learning and to embark upon retraining as and when necessary. The moral of this for universities is that, except for a small proportion of high specialists who will mainly be in the postgraduate field or in professional schools, curricular rigidities should be avoided and, equally, physical plant must be planned in such a way that it can be adapted for varying uses as needs change. The achievement of this flexibility is going to be very difficult when higher education is not expanding and this raises a series of issues the discussion of which could occupy a session in itself.

VI. *Influential Trends in Western Society*

In the previous two sections I have mentioned the government in its role of paymaster and scientific manpower planner but it is also a significant force shaping and reflecting trends in modern society, of which the universities must take cognisance. Two such trends could have powerful effects on the directions which different institutions of higher education might take, and both trends are derived from a supposed alienation of citizens in large countries from central government and represent attempts to bring power nearer to the people.

The first of these is the tendency of governments to devolve power for certain of their functions to regional authorities and there is no doubt that some of the protagonists of this devolution of authority consider that universities should be owned, financially supported and managed on a local basis. Whilst this may be satisfactory for institutions of higher education that serve purely local purposes and train people who will spend most of their lives working locally, it is entirely unsuitable for institutions like universities for whose graduates the world is their oyster and which have international responsibilities to research and scholarship. To attempt to brigade universities in this way would be highly damaging, by forcing them into a parochialism of outlook which is the antithesis of the university ethos. It is better that the universities should be part of a national system. However this is not to say that the universities should not co-operate locally with other institutions of higher education. Indeed this is highly desirable and many benefits are to be derived therefrom, but the universities should enter co-operative agreements freely of their own will and only enter those which do not impair the performance of their national and international roles.

The second trend is that towards participatory democracy in the management of any enterprise by involving employees in decision making. Insofar as it erodes any excessive authoritarianism it helps to confer dignity and sense of self-determination on employees and can increase their commitment to the institution. But in the institutions of higher education there is a danger here of throwing out the baby with the bathwater. In the first place there is often a confusion as to where employees' inputs can be best directed and most effective. It is to my mind very unlikely that the generality of technicians and students can make a significant contribution to questions of curriculum and assessment as compared with their seniors who have studied both questions for much longer and have a lifelong commitment to teaching and certification. Moreover there is no evidence to suggest that where participatory democracy has been put into practice at the highest levels of the university (*e.g.* the Dreigruppenprinzip of German and Dutch universities) the decisions have been more rationally arrived at than under the present imperfect systems of governance. On the contrary such procedures have often led to interminable and inconclusive meetings at which voting is by sectional interest and consensus judgement rarely reached.

Nevertheless universities could derive more benefit from the very useful contributions which their employees in particular and students can make to the working of the university. Both these groups have legitimate interests in the governance of the university because this can affect them intimately, whether it affects the career development, terms of service and job satisfaction of the former or promotes or retards the approach of the students to their work. It is in the nature of these problems that they impinge more at the departmental level where many of them can be resolved by sympathetic management but there will still be a residue of issues which call for discussion and perhaps even decision at the central and highest levels of the universities.

There is nothing in the direction of these trends which distinguishes one institution of higher education from another. But those institutions which are autonomous and do not handle these problems imaginatively and successfully will strengthen the case for direct government intervention and by so doing erode their own autonomy.

VII. *Functional Symbioses and Antagonisms*

In a one-man dialectical analysis Peter Karmel (p. 504) has listed various seeming opposites. I would now like to make a few comments on some of these and add one or two more for good measure.

(i) There are many examples of single-faculty institutions, whether colleges of education or agriculture. In my experience these all suffer through lack of contact with other subjects and disciplines which is so easily avoided in a multifaculty institution. Whilst I do not share the sour critic's comment that the colleges of education admirably fulfil the purpose of training their graduates to teach successfully that which is wrong, there is some force in the criticism and it seems to me there is every advantage to be gained from having easily accessible colleagues whose business is being a specialist in a certain subject, just as it is useful for university teachers in performing their tasks to have some understanding of modes of presentation of material which facilitate rather than impede the understanding of their students.

(ii) There are some who would argue that the business of teaching 18-year-olds is so different from that of teaching adults that a different institution is required for each of these two purposes. Whilst it can reasonably be argued that people differ in their abilities to teach each of these two groups I believe that skills can often be acquired for teaching both successfully, and that the most important difference between the two is the geographical limitation which compels the adult to receive the face-to-face teaching near where he lives and therefore that adult teaching requires the use of peripatetic teachers. This is the only practical reason I know for separating the two groups. Somewhat similar arguments apply to part-time students.

More difficult problems arise over the question of selection of students. If higher education is to provide a 'second chance' for adults who miss the first chance at 18 some would argue that a period of work should replace part of the intellectual entry qualification. A closely related argument is that people who have been disadvantaged by reason of parents' income, social environment or belonging to an ethnic minority should be admitted even at the age of 18 without the necessary qualifications. Those who proposed this idea are paying more attention to the promptings of their heart than their head. I have seen too many personal tragedies arising from persons embarking upon university courses without adequate preparation (in some cases possessing the formal qualification) to wish to add to their number. On the other hand there is no doubt that there are able and worthy people who ought to go to a university but lack the necessary preparation and the question then arises as to what institution should help them get the necessary qualification. Here I find myself somewhat ambivalent; some universities have shown that they are good at providing the necessary remedial courses but there are others which cannot compare in effectiveness with the local further education college. But I am quite certain that what we least need and indeed what would be positively harmful would be to establish special higher education institutions devoted exclusively to 'second chance' students other than those like the Open University.

A special problem. Academics tend to rank universities and their colleges in order of esteem according to the perceived value and distinction of their research activities. But research costs a great deal of money and continues to increase in cost so that it is inconceivable that governments would ever be willing to pay for that amount of research to which many universities aspire. This is an area within which selection *must* be made. Questions of differentiation therefore arise which I would list as follows:—

(a) Are institutions, areas of study or people or any combination of these to be selected for long-term support?

(b) On what criteria and by whom are these choices to be made?

(c) What is and what should be the relation of teaching and research to one another at the undergraduate level and the postgraduate level?

The maintenance of excellence in research is inherent in the first question. Excellence is a quality of performance of a person as a thinker or doer, and of the quality of resources for research, and the best of both must be brought together, especially in subjects like science where the best research annihilates the good and the better. Recognition of this fact has been the principal argument advanced in favour of 'centres of excellence'. The objections to trying to plan centres of excellence are firstly that researchers do not remain excellent for ever, and that young able people, whether staff or students, may be found anywhere in the university system, and their potential contribution should not be frustrated because they do not happen to be in the centre of excellence. Perhaps a better way forward would therefore be to encourage co-operation between researchers in different universities in much the same way that the communities of high energy nuclear physicists and radio astronomers and space scientists have already achieved. Perhaps also it would be worth considering more positive policies to identify young unusually gifted staff members and give them special support during their creative periods.

It seems to be generally true that the more participatory the governance of a university the greater the tendency to egalitarian distribution of resources and the more difficult it is to acknowledge and support the excellent work of individuals. But if universities do not take a more positive line on this question then they must expect that these necessary choices will be made increasingly by outside agencies.

Postgraduate teaching and research are in general strongly mutually supportive. Whether this is so at the undergraduate level is and will continue to be a hotly debated question on which we all have our own views. I do not propose to add now to the mass of verbiage which has already been published, but I would like to stress that arguments which are acceptable within a university context are not necessarily so acceptable to our political masters. The universities would be better able to persuade the politicians if the latter saw that the universities were seriously grappling with these problems. In particular what a university said about these issues would be much more credible if the university (a) had a genuinely influential research policy committee and (b) could show that its procedures for career development of its staff took full account of the quality of the staff member as a teacher as well as a researcher, or acknowledged that he was either one or the other. I know, of course, of the supposed objectivity of assessing research performance and of the difficulty of doing the same for teaching, but with the broadening of university education which seems inevitable universities will be at risk unless they really tackle this problem — again one of differentiation.

VIII. *Conclusion*

I realise that I have given few prescriptions for the development of higher education in the future and certainly not provided any 'blueprint'. I can certainly be charged with posing more problems than proffering solutions. However I would like to conclude by stressing my preference for polytechnic rather than monotechnic institutions, and that universities should urgently examine their roles and work towards conscious inter-institutional co-operation. We have a great diversity of institutions which are self-governing and staffed by intelligent people. They have within them the capacity to change in response to what they see as national and international needs and to work out their own contributions. Failure to do so is to invite government intervention. I hope that universities will initiate their own revolutionary change, altering their purposes in a way which will ensure their survival. That the rate of change will be slower than many people who want radical reform would wish seems to me to be almost certain in a free society. But those radical reformers should learn a lesson from natural history, namely, that successive small mutations are to be preferred to large mutations which are almost invariably lethal.

Professor P. H. KARMEL (*Chairman of the Tertiary Education Commission, Australia*):

Roles of Higher Education

In broad terms higher education is concerned with the conservation, transmission and extension of knowledge. The following basic functions of higher education emerge from this proposition: —

(1) the preservation of the cultural heritage, interpreted in both national and world terms;

(2) the provision of what is traditionally known as a 'liberal' education, which is both a foundation for good citizenship and a vehicle for personal satisfaction;

(3) the production of highly qualified manpower. The provision of a liberal education provides a basic education for certain vocations, for example, political or administrative activities; in other vocations advanced specialist courses are necessary, for example, in medicine, law, engineering, etc.; and

(4) scholarly activities and research, comprising problem-oriented research and development as well as pure research and scholarship.

The above functions, although derived from the broad purposes of higher education, by no means exhaust the roles of institutions of higher education as we understand them today. Institutions of higher education exist in a social context and through their place in the wider society they have acquired functions additional to the ones listed above. Perhaps the most significant of these are: —

(5) the critical evaluation of society. Universities in western countries, for example, are often referred to as 'the community's conscience', and it is expected that at least some academics will question and oppose accepted community values and established traditions and policies;

(6) the socialisation of the individual in the ways of the particular society. To some extent this function conflicts with the previous one, but the graduates of higher education are expected to be able to operate within society as it is;

(7) community service, in terms not only of serving the local community within which an institution is located, but also of providing expert services and advice at national level to both the public and private sectors. Community service also includes the outreach of institutions into the general community in the form of extension services and continuing liberal and professional education;

(8) the function of keeping young people occupied until they are able to obtain employment. This is a custodial role, not necessarily welcomed by the institutions themselves, but one which has grown in importance as the age of entry to employment has steadily risen.

When one speaks of the purpose of *universities* it is customary to emphasise the conservation, transmission and extension of knowledge. These are thought of as being 'objective' activities in which the universities are concerned with 'seeking out the truth'. While objective enquiry should be a central value in universities and academics have a responsibility to distinguish between objective knowledge and value judgements, the broad functions of universities in conserving, transmitting and extending knowledge are undoubtedly influenced by open and hidden values. This applies to the first four functions mentioned above and is most obvious in decisions as to what constitutes a 'liberal education' and in the selection of topics for applied research and development. The second four functions are much more patently value-laden, and would clearly be interpreted differently in different social contexts. It follows that the nature of universities in one country might turn out to be very different from their nature in another, although both still conform with the functions listed above.

Differentiation of Roles

Forty years ago institutions of higher education were in the main universities and were much more homogeneous than they are today. Since the second world war there has been a great proliferation of institutions of higher education together with an enormous expansion in the number of students and significant changes in their aspirations and motivations and their educational and social backgrounds. Higher education is now much more complex and heterogeneous. The differentiation of institutions of higher education may occur in terms of one or more of a number of characteristics.

Functions. Institutions differ because they place different emphases on the functions of higher education. Institutions may place an emphasis on liberal education or on vocational training—thus the contrast between liberal arts colleges and technical training institutions. Some institutions are concerned mainly with teaching (the transmission of knowledge) rather than its extension through research or its conservation through scholarship; some institutions therefore build up vast research libraries while others provide only working collections for undergraduates. Some institutions deliberately involve themselves in applied research, developmental work and problem solving; others concentrate on pure research and scholarship. Some institutions are committed to serve their local community, others make a profession of being remote and disinterested—thus the community college contrasts with the traditional 'ivory tower' view of a university. It follows that the relative emphases placed on the eight functions listed at the beginning of the paper can produce considerable variation between institutions, all of which are concerned with higher education in one sense or another.

Courses. Institutions differ in the range of courses they offer. One normally thinks of a university as being multi-faculty and including such faculties as arts, science, education, economics, agriculture, medicine, dentistry, veterinary science, engineering, etc. However the liberal arts college is basically an arts and science institution and is clearly different in its ethos from a large multi-faculty university. Similarly, some institutions concentrate on one major vocation, for example teachers' colleges, agricultural colleges, conservatoria of music; others, such as the polytechnics, provide education and training for a number of vocations. Further, some institutions concentrate on undergraduate courses while others offer mainly postgraduate degrees.

Size. Institutions of higher education range in size from a few hundred enrolments to tens of thousands. Size itself affects the nature of institutions in terms both of the relations between teachers and students and of the management structure.

Student body. The traditional university provided full-time education. Many universities now offer courses on a part-time basis (in Australia, for example, part-time studies have been customary since the foundation of the universities). The full-time/part-time mix of the student body may be an important characteristic in differentiating institutions. Similarly some institutions offer off-campus courses (external studies) — indeed, some enrol only external students, for example, the UK Open University. Another source of differentiation relates to the age of students. Traditionally universities enrolled school-leavers and the student body was almost entirely in the age range of 17 to 22 years. Many institutions, however, enrol older students; for example, in Australia, 42% of university students are aged 23 years or over. Furthermore, some institutions enrol students who undertake their courses under contractual arrangements with employers; for example, military academies, some teachers' colleges, etc.

Modes of study. In traditional universities students studied through lectures, tutorials and supervised work. In recent years there has been differentiation in the modes of study. Perhaps the development of off-campus studies, as illustrated in the major external studies programmes of several Australian universities and, more dramatically, through the work of the Open University in the UK, has been the most significant contribution in this area in recent years. Other variations in modes of study involve arranging studies through learning contracts, or recognising life or work experiences as contributing to the academic work of the student.

Entry requirements. Access to institutions of higher education varies greatly from country to country and from institution to institution. Traditionally universities have employed strict prerequisites to the entry of students, but increasingly there has been a liberalisation of entry requirements and many institutions are prepared to admit students on bases other than prior academic record. Some have had completely open entry, as, for example, in the case of City University of New York; similarly the technical colleges in Australia have virtually open entry. Whether or not they have strict academic prerequisites to entry, some institutions have quotas on entry to particular courses. The nature of entry requirements and the openness of access are thus further factors differentiating institutions of higher education. This is not unrelated to the background of students; quite apart from previous academic record, some institutions attract students from higher socio-economic levels than others. Likewise some faculties attract different classes of students from others. Since certain kinds of students may find certain kinds of institutions more congenial than others, the differentiation of institutions may itself improve access to higher education.

Staff. Different institutions place different emphases on the qualities required of staff; some require a major commitment to teaching, others to research. The extent to which academic staff are appointed through competitive arrangements involving open advertisement affects the nature of staff and the degree to which institutions are open to new people with new ideas. In some systems of higher education there may be restrictions on who are eligible for appointment as staff; for example, appointments may be restricted to nationals of the country concerned.

Nature of institution. Some institutions are committed to particular values or have a particular ethos; for example, some are operated under the aegis of religious orders and therefore have commitments to particular religious points of view. Private institutions differ from those that are wholly supported by public funds. Some institutions constitute elements in state systems of higher education and the staff of these institutions are, in effect, public servants. Whether or not students are expected to pay fees, and the level of those fees, are important considerations in differentiating institutions.

Academic freedom. The ideal of an institution's being free to select its staff, students and the courses it teaches, is not met in all institutions. Some are subject to controls from co-ordinating bodies or governments; and these may place constraints on academic freedom. By the same token the extent to which institutions are accountable for the way they distribute their resources (and their ability to do this free from bureaucratic interference) varies from institution to institution. Likewise the emphasis placed on accountability in terms of the outputs of institutions and their effectiveness in meeting the institutions' objectives varies a great deal.

General Conclusions

It is clear that all institutions of higher education do not perform all the eight functions which were set out at the beginning of the paper, but they all perform some of these functions. The varying emphases placed on them by different institutions consti'ute an important element in the differentiation between them. The complexity of the functions of higher education and the large number of possible points of difference mean that a simple classification of institutions is not possible. There are no theoretical bases for distinguishing groups of institutions in a way which would enable one to say that universities have these functions and polytechnics have those. Institutions of higher education generally have certain characteristics in common, and differentiation of one group of institutions from another can only be made by recognising on the one hand the commonalities and on the other the differing emphases in their roles, modes of operation and institutional characteristics. An example of this, drawn from Australian experience, are the distinctions that can be made between universities and colleges of advanced education; the latter constitute a sector of higher education which has been developed since the mid-1960s as an alternative stream to the university sector.

In the words of the then Universities Commission: —

'While it may be difficult to define universities and colleges in generic terms, it is possible to list typical characteristics which reflect differences in definition and purpose of colleges compared with universities. These characteristics are:

(*a*) College courses tend to have a more applied emphasis and to be more vocationally oriented;

(*b*) College students could be expected to have vocational rather than academic or scholarly interests;

(*c*) Colleges have more flexible entrance requirements;

(*d*) Colleges have a more direct relationship with industry, commerce and other employing authorities;

(*e*) Colleges provide greater opportunities for part-time studies;

(*f*) The academic staffs of universities have a commitment to research in that their academic duties include teaching *and* research and they are expected to spend a substantial portion of their time on research and scholarship. Although some research activities occur in colleges, the staff's commitment is strongly to teaching;

(*g*) Universities offer higher degrees by research work. Generally, colleges do not offer such degrees, although in some specialised areas some colleges offer masters degrees by this route and by course work;

(h) The commitment of universities to scholarship and research implies that they should have more substantial library facilities and scientific research facilities than colleges;

(i) While the distribution of enrolments as between those in scientifically oriented courses and those in non-scientifically oriented courses is in the aggregate similar in universities and colleges, the colleges do not offer many courses in the humanities;

(j) Although colleges are offering an increasing number of degree courses, a significant commitment of colleges is to three-year diplomas following a full secondary education. In addition, in some disciplines, some colleges offer lower-level two-year diplomas. Some colleges also offer pre-tertiary courses.

Although a particular college may not differ from a particular university in respect of each of the above factors, taken as a whole they enable a broad distinction to be drawn between universities and colleges.

'It should be clear from the above considerations that in terms of educational offerings, with the possible exception of the humanities, the colleges provide a wider spectrum of tertiary education than do the universities. This makes them particularly appropriate as institutions of higher education in country areas where the regional population is not sufficient to support both a university and a college of reasonable size. A college in such an area can offer a range of courses to lower diploma level and meet local demand for tertiary education over a wide range. It may, in fact, satisfy the needs of the area more adequately than a more specialised institution'.*

In the light of the above comments, do universities have essential characteristics which distinguish them from other institutions of higher education? Universities usually claim to place an emphasis on liberal education, pure research and scholarship, the critical evaluation of society, academic freedom, strict standards in academic staff selection, and international recognition. Other institutions of higher education display some of these characteristics, but the essence of the university is the weight which it places on these functions, within the total mix of the roles of higher education. One practical problem is that most communities cannot afford to

---

* *Report on the Proposal of the Government of Victoria for a Fourth University in Geelong, Ballarat and Bendigo*, Australian Government Publishing Service, Canberra, 1974, paras. 3.4 and 3.5.

support many institutions of the 'pure' university kind; consequently institutions that are called universities often include in their activities elements which go well beyond those that are usually claimed to be the essential characteristics of universities.

The differentiation among institutions of higher education occurs through the varying emphases on functions and through a diversification of courses offered, modes of learning, modes of entry, etc. This has two consequences, which to some extent are in opposition to each other. First, differentiation of higher education, through diversification, increases access to, and thereby raises the demand for, higher education. Secondly, it fragments higher education and tends to erode its unity of purpose so that tensions develop between, for example, the pursuit of excellence and the maximisation of access.

The trend towards placing an emphasis on vocational education, which is commonly found today in many parts of the world, is itself a part of the process of diversification of institutions of higher education as well as being a result of the phase of general disillusionment with education through which we are passing at present. The diversification of course offerings tends to result in increasing specialisation and to produce graduates tailor-made to particular occupations. This tendency may not only be destructive of some of the basic values of higher education as it places an undue emphasis on the production of skilled manpower defined in narrower and narrower terms, but may also be self-defeating in its attempt to gear educational outputs to market demands for particular categories of skilled manpower. There may be disadvantages in training people with highly specific skills in a world of changing job requirements. What we need are people who can adapt to changes in industrial and commercial conditions. This is probably best achieved by emphasising general education, in whatever discipline is under consideration, rather than in the acquisition of specific skills which can be learned subsequently in short specialised courses or on the job. It is thus important to ensure that the increasing differentiation of higher education does not prove destructive of the essential purposes which higher education has traditionally served.

Professor J.-G. PAQUET (*Rector of Laval University*): It is generally agreed that institutions of higher education are often the expression of nationality, religion, philosophy, politics, language;

they are often the result of a 'mentality' and of a nation's genius. This statement is illustrated by the orientation and progress of North American universities.

American universities and anglophone universities in Canada have a cultural tradition and scientific achievements which it is needless to demonstrate here. On the other hand francophone universities in Quebec evolved along the lines of the French tradition, and were characterized by the classical literary humanism before their involvement, less than fifty years ago, in sciences and scientific research.

However it is also obvious that institutions of higher education in the western world, and very likely in the entire world, come under major changes for reasons that go beyond those previously mentioned. Present-day universities are influenced by other forces generated by an everchanging world. In order to make this phenomenon explicit I will try, first, to mention a few factors of differentiation between institutions of higher education; secondly, I will use Canadian universities as examples to illustrate my statements.

Factors of Differentiation

Our universities are at the crossroads of forces which, in their origin, have nothing to do with either the university itself or the values which it is its mission to examine thoroughly and to diffuse.

One of the factors which could have a wide influence on the future of institutions of higher education, and which is capable of determining their specific orientations, is precisely *the increasing responsibility assumed by the governments*. This is a relatively new phenomenon, corresponding to the setting up of an integrated system for national education, whose consequences are not completely known.

These consequences could be of importance, not only as regards the duties assigned to the educational system, but also for the survival of the institutions covered by the system. The percentage of the national budget devoted to education is in question at a time when rate of increase of the education budget is higher than that for the gross national product; the regional population becomes, in this way, a determining factor in the geographic distribution of institutions and the result is a network of institutions with variable sizes.

Awareness of the dynamics which contribute to differentiation indicates that the way institutions have developed during the last few centuries, in our western world at least, is a souvenir. For example, *differentiation due to research activities* is now a fact.

Experimental sciences are a good example of this statement. Choices have to be made because technology, with its diversity, influences the orientation of research and, conversely, scientific discoveries condition technology.

World-wide *co-operation between institutions* of higher education is sometimes a dream that collides with political or economic orientations. However co-operation with developing countries has given universities the chance to expand and diffuse their contribution, and so to differentiate their personality.

Diversification of clienteles is also another factor of differentiation. Until recently the university population was mainly composed of young students in professional schools. But a trend towards continuing education, spread in time, the interest of adults for education, the insertion of the university in its milieu, the efforts for an individualized pedagogy, all shape new clienteles for which age is no longer a valid criterion of distinction.

Canadian Universities

How have Canadian universities faced these factors and how are they preserving their individuality within systems of which they are integral parts, while keeping their fundamental concerns as institutions of higher education?

The post-war period, in Canada, has witnessed a generalized effort to study the orientation and organization of education systems. Commissions have been set up for inquiries and have given birth to reports having sometimes, at the provincial level, the value of charters for education. Many universities have also created their own commissions to study institutional policies and internal functioning mechanisms.

I will limit my remarks to recommendations from reports written by commissions set up by the provinces of Alberta and Quebec. From Alberta *A Future of Choices, a Choice of Futures* (1972) is probably the one which presents, in a coherent way, the precise functions for its higher education system and for its constituents. From Quebec *Le Rapport de la Commission royale d'enquête sur l'enseignement* (1964–66), and from Ontario that of the commission on post-secondary education (*The Learning Society*, 1972), reflect similar considerations for these provinces.

In Alberta. The Worth Commission in Alberta has established the principle of diversification and differentiation for institutions, their roles and their necessary co-ordination.

> 'The response to this challenge of expansion in both quantity and quality must be increasingly diversified and coordinated.

Within higher education the particular role of each sector, institution and program must be clearly specified. Every institution must also assume responsibility for developing a high degree of competence and effectiveness in its role. Concurrently, there needs to be effective role coordination to avoid gaps as well as unwarranted duplication, to eliminate mutually destructive warfare between divided faculties, and to facilitate student transfer and continuity in learning. Planned differentiation in mission, size and character is the path that higher education must follow if it is to maximize its contribution to the general goals of education. This concept of planned differentiation demands that the functions of higher education be subjected to continuing re-examination.'

'The colleges of the future must have parity in higher education. They ought not to be institutions with a junior partner role. Rather they should have a distinctive mission of their own which they carry out in accordance with the principle of quality. In this way, the colleges can attain their own integrity and stop conducting their affairs as though they were on the lower rungs of a status ladder.'

'The career function of the institutes should continue to focus on the development of specialized technical knowledge and skills.'

'.... [the universities'] involvement in research gives them opportunities to make some very different contributions to the larger society, as well as to the educational goals of the province.'

In Quebec. Prior to the publication of the report of the commission on higher education in the province of Quebec (1966), post-secondary education was the responsibility of private institutions. Classical colleges, most of them belonging to religious corporations, composed the college system leading to the classical BA, a condition for admission to the university. The curriculum was mostly oriented towards humanities, some sciences and philosophy. Technical education was the responsibility of technical schools controlled by the government. Six private universities were responsible, to various degrees, for higher education.

Educational reform has led to a new bill, to the creation of the Department of Education and to the organization of an integrated system. Democratization of education, necessary specialization, polyvalent programmes, are some of the fundamental principles of these changes.

The most original element of the new system in Quebec is probably the setting up of general and professional colleges, corresponding to the American 'junior colleges'. After a five-year course at the secondary level the student, at the college level, can choose between two directions; a vocational (technical) education leading after a three-year programme to professional practice; or a general education leading after a two-year programme to the university.

At the university level these changes had not very much influenced the system until, in 1968, the government established a new university, with constituents, each of them having regional priorities and specific responsibilities.

It is important to mention that the specification phenomenon for an institution of higher education is sometimes more the result of the needs expressed by a region than the conclusion of theoretical views on the relations between an institution and its environment.

However the differentiation mechanisms in Quebec have been particularly influenced by the Council of Quebec Universities, which submits 'recommendations to the Minister of Education on the needs of higher education and university research'. In February, 1973, this Council presented to the universities a planning project 'with guidelines for each university during the next five years' based on a rationalized development for the university network and 'on the preservation of characteristics which make the originality of each institution'.

Conclusion

All institutions of higher education influenced by a trend of service to community must be sensitive to the needs of society corresponding to a geographical area. In so doing their functions are diversified and a certain co-ordination is necessary. Continuing education, which appears to be an irreversible movement, will also be in the future a factor determining the specificity of the role played by each institution of higher education.

DISCUSSION
See page 567

Sub-Topic 5 (b)

PROBLEMS OF CHOICE BETWEEN DIFFERENT INSTITUTIONS

Chairman: Dr. C. R. MITRA
Director of the Birla Institute of Technology and Science

Rapporteur: Dr. R. O. H. IRVINE
Vice-Chancellor of the University of Otago

Tuesday, 22 August

The Derivation of a Model System

Sir WALTER PERRY (*Vice-Chancellor of the Open University*): The title of this sub-topic is quite clearly capable of two very different interpretations. In the first place, I could have chosen to discuss the problems facing a putative student in choosing which of the various kinds of institution of tertiary education currently available to him he should attend. In the second place, I could have chosen to discuss the problems facing a minister of education in choosing the kinds of institutions to set up in his country. I chose the latter largely because my ignorance of the different forms of institution available in different Commonwealth countries precluded a choice of the former. I decided, therefore, to put myself in the hypothetical situation that I was minister of education of a Commonwealth country which had no pre-existing system of tertiary education whatsoever. I would have to derive a model system — hence the title of this paper. I would be wholly free to establish whatever institutions I wished to serve the needs of my country. I could even choose to create new kinds of institution which had no pre-existing counterparts in any real-life situation. Iconoclasm has no place in educational development. None of us can tear down that which exists in order to replace it with something that we think would be better. All we can hope to do is to modify our existing systems slowly and piecemeal to arrive at a situation that we judge to be comparably better. Such constraints do not apply in my hypothetical situation.

Primary Objectives of a Model System

How then would I, in my new role as minister of education, start to plan my model system of tertiary education? I would have to begin by defining my primary objectives. There seem to me to be only two such primary objectives.

1. The system should make it possible to equip every individual to make his or her maximum contribution to the needs of society so as to satisfy those needs.

2. The system should enable every individual to achieve the maximum degree of self-fulfilment.

These are ideals, goals that we must aim at. Like all ideals they are virtually unachievable in practice. There are two major constraints that prevent us reaching the desired goal. The first is that in no society is the fraction of the gross national product that can be spent on education sufficient to enable us to achieve all that we would like to do. The second is that the needs of society as perceived by the individual members of that society may not match the needs as perceived by society as a whole. For example, society as a whole, through its elected representatives, may perceive a need for the education of a particular number of doctors; but the number of individuals who see their maximum contribution to the needs of society as being made through their qualification as doctors may fall far short of, or grossly exceed, that particular number. Consequently, in planning and creating a model system I must build a number of medical schools calculating the places available in them on the basis of an estimate of need derived from a manpower planning exercise. Although such exercises have, historically, often led to outrageously erroneous predictions, I have no choice but to continue to use them, for if I respond solely to demand from individuals I may, while satisfying my second primary objective — to allow individuals to achieve maximum self-fulfilment — wholly fail to satisfy my first objective — to satisfy the needs of society by equipping each individual to make his or her maximum contributions to them. Clearly an excess of qualified doctors are not making their maximum contribution to society; they might have done so had they been educated to fill vacant jobs as engineers.

It is inevitably true that the more democratic any regime becomes the more it will be influenced by the political pressures that derive from the ambitions of its individual constituents for self-fulfilment;

and the less will calculated national need be acceptable as the overriding factor in planning. Political pressure groups seldom take the long view. It is the art of the statesman to try to ensure that the long view prevails despite the short-term political pressures.

Principles Guiding the Design of a Model System

Accepting the two major objectives of my model system, and realising that there are practical constraints that will operate to prevent my achieving them, I must proceed to adopt certain principles that will guide me in my design.

1. My first principle would be that all members of a particular group in society will not be of equal intellectual capacity, but that all should have an equal educational opportunity. This sounds like a truism but it perhaps bears a rather closer scrutiny. The idea of providing equal educational opportunity is closely related to the effects of the environment upon intellectual capacity; and many educationists have been preoccupied with these problems. I imagine that no one would argue that the penalty of being brought up in an impoverished home, in the absence of books, by parents with no interest in education, is very great and is bound to be a disadvantage to the children emanating from this background. It is also quite clear that the only way of mitigating the disadvantage induced by such factors is to change the social structure of society. It is not a disadvantage that can be overcome by any system of education itself. Consequently the idea of providing a system of higher education that provides total equality of opportunity is itself a mirage and to admit this fact is not in any sense to argue that it is not a wholly desirable goal. It is merely to be realistic and recognise that no tinkering with the educational system can reach that goal. This is an important differentiation because it seems to me that preoccupation with the idea of achieving equality of opportunity has led to the adoption of the fallacious idea that there is merit in seeking a uniformity of treatment of all those in any educational cohort. It is a fallacious idea because it ignores the fact that, even in the ideal situation where equality of opportunity has been achieved, hereditary factors will, of themselves, have determined that some members of the cohort will have a greater intellectual capacity than others. I am aware that this view has been challenged, especially in relation to racial or ethnic differences, but it would be a break with all biological laws if it were not true.

The fact is that in most societies differences in intellectual capacity, from whatever cause, are recognised in respect of backward children and, for them, the idea of uniformity of treatment is abandoned. Thus extra time, trouble and money is spent on creating special educational provision for backward children. Here there seems to be little argument that there exists a segment of the population that falls perhaps so far outside the normal distribution of ability that very special provision has got to be made to try to cater for its particular needs. Yet these same societies do very little to cater for those in the opposite tail of the distribution of ability — for the most gifted children. They, it is argued, must be given the same uniform treatment that is offered to all the rest. The main argument in favour of uniformity of treatment is that to move children out of the mainstream or out of their age group by segregating them for special educational opportunities is to impose upon them social and emotional strains. While this is almost certainly true, the intellectual strains imposed by *not* segregating them are often ignored. Furthermore the very large potential contribution of such children to the needs of society may be seriously reduced. There is also, of course, a fear that segregation may produce a new élite — based not upon class or upon wealth but upon intellect. I have no such fear — I am unashamedly an intellectual élitist and I believe that society will depress its intellectual élite at a very great price to itself.

I can hold this view without any discomfort while still subscribing to the concurrent view that the idea of comprehensive schools is a good one, for I am not suggesting dividing the normal distribution of ability somewhere down the middle at near maximum frequency; I am advocating the segregation of the extreme tail of the distribution — of less than 0.5% who lie 3 or more standard deviations above the mean.

2. The second principle that I would adopt in designing my new system is that society has a far greater need for the generalist than for the hyper-specialist. This is a theme that I have developed many times in the past and I am by no means alone in doing so. There are many others who have argued very cogently in favour of the same general principle. It seems to me that in England we have a prime example of a system that has gone wrong in this sense. We have a school system which is geared, under pressure from the universities, to the needs of preparing students to embark on a 3-year honours degree programme, a programme that has few counterparts elsewhere in the world. This has led to the situation where children are forced from an early age to choose 2 or 3 subjects on which they spend the bulk of their time at school in order to achieve, at the age of 18 or 19, a level of excellence in the chosen subjects which will enable them to gain entrance to the highly selective universities. The system works very well as measured by the success rate of those who enter university; but the corollary is that all the other children

attending school up to the age of 18 are being offered a course of study that is wholly inappropriate to their needs.

Those who go to university often study for 3 years, in one particular honours school, little more than a series of courses in one discipline. They will have had little or no exposure to education in any subject outside their chosen field since they were about 15. Furthermore, those who go on to a PhD will study, for 3 further years, one small facet of their chosen discipline in very great depth — indeed to the very frontiers of knowledge. By the time they reach the age of 24 or 25 some will have become totally unable to contribute to ordinary conversation in any area outside their own chosen field. We are producing illiterate scientists and innumerate arts graduates. This is the root cause of Lord Snow's two cultures. It is a system admirably geared to what Lord Ashby called 'the thin clear stream of excellence', to produce the new generation of specialist scholars. This is a goal to which I wholly subscribe, an admirable goal, something which we must achieve at all cost; but not a goal which so colours our whole educational system as to penalise all those who are not excellent and are not going to be the scholars of the future. It seems to me that it is this kind of example that shows just how difficult it is to design any sort of system that does in fact meet the needs of society. There is no way in which a uniform system can meet all the needs. If it satisfies the needs of one kind of group it will tend to put other groups at a disadvantage. If it meets the need of the other groups it will neglect the first. It is in the balance of provision that takes account of these differing needs that the skill in planning an overall system lies. It is on the recognition of these different needs that the argument against uniformity rests. Uniformity of treatment, whether at school or at university, is an idea that in fact one single system can cater for all the diverse needs. It is my contention that it cannot do so, or at least that it cannot do so adequately.

3. The third of the principles that I would adopt in planning my new system would be that the pace of acquisition of new knowledge in this modern world has accelerated over the last few years to such a degree that no system based on initial education alone is any longer adequate. For many graduates much of the information and knowledge that they have painfully acquired is out of date before they have finished their final examinations. No longer is it possible for initial education to fit a man for the practice of his chosen profession or trade for the whole of his career. It is inevitable that updating, refresher and retraining courses will be required at ever-increasing intervals. I do not intend to introduce evidence in support of this contention. It is now popularly conceded that it is

bound to be the case. What is not popularly conceded is that there is an inevitable corollary, namely that much of what is now included in the curricula of initial education is in fact a waste of time and effort. It would be far better ruthlessly to prune the curricula of initial education, accepting that much of the detail will be outdated very rapidly and that therefore there is no call to ask the graduate to comprehend and reproduce such information. What he should be expected to do is to master those basic principles that will enable him to cope as well as possible with the new knowledge that will come into existence during his career. I have seen very little sign that there is any widespread acceptance of this corollary in our existing educational systems. It is very easy to add to curricula, to add to the burden on students; it is much more difficult to prune out the unnecessary. Nevertheless it is essential that we do this if we are going to be able to afford to add continuing education to the total educational provision of our countries. The cost of initial education is already vast. To add to it, without pruning it, the costs of continuing education will be beyond the means even of the richest of our Commonwealth countries. It would therefore be graven on my heart as minister for education in my hypothetical country that I must keep the costs of initial education down, reduce the length of initial education and devote a much higher proportion of my total available cash to the provision of an adequate continuing education programme.

Redesigning the Secondary Education System

These then would be my starting points. Let me get down to brass tacks. What would I actually do? Before I started looking at the system of tertiary education that I would create, I would want to take a very long and hard look at the secondary education system that existed. I am assuming for the sake of argument that secondary education is compulsory to the age of 16. My first iconoclastic decision would be that I would have no secondary education beyond the age of 16. I believe that children nowadays mature younger than they did some years ago; and that by the age of 16 most of them are ready for an ambience different from that which is common in many schools. I would therefore plan for education beyond the age of 16 to take place in colleges rather than in schools. Signs of a move in this direction are already apparent in England. An increasing number of children move from fifth forms in schools to study for 'A' (Advanced) levels in further education colleges, and find the relative freedom of taking classes at college much more acceptable than sitting in school classrooms. It may, of course, be more expensive to teach 16–18-year-olds in such a system. Yet the extra cost could be minimised by ensuring that most college students lived at home; and by using core teaching materials more widely. The enormous advantage of finishing secondary education at 16 is not, however, to be found in the effect it has upon those who go on at that age into tertiary education. Rather is it to be found in the effect upon the school experience of all those whose initial education will end, as it does at present, at 16. The influence of the universities upon the school curriculum would be greatly reduced—for it would become a curriculum designed for all children not just for those going to university.

I would want to emphasise the principle that society needs generalists by discouraging specialisation; and this could impose a uniformity of curriculum on all children. At the same time I would want to emphasise the principle that some children are more able than others; so that in each subject of the curriculum I would stream (or set) the children, allowing the more able to proceed faster than the less able. I would expect to achieve a social, class and emotional mix through the facts that children in the A stream in mathematics might well be in the C stream in history and that children in the A stream in all 'academic' subjects might well be in the C stream in art, music or physical education.

I would also want to recognise that school is a preparation not only for work but also for leisure. I would be aware that many factors were likely over the next few decades to increase the leisure time available to most people. The microprocessor, the silicon chip, would reduce the demand for unskilled and repetitive labour so that the working week would become shorter; early retirement and increased longevity would lengthen the period when work had ended. Our present school curricula were developed in an era when preparation for work was the primary motive. This would change, for many people are ill-prepared to use leisure constructively or to their satisfaction. I would include, for all children, a much wider exposure to craftsmanship which can be a lasting source of satisfacttion, to music and the visual arts for the same reasons, and to more directed attempts to instil a comprehension of the written word in all its forms.

Designing the Tertiary Education System

I would thus be trying to plan my tertiary education system to cope with the outflow of the whole cohort aged 16 from the secondary education system that I had created. I have already argued that no uniform system can adequately cater for all the diverse needs of society. Consequently my choice of institutions of tertiary education must be such as to provide a variegated series of options for the students with differing ability, differing skills and differing levels of achievement who emerge from the secondary education system. I must also provide for those who proceed end-on in an initial education programme, for those who go to work and come back, some years later, into what I have called deferred initial education, and for a programme of continuing education.

Nevertheless I believe that all these multifarious needs could be met by choosing only three kinds of institution of tertiary education which I have called colleges, universities and distance-learning institutions respectively. Rather than start by describing each of the three, I have looked instead first at the flow of the cohort of 16-year-old school-leavers into the various institutions or into work; and, second, at the flow back from work of people into the various institutions.

In essence the cohort emerging from school would follow one of three streams. The first stream is the familiar one that begins work at the age of 16. This will almost certainly remain the largest single stream in most countries, being at least 50% of the whole. It will remain so because of the pressure of economic circumstances which will drive many children to seek remunerated occupations at as early a date as possible. It will also remain a large stream, I think, because many children at the age of 16 are sufficiently mature to want to become independent of their families and of the state—the only sources of the support that is necessary to continue in full-time initial education. Such children will seek jobs and go out into the world without any further end-on education.

The second main stream would be that proceeding to what I would call colleges, and the third would proceed straight to the universities. The university stream would be the smallest of all and I would guess it would amount to no more than 1% of the total cohort. These would be the children who were brightest and most advanced in their achievements at school. They would proceed directly from secondary school at 16 to university and I shall return to discuss their progress a little later.

The Colleges

Let me consider first the second stream of the cohort, the college stream, which would embody something rather more than 45% of the total cohort. The colleges would provide for three different kinds of initial educational experience; in other words, the college stream would be sub-divided into three groups. The first very small group would be that which would take care of children emerging from secondary school with the lowest levels of achievement, even lower than those who would normally proceed to work. I call this the remedial stream and it would provide an opportunity for improving the level of general education achieved by these children at school. It would be essentially a fail-safe mechanism for school drop-outs who wanted, voluntarily, to drop in again in a new ambience. I imagine that the size of this particular group would be little more than 1 or 2% of the cohort. Students who entered the remedial stream in college would, of course, transfer across to other college streams if they turned out to be late developers and overcame the handicap of failure at secondary school.

The second sub-stream would be a large one which would probably account for something like 20–25% of the total cohort, and it would move into a series of college courses which resembled very closely the sort of further education course that is offered in Britain for 16–18-year-olds in technical colleges and similar institutions. Much of the work would thus be training for specific vocational jobs. This would include a range of technician training, training for clerical and secretarial posts and training for specific trades and crafts. I can see such programmes lasting anything up to 2 years on a full-time basis. Students would emerge from this stream into jobs and would join the pool of those at work.

My third sub-stream of the college stream would be that which entered into a programme of general education beyond secondary school level. It would be a fairly large stream amounting perhaps to some 20% of the total cohort. This programme would differ from the community college system in the United States in that it would be a programme that would go on for a full 4 years, leading ultimately to a first degree. This degree programme would be a modular one so that students could obtain credits each year and opt to leave to go to work after 1, 2 or 3 years, without completing a full degree programme. Furthermore, after 2 years of study students who were performing well and showing signs of significant advance in their intellectual achievement would transfer across to the universities. Here they would join, in an honours degree programme, the students who had gone direct to university from secondary school. I would imagine that, after 2 years in the general education programme at college, students who so transferred to university would enter the honours degree programme in the second year. In other words they would tend to be a year older than the students who had gone direct to the university from secondary school. I do not conceive of this transfer as an unusual phenomenon; I regard it instead as the main route from school to an honours degree. It would be the exceptional students only who would have entered the university stream directly. Thus of the 20% of the total cohort who entered the general education stream in college about one in three would in fact transfer in this way. This would mean that the fraction of the cohort obtaining a full university education would rise to some 7–8% in all.

I am thus choosing to maintain full university education for a highly selected group. Given that the main purposes of the university are the pursuit of scholarship, the education of scholars and the training of vocational specialists, the numbers of students at universities should not increase. Indeed there are cogent reasons why the reduction in the size of the total cohort due to the fall in the birth rate should be used to reduce the size of the universities and to re-emphasise their concern with scholarship rather than with mass higher education.

Mass higher education should properly be the concern of the colleges. Hence the unique feature of the college stream—the 20% of the cohort in the general education sub-stream that can proceed through a 4-year first degree programme.

This programme would be general in its nature, much more general than many current degree programmes. It would, however, especially in its last two years, lead to a partial specialisation. I would eschew as far as possible all monotechnics, all single-faculty colleges. In other words most teacher training, most business training, would take place within the college stream; moreover it would turn out many graduates who had studied combinations of courses in science, arts and social science, who would be the managers, the civil servants and the social workers of the future. This would be the great training ground of those who were to be the doers in society rather than the thinkers in society. They would receive an education that was not geared to the needs of the hyper-specialist, that was not in any sense meant to turn out scholars in the image of the teacher, that was instead designed specifically for those who wanted to be generalists, who did not want to be specialists.

In setting up colleges of this kind it is quite clear that, looking to the financial implications of the system, they would be run as non-research-based institutions, with the prime purpose of teaching. They would be able to cope with large numbers of students with a lower staff/student ratio than would be normal for universities. There would be a college in every township so that as many students as possible could live at home and the costs of residence would not fall upon the nation. They would furthermore make wide use of teaching materials prepared centrally that could back up the efforts of the staff employed in the institutions themselves.

The Universities

What then of the third, the university, stream? I have already explained the way I would try to arrange the intake to the stream, first direct from school for a small fraction of the cohort and, secondly, from transfer from the college stream, after 2 years of college, at the age of 18. The basic programme in the universities would be the honours degree, which would take 4 years of study. Consequently those entering straight from secondary school would complete an honours degree at the age of 20, those who entered through college at 21. There would, however, be a sub-sream in the universities that was entered after 1 or 2 years of university experience. I have called this the specialist school stream. I am thinking here of the vocational schools of medicine, veterinary medicine, dentistry, law, divinity, music and drama. These are disciplines where an advanced level of research-based teaching is required, but where the normal honours degree programme may be inappropriate. Nevertheless such specialist schools would, wherever possible, be incorporated within the university itself and should not exist separately as uni-disciplinary schools of study. I am, indeed, in favour of having some exposure, even for the specialist of the future, to disciplines other than the chosen one during university education. Finally, the university would at the completion of the honours degree programme provide a graduate school of the kind that is currently common in the British universities, where students can proceed from an honours degree to a PhD or other higher qualification. This will provide for the thin clear stream of excellence which I have argued already must be preserved at all costs within any tertiary education system.

Part-Time Initial Education

I have, then, discussed the sort of choice I would make as minister of education in setting up completely new institutions to meet the needs of the community and the needs of the individual. I have however discussed it solely from the point of view of full-time initial education programmes. I am quite clear that, in the colleges, provision would have to be made for part-time study which would, of course, take correspondingly longer but which would follow the same courses as were provided for the full-time student. It would thus be possible in the college system for anyone at work to study part-time for all the various qualifications that were available for full-time students in that system. The distribution of colleges locally in centres of population would provide a means of part-time study for the bulk of the population, although special provision might be made, for those who lived too far away from any individual college, to undertake study through a distance-learning institution.

Deferred Initial Education

As I indicated earlier, no system of tertiary education would be complete if it dealt solely with the problem of initial education. As we have seen, many school-leavers will continue to go straight into work and many others will leave initial end-on education without completing as much of the programme as they are competent to do. Provision must be made for a return from work to continue or complete an initial education. This sort of provision has often been regarded as a part of continuing education, but I think it is easier to consider it as a separate need, a separate system. I have coined for it the name 'deferred initial education'. The first degree programmes of the Open University are a splendid example of this stream. To cope with it fully we require the possibility of feeding mature students back into the colleges and the universities; but we also need to establish distance-learning institutions which, like the Open University, can cater for those mature students who cannot, because of their circumstances, attend either the colleges or the universities on either a full-time or a part-time basis. Such people embrace those whose work or family circumstances make this difficult, those who live too far from any college or university campus, those who are physically disabled, those who are institutionalised, those whose work entails constant travelling.

It may be that, whether mature students return to colleges or universities or whether they study through distance-learning institutions, they will require courses that are different in style and structure from those offered to school-leavers. It may be that courses based upon subjects that concern adults can be structured to introduce the same sort of basic education that is usually offered in discipline-based courses. Thus courses in 'taxation' or in 'insurance' could incorporate much of the content of courses normally labelled 'mathematics'.

Continuing Education

The last major problem is to provide continuing education, the very special refresher, updating and retraining courses that will be required because of the rate of acquisition of new knowledge. There is no reason why such courses should not also be offerd in the college system and indeed in the university system. It is however an extremely expensive undertaking to mount such courses in the multiplicity of colleges all over the country and I would therefore be very likely to plan my continuing education system much more on the basis of distance-learning institutions. Such systems are being started all over the world as a necessary feature of a complete tertiary education system. There are some 16 open universities already in existence if one defines them as institutions which were set up wholly or partly with the objective of providing distance learning. If one includes also those conventional institutions which have added a distance-learning programme to their other provisions one gets a total of about 40, and more are appearing almost daily.

There are many reasons why countries are creating distance-learning institutions, not all of which are related to the need to provide continuing education. Nevertheless it is in that particular area where the enormous merits and advantages of the distance-learning system most clearly appear. It is possible to update, refresh or retrain people without taking them away from their productive work, without eliminating their contribution to the gross national product of the country. It is possible for them to study at home without disrupting their family lives. It is possible to do all this at a very low cost provided that the number of students following a particular course is relatively large.

It is perhaps also worth mentioning that updating and refresher courses demand teachers who are extremely well informed and up to date in their subjects, and such teachers are rare. It is only by using centralised production of teaching materials and offering these by distance-learning methods that one allows such teachers to reach a wide audience.

You will all be aware that I am biased in favour of distance-learning methods. This is inevitable when one has spent 10 years building a very large and successful system of distance learning. I would, however, like to make three things perfectly plain. First, there are some things that distance-learning systems cannot do. They cannot provide the sort of apprenticeship training that is needed in clinical medical education or in plumbing. Second, they cannot be used economically for the education of small numbers of students. It would never make sense to train marine architects or to teach Sanskrit by such methods; it would always be cheaper to use traditional systems. Third, and much the most important, distance-learning systems should not in any sense replace the traditional college and university system for end-on initial education. I do not believe that children at 18, far less at 16, are capable of study by themselves in what is a very difficult learning situation. I think it is absolutely essential that we should be clearly aware of this fact and that we do not allow the beguiling prospect of doing things more cheaply to tempt us to offer a less than adequate system for young people. I am often assured when I visit some of the developing countries of the world that things are different there; that the problem of motivation of the younger student is not nearly so real; that opportunities for traditional kinds of education do not exist and cannot be made to exist; that the problem of higher education cannot be solved unless ways can be found of making the whole programme very much cheaper. In such cases distance learning may be used for end-on initial education with success, but it should nevertheless be realised that this is very much a second-best.

Problems of Introducing the Model System

That completes my choice of institutions for a system of tertiary education. I would hope that it would provide for the needs that I have outlined and meet the objectives I have set forth. What then are the snags and difficulties in achieving a satisfactory overall provision by such a programme? Let me end by examining just a few of them.

The first difficulty in achieving a system of the sort that I have described is undoubtedly that of building the necessary bridges to allow the transfer of people from one part of the system to the other without any loss of credit. We are all aware of the very great difficulties that exist in most countries in achieving such transfer—in building such bridges. It is perhaps particularly true in Britain where the development of modular-type courses has been very slow. I am sure that without modular programmes no such bridges are really possible. I can therefore hear in advance the arguments against the system that I have proposed. The fact that most students would enter the university honours degree programme with advanced standing obtained in colleges would be held up to ridicule; it would be regarded as a system impossible to operate without loss of quality. I reject these arguments. When I was dean of medicine I once admitted a student directly to 2nd MB studies because he had 3 'A' levels at grade A. I made a mistake because they were in chemistry, physics and mathematics. He had never studied biology—but he was exempted from 1st MB biology. He never seemed to miss it, for in his first year he got the medal in physiology. I am quite sure that we lay far too much stress on our ability to plan coherent sequential programmes of study; and that we would do little harm by admitting students to these programmes in second or even third year, even if their previous studies have not been planned to achieve that coherence or that sequence. We would give students a chance to catch up for themselves and this could be a real stimulus. We would certainly not frustrate them as badly as we do at present by insisting that they go back to the beginning of our course, that they cannot count for credit what they have studied elsewhere.

Then there are those who argue that modular systems leave the students too free to select their own courses, leading to degrees composed of what has been called 'a miscellaneous hodge-podge of credits'. In the Open University, where students are wholly free to choose courses to suit themselves, it is quite remarkable how conservative they are. Very very few select programmes which are not coherent and when indeed one finds a student who has taken what looks like a strange combination of credits and enquires why, one usually finds that there are very good reasons for the choice, strange as it may seem on the surface. The student may have, in the course of his employment, acquired knowledge and skills that allow him to jump perfectly satisfactorily to an advanced course without taking the preceding course which we would consider a prerequisite. Yet he has sound reasons indeed for his choice. No doubt adult students are better placed to make the correct choices; and students at the age of 16 may well be less able and more likely to be swayed by bush telegraph messages about which courses are relatively easy to pass. I therefore subscribe in part to the idea that sometimes 'teacher knows best'. On the other hand I think we often overact our parts and I have no real fear that modular courses would really produce many degrees composed of the miscellaneous hodge-podge of credits. Nevertheless one important safeguard lies in determining the size of the modules that are offered. Each module will tend to be controlled by a different group of academic staff and very small modules may have little more than an internal coherence; they will not necessarily interdigitate with other small modules. It is safer to work with larger modules. Thus an honours degree programme in the Open University is made up of a maximum of 14 modules; whereas in the United States a 4-year degree programme can be made up of as many as 40 or more modules. I think that we in the Open University have adopted the wiser tactic.

The third major criticism that I can see being levelled at the scheme is that there would be difficulties imposed by the fact that a degree obtained in this college system would be regarded as inferior to a degree obtained in the university system. I think this is undoubtedly true. It *would* be so regarded to begin with — and, in a sense, properly so; for a degree in the college system would not be such a challenge to the intellectual capacity of the individual as a degree in the university. In time a degree in the college system, although not so intellectually challenging, would turn out to be of far more practical value to the individual in society during the rest of his life. I think we waste a great deal of time and energy in trying to pretend that all degrees are of equal intellectual stature. They should not be, and there is no reason why this differentiation should not be recognised. Everyone is not equal in intellectual capacity, and sooner or later every member of the community must come to recognise at what level his intellectual capacity places him in the spectrum. Sooner or later we must realise we are not as good as some and that we are better than others. Sooner or later we must come to recognise wherein lies our particular strength and our particular skill. Society has a much greater need for people with a general education than for people with a specialised education, but we have failed, at least in Britain, to get this message across to our students or to our colleagues in university teaching. Basically, the deeply engrained instinct of the university academic to reproduce his own kind has been allowed to overshadow everything else. The system that I have devised, the choice that I have made, of the different kinds of institution of tertiary education would, I believe, go far to correct this imbalance.

The Economics of the Model System

Finally, let me look at the system that I have devised in terms of its economics. This I can do only in general terms. It achieves a reduction in the average length of initial education; this reduction must reduce the total cost and such a reduction is absolutely vital if we are going to provide a new system of continuing education and still keep the total education budget within bounds. The cost of secondary schooling would go down because it would end at 16. The cost of university education would go down since only $0 \cdot 5\%$ of the cohort would actually be at university for 4 years and $7-8\%$ of the cohort would be at university for only 3 years. No other institutions would be research-based and consequently the cost of the whole college system could be kept within reasonable bounds. Furthermore, from the national point of view, students would emerge with first degrees at the age of $20-21$, which is significantly younger than is at present the case, and would in fact be able to contribute to the gross national product at a correspondingly earlier time. There would be a reduction in the overall cost of residence in the higher education sphere, since nearly all the students in the college system would be resident at home. There would be, of course, one increase in the cost of the college system because of the fact that students who are currently studying in sixth forms at school would be transferred to the slightly more expensive college system. The bulk of continuing education would be operated through a distance-learning mechanism supplemented by the entry of mature students on a part-time basis into the college system. Overall it seems to me that the system could be operated within the current educational budget and would achieve very much more of the objective of fitting each individual to make his maximum contribution to society and of meeting the needs of individuals for self-fulfilment.

The Situation As It Is

I started off by pointing out that my hypothetical situation was not one that existed in practice. There is no country that can start with a clean sheet, and build a tertiary education system from scratch. All of us have to live with the practical realities that pre-exist in our own countries. There is no way in which we can wipe the slate clean. Nevertheless I think that if our aims are clear we can make changes slowly and in a piecemeal fashion, so that the system that pre-exists comes more closely to approximate to whatever ideal we have in mind. If I may take just a few more moments to translate this philosophy into the situation in Britain, I would say that I would certainly stop any further expansion of the university system. I would provide no research facilities in any institution other than the universities. I would begin to put pressure on all institutions to move towards a modular structure of courses and credits. I would encourage the technical colleges and other colleges to offer an alternative route to sixth-form studies. I would concurrently move towards broadening the secondary school curriculum, making it less and less specialised. Many of these changes would meet with very great resistance from the vested interests concerned in maintaining the status quo. But, nevertheless, movement in this direction will be quite essential if we are to achieve anything like the ideal state.

The most critical change of all would come when 'A' levels were abandoned and when the 3-year honours degree programme was extended to a 4-year honours degree programme. This, of course, would be a very expensive undertaking in the first instance. It would however pay off in the end. The problem would be to persuade government to spend the additional money in order to make later savings. The forward planning of government is not always as clear thinking as that. Yet this would be an essential prerequisite to implementing anything like the sort of system I have outlined. One cannot abandon 'A' levels and maintain the 3-year honours degree of the English universities. The two must go together. Unless they

SUB-TOPIC 5(B): PROBLEMS OF CHOICE [Perry]

are changed I see little way of escaping from the dilemma in which we find ourselves. I would hope that in other Commonwealth countries, at an earlier stage of developing their systems of tertiary education, people will be too wise to allow themselves to fall into a similar dilemma.

Mr. W. G. PITMAN (*President of Ryerson Polytechnical Institute*): A successful businessman returned to his alma mater for a visit with his former economics professor. For reasons of personal interest and amusement he wanted to see how well he could do on a current exam. He asked to see a copy of one and was amazed to find that the questions were exactly the same as in his own student days. The professor, sensing the reason for his visitor's bewilderment, cheerfully explained: 'Of course the questions are the same as always, but in economics we keep changing the answers'.

Today the economics of higher education has educators looking for new answers—and the question of choices between institutions of higher learning is a constant source of frustration both for educators and the society looking for more practical results of these choices. Shifts of interest from liberal arts to career-oriented education overcrowd certain facilities while emptying others, overworking certain professors while leaving other faculty under- or unemployed.

There was a time many years ago when the classical university dominated the post-secondary education field in most countries. There were a few other institutions such as teachers' colleges, nursing schools, technical and business colleges—but when one talked of education after the secondary level one was normally talking about a university experience. At that time the clientele was a very small percentage of the youth population largely drawn from upper income families and particularly from families in which the parents had attended a university.

Today we see before us a much more sophisticated tertiary sector. Throughout the world there has been a major development of the community college or colleges associated with applied rather than liberal arts, and associated with technology and business rather than languages, humanities and social sciences. These institutions engage in educational activity at a variety of levels from the upgrading of basic skills to a rather sophisticated level of career-oriented education. In the United Kingdom we have seen the development of the polytechnic sector which puts its emphasis on career-oriented education with a liberal arts component. As well, this sector seeks to achieve an intellectual rigour comparable to the university experience. And of course we have the extraordinary expansion of the university system in most countries in terms of numbers of students, in variety of functions and in new disciplines or inter-disciplinary areas.

Students who come to all these institutions have a far greater difficulty with choice. There is so much more to choose from and there is often less sophistication on the part of the potential student and his parents. They are often forced back upon their own resources to discover what opportunities lie before them either through counselling at the secondary school or through the information programme provided by these various institutions, either individually or collectively.

The problem of choice would be less difficult if there was more flexibility in the relationships between all the institutions devoted to tertiary education. There has been a tremendous change in attitude over the past number of years and very sincere efforts have been made to discover means of giving credit for work carried out in one institution, of allowing flexible arrangements for joint programmes in more than one institution—all of these are impressive and worthwhile. Further, there has been a considerable overlapping of functions and students who wish to pursue a particular field of interest may do so with integrity at a community college, a polytechnic or a university. Universities are providing programmes now which are almost entirely professional and career-oriented. At the same time polytechnics offer programmes of liberal arts.

Yet, for reasons which are evident—the period of time necessary to secure qualification, the level of academic education, the previous scholastic record—we still expect students to choose *either* a university *or* a college *or* a polytechnic. We still expect students to carry out a two- or three- or four-year continuous programme leading to a certificate or degree in one of these kinds of institutions. Less often do we see the legitimacy of assisting the student who moves from one type of institution to the other acquiring relevant educational experience that creates a holistic pattern in the light of the students' personal and career goals.

There is a rationale behind this expectation as one can make a very strong argument that formal education is more than a collection of fragments from various institutions and that there should be some kind of integrated development based on a curriculum which has specific goals. The argument would be that this integration comes as a result of years of attendance and of credit accumulation within a defined programme of studies. This achievement is symbolized by the paper of qualification which the student receives, but it has a reality which is basic to the purpose of every reputable institution.

In the 1980s, during which there will be fewer resources devoted to 'institutionalized' education, one must question (*a*) whether we must solve this issue in the context of education as a youth activity, and whether life-long learning is a more satisfying context, and (*b*) whether education must be seen as something associated with formalized, institutionalized process, or whether the increased access to learning by people of all ages should more pervasively affect our thinking. It would be my perception that although we will give lip service to the evidence for need to change our learning styles, we tend to organize our institutional affairs as though these changes are not as essential to the issue of choice as they surely are. Each one of us knows that the amount of information available to individuals in our society has risen exponentially. We know that — through the development of radio and television, the paperback book evolution, the extension of library services — an individual in our society may have a much greater opportunity of integrating his or her own individual educational learning experience within a society in which a valid learning experience is much more widely accessible. Quite simply there are a great many opportunities for continuing education outside the formal educational process — quite isolated from the traditional institutional format.

If so, the problem of choice should be less between institutions, less associated with paper qualifications and more associated with personal, intellectual and spiritual needs of the individual at any age, and with the needs of society for people with skills and capabilities if that society is going to be able to maintain a decent standard of living for its citizens. These are but two criteria — and there are others. But, in a world in which the entire industrial growth-oriented path to prosperity is being questioned, the need for sensitive, aware, socially responsible, intelligent people who can find alternative technologies, more satisfying lifestyles, indeed, more rational value patterns, is absolutely essential. The style of education which appears to have some relevance for the eighties (assuming that individuals have competence at the secondary level) is one of interrupted education, a process of learning and work experience which are complementary and lead to individual growth and greater collective economic well-being. The individual might well take a year or two at a college to secure a skill which is obviously needed in the community in which he lives. After using such a skill for a while the individual might well decide that he or she needs a liberal arts education and might spend a year or two at a university. This new experience might lead this person to believe that a greater contribution might be made with a higher level of technological skill and thus a move to a polytechnic for a year or two would seem appropriate, or, indeed, a change in career directions might occur as a result of either academic or work experience.

It would seem to me that such an educational style would have more relevance in a changing society in which career opportunities seem to widen and narrow precipitately. Not only would it provide a wider opportunity for individuals to fulfil a variety of personal goals, it would also be possible for young people to shift their careers and make real contributions to the needs of society throughout a flexible and interactive process, relieving that society of the embarrassment of having an educational system producing graduates in areas where their talents are not needed, and having a dramatic shortfall of skilled people in other sectors of the economy where the needs are not being supplied by the educational system.

It is obvious that the educational sector cannot be expected to accommodate raw manpower needs. However it is appalling to think that nations will, over the next few decades, doom their young people to unprecedented levels of both unemployment and underemployment. The implications of such a disillusioning state of affairs on the political, social and economic life of various nations is absolutely terrifying. By adopting a commitment to life-long learning, by assisting both management and the trade union movement to understand the value of such a learning style (and helping both to see education as much more than either an elegant form of on-the-job training or training in the care and nurture of trade unionism), the linkage between manpower needs of society and the legitimate educational system can be devised. Thus wider and more rewarding choice is neither negated by institutional structure nor is it made irrelevant by the spectre of unacceptable and unavoidable distress coming as a result of choices made too early in life on the basis of too little information and as a result of a system which locks individuals into the implications of their choices too soon.

For the university it might mean far more than greater attention to transfer of credits from one institution to another as fewer students perceive a continuous process to a degree as a necessarily legitimate ambition. Certainly curriculum design will be profoundly influenced by this style of learning. Certainly the focus of the institution's research and scholarship will be affected.

However, unless there is accommodation to these pressures for making effective choices possible in the light of social and economic change, the universities will be pressured or forced by government to perceive their societal role more consciously. This pressure can be applied in many ways—by government financial support of alternative educational opportunities and by severely reducing support for the traditional university—or more directly, through legislation. It would be my perception that the universities themselves could maintain autonomy, teach in an atmosphere of academic freedom, support research free from political restraint and yet provide the flexibility which will allow choices which are personally satisfying and societally necessary in a world which must move from industrial expansion, high technologies on a wasteful consumer economic style, to a world of steady-state, appropriate technology and conservation. To talk of choice unconnected to these world-wide developments is to court disaster.

The threat of government control is a serious one. But the other possibility is that universities, polytechnics and colleges of various kinds may seek to accommodate the broad desire for choice by expanding their own roles. Quite often the funding mechanisms of government encourage this frantic effort to be all things to all men. If universities perceive their own roles clearly they will make only changes which have academic integrity, recognizing and applauding the complementary commitments of other institutions. Thus the choice of students to move from institution to institution becomes the solution for the wider variety of educational needs throughout a career and a lifetime—rather than the irrational and dissipative expansion of functions by any one institution.

Finally, enabling choices to be made more flexibly between institutions with contrasting roles over a lifetime would soften the interface between the liberal arts education designed to make life intelligible and the skill/information-oriented education leading to employment. In a world in which technology and business style have created environmental problems of massive proportions, we cannot allow ourselves the danger of having individuals involved in either business or technology without that essential liberalization emanating from an experience which emphasizes man as a spiritual and intellectual being rather than as an acquisitive creature.

In spite of the difficulties faced by universities throughout the world, there is the basic reality that in the long run we are moving towards a learning society. Since world war two the attention of man has been pre-eminently focused on gross national product patterns, world trade competition and the illusion of the good life based on consumption. The rest of this century must be devoted to the sharing of what is now seen as the fruits of a finite planet, and the conserving of resources for future generations. The need for young people who are not wedded to the style of the past, who have a capacity to translate their commitment to holistic personal patterns of behaviour to the needs of their communities, provides a strong argument for the growth and refinement of the educational process. Intellectual and spiritual growth are almost unique in their capacity to be non-pollutive and non-exploitive. But if the institutions which have served mankind well for many hundreds of years are to serve this kind of future they must make it possible for individuals to make choices which have integrity, both in personal and societal terms. That is the challenge facing the universities in the eighties.

DISCUSSION
See page 567

Sub-Topic 5(c)

PROBLEMS OF TRANSFER AND COMMUNICATION AMONG DIFFERENT INSTITUTIONS

Chairman: Mr. M. T. MASHOLOGU
Vice-Chancellor of the National University of Lesotho

Rapporteur: Dr. J. A. MARAJ
Vice-Chancellor of the University of the South Pacific

Tuesday, 22 August

Sir CHARLES CARTER (*Vice-Chancellor of the University of Lancaster*): Very occasionally a system of higher education is planned as a whole, at the same time, by a single central authority. More usually the parts of higher education in a country have different historical origins, have grown up under different arrangements for control and administration, and are brought together as a true 'system' when already possessing strong individual characteristics: or are not really a co-ordinated system at all, except perhaps in the rhetoric of occasional commission reports and the dreams of politicians. Thus there is no system of higher education in the United Kingdom, except in the rudimentary sense that most of the providers are competitors for help from the public purse, and the Treasury therefore has to take a broad view of the allocation between them. There are universities, autonomous institutions protected by their royal charters, which (despite their overwhelming reliance on public funding) act in an independent competitive manner like private firms. There are local authority colleges, ranging from polytechnics, colleges of higher education and teacher training colleges whose interests are mainly or entirely in degree work to colleges of further education which have developed some degree-level work as a minority interest to add to their main function in lower-level education. There are 'voluntary' (typically church) colleges doing both teacher training and other degree-level work. There are professional institutions whose qualifications are rated as equivalent to a degree, and these qualifications can sometimes be obtained through private study and correspondence courses. There is the Open University, providing a national system of correspondence courses backed by local tutors and by radio and television broadcasts. There are some specialist institutions which fall into none of the above classes—and, inevitably, the arrangements in Scotland are rather different.

This diversity can be seen either as a sign of vigorous life or as a source of waste and confusion: indeed both conclusions are valid simultaneously, and the challenge is to minimise the waste and lessen the confusion without losing the advantages which come from diverse sources of decision. One problem which is often mentioned is the difficulty, in an unco-ordinated system, of arranging the transfer of students from one institution to another—to put right a wrong choice of course or place, to provide a second chance after failure, or to allow access to special facilities or to graduate study. People refer, with a nostalgia uncontaminated by much factual knowledge, to the German tradition of the 'wandering student', or to the supposedly simple transferability of credits between colleges in the United States.

But this problem is not quite what it seems, and it has very little to do with the diversity of institutions. One suspects that, all the world over, the enthusiasm of colleges for the acceptance of someone else's failures is very limited, and in Britain such acceptance is often prevented by the difficulty of extending a student's grant for extra years. So the interesting question relates to the transfer of students 'in good standing', either to get a better undergraduate experience or to undertake graduate study. In Britain diversity is no real obstacle to entry to graduate study: this usually depends on having a good first degree (or an equivalent professional qualification), and I know of no discrimination in this matter between the degrees offered by universities and by other institutions, or between those degrees and the professional qualifications which have received recognition as degree-equivalent. Movement *during* undergraduate studies is, however, difficult: but this is not because of differences in the government of institutions, but because of differences of course-structure. The tightly-packed three-year degree contains, at each stage, prerequisites from the earlier stages, and it is a matter of luck if the first year of polytechnic A can be accepted as adequate preparation for the second year of university B. Thus many transfers involve a loss of a year, and come up against the problem of extending the student's grant. The will to allow transfers is certainly present, and is evidenced in the agreements which a number of institutions have made with the Open University for movement in both directions between its part-time courses and full-time work.

Problems of staff transfer in Britain arise also from simple practical considerations. At the younger ages, the 'public sector' institutions (polytechnics, colleges of education, etc.) have tended to pay higher salaries, and to offer longer holidays and lower expectations of effort, than the universities. They also have a research interest which is smaller, and in some cases negligible: in consequence they do not normally produce candidates capable of transfer to senior university posts, in which an established record in research is normally essential. A young university lecturer might find it financially attractive to have a few years' work in the public sector, but he would run the risk of cutting himself off from all higher university posts. Thus exchanges of staff, and indeed transfers of all kinds across the 'binary divide', are quite rare. In fifteen years' experience I can recall only one member of staff who moved from a public sector college to my university without a drop of salary.

This lack of cross-fertilisation is of course a disadvantage which can be in part attributed to the diverse structure. But it would be difficult to remove it — different unions are involved — and it is not clear that it would be possible or desirable to have a single salary structure for the whole of higher education. Even if all institutions had the same system of management there would be some mainly or entirely concerned with undergraduate (or lower-level) teaching, some with graduate interests, and some with heavy research commitments. No one in their senses would want to spread research evenly over the two hundred or so institutions in British higher education. The different interests of institutions (not all of which *need* to employ Fellows of the Royal Society or of the British Academy) would naturally produce differences of salary structure and job specification, which would impede movement.

The critics of waste, however, often have in mind another point. There appears to be no way of preventing the appearance of competing courses in the same subject, even though most of these courses may be undersubscribed: and expensive facilities such as libraries, computers and electron microscopes are provided in parallel, even for institutions which are very close to each other. In the British scene this lack of co-ordination exists between universities, and the existence of the public sector institutions only complicates a problem which is already there. It is an illusion to suppose that the University Grants Committee can control, or wishes to control, the details of a university's curriculum, except where a specialist building is involved or where there is a firm national plan (as with medicine).

I happen to believe that British universities are rather good at their job, and that part of their strength comes from the 'free enterprise' spirit—the unfettered ability to use their resources according to their own judgement. But this particular form of free enterprise is not subject to the discipline of the market: a university which makes a silly decision, to increase still further the excess of places for some subject, suffers no penalty except the internal stress produced by the misallocation of resources. Unfortunately the polytechnics and the colleges of higher education suffer, to some extent, from a tendency to seek academic status by copying the universities, so that errors, once begun, tend to be magnified.

But the significance of these misallocations must not be overemphasized. Some are due to shifts in student preference or national need which were quite unforeseeable, and which produce waste simply because the numbers of tenured staff cannot be reduced in line with demand. Some apparent overlapping is an illusion produced by using broad categories: two neighbouring institutions with degrees in engineering or chemistry or German may in fact teach these subjects on syllabuses so different that they are not genuinely competitive at all. I am inclined to think that the harm to be expected from any kind of central or regional control of activities would far exceed any benefit from the avoidance of waste. At least three activities in my university which provide a distinguished and special contribution to national needs would, I suspect, have been stopped by any system of 'planning'.

However, even if overlapping, undertaken after due consideration, can be justified, it ought not to be allowed to arise through ignorance. I do not put much reliance on the idea of a national bank of information about activities, plans and resources: I think it would get an unmanageable amount of material, and would be little used (except perhaps for sinister purposes of national control). But I would like to see much better *regional* exchanges of information, coupled with administrative systems which allow institutions to buy resources from each other and to set up joint facilities (*e.g.* computers). This development of common sense between neighbours is commonly prevented, partly by the suspicion of the local authority colleges that the universities want to control them and partly by the great difficulty of getting a flexible response from local authority administration. I suggested some time ago that my University council and the governing body of the nearest polytechnic should have an overlapping membership, so that at least a few people would know the plans and resources of both institutions. The suggestion was greeted with a stunned silence.

SUB-TOPIC 5(C): TRANSFER AND COMMUNICATION [Carter]

The British polytechnics and other public-sector colleges assert, quite rightly, that they are doing something different from the universities. They often, however, define the difference wrongly, believing their contribution to be more 'practical' or 'relevant' — an assertion which is readily disproved by looking at what is actually done. The real difference is that they have (potentially, at least) a wider range of work, with many activities other than degree courses: and that they are specialist teaching institutions, with much less interest in research. Two bodies doing different jobs could be equally honoured; but unfortunately many of the public-sector colleges have become exceedingly defensive about their 'status', and do not like anything which suggests co-operation with the universities lest an appearance of difference of status should be created. This is a pity, because there are common-sense things which could be done. In the north-west of England we have perhaps retained rather better links than elsewhere, since my University has close relations with six former colleges of education, two of which are now the education section of a polytechnic while three have diversified into degree courses other than those for teachers. The decisions about courses and academic policies are made jointly, admittedly with considerable calls on university expertise, but in committees in which the associated colleges have an equal (or majority) representation: and the colleges are represented on the university senate, which has to provide the final authority for the grant of degrees. However this system is an historical survival from the times when universities were the usual 'validating' authorities for teacher training, and it is partly accidental that Lancaster has been able not only to enlarge its group of associates but to go so far with the development of non-teaching degrees in the other colleges. There are other areas in which joint action would have been sensible — for instance, the University and the neighbouring Polytechnic would have done well to act jointly in developing social work training; but any suggestion of using the University as sole validating authority in that area would have been resented.

I conclude that the problems which arise in this area of transfer and communication among different institutions are in part the consequence of natural differences of structure and administration, but are aggravated by uncertainties of status and by the growth of defensive attitudes among those who imagine themselves to be regarded as inferior. There is no way of giving institutions 'parity of esteem' by declarations from ministers — indeed, public assertions of the equal excellence of different institutions tend to be counterproductive: they suggest that a special defence is needed, and that the case being made may be weak. But where relations can be at a personal, human level the difficulties usually disappear. The differences of function tend to be recognised as natural, and common sense begins to take over. I would therefore suggest dealing with the problem by multiplying the points of personal contact.

Dr. L. ISABELLE (*President of Algonquin College of Applied Arts and Technology*)*: Today I am effecting a *transfer* (the subject of our group discussion is transferability, is it not?) from my first half-century to what I pray will be a full second half! I'm 50 today!

It's therefore a *transfer*, a transfer from that group of people in their prime to that group, some of whom feel, are on the decline. Or, as some critics might have it, I am effecting a transfer from the 'group on the make' to that group whom the younger members of our society sometimes call 'on the take'.....

Introduction

If we were to ask each other which political, social or philosophical principles bind us, as participants at this Twelfth Commonwealth Universities Congress, we would probably hear égalité, fraternité et liberté! No?

If we were to ask each other, as college or university presidents (or vice-chancellors, as I hear it at this conference) which 'educational' or 'managerial' principles guide us, we would probably hear accessibility, flexibility, equity, transferability and accountability, all in a context of diversity, efficiency, economy and viability. Yes?

Transferability is the topic of our panel presentation for group discussion. Allow me to define the term transferability by quoting and paraphrasing the report of the Commission on Post-Secondary Education in Ontario. Transferability means ideally 'an accessible hierarchy of educational services—from on-the-job skill training to professional schools, from extension studies to graduate laboratory research—with screens but not closed barriers between the different levels'[1] leading to opportunities to transfer from institution to institution or from programme to programme. If this definition were

---

*This is a revised version of the paper that Dr. Isabelle presented at the Congress.
1. Ontario. Commission on Post-Secondary Education in Ontario. *The Ontario Colleges of Applied Arts and Technology*. A Study Prepared for the Commission, Toronto: Queen's Printer, 1972, p. 34.

SUB-TOPIC 5(C): TRANSFER AND COMMUNICATION [Isabelle]

accepted we would seek (i) 'to facilitate transfer between professions and from one level to another within a profession'[2] in order to break the constraint between educational credits for studies or programmes taken and professional licensing for admission to practice (the current practices assume as fact that there is a near perfect relationship between educational credits and requirements for the practice of the trade or profession); if this definition were accepted we would seek (ii) 'to provide orderly procedures for the transfer of abilities, aptitudes and skills from one post-secondary enterprise to another and, indeed, from one activity in an individual's life relevant to the educational process.'[3]

If we portray our educational systems as a ladder, narrower at the top than at the foot, transferability would mean movement 'upwards', step by step, from K to PhD (I hope that the image I am using applies to the more than 30 countries represented here).

Years	Level
1 – 8	PhD (2) Master (2) Bachelor (3 – 4) universities
1 – 3	Community College (in Ontario)
9 – 13	secondary (in Ontario)
7 – 8	intermediate (in some countries)
1 – 6	elementary
	pre-kindergarten kindergarten

Numbers refer to approximate years of study

If we portray occupations and families of occupations as ladders, again narrower at the upper end, as for example occupations in the health field, we find such distributions

2. Ibid., p. 34.
3. Ibid., p. 34.

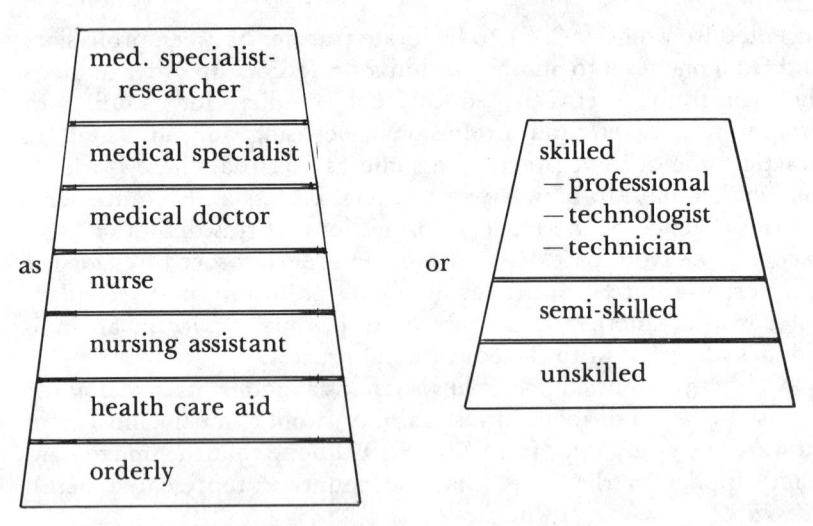

[Isabelle]   TOPIC 5: UNIVERSITIES AND OTHER INSTITUTIONS

```
                  ┌─────────────────┐
                  │ med. specialist-│
                  │   researcher    │
                  ├─────────────────┤
                  │medical specialist│              ┌──────────────────┐
                  ├─────────────────┤               │    skilled       │
                  │ medical doctor  │               │  — professional  │
            as    ├─────────────────┤       or      │  — technologist  │
                  │     nurse       │               │  — technician    │
                  ├─────────────────┤               ├──────────────────┤
                  │nursing assistant│               │   semi-skilled   │
                  ├─────────────────┤               ├──────────────────┤
                  │ health care aid │               │    unskilled     │
                  ├─────────────────┤               └──────────────────┘
                  │    orderly      │
                  └─────────────────┘
```

where we would also observe ever-decreasing numbers of persons as we 'move up' the occupation scale.

Egalitarians argue that we can all be MDs..... PhDs....., and if not it is because 'society' or 'the system' has failed us. But research in vocational psychology reveals to me that differences exist, differences in both *potential* and *actualization*, differences in abilities, aptitudes, interests, personality characteristics, differences in motivation, in 'drive'..... Equal before God, *yes*, but not equals in intelligence, in aptitude, in skill, in achievement. Just as we are not equals in size, weight, colour, agility, strength..... Should we not praise and thank *him* or *her* for these shades or variations? 'Vive la différence' est un vieux dicton.....

Research in psychology reveals, to me at least, 'normal distributions' of human characteristics, and the bell-shaped curve is indeed a well-known illustration. University graduates are found to come from the top 16% of the general population, or from the top 12% of a grade one entrance class. (I shaded in a different style that right-hand portion of the distribution, to illustrate the data better). MAs and PhDs usually are those at the top 3 or 4%. 'Élitist' shout the egalitarians! I'm sure you hear them too, don't you?

The same research reveals that colleges like Algonquin College, a CCAATT (you have never seen such poor spelling!)—that is, a Community College of Applied Arts, Technology and Trades— offer programmes that are designed to cover 84 to 96% of that 'normal distribution'. Such colleges offer programmes designed for manpower upgrading or retraining, apprentices, 1-, 2- and 3-year post-secondary programmes in a wide spectrum of endeavours

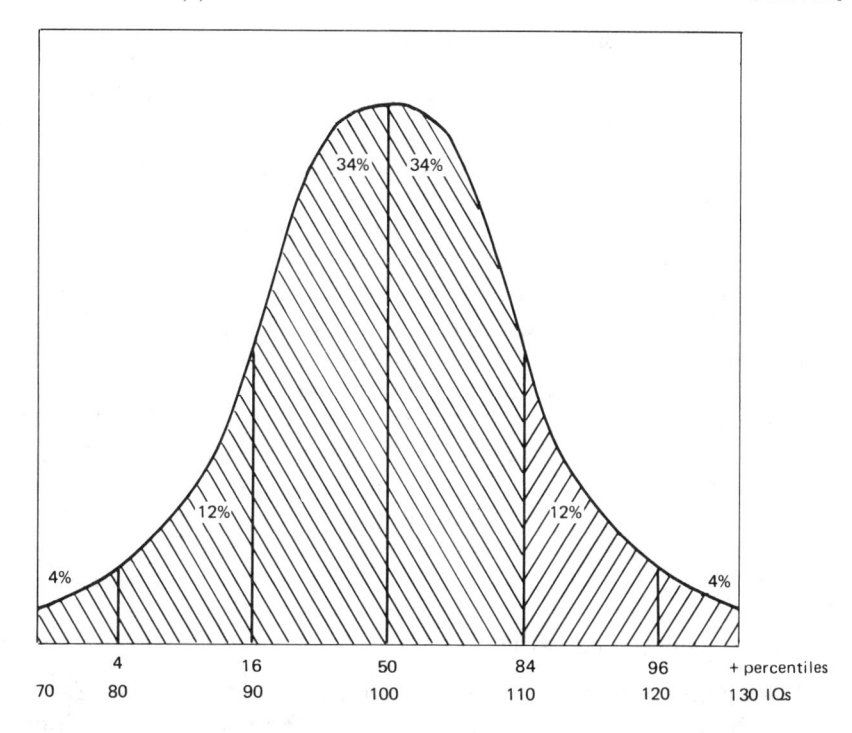

SUB-TOPIC 5(C): TRANSFER AND COMMUNICATION   [*Isabelle*]

[Bell curve figure showing normal distribution with percentages 4%, 12%, 34%, 34%, 12%, 4% under the curve; percentiles 4, 16, 50, 84, 96 + percentiles; IQs 70, 80, 90, 100, 110, 120, 130]

Percentages under the curve refer to proportions of the general population within that part of the distribution. Bottom scores refer to traditional measures of intelligence (IQs)

including health sciences, training in business and industry, management development programmes, community education, and others too numerous to list here.

Transferability, in the light of such data, suggests that MAs and PhDs are very gifted or talented indeed, that at best we can expect the resource pool to be 3 or 4% of any broad general distribution of human beings, that undergraduates undertaking studies at the honours level are normally drawn from a reserve pool of approximately 16% of a general population. In concrete terms, it is clear to me that not all community college or polytechnic students are 'university material'; nor in social and philosophical terms should they be led or misled to think they are. That does not mean that I consider these students to be 'poorer than' or 'better than' university-bound students. To me it means they are 'equal to' and 'different'. Old clichés, some of you might say..... Well, not to my understanding. To me, it's 'parity of esteem'; it's *different* but *equal*.....

But transferability must not just be a concept of *upward* mobility, as if upward always meant better. Transferability must also apply to *lateral* mobility, that is, movement from one programme of study to

547

another or from one occupation to another at approximately the same levels of demands on talent, drive and motivation.

Transferability implies a recognition of 'transfer of learning', that is, recognition that learning this particular subject has enabled the learner to discover *how to* learn. Transferability implies recognition of experiential learning and not just recognition of 'paper credentials'. And we all know that this is, however, difficult to measure. It is indeed a challenge!

The CCAATTs of Ontario, one of Canada's 10 provinces (forgive the parochialism!), as institutions of learning and skill development, are clear alternatives to the universities in the province. They are not half-way houses. There are no formal transfer routes. As a matter of fact we shun them, we do not want them. *But* all these colleges will encourage individual students who have demonstrated talent and achievement and who want to go on to university, or to *transfer* to the university in mid-stream or at the end of their college programme, to do so. We will encourage the universities to recognize merit on an individual basis. But we will not seek their accreditation of our programmes. Allow me to quote a passage from a report I mentioned earlier:

> 'Although the present system of haphazard and uncertain transfers from colleges of applied arts and technology to universities clearly brings hardships to individual students, a formal, uniform system of transfers would, in our view, diminish the variety present in our post-secondary educational system. If a transfer policy stipulated that X credits in a college were worth Y university credits, X and Y could be either equal or unequal. If they were equal, then the colleges of applied arts and technology would actually become junior colleges, a policy rejected by the Ontario government and equally by this Commission. If they were not equal, this would imply that the colleges' courses were either inferior or superior to university courses. But that implication is unacceptable; while these courses may or may not be "equal", they should be different. Furthermore, a uniform transfer policy would very likely be followed by a uniform syllabus or by a tendency of colleges of applied arts and technology to imitate university undergraduate courses.'[4]

This is a good illustration of what I meant earlier when I said 'parity of esteem'.

A final and touchy point on this topic of transferability. Some among this assembly may be surprised and perhaps offended by my

---

4. Ibid., p. 50

SUB-TOPIC 5(C): TRANSFER AND COMMUNICATION [*Isabelle*]

abuse of the word 'transferability'..... and it is perhaps a risk that I'm taking!

CCAATTs in Ontario—22 of them—(and perhaps similar institutions in other provinces and countries) are clear alternatives to the province's 15 universities. Their objectives are, in summary, short, career-oriented programmes—both full- and part-time—whose programme contents are roughly defined as 70% 'vocational' and 30% 'general education', or 60 – 70% 'practical' and 40 – 30% 'theoretical'. Whereas universities' objectives *were*, and perhaps *are* (if not, I think they should be), the maintenance of a thriving and existing community of scholars dedicated to the extension, dissemination and preservation of knowledge. The colleges and the universities are different, but equal, and therefore complementary to each other, and not just competitors for bodies as is increasingly the case these days in countries hard-pressed for funds.

I have portrayed their differences and their similarities in geometric terms[5] in the illustration below. Assuming the same base, namely, high school graduation, the colleges' curricula may be represented by a trapezoidal structure (broader at the top than at

FIGURE 1: DISTINCTION BETWEEN UNIVERSITY AND COMMUNITY COLLEGE EDUCATION BY MEANS OF GEOMETRIC REPRESENTATION

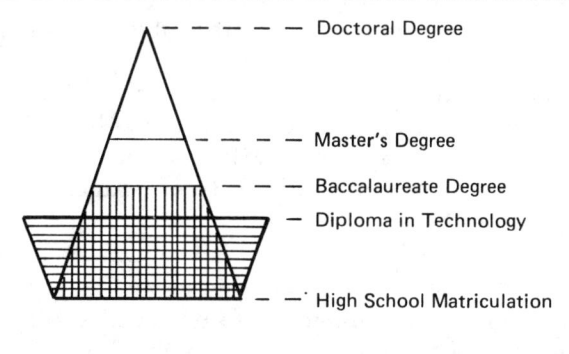

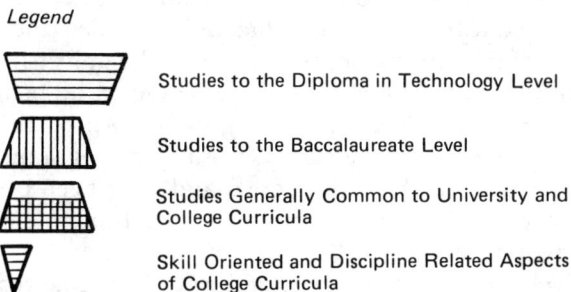

– – – – Doctoral Degree

– – – – Master's Degree

– – – Baccalaureate Degree
– Diploma in Technology

–· High School Matriculation

Legend

Studies to the Diploma in Technology Level

Studies to the Baccalaureate Level

Studies Generally Common to University and College Curricula

Skill Oriented and Discipline Related Aspects of College Curricula

5. Ryant, Maurice A. and Isabelle, Laurent, *Colleges, Universities and Society in Interaction*, unpublished paper, 1978.

the base), whereas the universities' curricula should be represented by a triangular form (see Figure 1, above). In the case of universities, as the student moves towards a baccalaureate degree a measure of specialization begins to take place and, consequently, his or her horizons begin to narrow. In moving towards the master's degree further specialization occurs so that the structure of the triangle becomes more apparent. With the attainment of the doctoral degree the triangle is completed, with the student having demonstrated expertise in a particular aspect of his or her discipline.

Within given disciplines in the community colleges, however, the programmes are designed to broaden the scope of the student's knowledge and skills and so prepare him/her for the diverse demands which would be made of him or her on employment after graduation. Theoretical development in the major discipline does not proceed to the depth studied in the university. Far more time, however, is spent in developing laboratory and shop skills in situations replicating those which would be experienced at work. Moreover theoretical, laboratory and shop skills are provided in the related disciplines to ensure further that the graduate is immediately utilizable on employment with minimal time spent on on-the-job training. The college student's range of knowledge and practice is broader—but shallower than that of the student from the university.

These distinctions are fundamental and essential. *If I am right* I should add that in my estimation some univerities have lost sight of their objectives; and others, particularly now, at least in Canada, because we are facing pressures arising from financial constraint, will surely lose sight of their objectives.

In the last 50 years, perhaps more, an era which was characterized by a rapidly expanding school population as well as by favourable systems of government formula grants to universities, we have seen the basic direction of the universities change. (Grave disquiet has been voiced about the quality of education provided and about the raison d'être of the universities themselves.) The universities seem to have attempted, in recent years, to be all things to all people. Their range of programmes has expanded greatly and to an increasing extent they have tended to become job-oriented programmes. While such programmes may have developed and have been presented in an atmosphere of excellence, they make no fundamental contribution to existing knowledge.

The universities of the future, cognizant of the role that is being played by the community colleges and of the nature of excellence of the services rendered by these institutions, will have opportunities to redefine their roles and, in doing so, maintain the primacy of research and creative endeavour. Legitimate questions will have to be asked as to the place of existing programmes in the armamentary of the universities. For example, the place of programmes such as library science, business administration, physiotherapy, physical education, teacher training, journalism, and perhaps many others, must be questioned. Do they not belong in the community colleges or polytechnics, institutions capable of handling such challenges, thus enabling the universities to utilize their financial and physical resources in areas desperate for the funds so necessary to support research activities? Thus a criterion for the retention of a programme in the university of the future could be whether or not the programme has a significant research component associated with it. Only in such instances will the frontiers of knowledge be advanced, new knowledge and insights acquired and new concepts developed to a degree commensurate with the resources available for this purpose.

REFERENCES

British Columbia, Department of Education, Research and Development Division, Task Force on the Community College in British Columbia. *Towards the Learning Community: Report*, Victoria: Queen's Printer, 1974.

Campbell, Gordon. 'Community Colleges of Canada'. In *Universities and Colleges of Canada, 1976*, pp. 36 – 44, Ottawa: Statistics Canada in co-operation with the Association of Universities and Colleges of Canada, 1977.

Campbell, Gordon. 'Some Comments on Reports of Post-Secondary Commissions in Relation to Community Colleges in Canada'. *Canadian Journal of Higher Education* 5, no. 3 (1975): 55 – 68.

Colvin, James; Isabelle, Laurent; and Rowless, Dorothy. 'The CAAT's Next Decade: A View from the Top'. *OCLEA*, no. 7 (May 1976): 3 – 5.

Cooke, R. H. and Harper, D. C. College-University Transfer: *Evolving a Province-wide Solution*. CAUT Bulletin ACPU, 23, no. 3 (1974): 21 – 22.

Dennison, John D. 'The Colleges of British Columbia: Some Basic Issues'. *Stoa* 1, no. 1 (1971): 27 – 33.

Dennison, John D., and others. *The Impact of Community Colleges: A Study of the College Concept in British Columbia*. Vancouver: B. C. Research, 1975.

Jardine, D. K. *Transferability: a Matter of Integrity*, CAUT Bulletin ACPU, 23, no. 3 (1974): 15 – 16.

Konrad, Abram G., ed. *Clientele and Community: The Student in the Canadian Junior College*. Toronto: Association of Canadian Community Colleges, 1974.

[*Isabelle*]   TOPIC 5: UNIVERSITIES AND OTHER INSTITUTIONS

Long, John C. *The Ontario CAATs 1965 – 73 – A Case Study of The Transfer Issue in College-University Relationships,* unpublished paper, 1974.

McIntosh, R. G., ed. *The Community College in Canada: Present Status, Future Prospects.* Edmonton: University of Alberta, Department of Educational Administration, 1971.

Manitoba. Task Force on Post-Secondary Education in Manitoba, *Report,* Winnipeg, 1973.

Ontario. Commission on Post-Secondary Education in Ontario. *The Ontario Colleges of Applied Arts and Technology.* A Study Prepared for the Commission, Toronto: Queen's Printer, 1972.

Ryant, Maurice A. and Isabelle, Laurent. *Colleges, Universities and Society in Interaction,* unpublished paper, 1978.

Sheffield, Edward F. 'A Coherent System for Manitoba'. *Stoa* 4, no. 1 (1974): 111 – 16.

Thiemann, Francis C., and Mowat, Gordon L., eds. *Report of the Hearing by the Canadian Commission for the Community College,* Toronto: Canadian Commission for the Community College; Edmonton: University of Alberta, Department of Educational Administration, 1969.

Whitelaw, James H. 'From CEGEP to University: Problems of Articulation in Quebec'. *Canadian University and College* 6, no. 2 (March – April 1971): 52 – 55.

Special thanks to Wayne Smith, Reference Section, Resource Centre, Algonquin College of Applied Arts and Technology, Ottawa, for his identification of appropriate resources for the preparation of this paper.

Mr. A. Z. PRESTON (*Vice-Chancellor of the University of the West Indies*): My special assignment today is to discuss the subject 'Problems of Transfer and Communication among Different Institutions'. I would like to say at the outset that I am not an expert on this subject, and because of this limitation I propose dealing with it mainly from the point of view of the University of the West Indies (UWI).

The UWI continues to be the major indigenous university institution serving most of the territories of the English-speaking Caribbean. This represents a geographical spread of some fourteen island territories, five of which are independent territories within the Commonwealth, and two mainland territories, one of which is independent with its own universty (the University of Guyana) established in 1963 and working in close collaboration with the UWI.

The inter-university relationship, though it took some time to be realised, has been achieved with relative ease largely on the basis of the parity deemed to exist between higher educational institutions that are similar not only in name but in stated objectives and levels of operation. Relationships are not always as easily forged with other tertiary educational institutions which embrace a wide variety of types from national 'global' colleges (such as the recently established College of the Bahamas and the projected College of Jamaica) and technical colleges (*e.g.* the College of Arts, Science and Technology (CAST) in Jamaica, and the John Donaldson Technical Institute in Trinidad), through professional schools (such as teacher training colleges, schools of agriculture, theological colleges) to cultural training institutions (such as the newly established Cultural Training Centre in Jamaica housing the national schools of art, music, dance, and drama). A further complication is the fact that, while the UWI is a regional institution, most if not all of the other tertiary institutions are national ones fully financed and controlled by the individual territorial government.

The problems that have attended, and still attend, efforts at transfer and communication between such institutions on the one hand and the UWI on the other may be examined from three points of view — the *philosophical*, the *technical* and the *structural*. They represent dimensions which are all inter-connected. But a recognition of their separate existence and the peculiar emphases each carries has helped immensely in coming to grips with some of the problems.

The Philosophical Dimension

In a society where education remains one of the key instruments of social mobility, university and other tertiary-level education has been at a premium. The pre-independence legacy of an elitist tertiary-level education for the training of 'leaders' still lingers in the Commonwealth Caribbean situation, though there has been a tremendous move away from this through the increased opportunities that have existed since the late forties for West Indians of all classes to receive higher education in an ever widening variety of specialisms. But even within this new range of choice old prejudices die hard. The primacy of the university over other tertiary institutions presents psychological problems in the assessing of courses offered by the latter, and in according due academic worth to their 'graduates'. There is also a problem outside the university of assessing university degrees in terms of the use for which they were designed, as distinct from the use to which necessity might dictate they should in particular circumstances be put.

The right of the university to exist as a special and unique type of higher education institution is not openly challenged. This right continues to survive because most people believe in it; and the university plays its part by not being absent from scenes where new third-level institutions are being produced, by never failing to help shape the new creations, and by continually subjecting to review its own conception of what is or is not a university subject.

Some of the policy utterances of popularly elected governments described as progressive or enlightened and pledged to fight the deleterious consequences of colonialism and imperialism are a reaction to the primacy of the university among tertiary institutions. The aim is for the democratisation not only in terms of making higher education accessible to more people and in having more people involved in the management of education, but also in terms of de-mystifying the hegemonic role of the university (especially that of the classical type) in the overall and the more popular system of education.

Moreover, with the increasing emphasis on development and the impact of growth theories on Caribbean and third world public policy strategies, greater encouragement is being given to appropriate or intermediate technology; and tertiary-level training with strong practical inputs has been promoted ever since the early sixties by the bigger territories like Trinidad and Jamaica. The notion that the university is the sole repository of higher wisdom and knowledge is therefore ideological anathema to many political leaders and others who are more interested in the production of manpower to meet needed levels for the management and development of the economy. The urgency of the development process and the shortage of time dictate to them the need for a plurality of 'production agencies' and a fusion of aims to fill the gap. Some tend to consider that the university community holds on to what it regards as the standards, academic life-style and mores of metropolitan model institutions—often in vigilant defence of intellectual freedom and academic excellence. Some tend to see the university as an anachronism and demand that it be relevant. It is particularly in this situation that the difficulty of communication plays so critical a part. And here I am speaking of a two-way communication process. A polarisation of views is unnecessary and wasteful. The situation requires rational and sane assessment by the university itself of the justifiable claims made on it by the society it serves and an examination of the ways of meeting these. This does no violence to the commitment which it must preserve in respect of professional competence, intellectual integrity and academic excellence. Indeed without this commitment its role as an agent of development is minimised.

There persists that ambivalence which still places the university at the peak of the pinnacle while questioning the university's claim to that position. The university 'degree' still carries a great psychic pull and the desire to up-grade certificates and diplomas to 'graduate status' remains a feature of the relationship between university and other tertiary-level institutions. In some ways this is a non-question since it is the quality of the product and not the name it goes by which counts. But the creative tension that therefore exists between the university and other tertiary institutions in the region provides the basis for a continuing dialogue, sometimes heated and even irrational, but never without the possibility of discovering solutions suited to the special problems.

The Technical Dimension

A necessary approach to the problem is through the technical dimension—that is by way of accrediting courses pursued in other tertiary institutions and determining the status of the graduates. The early years of the UWI did not afford the University the opportunity to do this since it was itself a college in special relationship with the University of London. It has sought positively to address the problem since its own independence. Notwithstanding the concern as to standards (and academic jurisdiction) and the habitual conservatism on the part of some University academics, the need to provide opportunity for economic advancement has been fully accepted and the UWI has agreed on schemes of accreditation covering matriculation, exemption from a year of a degree course, and even individual first-year courses, and we are now discussing the mixed exemption from year 1 and year 2 courses.

The general approach adopted has been that just as students with 'O' (ordinary) levels follow two-year 'A' (advanced) level courses in the sixth form, so students who complete two years at a tertiary institution from basic 'O' level admission should be considered for normal matriculation and those who do more should be considered for exemption from courses in the degree programme where this is appropriate.

1. *Matriculation.* Certificates or diplomas from the schools of agriculture, colleges of technology and teacher training colleges are generally recognised and specific recognition is given to others. In addition, passes at an agreed level in certain subjects in the institutions' examinations are recognised as equivalent to passes in the

appropriate 'O'- or 'A'-level examination in order to satisfy specific requirements. The University usually prescribes passes in four subjects at 'O' level or the equivalent in order to ensure that a range of subjects has been covered at this level.

2. *Exemption from part of degree course.* (i) BSc(Agric) part I: applicants holding the Associateship of the Jamaica School of Agriculture or equivalent qualifications are exempted from part I (year 1) of the degree and admitted directly to part II.

(ii) BSc(Eng) part I: studies pursued and examinations passed elsewhere may be accepted in lieu of studies and examinations for part I (year 1). This is now done for the Diploma in Engineering Technology at CAST and for the University of Guyana's Higher Diploma in Technology.

In these cases the University accepts the qualification from the other institutions without any attempt to control or supervise syllabus, staffing, etc., though a pass at a stated minimum grade may be required.

(iii) A special case of this kind is that of the University's 2-year BEd degree which was designed for qualified teachers with at least 5 years' approved teaching experience who hold or are likely to hold posts of special responsibility and perform satisfactorily in an entrance examination. The University's senate in approving the programme accepted the view that the special students to be admitted had acquired advanced status by virtue of their teacher training certificate plus job experience. A modified form of this programme has now been introduced at the College of the Bahamas whereby the first year is done as a 2-year part-time course.

(iv) Special arrangements for exemption from year 1 of the BSc in social sciences in relation to admission to the degree in hotel management. A new approach has recently been adopted in relation to the associate degree of the College of the Bahamas which will be accepted for granting exemption from part I (year 1) of the UWI degree in hotel management. The College is relatively new and the course specially constructed, and while there is no requirement that University examinations should be taken the faculty of social sciences will be involved in vetting the courses and monitoring the examinations. No students have yet been presented however. This scheme is particularly interesting since it assumes that students at the College of the Bahamas will be prepared for first-year university examinations in 2 years from 'O'-level standard, just as is now done within the University.

(v) *Exemption from individual first-year courses.* The faculty of social sciences has also agreed to grant credit for first-year courses taken at other institutions. Such accreditation has so far only been given in accounting I but the possibility of other exemptions exists.

(vi) *Mixed exemption from year 1 and 2 courses.* A case under consideration at present is that of students who complete a diploma course at the Bahamas Hotel Training College or at similar institutions for middle management training in the industry. Such students would not have covered all the first-year social science requirements of the University's programme, but will have covered some of the courses which would normally be done in our second year. The proposal now under consideration is that of exempting them, on an experimental basis, from the appropriate courses and then requiring them to make up the first- and second-year deficiencies in their first year at the University.

As might be expected the UWI academics continue to entertain much concern about these admissions and it is therefore interesting to examine the performance statistics given in Tables 1, 2 and 3, below. Table 1 compares the performance of students admitted from 1971 to 1973 to arts at the Mona Campus with 2 'A' levels and with the teachers' diploma; Table 2 compares performance of students admitted in the same period with different qualifications to the 3-year agriculture degree and that of students admitted from 1972 to 1974 with the associateship to the 2-year degree; Table 3 does roughly the same as Table 2 but for engineering.

The following conclusions appear reasonable:—

(i) In general the 2-'A'-level admissions perform better than the diploma admissions both in terms of percentage passes and percentage obtaining firsts and upper seconds.

(ii) The performance of the diploma admissions is quite satisfactory.

(iii) The performance of the students exempted from year 1 is very good and in general even better than the 'A'-level admissions. However since the number of such admissions is small the safest conclusion probably is that the present selection requirements could probably be relaxed somewhat.

The shortage of qualified 'A'-level applicants in the science-based areas in some of the territories has encouraged the University to introduce a 1-year preliminary science course to which students with good grades in 5 'O' levels may be admitted, although many students with 1 'A' level or even with 2 'A' levels but lacking certain prerequisites are also admitted. Not surprisingly some of the other institutions claim that they could also offer the equivalent of such a programme, thus enabling their students to reach first-year degree level in 2 years.

This is essentially the significance of the agreement to allow students at the College of the Bahamas to do part I social sciences

TABLE 1: DEGREE PERFORMANCE OF ARTS STUDENTS BY QUALIFICATION AT ADMISSION
Mona Campus, UWI — 1971 – 1973 Admissions

Yr. of Admission	Qualifs.	No.	Dropouts Yr. 1	Yr. 2	Later	Graduated in Four Years Yr. 3*	Yr. 4*	Total*	%	Ongoing after 4 Yrs.
1971	2 'A's	76	1	4	1	61(13)	8(1)	69(14)	91	1
	†Diplomas	40	5	1	1	19(3)	11(—)	30(3)	75	1
	‡Other	11	—	1	—	8(2)	1(—)	9(2)	82	1
	Total	127	6	6	2	88(18)	20(1)	108(19)	85	3
1972	2 'A's	60	—	2	2	47(14)	6(—)	53(14)	88	3
	Diplomas	72	—	8	2	40(1)	15(—)	55(1)	74	7
	Other	15	1	1	1	8(2)	2(—)	10(2)	67	2
	Total	147	1	11	5	95(17)	23(—)	118(17)	80	12
1973	2 'A's	74	—	3	1	49(8)	17(1)	66(9)	89	4
	Diplomas	57	3	1	—	38(6)	13(—)	51(6)	89	2
	Other	5	1	1	—	3(—)	—	3(—)	60	—
	Total	136	4	5	1	90(14)	24(1)	120(15)	88	6

*Numbers in brackets refer to those obtaining first- or upper second-class degrees.
†These refer almost exclusively to teacher training colleges.
‡These refer mainly to students admitted under the mature clause.

SUB-TOPIC 5(C): TRANSFER AND COMMUNICATION [Preston]

TABLE 2: COMPARISON OF DEGREE PERFORMANCE OF UWI AGRICULTURE STUDENTS BY ADMISSIONS CATEGORIES

(a) Three-Year Degrees—1971–1973 Admissions

Year	Category	No. Admitted	Drop-out	Graduated in Four Years					Ongoing after 4 Yrs.
				3 Yrs.*	4 Yrs.*	3 or 4 Yrs.*	% of Adm.	
1971	†D.E.: 'A' Levels	20	3	15(3)	2(—)	17(3)	85.0	—
	†D.E.: Diplomas	21	6	8(2)	7(—)	15(2)	71.4	—
	‡Transfers	12	2	6(3)	3(—)	9(3)	75.0	1
	Total	53	11	29(8)	12(—)	41(8)	77.4	1
1972	D.E.: 'A' Levels	20	1	15(8)	3(1)	18(9)	90.0	1
	D.E.: Diplomas	27	6	14(2)	7(1)	21(3)	77.8	—
	Transfers	23	2	15(1)	6(—)	21(1)	91.3	—
	Total	70	9	44(11)	16(2)	60(13)	85.7	1
1973	D.E.: 'A' Levels	35	1	29(11)	2(—)	31(11)	88.6	3
	D.E.: Diplomas	28	4	12(3)	7(—)	19(3)	67.9	5
	Transfers	16	4	12(6)	—	12(6)	75.0	—
	Total	79	9	53(20)	9(—)	62(20)	78.5	8

continued overleaf

TABLE 2 (continued)

(b) Two-Year Degrees—1972–1974 Admissions

Year	No. Admitted	Dropout	Graduated in Three Years			Ongoing after 3 Yrs.
			2 Yrs.*	3 Yrs.	Total*	% of Adm.	
1972	6	—	6(3)	—	6(3)	100	—
1973	2	—	2(—)	—	2(—)	100	—
1974	4	—	4(2)	—	4(2)	100	—

*Numbers in brackets refer to those obtaining first- or upper second-class degrees.
†D.E. = Direct entry to the University for 3-year degree.
‡Usually refers to students who transfer from preliminary or part I science.

TABLE 3: COMPARISON OF DEGREE PERFORMANCE OF UWI ENGINEERING STUDENTS BY ADMISSIONS CATEGORIES

(a) Three-Year Degrees—1971–1973 Admissions

Year	Category	No. Admitted	Drop-out	Graduated in Four Years					Ongoing after 4 Yrs.
				3 Yrs.*	4 Yrs.*	Total*	% of Adm.	
1971	Direct entrants	79	12	54(24)	5(—)	59(24)	74.7	8
	†Transfers	37	9	7(3)	14(—)	21(3)	56.8	7
	Total	116	21	61(27)	19(—)	80(27)	69.0	15
1972	Direct entrants	54	9	28(16)	12(—)	40(16)	74.1	5
	Transfers	47	12	16(2)	13(1)	29(3)	61.7	6
	Total	101	21	44(18)	25(1)	69(19)	68.3	11
1973	Direct entrants	69	13	43(21)	12(3)	55(24)	79.7	1
	Transfers	49	8	28(5)	13(—)	41(5)	83.7	—
	Total	118	21	71(26)	25(3)	96(29)	81.4	1

continued overleaf

TABLE 3 (continued)
(b) Two-Year Degrees—1972–1974 Admissions

| Year | No. Admitted | Dropout | Graduated in Three Years |||| Ongoing after 3 Yrs. |
			2 Yrs.*	3 Yrs.*	Total*	% of Adm.	
1972	9	1	7(4)	1	8(4)	89	—
1973	7	—	6(—)	—	6(—)	86	1
1974	9	—	6(1)	3(2)	9(3)	100	—

*Numbers in brackets refer to those obtaining first- or upper second-class degrees.
†Usually refers to students who transfer from preliminary or part I science.

and a similar proposal has been made by CAST in relation to the degree in engineering. Such proposals will receive very careful scrutiny, however, as there is a body of opinion which jealously advocates unrelieved custodial care over all courses which bear the seal of UWI accreditation. In addition, we are ourselves well aware that the preliminary science approach also has some disadvantages.

Similar arguments have been put forward for a joint 4-year degree with the teacher training colleges and there is a distinct possibility that if the University does not seek to accommodate such requests the institutions in one country may be given the power to award degrees.

Of course our situation is aggravated by our proximity to the USA as students completing courses in some of the other institutions can usually obtain equivalent credits at *some* American university. Herein lies one of our problems, however, as the one University must be 'all things to all men'. It must seek to maintain and even improve on the standards bequeathed by London University and at the same time to accommodate all the varieties of transfer arrangements which may be available from the full and significantly wider range of North American universities.

The Structural Dimension

Such problems, or rather 'fears', can be and are met by yet another approach which may be described as structural — and is by way of the more direct *association of the staff in the two sets of institutions* (as opposed to individuals). This involves a high level of communication, general consultation, planning of curricula, examining and even participating in joint degree programmes through one of the mechanisms described below.

A standard though important form of link is that of affiliation. In our case we have affiliated four theological colleges through which programmes for the licentiate and the BA degree in theology are awarded. The students are registered in the colleges but the teachers and examiners need to be approved by the University faculty. The examinations are handled like other University examinations.

A different arrangement exists with the affilated Caribbean Meteorological Institute which offers degree courses in meteorology to our students as part of the BSc programme at the Cave Hill campus in Barbados. Teachers and examiners have to be approved as mentioned before.

In the case of the Institute of International Relations the UWI has gone one stage further. The Institute, which is mainly funded by the Trinidad and Tobago government but is also supported by other regional governments, offers diploma, MSc and PhD programmes for University qualifications but the students are officially registered with the institution and not with the University.

Conditions for affiliation are stringent and senate must 'satisfy itself that the college or other institution has attained an appropriate standard of educational efficiency' before recommending affiliation.

Secondly, the *closer working association between the University and other tertiary institutions*. As in other countries, the Institute of Education was established for the specific purpose of assisting with the development of teacher training colleges and more generally 'reaching out' in education. It has thus been involved with them in curriculum development, upgrading of and to a certain extent standardising the teacher training programmes and in consultancy and research programmes in response to specific requests. The school of education has taken over the work of the Institute and is also directly involved in the monitoring of the examinations taken in the colleges through the provision for joint boards of teacher education.

Extensive discussions have taken place at varying stages in relation to a closer link between the school of agriculture in Jamaica and the faculty of agriculture in Trinidad. As a result of the discussions it was agreed that the faculty would assist the school in enabling it to mount the first year of the degree programme by providing very limited staff and this was done for about 3 years. However the school found the scheme too costly for the number of students involved and it was abandoned in favour of exemption from the first year via the associate degree mentioned above.

A third structural approach has over the past decade earned the designation 'outreach'. The increasing desire to rationalise a wish into formal policy for implementation is a function of the geographical realities of the island archipelago with separate communities in the Leeward and Windward Islands eager for continuous educational activity at levels other than the primary and secondary. The old public relations and 'intellectual enrichment' programmes of the extra-mural department, the official outreach arm of the University, are no longer regarded as adequate for the development needs of these territories which are independence-bound. The problem of inadequate funds notwithstanding, territorial governments are demanding stronger outreach programmes by the University in helping them to build up tertiary-level educational capabilities within the territories.

It was in response to this articulated need that a recent intergovernmental committee charged with examining the problems recommended to the Commonwealth Caribbean heads of government that there is a need for 'greatly increased emphasis on "outreach" and extension programmes in all teaching and research activities of the University'. 'In this connection', concludes the committee, 'the role, scope and functions of the Extra-Mural Department should be re-oriented'.

Other recommendations which have been accepted as guidelines by the heads of government conference but subject to examination of costs and the necessary funding are that:—

(1) the University should develop systems of accreditation so as to allow students from other tertiary institutions to enter the University at an appropriate point;

(2) consideration should be given to the introduction of the teaching of university courses in non-university tertiary institutions up to full first degree levels using qualified staff in these institutions supervised by the University;

(3) the University should play a positive role in the development and improvement of other tertiary institutions;

(4) the University should be regarded as part of the entire system of tertiary education and a right balance should be struck between the University and the non-university components of the tertiary system.

It will be seen that these guidelines formalise and give official blessing to policies which the University has sought to pursue. The College of the Bahamas is already collaborating with the UWI on lines suggested by the second recommendation above, and the University both institutionally and through its individual members has played and continues to play a positive role in the development and improvement of other tertiary institutions (colleges of technology, teacher training colleges, cultural training centres in Jamaica, College of the Bahamas, the Morne complex comprising tertiary institutions in St. Lucia).

One area in which the need for the University's assistance is constantly mentioned is the post-'O'-level work in the smaller territories. The approach in the past has been through the traditional sixth form but there is a move now towards community college or junior college organisation merging the traditional sixth form, the teacher training college and the technical college, plus general educational development of the community through evening or day-release classes. The University has pledged its co-operation with such developments but the problems of size and economics loom large. Here the voluntary public service by individual members of the UWI staff operating all over the region cannot be underestimated. The presence of the University affords the opportunity for consultancy service in the field of education. But more important is the evidence of widespread voluntary advisory service rendered by individual members of the University staff in development plans (physical planning, curriculum design, policy refinements) for other tertiary educational institutions.

On the fourth recommendation (above) the University is increasingly being regarded as part of the entire system of tertiary education. The old prejudices and caution surrounding sometimes legitimate concerns about standards can still be detected, although to a lesser degree, while the conservative indulgences on status are disappearing fast, if not altogether. The major problem has been, and continues to be, limited resources—financial and manpower, and the University has not been able to move ahead as would have been desirable; nor in a world of decreasing money resources does it seem likely there will be much improvement in the foreseeable future. But perhaps the greatest problem is still a case of the will on the part of the UWI to effect creative interface with other institutions of tertiary education galloping ahead of the material means to implement meaningful and productive schemes. How we close the gap, and how soon, are questions of increasing significance.

DISCUSSION
See page 567

Topic 5

UNIVERSITIES AND OTHER INSTITUTIONS OF TERTIARY EDUCATION

Discussion

Chairman: Sir HARRY PITT
Vice-Chancellor of the University of Reading

Rapporteur: Mr. J. HOLMES
Director of the Education, Science and Culture Division of Statistics Canada

Thursday, 24 August

For the fourth discussion period on Topic 5 there were no opening speakers/papers; the entire session was devoted to discussion, which is covered in the account given below.

DISCUSSION
(covering all four sessions)

The topic was divided into three sub-topics: (*a*) differentiation of roles between different institutions of higher education; (*b*) problems of choice between different institutions; (*c*) problems of transfer and communication among different institutions. A session was devoted to each of these sub-topics, which were introduced by the eight speakers whose papers are printed in the preceding pages, and there was also a final session devoted entirely to further discussion. At all four sessions the discussions were lively and despite differences in the viewpoints that were expressed a true *esprit de corps* prevailed.

Throughout the discussions one thing came out loud and clear, namely the existing diversity of the universities in the Commonwealth. Indeed as the discussions veered here and there identifying specific points there seemed to be no agreement as to the roles of a university. The diversity

TOPIC 5: UNIVERSITIES AND OTHER INSTITUTIONS

therefore came to be accepted as inevitable, although not before exhaustive discussions. One thing which emerged unanimously was that the ACU ought to play a more leading role in arranging exchange of information, persons, etc., not only between universities in developed and developing countries but also between universities in the different developing countries of the Commonwealth.

In the discussion on the first sub-topic—differentiation of roles between different institutions of higher education—the group noted the rapid expansion in facilities for higher education that had taken place during the preceding decades in almost every part of the Commonwealth. At the same time the group noted that there was at present a certain element of disenchantment in many parts of the Commonwealth with the universities and their role. This in some parts of the Commonwealth has led to fewer people seeking entry into the university. That apart, demographic trends alone suggested that in some countries some years from now there would be fewer university entrants. Another significant factor hindering further expansion of the university system was that, in some countries, wherever national priorities dictated a cut in allocations it was invariably sought to levy that cut on the university system.

Against this background the group accepted the eight possible roles of institutions of higher education described by Sir Frederick Dainton (University Grants Committee, U.K.), namely: (i) liberal education for selected 18-year-olds; (ii) continuing education of adults; (iii) professional and vocational training; (iv) certification of students; (v) additional goals that may be set by some countries, *e.g.* the relief of social stresses and personal injustice to disadvantaged minorities; (vi) research; (vii) home of scholarship; (viii) service to community. These eight roles have evolved over the years, as tertiary education has developed. The university's role has changed in response to newer and emerging needs, and this evolution has sufficed to show that universities could adapt and change. Wherever such adaptation did not take place in relation to express and felt needs there was evidence that change was forced on the university system more often by political will and quite often to the dislike, if not detriment, of the university system itself. It was therefore clear to the group that universities had to be responsive to the needs of society, if they were to survive as viable institutions offering quality education and training at the tertiary level.

Although eight possible roles could be identified, it could not be said that universities all over the Commonwealth had all these roles. The roles of institutions in the developing countries were not identical with those of universities in the developed parts of the world.

Even in the growth of universities, while some countries had faith in manpower planning others had not attempted this approach. In countries adopting manpower planning there were restrictions on intake. Such restrictions were inbuilt in the strategy of manpower planning. This again led the universities to take on a role different from the one that they had been following hitherto.

The discussions went on to the factors differentiating universities from other types of institution such as mono-technics, polytechnics, and the

DISCUSSION

institutions of further education that had come to be established. The group itself, in its efforts to identify criteria by which tertiary-level institutions could be differentiated, mentioned the following: (i) courses offered; (ii) attitude to research; (iii) level of entry; (iv) methods of teaching; (v) general freedom enjoyed. Yet another factor contributing to differences between the types of institution in the tertiary sector was cultural background—for example, the francophone and anglophone universities in Canada. Such a diversity of institutions operating in the same country at the tertiary level created its own problems for society. The group therefore felt that, at least in the future, such variety should evolve on a planned basis rather than arise from responses to the immediate needs of a local area. In this kind of planning intermediary bodies like the university grants commissions/committees had a role to play.

The group noted that in the experience of some universities, especially in North America, it was easier to derive support for a community-college type of education than for a university. This was because the local community required an answer to its local needs, as opposed to national issues. Besides other factors, the ability of community colleges to attract greater resources made universities vulnerable. However as these are transient phenomena there was a tendency towards an 'upward drift', and wherever such upward drift occurred there was a danger of gaps emerging. The only way to prevent this upward drift, in the opinion of the group, was to establish 'parity of esteem' between institutions. No concrete proposals emerged as to the mechanics for establishing this parity, although faculty salaries were mentioned as one indicator of esteem.

There was also the problem of a proper mix of the different types of institution functioning at the level of tertiary education. The group could not identify any formula for this mix, mainly because the needs of different parts of the Commonwealth were not identical.

Discussions then turned to the role of research. It was clear that there was no evidence of proper planning, even within the institutions, although it was increasingly necessary to plan especially since research had come to mean the acquisition of more and more expensive and sophisticated equipment. The resources required for this did not always match the needs. Unless there was proper planning expectations might be aroused in the faculty which, if not fulfilled, could lead to frustration. One way of allocating scarce resources could be to build up 'centres of excellence' with all facilities for research. This, however, might cause young talented staff to move to these centres. A proper policy would have to be evolved for this purpose. Also, building such centres might mean building a hierarchy of institutions. Moreover, in some countries there were fully-equipped laboratories functioning outside the university system providing excellent facilities even in expensive areas of research. In such situations perhaps inter-institutional collaboration could be an answer. Also, the group felt that there was a definite need to monitor research.

Thus the kinds of programme that a university should offer would not depend on the definition of a university but on the ethos and needs of the society in which the university was functioning. Universities need not,

TOPIC 5: UNIVERSITIES AND OTHER INSTITUTIONS

therefore, feel diffident about stating in clear terms what they believe in. In other words the universities need not underestimate their own power to influence events. Also, since research had become international in character there ought to be more active collaboration between universities in developed and developing countries. Such collaboration could only be on the basis of an equal partnership at all levels.

Sir Harry Pitt in his contribution to the sub-group on 'problems of choice between different institutions' stressed two aspects of higher education. One was entry after completing school, say at the age of 18 or some other appropriate age, and the other was access to professions through education. The latter was prestigious inasmuch as it gave individuals an opportunity to acquire a position of responsibility and a power to influence.

Sir Walter Perry (Open) dwelt at length in his paper on the 'ability spectrum' model of tertiary education, while Mr. W. G. Pitman (Ryerson) focused his attention on the concept of 'interrupted education'. There was an apparent conflict between the two theses. The 'ability spectrum' model implied streaming into different types of tertiary institution on the basis of differing levels of ability. Only this would ensure the desired results. Mr. Pitman, on the other hand, pointed out the need for universities to accept transfers and credits of students coming from different kinds of tertiary-level institution. However the group felt that each of the speakers was basing his thesis on experience gained in a developed country. Ultimately it was opined by the speakers themselves that the interpretation of the model would have to depend on and relate to the background of a particular society. The educational system had to be linked to the economic structure. The differences between developed countries and developing countries were accentuated in these discussions. For example, the work ethic differs: in the developing societies education is taken as the training ground for work, and certainly not for enjoyment of leisure.

In discussing 'problems of transfer and communication among different institutions' the three papers presented to the group included one by Sir Charles Carter (Lancaster). He, in the context of the north of England situation, drew attention to the diversity of institutions, their objectives and their functions. The transfer of students of 'good standing' was not beset with many difficulties. However there were a number of practical difficulties in staff transfers. At the same time universities, as validating institutions, had a predominant role to play. Transfers became necessary for various reasons. To facilitate such transfers personal contact rather than structural reform was best suited, according to the speaker.

Dr. L. Isabelle (Algonquin), drawing on the Canadian experience, pointed out that whereas colleges are occupation-oriented, universities should be a 'community of scholars' and should not try to mean all things to all people. Explaining the 'bell-shaped curve' of ability, he was of the opinion that only a very small number would seek transfer to universities. However wherever such transfer was sought it had to be facilitated.

Mr. A. Z. Preston (West Indies), illustrating his paper with examples from the situation in the West Indies, drew attention to various facilitating

DISCUSSION

mechanisms evolved for the transfer of students from one institution to another. Such transfer, he said, was a fact of life so far as the West Indies was concerned, and arose from necessity. Not the least important of the contributing factors were the flexible approach and immense opportunities available in institutions in North America. The facilitating mechanisms evolved in the West Indies include advanced placement of students, giving of credit, affiliation and exemptions.

Once again it became clear in the discussions that followed that there were fundamental differences between the situation in the developing countries and that in the developed countries. To facilitate transfer it was necessary to build bridges both between universities and between universities and non-university institutions in the tertiary sector. Such bridges could either be informal and through personal contact, or through structural arrangements. What was important, however, was that there should be information dissemination amongst various institutions.

In the final session nomenclature, definition and the concept of access were discussed, because the discussions in the previous sessions appeared to have revolved around these major items. So far as definition was concerned, the various roles of the university, already identified, could form a basis. It was, however, felt that a university without research could not be a university.

Access to education implied not only access to higher education but through education to professional life and to positions of power and influence.

The extent of research needed in a university occupied quite a large part of the discussions. No clear-cut decisions could be taken in the matter. Everything depended upon the kind of society, the kind of faculty in the institution, the kind of ethos that a particular institution had built up, and the facilities available. Abstract research, it was felt, was useful, for it added to the sum total of knowledge. At the same time developing countries had to do research which was more relevant to their immediate needs. There could thus be no agreement either on the quality or on the amount of research that was needed in a university. Research capability and teaching capability were two different types of capability. Both were not always present in the same person, but both were needed in a university.

The group concluded that there was a greater need for exchange and assistance between developed and developing countries and amongst developing countries. It was unanimously agreed that the Association of Commonwealth Universities should do more in this field.

The Topic Chairman (Dr. C. -M. Li), in summing up the discussions, pointed out how they enabled us to learn from one another about the divergent situations prevailing in different parts of the Commonwealth, and how difficult it was to evolve any common formula for the Commonwealth as a whole. He re-emphasised, however, the one concrete and unanimous suggestion: that exchange was needed and that in this the ACU had a positive role to play.

SECOND PLENARY SESSION AND CLOSING CEREMONY
Friday, 25 August

At the Second Plenary Session Topic Chairmen summarised the main points made in the course of the group discussions relating to their Topics.

The Second Plenary Session was followed by a Closing Ceremony under the chairmanship of Dr. H. E. Duckworth (Chairman of the Congress) in which Dr. J. Steven Watson (Chairman of the Congress Organising Committee) expressed warm thanks to all who had contributed to the success of the Congress, and the Chairman thanked Dr. Steven Watson for his work as Chairman of the Organising Committee.

A valedictory address was given by Dr. Lacoste.

Dr. P. LACOSTE (*Rector of the University of Montreal and President of the Association of Universities and Colleges of Canada*): Allow me, as president of the Association of Universities and Colleges of Canada, to repeat how much Canadian universities are pleased and proud to have hosted the Twelfth Commonwealth Universities Congress. It has been a very successful gathering. Twenty years ago, in 1958, the first Congress held outside the United Kingdom chose Montreal as its site. This past week, and this time in the beautiful surroundings of Vancouver and the University of British Columbia, another significant experience has been added to the history of Canadian higher education.

Your Congress documentation contains a Statistics Canada special report entitled *From the Sixties to the Eighties: A Statistical Portrait of Canadian Higher Education.** In a fairly detailed overview, this document outlines the dramatic changes which have affected universities in Canada. The tables and figures define how material and human resources grew and expanded, how quickly graduate studies and research developed, and this reflects how confident and proud the Canadian people were of their university community. One can also detect, alas, how in the later years of the two decades covered by the report growth is being reduced, how

---

* *See* Appendix III

resources are being restricted. In Canada, as in so many countries, criticism and scepticism is being directed at those same universities.

At the same time, within the university, relations among constituencies also evolved. Faculty demanded and obtained a larger share in the management of the institution; so to a certain degree did students and, in some instances, non-academic staff. Every university has suffered some form of unrest; faculty at an increasing number of institutions are being unionized.

To add one final item to this summary and incomplete picture, the relations of the universities to the state have changed markedly; the universities seek a balance between increasing interventions by governments and the pursuit of their traditional autonomy. The Canadian system of higher education has always operated under a rather particular form of pluralism. Under our federative system of government, education is a domain of provincial jurisdiction. The universities serve two officially recognized linguistic groups, one English-speaking, the other French, and there exist English-language, French-language and a few bilingual institutions. Canadians are proud, incidentally, that two international associations, the Association of Commonwealth Universities and the Association des universités partiellement ou entièrement de langue française (AUPELF), consider themselves equally at home in our country. I would be remiss if I did not underline the recognition afforded by the ACU to the bilingual character of Canada in the introductory pages of the programme for the Twelfth Congress.

In this diversity, which does not exist without some healthy tensions, there is an opportunity for substantial and important inter-university co-operation, based on the respect of common values and of shared objectives. This mention of a very positive aspect of Canadian reality brings us back to the ACU Congress which is ending.

Under the very fundamental yet contemporary theme of 'Reconciling national, international and local roles of universities with the essential character of a university', the Association of Commonwealth Universities has recognized the need to reaffirm the responsibility of the university. Indeed the first topic, 'The World Food Problem and the Universities', indicates very clearly that we are very far from the ivory tower concept. The whole programme of addresses and discussions has aptly delimited the essential and central aspects of so vast a subject; speakers and discussants have pinpointed the common basic preoccupation of reconciling the service to society and the intellectual values which are proper to the university. There have been inevitable confrontations of ideas and ideals encouraged by the twin aspects of the theme. Some participants inclined to the concept of classical disinterested knowledge, while others opted for the more modern concept of 'engagement'.

The discussions have indeed been an illustration of the great diversity of circumstances known to the Congress participants. The issues stand in very different contexts in industrially and technically developed and in developing countries. Priorities are not similar and the 'service' concept is stronger in developing areas. Priorities vary also according to the philosophies underlying the relations between the state and the university. In countries already developed there may be a greater flexibility and more opportunities to undertake undirected studies and research, while in other countries governments insist more strenuously on applied studies and research whose purpose is to satisfy the pressing socio-economic needs as they are perceived.

Finally, within certain societies and within single systems, there exists a variety of institutions, each with its own traditions; universities which have recently been created often have a tendency to lean to stronger 'engagement' and to greater sensitivity to needs expressed by governments.

The Commonwealth offers an extraordinary combination of such varied realities. The ACU is privileged, in that it can bring into focus discussions that take account of the variety, and allow for a thorough analysis of these components. This Congress has benefited also by the interventions of observers and guests from outside the Commonwealth. The animating spirit of ACU is one which accepts many cultures and encourages unfettered dialogue, in the context of a few shared and cherished traditions. It is one of the great strengths of ACU that it makes possible the discussion of university and universal problems without politicizing them, particularly in a congress such as this one where the issues are substantial and concrete. This reflects a respect for what is most precious in the spirit of the university and helps to guarantee its survival.

It is this spirit which allows us to place issues in perspective and to formulate them, as it were, from a distance. In fact, none of the issues are new; the university is regularly put to the question on the matters of intellectual versus service content, tradition and relevance, etc. If one looks at the history of the university, various institutions have had different orientations; in the middle ages Italian universities were more 'professional' than English or French universities. Recurrently the universities have been accused of transmitting a soulless and outdated culture. Periodically, parallel institutions have been created, like the Collège de France in the sixteenth century or later academies, professional schools or research organizations independent of universities. One need not mention new types of universities in the nineteenth or twentieth century, the draconian reforms imposed on universities on certain occasions, or even their closure. Politics have often been more important than intellectual considerations in reaching decisions affecting universities.

Throughout, one must insist, however, there has also been an evolution of the university from within, because it has possessed its own dynamic and has usually found within itself the ability to adapt to new circumstances.

There has been chronic tension between the university and society. Too often external pressures have been needed to bring the universities to recognize certain needs, particularly when the institutions seemed too easily satisfied with perpetuating their own tradition. But there normally exists within the universities themselves a capacity for self-criticism and renewal.

A condition qu'ils se mettent à l'écoute de la société qu'ils dovient servir, les universitaires sont les plus capables de concevoir et d'apprécier les changements qui s'imposent, de rénover les programmes d'études et les méthodes d'enseignement, et cela sans les inconvénients et les risques de réformes imposées de l'extérieur. C'est cette faculté d'adaptation et de dynamisme qui nous permettront de répondre aux besoins changeants du monde actuel, tout en sauvegardant ce qui constitue le caractère propre de l'enseignement supérieur.

I am convinced – and I know I reflect the common sentiment – that our speakers' contributions, our discussions and private conversations have contributed to enrich our experience and to stimulate our reflection and research. We leave this conference perhaps a little more prepared to face the most difficult challenge of reconciling the manifold aspects of the role of the universities.

I hope we will be together again in 1983 in the United Kingdom for the next Congress of ACU.

Au revoir et bon voyage.

APPENDICES

I
QUINQUENNIAL REPORT OF THE SECRETARY GENERAL
page 579

II
GENERAL MEETING OF THE ASSOCIATION OF COMMONWEALTH UNIVERSITIES
(Western Ontario, 16 August 1978)
614

III
A STATISTICAL PORTRAIT OF CANADIAN HIGHER EDUCATION
625

APPENDIX I

THE ASSOCIATION OF COMMONWEALTH UNIVERSITIES
QUINQUENNIAL REPORT 1973−1978
OF THE
SECRETARY GENERAL

TO THE TWELFTH COMMONWEALTH UNIVERSITIES CONGRESS

CONTENTS	
REPORT	
Edinburgh Congress	*page* 581
Last Quinquennium's Innovations	581
This Quinquennium's Changes	582
Membership and Meetings	584
Staff and Premises	584
Publications and Information	587
Appointments Service	590
ACU/Commonwealth Foundation Administrative Travelling Fellowships	592
Academic Exchange Programme	593
Times Higher Education Supplement Third World Fellowship	595
Commonwealth Scholarship and Fellowship Plan	595
Other Scholarships	598
Relations with other Organisations	599
Obituary	599
APPENDICES	
I Member Institutions	600
II Members of Council	603
III Members of Executive Committee	605
COMPARATIVE FINANCIAL TABLES	
Note by Honorary Treasurer	607
Income and Expenditure Accounts: Five years' Comparative Statements	608
Summary of Balance Sheets	610
Five years' Comparative Analysis according to Activities	610
LIST OF PUBLICATIONS	612

QUINQUENNIAL REPORT OF THE SECRETARY GENERAL

FOR THE PERIOD AUGUST 1973 TO JULY 1978

THE EDINBURGH CONGRESS

The first major event of the quinquennium was, of course, the Eleventh Commonwealth Universities Congress at Edinburgh in August 1973, which was immediately followed by the Conference of Executive Heads and the Statutory General Meeting in Exeter in the same month. By unanimous consent the Edinburgh Congress was a great success, as in its different way was the Exeter occasion. The printed Report of the Congress and its associated meetings was published and distributed to members in 1974.

The next event, alas! was the oil crisis; and financial constraints have been a continuous and dominant feature of the quinquennium, no less for all our members than for the Association itself. Growth has virtually ceased, and in at least one member country, where towards the end of the previous quinquennium the curve of expansion was already levelling off, enrolment now shows signs of decline.

LAST QUINQUENNIUM'S INNOVATIONS

The last *Quinquennial Report* (for 1968–73) recorded a number of constitutional and other changes of policy and practice, some initiated as a result of recommendations of the Policy Review Committee which the Council had appointed on the occasion of the Tenth Quinquennial Congress (Australia 1968), others resulting from the Council's own subsequent deliberations. All were designed to enable the Association both to move with the times and to improve the quality of its services to its members. Chief among them were the expansion of the Council, to take account of the altered composition of the membership, and the change in the basis of subscription from number of students to size of income. The latter was brought into force by resolution of the Special General Meeting held at Exeter for that purpose after the Congress in 1973.

The experience of the quinquennium now closing has confirmed the wisdom and proved the timeliness of these innovations. There is no doubt that they have contributed in large measure to the ability of the Association to come safely through a period in which its member institutions have been exposed to grave financial and other difficulties.

Also worthy of note is an innovation of a different sort. For the Edinburgh Congress to facilitate discussion in groups, the number of topics was increased over that of previous Congresses and they were sub-divided. Moreover for the first time outward-looking topics—'The problem of the environment and the universities', 'Contemporary culture and the universities'—were introduced. These measures proved successful at Edinburgh and will be repeated at the Vancouver Congress.

THIS QUINQUENNIUM'S CHANGES

Budget Review Committee

By contrast the period under review has provided few changes to record. The most important was the creation in 1975 of the Budget Review Committee. The Council's response to financial pressure transmitted from our members, it has already become an indispensable part of our management machinery.

Honorary Deputy Treasurer

Also on the constitutional front, the Charter was amended to provide for the appointment of an Honorary Deputy Treasurer. The purpose of this innovation (proposed by the then Honorary Treasurer, Sir Douglas Logan) was to enable the office of Honorary Treasurer to be held by a person not resident in the United Kingdom without loss of attention to the day-to-day duties of the Treasurer's office. Accordingly in 1974 Professor T. H. B. Symons (formerly President of Trent University, Peterborough (Ontario) and Chairman of the Association in 1971–72) was appointed Honorary Treasurer and Sir Douglas Logan became the first Honorary Deputy Treasurer, having served as Honorary Treasurer since 1967.

The Symons Award

Another innovation worthy of note is the Symons Award, made possible by a generous endowment by Professor Symons. It was inaugurated in 1973 for the purpose of honouring persons who have made outstanding contributions to the Association and to Commonwealth universities. It has up to now taken the form of a small gift of silver, and has been presented on the occasion of four successive Annual General Meetings: to Sir Charles Wilson and Sir Douglas Logan in 1973; to Professor James Auchmuty, Vice-Chancellor of the University of Newcastle (New South Wales) and a member of the Council of the Association, in 1974; in 1975 posthumously to Dr. John Foster; and in 1976 to Mr. Stephen Stackpole, recently retired Executive Director of the Commonwealth Programme of the Carnegie Corporation of New York. No award was made in 1977.

Dr. John Foster

Although not marked by much change in the Association's rules and practices, the quinquennium has seen two important personal changes. In 1975 we mourned the death of Dr. John Foster, who had been Secretary, and later Secretary General, of the Association under its changing names from 1947 to 1970. He drifted away from us gradually over the last year of his life and finally went peacefully on the 24th of September.

The Association he took over in 1947 had been born on the eve of the first world war and had passed its whole life till then through two world wars separated by a world depression. It was his task to nurse an undernourished child to vigorous adulthood, and the Association as we know it today commemorates his success. The Association expressed its gratitude to him when he retired, and if he had lived would have presented him with the Symons Award in November 1975. His wife Margaret received it in his stead. At a well-attended memorial service in the London University Church of Christ the King his praise was eloquently and justly spoken by Sir Charles Wilson. The Council has agreed that the Association's headquarters shall be named John Foster House.

Sir Charles Wilson

Sir Charles Wilson is the subject of the other of the personal changes to which I have referred. He ceased to be a member of the Council in November 1975 after an unbroken period of sixteen years, during which he had been three times Chairman and five times Vice-Chairman. The Association owes him an enormous debt, and he has added to it by agreeing to deliver the keynote address at the Twelfth Quinquennial Congress.

APPENDIX I

MEMBERSHIP AND MEETINGS

Membership

In 1973 the number of members of the association was 191. In 1978 the number is 221. This represents seven times the rate of increase in membership during the previous quinquennium, which had been from 187 members in 1968 and 191 in 1973; but no subsequent growth can be expected to match the phenomenal increase that took place in the fifties and sixties. On the contrary, in view of the financial climate prevailing since 1973 it is a matter for sober satisfaction that the number of members has increased at all.

During the quinquennium the University of Botswana, Lesotho and Swaziland was dissolved and was succeeded by the National University of Lesotho and the University of Botswana and Swaziland.

Meetings

The Council met ten times during the quinquennium and the Executive Committee met fifteen times. In accordance with established practice three meetings of the full Council were held abroad, in Kuala Lumpur in 1975, in Wellington in 1976 and in Malta in 1977. The second inter-Congress Conference of Executive Heads took place in Wellington in 1976.

The Organising Committee for the 1978 Congress was appointed by the Council at its meeting in Kuala Lumpur in 1975. The Committee held its first meeting in conjunction with the Wellington Conference, as did the Canadian Committee for the Congress. These two committees, as well as the local committee of the universities of British Columbia, have met as often as necessary to carry forward the preparations for the Congress and its associated meetings of the Council in Quebec and the Conference of Executive Heads in London, Ontario. The Association is greatly indebted to the members of these committees and to the officers who have been engaged in the practical preparations for the devotion and skill with which they have organised the arrangements for the three meetings.

STAFF AND PREMISES

Staff

The Secretary General, who reached the normal age of retirement in 1978, has accepted the Council's invitation to continue in office until 1980.

QUINQUENNIAL REPORT OF SECRETARY GENERAL 1973 – 78

The Association has been fortunate in continuing to retain the services of its administrative staff. In the latter years of the quinquennium there was greater continuity of service among the secretarial staff also — an improvement which was achieved to some degree by the employment of part-time staff. With the Secretary General and the Assistant Secretaries General (formerly Assistant Secretaries; they received their present titles in 1973) there have been between 46 and 50 other officers, of whom 17 to 22 have been graduates. During the final year of the quinquennium 19 staff members completed between five and ten years' service, 5 between ten and fifteen years, 5 between fifteen and twenty years and 3 between twenty and twenty-five years. Mr. T. Craig, Assistant Secretary General (Publications) completed 28 years and Mrs. M. M. Hill, administrative officer in the Appointments department, who was awarded the Queen's Jubilee Medal in 1977, completed 30 years.

The Council has noted with regret the death, in November 1976, of Mr. S. E. D. Barff, OBE, administrative officer in charge of the Kennedy Memorial Scholarships and Frank Knox Memorial Fellowships since 1970, and, in December 1977, of Miss D. (Margaret) Tayler Cox, MA Camb., editorial and information officer in the Publications department since 1970. A donation received from Miss Cox's father will form part of a memorial fund, linked with the work on which she was engaged, to be administered by the Secretary General.

The Council also noted with regret the deaths of Sir Charles Harris, who was Medical Awards Administrator of the Association from 1966 to 1973, and Dr. Nicolas B. Malleson, for many years medical adviser to the Association.

In this quinquennium as in the last the Secretary General and the Assistant Secretaries General have kept contact with member universities by means of visits, making the fullest use of journeys occasioned by attendance at meetings abroad, whether convened by the Association or by other bodies with shared interests. The Secretary General took part in the celebration of the Centenary of the University of Adelaide in 1974 and attended also the Centenary Congregation of the University of Bristol and the 50th Anniversary Congregation of the University of Reading in 1976, and the Centennial celebrations of Lincoln College (Christchurch) in 1978. In 1977 he was guest speaker at a dinner held at St. John's College, Cambridge, as a part of the celebration of the 25th Anniversary of the University of Newcastle (NSW) and was among those who addressed the Congregation for the installation of the President of the University of Western Ontario. He attended three annual

585

conferences of the Association of Indian Universities, in 1974, 1975 and 1978, giving the inaugural address in 1974 and representing the Association, together with the Vice-Chairman, Dr. Steven Watson, at the AIU's 50th Anniversary seminar held in conjunction with the 1975 meeting. He attended the General Conference of the Association of African Universities in Nigeria in 1973. The Association was represented by the Assistant Secretary General (Publications) at the Conference of European Rectors at Bologna in 1974, at the General Conference of the AAU in Khartoum in 1976 and at the 1977 Conference of the Association of Universities and Colleges of Canada, and all the Assistant Secretaries General have represented the Association at other meetings and seminars.

The Commonwealth Prime Ministers at their meeting in Ottawa in 1973 appointed the Secretary General to be Chairman of the Commonwealth Foundation for the years 1974 and 1975 and his appointment was renewed for a second term, 1976 and 1977. He was among those who received the Queen's Jubilee Medal on the recommendation of the government of Barbados. He was President of the education section of the British Association in 1974–75 and received honorary degrees of DLitt from the universities of Warwick and Ulster in 1974, Heriot-Watt in 1975, Hong Kong in 1977 and The City (London) in 1978, and of LLD from the University of St. Andrews in 1977.

Premises

In the financial climate prevailing during recent years the Association's project to acquire alternative accommodation when the lease of 36–38 Gordon Square expired in 1977 had to be abandoned. Fortunately, however, the hope expressed in the last *Quinquennial Report,* that the University of London would renew the lease, has been realised and a new lease was duly signed in 1977. If the new rent is considerably higher than the old, this is a consequence of the fact that there had been no rent increase during twenty years of inflation. The new lease provides for rent increases at appropriate intervals. It is right that we should here record an expression of our gratitude to the University of London for past generosity and our hope that our good relations will continue unimpaired. The Association's headquarters continue to be in London because in the Commonwealth, as in Britain, all roads still lead to London. This fact creates special obligations for London and its institutions, which happily the University for one acknowledges.

QUINQUENNIAL REPORT OF SECRETARY GENERAL 1973 – 78

PUBLICATIONS AND INFORMATION

The Association provides factual information about Commonwealth universities and about access to them. It does so through some twenty publications (for a list, see pp. 612–613) and three information services: a personal information service, a documentation service and an awards information service.

With the exception of the Association's bulletin and newsletter (*ABCD* and *Acumen*), nearly all the publications are directories, lists or guides of one kind or another which are issued in regularly revised form for reference use by students and their parents, academic and administrative staff, and a wide range of other readers. They draw their authority from the universities that provide the basic material; and all the publications involve the collection of data from a variety of sources, by letter and personal contact, and careful editing by the ACU publications staff. The aim is to put basic facts at the disposal of enquirers throughout the Commonwealth, and elsewhere; and at least one free copy of each publication is sent to each member university for local reference.

Among the subjects covered, often in great detail, are: entrance requirements; courses available at first and higher degree levels; visiting professorships and scholarships and fellowships for inter-Commonwealth study travel; fields of research strength in universities; academic visitors from other countries; plus, in the *Commonwealth Universities Yearbook,* complete staff lists and much general information about each university of good standing.

Almost all the Association's publications are 'standard works' and its reputation for being good at this kind of 'university directory' publishing has led to the collaboration with other bodies that is described below.

Increased Productivity

The last Report recorded that the Publications and Information Department had grown to be the largest in the secretariat. The past five years have been remarkable for increased productivity. The Department has done noticeably more editorial, information and sales publicity work with the same number of staff. For example, the number of pages (now 2,600) in the annual *Commonwealth Universities Yearbook,* the principal publication of the Association, has increased by 16% in the quinquennium, the increase in content being actually greater, since the new typeface adopted for the 1976 edition packs more closely than the one used previously. Indeed almost all the regularly revised publications of the ACU have increased substantially in content during the period.

APPENDIX I

Yearbook Changes

Two major changes were made in the production of the Yearbook: (*a*) from hot-metal typesetting to a computer-assisted method; and (*b*) from one hard-covered volume to four limp-covered ones. The 1976 Yearbook was the first to appear in this new style, which saves money and makes the constantly expanding book easier to handle. Thus dignity has given way to convenience.

New Publications

Seven publications have been prepared by the ACU for the first time during the quinquennium, some of them (marked with an * below) produced in collaboration with other organisations on a basis that fully covers costs. The following were compiled and published by the Association:—

Research Strengths of Universities in the Developing Countries of the Commonwealth (at the request of the Commonwealth Secretariat) (first edition 1976, second edition mid-1978)

Financial Aid for First Degree Study at Commonwealth Universities (1974, 1975, 1977)

Who's Who at Executive Heads Conferences (1973, 1976, 1978)

Acumen A newsletter for executive heads of member universities of the ACU; at least four issues a year (first: January 1978).

The ACU collaborated with the organisations indicated in the publication of the following:

**Guide to Education and Training Resources in the Developing Countries of the Commonwealth* The first edition (1974) was compiled by ACU and published by the Commonwealth Secretariat. The second edition (1977) was published by the Commonwealth Secretariat, the ACU supplying only the raw material for the university section.

All of these were completely new publications. In addition, the Department took over from the UK Vice-Chancellors' Committee the editing of two already established handbooks:—

**The Compendium of University Entrance Requirements for First Degree Courses in the United Kingdom* This annual publication has been compiled and sold since the 1974–75 edition (issued in 1973) by the ACU on behalf of the Committee of Vice-Chancellors and Principals of the Universities of the United Kingdom.

**Schedule of Postgraduate Courses in United Kingdom Universities* This annual publication has been compiled and sold since the 1973–74 edition (issued in 1973) by the ACU on behalf of the Committee of Vice-Chancellors and Principals of the Universities of the United Kingdom.

We have also continued the collaboration with the British Council, which dates back to before the war, on the two-yearly *Higher Education in the United Kingdom; a Handbook for Students from Overseas and their Advisers* which is published by Longman's for the British Council and the ACU.

Sales

The financial cutbacks applied by governments during the period have affected the sales of our publications—as of many similar reference works throughout the world—since many of our customers, for example, universities and public libraries, have had less money to spend on books. So that, after a period of steady increase, sales have dropped somewhat. To counteract the trend we undertook a vigorous publicity campaign of direct-mailing to likely customers and of announcements within universities. More effective distribution arrangements in the USA and India were made with commercial firms; and paid advertisements (including some for chair vacancies) have become a regular feature of ABCD.

Library

The number of books and pamphlets in the one-man ACU Reference Library rose from 6,000 to 10,000 during the period. The Library badly needs more space for both books and readers (who include not only members of staff but many students and other visitors).

Attestations Service

The Association has continued to issue attestations, though on a reduced scale. Attestations are statements under seal provided to qualified applicants under a long-standing arrangement with the French Ministry of Education by which academic qualifications obtained in certain Commonwealth countries which satisfy the minimum entrance requirements of United Kingdom universities, upon being so certified by the ACU, are accepted by the authorities in France as equivalent to the baccalaureat for the purpose of admission to universities there. Since 1973, 608 attestations were issued, mainly to students from Mauritius.

APPENDIX I

Information Services

As well as the production of these publications, the personal information service provides information on a variety of subjects to individual enquirers who contact us by letter, telephone or personal visit. The number of enquiries rose from 3,000 to more than 5,000 a year. For those seeking money for study travel abroad there is the awards information service whose publications are listed on p. 612. A documentation service produces the *ACU Bulletin of Current Documentation* (ABCD), *Acumen* a newsletter for executive heads, and the long bibliography in the Yearbook; and can undertake bibliographical searches for senior officers of member institutions.

All three services draw strength from the constant stream of information sent to us by universities and the wide range of personal contacts between their staff and those of the ACU.

APPOINTMENTS SERVICE

It is some sign of depth to which the Association is drawn into the affairs and counsels of its member universities, that its own fortunes so closely reflect theirs. Such a correspondence is particularly evident in the work of the Appointments service in which, during the last quinquennium, there has been a quite significant reduction due to the financial straits into which universities throughout the world have entered. Nevertheless the style of the department's work has remained unchanged, and in certain senses its involvement with the affairs of the universities which it serves has become deeper.

Nature of the Service

It has never been a service of which all members avail themselves though all of course have a right to do so. It provides members with facilities to announce vacancies, to distribute information about them to enquirers and prospective applicants, and, when they wish it, to have shortlisted candidates interviewed or assessed by independent and expert advisers. In its Appointments work the Association serves each member university not according to a single procedural stereotype but in a style matched to that university's own internal procedures and requirements.

The costs of the service are met by the universities which use it, not out of subscription income, and, though inflation has enforced some increase in cost, service fees remain modest, not least because the Association has been able to negotiate with the press rates of discount from which the accrued income is largely used to offset some of the costs of the service.

Coping with Restraints and Limitations

The first year of this quinquennium was also the first in which the Association did not provide Appointment services for former member universities; even so there was at first a notable growth (to nearly 2,000 in 1973–74) in the number of appointments which it was asked to advertise. Since that time, however, there has been a general reduction in the number of appointments announced from 1,980 in 1973–74 to 1,356 in 1976–77, and at the time of writing no prospect of a greater figure for 1977–78. The average number of enquirers for each advertised post, however, has not diminished and the average number of applications has if anything slightly risen; and there has been, relatively speaking, an increase in the extent to which universities which use the service exploit its ability to arrange, often at short notice, for candidates in whom they are interested to be interviewed. Interviews are conducted not just by the Association's own officers, but by *ad hoc* panels of independent experts in the appropriate subject who can inform the university's own decision about a post by making to it an objective and descriptive (rather than prescriptive) report on a candidate's qualifications and weaknesses. It is perhaps this aspect of the Appointments work which most readily commended the service to those colleges of advanced education in Australia which, with the permission of member universities there, have been given access to the service. This does not, of course, constitute an especially large sector of the department's work, but the colleges which have sought help from it have expressed themselves gratified with the quality and efficacy of the service; the Association for its part has welcomed and continues to welcome the opportunity of extending to the sister-sector of tertiary education a set of skills and insights which were first developed in response to member universities' statements of their own needs; this extension at the very least eases the burden of cost to member universities themselves because of the diffusion of overheads which it permits.

Advisers

The Council does not cease to admire or be grateful for the generosity with which senior academics in the United Kingdom, or on leave in the United Kingdom from member universities overseas, give time and effort to the task of acting as members of the interviewing and advisory panels which the office is asked to set up. They do so always at some sacrifice of time and convenience, rewarded only by the knowledge that they are contributing to the development and health of their subject in sister institutions. That the service enjoys among member universities so cordial a reputation is due in very large measure to the sense of responsibility, and to the generosity of outlook, of the senior academics and research workers who play so important a part in one of the Association's key activities.

ACU/COMMONWEALTH FOUNDATION ADMINISTRATIVE TRAVELLING FELLOWSHIPS

In each year of this quinquennium the Association has been able to announce a competition for this extended scheme of awards, promoted with the help of generous grants from the Commonwealth Foundation. The object of the scheme is each year to provide at least one administrator from each of the Association's constituent regions with an opportunity to travel to another part or other parts of the Commonwealth, and study in one or more of the universities there problems which they have recognised to be of importance to their own university and country, and on which the experience of other institutions has some bearing. In the course of the quinquennium the Association has made no less than 84 awards, from fields of candidates which have proved in most years to be embarrassingly rich. It has been some testimony to the esteem which this programme has now earned among member universities, that nearly all applications from the developed parts of the Commonwealth, as well as a number of those from the developing parts, carry an offer of actual financial sponsorship from the nominating university. The many administrative sub-groups from which fellows have been drawn include staff from registries, council secretariats, finance offices, estates or buildings offices, information offices and university presses.

There is no doubt that the scheme has helped establish between administrators in many parts of the Commonwealth a complex and invaluable network of personal and professional relationships, as well as improving skills and generating, for both host and nominating institutions, valuable insights into a great diversity of problems.

The Association once again expresses to the Commonwealth Foundation its profound gratitude for the continuing generosity which has made this programme possible. It is an additional pleasure to be able to report that early in 1978 the Canadian International Development Agency announced its willingness to supplement the scheme by three annual and munificent grants intended particularly to support administrative fellows from the developing parts of the Commonwealth. The Council sees this development as enhancing immeasurably the value of the scheme through the greater richness of contact which it will enable administrators from those parts of the world to make.

ACADEMIC EXCHANGE PROGRAMME

Since 1973 the Association has been active in its work on the Academic Exchange Programme, which it administers jointly with, and on behalf of, the Commonwealth Fund for Technical Cooperation. This scheme is designed especially to promote movement and contact, of developmental import and value, among member universities in the developing countries, complementing the existing formal schemes of academic exchange whose emphasis is on movement between developed and developing parts of the Commonwealth. The scheme provides *ad hoc* support for:

(*a*) attachments of university staff, both academic and administrative, to other universities in Commonwealth developing countries to obtain greater experience and training;

(*b*) short study-tours of university staff in Commonwealth developing countries to enhance their ability to contribute to national development;

(*c*) exchanges of staff between universities in developing countries of the Commonwealth with a specific developmental objective in view;

(*d*) university-sponsored seminars with a national or regional developmental orientation, for which support could be provided in organisation and in assisting teachers or students to attend.

In this quinquennium the Association has promoted a great diversity of programmes of contact and movement from one to other parts of the Commonwealth, to an extent that there is no developing country which has not had the benefit either of sponsoring or receiving a research worker, teacher or administrator under this programme.

The following list shows examples of the kinds of project which have been funded by the programme: —

Swaziland/Kenya/Nigeria

A lecturer in extra-mural studies has been supported in a visit to Kenya and West Africa to study methods of adult education.

Bangladesh/West Africa

A population geographer from Jahangirnagar University has been supported in visits to demographic research institutions in West Africa.

Bangladesh/Malaysia

An assistant professor in agriculture, University of Dacca, has been supported in the study of rubber planting and extraction/processing technology in Malaysia.

Sri Lanka/India/Malaysia

A professor of chemistry from the University of Sri Lanka has been supported in a visit to India and Malaysia to study control of aquatic weeds.

Malaysia/Tanzania

A lecturer in the department of economic development and planning, National University of Malaysia, is to be supported in a study of Ujamaa villages in Tanzania.

Malawi/Zambia/Tanzania/India

A senior lecturer in mechanical engineering, University of Malawi, has been supported in a study tour to enable him to examine the use of alternative sources of energy with particular application to small-scale rural industries.

West Indies/Fiji

A lecturer in biology, University of the West Indies, is being supported in the study of techniques of mariculture at the University of the South Pacific.

Nigeria/East Africa

A lecturer in African languages, Ahmadu Bello University, is being supported in a study in Tanzania and East Africa generally of the development of regional and national languages.

QUINQUENNIAL REPORT OF SECRETARY GENERAL 1973 – 78

The Association is willing at any time to receive applications from member universities for the support, under this programme, of individual projects or attachments which they wish to sponsor.

The programmes which the Association proposes to the Commonwealth Fund for Technical Co-operation have always been handled by the officers of that Fund with expedition and sympathy. The Association is glad to have this public opportunity of expressing its grateful thanks to them.

TIMES HIGHER EDUCATION SUPPLEMENT
THIRD WORLD FELLOWSHIP

In 1973 the Times Higher Education Supplement made the first of what have since become annual grants to the Association to promote a fellowship designed for developmental purposes closely akin to those set out at (a) to (c) above. The number of applications for this award has grown annually, and the elector's task of choosing between them has grown thereby annually more difficult. Since the award was inaugurated the Association has been able to help: —

(i) an engineer from Ghana to visit India to study the development of small-scale and cottage industry;

(ii) a university estates officer from Sierra Leone to visit East and West Africa to discuss optimal use of buildings, development schemes, programming of building extensions, etc.;

(iii) a teacher of developmental studies from the University of Sri Lanka to study the organisation of development studies in Tanzania;

(iv) a lecturer in geology from Hong Kong to study techniques of tin extraction in Malaysia;

(v) a professor of electrical engineering from Bangladesh to visit India and Malaysia to discuss and establish co-operative programmes of research.

The annual competition for this award has produced proposals of many projects of merit which the Association has not been able to fund from this source. It has, however, been able to secure support for many of them from alternative sources, notably and generously, the Commonwealth Fund for Technical Co-operation.

COMMONWEALTH SCHOLARSHIP AND FELLOWSHIP PLAN

The Association has continued to provide the secretariat for the Commonwealth Scholarship Commission in the United Kingdom, which is the statutory agency in Britain for the Commonwealth

Scholarship and Fellowship Plan. The Commission makes available six types of award in all: Commonwealth Scholarships (including Medical Scholarships); Academic Staff Scholarships and Fellowships; Medical Fellowships; Senior Medical Fellowships; and Visiting Professorships. The staff of this secretariat is concerned with the selection, placing and subsequent academic progress of the candidates nominated for United Kingdom awards by the designated Commonwealth Scholarship agencies and by Commonwealth universities overseas. They work closely with all British universities and, in matters affecting the award-holders' welfare, accommodation and travel arrangements, with the British Council. The secretariat also assists the Commission in discharging its responsibility for nominating United Kingdom candidates on the invitation of the other countries making awards available under the Plan. The Association is pleased to acknowledge the invaluable assistance of the Commission panel of academic advisers in assessing the merits of candidates, both incoming and outgoing, and the co-operation of the British universities in finding suitable places for the selected candidates and then providing every encouragement in their studies.

Chairman

Lord Garner, GCMG, a former British High Commissioner in Canada, who had given distinguished service as Chairman of the Commission since 1968, relinquished the chair in September 1977 and was succeeded by Sir Michael Walker, GCMG, formerly British High Commissioner in India.

Numbers

The number of award-holders in the United Kingdom has varied over the last five years, fluctuating between a monthly average of 530 and one of 611 (in 1975–76). The number each year has well exceeded the original target figure of 500 awards; and the total is now rising again, the number in residence in November 1977 being 595 (consisting of 5 Visiting Professors and Senior Medical Fellows, 83 Fellows and 507 Scholars). The average of the whole quinquennium, however, should not turn out to be markedly different from the preceding five-year period which saw the establishment of the Academic Staff Awards.

Regional Conferences

Regional conferences have been held every year, in collaboration with the British Council and the universities concerned, so as to provide opportunities for Scholars and Fellows to meet members of the Commission, their fellow award-holders and academic supervisors and to discuss the strengths and weaknesses of the scheme and exchange experiences. Conference centres have been chosen to make attendance possible for award-holders from as large a number of surrounding universities as possible. Generally the meetings are well-attended and are considered worthwhile.

Academic Staff Fellowships and Scholarships

The Academic Staff awards, which were instituted at the beginning of the last quinquennium and which the Association administers in close co-operation with the Inter-University Council for Higher Education Overseas, are now well established. They continue to provide the means by which selected members of staff of universities in the developing Commonwealth are enabled to obtain work-related experience and training in universities or other appropriate institutions in the United Kingdom.

Typically, candidates are nominated by their vice-chancellor either directly or through their local Commonwealth Scholarship agency. The number of Academic Staff Scholarships originally made available proved to be well below demand and it was agreed by the Commission in December 1973 that for as long as possible the annual intake of Academic Staff Scholars should be maintained at a level of 48. By the end of the period under review over 90 Scholars were holding awards. Fellowships, which are tenable for one academic year and are normally awarded at postdoctoral level, continue to attract sound candidates for the 45 awards which the Commission has at its disposal.

Medical Fellowships

Awards for training at various levels in the field of medicine continued to be made as before. There was however a notable change in procedure, designed by the Commission to enable medical schools overseas to plan their academic releases more effectively. Instead of *ad hoc* consideration of candidates for the one-year Medical Fellowships and three-month Senior Medical Fellowships a twice-yearly selection is now in force.

APPENDIX I

From the United Kingdom to other Countries

The Commission has continued to invite applications and organise the preliminary selection, including interviews, for the Commonwealth Scholarships offered by eleven other countries under the Plan. Each year about 300 British graduates apply, of whom over 50 candidates secure nomination by the United Kingdom. Perhaps a third of the candidates nominated take up awards; for instance, of the candidates nominated in 1976, 17 are known to have taken up awards in six different countries.

Commonwealth Education Conferences and Reports

In this quinquennium have occurred two Commonwealth Education Conferences, each of which the Secretary General attended by invitation (the head of the ACU Commonwealth Scholarship section being present also as a member of the British delegation). The Sixth Commonwealth Education Conference was held in Jamaica in 1974; and had before it the Ten-Year Review (1960–1970) of the Commonwealth Scholarship and Fellowship Plan prepared by the ACU. After thorough discussion the Jamaica Conference recorded its clear endorsement of the value of the Plan and of its basic purposes and mode of operation. In the discussions at the Seventh Conference held in Accra, Ghana, in 1977 the Plan was again prominent as a major Commonwealth activity.

By long-standing arrangement the Commonwealth Secretariat seeks the assistance of the ACU in its preparation for Commonwealth Education Conferences, in compiling the Administrative Handbook relating to the Plan, and in drawing up annual reports on the operation of the Plan throughout the Commonwealth. Since the Accra Conference collection of the material for the annual reports has continued but with the intention of publication only at three-yearly intervals.

OTHER SCHOLARSHIPS

The Association has continued to provide the Secretariat for the Marshall Aid Commemoration Commission and Kennedy Memorial Trust as well as to organise, at the request of the UK Committee of Vice-Chancellors, the competition for the Knox Fellowships; and help has continued to be given to the Drapers' Company by the Assistant Secretary General (Commonwealth Scholarships) in the selection and placement of scholars from Britain in universities in Canada, Australia and New Zealand, as well as in relation to the Company's scheme of Visiting Lectureships.

QUINQUENNIAL REPORT OF SECRETARY GENERAL 1973−78

The Association of Commonwealth Universities has accepted a request to help in the administration of a Government of Alberta Graduate Scholarship in Petroleum Engineering tenable at the University of Alberta by a British student. The first holder took up his award in 1976, and a competition is in progress for the 1978 Scholar.

RELATIONS WITH OTHER ORGANISATIONS

In addition to its intimate family ties with the national committees of vice-chancellors and associations of universities in the larger Commonwealth countries—Britain, Canada, India, Australia, New Zealand, Nigeria, Bangladesh—the Association has maintained close and mutually helpful relations with a number of bodies with cognate interests and spheres of operation, both national and international and both within and outside the Commonwealth, especially the Inter-University Council for Higher Education Overseas, the British Council, the Commonwealth Secretariat and the Commonwealth Foundation. The Secretary General and the Assistant Secretary General (Commonwealth Scholarships) have regularly attended meetings of the Commonwealth Education Liaison Committee and they were both present at the Sixth and Seventh Commonwealth Education Conferences in Jamaica in 1974 and in Ghana in 1977. The Secretary General continues to be the Barbados member of the Board of Trustees of the Commonwealth Foundation, having ceased to be Chairman on 31 December, 1977.

The Association, as an associate member of the International Association of Universities, was represented by the Secretary General at the latter's General Conference in Moscow in 1975 and at four meetings of its Administrative Board. Two of its seminars were attended by two different Assistant Secretaries General. The Association was also represented at one of the two General Conferences of UNESCO held during the period, and at one other of its meetings; the ACU continues to be a 'non-governmental organisation in information and consultative relationship' (category B).

OBITUARY

The Council has noted with regret the deaths which have occurred since the last Congress of the following of its former members: Sir Raymond Priestley, MC (Vice-Chairman 1947−51), Sir James Cook, Dr. James Williams and Sir Hugh Robson.

June 1978

HUGH W. SPRINGER
Secretary General

APPENDICES TO QUINQUENNIAL REPORT

I. MEMBER INSTITUTIONS OF THE ASSOCIATION OF COMMONWEALTH UNIVERSITIES

(Unless otherwise indicated the names are of universities and membership is continuous throughout 1973–78)

ORDINARY MEMBERS

United Kingdom

Aberdeen
Aston
Bath
Queen's, Belfast
Birmingham
Bradford
Bristol
Brunel
Cambridge
City
Dundee
Durham
East Anglia
Edinburgh
Essex
Exeter
Glasgow
Heriot-Watt
Hull
Keele
Kent
Lancaster
Leeds

Leicester
Liverpool
London
Loughborough
Manchester
Newcastle upon Tyne
Nottingham
Open
Oxford
Reading
St. Andrews
Salford
Sheffield
Southampton
Stirling
Strathclyde
Surrey
Sussex
Ulster
Wales
Warwick
York

Canada

Acadia
Alberta
Athabasca (from 1978)
Bishop's (from 1977)
Brandon
British Columbia
Brock
Calgary
Carleton
Concordia (from 1974)
Dalhousie

Guelph
King's College
Lakehead
Laval
Lethbridge
McGill
McMaster
Manitoba
Memorial, Newfoundland
Moncton (until 1977)
Montreal

600

QUINQUENNIAL REPORT OF SECRETARY GENERAL 1973 – 78

Mount Allison
Mount Saint Vincent
New Brunswick
Ottawa
Prince Edward Island
Quebec
Queen's, Kingston
Regina (from 1974)
St. Francis Xavier
St. Mary's
Saskatchewan
Simon Fraser
Sir George Williams (until 1974)
Toronto
Trent
Victoria (B.C.)
Waterloo
Waterloo Lutheran (until 1973)
Western Ontario
Wilfrid Laurier (from 1973)
Windsor
Winnipeg
York

Australia

Adelaide
Australian National
Deakin (from 1975)
Flinders
Griffith
James Cook
La Trobe
Macquarie
Melbourne
Monash
Murdoch (from 1973)
Newcastle
New England
New South Wales
Queensland
Sydney
Tasmania
Western Australia
Wollongong (from 1975)

New Zealand

Auckland
Canterbury
Massey
Otago
Victoria, Wellington
Waikato

India

Aligarh Muslim
Allahabad (from 1978)
Andhra
Annamalai
Banaras Hindu
Baroda
Berhampur (from 1974)
Bhagalpur
Birla Institute of Technology and
    Science (from 1975)
Bombay
Burdwan
Calcutta
Calicut (from 1978)
Delhi
Dibrugarh (from 1974)
Gorakhpur (until 1974)
Guru Nanak Dev (from 1975)
Indian Institute of Technology,
    Delhi
Indian Institute of Technology,
    Kharagpur (from 1978)
Indian Institute of Technology,
    Madras (from 1978)
Indore (from 1977)
Jadavpur
Jammu (from 1974)
Jawaharlal Nehru (from 1976)
Jodhpur
Kalyani (from 1976)
Karnatak
Kashmir

APPENDIX I

Kerala
Kurukshetra
Madras
Madurai
Magadh (from 1976)
Marathwada (until 1977)
Mysore
North-Eastern Hill (from 1977)
Osmania
Panjab, Chandigarh
Patna
Punjabi

Rajasthan
Rohilkhand (from 1976)
Roorkee (until 1973)
Saugar (until 1976)
S.N.D.T. Women's (from 1978)
Sri Venkateswara
Tamil Nadu Agricultural (from 1975)
Udaipur
Utkal
Vikram
Visva-Bharati

Nigeria

Ahmadu Bello
Benin
Calabar (from 1977)
Ibadan
Ife
Ilorin (from 1978)

Jos (from 1978)
Lagos
Nigeria (Nsukka)
Port Harcourt (from 1978)
Sokoto (from 1978)

Bangladesh

Bangladesh Agricultural
Bangladesh Engineering
Chittagong

Dacca
Jahangirnagar
Rajshahi

Other Parts of the Commonwealth

U. of Agriculture, Malaysia
Botswana, Lesotho and Swaziland
 (until 1977)
Botswana and Swaziland
 (from 1977)
Cape Coast
Chinese U. of Hong Kong
Dar es Salaam
Ghana
Hong Kong
Kumasi
Makerere
Malawi
Malaya
Malta
Mauritius
Nairobi
Nanyang

National U. of Lesotho
 (from 1977)
National U. of Malaysia
Papua New Guinea
Papua New Guinea U. of Technology
 (from 1974)
Rhodesia
U. of Science, Malaysia
 (from 1974)
Sierra Leone
Singapore
South Pacific
Sri Lanka
U. of Technology Malaysia
 (from 1973)
West Indies
Zambia

QUINQUENNIAL REPORT OF SECRETARY GENERAL 1973–78

ASSOCIATE MEMBERS

U. of Manchester Institute of
 Science and Technology
 (from 1974)
U.C. Aberystwyth
U.C. Bangor
U.C. Cardiff
U.C. Swansea
Welsh National School of Medicine
 (from 1977)

St. David's U.C., Lampeter
College of Cape Breton (Canada)
 (from 1977)
Lincoln College (N.Z.)
U.C. Botswana (from 1977)
Kenyatta U.C. (Kenya) (from 1975)

ADDITIONAL MEMBERS

Cranfield Institute of Technology
U. of Manchester Institute of Science
 and Technology (until 1974)
Nova Scotia Technical College

Royal Military College of Canada
Ryerson Polytechnical Institute
Birla Institute of Technology and
 Science (until 1975)

II. MEMBERS OF THE COUNCIL OF THE ACU DURING THE QUINQUENNIUM 1973-78

Aboyade, Professor O. (Nigeria)	1976–77
Abubakar, Professor I. (Nigeria)	1977–78
Adinarayan, Dr. S. P. (India)	1973–74
Ahmed Choudhury, Dr. U. (Bangladesh)	1973–74
Ainuddin bin Wahid, Tan Sri (Other Parts)	1975–76
Ajayi, Professor J. F. Ade (Nigeria)	1973–74
Anuwar bin Mahmud, Datuk Dr. (Other Parts)	1977–78
Armitage, Professor Sir Arthur (United Kingdom)	1973–78
Auchmuty, Professor J. J. (Australia)	1973–74
Aziz, Professor Ungku A. (Other Parts) (*Vice-Chairman* 1973–74, *Chairman* 1974–75)	1973–76
Back, Professor K. J. C. (Australia)	1977–78
Bekoe, Professor D. A. (Other Parts)	1977–78
Borg Costanzi, Professor E. J. (Other Parts) (*Chairman* 1976–77)	1973–74, 1976–78
Bose, Dr. A. N. (India)	1976–77
Boyle of Handsworth, Rt. Hon. Lord (United Kingdom)	1977–78
Bullayya, Mr. L. (India)	1974–75
Burrenchobay, Mr. R. (Other Parts)	1974–77
Choudhury, Professor F. H. (Bangladesh)	1977–78
Cowen, Professor Sir Zelman (Australia)	1975–77

APPENDIX I

Das, Mr. J. N. (India) 1975–76
Deo, Mr. P. G. (India) 1977–78
Derham, Professor Sir David (Australia) 1974–76
Duckworth, Dr. H. E. (Canada) (*Chairman* 1977–78) 1973–78
Dutta, Dr. S. K. (India)... 1975–76

Ewusie, Professor J. Y. (Other Parts) 1975–76

Fazal, Professor A. (Bangladesh) 1975–76

Goma, Professor L. K. H. (Other Parts) 1973–74
Gris, Dr. G. B. (Other Parts) 1975–76

Habakkuk, Sir John (United Kingdom) 1976–77
Hsueh, Professor S. S. (Other Parts) 1973–75
Huang, Professor R. L. (Other Parts) 1975–76
Hunnings, Professor G. (Other Parts) 1976–77

Inglis, Professor K. S. (Other Parts) 1973–74
Irvine, Dr. D. H. (Other Parts)... ... ... 1973–75, 1977–78

Javare Gowda, Professor D. (India) 1975–76

Kaduma, Mr. I. M. (Other Parts) 1977–78
Karanja, Dr. J. N. (Other Parts) 1976–77
Karim, Professor A. (Bangladesh) 1975–76
Kerwin, Dr. L. (Canada) 1973–75
Kwakye, Dr. E. B. (Other Parts) 1976–77
Kwan, Mr. Sai Kheong (Other Parts) 1976–77
Kwapong, Professor A. A. (Other Parts) 1973–74

Lacoste, Dr. P. (Canada) 1977–78
Li, Dr. Choh-Ming (Other Parts) 1973–74, 1976–77
Logan, Sir Douglas (United Kingdom) (*Hon. Treasurer* 1973–74,
   Hon. Deputy Treasurer 1974–78) 1973–78
Lutwama, Professor J. S. W. (Other Parts) 1975–76

Maiden, Dr. C. J. (New Zealand) 1975–78
Maraj, Dr. J. A. (Other Parts) 1976–78
Mehrotra, Dr. R. C. (India) 1978
Mitra, Dr. C. R. (India) 1974–75
Morgan, Dr. M. O. (Canada) 1977–78
Msekwa, Mr. P. (Other Parts) 1974–75
Mukherji, Dr. R. (India) 1976–77
Mwanza, Dr. J. M. (Other Parts) 1977–78
Myers, Professor R. H. (Australia) 1976–78

Naser, Professor M. A. (Bangladesh) 1974–75
Noble, Sir Fraser (United Kingdom) 1973–78

O'Brien, Dr. J. W. (Canada) 1975–78
Oliver, Dr. M. K. (Canada) 1974–77

QUINQUENNIAL REPORT OF SECRETARY GENERAL 1973−78

Phillips, Professor N. C. (New Zealand)	1973−74
Pitt, Sir Harry (United Kingdom)	1974−78
Porter, Dr. A. T. (Other Parts)	1974−75
Preston, Mr. A. Z. (Other Parts)	1975−78
Rahim, Professor Quazi M. F. (Bangladesh)	1973−74
Rangaswami, Dr. G. (India)	1977−78
Robson, Professor Sir Hugh (United Kingdom)	1973−76
Rogers, Professor C. A. (Other Parts)	1973−76
Samundri, Sardar B. S. (India)	1976−77
Sen, Professor S. N. (India)	1973−74
Sendut, Tan Sri Professor Hamzah (Other Parts)	1974−75
Siddiqui, Professor Z. R. (Bangladesh)	1976−77
Singh Suman, Dr. S. N. (India)	1973−75
Siriwardene, Professor P. P. G. L. (Other Parts)	1977−78
Sumanadasa, Mr. L. H. (Other Parts)	1974−75
Sundaravadivelu, Mr. N. D. (India)	1974−75
Swani, Professor N. M. (India)	1977−78
Symons, Dr. T. H. B. (Canada) (*Hon. Treasurer* 1974−78)	1973−78
Taylor, Dr. D. B. C. (New Zealand) (*Chairman* 1975−76)	1974−77
Thomas, Professor H. O. (Nigeria)	1974−75
Tope, Mr. T. K. (India)	1975−76
Wallace, Sister Catherine (Canada)	1973−74
Watson, Dr. J. Steven (United Kingdom) (*Vice-Chairman* 1974−78)	1973−78
Watts, Dr. R. L. (Canada)	1977−78
Williams, Professor B. R. (Australia)	1973−75
Williams, Dr. D. C. (Canada)	1973−74
Wilson, Sir Charles (United Kingdom) (*Chairman* 1973−74)	1973−75
Yesufu, Professor T. M. (Nigeria)	1975−76

III. MEMBERS OF THE EXECUTIVE COMMITTEE OF THE ACU 1973-78

Aboyade, Professor O.	1976−77
Ajayi, Professor J. F. Ade	1973−74
Anuwar bin Mahmud, Datuk Dr.	1977−78
Armitage, Professor Sir Arthur	1974−78
Auchmuty, Professor J. J.	1973−74
Aziz, Professor Ungku A. (*Vice-Chairman* 1973−74, *Chairman* 1974−75)	1973−76
Borg Costanzi, Professor E. J. (*Chairman* 1976−77)	1976−78
Bose, Dr. A. N.	1976−77

APPENDIX I

Derham, Professor Sir David 1975–76
Duckworth, Dr. H. E. (*Chairman* 1977–78) 1975–78

Logan, Sir Douglas (*Hon Treasurer* 1973–74,
   Hon. Deputy Treasurer 1974–78) 1973–78

Mitra, Dr. C. R. 1974–75
Myers, Professor R. H. 1977–78

Noble, Sir Fraser 1973–78

Pitt, Sir Harry 1976–78
Porter, Dr. A. T. 1974–75

Robson, Professor Sir Hugh 1973–76

Swani, Professor N. M. 1977–78
Symons, Dr. T. H. B. (*Hon. Treasurer* 1974–78) 1973–78

Taylor, Dr. D. B. C. (*Chairman* 1975–76) 1974–77

Wallace, Sister Catherine 1973–74
Watson, Dr. J. Steven (*Vice-Chairman* 1974–78) 1973–78
Wilson, Sir Charles (*Chairman* 1973–74) 1973–75

Yesufu, Professor T. M. 1975–76

QUINQUENNIAL REPORT OF SECRETARY GENERAL 1973-78

COMPARATIVE FINANCIAL TABLES
Note by the Honorary Treasurer

As envisaged in the financial note in the last Quinquennial Report, the General Meeting in August 1973 approved the introduction of a new system of variable assessments of annual subscriptions on the basis of member institutions' recurrent incomes instead of the less flexible quinquennial basis of student numbers which had previously been used. This new system, together with continuing annual reassessments of administration fees for separately financed scholarship schemes, has enabled the Association to match income with expenditure throughout the quinquennium now under review.

The most striking feature of the financial position of the Association over the past five years is the increase in total expenditure from £247,557 in 1973-74 to an estimated £457,000 in 1977-78. The work of the Association has continued to expand, particularly in publications and appointments services, but, as in the previous quinquennium, the main cause of the increase has been continuing financial inflation in the United Kingdom. This is, again, reflected in several items but particularly in the rising cost of salaries and superannuation (the latter also reflecting the introduction, in 1975-76, of improved pension schemes requiring higher rates of employer's contributions). Staff in post has remained virtually unchanged over the period (again between 50 and 52) whereas expenditure under these items has risen from £180,840 in 1973-74 to an estimated £307,700 in 1977-78. The other main increase, during the last two years of the quinquennium, has occurred under the item of rent and rates. The former lease, which was granted by the University of London in 1955 and expired in 1977, required a very modest annual rent of £3,200, with no provision for periodic reviews. The economic rent, which the university is obliged to charge in accordance with UK University Grants Committee policy (with no net financial benefit to the University itself), for the new 21-year lease from June 1977 is £31,750 per annum and will be subject to quinquennial reviews.

T.H.B.S

APPENDIX I

INCOME AND EXPENDITURE ACCOUNTS

EXPENDITURE	1973/74 £	1974/75 £	1975/76 £	1976/77 £	1977/78 (Est.) £
ADMINISTRATION					
Salaries, national insurance, graduated pensions and luncheon vouchers	169,789	201,399	238,048	258,789	282,500
Superannuation	11,051	11,319	18,044	21,333	25,200
Provision for supplementation of FSSU retirement benefits	1,500	1,500	750	350	—
Pension and FSSU supplementation	2,067	2,652	564	100	385
Staff vacancies: advertising, fares, etc.	1,015	2,212	1,482	563	1,650
Stationery and printing (other than publications)	8,178	7,353	7,602	7,320	10,150
Postage and telegrams	6,756	7,900	9,540	8,479	9,500
Telephone	1,774	2,445	3,418	3,446	4,000
Expenses—conferences and meetings	385	354	1,068	688	800
Hospitality	767	1,103	1,340	1,093	1,625
Travelling: Executive Committee	—	238	5,051	4,965	6,000
Travelling: staff members	4,830	6,710	9,177	7,004	7,700
Visiting administrator's expenses	999	—	819	—	500
Books and newspapers	576	924	957	926	1,150
Miscellaneous	1,114	1,098	1,492	1,529	1,600
Audit fee	441	386	508	512	615
Professional charges	789	391	807	171	5,300
Bank charges	562	941	140	290	105
Kennedy Scholars' expenses	738	834	813	925	1,100
Repairs to office furniture and equipment	485	880	1,079	894	1,100
Provision for purchase of office furniture and equipment	1,000	1,000	3,200	5,000	5,000
File storage charges	—	—	—	99	70
	214,816	251,639	305,899	324,476	366,050
MAINTENANCE OF PREMISES					
Rent and rates	5,836	6,474	7,662	10,596	37,350
Insurance	321	488	595	652	700
Heating and lighting	1,963	2,851	3,137	3,827	4,300
Repairs, alterations and redecoration	1,053	2,009	1,637	5,525	3,400
Caretaking, cleaning, etc.	4,373	6,051	6,965	7,091	8,650
Fire escape adaptations	—	—	6,531	1,499	—
Provision for exterior redecoration	1,000	1,200	1,440	1,460	1,600
22 Kensington Court Gardens: ground rent, rates, heating and service charges	1,763	1,613	2,543	2,357	3,500
	16,309	20,686	30,510	33,007	59,500
Bad debts	92	3,177	5,502	2,232	2,300
Deficit on publications	2,740	—	—	—	—
Provision for Council meetings	5,000	5,000	36,000	15,000	15,000
Provision for 1978 Congress	5,000	5,000	6,000	8,000	8,000
Provision for ACU/Commonwealth Foundation Travelling Fellowships	1,500	1,500	1,800	2,000	2,000
Provision for special studies	1,600	1,600	50	50	50
Provision for Inter-University Travel Fund	500	500	100	100	100
Dilapidations fund	—	—	—	—	1,000
Premises fund	—	—	3,335	3,335	3,000
Total expenditure	247,557	289,102	389,196	388,200	457,000
Balances, income over expenditure	15,669	14,173	16,735	49,812	50,386
	263,226	303,275	405,931	438,012	507,386

QUINQUENNIAL REPORT OF SECRETARY GENERAL 1973 – 78

FIVE YEARS' COMPARATIVE STATEMENTS

INCOME	1973/74 £	1974/75 £	1975/76 £	1976/77 £	1977/78 (Est.) £
Subscriptions	132,291	154,014	214,257	239,449	265,186
Donations	1,645	160	—	320	—
Administration fees:					
Marshall Scholarship Scheme	8,500	11,200	14,000	14,550	20,600
Commonwealth Scholarship Scheme	54,667	62,667	88,467	91,267	116,000
Frank Knox Memorial Fellowships	50	506	998	1,264	1,600
Kennedy Memorial Scholarships	5,700	7,100	10,100	11,200	15,200
Drapers' Company	800	900	700	950	900
Surplus on publications	—	4,260	8,805	4,746	4,000
Editorial services	3,518	3,320	2,967	3,917	5,000
Appointments fees from overseas universities	56,055	52,867	60,120	62,560	63,000
Refund of proportion of Appointments Service advertising expenditure	—	6,281	5,517	7,213	15,300
CFTC handling charge	—	—	—	576	600
	263,226	303,275	405,931	438,012	507,386

APPENDIX I

BALANCE

LIABILITIES	1973/74 £	1974/75 £	1975/76 £	1976/77 £	1977/78 (Est.) £
Capital reserve	84,479	70,374	77,468	77,468	77,468
General revenue reserve	73,130	105,600	147,851	222,697	280,000
Premises fund	36,677	38,510	43,771	49,295	54,760
Staff benefit fund	14,232	15,253	8,714	10,048	10,700
Special funds	5,571	10,516	8,295	11,608	10,000
Provision for exterior redecoration	946	2,146	3,586	3,675	1,000
Provision for supplementation of FSSU retirement benefits	15,500	17,000	17,750	18,100	18,100
Provision for Council meetings	8,986	−17,947	12,455	−184	10,500
Provision for 1973 Congress	29	—	—	—	—
Provision for 1978 Congress	—	5,000	11,000	18,927	20,000
Dilapidations fund	25,641	26,923	28,269	29,682	32,166
Provision for purchase of office furniture and equipment	134	496	159	3,706	5,000
Provision for ACU/Commonwealth Foundation Travelling Fellowships	10,658	9,799	14,700	15,907	24,000
Provision for special studies	4,800	6,400	6,450	6,500	6,550
Provision for Inter-University Travel Fund	1,500	2,000	2,100	2,200	2,800
Symons Award Fund	117	245	617	942	942
Subscriptions in advance	317	1,030	101	818	600
Sundry creditors	29,520	48,343	48,711	38,374	35,000
	312,237	341,688	431,997	509,763	589,586

FIVE YEARS' COMPARATIVE ANALYSIS OF INCOME AND EXPENDITURE ACCORDING TO ACTIVITIES OF THE ASSOCIATION

GENERAL (for all member institutions)	Income £	Expenditure £	Balance £
1973/74	207,171	195,653	+11,518
1974/75	244,127	229,954	+14,173
1975/76	340,294	323,559*	+16,735
1976/77	367,663	317,851*	+49,812
1977/78 (Est.)	428,486	378,100	+50,386

APPOINTMENTS SERVICES (for various overseas universities)			
1973/74	56,055	51,904	+ 4,151
1974/75	59,148	59,148	—
1975/76	65,637	65,637*	—
1976/77	70,349	70,349*	—
1977/78 (Est.)	78,900	78,900	—

*Includes non-recurrent items

QUINQUENNIAL REPORT OF SECRETARY GENERAL 1973 – 78

SHEETS

ASSETS	1973/74 £	1974/75 £	1975/76 £	1976/77 £	1977/78 (Est.) £
Investments at cost	151,394	141,771	142,185	138,195	140,000
Premises at 22 Kensington Court Gardens, London W8	23,400	23,400	23,400	29,041	29,041
Subscriptions in arrears	21,957	19,274	10,234	17,253	20,000
Appointments Service charges and expenses	42,940	71,901	59,779	103,804	95,000
Sundry debtors	44,232	77,267	69,978	107,707	175,545
Short-term loans	20,000	—	100,000	90,000	100,000
Cash at bank, etc.	8,314	8,075	26,421	23,763	30,000
	312,237	341,688	431,997	509,763	589,586

PUBLICATIONS OF THE ASSOCIATION 1973-78

Obtainable (unless otherwise indicated) by direct order from
ACU, 36 Gordon Square, London, England WC1H 0PF

Commonwealth Universities Yearbook. Annual. 2600 pages. £25 (£16.25 to staff of member universities). A guide to the facilities, organisation, staff and activities of universities of good standing in the Commonwealth. A chapter on each of 280 universities contains general information including details of first and higher degrees and a complete list of teaching staff arranged by subjects. Major bibliography; 155,000-names index, general index and 21 other indexes to study facilities.

(A Register of) *Research Strengths of Universities in the Developing Countries of the Commonwealth.* 1976, 1978. 200 pages. £3.50. Provides brief information about 1840 research areas in which 96 universities in developing countries of the Commonwealth have said they can offer facilities to academic staff and postdoctoral or graduate students from other Commonwealth developing countries who wish to undertake advanced study or research.

Awards for Commonwealth University Staff. 1973, 1975, 1977. 227 pages. £2.75. Describes more than 720 separate schemes of fellowships, visiting professorships, travel grants, etc., open to university staff in one Commonwealth country who wish to carry out research, make study visits, or teach for a while at a university in another Commonwealth country.

Scholarships Guide for Commonwealth Postgraduate Students. 1974, 1976. 346 pages. £3.75. Describes more than 1,250 separate scholarships, grants and other forms of financial aid open to graduates of Commonwealth universities who wish to undertake postgraduate study or research at a Commonwealth university outside their own country.

Financial Aid for First Degree Study at Commonwealth Universities. 1974, 1975, 1977. 32 pages. 85p. Describes about 100 separate schemes for Commonwealth students who wish to study for a first degree at a Commonwealth university outside their own country.

Acumen. Began January 1978. At least 4 issues a year. A newsletter for executive heads of ACU member universities.

ACU Bulletin of Current Documentation (ABCD). 5 times a year. 32 pages. Annual subscription: UK £1.90; elsewhere £2.60. Extracts, summaries and notes relating to important books, reports and other documents on matters affecting universities and of more than local interest. Occasional original articles. Notes on ACU services. List of chair vacancies.

ABCD Extra, July 1978. *The Role of Universities in National Development,* by Prof. R. P. Dore. An ACU Occasional Paper.

Who's Who at Executive Heads Conferences. 1973, 1976, 1978.

Commonwealth Universities and Society. 1974. 490 pages. £3. The report of the proceedings of the Eleventh Commonwealth Universities Congress, Edinburgh, 1973.

List of University Institutions in the Commonwealth. Annual. 36 pages. As well titles and postal addresses of institutions, this list gives for each the name of the executive head and of the officer to whom general enquiries should be sent.

QUINQUENNIAL REPORT OF SECRETARY GENERAL 1973-78

Higher Education in the United Kingdom: a handbook for students from overseas and their advisers. 1974, 1976, 1978. 308 pages. £3.25. Lists courses (150-subject directory of study facilities) and gives information on entrance requirements and procedures, costs, etc. Longman's for British Council and ACU.

Report of the Council of the ACU. Annual. 52 pages.

List of Academic Visitors to the United Kingdom. 3 times a year. 83rd issue: 38 pages. Each issue has more than 1,000 name entries.

The Association of Commonwealth Universities: What it is and what it does. Annual. 4 pages.

The Compendium of University Entrance Requirements for First Degree Courses in the United Kingdom*. Annual. 340 pages. £3.75. Obtainable only from Lund Humphries (ACU), The Country Press, Drummond Rd., Bradford, England BD8 8DH. Describes minimum (GCE) requirements for entry to each of the 5,000 first degree courses at the 87 UK universities and university colleges. Also profiles of each admitting institution.

Schedule of Postgraduate Courses in United Kingdom Universities*. Annual. 108 pages. £2.10. Gives title of taught courses, duration and qualification awarded.

Safety in Universities: Code of Practice Part 1, General Principles*; Notes of Guidance Part 2: 1—Lasers*. Code: 1977 reissue with revisions; 38 pages; 90p. Notes: 1978; 45 pages; 70p. Both obtainable only from CVCP.

PREPARED BY ACU BUT OBTAINABLE ONLY FROM PUBLISHERS NAMED

Directory of Education and Training Resources in the Developing Countries of the Commonwealth. 1974. 430 pages. £3. This guide to institutions at post-secondary level was edited by the ACU for the Commonwealth Fund for Technical Co-operation and published by the Commonwealth Secretariat, London. The ACU also contributed material for a revised edition (1977).

Commonwealth Scholarship and Fellowship Plan: Report. Annual to 1976. (Commonwealth Secretariat, London).

Commonwealth Scholarship Commission in the United Kingdom: Annual Report. (H.M. Stationery Office, London).

Marshall Aid Commemoration Commission: Annual Report. (H.M. Stationery Office, London).

Choosing a British University by Sir Robert Aitken, 1973. A guide for candidates in the USA for Fulbright Awards and Marshall Scholarships. (Marshall Aid Commemoration Commission and US—UK Educational Commission, for distribution only in the USA). New edition, by Sir Frederick Dainton, in preparation.

**Published for Committee of Vice-Chancellors and Principals of the Universities of the United Kingdom (CVCP).*

APPENDIX II

GENERAL MEETING

OF

THE ASSOCIATION OF COMMONWEALTH UNIVERSITIES

Minutes of a General Meeting of members of the Association held at 2.30 p.m. on Wednesday, 16 August 1978, in Room 40 of the School of Business Administration at the University of Western Ontario.

Present:

The Chairman, Dr. H. E. DUCKWORTH
The Vice-Chairman, Dr. J. STEVEN WATSON
The Honorary Treasurer, Dr. T. H. B. SYMONS
The Honorary Deputy Treasurer, Sir DOUGLAS LOGAN

Professor O. ABOYADE (Ife)
Professor W. AHMAD (Bangladesh Engineering and Technology)
Professor J. F. ADE. AJAYI (Lagos)
Dr. O. O. AKINKUGBE (Ilorin)
Dr. J. M. ANDERSON (New Brunswick)
Mr. M. R. APPAROW (Andhra)
Professor Sir ARTHUR ARMITAGE (Manchester)
Professor E. A. AYANDELE (Calabar)
Professor K. J. C. BACK (James Cook)
Dr. L. I. BARBER (Regina)
Professor A. BEACHAM (Murdoch)
Dr. W. E. BECKEL (Lethbridge)
Dr. R. W. BEGG (Saskatchewan)
Professor D. A. BEKOE (Ghana)
Professor L. M. BIRT (Wollongong)
Dr. A. N. BOSE (Jadavpur)
Dr. A. N. BOURNS (McMaster)
Rt. Hon. Lord BOYLE OF HANDSWORTH (Leeds)
Dr. G. M. BURNETT (Heriot-Watt)
Mr. J. B. BUTTERWORTH (Warwick)
Dr. D. F. CAMPBELL (Cape Breton)
Dr. D. R. CAMPBELL (Manitoba)
Professor D. E. CARO (Tasmania)
Dr. D. O. CARRIGAN (St. Mary's)
Sir CHARLES CARTER (Lancaster)
Dr. S. CHANDRASEKHAR (Annamalai)
Sir DERMAN CHRISTOPHERSON (Durham)

GENERAL MEETING OF THE ACU

Dr. W. A. COCHRANE (Calgary)
Dr. W. H. COCKCROFT (Ulster)
Dr. G. E. CONNELL (Western Ontario)
Sir ALAN COTTRELL (Cambridge)
Dr. W. A. CRAMOND (Stirling)
Dr. W. S. H. CRAWFORD (Mount Allison)
Sir SAMUEL CURRAN (Strathclyde)
Dr. J. R. DACEY (Royal Military)
Sir GORONWY DANIEL (Wales)
Professor G. N. DAVIES (Queensland)
Professor S. R. DENNISON (Hull)
Professor Sir DAVID DERHAM (Melbourne)
Dr. A. K. DHAN (North-Eastern Hill)
Dr. A. J. EARP (Brock)
Dr. J. Y. EWUSIE (Cape Coast)
Dr. P. FROGGATT (Queen's, Belfast)
Dr. E. MARGARET FULTON (Mount Saint Vincent)
Professor D. W. GEORGE (Newcastle, NSW)
Professor R. C. GATES (New England)
Mr. M. A. M. GILANI (Bhagalpur)
Dr. J. F. GODFREY (King's College)
Professor S. C. DUBE (Jammu)
Professor D. E. U. EKONG (Port Harcourt)
Professor L. C. B. GOWER (Southampton)
Rev. Father R. GUINDON (Ottawa)
Dr. S. M. GUMA (Botswana and Swaziland)
Dr. P. D. HAJELA (Allahabad)
Professor J. M. HAM (Toronto)
Tan Sri Datuk Haji HAMDAN B. SHEIKH TAHIR (U. of Science, Malaysia)
Dr. G. A. HARROWER (Lakehead)
Professor R. N. HASZELDINE (UMIST)
Rt. Hon. Lord HUNTER OF NEWINGTON (Birmingham)
Dr. D. H. IRVINE (Guyana)
Dr. R. O. H. IRVINE (Otago)
Professor F. R. JEVONS (Deakin)
Professor RAM JOSHI (Bombay)
Mr. I. M. KADUMA (Dar es Salaam)
Mr. W. S. KAJUBI (Makerere)
Dr. J. N. KARANJA (Nairobi)
Dr. P. N. KAWTHEKAR (Vikram)
Dr. HARRY KAY (Exeter)
Dr. A. M. KHUSRO (Aligarh Muslim)
Dr. DAVID KIMBLE (Malawi)
Mr. J. K. KOINANGE (Kenyatta UC)
Dr. V. C. KULANDAISWAMY (Madurai)
Dr. E. B. KWAKYE (Kumasi)
Mr. KWAN SAI-KHEONG (Singapore)
Dr. PAUL LACOSTE (Montreal)
Mr. HARDWARI LAL (Maharshi Dayanand)
Professor SHANKAR LAL (IIT, Kharagpur)
Dr. J. F. LEDDY (Windsor)
Dr. CHOH-MING LI (Chinese U. of Hong Kong)
Dr. D. R. LLEWELLYN (Waikato)

Mr. R. R. LOHIA (Papua New Guinea)
Professor D. A. LOW (Australian National)
Dr. H. I. MACDONALD (York, Canada)
Mr. R. A. MCKINLAY (Bradford)
Rev. G. A. MACKINNON (St. Francis Xavier)
Dr. C. J. MAIDEN (Auckland)
Dr. J. A. MARAJ (South Pacific)
Professor R. L. MARTIN (Monash)
Mr. M. T. MASHOLOGU (Lesotho)
Dr. B. C. MATTHEWS (Waterloo)
Dr. R. C. MEHROTRA (Delhi)
Dr. P. P. M. MEINCKE (Prince Edward Island)
Dr. B. MISRA (Utkal)
Dr. C. R. MITRA (Birla ITS)
Dr. M. O. MORGAN (Memorial, Newfoundland)
Dr. J. P. D. MOUNSEY (Welsh National School of Medicine)
Dr. N. A. NOOR MUHAMMAD (Calicut)
Dr. S. K. MUKHERJEE (Calcutta)
Dr. R. MUKHERJI (Burdwan)
Dr. K. S. MURTY (Sri Venkateswara)
Dr. J. M. MWANZA (Zambia)
Professor R. H. MYERS (New South Wales)
Dr. B. D. NAG CHAUDHURI (Jawaharlal Nehru)
Dr. V. K. S. NAYAR (Kerala)
Professor R. G. NARAYANAMURTHI (IIT, Madras)
Professor A. M. NEVILLE (Dundee)
Professor T. E. W. NIND (Trent)
Sir FRASER NOBLE (Aberdeen)
Dr. J. W. O'BRIEN (Concordia)
Dr. M. K. OLIVER (Carleton)
Professor G. O. ONUAGULUCHI (Jos)
Dr. E. W. PARKES (City)
Professor R. C. PAUL (Panjab)
Dr. H. J. PERKINS (Brandon)
Sir WALTER PERRY (Open)
Dr. H. E. PETCH (Victoria, BC)
Mr. W. G. PITMAN (Ryerson Polytechnical Institute)
Sir HARRY PITT (Reading)
Dr. A. T. PORTER (Sierra Leone)
Mr. A. Z. PRESTON (West Indies)
Professor G. RAM REDDY (Osmania)
Professor T. RATHO (Berhampur)
Sir REX RICHARDS (Oxford)
Professor R. W. RUSSELL (Flinders)
Sardar B. S. SAMUNDRI (Guru Nanak Dev)
Professor J. F. SCOTT (La Trobe)
Dr. N. O. H. SETIDISHO (Botswana UC)
Dr. (Mrs.) MADHURI R. SHAH (SNDT)
Mr. M. SHOCK (Leicester)
Professor Z. R. SIDDIQUI (Jahangirnagar)
Professor G. D. SIMS (Sheffield)
Dr. AMRIK SINGH (Punjabi)
Dr. P. P. G. L. SIRIWARDENE (Sri Lanka)

GENERAL MEETING OF THE ACU

Dr. A. E. Sloman (Essex)
Dr. W. A. S. Smith (Athabasca)
Professor R. W. Steel (Swansea UC)
Dr. A. Stewart (Massey)
Professor J. D. Stewart (Lincoln)
Professor W. A. C. Stewart (Keele)
Professor D. R. Stranks (Adelaide)
Professor R. Street (Western Australia)
Professor T. N. Tamuno (Ibadan)
Dr. N. H. Tayler (Wilfrid Laurier)
Dr. D. B. C. Taylor (Victoria, Wellington)
Dr. G. Templeman (Kent at Canterbury)
Dr. F. Thistlethwaite (East Anglia)
Mr. D. V. Urs (Mysore)
Dr. R. L. Watts (Queen's, Kingston)
Professor E. C. Webb (Macquarie)
Dr. B. C. L. Weedon (Nottingham)
Professor R. F. Whelan (Liverpool)
Sir Denys Wilkinson (Sussex)
Professor F. J. Willett (Griffith)
Dr. A. Williams (Glasgow)
Professor B. R. Williams (Sydney)
Mr. S. S. Wodeyar (Karnatak)
Professor T. M. Yesufu (Benin)

By invitation:
Mr. R. C. Griffiths (Inter-University Council for Higher Education Overseas)
Mr. F. S. Hambly (Australian Vice-Chancellors' Committee)
Mr. B. P. Hampton (New Zealand Vice-Chancellors' Committee)
Dr. J. R. Keyston (Association of Atlantic Universities)
Mr. E. K. Kigozi (Inter-University Committee for East Africa)
Sir Roy Marshall (Committee of Vice-Chancellors and Principals of the Universities of the UK)
Dr. E. J. Monahan (Council of Ontario Universities)
Mr. R. Pérusse (Conference of Rectors and Principals of Quebec Universities)
Mr. M. S. Ramamurthy (Association of Indian Universities)
Mrs. Ayodele F. Sanwo (Committee of Vice-Chancellors of Nigerian Universities)
Mr. M. K. Hussain Sirkar (Association of Universities of Bangladesh)
Mr. B. H. Taylor (Committee of Vice-Chancellors and Principals of the Universities of the UK)
Dr. C. J. Thibault (Association of Universities and Colleges of Canada)

Sir Hugh W. Springer (Secretary General)
Mr. T. Craig
Mr. P. B. Hetherington
Mr. J. A. Whittingham
Mrs. D. Blanche Gubertini

The Chairman, Dr. Duckworth, welcomed members and gave a brief account of Association meetings. The Annual General Meeting of the Association was held each November in London; the Council of the Association, which now consisted of 29 members and was representative of all member institutions, met annually; and between meetings of the Council the Executive Committee (consisting of 5 officers and 6 elected members, 3 from the United Kingdom and 3 from overseas), met three times. The Secretary General also seized any opportunity of putting before members ideas for the purpose of advice, information and criticism. At Vancouver during the Congress there would be a session on the domestic affairs of the Association which would be open to all delegates.

Prior to this meeting the Council had met in Quebec City and there would be a report on matters arising there.

1. THE QUINQUENNIAL REPORT 1973 – 78 [see Appendix I]

The Honorary Treasurer, Dr. T. H. B. Symons, reminded members that in August 1973 a new system of assessment was introduced under which subscriptions were based on the annual income of institutions and not on student numbers as had previously been the case. The new system had worked well and had enabled the Association to meet its obligations and distribute the burden of costs in a way acceptable to its membership. It had been agreed that the structure of subscriptions assessments would be reviewed at the next meeting of the Executive Heads in 1981.

The most striking single feature over the past five years had been the rise in the level of expenditure from £247,557 in 1973 – 74 to a nearly final figure of £470,800 for the year just ended (1977 – 78). This reflected a steady expansion but there had been virtually no change in the numerical strength of the staff of just over 50 members during this period. The increase had been caused by the expansion of activities and by inflation, of which the rise in salaries and pension arrangements together with the new lease had formed the major part. The Honorary Treasurer reviewed the history of the lease of the Association's offices, saying that the University of London had, until 1977, leased the buildings at the very low figure of £3,200. A review of this situation had been enforced by the government and the resulting economic rent had been fixed at approximately £32,000 and was subject to quinquennial review. Fortunately the inevitability of increase had been foreseen and provision had been made.

He referred to the formation of the Budget Review Committee which had been decided on at the Council meeting in Malaysia in 1975. The Committee had met in New Zealand in 1976, in Malta in 1977, and in the current year in London in June and at Quebec City earlier in August, to review in detail the budget which had been recommended to the Council. The membership was designed to be representative and consisted of the Honorary Treasurer, who served as Chairman, the Chairman of the Association, the Honorary Deputy Treasurer and the Secretary General as officers, together with three elected overseas members. The Vice-Chairman had also taken an interest and attended the last two meetings. He expressed appreciation of the services of the members of the Committee.

The Honorary Treasurer reported that the budget for 1977 – 78 was expected to produce a surplus of some £32,000. Over 98% of the year's subscriptions had been received which compared with a figure of 93% in 1976 – 77.

In the budget for 1978 – 79 the total expenditure was expected to be £508,000. Expenditure would be met by income from subscriptions, administrative fees and fees from the Appointments Service. The revenue from subscriptions would be approximately £278,000, from administration fees £166,000, which would cover completely the cost of the services provided, and £90,000 would come from the Appointments Service. The total income for the year of £534,000 thus provided for a preliminary surplus of some £26,000. He expressed his appreciation of the work of the Honorary Deputy Treasurer who was available both to sign documents and to give advice in the UK, and because of his and the secretariat's work and the support of the membership the financial affairs of the Association were in good order.

Prompted by an enquiry from the floor, the Meeting discussed the Association's custom of many years of not recording the income received from the Association's investments in the balance sheet separately, and it was decided that in future such income would be shown clearly in the Income and Expenditure account. The Honorary Treasurer indicated that he particularly welcomed this suggestion.

The Secretary General reported on the quinquennium, saying that the report tended to fall into a pattern. Looking back over the past five years the first major event was the oil crisis which had occurred shortly after the Edinburgh Congress and had gravely affected the finances of member universities. The quinquennium just ended had justified the changes in the method of calculating subscriptions which had been taken at Exeter in 1973. There had been few other major changes apart from the setting up of the Budget Review Committee on which the Honorary Treasurer had commented. The other principal innovation had been the institution of the office of Honorary Deputy Treasurer which had enabled the post of Honorary Treasurer to be held outside Britain.

APPENDIX II

A feature of the quinquennium which deserved mention was the institution of the Symons Award. This award, which was usually made after the Annual General Meeting in November, had been made possible by the generosity of the Honorary Treasurer who had provided funds which enable a piece of silver to be presented to persons who had made outstanding contributions to the Association and to the universities of the Commonwealth.

He also reported that the Council had agreed that the headquarters of the Association at 36 Gordon Square should be renamed John Foster House.

There had been a gratifying increase in the membership of the Association from 191 in 1973 to 221 in 1978, which represented an increase of 16%, as compared with an increase in number of members of 4 during the previous quinquennium, or 2%. Of the 221 members, 125, or 58%, were in developed countries and 96, or 42%, in developing countries. In 23 Commonwealth countries there was 100% membership. The pattern of meetings provided for the Council to go outside Britain three times during the quinquennium, and the Council had met in Kuala Lumpur in 1975, in Wellington in 1976 and in Malta in 1977. He made mention of visits to universities in other parts of the Commonwealth by the Secretary General and the Assistant Secretaries General. It was hoped that universities not yet visited would be included in travel in the near future but long journeys were not usually undertaken just for the purpose of such visits; they were made as far as possible when opportunities arose to include them.

The Assistant Secretary General (Publications and Information), Mr. T. Craig, described the work of his department and the way in which it had been developing. The work centred on a *Publications Service* and *three free Information Services* (a Personal Information Service, an Awards Information Service and a Documentation Service). There was also an Attestation Service for students from certain Commonwealth countries (mainly used by Mauritian students) who wished to study at a French university and had qualifications that met the entry requirements of a UK university.

Most of the 18 or so titles issued by the Association were reference directories—including the large *Commonwealth Universities Yearbook*—but two were 'news' periodicals: *Acumen,* a newsletter for vice-chancellors, and the *ACU Bulletin of Current Documentation* (ABCD). Most universities submitted material promptly and in the form requested for the *Yearbook* and other publications.

The Personal Information Service was used mainly by students. It dealt with about 5,000 enquiries a year by correspondence or interview or by telephone. The Awards Information Service provided, mostly through publications, information about fellowships, scholarships, grants, visiting lectureships, etc. It was as a result of monitoring by the Documentation Service of commission reports, university gazettes and a wide range of other material that *ABCD*, *Acumen* and the *Yearbook* Bibliography were produced. Central to that Service was the ACU Reference Library of 10,000 volumes whose resources were available to the staff of member universities.

It was the ACU office staff who provided the three Information Services who also compiled the publications. They could thus continuously and constructively adapt the various handbooks in a practical way, to take account of the questions people were actually asking. While the department still tried to maintain high editorial standards, considerable emphasis was being given to making the ACU publications better known throughout the world (mainly by direct mailing of leaflets) with a view to increasing sales. In the production of publications there was now a good deal of co-operation with other bodies, especially with the Commonwealth Secretariat and the UK Vice-Chancellors' Committee. In effect, the ACU sold its expertise for the benefit of its member universities.

The department would be glad, Mr. Craig concluded, to undertake work for any group of member universities or (providing the operation was approved by the members) for other bodies of good standing.

The Assistant Secretary General, Mr. P. B. Hetherington, reported that he carried four portfolios, all dealing with that part of the Association's raison d'être which was concerned with the movement of people from member universities.

(a) The *Appointments Service* had been part of the Association's activities since its inception, and though originally concerned exclusively with the movement of staff from the United Kingdom to other parts of the Commonwealth had, over the years, assumed something of a more comprehensive character. There had since the last meeting been something of a reduction from as many as 2,000 to about 1,300 in the number of academic positions announced each year, but the service was still dealing annually with over 10,000 enquiries from the academic public about overseas vacancies, and there had been no drop in the calls made by member universities on the interviewing facilities offered by the service. The service helped to establish very strong and personal links between the office and those universities which used it most (primarily those in Australia, New Zealand, Hong Kong, Malaya and Papua New Guinea). It was not the general membership which maintained the service but rather the universities which used it. The levy which the Association had to make on these member universities fell below the economic cost,

APPENDIX II

since the service had each year been able to negotiate with the press substantial discounts which had generated for the Association sums equivalent to as much as one-fifth of departmental costs.

(*b*) *Administrative Travelling Fellowships.* Under this scheme the Association was able to provide career administrators in member universities with opportunities to make study visits to universities in other parts of the Commonwealth, there to examine problems of professional importance to themselves and their universities. The scheme was funded by the Association itself and the Commonwealth Foundation, and for the first time this year by the Canadian International Development Agency, who had particularly earmarked funds for awards to Fellows from the developing countries of the Commonwealth. The Assistant Secretary General reported, with gratification, on the number of former holders who had now achieved significant advance within their own university systems.

(*c*) *Academic Exchange Fellowships Programme.* The Association assisted the Commonwealth Fund for Technical Co-operation in the administration of funds permitting interchange, contact and movement between academics in developing countries of the Commonwealth. Since its inception the scheme had supported over 70 scholars and research workers in study tours and attachments to other universities in the developing world, with a view to sharing, acquiring or imparting expertise of developmental importance. The Assistant Secretary General paid tribute to the generosity and the helpfulness of the CFTC and its staff.

(*d*) *THES Third World Fellowship.* This award had been established by the Association with an initial, now an annual, grant from the Times Higher Education Supplement, aimed specifically at providing support each year for a scholar from a developing country to make to another such country a visit for purposes akin to those outlined in (*c*) above. As a named award, this Fellowship attracted candidates of a high quality, for whom the Association was often able to elicit support from other sources as well as these. He wished to offer the Association's thanks for its generous maintenance of this grant.

2. POINTS ARISING FROM THE COUNCIL MEETING IN QUEBEC ON 12 AND 14 AUGUST

It was reported that much of the time had been spent reviewing work done in the quinquennium and reported by the Secretary General. The following points had arisen at the meetings:

(*a*) The Council had authorised the Executive Committee to take steps in the not too distant future to establish a search committee to replace the Secretary General when he retires in September 1980, two years beyond normal retirement date.

(*b*) The venue for the next meeting of Executive Heads in 1981 was discussed. The matter was still under consideration and member institutions would be informed when a decision was taken.

(*c*) Margaret Cox Memorial Fund: the Secretary General reported that at the Malta Council meeting he had been asked to consider the possible use of money which had accumulated in the Association's balance sheet under the heading of 'Inter-University Travel Fund'. He had intended to recommend that the money should be used as an emergency fund to help deserving cases which did not come within the terms of existing schemes. The use of the fund would be at the discretion of the Secretary General who would report to the Council on action taken. Miss M. Cox, one of the senior editors of the Publications Department, had died suddenly at the end of 1977 and, when her pension contributions were sent to her father, in gratitude he had sent the sum of £500 to the Finance Officer. With Mr. Cox's agreement this sum was added to the accumulated figure and the Council had agreed to accept the Secretary General's recommendation and institute the Margaret Cox Memorial Fund.

3. Venue of Thirteenth Commonwealth Universities Congress

The Secretary General explained that before the second world war all Congresses had been held in the UK. In 1948 it was decided that Congresses should be held alternately in Britain and in other parts of the Commonwealth and in 1958 the first 'overseas' Congress had been held in Montreal. Since then they had alternated between Britain and other countries, the next being due to take place in Britain in 1983.

Lord Hunter of Newington, Vice-Chancellor of the University of Birmingham, extended a firm invitation that the Thirteenth Congress, in 1983, should be held at his university.

Sir Goronwy Daniel, Vice-Chancellor of the University of Wales, then extended an invitation that the Conference of Executive Heads should meet in Wales in the same year of 1983. He was joined by Professor Steel, Principal of the University College of Swansea, who formally invited the Association to make the campus at Swansea the venue of the meeting.

The Chairman reported that the Council was aware of these invitations and had accepted them on behalf of members of the Association.

4. ANY OTHER BUSINESS

The Vice-Chairman briefly reported the discussion about the present situation in Malta vis-à-vis the University which had taken place at the Council meetings in Quebec, at which the Secretary General had read a letter from the Rector of the University (the Immediate Past Chairman of the Association) apologising for not attending. After discussion it was agreed that the Secretary General should send a personal reply to the Rector expressing the Association's regret at his absence and for the reasons which had occasioned it.

There being no further business the meeting closed at approximately 5 p.m.

APPENDIX III

The Education, Science and Culture Division of Statistics Canada prepared a publication specially for the Vancouver Congress. It was called *From the Sixties to the Eighties: a Statistical Portrait of Canadian Higher Education*. A copy was given to each Congress participant.

The ten chapters are headed: —
1. Introduction
2. The Structure of Education
3. Past and Future Demographic Trends
4. Education Finance
5. University Enrolment Patterns
6. University Student Characteristics
7. Foreign Students and Canadian Students Abroad
8. Degrees Awarded
9. Faculty Characteristics
10. Research and Development

There is a selected bibliography.

The 119-page report was compiled and written by Dr. M. von Zur-Muehlen, with the assistance of Miss Jo-Anne Belliveau, Ms. M. S. Devereaux, Mr. J. Godin, Mrs. Christine Jolicoeur and Mrs. E. Kealey. Enquiries may be addressed to Dr. von Zur-Muehlen or to Mr. J. Holmes, Director, Education, Science and Culture Division, Statistics Canada, Ottawa.

Council of the Association 1977 – 78

Dr. H. E. Duckworth (Winnipeg), *Chairman, Chairman of the Congress*
Dr. J. Steven Watson (St. Andrews), *Vice-Chairman*
Dr. T. H. B. Symons (Canada), *Honorary Treasurer*
Sir Douglas Logan (U.K.), *Honorary Deputy Treasurer*
Professor E. J. Borg Costanzi (Malta), *Immediate Past Chairman*

Professor I. Abubakar (Ahmadu Bello)
Tan Sri Datuk Professor Anuwar bin Mahmud (National U., Malaysia)
Professor Sir Arthur Armitage (Manchester)
Professor K. J. C. Back (James Cook)
Dr. D. A. Bekoe (Ghana)
Rt. Hon. Lord Boyle of Handsworth (Leeds)
Professor F. H. Choudhury (Dacca)
Dr. D. H. Irvine (Guyana)
Mr. I. M. Kaduma (Dar es Salaam)
Dr. P. Lacoste (Montreal)
Professor P. J. Madan (Baroda)
Dr. C. J. Maiden (Auckland)
Dr. J. A. Maraj (South Pacific)
Dr. R. C. Mehrotra (Delhi)
Dr. M. O. Morgan (Memorial, Newfoundland)
Dr. J. M. Mwanza (Zambia)
Professor R. H. Myers (New South Wales)
Sir Fraser Noble (Aberdeen)
Dr. J. W. O'Brien (Concordia)
Sir Harry Pitt (Reading)
Mr. A. Z. Preston (West Indies)
Dr. G. Rangaswami (Tamil Nadu Agricultural)
Professor P. P. G. L. Siriwardene (Sri Lanka)
Dr. R. L. Watts (Queen's, Kingston)

Sir Hugh W. Springer, *Secretary General*

Members of the Congress

PATRONS
His Excellency The Rt. Hon. Jules Léger, CC, CMM, CD, Governor General of Canada
The Rt. Hon. Bora Laskin, MA, LLM, DCL, LLD, FRSC, Chief Justice of Canada
The Hon. R. Steinhauer, OC, Lieutenant Governor of Alberta
Brigadier General The Hon. Henry P. Bell-Irving, DSO, OBE, ED, Lieutenant Governor of British Columbia
The Hon. F. L. Jobin, BA, LLD, Lieutenant Governor of Manitoba
The Hon. Hedard J. Robichard, PC (Can.), Lieutenant Governor of New Brunswick
The Hon. Gordon A. Winter, OC, LLD, Lieutenant Governor of Newfoundland
The Hon. Clarence L. Gosse, MD, Lieutenant Governor of Nova Scotia
The Hon. Pauline M. McGibbon, OC, BA, LLD, DU, DHumL, BAA (Theatre), Hon. FRCPS(C), Lieutenant Governor of Ontario
The Hon. Gordon L. Bennett, MA, Lieutenant Governor of Prince Edward Island
The Hon. Hugues Lapointe, PC(Can.), QC, Lieutenant Governor of Quebec
The Hon. George Porteous, Lieutenant Governor of Saskatchewan

The Hon. N. T. Nemetz, LLD, Chief Justice of Supreme Court of British Columbia

CANADIAN GOVERNMENT MINISTERS
Minister of State for Science and Technology
The Hon. Judd Buchanan represented by H. R. Wynne-Edwards, DSc, PEng, Assistant Secretary, University Branch

Secretary to the Cabinet
Mr. R. G. Robertson represented by B. F. J. Neville, MA, Director, Policy and Programme Review, Federal-Provincial Relations

Department of Secretary of State for Canada
J. Desroches, MA, PhD, Senior Policy Adviser

HIGH COMMISSIONERS IN CANADA OF OTHER COMMONWEALTH COUNTRIES AND THE COMMONWEALTH SECRETARY GENERAL
AUSTRALIA
P. B. Clare, Consul General in Vancouver, representing the High Commissioner
BRITAIN
J. F. C. Springford, OBE, MA, Counsellor (Cultural Affairs), representing the High Commissioner
INDIA
N. R. Verma, MA, Deputy High Commissioner
LESOTHO
H.E. Mr. J. K. Mollo, BA(Admin) MCEd
TRINIDAD AND TOBAGO
H.E. Mr. S. S. Lutchman, BA

MEMBERS OF CONGRESS

UGANDA
H.E. Mr. L. E. Akong'O, BA

THE COMMONWEALTH
R. E. O. Akpofure, Director of Education Division, Commonwealth Secretariat, representing the Commonwealth Secretary General

CANADIAN ORGANISATIONS

Canadian International Development Agency
Dr. L. A. Dorais, Senior Vice-President
Dr. L. Perinbam, Vice-President, Special Programmes Branch

International Development Research Centre
J. King Gordon, CM, MA, LLD, Senior Adviser, University Relations

Statistics Canada
J. Holmes, Director, Education, Science and Culture Division

Social Sciences and Humanities Research Council Canada
A. Fortier, President

Canadian Bureau for International Education
J. R. McBride, MA, Executive Director

Canadian Education Association
J. H. M. Andrews, MA, PhD, Dean of Education, University of British Columbia

World University Service of Canada
W. McNeill, BA, Executive Director

Donner Canadian Foundation
D. Rickerd, QC, MA, President

CANADIAN PROVINCIAL GOVERNMENT DEPARTMENTS

Ministry of Education, Victoria, B.C.
A. E. Soles, BA, MEd, Associate Deputy Minister

Department of Education, Winnipeg, Man.
W. C. Lorimer, MA, EdD, LLD, Deputy Minister

Government of Northwest Territories, Yellowknife, N.W.T.
R. D. Sparham, Policy Consultant: Further Education Study

Minister of Education and Continuing Education, Regina, Sask.
Hon. D. Faris, BA, BD, PhD

Delegates of Member Institutions

AUSTRALIA

ADELAIDE
Professor D. R. Stranks, PhD, MSc, FRACI, Vice-Chancellor
Professor T. G. C. Murrell, MD, DTM&H, FRACGP, Head of Department of Community Medicine
R. E. Bogner, PhD, DIC, ME, Professor and Chairman of Department of Electrical Engineering

AUSTRALIAN NATIONAL UNIVERSITY
Sir John Crawford, AC, CBE, DSc, DEc, DScEcon, LLD, Chancellor
Professor D. A. Low, MA, DPhil, FAHA, FASSA, Vice-Chancellor

DEAKIN
P. N. Thwaites, OBE, MA, BEd, FACE, Chancellor
Professor F. R. Jevons, MA, PhD, DSc, Vice-Chancellor
L. R. Baker, MEngSc, BCE, AGInstTech, Senior Lecturer in Civil Engineering

FLINDERS, SOUTH AUSTRALIA
Professor R. W. Russell, MA, PhD, DSc, Vice-Chancellor and Professor of Psychobiology
Professor G. J. Fraenkel, MA, BM, MCh, FRCS, FRACS, FACMA, Dean of School of Medicine
R. J. Paddick, MA, Senior Lecturer in Education

GRIFFITH
Sir Theodor Bray, CBE, DGU, Chancellor
Professor F. J. Willett, DSc, MA, MBA, LLD, Vice-Chancellor
G. D. Saunders, BA, DU, Senior Lecturer, School of Humanities

JAMES COOK, NORTH QUEENSLAND
The Hon. Mr. Justice J. P. G. Kneipp, LLB, Chancellor
Professor K. J. C. Back, MSc, PhD, Vice-Chancellor
G. T. Steadman, MEc, FASA, Senior Lecturer, Department of Commerce
K. N. P. Chester, BComm, AAUQ, Registrar

LA TROBE
Professor J. F. Scott, MA, FIS, Vice-Chancellor
E. K. Braybrooke, LLM, Professor of Legal Studies

MACQUARIE
Professor P. H. Partridge, MA, Chancellor
Emeritus Professor E. C. Webb, MA, PhD, DSc, FRACI, Vice-Chancellor
C. D. Throsby, MScAgr, PhD, Professor of Economics
D. J. S. Rutledge, MA, MSc, PhD, Associate Professor of Economics

MELBOURNE
Professor Sir David Derham, KBE, CMG, BA, LLD, Vice-Chancellor and Principal
The Hon. J. G. Norris, ED, QC, LLM, Member of Council
J. W. Watson, PhD, MVSc, QDAH, Reader in Veterinary Anatomy and Member of Council
D. O. White, MD, BS, PhD, MSc, FRCPA, Chairman of Professorial Board and Professor of Microbiology

MEMBERS OF CONGRESS

MONASH
Professor R. L. Martin, PhD, ScD, DSc, FRACI, FRIC, FAA, Vice-Chancellor
R. F. C. Brown, MSc, PhD, FRACI, Reader in Chemistry

MURDOCH
Professor A. Beacham, OBE, MA, PhD, LLD, Acting Vice-Chancellor
A. P. Robertson, MA, PhD, FIMA, FRSE, Professor of Mathematics
Observer: Ann Macbeth, BA, Member of Senate

NEWCASTLE, NEW SOUTH WALES
Sir Bede Callaghan, CBE, DSC, FAIM, FBIA, Chancellor
Professor D. W. George, BE, BSc, PhD, Vice-Chancellor

NEW ENGLAND
R. C. Robertson-Cuninghame, BScAgr, DPhil, Deputy Chancellor
Professor R. C. Gates, AO, BCom, MA, DEcon, FASSA, Hon. FRAPI, Vice-Chancellor
Professor P. K. Elkin, BA, BLitt, DPhil, Pro Vice-Chancellor
R. B. Ward, MA, PhD, DipEd, Professor of History

NEW SOUTH WALES
The Hon. Mr. Justice G. J. Samuels, MA, Chancellor
Professor R. H. Myers, CBE, PhD, DSc, LLD, Vice-Chancellor and Principal
Professor D. M. McCallum, MA, BPhil, Chairman of Professorial Board and Head of School of Political Science
A. J. Wicken, BSc, MA, PhD, FNZIC, MASM, Associate Professor of Microbiology

QUEENSLAND
The Hon. Mr. Justice W. B. Campbell, MA, LLB, Chancellor
Professor G. N. Davies, DDS, FDSRCS, FACD, Acting Vice-Chancellor
Professor L. C. Holborow, MA, BPhil, Deputy President of Professorial Board

SYDNEY
Sir Hermann Black, MEc, DLitt, FCIS, Chancellor
Professor B. R. Williams, MA, MA(Econ), DLitt, Vice-Chancellor and Principal
J. M. Ward, MA, LLB, FAHA, FASSA, Professor of History

TASMANIA
Sir John Cameron, CBE, MA, Chancellor
Professor D. E. Caro, OBE, MSc, PhD, LLD, FIP, FAIP, Vice-Chancellor
R. C. Porter, BA, DPE, MACE, Master of Hytten Hall

WESTERN AUSTRALIA
Emeritus Professor R. Street, PhD, DSc, FAA, FIP, FAIP, MIEE, CEng, Vice-Chancellor
Professor A. L. Blakers, BSc, MA, PhD, Chairman of Department of Mathematics
N. F. Dufty, AMet, MA, MEd, PhD, Warden of Convocation

WOLLONGONG
Mr. Justice R. M. Hope, LLB, Chancellor
Emeritus Professor L. M. Birt, BAgrSc, BSc, PhD, DPhil, Vice-Chancellor
R. F. Stewart, BComm, DipEd, Registrar

DELEGATES OF MEMBER INSTITUTIONS

BANGLADESH
BANGLADESH U. OF ENGINEERING AND TECHNOLOGY
Professor W. Ahmad, PhD, MIE, Vice-Chancellor

JAHANGIRNAGAR
Professor Z. R. Siddiqui, MA, Vice-Chancellor

BOTSWANA, SWAZILAND
BOTSWANA AND SWAZILAND
Professor S. M. Guma, MA, DLitt&Phil, Rector of University College of Swaziland, and Chairman of Senate of University for 1977 – 78
C. B. Mackay, QC, BA, DCL, LLD, DèsL, Member of Governing Committee

UNIVERSITY COLLEGE OF BOTSWANA
Professor N. O. H. Setidisho, BSc, MEd, PhD, Rector
O. M. Gaborone, BA, Assistant Registrar

BRITAIN
ABERDEEN
Sir Fraser Noble, MBE, MA, LLD, FRSE, Principal and Vice-Chancellor
K. Walton, MA, PhD, FRSE, FRSGS, Vice-Principal and Professor of Geography
Professor Elizabeth D. Fraser, MA, EdB, PhD, Dean of Arts and Social Sciences

ASTON IN BIRMINGHAM
Professor M. Holmes, DSc, PhD, FICE, Pro Vice-Chancellor

QUEEN'S, BELFAST
P. Froggatt, MD, PhD, FRCPI, President and Vice-Chancellor
Professor A. E. Astin, MA, MRIA, Pro Vice-Chancellor
Professor G. Owen, DSc, MRIA, FIBiol, Pro Vice-Chancellor
C. H. G. Kinahan, CBE, DL, JP, Non-Academic Member of Senate and Chairman of Buildings Committee

BIRMINGHAM
The Rt. Hon. Lord Hunter of Newington, MBE, DL, LLD, FRCP, FRSE, Vice-Chancellor
Professor J. M. Samuels, BCom, Dean of Faculty of Commerce
E. J. Hathaway, BA, Chev. de l'Ordre Nat. du Mérite, Senior Tutor, Combined Honours
H. Harris, BSc(Econ), LLB, DPA, FCIS, Secretary

BRADFORD
R. A. McKinlay, MA, BCom, Acting Vice-Chancellor

BRUNEL
Professor J. D. Gillett, OBE, PhD, DSc, FIBiol, Pro Vice-Chancellor and Head of School of Biological Sciences

CAMBRIDGE
Sir Alan Cottrell, PhD, ScD, FRS, Vice-Chancellor and Master of Jesus College
Dame Rosemary Murray, DBE, JP, DPhil, President of New Hall
Professor Sir Peter Swinnerton-Dyer, MA, FRS, Master of St. Catharine's College

MEMBERS OF CONGRESS

CITY
The Rt. Hon. Lord Alport, PC, TD, DL, MA, Pro Chancellor
E. W. Parkes, MA, PhD, ScD, FIMechE, Vice-Chancellor
Professor J. C. Levy, MS, PhD, FIMechE, Pro Vice-Chancellor

CRANFIELD INSTITUTE OF TECHNOLOGY
Sir Henry Chilver, MA, PhD, DSc, Vice-Chancellor
M. D. Geddes, BA, Development and Estates Officer

DUNDEE
Professor A. M. Neville, DSc, FIStructE, Principal and Vice-Chancellor (Designate)
R. Seaton, MA, LLB, Secretary

DURHAM
Sir Derman Christopherson, OBE, DPhil, LLD, DCL, DSc, FRS, FIMechE, Vice-Chancellor

EAST ANGLIA
F. Thistlethwaite, MA, LHD, FRHistS, Vice-Chancellor

EDINBURGH
Professor A. G. Mackie, MA, PhD, FRSE, Vice-Principal
C. H. Stewart, OBE, JP, MA, LLB, CA, Secretary

ESSEX
A. E. Sloman, MA, DPhil, DU, Vice-Chancellor
G. E. Chandler, BA, Registrar

EXETER
H. Kay, MA, PhD, Vice-Chancellor

GLASGOW
A. Williams, PhD, DSc, FRSE, MRIA, FGS, FRS, Principal and Vice-Chancellor

HERIOT-WATT
Professor G. M. Burnett, PhD, DSc, FRIC, FRSE, Principal and Vice-Chancellor
Professor J. R. Small, BSc(Econ), Vice-Principal

HULL
Professor S. R. Dennison, CBE, MA, Vice-Chancellor
T. H. F. Farrell, TD, DL, LLB, Treasurer
F. T. Mattison, MA, LLB, Registrar

KEELE
Professor W. A. C. Stewart, DL, MA, PhD, DLitt, Vice-Chancellor

KENT AT CANTERBURY
G. Templeman, MA, PhD, DTech, Vice-Chancellor

LANCASTER
Sir Charles Carter, DEconSc, FBA, Vice-Chancellor

DELEGATES OF MEMBER INSTITUTIONS

LEEDS
The Rt. Hon. Lord Boyle of Handsworth, MA, LLD, DSc, DLitt, Vice-Chancellor
F. W. Chattaway, MSc, PhD, Senior Lecturer in Biochemistry
I. G. K. Fenwick, BA, PhD, Adviser to Overseas Students and Lecturer in Education
J. MacGregor, BA, MEd, PhD, Registrar

LEICESTER
His Honour Judge H. A. Skinner, QC, MA, Treasurer (Honorary)
M. Shock, MA, Vice-Chancellor
Professor R. Kilpatrick, MD, FRCP, FRCPEd, Dean of Medicine
M. Baatz, MA, Registrar

LIVERPOOL
A. W. Beeston, JP, MSc, PhD, FRIC, CPA, Senior Pro-Chancellor
H. B. Chrimes, DL, MA, President of the Council
Professor R. F. Whelan, MD, PhD, DSc, FRACP, FAA, Vice-Chancellor
R. C. Connolly, BSc, Senior Lecturer in Anatomy
Observer: J. M. Meek, CBE, DEng, DSc, FIP, FIEE, Professor of Electric Power Engineering

LONDON
Sir Frank Hartley, CBE, BSc, PhD, CChem, FRIC, FPS, Vice-Chancellor
Professor N. F. Morris, MD, FRCOG, Deputy Vice-Chancellor
Professor F. R. Crane, LLB, Chairman of Academic Council
J. R. Stewart, CBE, MA, Clerk of the University Court

LOUGHBOROUGH
D. B. Collett, FPRI, Senior Pro-Chancellor
Professor L. M. Cantor, MA, Senior Pro Vice-Chancellor
F. L. Roberts, JP, BA, Registrar

MANCHESTER
Sir George Kenyon, DL, BSc, Chairman of Council
Professor Sir Arthur Armitage, MA, LLD, Vice-Chancellor
D. S. R. Welland, MA, PhD, Professor of American Literature and Dean of Faculty of Arts
Vincent Knowles, OBE, MA, Registrar

MANCHESTER, INSTITUTE OF SCIENCE AND TECHNOLOGY
G. H. Sugden, MC, Deputy Chairman of Council
Professor R. N. Haszeldine, MA, DSc, ScD, FRIC, FRS, Principal
K. M. Entwistle, MSc, PhD, FIM, Professor of Metallurgy
D. H. McWilliam, BA, Registrar

NOTTINGHAM
B. C. L. Weedon, CBE, PhD, DSc, DTech, FRIC, FRS, Vice-Chancellor
W. F. Nash, MSc, PhD, FIP, Pro Vice-Chancellor and Professor of Physics
D. Rees, BSc, PhD, DIC, ARCS, Warden of Hugh Stewart Hall and Lecturer in Mathematics
J. E. Madocks, CBE, BA, Bursar

MEMBERS OF CONGRESS

OPEN
Sir Walter Perry, OBE, MD, DSc, FRCPEd, Vice-Chancellor
Professor L. J. Haynes, BSc, PhD, FRIC, Pro Vice-Chancellor (Academic)
A. Christodoulou, CBE, MA, Secretary

OXFORD
Sir Rex Richards, MA, DPhil, DSc, FRS, Vice-Chancellor and Warden of Merton College
Sir John Habakkuk, MA, FBA, Former Vice-Chancellor, and Principal of Jesus College
D. M. Stewart, MA, Vice-Chairman of General Board of Faculties
G. K. Caston, MA, MPA, Registrar

READING
Sir Harry Pitt, PhD, LLD, FRS, Vice-Chancellor

ST. ANDREWS
Dr. J. Steven Watson, MA, DLitt, DHL, DH, FRHistS, Principal and Vice-Chancellor
Professor D. J. Gifford, TD, MA, BLitt, Director of Centre for Latin-American Linguistic Studies

SALFORD
Rt. Rev. Dr. E. R. Wickham, BD, DLitt, Pro Chancellor and Chairman of Council
Professor T. Constantine, BSc, PhD, CEng, FICE, FIMunE, Pro Vice-Chancellor
J. H. Calderwood, MEng, PhD, DSc, FIEE, FIP, Professor of Electrical Engineering
S. R. Bosworth, BA, Registrar

SHEFFIELD
Professor G. D. Sims, OBE, MSc, PhD, CEng, FIEE, FIERE, Vice-Chancellor
B. B. Argent, BMet, PhD, FIM, Professor of Metallurgy
G. A. Taylor, MA, DPhil, Senior Lecturer in Chemistry

SOUTHAMPTON
Professor L. C. B. Gower, MBE, LLD, FBA, Vice-Chancellor

STIRLING
W. A. Cramond, OBE, MD, FRCPsych, FRANZCP, FRACP, FRSE, Principal and Vice-Chancellor
Professor J. Trainer, MA, PhD, Deputy Principal
D. A. G. Waddell, MA, DPhil, FRHistS, Professor of Modern History
R. G. Bomont, JP, BSc(Econ), IPFA, Secretary

STRATHCLYDE
Sir John Atwell, CBE, CEng, LLD, FIMechE, FRSE, Chairman of Court
Sir Samuel Curran, DL, DSc, ScD, LLD, FRS, Principal and Vice-Chancellor
Professor A. M. North, PhD, DSc, FRSE, Vice-Principal
D. W. J. Morrell, MA, LLB, Registrar

SURREY
Professor V. S. Griffiths, PhD, FRIC, FIP, Pro Vice-Chancellor
P. J. Timms, IPFA, DPA, Secretary

DELEGATES OF MEMBER INSTITUTIONS

SUSSEX
L. Farrer-Brown, CBE, BSc(Econ), LLD, DSc, Chairman of Council and Senior Pro-Chancellor
Sir Denys Wilkinson, MA, PhD, ScD, DSc, FRS, Vice-Chancellor

NEW U. OF ULSTER
R. S. McCulloch, BSc, Pro-Chancellor and Chairman of Council
W. H. Cockcroft, MA, DPhil, Vice-Chancellor
W. T. Ewing, JP, MA, LLB, Registrar

WALES
The Rt. Hon. Lord Edmund-Davies, LLD, BCL, Pro Chancellor
Sir Goronwy Daniel, KCVO, CB, DPhil, Vice-Chancellor and Principal of University College, Aberystwyth
The Rt. Hon. Lord Heycock, CBE, CStJ, JP, DL, LLD, Chairman of Finance and General Purposes Committee and other Committees
J. Gareth Thomas, MA, Registrar

UNIVERSITY COLLEGE, BANGOR
E. Hughes, BA, Secretary and Registrar

UNIVERSITY COLLEGE, CARDIFF
Professor L. A. Moritz, MA, DPhil, Vice-Principal (Administration) and Registrar

UNIVERSITY COLLEGE, SWANSEA
Professor R. W. Steel, MA, DSc, Principal
D. J. Young, CBE, CA, Vice-President and Treasurer
A. Davies, MA, Registrar/Secretary

WELSH NATIONAL SCHOOL OF MEDICINE
J. P. D. Mounsey, MA, MD, FRCP, Provost
T. R. Saunders, BA, Registrar and Secretary

WARWICK
J. B. Butterworth, JP, DL, MA, DCL, Vice-Chancellor

CANADA

ALBERTA
J. L. Schlosser, Chairman of Board of Governors
M. Horowitz, BA, MEd, EdD, FCCT, Vice-President (Academic)
F. V. MacHardy, BSc, MS, PhD, Professor of Agricultural Engineering

ATHABASCA
W. A. S. Smith, MA, PhD, President
A. G. Meech, MA, Director of Regional and Student Services

BISHOP'S
C. I. H. Nicholl, BSc, MASc, PhD, Principal and Vice-Chancellor
C. B. Haver, BSA, MS, PhD, Dean of Faculty

BRANDON
H. J. Perkins, BA, MSc, PhD, President and Vice-Chancellor

MEMBERS OF CONGRESS

BRITISH COLUMBIA
D. T. Kenny, MA, PhD, President and Vice-Chancellor
M. Shaw, PhD, DSc, FAPS, FLS, FRSC, Vice-President, Academic Development
W. White, FCGA, Vice-President and Bursar
C. J. Connaghan, MS, Vice-President, Administrative Services

BROCK
A. J. Earp, MA, MLitt, LLD, President and Vice-Chancellor
J. M. McEwen, MA, PhD, Dean of Humanities
T. B. Varcoe, MBA, CA, Comptroller
P. E. Bartram, BA, MEd, Registrar

CALGARY
Professor P. J. Krueger, MSc, DPhil, FCIC, FRIC, Vice-President (Academic)
F. Terentiuk, BSc, MA, PhD, Provost of University College
U. F. J. Eyck, MA, BLitt, FRHistS, Professor of History

CARLETON
M. K. Oliver, MA, PhD, LLD, DU, President and Vice-Chancellor
J. Porter, DSc, LLD, DLitt, Vice-President (Academic)
G. R. Love, MA, PhD, Director, Academic Staff Relations

CONCORDIA
J. W. O'Brien, MA, PhD, DCL, LLD, Rector and Vice-Chancellor
Professor J. Bordan, MSc, Vice-Rector, Academic
Professor J. H. Whitelaw, MA, Associate Vice-Rector, Academic Planning

DALHOUSIE
H. D. Hicks, CC, QC, BSc, MA, DEd, DCL, LLD, President and Vice-Chancellor
Professor W. A. MacKay, QC, BA, LLD, Vice-President
P. D. Pillay, BA, PhD, Professor of History
A. J. Tingley, MA, PhD, Registrar and Professor of Mathematics
Observer: I. C. Bennett, DDS, MSD, FACD, FICD, Dean of Faculty of Dentistry

KING'S COLLEGE
J. F. Godfrey, BA, DPhil, President and Vice-Chancellor

LAKEHEAD
G. A. Harrower, MSc, PhD, President

LAVAL
Professor J.-G. Paquet, DSc, FRSC, Rector
L. Kerwin, OC, DSc, LLD, DCL, FRSC, Professor of Physics and Past Rector
J. Desautels, BA, BPh, LèsL, DU, Vice-Rector
Professor G.-B. Martin, DSc, Vice-Dean, Faculty of Agriculture and Food Sciences

LETHBRIDGE
W. E. Beckel, BA, MSc, PhD, President and Vice-Chancellor

McGILL
R. E. Bell, CC, MA, PhD, DSc, LLD, DCL, FRSC, FRS, Principal and Vice-Chancellor
E. J. Stansbury, MA, PhD, Vice-Principal (Planning)
W. F. Hitschfeld, PhD, FRMetS, FRSC, Vice-Principal (Research)
L. E. Lloyd, MSc, PhD, Dean of Faculty of Agriculture and Vice-Principal (Macdonald Campus)

DELEGATES OF MEMBER INSTITUTIONS

McMASTER
A. N. Bourns, PhD, DSc, FRSC, FCIC, President and Vice-Chancellor
A. A. Lee, BD, MA, PhD, Vice-President (Academic)
R. C. McIvor, MA, PhD, FRSC, Dean of Social Sciences
D. R. McCalla, MSc, PhD, FCIC, Professor of Biochemistry

MANITOBA
D. R. Campbell, MA, LLD, DFC & bar, President
D. J. Lawless, MA, PhD, Vice-President (Academic)

MEMORIAL, NEWFOUNDLAND
F. W. Russell, CD, LLD, Chairman of Board of Regents
M. O. Morgan, CC, MA, LLD, DCL, President and Vice-Chancellor
L. Harris, BA(Ed), MA, PhD, Vice-President (Academic)
A. A. Bruneau, BASc, DIC, PhD, Vice-President (Professional Schools and Community Services)

MONTREAL
P. Lacoste, OC, LLL, DU, Rector
Professor J. St.-Pierre, MSc, PhD, Vice-Rector, Planning
J. L'Ecuyer, MSc, PhD, Professor of Physics

MOUNT ALLISON
H. S. Sutherland, MSc, PhD, LLD, Chairman of Board of Regents
W. S. H. Crawford, MA, PhD, President

MOUNT SAINT VINCENT
E. Margaret Fulton, MA, PhD, President

NEW BRUNSWICK
J. M. Anderson, BScF, PhD, LLD, DPed, President
Professor D. C. Blue, MA, MEd, University Secretary

OTTAWA
Rev. Father R. Guindon, CC, BA, LPh, DTh, LLD, Rector
A. D'Iorio, BSc, PhD, MSRC, Vice-Rector (Academic Affairs)
A. K. Gillmore, BA, Vice-Rector (Administration)

PRINCE EDWARD ISLAND
W. C. McInnis, BA, Member of Board of Governors
P. P. M. Meincke, BSc, MA, PhD, President
Professor R. J. Baker, MA, LLD, former President

QUEBEC
C.-E. Beaulieu, BA, BScA, DSc, Vice-President, Academic Affairs and Research
Professor G. Boulet, BTh, LTh, MèsL, LPh, Rector at Trois-Rivières
Observers: F. Soumis, LScCom, Vice-Rector, Administration, at Trois-Rivières
J.-G. Béliveau, BA, BPed, LPed, Vice-Rector, Communications, at Trois-Rivières
A. Brousseau, BA, BPed, LPed, Vice-Rector and Secretary General at Trois-Rivières
S. de La Rochelle, APR, Public Relations General Manager
R. Normandeau, Administrative Director, Tele-University

MEMBERS OF CONGRESS

QUEEN'S, KINGSTON
R. L. Watts, MA, DPhil, Principal and Vice-Chancellor
H. M. Love, BSc, PhD, Vice-Principal (Services)
Professor R. J. Uffen, PhD, DSc, FRSC, Dean of Faculty of Applied Science
Professor Alice J. Baumgart, BScN, MSc(A), Dean of School of Nursing

REGINA
L. I. Barber, OC, BA, BComm, MBA, PhD, President
E. B. Tinker, BE, MSc, PhD, Vice-President

ROYAL MILITARY COLLEGE
Professor J. R. Dacey, MBE, MSc, PhD, FCIC, Principal

RYERSON POLYTECHNICAL INSTITUTE
W. G. Pitman, MA, President
Professor J. L. Packham, BASc, MBA, Vice-President Academic

ST. FRANCIS XAVIER
Rev. G. A. MacKinnon, STD, PhD, President
Professor W. J. Kontak, MA, Chairman of Department of Political Science

ST. MARY'S
D. O. Carrigan, MA, PhD, President
J. B. Owen, BSc, MA, DPhil, FRHistS, Academic Vice-President

SASKATCHEWAN
R. W. Begg, OC, MD, DPhil, DCL, LLD, FRCPCan, President
J. A. Pringle, ED, CD, BAcc, Vice-President (Administration)

SIMON FRASER
Pauline Jewett, MA, PhD, President
D. R. Birch, MA, PhD, Associate Vice-President (Academic)
I. R. Whitaker, MA, DrPhil, Professor of Anthropology

TORONTO
Mrs. Marnie S. Paikin, BA, Chairman of Governing Council
Professor J. M. Ham, BASc, ScD, DScA, DSc, FIEE, President
J. H. Sword, MA, LLD, Special Assistant to President, Institutional Relations

TRENT
Professor T. E. W. Nind, MA, President and Vice-Chancellor
Professor Marion G. Fry, MA, BLitt, Vice-President
G. F. Hamilton, PhD, Dean of Arts and Science

VICTORIA, BRITISH COLUMBIA
R. T. Wallace, MA, LLD, Chancellor
H. E. Petch, PhD, DSc, FRSC, President
Professor K. G. Pedersen, MA, PhD, Vice-President

WATERLOO
B. C. Matthews, BSA, AM, PhD, President and Vice-Chancellor
Rev. C. L. Siegfried, BA, MSc, LLD, President of St. Jerome's College
A. B. Gellatly, BA, CGA, Vice-President Finance and Operations
L. A. K. Watt, BSc, MS, PhD, Dean of Graduate Studies

DELEGATES OF MEMBER INSTITUTIONS

WESTERN ONTARIO
G. E. Connell, BA, PhD, FRSC, President and Vice-Chancellor
Angela M. Wellman, BSc, PhD, Associate Dean of Science
Professor D. E. Gerber, MA, PhD, Chairman of Department of Classical Studies and Vice-Chairman of Senate
Professor R. N. Shervill, MA, PhD, Chairman of Department of Spanish and Italian

WILFRID LAURIER
N. H. Tayler, MA, PhD, President and Vice-Chancellor

WINDSOR
J. F. Leddy, OC, DPhil, DLitt, DèsL; DLit, LLD, DCL, FRHistS, President
F. A. DeMarco, MASc, PhD, FCIC, Senior Vice-President

WINNIPEG
W. J. A. Bulman, Chairman of Board of Regents
H. E. Duckworth, OC, BA, PhD, DSc, LLD, FRSC, President and Vice-Chancellor
D. W. Kydon, BA, MSc, PhD, Dean of Arts and Science (elect)
R. M. Bellhouse, BSc, Registrar

YORK
H. I. Macdonald, OC, BCom, MA, BPhil, LLD, President and Vice-Chancellor
G. G. Bell, MBE, CD, BS, MA, PhD, Executive Vice-President, International Relations and Public Administration
C. M. Lanphier, AM, PhD, Chairman of Senate and Professor of Sociology
W. C. Found, MA, PhD, Director, Office of Research Administration
Observer: O. R. Lundell, BA, PhD, Professor of Chemistry and Dean of Faculty of Science

GHANA

CAPE COAST
F. K. Buah, BA, FHSG, FIBA, Pro Chancellor and Chairman of Council
Professor J. Y. Ewusie, BSc, PhD, Vice-Chancellor
Professor S. K. Odamtten, MA, Head of Department of Educational Foundations

GHANA
D. A. Bekoe, BSc, DPhil, Vice-Chancellor
Professor E. Laing, BSc, PhD, Pro Vice-Chancellor
S. B. Mfodwo, BA, Deputy Registrar

KUMASI, U. OF SCIENCE AND TECHNOLOGY
Professor E. Bamfo Kwakye, DrIng, Vice-Chancellor
Professor E. O. Asare, MSc, PhD, Dean of Faculty of Agriculture
A. S. Y. Andoh, MA, Registrar

GUYANA

GUYANA
Cecilene L. Baird, MEd, Pro Chancellor
D. H. Irvine, CCH, BSc, PhD, Vice-Chancellor and Principal

MEMBERS OF CONGRESS

HONG KONG

CHINESE U. OF HONG KONG
C. -M. Li, KBE(Hon.), MA, PhD, LLD, DSSc, Vice-Chancellor
L. Ma, BSc, PhD, Professor of Biochemistry

HONG KONG
Sir Albert Rodrigues, CBE, ED, JP, MB, BS, LLD, Pro Chancellor and Chairman of Council
R. L. Huang, CBE, JP, DPhil, DSc, Vice-Chancellor
P. C. Y. Lee, JP, MB, BS, LLD, Member of Council and Chairman of Convocation
Mrs. Kit Ching Chan, BA, PhD, Senior Lecturer in History

INDIA

ALIGARH MUSLIM
Professor A. M. Khusro, MA, PhD, Vice-Chancellor
Professor M. Shafi, MSc, PhD, Pro Vice-Chancellor

ANDHRA
M. R. Apparow, MA, Vice-Chancellor
K. V. Sivayya, MBA, PhD, Professor and Head of Department of Commerce and Business Administration

ANNAMALAI
Professor S. Chandrasekhar, PhD, DSc, DLitt, MD, LLD, Vice-Chancellor

BANARAS HINDU
Professor T. R. Anantharaman, MSc, DIISc, DPhil, Rector
Professor S. S. Saluja, MS, PhD, Director of Institute of Technology

BERHAMPUR
Professor T. Ratho, MSc, DPhil, Vice-Chancellor

BHAGALPUR
M. A. M. Gilani, MA, Vice-Chancellor

BIRLA INSTITUTE OF TECHNOLOGY AND SCIENCE
C. R. Mitra, SM, EngScD, Director

BOMBAY
Professor R. Joshi, MA, Vice-Chancellor
K. S. Kolge, BA, DipLib, Registrar

BURDWAN
Professor R. Mukherji, MA, DPhil, DLitt, Vice-Chancellor

CALCUTTA
S. K. Mukherjee, DSc, FNA, Vice-Chancellor

CALICUT
Haji N. A. Noor Muhammad, MA, LLM, JSD, Vice-Chancellor

DELEGATES OF MEMBER INSTITUTIONS

DELHI
Professor R. C. Mehrotra, DPhil, PhD, DSc, FNASc, FASc, FNA, Vice-Chancellor

GURU NANAK DEV
Sardar B. S. Samundri, MSc, MEd, Vice-Chancellor

INDIAN INSTITUTE OF TECHNOLOGY, DELHI
N. M. Swani, PhD, FTI, Professor of Textile Technology

INDIAN INSTITUTE OF TECHNOLOGY, KHARAGPUR
Professor S. Lal, PhD, Director

INDIAN INSTITUTE OF TECHNOLOGY, MADRAS
Professor R. G. Narayanamurthi, BE, DIC, Director

JADAVPUR
Professor A. N. Bose, MSc, PhD, Vice-Chancellor

JAMMU
Professor S. C. Dube, PhD, Vice-Chancellor

JAWAHARLAL NEHRU
B. D. Nag Chaudhuri, PhD, DSc, Vice-Chancellor
Professor K. J. Mahale, MA, LLB, PhD, Rector (Humanities)

KALYANI
T. B. Mukherjee, MA, BL, PhD, DLitt, Vice-Chancellor

KARNATAK
S. S. Wodeyar, MA, LLB, Vice-Chancellor

KERALA
Professor V. K. S. Nayar, MA, PhD, Vice-Chancellor

MADURAI
V. C. Kulandaiswamy, BE, MTech, PhD, DSS, Vice-Chancellor

MAHARSHI DAYANAND
H. Lal, MA, Vice-Chancellor

MYSORE
D. V. Urs, MA, Vice-Chancellor
M. N. Viswanathiah, MSc, PhD, Professor and Head of Department of Geology, Director of Mineralogical Institute and Dean of Faculty of Science

NORTH-EASTERN HILL
A. K. Dhan, MA, PhD, Vice-Chancellor

OSMANIA
Professor G. R. Reddy, MA, PhD, MSc(Econ), Vice-Chancellor
Professor B. Krishnamurti, AM, PhD, Head of Department of Linguistics

PANJAB
Professor R. C. Paul, ScD, PhD, Vice-Chancellor

PATNA
V. A. Narain, MA, PhD, Professor of History

PUNJABI
Amrik Singh, MA, PhD, Vice-Chancellor
B. S. Sood, MSc, PhD, Professor of Physics

S.N.D.T. WOMEN'S
Professor (Mrs.) Madhuri R. Shah, PhD, Vice-Chancellor
Mrs. Kallolini P. Hazarat, BA, Member of Senate

SRI VENKATESWARA
Professor K. Satchidananda Murty, MA, PhD, Vice-Chancellor
M. J. K. Murthy, MSc, PhD, Reader in Physics and Registrar

TAMIL NADU AGRICULTURAL
G. Rangaswami, PhD, Vice-Chancellor

UTKAL
B. Misra, MA, PhD, Vice-Chancellor

VIKRAM
P. N. Kawthekar, MA, PhD, Vice-Chancellor

KENYA
NAIROBI
B. M. Gecaga, Barrister at Law, Chairman of Governing Council
J. N. Karanja, MA, PhD, Vice-Chancellor
E. N. Gicuhi, BA, Registrar

KENYATTA UNIVERSITY COLLEGE
J. K. Koinange, BA, Principal
L. Mungai, LLB, Registrar

LESOTHO
NATIONAL U. OF LESOTHO
M. T. Mashologu, BA, Vice-Chancellor
J. M. Putsoane, BA, Assistant Registrar (Academic)

MALAWI
MALAWI
D. Kimble, OBE, BA, PhD, Vice-Chancellor
R. B. Mbaya, BA, DPA, Registrar

MALAYSIA
MALAYA
Tan Sri Dato' Haji Abdul Majid Ismail, PSM, JMN, MB, BS, MChOrth, FRCSEd, FRACS, Chairman of University Council
Professor Ungku A. Aziz, BA, DEcon, DLittH, Vice-Chancellor
Datuk Professor Mokhzani b. Abdul Rahim, DPMP, MA, PhD, Deputy Vice-Chancellor

DELEGATES OF MEMBER INSTITUTIONS

NATIONAL U. OF MALAYSIA
Tan Sri Datuk Professor Anuwar bin Mahmud, PSM, JMN, PGDK, AK, GVSc, MSc, FSc(M), Vice-Chancellor

U. OF SCIENCE, MALAYSIA
Tan Sri Datuk Haji Hamdan bin Sheikh Tahir, PSM, KMN, DMPN, DipArts, BA, PCE, CYL, LLD, Vice-Chancellor

NEW ZEALAND

AUCKLAND
The Hon. Mr. Justice G. D. Speight, LLB, Chancellor
C. J. Maiden, ME, DPhil, Vice-Chancellor
A. MacCormick, BSc, MA, MCom, PhD, Senior Lecturer, Economics/Management Studies
D. W. Pullar, BCom, Registrar

CANTERBURY
B. F. Anderson, BCom, Chancellor
J. A. Ritchie, MusB, LMusTCL, LTCL, Professor and Head of Department of Music
G. G. Turbott, MC, JP, BA, BCom, FCA(NZ), Registrar

LINCOLN COLLEGE
D. W. Bain, MBE, MA, DipJourn, LLD, Chairman of Council
Professor J. D. Stewart, MA, PhD, Principal
D. S. Hart, MA, PhD, Reader in Animal Science

MASSEY
A. H. Ward, OBE, ACA, Chancellor
A. Stewart, CBE, MAgrSc, DPhil, Vice-Chancellor
J. C. Hawke, MSc, PhD, Reader in Biochemistry

OTAGO
The Very Rev. J. S. Somerville, CMG, MC, MA, DD, Chancellor
R. O. H. Irvine, MD, Drh.c., FRCP, FRACP, Vice-Chancellor
Professor J. S. Loutit, BSc, PhD, Chairman of Department of Microbiology
D. W. Girvan, MA, LLB, Registrar

VICTORIA, WELLINGTON
D. B. C. Taylor, MA, MSc, PhD, FIMechE, Vice-Chancellor
C. W. Dearden, BA, PhD, Professor of Classics
J. D. Gould, MA, Professor of Economic History

WAIKATO
H. R. Bennett, MB, ChB, DPM, FRANZCP, Chancellor
D. R. Llewellyn, JP, DPhil, DSc, FNZIC, FRIC, FRSA, Vice-Chancellor
J. E. Ritchie, MA, DipEd, PhD, FNZPsS, FBPsS, FAAA, Professor of Psychology and Dean of Social Sciences
I. T. Snowdon, BCom, MA, Registrar

NIGERIA

BENIN
Professor T. M. Yesufu, BA, BSc(Econ), PhD, Vice-Chancellor

MEMBERS OF CONGRESS

CALABAR
Alhaji Shettima A. Monguno, Pro Chancellor
Professor E. A. Ayandele, BA, PhD, Vice-Chancellor
S. M. Essang, MSc, PhD, Professor and Head of Department of Economics

IBADAN
Alhaji A. Y. Okene, Pro Chancellor
Professor T. N. Tamuno, JP, PhD, Vice-Chancellor
Professor S. O. Olayide, MSc, PhD, Deputy Vice-Chancellor
S. J. Okudu, BA, Registrar

IFE
Professor O. Aboyade, BSc, PhD, Vice-Chancellor

ILORIN
Professor O. O. Akinkugbe, MD, DPhil, FRCPEd, Vice-Chancellor
Professor J. O. O. Abiri, MEd, PhD, Dean of Education
O. Daramola, MA, Registrar

JOS
Professor G. O. Onuaguluchi, BSc, PhD, FRCPEd, FRCPGlas, Vice-Chancellor

LAGOS
Mallam M. N. Bayero, Pro Chancellor and Chairman of Council
Professor J. F. Ade Ajayi, BA, PhD, LLD, Vice-Chancellor
Professor E. A. Elebute, MA, MD, FRCS, FRCSEd, Provost of College of Medicine
M. O. Eperokun, MA, Registrar and Secretary to Council

NIGERIA
C. E. Abebe, LLD, Pro Chancellor
Professor J. O. C. Ezeilo, MSc, PhD, FAS, Vice-Chancellor

PORT HARCOURT
Professor D. E. U. Ekong, BSc, DrRerNat, Vice-Chancellor
Professor C. Ake, BSc, PhD, Dean of Social Sciences
M. E. Akpe, MA, Registrar

PAPUA NEW GUINEA

PAPUA NEW GUINEA
R. R. Lohia, MA, DipEd, Vice-Chancellor

SIERRA LEONE

SIERRA LEONE
A. T. Porter, MA, PhD, LHD, LLD, Vice-Chancellor
T. F. Hope, OBE, DSc, FICE, Deputy Chairman of Court
A. I. Kamara, MS, PhD, Dean of Faculty of Education

SINGAPORE

NANYANG
K. P. Ang, BA, PhD, Dean of Arts

DELEGATES OF MEMBER INSTITUTIONS

SINGAPORE
S. K. Kwan, PPA, PJG, BA, ARCA, DLitt, DEd, OrdPalmesAcad, Vice-Chancellor
Professor M. H. E. Tay, BDS, FDSRCS, Dean of Faculty of Dentistry
S. K. Cheong, BSc(Eng), Council Member

SOUTH PACIFIC

SOUTH PACIFIC
J. A. Maraj, MOM, BA, PhD, Vice-Chancellor

SRI LANKA

SRI LANKA
Professor P. P. G. L. Siriwardene, PhD, FRIC, FINucE, FIM, Vice-Chancellor

TANZANIA

DAR ES SALAAM
I. M. Kaduma, BSc, BPhil, Vice-Chancellor
Professor G. R. V. Mmari, MA, PhD, DipEd, Dean of Faculty of Arts and Social Sciences

UGANDA

MAKERERE
W. Senteza Kajubi, MSc, Vice-Chancellor
Professor E. H. Rukare, MEd, EdD, Dean of Education

WEST INDIES

WEST INDIES
A. Z. Preston, JP, LLB, FCA, FCCA, FCIS, FREconS, Vice-Chancellor
Professor L. E. S. Braithwaite, BA, Pro Vice-Chancellor and Principal, St. Augustine, Trinidad
S. L. Martin, ARCS, DIC, MSc, FRIC, Pro Vice-Chancellor and Principal, Cave Hill, Barbados
Professor L. R. B. Robinson, MA, Pro Vice-Chancellor (Planning)
Observers: J. A. Spence, BSc, PhD, DTA, DipAgrSc, Professor of Botany
C. E. Jackman, MA, DipEd, Registrar

ZAMBIA

ZAMBIA
J. M. Mwanza, PhD, Vice-Chancellor
Professor M. Mwanalushi, PhD, Dean of School of Humanities and Social Sciences

MEMBERS OF CONGRESS

Representatives and Guests

Organisations within the Commonwealth

Executive Officers of Commonwealth National and Regional Inter-University Bodies

AUSTRALIAN VICE-CHANCELLORS' COMMITTEE
F. S. Hambly, BEc, Secretary

ASSOCIATION OF UNIVERSITIES OF BANGLADESH
M. K. Hussain Sirkar, MSc, BT, MS, Secretary

ASSOCIATION OF UNIVERSITIES AND COLLEGES OF CANADA
C. J. Thibault, PhD, Executive Director
G. D'Auray, Director, International Programmes
A. M. Kristjanson, MA, PhD, FCIC, Director, National Programmes
Mrs. Rosemary A. Cavan, BA, Director of Information
Joan Rondeau, Director of Administration
Denise M. Michaud, Executive Assistant (Special Projects)

INTER-UNIVERSITY COMMITTEE FOR EAST AFRICA
E. K. Kigozi, BA, Executive Secretary

ASSOCIATION OF INDIAN UNIVERSITIES
M. S. Ramamurthy, BA, BL, GDCS, Secretary

NEW ZEALAND VICE-CHANCELLORS' COMMITTEE
B. P. Hampton, BA, Secretary

COMMITTEE OF VICE-CHANCELLORS OF NIGERIAN UNIVERSITIES
Mrs. Ayodele F. Sanwo, BSc, Acting Secretary

COUNCIL OF ONTARIO UNIVERSITIES
E. J. Monahan, MA, PhD, Executive Director

CONFERENCE OF RECTORS AND PRINCIPALS OF QUEBEC UNIVERSITIES
R. Pérusse, BA, Director General

COMMITTEE OF VICE-CHANCELLORS AND PRINCIPALS OF THE UNIVERSITIES OF THE UNITED KINGDOM
Sir Roy Marshall, CBE, MA, PhD, LLD, Secretary General
B. H. Taylor, BSc(Econ), Executive Secretary

INTER-UNIVERSITY COUNCIL FOR HIGHER EDUCATION OVERSEAS
R. C. Griffiths, CMG, MA, Director

University Grants Committees or Equivalent Bodies

TERTIARY EDUCATION COMMISSION, AUSTRALIA
Professor P. H. Karmel, AC, CBE, PhD, Chairman
Professor D. N. F. Dunbar, PhD, Chairman, Universities Council

REPRESENTATIVES AND GUESTS

UNIVERSITY GRANTS COMMITTEE, UNITED KINGDOM
Professor Sir Frederick Dainton, ScD, FRS, Chairman

UNIVERSITIES COUNCIL OF BRITISH COLUMBIA
W. C. Gibson, MD, DPhil, Chairman

ONTARIO COUNCIL ON UNIVERSITY AFFAIRS
W. C. Winegard, MASc, PhD, LLD, DEng, Chairman

NATIONAL COUNCIL FOR HIGHER EDUCATION, GHANA
C. M. O. Maté, BA, DipEd, Chairman

UNIVERSITY AND POLYTECHNIC GRANTS COMMITTEE, HONG KONG
S. F. Bailey, CBE, Secretary

UNIVERSITY GRANTS COMMISSION, INDIA
R. K. Chhabra, BSc, Secretary

UNIVERSITY GRANTS COMMITTEE, NEW ZEALAND
A. T. Johns, PhD, DSc, FRS(NZ), Chairman

NATIONAL UNIVERSITIES COMMISSION, NIGERIA
Mr. Justice M. Balonwu, Chairman
J. Aminu, MB, BS, PhD, MRCP, Executive Secretary
A. Osuntokun, BA, PhD, Director, Ottawa Office

UNIVERSITY GRANTS COMMITTEE OF THE UNIVERSITY OF THE SOUTH PACIFIC
T. Bhim, CA, Chairman

Other Organisations
BRITISH COUNCIL
Sir John Llewellyn, KCMG, DSc, LLD, Director-General
J. F. C. Springford, OBE, MA, Representative in Canada

COMMONWEALTH EDUCATION LIAISON COMMITTEE
Sir Roy Marshall, CBE, MA, PhD, LLD, Chairman

COMMONWEALTH FOUNDATION
J. Chadwick, CMG, MA, Director

COMMONWEALTH HUMAN ECOLOGY COUNCIL
Mrs. Zena Daysh, Secretary-General

CANADIAN COMMONWEALTH SCHOLARSHIP AND FELLOWSHIP COMMITTEE
Professor A. Brebner, PhD, Chairman

COMMONWEALTH SCHOLARSHIP COMMISSION IN THE UNITED KINGDOM
Sir Michael Walker, GCMG, Chairman

COMMONWEALTH SECRETARIAT
R. E. O. Akpofure, Director, Education Division
L. S. Perera, BA, PhD, Senior Education Officer

MEMBERS OF CONGRESS

COUNCIL FOR NATIONAL ACADEMIC AWARDS, UNITED KINGDOM
E. Kerr, BSc, PhD, Chief Officer

LEVERHULME TRUST FUND
R. C. Tress, CBE, DSc, Director

NUFFIELD FOUNDATION
J. Maddox, Director

International Organisations
(including those with a partial Commonwealth membership)

ADMINISTRATIVE BOARD OF THE INTERNATIONAL ASSOCIATION OF UNIVERSITIES
R. Gaudry, CC, DSc, FRSC, President (former Rector, University of Montreal)
Professor M. L. Dowidar, DCh (President Emeritus, University of Alexandria)
Sir John Habakkuk, MA, FBA (former Vice-Chancellor, University of Oxford, and Principal of Jesus College)
Professor G. A. Johnson, Dr (Rector, Université du Bénin)
Professor F. Luchaire (Honorary President, University of Paris I)
Dr. M. Meyerson (President, University of Pennsylvania)
D. J. Aitken, Secretary-General, IAU

ASSOCIATION OF AFRICAN UNIVERSITIES
Professor L. Makany, DrSc, Secretary General

ASSOCIATION OF PARTLY OR WHOLLY FRENCH-SPEAKING UNIVERSITIES (AUPELF)
P. Lacoste, OC, LLL, DU, Member, Administrative Council

STANDING CONFERENCE OF RECTORS AND VICE-CHANCELLORS OF THE EUROPEAN UNIVERSITIES (CRE)
Professor F. Luchaire, Vice-President (Honorary President, University of Paris I)

ASSOCIATION OF SOUTH EAST ASIAN INSTITUTIONS OF HIGHER LEARNING
C.-M. Li, KBE(Hon), MA, PhD, LLD, DSSc, Past President and current second Vice-President (Vice-Chancellor, Chinese University of Hong Kong)

COMMISSION OF THE EUROPEAN COMMUNITIES
A. A. Bath, BSc(Econ), Director, Education and Training

UNESCO
Professor J. K. Balbir, Chief, Section of Higher Education, Division of Higher Education and Training of Educational Personnel

Organisations Outside the Commonwealth

ASSOCIATION OF AMERICAN UNIVERSITIES
T. A. Bartlett, MA, PhD, LLD, President
Professor R. Christy, MA, PhD, Acting President, California Institute of Technology
A. Dykes, MA, EdD, Chancellor, University of Kansas
F. H. T. Rhodes, PhD, LLD, DSc, President, Cornell University
C. E. Young, PhD, Chancellor, University of California—Los Angeles

REPRESENTATIVES AND GUESTS

AMERICAN COUNCIL ON EDUCATION
J. W. Peltason, MA, AM, PhD, President
E. L. Johnson, PhD, LLD, LittD, LHD, Chairman, Overseas Liaison Committee

CARNEGIE CORPORATION OF NEW YORK
D. R. Hood, JD, Director, Commonwealth Programme

CONFERENCE DES RECTEURS DES UNIVERSITES FRANCOPHONES D'AFRIQUE
Université du Bénin, Professor K. Adotevi-Akue, Dean of Engineering

UNION DE UNIVERSIDADES DE AMERICA LATINA
D. J. Aitken (Secretary-General, International Association of Universities)

INTERNATIONAL COUNCIL FOR EDUCATIONAL DEVELOPMENT
J. A. Perkins, MA, PhD, LHD, LLD, Chairman of the Board

Other Observers

ASSOCIATION OF COMMUNITY COLLEGES OF CANADA
A. H. Cameron, MA, PhD, Liaison Officer
S. R. Gilbert, MA (Associate Dean, Academic Studies, Capilano College)

LESTER B. PEARSON COLLEGE OF THE PACIFIC
J. E. Matthews, BA, Director

THE TIMES HIGHER EDUCATION SUPPLEMENT
P. Scott, Editor
C. Cookson, MA
D. Walker, MA

Special Guests

G. C. Andrew, MA, DCL, DèsL, former Executive Director, Association of Universities and Colleges of Canada
J. A. Corry, CC, BCL, LLD, former Principal, Queen's University at Kingston
G. F. Curtis, QC, LLD, Dean Emeritus, University of British Columbia
N. A. M. MacKenzie, CC, CMG, MM & bar, QC, CD, DCL, LLD, LittD, DScSoc, FRSC, President Emeritus, University of British Columbia
P. M. Roberts, Assistant Under Secretary of State (Cultural Affairs), Government of Canada
Sir Charles Wilson, MA, LLD, DLitt, DCL, Principal Emeritus, University of Glasgow

Congress Speakers (not included above)

W. D. Borrie, OBE, MA, DLitt, Professor of Demography, Research School of Social Sciences, Australian National University
A. G. Dickson, CBE, LLD, MA, Founder/Director, Community Service Volunteers (United Kingdom)

MEMBERS OF CONGRESS

Dr. L. Isabelle, FCPA, President, Algonquin College of Applied Arts and Technology

R. S. Musangi, MSc, PhD, Professor and Head of Department of Animal Production, University of Nairobi

H. P. Oberlander, PhD, Professor of Regional Planning and Director, Centre for Human Settlements, University of British Columbia

A. Omololu, DPH, DCH, FWACP, FRCPI, FNMCPH, Professor of Nutrition and Director, Department of Human Nutrition, University of Ibadan

L. H. Shebeski, OC, DSc, LLD, FRSC, FAIC, Dean of Faculty of Agriculture, University of Manitoba

Professor C. M. Switzer, MSA, PhD, PAg, Dean, Ontario Agricultural College, University of Guelph

R. Toomey, BA, Under Secretary, Higher and Further Education, Department of Education and Science, Britain

Congress Committees, Officers and Secretariat

CONGRESS ORGANISING COMMITTEE

J. Steven Watson, MA, DLitt, DHL, DH, FRHistS, *Chairman*
Professor Ungku A. Aziz, BA, DEcon, DLittH
Professor Sir David Derham, KBE, CMG, BA, LLD
H. E. Duckworth, OC, BA, PhD, DSc, LLD, FRSC
Pauline Jewett, MA, PhD
D. T. Kenny, MA, PhD
Professor L. Kerwin, OC, DSc, LLD, DCL, FRSC
Sir Douglas Logan, DPhil, MA, DCL, DLitt, LLD, FDSRCS, FRIBA, ChevLégd'Hon
C. R. Mitra, SM, EngScD
Sir Fraser Noble, MBE, MA, LLD, FRSE
M. K. Oliver, MA, PhD, LLD, DU
H. E. Petch, PhD, DSc, FRSC
A. T. Porter, MA, PhD, LHD, LLD
T. H. B. Symons, OC, LLD, DU, FRSC
D. B. C. Taylor, MA, MSc, PhD, FIMechE
C. J. Thibault, PhD
D. C. Williams, MA, PhD, LLD
Sir Charles Wilson, MA, LLD, DLitt, DCL

Sir Hugh W. Springer, KCMG, CBE, MA, DScSoc, LLD, DLitt, *Secretary*
E. W. Vogt, OC, MSc, PhD, FRSC, *Chairman, Local Organising Committee*
J. E. D. Pearson, CD, BCom, *Administrator and Deputy Chairman, Local Organising Committee*
T. Craig, MA, *Editor of Congress Proceedings*
J. A. Whittingham, MA, *ACU Finance Officer*
Mrs. D. Blanche Gubertini, BA, *Personal Assistant to Secretary*

CANADIAN COMMITTEE FOR THE CONGRESS

H. E. Duckworth, OC, BA, PhD, DSc, LLD, FRSC, *Chairman (from 16/4/77)*
D. C. Williams, MA, PhD, LLD, *Chairman until 16/4/77, Co-Chairman thereafter*
D. T. Kenny, PhD
Professor L. Kerwin, OC, DSc, LLD, DCL, FRSC
Joy S. McDiarmid, BA
C. B. Mackay, QC, BA, DCL, LLD, DèsL, *Secretary (until 16/4/77)*
M. O. Morgan, CC, MA, LLD, DCL
M. K. Oliver, MA, PhD, LLD, DU
Professor R. N. Shervill, MA, PhD
C. J. Thibault, PhD
E. W. Vogt, OC, MSc, PhD, FRSC

CONGRESS COMMITTEES AND STAFF

LOCAL ORGANISING COMMITTEE FOR THE CONGRESS

E. W. Vogt, OC, MSc, PhD, FRSC, *Chairman*
J. E. D. Pearson, CD, BCom, *Administrator and Deputy Chairman*
Dean G. M. Volkoff, MBE, MA, PhD, DSc, FRSC
Ann Chasmar, BA
J. Currie, BCom, MBA
M. Davis, BA, MBA
Betty Fata
Mrs. M. Stovell
Mrs. B. Vogt, BA
Mrs. Alison Watt, BA

CONGRESS SECRETARIAT

Sir Hugh W. Springer, KCMG, CBE, MA, DScSoc, LLD, DLitt, *Secretary, Congress Organising Committee (Secretary General, ACU)*
E. W. Vogt, OC, MSc, PhD, FRSC, *Chairman, Local Organising Committee (Vice-President, University of British Columbia)*
T. Craig, MA, *Editor of Congress Proceedings (Assistant Secretary General, ACU)*
Mrs. D. Blanche Gubertini, BA, *Personal Assistant to the Secretary General, ACU*
P. B. Hetherington, MA, *Assistant Secretary General, ACU*
Joy S. McDiarmid, BA, *Executive Assistant to the Congress Chairman*
J. E. D. Pearson, CD, BCom, *Administrator and Deputy Chairman, Local Organising Committee*
E. E. Temple, BA, *Assistant Secretary General, ACU*
J. A. Whittingham, MA, *Finance Officer, ACU*

MEMBERS OF THE UNIVERSITIES OF BRITISH COLUMBIA ASSISTING WITH THE ORGANISATION OF THE CONGRESS

UNIVERSITY OF BRITISH COLUMBIA

Ladies Committee
Barbara Vogt, *Chairman*
Eileen Milsum
Joan Stager
Jo Robinson
Marion Nodwell

Ginny Russell
Helen Chitty
Margaret McTaggart
Marilyn Webber
Jean Shaw
Eileen Kitts

Sheila White
Meg Kenny

Special Projects
Grace Briggs
T. Moore

SIMON FRASER UNIVERSITY

C. Buchanan, Director of Ancillary Services
Ms. D. Laws, Assistant to the President
B. Li, Director of Food Services
Ms. J. McLeod, Catering Manager
D. Roberts, Director of University News Service
C. Smith, Director of Traffic and Security

UNIVERSITY OF VICTORIA

Professor W. A. W. Neilson, Faculty of Law
Dean P. L. Smith, Faculty of Fine Arts
Professor D. E. Kennedy, Chairman of Ceremonies Committee
F. A. Fairclough, Director, University Relations
J. K. Watson, Director, Food Services
D. Connell, President, Alma Mater Society
T. W. O'Connor, Superintendent, Traffic and Security

NAMES INDEX

Abdul Majid Ismail, 644
Abebe, C. E., 206, 646
Abiri, J. O. O., 206, 646
Aboyade, O., 206, 281, 603, 605, 614, 646
Abubakar, I., 603, 627
Adinarayan, S. P., 603
Adotevi-Akue, K., 651
Ahmad, W., 452, 614, 633
Ahmed Choudhury, U., 603
Ainuddin bin Wahid, 603
Aitken, D. J., 650, 651
Ajayi, J. F. Ade, 11, 245, 279, 603, 605, 614, 646
Ake, C., 449, 646
Akinkugbe, O. O., 614, 646
Akong'O, L. E., 630
Akpe, M. E., 646
Akpofure, R. E. O., 317, 384, 630, 649
Alport, Lord, 451, 634
Aminu, J., 206, 243, 649
Anantharaman, T. R., 642
Anderson, B. F., 645
Anderson, J. M., 614, 639
Andoh, A. S. Y., 641
Andrew, G. C., 651
Andrews, J. H. M., 630
Ang, K. P., 646
Anuwar bin Mahmud, 603, 605, 627, 645
Apparow, M. R., 415, 614, 642
Argent, B. B., 636
Armitage, Sir A., 8, 603, 605, 614, 627, 635
Asare, E. O., 641
Astin, A. E., 343, 357, 633
Atwell, Sir J., 636
Auchmuty, J. J., 583, 603, 605
Ayandele, E. A., 243, 614, 646
Aziz, A., 4, 8, 55, 603, 605, 644, 653

Baatz, M., 285, 635
Back, K. J. C., 603, 614, 627, 631
Bailey, S. F., 649
Bain, D. W., 416, 484, 645
Baird, Cecilene L., 641
Baker, L. R., 631
Baker, R. J., 243, 639
Balbir, J. K., 650
Balonwu, M., 649

Barber, L. I., 614, 640
Barff, S. E. D., 585
Bartlett, T. A., 650
Bartram, P. E., 638
Bath, A. A., 650
Baumgart, Alice J., 640
Bayero, M. N., 646
Beacham, A., 614, 632
Beaulieu, C.-E., 418, 450, 639
Beckel, W. E., 614, 638
Beeston, A. W., 635
Begg, R. W., 158, 614, 640
Bekoe, D. A., 603, 614, 627, 641
Béliveau, J.-G., 639
Bell, G. G., 641
Bell, R. E., 638
Bellhouse, R. M., 641
Bell-Irving, H. P., 11, 629
Bennett, G. L., 629
Bennett, Mrs. H., 645
Bennett, I. C., 638
Bhim, T., 649
Birch, D. R., 640
Birt, L. M., 450, 614, 632
Black, Sir H., 343, 632
Blakers, A. L. 632
Blue, D. C., 639
Bogner, R. E., 483, 631
Bomont, R. G., 636
Bordan, J., 638
Borg Costanzi, E. J., 603, 605, 627
Borrie, W. D., 92, 651
Bose, A. N., 92, 603, 605, 614, 643
Bosworth, S. R., 636
Boulet, G., 639
Bourns, A. N., 418, 614, 639
Boyle of Handsworth, Lord, 343, 357, 603, 614, 627, 635
Braithwaite, L. E. S., 647
Bray, Sir T., 486, 631
Braybrooke, E. K., 631
Brebner, A., 649
Briggs, Grace, 654
Brousseau, A., 639
Brown, R. F. C., 632
Bruneau, A. A., 318, 340, 342, 343, 639
Buah, F. K., 641
Buchanan, C., 654
Bullayya, L., 603
Bulman, W. J. A., 641
Burnett, G. M., 614, 634

Burrenchobay, R., 603
Butterworth, J. B., 614, 637

Calderwood, J. H., 636
Callaghan, Sir B., 632
Cameron, A. H., 651
Cameron, Sir J., 632
Campbell, D. F., 614
Campbell, D. R., 343, 614, 639
Campbell, W. B., 632
Cantor, L. M., 635
Caro, D. E., 614, 632
Carrigan, D. O., 614, 640
Carter, Sir C., 539, 570, 614, 634
Caston, G. K., 636
Cavan, Mrs. R. A., 385, 648
Chadwick, J., 482, 649
Chan, Mrs. K. C., 642
Chandler, G. E., 634
Chandrasekhar, S., 104, 614, 642
Chasmar, Ann, 9, 654
Chattaway, F. W., 635
Cheong, S. K., 647
Chester, K. N. P., 631
Chhabra, R. K., 244, 280, 649
Chilver, Sir H., 634
Chitty, Helen, 654
Choudhury, F. H., 603, 627
Chrimes, H. B., 635
Christodoulou, A., 281, 636
Christopherson, Sir D., 614, 634
Christy, R., 650
Clare, P. B., 629
Cochrane, W. A., 8, 615
Cockcroft, W. H., 452, 615, 637
Collett, D. B., 635
Connaghan, C. J., 638
Connell, D., 654
Connell, G. E., 7, 486, 615, 641
Connolly, R. C., 357, 635
Constantine, T., 636
Cookson, C., 651
Corry, J. A., 484, 651
Cottrell, Sir A., 428, 449, 450, 451, 615, 633
Cowen, Sir Z., 603
Cox, Miss D. T., 585
Craig, T., 4, 585, 617, 620, 653, 654

655

NAMES INDEX

Cramond, W. A., 615, 636
Crane, F. R., 342, 635
Crawford, Sir J., 11, 12, 26, 53, 182, 631
Crawford, W. S. H., 615, 639
Curran, Sir S., 126, 615, 636
Currie, J., 9, 654
Curtis, G. F., 651

Dacey, J. R., 615, 640
Dainton, Sir F., 491, 568, 649
Daniel, Sir G., 92, 615, 623, 637
Daramola, O., 646
Das, J. N., 604
D'Auray, G., 648
Davies, A., 206, 637
Davies, G. N., 615, 632
Davis, M., 9, 654
Daysh, Mrs. Z., 649
Dearden, C. W., 645
De La Rochelle, S., 639
DeMarco, F. A., 641
Dennison, S. R., 615, 634
Deo, P. G., 604
Derham, Sir D., 4, 8, 26, 358, 359, 382, 604, 606, 615, 631, 653
Desautels, J., 638
Desroches, J., 629
Dhan, A. K., 317, 615, 643
Dickson, A. G., 387, 415, 651
D'Iorio, A., 639
Dorais, L. A., 630
Dowidar, M. L., 650
Dube, S. C., 615, 643
Duckworth, H. E., 4, 8, 9, 11, 12, 15, 19, 573, 604, 606, 614, 617, 627, 641, 653
Dufty, N. F., 632
Dunbar, D. N. F., 648
Dutta, S. K., 604
Dykes, A., 650

Earp, A. J., 484, 615, 638
Edmund-Davies, Lord, 637
Ekong, D. E. U., 615, 646
Elebute, E. A., 415, 646
Elkin, P. K., 632
Entwistle, K. M., 635
Eperokun, M. O., 646
Essang, S. M., 646
Ewing, W. T., 637
Ewusie, J. Y., 416, 604, 615, 641
Eyck, U. F. J., 383, 638
Ezeilo, J. O. C., 646

Fairclough, F. A., 654
Faris, D., 630
Farrell, T. H. F., 634
Farrer-Brown, L., 637
Fata, Betty, 9, 654
Fazal, A., 604
Fenwick, I. G. K., 635
Fortier, A., 630
Foster, J., 583
Found, W. C., 641
Fraenkel, G. J., 357, 631
Fraser, Elizabeth D., 633
Froggatt, P., 615, 633
Fry, Marion G., 640
Fulton, E. Margaret, 615, 639

Gaborone, O. M., 633
Garner, Lord, 596
Gates, R. C., 615, 632
Gaudry, R., 650
Gecaga, B. M., 644
Geddes, M. D., 634
Gellatly, A. B., 640
George, D. W., 126, 155, 156, 615, 632
Gerber, D. E., 641
Gibson, W. C., 649
Gicuhi, E. N., 644
Gifford, D. J., 344, 355, 356, 636
Gilani, M. A. M., 615, 642
Gilbert, S. R., 651
Gillett, J. D., 158, 180, 633
Gillmore, A. K., 639
Girvan, D. W., 645
Godfrey, J. F., 615, 638
Goma, L. K. H., 604
Gordon, J. K., 630
Gosse, C. L., 629
Gould, J. D., 645
Gower, L. C. B., 615, 636
Griffiths, R. C., 384, 617, 648
Griffiths, V. S., 636
Gris, G. B., 604
Gubertini, Mrs. D. B., 4, 617, 653, 654
Guindon, R., 8, 615, 639
Guma, S. M., 615, 633

Habakkuk, Sir J., 604, 636, 650
Hajela, P. D., 615
Ham, J. M., 486, 615, 640
Hambly, F. S., 53, 617, 648
Hamdan bin Sheikh Tahir, 615, 645
Hamilton, G. F., 640
Hampton, B. P., 617, 648
Harris, Sir C., 585
Harris, H., 633
Harris, L., 639

Harrower, G. A., 615, 638
Hart, D. S., 645
Hartley, Sir F., 451, 483, 635
Haszeldine, R. N., 449, 450, 482, 615, 635
Hathaway, E. J., 633
Haver, C. B., 637
Hawke, J. C., 645
Haynes, L. J., 636
Hazarat, Mrs. K. P., 644
Hetherington, P. B., 185, 617, 621, 654
Heycock, Lord, 637
Hicks, H. D., 318, 638
Hill, Mrs. M. M., 585
Hitschfeld, W. F., 485, 638
Holborow, L. C., 450, 632
Holmes, J., 567, 625, 630
Holmes, M., 633
Hood, D. R., 651
Hope, R. M., 632
Hope, T. F., 646
Horowitz, M., 342, 637
Hsueh, S. S., 604
Huang, R. L., 387, 416, 486, 604, 642
Hughes, E., 637
Hunnings, G., 604
Hunter of Newington, Lord, 484, 615, 623, 633

Inglis, K. S., 604
Irvine, D. H., 317, 342, 359, 604, 615, 627, 641
Irvine, R. O. H., 516, 615, 645
Isabelle, L., 544, 570, 652

Jackman, C. E., 647
Javare Gowda, D., 604
Jevons, F. R., 615, 631
Jewett, Pauline, 4, 8, 11, 640, 653
Jobin, F. L., 629
Johns, A. T., 649
Johnson, C. B., 8
Johnson, E. L., 651
Johnson, G. A., 650
Joshi, R., 206, 449, 615, 642

Kaduma, I. M., 604, 615, 627, 647
Kajubi, W. S., 357, 384, 615, 647
Kamara, A. I., 646
Karanja, J. N., 604, 615, 644
Karim, A., 604
Karmel, P. H., 504, 648
Kawthekar, P. N., 615, 644
Kay, H., 486, 615, 634

NAMES INDEX

Kennedy, D. E., 654
Kenny, D. T., 4, 8, 9, 11, 13, 15, 348, 356, 357, 638, 653
Kenny, Meg, 654
Kenyon, Sir G., 452, 481, 482, 483, 486, 635
Kerr, E., 650
Kerwin, L., 4, 8, 9, 253, 279, 280, 604, 638, 653
Keyston, J. R., 617
Khusro, A. M., 384, 615, 642
Kigozi, E. K., 617, 648
Kilpatrick, R., 635
Kimble, D., 383, 615, 644
Kinahan, C. H. G., 633
Kitts, Eileen, 654
Kneipp, J. P. G., 631
Knowles, V., 635
Koinange, J. K., 437, 615, 644
Kolge, K. S., 244, 642
Kontak, W. J., 640
Krishnamurti, B., 643
Kristjanson, A. M., 648
Krueger, P. J., 638
Kulandaiswamy, V. C., 416, 485, 615, 643
Kwakye, E. B., 449, 461, 481, 482, 485, 604, 615, 641
Kwan, S. K., 287, 604, 615, 647
Kwapong, A. A., 604
Kydon, D. W., 641

Lacoste, P., 12, 385, 416, 573, 604, 615, 627, 639, 650
Laing, E., 641
Lal, H., 615, 643
Lal, S., 342, 615, 643
Lanphier, C. M., 415, 416, 641
Lapointe, H., 7, 629
Laskin, B., 10, 15, 629
Lawless, D. J., 639
Laws, Ms. D., 654
L'Ecuyer, J., 639
Leddy, J. F., 12, 615, 641
Lee, A. A., 639
Lee, P. C. Y., 642
Léger, J., 10, 629
Levy, J. C., 482, 634
Li, B., 654
Li, C.-M., 12, 489, 491, 571, 604, 615, 642, 650
Llewellyn, D. R., 615, 645
Llewellyn, Sir J., 207, 243, 649
Lloyd, L. E., 638
Logan, Sir D., 4, 8, 243, 582, 583, 604, 606, 614, 627, 653

Lohia, R. R., 616, 646
Lorimer, W. C., 630
Loutit, J. S., 645
Love, G. R., 638
Love, H. M., 640
Low, D. A., 384, 616, 631
Luchaire, F., 650
Lundell, O. R., 641
Lutchman, S. S., 629
Lutwama, J. S. W., 604

Ma, L., 642
Macbeth, Ann, 632
McBride, J. R., 630
McCalla, D. R., 639
McCallum, D. M., 632
McCarthy, Grace, 11
MacCormick, A., 645
McCulloch, R. S., 637
McDiarmid, Joy S., 9, 653, 654
Macdonald, H. I., 187, 205, 616, 641
McEwen, J. M., 638
McGeer, P., 12
McGibbon, Pauline M., 7, 629
MacGregor, J., 635
MacHardy, F. V., 637
McInnis, W. C., 639
McIvor, R. C., 639
Mackay, C. B., 9, 633, 653
MacKay, W. A., 387, 638
MacKenzie, N. A. M., 651
Mackie, A. G., 634
McKinlay, R. A., 616, 633
MacKinnon, G. A., 616, 640
McLeod, Ms. J., 654
McNeill, W., 630
McTaggart, Margaret, 654
McWilliam, D. H., 635
Madan, P. J., 627
Maddox, J., 650
Madocks, J. E., 484, 635
Mahale, K. J., 643
Maiden, C. J., 126, 604, 616, 627, 645
Makany, L., 650
Malleson, N. B., 585
Maraj, J. A., 11, 539, 604, 616, 627, 647
Marshall, Sir R., 617, 648, 649
Martin, G.-B., 638
Martin, R. L., 616, 632
Martin, S. L., 451, 647
Mashologu, M. T., 539, 616, 644
Maté, C. M. O., 649
Matthews, B. C., 471, 481, 482, 483, 485, 616, 640
Matthews, J. E., 651
Mattison, F. T., 634
Mbaya, R. B., 644

Meech, A. G., 637
Meek, J. M., 635
Mehrotra, R. C., 243, 245, 604, 616, 627, 643
Meincke, P. P. M., 486, 616, 639
Meyerson, M., 650
Mfodwo, S. B., 641
Michaud, Denise M., 648
Milsum, Eileen, 654
Misra, B., 616, 644
Mitra, C. R., 4, 8, 11, 383, 516, 604, 606, 616, 642, 653
Mmari, G. R. V., 384, 647
Mokhzani b. Abdul Rahim, 644
Mollo, J. K., 629
Monahan, E. J., 617, 648
Monguno, A., 646
Moore, T., 654
Morgan, M. O., 9, 604, 616, 627, 639, 653
Moritz, L. A., 637
Morrell, D. W. J., 636
Morris, N. F., 635
Mounsey, J. P. D., 616, 637
Msekwa, P., 604
Mukherjee, S. K., 616, 642
Mukherjee, T. B., 643
Mukherji, R., 344, 356, 604, 616, 642
Mungai, L., 644
Murray, Dame Rosemary, 633
Murrell, T. G. C., 631
Murthy, M. J. K., 644
Murty, K. S., 207, 616, 644
Musangi, R. S., 55, 652
Mwanalushi, M., 342, 415, 416, 647
Mwanza, J. M., 324, 341, 604, 616, 627, 647
Myers, R. H., 242, 269, 280, 604, 606, 616, 627, 632

Nag Chaudhuri, B. D., 137, 156, 616, 643
Narain, V. A., 644
Narayanamurthi, R. G., 616, 643
Naser, M. A., 604
Nash, W. F., 635
Nayar, V. K. S., 486, 616, 643
Neilson, W. A. W., 654
Nemetz, N. T., 11, 15, 629
Neville, A. M., 616, 634
Neville, B. F. J., 629
Nicholl, C. I. H., 317, 637
Nind, T. E. W., 616, 640
Noble, Sir F., 4, 8, 405, 415, 417, 604, 606, 616, 627, 633, 653

657

Nodwell, Marion, 654
Noor Muhammad, N. A., 206, 616, 642
Normandeau, R., 639
Norris, J. G., 631
North, A. M., 636

Oberlander, H. P., 117, 652
O'Brien, J. W., 484, 604, 616, 627, 638
O'Connor, T. W., 654
Odamtten, S. K., 641
Okene, A. Y., 646
Okudu, S. J., 646
Olayide, S. O., 646
Oliver, M. K., 4, 8, 9, 218, 243, 383, 604, 616, 638, 653
Omololu, A., 175, 180, 652
Onuaguluchi, G. O., 616, 646
Osuntokun, A., 649
Owen, G., 633
Owen, J. B., 640

Packham, J. L., 640
Paddick, R. J., 631
Paikin, Mrs. M. S., 640
Paquet, J.-G., 7, 511, 638
Parkes, E. W., 616, 634
Parrott, H. C., 8
Partridge, P. H., 631
Paul, R. C., 616, 643
Pearson, J. E. D., 4, 9, 13, 653, 654
Pedersen, K. G., 640
Peltason, J. W., 651
Perera, L. S., 649
Perinbam, L., 630
Perkins, H. J., 616, 637
Perkins, J. A., 244, 283, 365, 382, 651
Perry, Sir W., 516, 570, 616, 636
Pérusse, R., 617, 648
Petch, H. E., 4, 8, 12, 616, 640, 653
Phillips, N. C., 605
Pillay, P. D., 638
Pitman, W. G., 533, 570, 616, 640
Pitt, Sir H., 567, 570, 605, 606, 616, 627, 636
Porteous, G., 629
Porter, A. T., 4, 8, 12, 285, 342, 605, 606, 616, 646, 653
Porter, J., 638
Porter, R. C., 632
Preston, A. Z., 552, 570, 605, 616, 627, 647
Pringle, J. A., 640

Pullar, D. W., 645
Putsoane, J. M., 644

Rahim, M. F., 605
Ramamurthy, M. S., 489, 617, 648
Rangaswami, G., 158, 605, 627, 644
Ratho, T., 616, 642
Reddy, G. R., 616, 643
Rees, D., 635
Rhodes, F. H. T., 650
Richards, Sir R., 616, 636
Rickerd, D., 630
Ritchie, J. A., 645
Ritchie, J. E., 645
Roberts, D., 654
Roberts, F. L., 635
Roberts, P. M., 651
Robertson, A. P., 632
Robertson-Cuninghame, R. C., 632
Robichard, H. J., 629
Robinson, Jo, 654
Robinson, L. R. B., 647
Robson, Sir H., 599, 605, 606
Rodrigues, Sir A., 642
Rogers, C. A., 605
Rondeau, Joan, 648
Rukare, E. H., 647
Russell, F. W., 639
Russell, Ginny, 654
Russell, R. W., 616, 631
Rutledge, D. J. S., 631

St.-Pierre, J., 639
Saluja, S. S., 642
Samuels, G. J., 342, 632
Samuels, J. M. 633
Samundri, B. S., 63, 605, 616, 643
Sanwo, Mrs. A. F., 617, 648
Saunders, G. D., 485, 631
Saunders, T. R., 637
Schlosser, J. L., 637
Scott, J. F., 316, 343, 383, 616, 631
Scott, P., 651
Seaton, R., 634
Sen, S. N., 605
Sendut, H., 605
Setidisho, N. O. H., 616, 633
Shafi, M., 642
Shah, Mrs. M. R., 317, 383, 616, 644
Shaw, Jean, 654
Shaw, M., 638
Shebeski, L. H., 77, 652
Shervill, R. N., 8, 9, 641, 653

Shock, M., 318, 616, 635
Siddiqui, Z. R., 287, 314, 605, 616, 633
Siegfried, C. L., 640
Sims, G. D., 491, 616, 636
Singh, A., 207, 616, 644
Singh Suman, S. N., 605
Siriwardene, P. P. G. L., 344, 605, 616, 627, 647
Sirkar, M. K. H., 617, 648
Sivayya, K. V., 416, 450, 482, 642
Skinner, H. A., 635
Sloman, A. E., 383, 617, 634
Small, J. R., 634
Smith, C., 654
Smith, P. L., 654
Smith, W. A. S., 617, 637
Snowdon, I. T., 645
Soles, A. E., 630
Somerville, J. S., 645
Sood, B. S., 644
Soumis, F., 639
Sparham, R. D., 630
Speight, G. D., 645
Spence, J. A., 647
Springer, Sir H. W., 4, 8, 9, 13, 584, 586, 617, 619, 627, 653, 654
Springford, J. F. C., 629, 649
Stackpole, S., 583
Stager, Joan, 654
Stansbury, E. J., 638
Steadman, G. T., 631
Steel, R. W., 617, 623, 637
Steinhauer, R., 629
Stewart, A., 617, 645
Stewart, C. H., 634
Stewart, D. M., 636
Stewart, J. D., 55, 617, 645
Stewart, J. R., 635
Stewart, R. F., 632
Stewart, W. A. C., 358, 617, 634
Stovell, Mrs. M., 9, 654
Stranks, D. R., 450, 485, 617, 631
Street, R., 617, 632
Sugden, G. H., 635
Sumanadasa, L. H., 605
Sundaravadivelu, N. D., 605
Sutherland, H. S., 639
Swani, N. M., 332, 341, 384, 482, 483, 605, 606, 643
Swinnerton-Dyer, Sir P., 633
Switzer, C. M., 146, 156, 652
Sword, J. H., 640
Symons, T. H. B., 4, 8, 287, 582, 605, 606, 614, 618, 627, 653

NAMES INDEX

Tamuno, T. N., 187, 617, 646
Tay, M. H. E., 647
Tayler, N. H., 617, 641
Taylor, B. H., 617, 648
Taylor, D. B. C., 4, 8, 418, 605, 606, 617, 645, 653
Taylor, G. A., 636
Temple, E. E., 359, 384, 654
Templeman, G., 617, 634
Terentiuk, F., 638
Thibault, C. J., 4, 8, 9, 617, 648, 653
Thistlethwaite, F., 372, 381, 617, 634
Thomas, H. O., 605
Thomas, J. G., 637
Throsby, C. D., 631
Thwaites, P. N., 631
Timms, P. J., 636
Tingley, A. J., 638
Tinker, E. B., 640
Toomey, R., 291, 315, 652
Tope, T. K., 605
Trainer, J., 636
Tress, R. C., 650
Turbott, G. G., 645

Uffen, R. J., 640
Urs, D. V., 617, 643

Varcoe, T. B., 638
Verma, N. R., 629

Viswanathiah, M. N., 643
Vogt, Mrs. B., 9, 654
Vogt, E. W., 4, 9, 13, 653, 654
Volkoff, G. M., 9, 654
Von Zur-Muehlen, M., 625

Waddell, D. A. G., 384, 636
Walker, D., 651
Walker, Sir M., 596, 649
Wallace, Sr. C., 605, 606
Wallace, R. T., 640
Walton, K., 633
Ward, A. H., 645
Ward, J. M., 632
Ward, R. B., 632
Watson, J. K., 654
Watson, J. S., 4, 8, 12, 19, 185, 205, 243, 282, 573, 586, 605, 606, 614, 627, 636, 653
Watson, J. W., 631
Watt, Mrs. A., 9, 654
Watt, L. A. K., 640
Watts, R. L., 187, 205, 605, 617, 627, 640
Webb, E. C., 617, 631
Webber, Marilyn, 654
Weedon, B. C. L., 450, 671, 635
Welland, D. S. R., 635
Wellman, Angela M., 641
Wettlaufer, J. J., 8

Whelan, R. F., 299, 316, 342, 617, 635
Whitaker, I. R., 640
White, D. O., 631
White, Sheila, 654
White, W., 638
Whitelaw, J. H., 357, 638
Whittingham, J. A., 4, 617, 653, 654
Wicken, A. J., 632
Wickham, E. R., 342, 485, 636
Wilkinson, Sir D., 317, 343, 617, 637
Willett, F. J., 245, 617, 631
Williams, A., 617, 634
Williams, B. R., 200, 205, 605, 617, 632
Williams, D. C., 4, 8, 9, 605, 653
Wilson, Sir C., 4, 8, 11, 19, 583, 605, 606, 651, 653
Winegard, W. C., 485, 649
Winter, G. A., 629
Wodeyar, S. S., 617, 643
Wynne-Edwards, H. R., 629

Yesufu, T.-M., 231, 243, 605, 606, 617, 645
Young, C. E., 384, 650
Young, D. J., 637

659

ACKNOWLEDGMENT

I want to thank Bob Oller of Oller Studios in Williamsburg, Virginia for his excellent illustrations and his assistance in all things electronic. Without his assistance I'm not sure I would have gotten the manuscript off to the publisher.

And I especially want to thank my wife, Anne-Liss. She encouraged me to write about the Korean War, and even bought me a computer, and then sent me off to my room every day to work on my manuscript.